R. Gupta's®

POPULAR MASTER GUIDE

BIHAR

D.El.Ed.

DIPLOMA IN ELEMENTARY EDUCATION

Combined Entrance Exam

Conducted by

Bihar School Examination Board (BSEB)

by

RPH EDITORIAL BOARD

2027
EDITION

RAMESH PUBLISHING HOUSE, NEW DELHI

Published by

O.P. Gupta *for* Ramesh Publishing House

Admin. Office

12-H, New Daryaganj Road, Opp. Officers' Mess,
New Delhi-110002 ✆ 23275224, 23245124

E-mail: info@rameshpublishinghouse.com

For Online Shopping: www.rameshpublishinghouse.com

Showroom

- Balaji Market, Nai Sarak, Delhi-110006 ✆ 23282525 📱 9354373464
- 4457, Nai Sarak, Delhi-110006

Book Code: R-2799

ISBN: 978-93-5477-664-9

Price: ₹ 320

Printed at: Deepak Offset, Delhi

CONTENTS

Work and Wages; Speed, Time and Distance; Average; Partnership; Mixture and Alligation; Mensuration; Algebraic Identities; Surds; Triangles and its Various Kinds; Similarity of Triangles; Circle and Tangents; Trigonometry; Data Tables; Bar Graphs; Frequency Polygon; Pie Charts; Miscellaneous Questions.

Scheme of Entrance Test

The entrance examination will be conducted through online mode (Computer Based Test). There will be 120 questions in this exam which will be objective and multiple choice.

Duration of Entrance Test: The duration of the entrance exam will be of 150 minutes (2:30 hours).

Pattern of Entrance Test

Sr. No.	Subject	No. of Questions	Total Number
1.	General Hindi/Urdu	25	25
2.	Mathematics	25	25
3.	Science	20	20
4.	Social Studies	20	20
5.	General English	20	20
6.	Logical & Analytical Reasoning	10	10
	Total	**120**	**120**

01 (one) mark will be given for each correct answer.

Previous Years' Paper

Bihar School Examination Board, Patna

Diploma in Elementary Education (D.El.Ed.)

Common Recruitment Exam-2025

(Exam held on 06-09-2025)

सामान्य हिन्दी

1. निम्नलिखित प्रश्न में से दिये गये पद्यांश में विद्यमान छन्द का निर्देश कीजिए :
शोभित मंच की अवली बजदन्त मयी छवि उज्जलु छाई।

A. सुन्दरी B. मत्तगयन्द
C. रोला D. बरवे

2. 'इस बुढ़िया को न सताओ, यह तो निरी गाय है।'
इस वाक्य में किस शब्द-शक्ति का चमत्कार है?

A. अभिधा
B. लक्षणा
C. व्यंजना
D. व्यंजना प्रधान अभिधा

3. 'भाव जिसके हृदय में रहते हैं' उसे कहते हैं :

A. आश्रय
B. आलंबन
C. उद्दीपन
D. आलंबन जन्य उद्दीपन

4. *मैत्री की राह बताने को, सबको सुमार्ग पर लाने को*
दुर्योधन को समझाने को, भीषण विध्वंस बचाने को
भगवान हस्तिनापुर आए, पांडव का संदेशा लाए
दो न्याय अगर तो आधा दो, पर इसमें भी यदि बाधा हो
तो दे दो केवल पाँच ग्राम, रखो अपनी धरती तमाम
हम वहीं खुशी से खाएँगे, परिजन पर असि न उठाएँगे
दुर्योधन वह भी दे न सका, आशीष समाज का ले न सका
उलटे हरि को बाँधने चला, जो था असाध्य साधने चला
जब नाश मनुज पर छाता है, पहले विवेक मर जाता है।
'मनुज' का अर्थ है :

A. मानव B. मनुष्य
C. मनु की संतान D. उपर्युक्त सभी

5. *विकसते मुरझाने को फूल, दीप जलता होने को मंद।*
बरसते भर जाने को मेघ, उदय होता छिपने को चाँद।।
इस पंक्ति में कौन-सा अलंकार है?

A. रूपक B. विरोधाभास
C. श्लेष D. यमक

1. B **2.** B **3.** A **4.** D **5.** B

6. 'राम ने ऐसी कहानी सुनाई कि करन रो पड़ा।'
वाक्य का संयुक्त वाक्य में रूपांतरण है :
A. राम ने कहानी सुनाई क्योंकि करन रो रहा था।
B. राम ने ऐसी कहानी सुनाई जिसको सुन कर करन रो पड़ा।
C. राम ने कहानी सुनाई और करन रो पड़ा।
D. इनमें से कोई नहीं

7. निम्न में से रूपक का उदाहरण है :
A. आए महंत वसंत।
B. मन का मनका का फेर।
C. चरण कमल बंदों हरिराई।
D. उपर्युक्त सभी

8. निरस्त करना शब्द का अंग्रेजी पारिभाषिक शब्द होगा :
A. Void B. Revalidate
C. Routine D. Revoke

9. *पूत कपूत तो क्यों धन संचय।*
पूत सपूत तो क्यों धन संचय।।
उक्त पंक्तियों में अलंकार का प्रकार बताएँ :
A. छेकानुप्रास
B. लाटानुप्रास
C. वृत्यानुप्रास
D. श्लेष

10. जहाँ उपमेय में अनेक उपमानों की शंका होती है :
A. यमक B. अनुप्रास
C. श्लेष D. भ्रान्तिमान

11. 'पुत्र-पुत्री' में कौन-सा समास है?
A. बहुव्रीहि B. द्वन्द्व
C. तत्पुरूष D. द्विगु

12. वाच्य का शाब्दिक अर्थ क्या है?
A. वचन
B. बोली
C. बोलने का विषय
D. कहावत

13. *पुलक प्रकट करती है, धरती हरित तृणों की नोंक से।*
मानों झूम रहे हो तरू भी, मंद पवन की झोकों से।।
इस पंक्ति में कौन-सा अलंकार है?
A. रूपक B. उत्प्रेक्षा
C. यमक D. विभावना

14. 'मेरे चाहने के अनुसार सब कुछ हो रहा था।' वाक्य का मिश्र वाक्य में रूप होगा :
A. सब कुछ हो रहा था, वो भी मेरे चाहने के अनुसार।
B. मेरे चाहने पर ही सब कुछ हो रहा था।
C. मेरे अनुसार ही सब कुछ हो रहा था।
D. मैं जैसा चाह रहा था, वैसा ही सब कुछ होता जा रहा था।

15. *रहिमन जो गति दीप की, कुल कपूत गति सोय।*
बारे उजियारै लगै, बढ़ै अंधेरो होय।।
उपर्युक्त पंक्तियों में कौन-सा अलंकार है?
A. उपमा B. रूपक
C. यमक D. श्लेष

16. खड़ी बोली के सर्वप्रथम लोकप्रिय कवि माने जाते हैं?
A. रामधारी सिंह 'दिनकर'
B. सूर्यकांत त्रिपाठी 'निराला'
C. मैथिली शरण गुप्त
D. अयोध्या सिंह उपाध्याय 'हरिऔध'

6. C	**7.** D	**8.** D	**9.** B	**10.** D	**11.** B
12. C	**13.** B	**14.** D	**15.** D	**16.** D	

17. निम्न में कौन-सा वाक्य शुद्ध है?
A. इस परिश्रम का बदला अपने कार्य से मनुष्य को जो संतोष होता है, वही है।
B. उसने जोर-जोर से रोने लगा।
C. आप उस प्रतिज्ञा को न भूले होंगे।
D. इस किताब का क्या मूल्य है?

18. अंग्रेजी के पारिभाषिक शब्द 'ALLOTMENT' के लिए हिन्दी का समानार्थक शब्द है :
A. पंजीयन B. निस्तारण
C. आवंटन D. संशोधन

19. 'परीक्षा' का संधि-विच्छेद है :
A. पर + इच्क्षा B. परी + क्षा
C. परी + इचक्षा D. परि + ईक्षा

20. अन्वय की दृष्टि से कौन-सा वाक्य शुद्ध है?
A. गीता को सिलाई करनी नहीं आती।
B. गीता को सिलाई करने नहीं आता।
C. गीता को सिलाई करना नहीं आता।
D. गीता को सिलाई करना नहीं आती।

21. 'विषय-वारि मन-मीन भिन्न नहिं होत कबहुं पल एक।' में कौन-सा अलंकार है?
A. रूपक B. अतिश्योक्ति
C. मानवीकरण D. उपमा

22. 'आँसू पोंछना' मुहावरे का क्या अर्थ है?
A. दिलासा देना B. खिल्ली उड़ाना
C. रूलाना D. बहलाना

23. अशुद्ध वाक्य की पहचान कीजिए :
A. ये फल अच्छे नहीं हैं।
B. मुझे निबंध लिखना है।
C. राम और राम का पुत्र बाजार गया।
D. यह पुस्तक रोहन की है।

24. राहुल फुटबॉल खेलकर चला गया। रेखांकित शब्द में कौन पदबंध है?
A. क्रिया पदबंध
B. क्रिया-विशेषण पदबंध
C. संज्ञा पदबंध
D. सर्वनाम पदबंध

25. 'घुड़दौड़' का समास-विग्रह बताइए?
A. घोड़े जैसी तेज दौड़
B. घोड़े की दौड़
C. दौड़ने वाला घोड़ा
D. घोड़ा और दौड़

GENERAL ENGLISH

26. Fill in the blank with the suitable option:
The child looks .... if he were hungry.
A. and B. as
C. but D. or

27. Complete the statement:
The Preposition 'Beside' means ....
A. in addition to
B. by the side of
C. Both
D. None

28. Fill up the blank, with the correct option.
The ball rolled .... the lawn.
A. towards B. over
C. under D. across

17. D	**18.** C	**19.** D	**20.** C	**21.** A	**22.** A
23. C	**24.** A	**25.** B	**26.** B	**27.** B	**28.** D

29. Identify the correct word.

A. Summary B. Sammary
C. Sumary D. Samary

30. Select the most appropriate option to change the sentence from direct speech to indirect speech.

"She must apply for the job," he said.

He said that .... apply for the job.

A. She had to
B. He has to
C. They have to
D. I have to

31. Choose the correct phrase from the given option and make a conditional sentence.

You would manage it if you .... panic.

A. didn't B. weren't
C. don't D. haven't

32. By the time she was fifteen, she .... a beautiful singer.

A. shall become B. become
C. had become D. has becoming

33. Fill in the blanks with suitable conjunction.

.... our constant disagreements, we remained fast friends.

A. Although B. Despite
C. Unless D. Due to

34. Identify the incorrect sentence:

A. You who are my friend, should not betray me.
B. He who is my friend, should not betray me.
C. Rani who is my friend, should not betray me.
D. Neeta who are my friend, should not betray me.

35. Select the alternative which best express the meaning of the idioms/ phrase.

Addicted to

A. Habituated to something
B. Under the pressure of someone
C. Under the control of
D. Blind to someone's fault

36. Fill in the blank with the past continuous tense form of the verb given in the bracket.

"Monica .... since last week" (Plan)

A. did plan
B. has been planning
C. had been planning
D. was planning

37. The sentence given below has a word/words underlined. Read the sentence carefully and find which word class the underlined word/ words belongs/belong to. Indicate your response accordingly.

<u>To swim</u> every day is good for health.

A. Participle
B. Infinitive verb
C. Gerund
D. Adjective

38. Identify the correct sequence for the following parts of a sentence.

(*i*) and forbade him
(*ii*) to returm
(*iii*) he ordered him
(*iv*) to leave the room

A. (*i*), (*ii*), (*iii*), (*iv*)
B. (*ii*), (*iii*), (*iv*), (*i*)
C. (*iii*), (*iv*), (*ii*), (*i*)
D. (*iii*), (*iv*), (*i*), (*ii*)

29. A	**30.** A	**31.** A	**32.** C	**33.** B
34. D	**35.** A	**36.** D	**37.** B	**38.** D

39. Select the most appropriate option to change the sentence from direct speech to indirect speech.
The salesman said, "Are you interested in the scheme?"
The salesman asked me if .... interested in the scheme.
A. they were B. you were
C. he was D. I was

40. Identify the Passive Voice of the given sentence.
The police arrested some thieves last night.
A. Some thieves have been arrested by police last night.
B. Last night some thieves were arrested by the police.
C. Some thieves were being arrested by the police last night.
D. Some thieves has been arrested by the police last night.

41. Select the appropriate option.
"If I forget her birthday, Ravi gets upset". Which conditional is this?
A. zero B. first
C. second D. third

42. We .... afford a new car this year.
A. should B. might
C. may D. can

43. Fill up the blank, with correct option.
.... Bracket is generally used to add in the middle of the sentence.
A. Round B. Square
C. Braces D. All of these

44. Which of the following statement is 'true'?
A. Listening and Reading are the Receptive Skills.
B. Listening and Speaking are the Receptive Skills.
C. Reading and Writing are the Productive Skills.
D. Listening and Speaking are the Productive Skilis.

45. Fill up the blank with the correct option.
An empty vessel .... much.
A. sounds B. have sound
C. sound D. were sound

MATHEMATICS

46. For what value of X will the mode of 1, 5, 3, 4, 7, 4, X, 7 be 4?
A. 4 B. 7
C. 3 D. 5

47. A chord of a circle with radius 10 cm subtends a right angle at the center. The area of the minor segment (given, $\pi = 3.14$) is:
A. 32.5 cm^2 B. 34.5 cm^2
C. 28.5 cm^2 D. 30.5 cm^2

48. If P is the midpoint of the chord AB in circle C(o, r), then the measure of ∠OPA will be:
A. 120° B. 160°
C. 90° D. 180°

49. If the sum of the zeros of the polynomial $f(x) = 2x^3 - 3kx^2 + 4x - 5$ is 6, then the value of k will be:
A. 4 B. –4
C. 2 D. –2

39. D	**40.** B	**41.** A	**42.** D	**43.** A	**44.** A
45. A	**46.** A	**47.** C	**48.** C	**49.** A	

50. The area of a parallelogram with length (l) and width (b) is:
A. ½ lb B. 2 lb
C. lb D. $(lb)^2$

51. The y-axis divides the line segment joining the points (–3, –4) and (1, –2) in the ratio:
A. 2 : 3 B. 3 : 1
C. 1 : 3 D. 3 : 2

52. In ΔABC, DE || AB. If CD = 3 cm, EC = 4 cm, BE = 6 cm, then DA is equal to ....
A. 7.5 cm B. 3 cm
C. 4.5 cm D. 6 cm

53. If the roots of the quadratic equation $ax^2 + bx + c = 0$ are $\sin \alpha$ and $\cos \alpha$, then b^2 =
A. $a^2 + 2ac$ B. $a^2 - 2ac$
C. $a^2 - ac$ D. $a^2 + ac$

54. If the roots of the quadratic equation $2x^2 - 6x + p = 0$ are real and unequal, then the value of p is:
A. $p < \frac{9}{2}$ B. $p \leq \frac{9}{2}$
C. $p > \frac{9}{2}$ D. $p \geq \frac{9}{2}$

55. The sides of a triangle are in the ratio 12 : 14 : 25 and its perimeter is 25.5 cm. The longest side of the triangle is:
A. 7 cm B. 14 cm
C. 12.5 cm D. 18 cm.

56. If a is a rational number, what is $1/a$?
A. Rational number
B. Irrational number
C. Prime number
D. Even number

57. In the given figure, a square OABC is inscribed in a quadrant OPBQ. If OA = 20 cm, then the area of the shaded region is (taking π = 3.14):

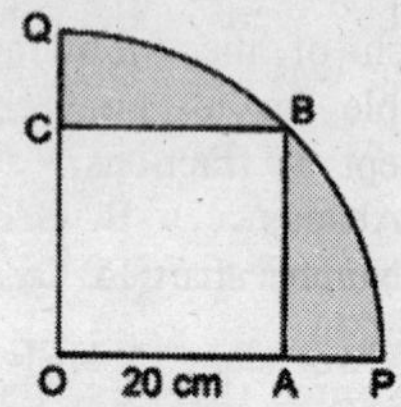

A. 214 cm^2 B. 228 cm^2
C. 242 cm^2 D. 248 cm^2

58. In how much time will ₹ 1600 increase to ₹ 1852.20 at 5% annual compound interest?
A. 2 years B. 3 years
C. 5 years D. None of these

59. Why are Roman numerals not commonly used in writing numbers like Hindu-Arabic numerals?
A. Roman numerals do not employ place value, so calculations using these numerals are difficult.
B. Roman numerals are difficult to remember.
C. Forming numbers using Roman numerals is a complex task.
D. Children get confused between the English alphabet and Roman numerals.

60. $9 \sec^2 A - 9 \tan^2 A$ = ...
A. 1 B. 9
C. 8 D. 0

50. C	**51.** B	**52.** C	**53.** A	**54.** A	**55.** C
56. A	**57.** B	**58.** B	**59.** A	**60.** B	

61. Raj's profit when selling a book to Simran is ₹ 63. Despite a 23% discount on the book, Raj managed to make a profit of 10%. What should be the list price of the book?
A. ₹ 1120 B. ₹ 560
C. ₹ 900 D. ₹ 750

62. Which of the following is most suitable for teaching children the concept of fractions?
A. Abacus B. Geoboard
C. Number chart D. Cuisenaire rods

63. If in two triangles DEF and PQR, angle D = angle Q and angle R = angle E, then which of the following is **not** true?
A. $\frac{EF}{PR} = \frac{DF}{PQ}$ B. $\frac{DE}{PQ} = \frac{EF}{RP}$
C. $\frac{DE}{QR} = \frac{DF}{PQ}$ D. $\frac{EF}{RP} = \frac{DE}{QR}$

64. In the given figure, $m \parallel n$ and l is a transversal, then $\angle 1$ will always be equal to:

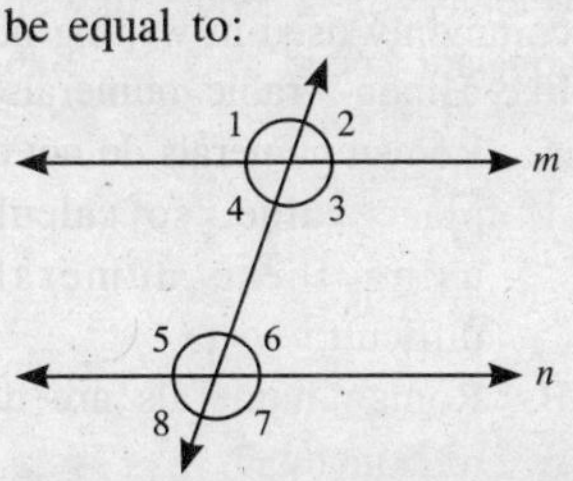

A. $\angle 2$ B. $\angle 4$
C. $\angle 5$ D. $\angle 8$

65. Bholu has a total of 40 coins of 30 paise and 10 paise denominations. Their total value is ₹ 9. How many 10 paise coins does he have?
A. 25 B. 35 C. 15 D. 20

66. If the probability of an event is p, then the probability of its complementary event is?
A. $p - 1$ B. p
C. $1 - p$ D. $1 - 1/p$

67. For what value of k will the pair of equations $x + 2y - 3 = 0$ and $5x + ky + 7 = 0$ have no solution?
A. 3 B. 10 C. 1 D. –1

68. $6\tan^2\theta - \frac{6}{\cos^2\theta} = ...$.
A. –1 B. 6 C. –6 D. 1

69. What type of number is $3 + 2\sqrt{3}$?
A. Irrational B. Rational
C. Prime D. Natural

70. The distance between the two points A (1, 1) and B (2, 3) in a plane will be ....
A. $\sqrt{6}$ B. $\sqrt{5}$
C. $2\sqrt{2}$ D. None of these

SCIENCE

71. What is the process of using natural resources without destroying them?
A. Sustainable management
B. Overexploitation
C. Mining
D. Extraction

72. Which of the following bacteria is associated with the roots of legumes?
A. Nostoc
B. Clostridium
C. Rhizobium
D. Spirogyra

61. C	**62.** D	**63.** B	**64.** C	**65.** C	**66.** C
67. B	**68.** C	**69.** A	**70.** B	**71.** A	**72.** C

73. Which of the following mirrors is used in the headlight of a car?

A. Concave mirror
B. Convex mirror
C. Plane mirror
D. Plane/Convex mirror

74. To which phylum does the cuttlefish belong?

A. Mollusca B. Echinodermata
C. Chordata D. Annelida

75. The study of the distribution of plants and animals worldwide is called:

A. Biogeography
B. Paleontology
C. Comparative anatomy
D. Molecular biology

76. When water freezes at 0°C to form ice at the same temperature of 0°C, it:

A. absorbs some heat
B. releases some heat
C. neither absorbs nor releases heat
D. absorbs 3.34×10^5 J/kg of heat

77. A student wants to extract energy from fossil fuels. Which process will help him extract energy from fossil fuels?

A. Burning
B. Crystallization
C. Condensation
D. Distillation

78. Which of the following gases is released when ethanol reacts with sodium?

A. CO_2 B. H_2
C. O_2 D. N_2

79. Which of these diseases is related to the Coronavirus?

A. MERS
B. SARS
C. Both
D. None of these

80. Name the organs that make up the excretory system in humans:

A. Two kidneys
B. Two ureters
C. Bladder and urethra
D. All of these

81. Identify the set of plant micronutrients (nutrients required by plants in small quantities) from the following:

A. Copper, Phosphorus, Calcium
B. Sulfur, Aluminum, Chlorine
C. Zinc, Iron, Manganese
D. Potassium, Magnesium, Copper

82. In a circle of radius r, the angular velocity of a body moving with constant speed v is given by:

A. $\frac{v^2}{r}$ B. $v.r.$
C. $\frac{v}{r}$ D. $\frac{r}{v}$

83. A pH value less than 7 indicates that the solution is:

A. Acidic B. Alkaline
C. Neutral D. No effect

84. Which of the following is **not** an element?

A. Marble B. Oxygen
C. Zinc D. Bromine

73. A	**74.** A	**75.** A	**76.** B	**77.** A	**78.** B
79. C	**80.** D	**81.** C	**82.** C	**83.** A	**84.** A

85. Dry ice on heating will turn into:
A. Liquid CO_2 B. Gaseous CO_2
C. Water D. Water vapor

86. Which of these are exothermic processes?
(*i*) Reaction of quicklime with water
(*ii*) Dilution of acid
(*iii*) Evaporation of water
(*iv*) Sublimation of camphor (crystals)
A. (*i*) and (*ii*) B. (*ii*) and (*iii*)
C. (*i*) and (*iv*) D. (*ii*) and (*iv*)

87. The currently accepted value of 'G' is approximately:
A. 6.673×10^{-11} Nm^2 kg^{-2}
B. 6.73×10^{11} Nm^2 kg^{-2}
C. 6.73×10^{11} Nm^2 kg^2
D. 9.8 ms^2

88. In which district of Bihar is the Valmiki Nagar Wildlife Sanctuary located?
A. West Champaran
B. East Champaran
C. Patna
D. Gaya

89. An object floats in water but sinks in coconut oil. The density of the object is:
A. Greater than the density of the oil..
B. Less than the density of water.
C. Both are true.
D. It is not possible to say anything based on the available information.

90. The oxides of aluminum and zinc are:
A. Acidic B. Amphoteric
C. Basic D. Neutral

SOCIAL STUDIES

91. Which of the following states has the largest area under permanent forests?
A. Nagaland
B. Assam
C. Madhya Pradesh
D. Kerala

92. When natural substances change form and become resources, they are called:
A. Renewable resources
B. Non-renewable resources
C. Man-made resources
D. Conventional resources

93. Which food industry is prominent among the agro-based industries in Bihar?
A. Spice industry
B. Pulses industry
C. Sugarcane industry
D. Grain-based industry

94. Which Governor General declared that Awadh was being misgoverned and that British rule was needed to ensure proper administration?
A. Lord Ripon
B. Lord Canning
C. Lord Dalhousie
D. Lord Mountbatten

85. B	**86.** A	**87.** A	**88.** A	**89.** C
90. B	**91.** C	**92.** C	**93.** D	**94.** C

95. The rearing of silkworms for the production of silk threads is known as:

A. Sericulture B. Aquaculture
C. Apiculture D. Pisciculture

96. Social outcomes cover areas such as:

(*i*) Dignity and freedom of citizens
(*ii*) Untouchability and discrimination
(*iii*) Gender equality
(*iv*) Prohibition of child labor

A. (*i*), (*iii*) and (*iv*)
B. (*ii*), (*i*) and (*iv*)
C. (*ii*) and (*iv*)
D. Only (*i*)

97. Where is the headquarters of East Central Railway located?

A. Hajipur
B. Gorakhpur
C. Bhubaneswar
D. Kolkata-Howrah

98. Columbus searched for someone to finance his westward journey for many years. Which country and leaders finally financed him?

A. His mother
B. King Ferdinand and Queen Elizabeth of Italy
C. Leif Erikson
D. King Ferdinand and Queen Isabella of Spain

99. When was the first non-Congress government formed at the Centre in India?

A. 1967 B. 1977
C. 1989 D. 1991

100. In which state is the Kakrapar Atomic Power Station located?

A. Maharashtra
B. Andhra Pradesh
C. Karnataka
D. Gujarat

101. What is the term of office of the members of the Rajya Sabha?

A. 4 years B. 5 years
C. 6 years D. 2 years

102. Who is the guardian of the Constitution in India?

A. President of India
B. Parliament
C. Election Commission
D. Supreme Court

103. The distinctiveness of tribal society is attributed to:

(*a*) The prevalence of the caste system
(*b*) The practice of various tribal religions, different from other prevalent religions
(*c*) The use of a distinct language
(*d*) The less pronounced presence of social hierarchy

Choose the correct answer:

A. (*b*), (*c*) and (*d*)
B. (*a*), (*b*) and (*d*)
C. (*a*), (*b*), (*c*) and (*d*)
D. (*a*), (*b*) and (*c*)

104. In which district of Bihar is the Durgavati Reservoir Project located?

A. Rohtas B. Kaimur
C. Gaya D. Patna

105. Where did the Enclosure Movement take place?

A. France B. Russia
C. England D. Germany

95. A	**96.** A	**97.** A	**98.** D	**99.** B	**100.** D
101. C	**102.** D	**103.** A	**104.** B	**105.** C	

106. In which year was the Imperial Ottawa Conference held?
A. 1928 B. 1929
C. 1930 D. 1932

107. The person who brought people from the villages, ensured jobs for them, helped them settle in cities, and provided them with money when needed, was called:
A. Stapler B. Fuller
C. Gomasta D. Jobber

108. Who was the owner of the land in the feudal system?
A. Feudal Lord B. Farmer
C. King D. Craftsman

109. Which of the following statements is true?
A. In a democracy, the opinions of the majority and the minority are not permanent.
B. In a democracy, it is also essential that the rule of the majority does not become the rule of the majority community based on religion, race, or linguistic group.
C. Democracy remains a democracy only as long as every citizen has the opportunity to be in the majority at some point.
D. All of the above

110. In which state is the Simlipal Biosphere Reserve located?
A. Bihar B. Jharkhand
C. Odisha D. Madhya Pradesh

LOGICAL AND ANALYTICAL ABILITY

111. Which letter is 4 letters to the right of the letter immediately preceding W?
A. R B. S
C. T D. U

112. If the LCM and HCF of two numbers are equal, then the numbers must be:
A. Prime numbers
B. Composite numbers
C. Equal
D. Co-prime numbers

113. Which letter is the 7th letter to the right of the letter that is the 13th letter to your left?
A. V B. U
C. T D. S

114. Aruna is 12th in a class of forty-six. What will be her rank from the last?
A. 33 B. 34 C. 35 D. 37

115. If in a code SPIDER is written as PSDIRE, then how will COMMON be written in the same code?
A. OCMMON B. OCMOMN
C. OCMMNO D. OCOMMO

116. Find the odd element from the options given below:
A. 11 B. 13 C. 15 D. 17

117. If in a code language DOG is called 4157, then what will MAN be called in the same language?
A. 13114 B. 131114
C. 14113 D. 13141

106. D	**107.** D	**108.** C	**109.** D	**110.** C	**111.** B
112. C	**113.** C	**114.** C	**115.** C	**116.** C	**117.** A

118. A girl counted the fingers of her left hand in this way: She started by calling the thumb 1, the index finger 2, the middle finger 3, the ring finger 4, the little finger 5, and then continued in the reverse direction calling the ring finger 6, the middle finger 7, and so on. She counted up to 1994. On which finger did she finish counting?
A. Thumb
B. Index finger
C. Middle finger
D. Ring finger

119. Choose the word that is different from the others.
A. Rooster
B. Snake
C. Swan
D. Crocodile

120. Which letter comes exactly in the middle of H and P?
A. K B. L C. M D. N

EXPLANATORY ANSWERS

1. दी गई पंक्ति *'शोभित मंच की अवली बजदन्त मयी छवि उज्जलु छाई।'* में मत्तगयन्द (सवैया) छन्द है।
मत्तगयन्द एक वर्णिक छन्द है। इसके प्रत्येक चरण में 23 वर्ण होते हैं। इस छन्द का गण-विधान सात भगण (S I I) और अंत में दो गुरु (S S) का होता है।
जब इस पंक्ति के वर्णों की गणना की जाती है, तो कुल 23 वर्ण प्राप्त होते हैं, जिससे यह स्पष्ट रूप से मत्तगयन्द सवैया सिद्ध होता है।

2. वाक्य *'इस बुढ़िया को न सताओ, यह तो निरी गाय है।'* में लक्षणा शब्द-शक्ति का प्रयोग हुआ है। यहाँ 'गाय' शब्द का अभिधा अर्थ (चौपाया पशु) अभिप्रेत नहीं है। यह शब्द बुढ़िया के सीधेपन, भोलेपन और अहिंसक स्वभाव को प्रकट करता है। जब मुख्य अर्थ में बाधा आने पर रूढ़ि या प्रयोजन के आधार पर दूसरा अर्थ ग्रहण किया जाता है, तब वहाँ लक्षणा शब्द-शक्ति होती है।

3. रस-सिद्धान्त के अनुसार *'भाव जिसके हृदय में रहते हैं'* उसे आश्रय कहा जाता है। आश्रय वही पात्र होता है जिसके भीतर स्थायी भाव स्थित रहते हैं, जैसे—नायक, नायिका या कोई भी भाववान पात्र। उसी के हृदय में भाव उत्पन्न होकर रस की निष्पत्ति करते हैं।

4. 'मनुज' शब्द का अर्थ मनुष्य है। शास्त्रीय दृष्टि से मनुष्य को मनु की संतान, मानव तथा मनुष्य—तीनों रूपों में परिभाषित किया गया है। इसलिए 'मनुज' के सभी दिए गए अर्थ सही हैं।

5. *'विकसते मुरझाने को फूल, दीप जलता होने को मंद।*
बरसते भर जाने को मेघ, उदय होता छिपने को चाँद।'
इस पंक्ति में परस्पर विरोधी स्थितियाँ एक साथ प्रस्तुत की गई हैं—जैसे विकसना-मुरझाना, जलना-मंद होना, उदय-छिपना। अर्थात् विरोध होने पर भी भाव की संगति बनी रहती है, इसलिए यहाँ विरोधाभास अलंकार है।

118. B **119.** A **120.** B

6. वाक्य *'राम ने ऐसी कहानी सुनाई कि करन रो पड़ा।'* में प्रधान वाक्य के साथ आश्रित उपवाक्य जुड़ा है।
संयुक्त वाक्य में दो स्वतंत्र वाक्य समुच्चय-बोधक अव्यय 'और' से जुड़े होते हैं। इसका सही संयुक्त रूप है—*राम ने कहानी सुनाई और करन रो पड़ा।*

7. रूपक अलंकार में उपमेय पर उपमान का सीधा आरोप होता है।
'आए महंत वसंत' (वसंत को महंत कहा गया),
'मन का मनका का फेर' (मन को मनका कहा गया),
'चरण कमल बंदों हरिराई' (चरण को कमल कहा गया) तीनों में रूपक अलंकार है।

8. *'निरस्त करना'* का अर्थ है किसी आदेश, निर्णय, अधिकार या वैधता को समाप्त करना या रद्द कर देना। प्रशासनिक एवं विधिक अंग्रेजी में इसके लिए Revoke शब्द का प्रयोग किया जाता है।
अन्य विकल्प जैसे Void (अवैध घोषित करना) या Revalidate (पुनः वैध करना) अर्थ की दृष्टि से उपयुक्त नहीं हैं।

9. *'पूत कपूत तो क्यों धन संचय।*
पूत सपूत तो क्यों धन संचय।'
इन पंक्तियों में पूत और धन संचय शब्दों की पुनरावृत्ति समान रूप में हुई है, किंतु भाव भिन्न है। शब्दों की आवृत्ति अर्थ-भेद के साथ होने के कारण यहाँ लाटानुप्रास अलंकार है।

10. जहाँ उपमेय को देखकर पाठक के मन में एक से अधिक उपमानों का भ्रम उत्पन्न हो जाता है, वहाँ भ्रान्तिमान अलंकार होता है। इस अलंकार में वास्तविक उपमान स्पष्ट नहीं होता और भ्रम की स्थिति बनी रहती है। यही इसकी प्रमुख पहचान है।

11. *'पुत्र-पुत्री'* में दोनों पद समान अधिकार वाले हैं और उनके बीच **और** का भाव निहित है। ऐसे समास में कोई भी पद प्रधान नहीं होता। इस प्रकार का समास द्वन्द्व समास कहलाता है।

12. व्याकरण में वाच्य का शाब्दिक अर्थ है—जो कहा जाए या जिस विषय में कथन किया जाए। यह बताता है कि वाक्य में कर्ता, कर्म या भाव में से किसकी प्रधानता है। इसलिए वाच्य का सही अर्थ बोलने का विषय है।

13. *'मानों झूम रहे हो तरु भी, मंद पवन की झोकों से।'*
यहाँ 'मानों' शब्द के द्वारा धरती और वृक्षों में मानवीय क्रिया की संभावना/कल्पना की गई है। जहाँ किसी वस्तु में *मानो, जैसे, जान पड़ता है* आदि शब्दों से कल्पना व्यक्त की जाए, वहाँ उत्प्रेक्षा अलंकार होता है।

14. वाक्य *'मेरे चाहने के अनुसार सब कुछ हो रहा था।'* का मिश्र वाक्य वह होगा जिसमें एक प्रधान और एक आश्रित उपवाक्य हो। *'मैं जैसा चाह रहा था, वैसा ही सब कुछ होता जा रहा था।'* में 'जैसा-वैसा' के माध्यम से आश्रित उपवाक्य जुड़ा है। इसलिए यही सही मिश्र वाक्य है।

15. *'रहिमन जो गति दीप की, कुल कपूत गति सोय।*
बारे उजियारै लगै, बढ़ै अंधेरो होय।'
इन पंक्तियों में 'बारे' (जलाने पर/बचपन में) और 'बढ़ै' (बुझने पर/बड़ा होने पर) शब्दों के एक से अधिक अर्थ निकलते हैं। ये दोनों अर्थ दीपक और कुपुत्र—दोनों पर समान रूप से लागू होते हैं। एक ही शब्द से अनेक अर्थ ग्रहण होने के कारण यहाँ श्लेष अलंकार है।

16. खड़ी बोली के सर्वप्रथम लोकप्रिय कवि के रूप में अयोध्या सिंह उपाध्याय 'हरिऔध' को माना जाता है। उन्होंने खड़ी बोली को साहित्यिक गरिमा और व्यापक लोकप्रियता प्रदान की। उनकी रचनाओं ने खड़ी बोली को काव्य-भाषा के रूप में सुदृढ़ आधार दिया।

17. वाक्य-शुद्धता की दृष्टि से विकल्पों का परीक्षण करने पर—

(A) में वाक्य-रचना अस्पष्ट और दोषपूर्ण है।

(B) में क्रिया-प्रयोग अशुद्ध है (रोने लगा के साथ *जोर-जोर से* का प्रयोग असंगत)।

(C) में *भूले होंगे* अनुमानसूचक है, जो संदर्भ में अशुद्ध है।

(D) *'इस किताब का क्या मूल्य है?'* सरल, स्पष्ट और व्याकरण की दृष्टि से पूर्णतः शुद्ध है।

18. अंग्रेजी का पारिभाषिक शब्द ALLOTMENT का अर्थ होता है—किसी वस्तु, भूमि या अधिकार का आवंटन/वितरण। हिंदी प्रशासनिक भाषा में इसके लिए सर्वमान्य शब्द आवंटन है। अन्य विकल्प अर्थ की दृष्टि से मेल नहीं खाते।

19. 'परीक्षा' शब्द का सही संधि-विच्छेद परि + ईक्षा है।

यहाँ परि उपसर्ग है और ईक्षा धातु से बना शब्द है, जिसका अर्थ है—देखना या निरीक्षण करना। स्वर संधि के नियम से परि + ईक्षा → परीक्षा बनता है।

20. अन्वय की दृष्टि से वाक्य में कर्ता-क्रिया का सामंजस्य आवश्यक होता है। यहाँ *'सिलाई करना'* क्रियापद है, जो पुल्लिंग एकवचन है, इसलिए उसके साथ **आता** का प्रयोग सही होगा। अतः *'गीता को सिलाई करना नहीं आता।'* व्याकरण की दृष्टि से शुद्ध वाक्य है।

21. *'विषय-वारि मन-मीन भिन्न नहिं होत कबहुं पल एक।'*

इस पंक्ति में 'विषय' को 'वारि (जल)' और 'मन' को 'मीन (मछली)' के रूप में प्रस्तुत किया गया है। यहाँ उपमेय और उपमान में कोई भेद नहीं दिखाया गया, बल्कि सीधा आरोप किया गया है। उपमेय पर उपमान का अभेद आरोप होने के कारण यहाँ रूपक अलंकार है।

22. *'आँसू पोंछना'* मुहावरे का अर्थ है—किसी दुःखी व्यक्ति को सांत्वना देना या दिलासा देना। इसका प्रयोग उस स्थिति में होता है जब कोई व्यक्ति दुःख या कष्ट में हो। अतः इसका सही अर्थ दिलासा देना है।

23. वाक्य-शुद्धता की दृष्टि से विकल्पों का परीक्षण करने पर—

(A) में *है* के स्थान पर *हैं* होना चाहिए।

(B) और (D) वाक्य शुद्ध हैं।

(C) में *राम और राम का पुत्र* में द्विरुक्ति और रचना-दोष है।

इसलिए (C) अशुद्ध वाक्य है।

24. वाक्य *'राहुल फुटबॉल खेलकर चला गया।'* में रेखांकित अंश 'फुटबॉल खेलकर चला गया' एक साथ मिलकर क्रिया का कार्य कर रहा है। यहाँ मुख्य क्रिया 'चला गया' है तथा 'फुटबॉल खेलकर' पूर्वकालिक/सहायक क्रिया के रूप में प्रयुक्त है। जब एक से अधिक पद मिलकर क्रिया का बोध कराते हैं, तब उसे क्रिया पदबंध कहा जाता है।

25. 'घुड़दौड़' शब्द में घोड़े और दौड़ के बीच संबंध 'की' का भाव है। अर्थात् घोड़े की होने वाली दौड़।

इसका सही समास-विग्रह है—घोड़े की दौड़।

26. The sentence *"The child looks ___ if he were hungry."* expresses a comparison or an imaginary condition.

The correct structure used to show such a condition is "as if".
Hence, the suitable word to fill in the blank is **as.**

27. The preposition "beside" means *next to* or *by the side of.* It is often confused with "besides", which means in addition to.
Therefore, the correct meaning of beside is by the side of.

28. In the sentence *"The ball rolled ___ the lawn.",* the action shows movement from one side of the lawn to the other. The preposition "across" is used to indicate movement over a surface covering the whole area.
Hence, across is the most appropriate option.

29. The question asks to identify the correctly spelled word. Among the given options, "Summary" is the standard and correct English spelling.
All other options contain spelling errors and are therefore incorrect.

30. In changing the sentence from direct to indirect speech, the modal verb "must" often changes to "had to" when reporting past statements.
The reporting verb "said" is in the past tense, so the tense must shift accordingly.
Thus, the correct indirect form is *"She had to apply for the job."*

31. The sentence is a second conditional, which is used for unreal or hypothetical situations in the present. In second conditional sentences, the simple past tense is used in the if-clause.
Therefore, *"didn't"* correctly completes the sentence.

32. The sentence *"By the time she was fifteen"* clearly refers to an action completed before a point in the past. For such situations, the past perfect tense is used. Therefore, *"had become"* is grammatically correct.

33. The sentence shows a contrast between disagreements and friendship. The word "Despite" correctly expresses contrast and is followed by a noun phrase *(our constant disagreements)*. Other options do not fit grammatically or semantically.

34. In this question, subject–verb agreement must be correct.
In option (D), *"Neeta"* is singular, but the verb "are" is plural, which makes the sentence incorrect.
All other options maintain proper agreement.

35. The phrase "addicted to" means having a habit or strong dependence on something. It is commonly used to describe repeated or compulsive involvement with an activity or substance.
Among the given options, "habituated to something" conveys the same meaning most accurately.

36. The question specifically asks for the past continuous tense form of the verb *"plan"*.
The past continuous tense is formed using was/were + present participle (-ing form).
Since *"Monica"* is a third-person singular subject, the correct auxiliary verb is was, and *plan* becomes *planning*.

37. In the sentence *"To swim every day is good for health.",* the underlined phrase *"To swim"* functions as a subject.

The structure "to + verb" is known as an infinitive.
Hence, the underlined words belong to the infinitive verb category.

38. To form a meaningful sentence, the main clause must come first, followed by the infinitive phrases. The correct logical order is: *"he ordered him"* → *"to leave the room"* → *"and forbade him"* → *"to return"*.
This sequence forms a grammatically and semantically correct sentence.

39. The direct question *"Are you interested in the scheme?"* changes into an indirect question using if/whether.
Since the reporting verb *asked* is in the past tense, "are" changes to "was", and "you" changes to "I". Thus, the correct indirect form is *"if I was interested in the scheme."*

40. The given sentence is in the simple past tense, so its passive form must also be in the simple past.
The correct passive structure is was/were + past participle, with the time expression last night retained. Hence, *"Last night some thieves were arrested by the police."* is the correct answer.

41. The sentence *"If I forget her birthday, Ravi gets upset."* expresses a general truth or habitual result.
Both the *if-clause* and the *main clause* are in the simple present tense.
Such sentences are classified as zero conditional.

42. The sentence *"We ____ afford a new car this year."* is most naturally completed with a modal showing ability/financial capacity.
"Can" expresses that ability (i.e., we have enough money / we are able to afford it).
"May/Might" indicate mere possibility, and "should" shows advice, not affordability.

43. **Round brackets** ( ) are most commonly used to add extra or explanatory information in the middle of a sentence.
Square brackets and braces are used in special or technical contexts.
Therefore, the generally used bracket for insertion is the round bracket.

44. In language learning, listening and reading involve receiving information. They do not require producing language, so they are called receptive skills.
Speaking and writing, on the other hand, are productive skills.

45. The sentence *"An empty vessel ____ much."* follows a well-known proverb and is in the simple present tense.
The subject *"An empty vessel"* is singular, so it requires a singular verb. Therefore, the correct verb form is "sounds".

46. The given data is: 1, 5, 3, 4, 7, 4, X, 7
Here, 'mode' means the number that appears most frequently.
Currently, 4 appears twice and 7 also appears twice. If the mode is to be 4, then the frequency of 4 must be the highest.
For this, if we take X = 4, then 4 will appear three times, while no other number will appear three times.
Therefore, the mode will be 4.

47. The radius of the circle $r = 10$ cm. The chord subtends a right angle at the center,
Therefore, the angle at the center $= 90°$
Area of the minor segment
= Area (sector) − Area (triangle)
Area of the sector

$$= \frac{90°}{360°} \times \pi r^2$$

$$= \frac{1}{4} \times 3.14 \times 100$$

$$= 78.5 \text{ cm}^2$$

Area of the triangle

$$= \frac{1}{2} \times r \times r = \frac{1}{2} \times 10 \times 10$$

$= 50 \text{ cm}^2$

Area of the minor segment
$= 78.5 - 50 = 28.5 \text{ cm}^2$.

48. In a circle C(o, r), P is the midpoint of the chord AB. It is a known property that the line joining the center to the midpoint of the chord is perpendicular to the chord. Therefore, OP ⊥ AB.
The angle between OP and PA is ∠OPA, which will be a right angle. Therefore, ∠OPA = 90°.

49. The polynomial is
$f(x) = 2x^3 - 3kx^2 + 4x - 5$
The sum of the zeros of a cubic polynomial $ax^3 + bx^2 + cx + d$ is $-\frac{b}{a}$

Here $a = 2$ and $b = -3k$

Sum of the zeros $= -\frac{(-3k)}{2} = \frac{3k}{2}$

Given that the sum of the zeros = 6

Therefore, $\frac{3k}{2} = 6$

$\Rightarrow \quad 3k = 12$

$\Rightarrow \quad k = 4$.

50. The area of a parallelogram
= base × height.
Here, the length is given as l and the width as b,
Therefore, Area $= l \times b$.

51. The ratio in which the line joining the points A(−3, −4) and B(1, −2) intersects the y-axis is found using the section formula for internal division.
Let the point P on the y-axis divide the line segment AB in the ratio $m : n$
The x-coordinate of any point on the y-axis is 0.

Therefore, $0 = \frac{m(1) + n(-3)}{m + n}$

$m - 3n = 0$

$\Rightarrow \quad m = 3n$

This gives the ratio $m : n = 3 : 1$.

52. In ΔABC, DE || AB.
Therefore, by Thales' theorem,

$$\frac{CD}{DA} = \frac{CE}{EB}$$

Given, CD = 3 cm, CE = 4 cm, BE = 6 cm.

$$\frac{3}{DA} = \frac{4}{6} = \frac{2}{3}$$

$$3 \times 3 = 2 \times DA$$

$$\Rightarrow \quad DA = \frac{9}{2}$$

$$= 4.5 \text{ cm.}$$

53. The roots of the quadratic equation $ax^2 + bx + c = 0$ are $\sin\alpha$ and $\cos\alpha$.

Sum of the roots $= \frac{-b}{a}$

$$\sin\alpha + \cos\alpha = \frac{-b}{a}$$

Squaring both sides:

$\sin^2 \alpha + \cos^2 \alpha + 2 \sin \alpha \cos \alpha$

$= \frac{b^2}{a^2}$

$$1 + 2 \sin \alpha \cos \alpha = \frac{b^2}{a^2}$$

Product of the roots

$$= \frac{c}{a} = \sin \alpha \cos \alpha$$

$$1+2\frac{c}{a} = \frac{b^2}{a^2}$$

$\Rightarrow \quad b^2 = a^2 + 2ac.$

54. For the quadratic equation $2x^2 - 6x + p = 0$ to have real and unequal roots, the discriminant must be positive.

$$D = b^2 - 4ac$$
$$= (-6)^2 - 4(2)(p)$$
$$= 36 - 8p$$

For real and unequal roots,

$$36 - 8p > 0$$
$$\Rightarrow \quad 8p < 36$$
$$\Rightarrow \quad p < \frac{9}{2}.$$

55. The sides of a triangle are in the ratio 12 : 14 : 25.

Let the sides be $= 12k, 14k, 25k$

Perimeter $= (12 + 14 + 25)k$
$= 51k = 25.5$

$$k = \frac{25.5}{51} = 0.5$$

The sides will be: 6 cm, 7 cm and 12.5 cm.

The longest side = 12.5 cm.

56. If a is a rational number, then a can be written as $a = \frac{p}{q}$ (where p and q are integers and $q \neq 0$). Then

$$\frac{1}{a} = \frac{q}{p}$$

Which is again the ratio of two integers.

Therefore, $\frac{1}{a}$ will also be a rational number.

57. In the given figure, OPBQ is a quadrant with center O and a square OABC is inscribed within it.

$$OA = 20 \text{ cm}$$

$\Rightarrow$ Side of the square = 20 cm.

Therefore, the radius of the quadrant,

$$r = OB$$
$$= \sqrt{20^2 + 20^2} = 20\sqrt{2} \text{ cm.}$$

Area of the quadrant $= \frac{1}{4}\pi r^2$

$$= \frac{1}{4} \times 3.14 \times \left(20\sqrt{2}\right)^2$$

$$= \frac{1}{4} \times 3.14 \times 800 = 628$$

Area of the square

$= 20 \times 20 = 400$

Shaded area

$= 628 - 400 = 228 \text{ cm}^2.$

58. Formula for compound interest:

$$A = P\left(1+\frac{r}{100}\right)^n$$

$$1852.20 = 1600(1.05)^n$$

$$\Rightarrow \quad \frac{1852.20}{1600} = 1.157625$$

$$(1.05)^3 = 1.157625$$

Therefore, $n = 3$ years.

59. There is no place value system in Roman numerals. This is why performing calculations with large numbers becomes difficult with Roman numerals, whereas calculations are simpler with Hindu-Arabic numerals due to their place value system.

Roman numerals do not utilize place value, therefore performing calculations using these numerals is difficult.

60. In the given expression,

$9\sec^2 A - 9\tan^2 A$

$= 9(\sec^2 A - \tan^2 A)$

According to the trigonometric identity,

$\sec^2 A - \tan^2 A = 1$

Therefore, the entire expression: 9×1 will be equal to 9.

61. Raj's profit is ₹ 63.

Let the cost price of the book be CP.

According to 10% profit,

Profit = 10% of CP

= 63

$\Rightarrow$ CP = 630

Selling price after 23% discount

= 77% of the marked price (MP)

Because Selling Price

= Cost Price + Profit

= 630 + 63 = 693

$0.77 \times MP = 693$

$\Rightarrow MP = \frac{693}{0.77} =$ ₹ 900.

62. To explain the concept of fractions to children, a teaching aid that allows parts to be seen and understood directly is most suitable. Cuisenaire rods are of different lengths and colors, which can provide a concrete and clear understanding of fractions.

63. $\frac{DE}{PQ} = \frac{EF}{RP}$

Step 1: Determine the corresponding vertices from the corresponding angles:

$\angle D = \angle Q \Rightarrow D \leftrightarrow Q,$

and $\angle E = \angle R \Rightarrow E \leftrightarrow R.$

Then the remaining vertex $F \leftrightarrow P$ (because the sum of the angles of a triangle is 180°).

Step 2: Therefore, the order of similarity is $\Delta DEF \sim \Delta QRP$

$(D \leftrightarrow Q, E \leftrightarrow R, F \leftrightarrow P)$

Therefore, the corresponding sides will be:

$DE \leftrightarrow QR, EF \leftrightarrow RP, DF \leftrightarrow QP$

Step 3: In similar triangles, the ratios of corresponding sides are equal:

$$\frac{DE}{PQ} = \frac{EF}{RP} = \frac{DF}{QP}$$

Now, in option (B), $\frac{DE}{PQ}$ is taken, whereas the corresponding side of DE is QR, not PQ. Therefore, the ratio in (B) does not follow the corresponding-ratio rule of similarity, and this statement is not true.

64. In the given figure, $m \,||\, n$ and l is a transversal. $\angle 1$ is the exterior angle on the left side of the transversal on the upper line m. Its corresponding angle on the line n below is $\angle 5$. If parallel lines are intersected by a transversal, then the corresponding angles are equal.

65. Let the number of 10 paise coins be x and the number of 30 paise coins be y.

Total coins, $x + y = 40$

Total value = ₹ 9 = 900 paise,

Therefore,

$10x + 30y = 900$

$\Rightarrow x + 3y = 90$

From the first equation,

$x = 40 - y$

$40 - y + 3y = 90$

$\Rightarrow 40 + 2y = 90$

$\Rightarrow y = 25$

$x = 40 - 25 = 15$

Therefore, the number of 10 paise coins = 15.

66. If the probability of an event is p, then the probability of its complementary event is obtained by subtracting p from the total probability 1.
Complementary probability $= 1 - p$

67. The equations are:

$$x + 2y - 3 = 0 \text{ and}$$
$$5x + ky + 7 = 0$$

The condition for no solution is:

$$\frac{a_1}{a_2} = \frac{b_1}{b_2} \neq \frac{c_1}{c_2}$$

Here, $\frac{1}{5} = \frac{2}{k}$

$\Rightarrow k = 10$

And $\frac{-3}{7} \neq \frac{1}{5}$

The condition is satisfied.

68. $6\tan^2\theta - \frac{6}{\cos^2\theta} = 6(\tan^2\theta - \sec^2\theta)$

We know, $\sec^2\theta - \tan^2\theta = 1$

$\Rightarrow \tan^2\theta - \sec^2\theta = -1$

Therefore, the value is

$$6(-1) = -6.$$

69. $\sqrt{5}$ is an irrational number. Adding $2\sqrt{5}$ an irrational number to a rational number 3 results in an irrational number.

70. According to the distance formula:

$$AB = \sqrt{(2-1)^2 + (3-1)^2}$$
$$= \sqrt{1+4} = \sqrt{5}.$$

71. The use of natural resources in a way that ensures their availability for future generations is called sustainable management. This process involves the judicious, balanced, and long-term use of resources. It maintains a balance between environmental protection and development.

72. Rhizobium is a bacterium that lives in the roots of legume plants. This bacterium fixes atmospheric nitrogen, making it available to the plants. This is why it helps in increasing soil fertility.

73. A concave mirror is used in car headlights. The concave mirror converts the light from the bulb into parallel rays. This allows the light to spread over a long distance with intensity.

74. Cuttlefish is an organism belonging to the phylum Mollusca. It has a soft body, a mantle, and a well-developed nervous system. It belongs to the class Cephalopoda, like octopuses and squids.

75. The study of the geographical distribution of plants and animals worldwide is called biogeography. This subject helps in understanding why and how different species are found in different regions. It is related to climate, topography, and evolutionary history.

76. When water freezes at 0°C and turns into ice at 0°C, its temperature does not change. During this phase transition, the water releases heat in the form of latent heat. This is called the latent heat of freezing.

77. To obtain energy from fossil fuels, they are burned. In the burning process, the chemical energy of the fuel is converted into heat and light energy. Therefore, the correct process for extracting energy from fossil fuels is combustion.

78. When ethanol (C_2H_5OH) reacts with sodium (Na), sodium ethoxide is formed, and hydrogen gas is released. This is a displacement reaction in which sodium displaces the hydrogen of ethanol. Therefore, the gas released is hydrogen (H_2).

79. Both MERS and SARS are diseases belonging to the coronavirus family. SARS (Severe Acute Respiratory Syndrome) and MERS (Middle East Respiratory Syndrome) affect the respiratory system. The viruses responsible for both these diseases are coronaviruses.

80. The human excretory system is made up of several organs. It includes two kidneys, two ureters, the bladder, and the urethra. All these organs work together to remove waste products from the body.

81. Plant micronutrients are those that plants need in very small quantities. Zinc (Zn), iron (Fe), and manganese (Mn) are examples of such micronutrients. They assist in enzyme activity, chlorophyll formation, and growth.

82. The angular velocity (ω) of a body moving at a constant speed v in a circle is determined by the ratio of the linear velocity and the radius.
The formula is: $\omega = v/r$
Therefore, the correct option is v/r.

83. A pH value less than 7 means that the solution has a higher concentration of hydrogen ions (H^+). Such a solution is called acidic.
pH = 7 is neutral, and a pH greater than 7 is alkaline.

84. An element is a substance that cannot be broken down into simpler substances by chemical methods.
Marble is a form of calcium carbonate ($CaCO_3$), which is a compound, not an element.
Oxygen, zinc, and bromine are all elements.

85. Dry ice is solid carbon dioxide (CO_2). When heated, it changes directly into gaseous CO_2 without becoming a liquid. This process is called sublimation.

86. An exothermic process is one in which heat is released. The reaction of quicklime (CaO) with water and the dilution of acid both release heat. Evaporation and the sublimation of camphor are endothermic processes.

87. 6.673×10^{-11} Nm^2 kg^{-2}.

88. Valmiki Nagar Wildlife Sanctuary is a major wildlife sanctuary in the state of Bihar. It is located near the India-Nepal border and is extremely important from the point of view of biodiversity. This sanctuary is located in the West Champaran district.

89. If an object floats in water, its density is less than that of water. And if the same object sinks in coconut oil, its density is greater than that of the oil. Therefore, both the given statements are correct.

90. Aluminum oxide (Al_2O_3) and zinc oxide (ZnO) both react with acids and bases. This type of oxide is called amphoteric. For this reason, they are neither purely acidic nor purely basic.

91. The largest area of reserved forests in India is found in Madhya Pradesh. Madhya Pradesh is also called the 'Forest State of India'. The extent of forest cover and the state of forest conservation here are greater than in other states.

92. When natural substances are transformed into usable forms by humans and become resources, they are called man-made resources. For example, furniture from wood, steel from iron ore.

93. Bihar is a major rice and wheat producing state. For this reason, grain-based industries related to rice and wheat milling have developed extensively here. Although the pulse and sugarcane industries are also important, the grain-based industry is considered dominant in terms of economic contribution and expansion.

94. Before the annexation of Awadh (1856), the British government alleged that there was misgovernance there. Lord Dalhousie declared on this basis that British rule was necessary for proper administration. On this same logic, Awadh was annexed into the British Empire.

95. The process of rearing silkworms for the production of silk thread is called sericulture. In Hindi, it is called रेशम उत्पादन (resham utpadan). It is an agro-based industry.

96. Social outcomes relate to areas that promote equality and justice in society. These include issues such as the dignity and freedom of citizens, gender equality, and the prohibition of child labor. These are all key indicators of democratic and social development.

97. The East Central Railway was formed in 2002. The headquarters of this zone is located in Hajipur (Bihar). The administrative operations of the various divisions of the East Central Railway are managed from Hajipur.

98. Christopher Columbus sought financial support for a long time for his expedition to reach India from the west. Finally, King Ferdinand and Queen Isabella of Spain provided him with financial assistance. This support made Columbus's famous sea voyage in 1492 possible.

99. The first non-Congress government at the center in India was formed in 1977. This government was formed after the Janata Party's victory in the elections held after the Emergency. Before this, the Congress party had dominated the central government.

100. The Kakrapar Atomic Power Station is one of India's important nuclear power plants. It is located on the banks of the Tapi River and uses nuclear fuel for electricity generation. This plant is located in the state of Gujarat and makes a significant contribution to Gujarat's energy needs.

101. The Rajya Sabha is the upper house of the Indian Parliament and is a permanent house. Its members have a term of 6 years. One-third of its members retire every two years, ensuring the continuity of the house.

102. In India, the responsibility for interpreting, protecting, and defending the Constitution is entrusted to the Supreme Court. Due to its power of judicial review, it ensures that the actions of Parliament and the executive are in accordance with the Constitution. Therefore, it is called the guardian of the Constitution.

103. The main reasons for the distinctiveness of tribal society are:

- The practice of various tribal religions and beliefs,
- The use of their own distinct languages and dialects,
- And the less prevalent presence of social hierarchy and caste discrimination in society.

The traditional caste system is not considered a fundamental characteristic of tribal society.

104. The Durgavati Reservoir Project is a major irrigation project in Bihar. This project is built on the Durgavati River. This reservoir is located in Kaimur district and plays a significant role in agricultural irrigation.

105. The Enclosure Movement took place in England, Europe. Under this movement, the common land of farmers was enclosed and converted into private property. As a result, many farmers became landless, and migration to industrial cities increased.

106. The Imperial Ottawa Conference was held in 1932. This conference was held to promote trade cooperation and preferential treatment among the countries of the British Empire. Its objective was to deal with the effects of the Great Depression.

107. A person who brought people from rural areas, arranged jobs for them in cities, helped them settle down, and also provided money when needed, was called a jobber. This system was especially prevalent during the Industrial Revolution.

108. In the feudal system, the king was the main and ultimate owner of the land. The king granted large portions of his land to feudal lords in exchange for loyalty and military service. The feudal lords had the land cultivated by peasants, but they were not the ultimate owners of the land. Thus, the supreme authority over the land was considered to belong to the king.

109. In a democracy, the positions of the majority and minority are not permanent, as public opinion keeps changing. Furthermore, democracy ensures that the rule of the majority does not become oppressive on the basis of religion, race, or language. The opportunity for every citizen to be part of the majority at some point is a fundamental condition of democracy. Therefore, all the given statements are correct.

110. Similipal Biosphere Reserve is one of the major biosphere reserves in India. This area is famous for its biodiversity, wildlife, and Sal forests. Similipal Biosphere Reserve is located in the state of Odisha.

111. In the English alphabet, V comes immediately before W.
Now let's count 4 letters to the right of V:
V → W (1) → X (2) → Y (3) → Z (4)
Therefore, the correct letter is Z.

112. If the LCM and HCF of two numbers are the same, it means that both numbers are the same. Because for different numbers, the LCM is always greater than or equal to the HCF.
LCM = HCF is only possible when both numbers are equal.

113. First, find the letter that is 13th from your left.
Let's assume that letter is M (13th when counting from A).
Now, the 7th letter to the right of M will be:
M → N (1) → O (2) → P (3) → Q (4) → R (5) → S (6) → T (7)

114. Total students = 46 and Aruna's rank from the beginning = 12th.
Formula to find the rank from the end:
Rank from the end
= Total students – Rank from the beginning + 1
Therefore, 46 – 12 + 1 = 35
So, Aruna will be 35th from the end.

115. In the code SPIDER → PSIDRE, it means the letters are being swapped in this order:
Position (1, 2, 3, 4, 5, 6) → (2, 1, 4, 3, 6, 5)
That is, reversing in pairs.
Apply the same to
COMMON (C O M M O N)
(2, 1) = O C,
(4, 3) = M M,
(6, 5) = N O
⇒ OCMMNO.

116. 11, 13, and 17 are prime numbers. But 15 is not prime (it is divisible by 3 × 5), i.e., it is composite. Therefore, the odd element is 15.

117. Here, the letters in the code language are written using the serial number of the English alphabet
(A = 1, B = 2, etc.).
In DOG, D = 4, O = 15, G = 7
⇒ 4 15 7 are combined to form 4157.
Similarly, in MAN, M = 13, A = 1, N = 14
⇒ 13 1 14 ⇒ 13114.

118. The finger counting sequence goes back and forth:
Thumb (1) → Index finger (2) → Middle finger (3) → Ring finger (4) → Little finger (5) → Ring finger (6) → Middle finger (7) → Index finger (8) → Thumb (9)...
This sequence repeats in a cycle of 8.
For 1994, (1994 – 1) = 1993, and the remainder when 1993 is divided by 8 is 1, which corresponds to the index finger.

119. Among the given options, snake, swan, and crocodile—all three are related to water or aquatic/semi-aquatic habitats.
Snakes and crocodiles can swim in water, and a swan is an aquatic bird.
Whereas a rooster is primarily a terrestrial bird and its life cycle is not connected to water. Thus, the rooster/chicken is different from others based on its habitat.

120. In the English alphabet, the position of H is 8 and the position of P is 16.
The middle letter is (8 + 16)/2 = 12, and the 12th letter is L.
Therefore, L is exactly in the middle of H and P.

Previous Years' Paper

Bihar School Examination Board, Patna

Diploma in Elementary Education (D.El.Ed.)

Common Entrance Exam-2024

(Exam held on 23 April, 2024)

सामान्य हिन्दी

1. 'उज्ज्वल' में प्रयुक्त संधि का नाम है :

A. स्वर संधि B. व्यंजन संधि

C. विसर्ग संधि D. इनमें से कोई नहीं

2. किस शब्द में द्विगु समास नहीं है?

A. महाजन B. अठन्नी

C. नवरत्न D. पंचतत्व

3. 'दोपहर' में समास है :

A. द्विगु B. द्वन्द्व

C. कर्मधारय D. तत्पुरुष

4. पहली बोलती फिल्म 'आलम आरा' बनाने वाले फिल्मकार अर्देशिर एम. ईरानी थे। वे ही सवाक सिनेमा के नए दौर की शुरूआत कराने वाले निर्माता-निर्देशक थे। उन्होंने हॉलीवुड की 'शो बोट' फिल्म से प्रेरणा लेकर इस फिल्म का निर्माण किया था। इस फिल्म ने भारतीय सिनेमा जगत में क्रांति ला दी थी। उस समय न तो कोई गीतकार था और न कोई संगीतकार। उन्होंने फिल्म के लिए गानों की धुनें स्वयं ही चुनीं। इस फिल्म के संगीत में केवल तीन वाद्यों—तबला, हारमोनियम और वायलिन का प्रयोग किया गया। अर्देशिर की कंपनी ने भारतीय फिल्म उद्योग के लिए डेढ़ सौ से अधिक मूक और लगभग सौ सवाक फिल्में बनाईं। इस फिल्म ने भविष्य के कई स्टार और तकनीशियन भी दिए। इस फिल्म की नायिका जुबैदा और नायक विट्ठल थे। इनके अतिरिक्त इस फिल्म से सोहराब मोदी, पृथ्वीराज कपूर, याकूब और जगदीश सेठी जैसे कलाकार भी थे, जो आगे चलकर फिल्म उद्योग को बहुत ऊँचाइयों तक ले गए।

इस फिल्म ने किस उद्योग को ऊँचाइयाँ प्रदान कीं?

A. लघु उद्योग

B. भारी उद्योग

C. फिल्म उद्योग

D. इलेक्ट्रॉनिक्स उद्योग

1. B	2. A	3. A	4. C

5. 'आप पानी पिएँगे अथवा जूस।' वाक्य का भेद है :

A. सरल वाक्य
B मिश्र वाक्य
C. संयुक्त वाक्य
D. प्रश्नवाचक वाक्य

6. 'वह ऐसा मेहनती है जो पराजय स्वीकार नहीं करता।' वाक्य का संयुक्त रूप है :

A. वह ऐसा मेहनती है, अतः वह पराजय स्वीकार नहीं करता।
B. वह इतना मेहनती है कि कभी भी अपनी पराजय स्वीकार नहीं करता।
C. वह पराजय स्वीकार नहीं करता क्योंकि वह बहुत मेहनती है।
D. वह मेहनती है किन्तु पराजय स्वीकार नहीं करता।

7. 'Whisper' अंग्रेजी शब्द के लिए सही हिन्दी शब्द है :

A. अधिपत्र B. समापन
C. कानाफूसी D. मजदूरी

8. 'SECONDARY' का हिन्दी समानार्थक नहीं है :

A. गौण B. द्वितीयक
C. माध्यमिक D. प्रस्तावक

9. 'कोसों दूर भागना' मुहावरे का अर्थ है :

A. साथ-साथ रहना
B. पैदल चलना
C. बहुत अलग रहना
D. बात करना

10. इनमें से कौन-सा वाक्य अशुद्ध है :

A. राम दिन-रात मेहनत करता है।
B. जैसा बोओगे उसी तरह काटोगे।
C. पुस्तक विद्वतापूर्वक लिखी गई है।
D. मैंने सारी पुस्तक पढ़ डाली।

11. उसका तोता <u>अत्यंत सुंदर</u> और <u>आज्ञाकारी</u> है।

उपरोक्त रेखांकित शब्दों में कौन-सा पदबंध है?

A. विशेषण पदबंध
B. संज्ञा पदबंध
C. सर्वनाम पदबंध
D. क्रिया पदबंध

12. इनमें से कौन-कौन से वाच्य के भेद हैं :

A. कर्तृवाच्य, कर्मवाच्य, भाववाच्य
B. संज्ञा, सर्वनाम
C. कारक, वचन
D. कर्ता का काल, क्रिया का काल

13. क्रिया के आधार पर वाक्य के .... भेद हैं।

A. चार B. तीन
C. दो D. सात

14. जब किसी पद में मुख्य अर्थ की बाधा होने पर अन्य अर्थ ग्रहण करते समय शब्द का अपना अर्थ कभी लुप्त नहीं होता, वहाँ शब्द शक्ति होती है :

A. साध्यवसान लक्षणा
B. उपादान लक्षणा
C. लक्षण-लक्षणा
D. प्रयोजनवती लक्षणा

5. C **6.** A **7.** C **8.** D **9.** C **10.** B **11.** A **12.** A **13.** B **14.** B

15. जब किसी शब्द का मुख्य अर्थ लेने में बाधा हो और अन्य अर्थ ग्रहण करते समय शब्द का अपना अर्थ लुप्त हो जाता है, तो कौन-सी शब्द शक्ति होती है :

A. साध्यवसान लक्षणा
B. उपादान लक्षणा
C. लक्षण-लक्षणा
D. प्रयोजनवती लक्षणा

16. जहाँ जड़ वस्तुओं या प्रकृति पर मानवीय चेष्टाओं को आरोपित किया जाता है, वहाँ कौन-सा अलंकार होता है?

A. अन्योक्ति B. मानवीकरण
C. दीपक D. प्रतीप

17. जो अलंकार शब्द और अर्थ दोनों के अधीन हो, उसे .... कहते हैं।

A. अर्थालंकार B. उभयालंकार
C. शब्दालंकार D. श्लेषालंकार

18. 'तरनि तनूजा तट तमाल तरुवर छाए' में कौन-सा अलंकार है?

A. अनुप्रास B. यमक
C. उत्प्रेक्षा D. उपमा

19. 'चरण कमल बंदौ हरिराई' में कौन-सा अलंकार है?

A. श्लेष B. उपमा
C. रूपक D. अतिशयोक्ति

20. 'आवत जात कुंज की गलियन रूप सुधा नित पीजै। गोपी पद-पंकज पावन की रज जामै भीजै।'
में कौन-सा अलंकार है?

A. अनुप्रास अलंकार
B. यमक अलंकार
C. उपमा अलंकार
D. रूपक अलंकार

21. 'देखि सुदामा की दीन दशा करुना करिके करुना निधि रोए।' में कौन-सा अलंकार है?

A. अनुप्रास अलंकार
B. यमक अलंकार
C. उपमा अलंकार
D. अतिशयोक्ति अलंकार

22. दोहे और रोले को क्रम से मिलाने पर कौन-सा छंद बनता है?

A. हरिगीतिका B. कुण्डलिया
C. सवैया D. बरवै

23. 'या लकुटी अरु कामरिया पुरा राज तिहूँ, पुर को तजि डारौ' प्रस्तुत पंक्तियों में कौन-सा छंद है?

A. कवित्त छंद B. सवैया छंद
C. बरवै छंद D. दोहा छंद

24. 'कठिन काव्य का प्रेत' किस कवि को कहा जाता है?

A. सेनापति को B. चिन्तामणि को
C. मतिराम को D. केशवदास को

25. 'पायो जी म्हें तो राम-रतन धन पायो। वस्तु अमोलक दी मेरे सतगुरु, करि किरपा अपणायो।
प्रस्तुत पंक्तियों में कौन-सा रस है?

A. वात्सल्य रस B. शांत रस
C. भक्ति रस D. अद्भुत रस

15. C	**16.** B	**17.** B	**18.** B	**19.** C	**20.** D
21. D	**22.** B	**23.** B	**24.** D	**25.** C	

Mathematics

26. Which one of the following can't be the square of a natural number?

A. 42437 B. 20164
C. 81225 D. 32761

27. There are 312, 260 and 156 students in class X, XI and XII respectively. Buses are to be hired to take these students to a picnic. Find the maximum number of students who can sit in a bus if each bus takes equal number of students.

A. 52 B. 56
C. 48 D. 63

28. The largest number which divides 60 and 75, leaving remainders 8 and 10 respectively, is:

A. 260 B. 75
C. 65 D. 13

29. If $x = 1$ and $y = 2$ are the solutions of equation $2x + by = 8$ and $ax - 3y = -4$ then the value of a and b be will be:

A. $a = 2$, $b = 3$
B. $a = -2$, $b = 3$
C. $a = 2$, $b = -3$
D. None of these

30. A pair of linear equations $a_1x + b_1y + c_1 = 0$; $a_2x + b_2y + c_2 = 0$ is said to be inconsistent, if

(a) $\frac{a_1}{a_2} \neq \frac{b_1}{b_2}$

(b) $\frac{a_1}{a_2} = \frac{b_1}{b_2} \neq \frac{c_1}{c_2}$

(c) $\frac{a_1}{a_2} = \frac{b_1}{b_2} = \frac{c_1}{c_2}$

(d) $\frac{a_1}{a_2} \neq \frac{c_1}{c_2}$

A. Option (*a*) is correct
B. Option (*b*) is correct
C. Option (*c*) is correct
D. Option (*d*) is correct

31. The father's age is six times his son's age. Four years hence, the age of the father will be four times his son's age. The present ages of the son and the father are, respectively:

A. 4 and 24 B. 5 and 30
C. 6 and 36 D. 3 and 24

32. Which of the following are the zeroes of polynomial $9x^2 - 4$:

A. $\frac{2}{3}, \frac{-2}{3}$ B. 4, –4
C. 9, –9 D. $\frac{3}{2}, \frac{-3}{2}$

33. Which of the following is the zeroes of polynomial $x^2 - 5x + 6$?

A. 6, –5 B. 1, –6
C. 2, 3 D. 3, –2

26. A **27.** A **28.** D **29.** A **30.** B **31.** C **32.** A **33.** C

34. The equation $12x^2 + 4kx + 3 = 0$ has real and equal roots, if

A. $k = \pm 3$ B. $k = \pm 9$
C. $k = 4$ D. $k = \pm 2$

35. Chandrika raised the price of their products by 40%. How much discount should they give so as to sell the products on no profit no loss basis?

A. 40% B. 28.5%
C. 22.5% D. 32.75%

36. Successive discounts of 20% and 15% are equivalent to a single discount of:

A. 68% B. 65%
C. 35% D. 32%

37. The distance of a point from the x-axis is called:

A. Ordinate B. Abscissa
C. Axis D. Graph

38. Two vertices of a triangle are (3, –5) and (–7, 4). If its centroid is (2, –1), then the third vertex is:

A. (10, 2) B. (–10, 2)
C. (10, –2) D. (–10, –2)

39. In triangle ABC, $\angle BAC = 90°$ and $AD \perp BC$. Then:

A. $BD \cdot CD = BC^2$
B. $AB \cdot AC = BC^2$
C. $BD \cdot CD = AD^2$
D. $AB \cdot AC = AD^2$

40. It is proposed to build a single circular park equal in area to the sum of areas of two circular parks of diameters 16 m and 12 m in a locality. The radius of the new park would be:

A. 10 m B. 15 m
C. 20 m D. 24 m

41. The perimeter of a circular field is 242 m. The area of the field is:

A. 9317 m^2 B. 18634 m^2
C. 4658.5 m^2 D. None of these

42. If r is the radius of the sphere, then the surface area of the sphere is given by:

A. $4\pi r^2$ B. $2\pi r^2$
C. πr^2 D. $4/3\pi r^2$

43. A right circular cylinder of radius r cm and height h cm $(h > 2r)$ just encloses a sphere of diameter:

A. r cm B. $2r$ cm
C. h cm D. $2h$ cm

44. The diameter of the base of a cone is 42 cm and its volume is 12936 cm^3. Its heights is:

A. 28 cm B. 21 cm
C. 35 cm D. 14 cm

45. If the sum of frequencies is 24, then the value of x in the observation: x, 5, 6, 1, 2, will be:

A. 4 B. 6
C. 8 D. 10

34. A	**35.** B	**36.** D	**37.** A	**38.** C	**39.** C
40. A	**41.** C	**42.** A	**43.** B	**44.** A	**45.** D

46. The cumulative frequency table is useful in determining the:

A. Mean B. Median

C. Mode D. All of these

47. Mode = ?

(*a*) $x_k + h.\left\{\frac{(f_{k-1} - f_k)}{(2f_k - f_{k-1} - f_{k+1})}\right\}$

(*b*) $x_k + h.\left\{\frac{(f_k - f_{k-1})}{(2f_k - f_{k-1} - f_{k+1})}\right\}$

(*c*) $x_k + h.\left\{\frac{(f_k - f_{k-1})}{(f_k - 2f_{k-1} - f_{k+1})}\right\}$

(*d*) $x_k + h.\left\{\frac{(f_k - f_{k-1})}{(f_k - f_{k-1} - 2f_{k+1})}\right\}$

A. Option (*a*) is correct
B. Option (*b*) is correct
C. Option (*c*) is correct
D. Option (*d*) is correct

48. If cos (α + β) = 0, then sin (α – β) = ?

(*a*) sin α (*b*) cos β

(*c*) sin 2α (*d*) cos 2β

A. Option (*a*) is correct
B. Option (*b*) is correct
C. Option (*c*) is correct
D. Option (*d*) is correct

49. $\frac{\cos 38° \text{ cosec } 52°}{\tan 18° \tan 35° \tan 60° \tan 72° \tan 55°} = ?$

(*a*) $\sqrt{3}$ (*b*) 1/3

(*c*) $1/\sqrt{3}$ (*d*) $2/\sqrt{3}$

A. Option (*a*) is correct
B. Option (*b*) is correct
C. Option (*c*) is correct
D. Option (*d*) is correct

50. If 2 cos 3θ = 1, then θ = ?

(*a*) 10° (*b*) 15°

(*c*) 20° (*d*) 30°

A. Option (*a*) is correct
B. Option (*b*) is correct
C. Option (*c*) is correct
D. Option (*d*) is correct

Science

51. The relation between the surface area of a solid with that of the particle size can be defined as:

A. The surface area of a solid is always equal to its particle size
B. The surface area of a solid is observed to increase with decrease in the particle size
C. The surface area of a solid doesn't depend on the particle size
D. The surface area of a solid is observed to increase with increase in the particle size

52. Most paramecium move with the help of _______.

A. Villi B. Oral grove

C. Cilia D. Stationary

46. B **47.** B **48.** D **49.** C **50.** C **51.** B **52.** C

53. This is not included in organic farming

A. crop rotation
B. chemical fertilizers
C. green manures
D. compost and farmyard manures

54. Through his experiments, Thomson discovered that every substance in the universe is made up of:

A. Neutrons B. Protons
C. Electrons D. Mass

55. If the mass of the body is doubled and its velocity becomes half, then the linear momentum of the body will:

A. become double
B. remain the same
C. become half
D. become four times

56. What are the primary forces acting on an object when it is submerged in water?

A. Five B. Three
C. Two D. One

57. Which of the following is an example of non-biodegradable waste?

A. Food waste B. Plastic
C. Paper D. Wood

58. Among the following compounds identify the compound that has all three bonds (ionic, covalent and coordinate bond).

A. Ammonia
B. Ammonium chloride
C. Sodium hydroxide
D. Calcium chloride

59. Which of the following statements about the rods and cones in the retina is true?

A. Rods are responsible for detecting color, while cones are responsible for detecting light.
B. Rods are more sensitive to light than cones.
C. Cones are more numerous in the retina than rods.
D. Rods are responsible for detecting fine details, while cones are responsible for detecting motion.

60. Which of the following statements is true about the cell wall?

A. The cell wall is mainly composed of lipid
B. The cell wall is mainly composed of starch
C. The cell wall is mainly composed of protein
D. The cell wall is mainly composed of cellulose

61. Diseases caused due to the inflammation of the vermiform appendix of the digestive system is known as ________.

A. Appendectomy
B. Appendicitis
C. Intestinal cancer
D. Amoebic dysentery

53. B **54.** C **55.** B **56.** C **57.** B **58.** C **59.** B **60.** D **61.** B

62. In which of the following groups of organisms are food materials broken down outside the body and absorbed?

A. Mushroom, green plants, amoeba
B. Yeast, mushroom, bread mould
C. Paramecium, amoeba, cuscuta
D. Cuscuta, lice, tapeworm

63. Which of the following is an anti-forest conservation activity?

A. preservation of wild animals
B. preservation of fires
C. clear felling
D. economy in lumbering

64. Entities exhibiting properties of both non-living and living are:

A. diatoms
B. lichens
C. bacteria
D. viruses

65. Place a solid object in a graduated cylinder with water and measure how much water is displaced to determine its:

A. Mass
B. Density
C. Volume
D. Weight

66. A charge of 10 coulomb flow through the conductor for 2 sec, the electric current flowing through the conductor is....

A. 2A B. 3A
C. 4A D. 5A

67. Electric bell works on which effect of electric current.

A. Heating effect
B. Chemical effect
C. Magnetic effect
D. None of these

68. Which of them serves as an indicator of atmospheric pollution?

A. fern
B. liverworts
C. hornworts
D. epiphytic lichens

69. Non-conventional sources of energy are ____________.

A. Exhaustible
B. Inexhaustible
C. Neither exhaustible nor inexhaustible
D. Too expensive

70. Which of the following option describes the achievements of Mendeleev's Periodic Table?

A. Prediction of noble gases
B. It eliminated the blank spaces left in the table
C. Predicting that the elements can be arranged based on their properties
D. An element in a trend has an average atomic mass of the elements above and below it

62. B **63.** C **64.** D **65.** C **66.** D **67.** C **68.** D **69.** A **70.** A

Social Studies

71. Louis XVI was 20 years old and married to the Austrian princess _____.

A. Catharina
B. Sophie
C. Marie Antoinette
D. Juliana

72. What was the main motive behind the establishment of "Reserved Forests" during colonial rule?

A. To create spaces for recreational activities of the British officers
B. To provide sanctuaries for endangered wildlife species
C. To ensure a steady supply of timber for the British industries
D. To settle displaced farmers from densely populated regions

73. Arrange the following in chronological order and choose the correct option:

I. Napoleonic wars
II. The Treaty of Vienna
III. Greek Struggle for Independence
IV. Slav Nationalism in Ottoman Empire

A. III, II, I and IV
B. I, II, III and IV
C. IV, III, II and I
D. IV, II, III and I

74. Who was the pioneer of the Chauri Chaura incident?

A. Shah Naim Ata
B. M.N. Roy
C. Bhagwan Ahir
D. Bhairo Nath

75. Which of the following innovations helped the weavers in increasing productivity and compete with the mill sector?

A. Spinning jenny
B. Fly shuttle
C. Cotton Gin
D. Roller

76. The southernmost point of the Indian mainland is:

A. Kanyakumari
B. Rameswaram
C. Cape Comorin
D. Thiruvananthapuram

77. Groundwater is polluted due to use of:

A. septic tanks
B. leaky underground gas tanks
C. sewage systems
D. all of these

78. The resources which can be used directly without any modification are called _____.

A. Non-renewable resources
B. Natural resources
C. Sustainable resources
D. Both Natural and Sustainable resources

71. C **72.** C **73.** B **74.** B **75.** B **76.** A **77.** D **78.** B

79. Which of the following is not the source of fresh water resources?

A. Ground water B. Ice sheet
C. River D. Oceans

80. Which of the following statements is NOT true about mangrove forests?

A. They grow along the coast especially in the river deltas
B. These plants are able to grow in a mix of saline and fresh water
C. They grow luxuriantly in muddy areas
D. All of these are wrong

81. _____ is an example of conventional energy sources.

A. Firewood B. Technology
C. Iron D. Silver

82. The first jute mill was set up in 1859 at Rishra, located near _______.

A. Mumbai B. Chennai
C. Kolkata D. Surat

83. As per census 2011, approximately what fraction of Bihar population is below 25 years of age.?

A. 0.25 B. 0.4
C. 0.6 D. 0.35

84. What is the territory under the immediate political control of another state called?

A. Communist state
B. Colony
C. Democratic state
D. None of these

85. Who was the permanent president of the Constituent Assembly?

A. J.L. Nehru
B. Dr. Rajendra Prasad
C. K.M. Munshi
D. B.R. Ambedkar

86. What is the term of office for the members of the Rajya Sabha in India?

A. 3 years B. 4 years
C. 5 years D. 6 years

87. The RTI application is addressed to______.

A. Chief Minister of the respective state
B. Prime Minister of India
C. President of India
D. Public Information Officer

88. A system of 'checks and balances' is another name for which one of the following power-sharing arrangements:

A. Power sharing among different social groups.
B. Vertical division of power or power shared among different levels of government.
C. Horizontal division of power or power shared among different organs of the government.
D. Power sharing in the form of political parties, pressure groups and governments.

79. D **80.** D **81.** A **82.** C **83.** C **84.** B **85.** B **86.** D **87.** D **88.** C

89. Which factors are required for the success of democracy in India?

A. The fundamental basis of democracy is election which is the procedure of selection of representatives.

B. Democracy cannot be established without education and political freedom.

C. The Judicial system is also a pillar of democracy.

D. All of these

90. Generally, all the suggestions or proposals about overcoming various challenges to democracy are called 'democracy reform' or ___.

A. Religious reform
B. Economic reform
C. Social reform
D. Political reforrm

General English

91. Find out the tense of this sentence:

Masons gather all the building materials before they construct a house.

A. Present tense
B. Past tense
C. Future tense
D. Present perfect

92. Name the correct tense form of the italicized word:

The light went out while I *was reading*.

A. Present continuous tense
B. Present perfect tense
C. Past continuous tense
D. Present tense

93. Select the most appropriate option to change the sentence from direct speech to indirect speech.

"I cannot take them home now", he said. He said that .... take them home ....

A. He could not/then
B. I could not/yesterday
C. they cannot/now
D. she cannot/today

94. Select the most appropriate option to change the sentence from direct speech to indirect speech.

They said to Geeta, "We are waiting for someone".

They said to Geeta that........ waiting for someone.

A. you were B. they were
C. we were D. he was

95. Pickout the Non finite verb/verbs in the sentence given below.

She is really good at confusing people.

A. She B. Good
C. Confusing D. People

89. D **90.** D **91.** A **92.** C **93.** A **94.** B **95.** C

96. Pickout the Non finite verb/verbs in the sentence given below

All the teachers have gone to the picnic together.

A. Have B. Gone
C. To D. Together

97. The money __________ stolen by the thieves if you leave it there.

A. Was B. Will be
C. Has been D. Is

98. Which of these is used to separate short co-ordinate clauses of a compound sentence?

A. Semicolon B. Comma
C. Full stop D. Colon

99. Choose the correct statement:

A. My aunt who lives in Mumbai is a doctor.
B. My aunt, who lives in Mumbai, is a doctor.
C. My aunt, who lives in Mumbai is a doctor.
D. My aunt who lives in Mumbai, is a doctor.

100. Fill up the blank, with the correct option

He was shocked..........the news of his father's death.

A. on B. at
C. with D. into

101. The Tajmahal was built .... Mumtaj.

A. in memory of
B. in the place of
C. though
D. in the face of

102. Combine the following pair of sentences into one simple sentence.

Robin is my friend. He is a journalist.

A. Robin who is a journalist and my friend.
B. Robin, my friend, is a journalist.
C. Robin is my friend but journalist.
D. Robin is my friend and journalist too.

103. Choose the correct option as your answer.

He made a promise. He kept it too.

A. He made a promise and kept it too.
B. Besides making a promise, he kept it.
C. Beside making a promise, he kept it.
D. He made a promise but he kept it.

104. Select the alternative which best express the meaning of the idioms/phrase.

Hit the nail in the head

A. To do or say something exactly right
B. To persuade someone
C. To misguide someone
D. To get the expected result

96. B **97.** B **98.** B **99.** B **100.** B **101.** A **102.** B **103.** A **104.** A

105. Select the alternative which best express the meaning of the idioms/phrase.

Call upon

A. To shout B. To order
C. To change D. To bother

106. Select the alternative which best express the meaning of the idioms/phrase.

Go by

A. To meet occasionally
B. To follow
C. To die
D. To force someone to do something

107. Choose the correct phrase from the given option and make a conditional sentence.

If he .... the best player in the team, he wouldn't have earned so much.

A. wasn't
B. won't be
C. hadn't been
D. haven't been

108. If you _______ lied to me before, I would have _______ you today.

A. Have- trusted
B. Hadn't- believe
C. Hadn't- believed
D. Hasn't- not believed

109. Fill up the blank with the correct option.

Every one....... rewarded.

A. Was B. Were
C. Have been D. Have

110. Fill up the blank with the correct option.

'Hammer and sickle'.......... there.

A. is B. were
C. are D. have

Logical & Analytical Reasoning

111. Find out the odd element from the given options:

A. HGF B. XWV
C. NML D. OPQ

112. If police is called teacher, teacher is called politician, politicaian is called doctor, doctor is called lawyer and lawyer is called surgeon, then who will teach children?

A. Politicaian B. Lawyer
C. Doctor D. Police

113. Shlok walked 5 km East, then turned to his right and walked 8 km. After that he took a left turn and walked 5 km, then in which direction is he walking?

A. North B. South
C. East D. West

105. B **106.** B **107.** C **108.** C **109.** A **110.** A **111.** D **112.** A **113.** D

114. Which letter is 4 letters to the right of the letter immediately preceding the letter W?

A. R B. S
C. T D. U

115. Directions: In a class there are seven students (including boys and girls) A, B, C, D, E, F and G. They sit on three benches I, II and III, such that at least two students on each bench and at least one girl on each bench. C who is a girl student, does not sit with A, E and D. F the boy student sits with only B. A sits on the bench I with his best friends. G sits on the bench III. E is the brother of C.

Who sits with C?

A. B B. D
C. G D. E

116. Which of the following is a Composite number?

A. 0 B. 19
C. 29 D. 91

117. In the following question, which one set of letters when sequentially placed at the gaps in the given letter series shall complete it?

b_d_ed_b_c_e

A. cedbc B. cecbd
C. ceabc D. cecdb

118. Look at this series:

8, 43, 11, 41, __, 39, 17, ...

What number should fill in the blank?

A. 8
B. 14
C. 43
D. 44

119. An application was received by the inward clerk in the afternoon of a weekday. Next day he forwarded it to the table of the senior clerk, who was on leave that day. The senior clerk the next evening put up the application to the desk officer. Desk officer studied the application disposed-off the matter on the same day i.e., Friday. Which day was the application received by the inward clerk?

A. Monday
B. Tuesday
C. Earlier week's Saturday
D. Wednesday

120. Find the missing number

54, 54, 46, 46, 38, 38, ?

A. 18
B. 20
C. 28
D. 30

114. B	**115.** C	**116.** D	**117.** B	**118.** B	**119.** D	**120.** D

EXPLANATORY ANSWERS

1. (B): 'उज्ज्वल' शब्द में प्रयुक्त संधि व्यंजन संधि है। यहाँ 'उज्' और 'ज्वल' शब्दों के मिलन से 'उज्ज्वल' बनता है, जहां 'ज्' व्यंजन की दोहराव होती है। स्वर संधि में स्वरों का मिलन होता है, विसर्ग संधि में विसर्ग का अन्य ध्वनियों में परिवर्तन होता है और इनमें से कोई नहीं उपयुक्त विकल्प नहीं है क्योंकि स्पष्ट व्यंजन संधि देखी जा सकती है।

2. (A): 'महाजन' शब्द में द्विगु समास नहीं है, बल्कि यह तत्पुरुष समास है जहाँ 'महा' (बड़ा) और 'जन' (व्यक्ति) मिलकर 'महाजन' (बड़े व्यक्ति) बनते हैं। अठन्नी, नवरत्न और पंचतत्व में द्विगु समास है, जहां संख्या और वस्तु का संयोग होता है।

3. (A): 'दोपहर' शब्द में द्विगु समास है, जिसमें 'दो' और 'पहर' मिलकर 'दोपहर' बनते हैं, जहां 'दो' दोनों पहरों (समयावधि) को संदर्भित करता है। द्वन्द्व समास में समानाधिकरण होता है, कर्मधारय में विशेषण और विशेष्य का मिलन होता है, और तत्पुरुष में उपसर्ग और शब्द का संयोग होता है।

4. (C): 'आलम आरा' फिल्म ने भारतीय फिल्म उद्योग में क्रांति ला दी थी। इस फिल्म ने नए तकनीकी और कलात्मक योगदान के साथ फिल्म उद्योग को नई दिशा दी। लघु उद्योग, भारी उद्योग, और इलेक्ट्रॉनिक्स उद्योग इस संदर्भ में उपयुक्त नहीं हैं क्योंकि प्रश्न विशेष रूप से सिनेमा के क्षेत्र की बात कर रहा है।

5. (C): 'आप पानी पिएँगे अथवा जूस।' यह वाक्य संयुक्त वाक्य है क्योंकि इसमें दो स्वतंत्र खंड हैं जो विकल्प को दर्शाते हैं। सरल वाक्य में केवल एक मुख्य क्रिया होती है, मिश्र वाक्य में मुख्य और उपवाक्य होते हैं, और प्रश्नवाचक वाक्य प्रश्न पूछता है, जो यहाँ लागू नहीं होता।

6. (A): वह ऐसा मेहनती है, अतः वह पराजय स्वीकार नहीं करता। यह वाक्य स्पष्ट रूप से व्यक्ति के मेहनती होने के कारण उसकी पराजय को न स्वीकारने की बात को दर्शाता है। यह सरल और सीधा संयोजन है जो कि मूल वाक्य का भाव पूर्णतः व्यक्त करता है। अन्य विकल्प इस भाव को या तो परिवर्तित कर देते हैं या अतिरिक्त सूचना जोड़ते हैं, जो मूल वाक्य में नहीं है।

7. (C): 'Whisper' का सही हिन्दी अनुवाद 'कानाफूसी' है। यह बहुत ही कम आवाज में बोलने की क्रिया को दर्शाता है, जिसे अंग्रेजी में 'whisper' कहा जाता है। अधिपत्र, समापन और मजदूरी शब्दों का 'whisper' से कोई सम्बन्ध नहीं है, ये विभिन्न अर्थ वाले शब्द हैं।

8. (D): 'SECONDARY' का हिन्दी समानार्थक 'प्रस्तावक' नहीं है। 'SECONDARY' का अर्थ होता है द्वितीयक या गौण, जिसका मतलब होता है किसी चीज का दूसरे स्थान पर होना या दूसरे महत्व का होना। 'माध्यमिक' भी इसी सन्दर्भ में प्रयोग होता है। 'प्रस्तावक' का अर्थ होता है वह व्यक्ति जो किसी प्रस्ताव को पेश करता है, जो 'SECONDARY' से संबंधित नहीं है।

9. (C): 'कोसों दूर भागना' मुहावरे का अर्थ है 'बहुत अलग रहना' या दूर जाना। यह अक्सर किसी से बहुत दूरी बनाकर रखने या संबंध तोड़ने को व्यक्त करता है। 'साथ-साथ रहना', 'पैदल चलना', और 'बात करना' इस मुहावरे के अर्थ से संबंधित नहीं हैं।

10. (B): जैसा बोओगे उसी तरह काटोगे : इस वाक्य में अशुद्धि है क्योंकि सही मुहावरा है 'जैसा बोओगे वैसा काटोगे'। 'उसी तरह' का प्रयोग इस मुहावर में अनुपयुक्त है और भाषा की शुद्धता को बिगाड़ता है। अन्य वाक्य राम दिन-रात मेहनत करता है, पुस्तक विद्वतापूर्वक लिखी गई है, और मैंने सारी पुस्तक पढ़ डाली व्याकरणिक रूप से सही हैं।

11. (A): 'अत्यंत सुंदर और आज्ञाकारी' विशेषण पदबंध है क्योंकि यह शब्द समूह तोता के गुणों का वर्णन करता है, जो विशेषण की भूमिका में हैं। संज्ञा पदबंध किसी वस्तु या व्यक्ति की पहचान दर्शाता है, सर्वनाम पदबंध किसी वस्तु या व्यक्ति की जगह लेता है, और क्रिया पदबंध क्रिया या गतिविधि संबंधी होता है।

12. (A): कर्तृवाच्य, कर्मवाच्य, भाववाच्य : ये तीनों हिंदी व्याकरण में वाच्य के प्रमुख भेद हैं। कर्तृवाच्य में कर्ता प्रधान होता है, कर्मवाच्य में क्रिया का कर्म प्रधान होता है, और भाववाच्य में क्रिया की स्थिति प्रधान होती है। संज्ञा, सर्वनाम, कारक, वचन और कर्ता का काल, क्रिया का काल वाच्य के भेद नहीं होते।

13. (B): हिंदी व्याकरण के अनुसार वाक्यों को क्रिया के आधार पर तीन भेदों में बांटा गया है : साधारण, यौगिक, और मिश्र। चार और सात विकल्प इस संदर्भ में नहीं आते। दो वाक्य भेद भी पर्याप्त नहीं होते।

14. (B): जब किसी पद में मुख्य अर्थ की बाधा होने पर अन्य अर्थ ग्रहण करते समय शब्द का अपना अर्थ कभी लुप्त नहीं होता, तब उपादान लक्षणा शब्द शक्ति का प्रयोग होता है। यह शब्द के द्वितीयक अर्थ को स्पष्ट करता है, जबकि मुख्य अर्थ भी बना रहता है। साध्यवसान लक्षणा और प्रयोजनवती लक्षणा अलग संदर्भों में प्रयुक्त होती हैं।

15. (C): जब किसी शब्द का मुख्य अर्थ लेने में बाधा हो और अन्य अर्थ ग्रहण करते समय शब्द का अपना अर्थ लुप्त हो जाता है, तो लक्षण-लक्षणा शब्द शक्ति प्रयोग होती है। इसमें मूल अर्थ के लुप्त होने पर एक नया अर्थ ग्रहण किया जाता है, जो व्यापक और प्रासंगिक होता है। साध्यवसान लक्षणा और उपादान लक्षणा मुख्य अर्थ को पूरी तरह से लुप्त नहीं होने देते।

16. (B): जब जड़ वस्तुओं या प्रकृति के तत्वों को मानवीय गुण, भावनाएं या चेष्टाएं दी जाती हैं, तो इसे मानवीकरण अलंकार कहते हैं। यह अलंकार गैर-मानवीय वस्तुओं को मानवीय विशेषताओं से सुसज्जित करता है, जिससे कविता या गद्य में रुचिकर और गहरी अभिव्यक्ति उत्पन्न होती है। अन्योक्ति, दीपक, और प्रतीप इस परिस्थिति में लागू नहीं होते हैं।

17. (B): जो अलंकार शब्द और अर्थ दोनों के अधीन होता है, उसे उभयालंकार कहते हैं। इसमें शब्दों की रचना और अर्थ का गहराई से सम्बन्ध होता है, जो कि काव्य को और अधिक सौंदर्यपूर्ण और अर्थपूर्ण बनाता है। अर्थालंकार, शब्दालंकार, और

'श्लेषालंकार' विशेष रूप से केवल अर्थ या शब्द पर केंद्रित होते हैं।

18. (B): 'तरनि तनूजा तट तमाल तरुवर छाए' में यमक अलंकार है। यमक अलंकार तब होता है जब एक ही शब्द का एक ही उच्चारण पर अलग-अलग अर्थों में प्रयोग होता है। इस पंक्ति में तत्सम ध्वनियाँ अलग-अलग अर्थों में प्रयुक्त होती हैं, जो यमक अलंकार की विशेषता है। अनुप्रास, उत्प्रेक्षा, और उपमा इस पंक्ति में नहीं पाए जाते।

19. (C): 'चरण कमल बंदौ हरिराई' में रूपक अलंकार है, जहाँ 'चरण' (पैर) को 'कमल' (कमल का फूल) के रूप में पूर्ण रूप से उपमित किया गया है। इसमें उपमेय और उपमान के बीच साम्यता इतनी अधिक होती है कि उपमेय लगभग उपमान में बदल जाता है। 'श्लेष, उपमा, और अतिशयोक्ति यहाँ लागू नहीं होते।

20. (D): 'आवत जात कुंज की गलियन रूप सुधा नित पीजै। गोपी पद-पंकज पावन की रज जामै भीजै।' में रूपक अलंकार है जहाँ 'रूप सुधा' (रूप की अमृत) और 'पद-पंकज' (पैर के फूल) का प्रयोग भावनात्मक और गहन अर्थ दर्शाने के लिए किया गया है। यहाँ विषय की गहराई और सौंदर्य को बढ़ाया गया है। अनुप्रास, यमक, और उपमा अलंकार इस विवरण में समावेशी नहीं हैं।

21. (D): 'देखि सुदामा की दीन दशा करुना करिके करुना निधि रोए।' में अतिशयोक्ति अलंकार है, जो भावनाओं और स्थितियों की अत्यधिक वृद्धि या विस्तार को दर्शाता है। इस पंक्ति में देवता के रूप में करुणा निधि (कृष्ण) का रोना भावनात्मक अतिरेक का सूचक है, जो उनकी असीम करुणा को प्रदर्शित करता है। अनुप्रास, यमक, और उपमा इस विशेष प्रसंग में प्रयुक्त नहीं हुए हैं।

22. (B): दोहे और रोले का संयोजन करने पर कुण्डलिया छंद बनता है। कुण्डलिया छंद में पहले एक दोहा होता है, उसके बाद एक रोला होता है, जो दोहे के पहले पद से प्रारम्भ होता है। यह विशेष रचनात्मक संरचना इस छंद की पहचान है। हरिगीतिका, सवैया, और बरवै यहाँ लागू नहीं होते हैं।

23. (B): 'या लकुटी अरु कामरिया पुरा राज तिहूँ, पुर को तजि डारो' में सवैया छंद है। सवैया छंद हिंदी कविता का एक जटिल छंद है जिसमें तुकांत और मात्राबद्ध शब्दों का कठोर नियम से पालन होता है। इसकी विशेषता है कि यह अक्सर गीतात्मक और लयबद्ध होता है। कवित्त, बरवै, और दोहा इस पंक्ति के लिए उपयुक्त नहीं हैं।

24. (D): 'कठिन काव्य का प्रेत' के रूप में केशवदास को जाना जाता है। केशवदास एक प्रमुख कवि थे जिन्होंने अपने काव्य में जटिलता और शास्त्रीयता का समावेश किया, जिससे उनकी रचनाएँ अत्यंत कठिन और गहन मानी जाती हैं। सेनापति, चिन्तामणि, और मतिराम इस उपनाम से संबद्ध नहीं हैं।

25. (C): 'पायो जी म्हें तो राम-रतन धन पायो। वस्तु अमोलक दी मेरे सतगुरु, करि किरपा अपणायो।' में भक्ति रस है। यह पंक्तियाँ भक्त की गहरी आध्यात्मिक अनुभूति और ईश्वर के प्रति समर्पण को दर्शाती हैं, जिसमें गुरु के प्रति कृतज्ञता और ईश्वरीय प्राप्ति की बात कही गई है। वात्सल्य रस, शांत रस, और अद्भुत रस इस कविता की मूल भावना से मेल नहीं खाते।

26. (A): (A) 42437 = ?

(B) 20164 = $(142)^2$

(C) 81225 = $(285)^2$

(D) 32761 = $(181)^2$

Hence, option (A) 42437 cannot be square of any natural number due to presence of 7 in its unit place.

27. (A): Maximum number of students who can sit in a bus

= HCF of 312, 260 and 156

= 52.

28. (D): Required number

= HCF of (60 – 8) and (75 – 10)

= HCF of 52 and 65 = 13.

29. (A): Given,

$$2x + by = 8 \quad \ldots(i)$$

and $ax - 3y = -4$ ...(*ii*)

Putting $x = 1$ and $y = 2$ in (*i*),

$$2 \times 1 + b \times 2 = 8$$

$$\Rightarrow \quad 2 + 2b = 8 \Rightarrow b = 3$$

Now putting value of x and y in (*ii*),

$$a \times 1 - 3 \times 2 = 4$$

$$\Rightarrow \quad a - 6 = -4$$

$$\Rightarrow \quad a = 6 - 4 = 2$$

$$\Rightarrow \quad a = 2$$

Hence, $a = 2$ and $b = 3$.

30. (B): Given Linear equation,

$$a_1x + b_1y + c_1 = 0 \quad \ldots(i)$$

and $a_2x + b_2y + c_2 = 0$ ...(*ii*)

are called inconsistent

When, $\frac{a_1}{a_2} = \frac{b_1}{b_2} \neq \frac{c_1}{c_2}$.

31. (C): Let present age of Father and son be $6x$ and x years respectively.

Then, after 4 years

$$4(x + 4) = 6x + 4$$

$$\Rightarrow \quad 4x + 16 = 6x + 4$$

$$\Rightarrow \quad 6x - 4x = 16 - 4$$

$$\Rightarrow \quad 2x = 12$$

$$\Rightarrow \quad x = 6$$

$\therefore$ Present age of son

$= x = 6$ years

Present age of father

$= 6x = 36$ years.

32. (A): Given, Polynomial $= 9x^2 - 4$

For Zeroes,

$$9x^2 - 4 = 0$$

$$\Rightarrow \quad x^2 = \frac{4}{9}$$

$$\Rightarrow \quad x = \pm\frac{2}{3}$$

$$\Rightarrow \quad x = \frac{2}{3}, \frac{-2}{3}$$

Hence, Zeroes of polynomial are $\frac{2}{3}, \frac{-2}{3}$.

33. (C): Given, Polynomial,

$P(x) = x^2 - 5x + 6$

$$\because \quad x^2 - 5x + 6 = 0$$

$$\therefore \quad x^2 - 2x - 3x + 6 = 0$$

$$\Rightarrow \quad x(x - 2) - 3(x - 2) = 0$$

$$\Rightarrow \quad (x - 2)(x - 3) = 0$$

$$\Rightarrow \quad x = 2,$$

$$x = 3$$

Hence, zeroes polynomial are 2, 3.

34. (A): Given equation,

$$12x^2 + 4kx + 3 = 0$$

Roots are real and equal.

$$\therefore \quad b^2 - 4ac = 0$$

$$\Rightarrow (4k)^2 - 4 \times 12 \times 3 = 0$$

$$\Rightarrow \quad 16k^2 - 12 \times 12 = 0$$

$$\Rightarrow \quad k^2 = \frac{12 \times 12}{16} = \frac{3 \times 12}{4}$$

$$\Rightarrow \quad k^2 = 3 \times 3 = 9$$

$$\Rightarrow \quad k = \pm 3.$$

35. (B): According to the question, Discount should be given,

$$= \frac{40}{100 + 40} \times 100 = \frac{40}{140} \times 100$$

$$= \frac{2}{7} \times 100 = \frac{200}{7} = 28.5\%.$$

36. (D): Single discount

$$= 100 - 100 \times \frac{100 - 20}{100} \times \frac{100 - 15}{100}$$

$$= 100 - 100 \times \frac{80}{100} \times \frac{85}{100}$$

$$= 100 - 80 \times \frac{17}{20}$$

$$= 100 - 68 = 32\%.$$

37. (A): The distance of a point from the x-axis is called ordinate.

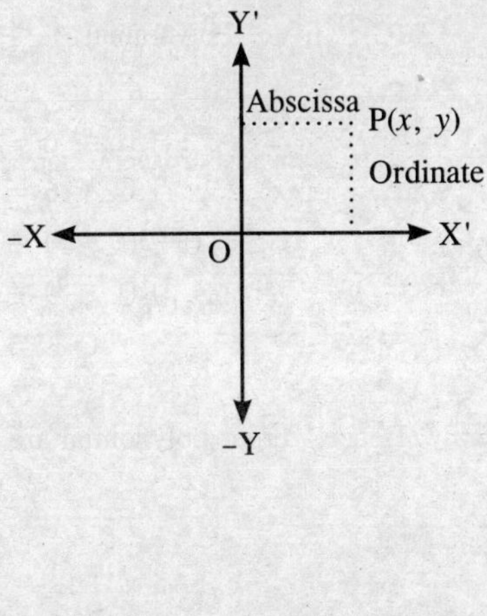

38. (C): Given two vertices of a triangle are (3, –5) and (–7, 4) and its centroid is (2, –1)

Let third vertex of this triangle be (x, y)

$$\text{Then,} \quad \frac{3 + (-7) + x}{3} = 2$$

$$\Rightarrow \quad -4 + x = 6$$

$$\Rightarrow \quad x = 10$$

$$\text{and} \quad \frac{-5 + 4 + y}{3} = -1$$

$$\Rightarrow \quad y - 1 = -3$$

$$\Rightarrow \quad y = -2$$

$\therefore$ Third vertex will be (10, –2).

39. (C): Given in ΔABC,

$\angle BAC = 90°$ and $AD \perp BC$

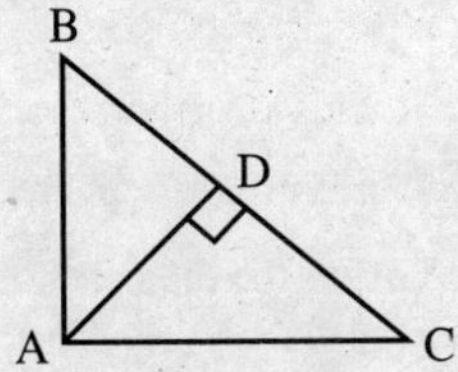

$$\therefore \quad BD \times CD = AB^2.$$

40. (A): The sum of areas of two circular parks of 16 m and 12 m

$$= \pi\left(\frac{16}{2}\right)^2 + \pi\left(\frac{12}{2}\right)^2$$

$$= \pi(8)^2 + \pi(6)^2$$

$$= 64\pi + 36\pi$$

$$= 100\pi$$

$\therefore$ Area of new park $= 100\pi \text{ m}^2$

$$\Rightarrow \quad \pi r^2 = 100\pi$$

$$\Rightarrow \quad r = 10 \text{ m}.$$

$\therefore$ Radius of new park = 10 m.

41. (C): Circumference of a circular park = 242 m

$\therefore \quad 2\pi r = 242$

$\Rightarrow \quad 2 \times \frac{22}{7} \times r = 242$

$\Rightarrow \quad r = 242 \times \frac{7}{2 \times 22}$

$= 11 \times \frac{7}{2}$ m

$\therefore$ Area of the field $= \pi r^2$

$= \frac{22}{7} \times \left(11 \times \frac{7}{2}\right)^2$

$= \frac{22}{7} \times 11 \times \frac{7}{2} \times 11 \times \frac{7}{2}$

$= 11 \times 11 \times 11 \times \frac{7}{2}$

$= 1331 \times \frac{7}{2} = \frac{9317}{2} = 4658.5 \text{ m}^2.$

42. (A): Radius of sphere $= r$

$\therefore$ Surface area of sphere $= 4\pi r^2$.

44. (A): Given, the diameter of the base of a cone = 42 cm.

$\Rightarrow \quad 2r = 42$

$\Rightarrow \quad r = 21$ cm

and volume of cone = 12936 cm^3

$\Rightarrow \quad \frac{1}{3}\pi r^2 h = 12936$

$\Rightarrow \frac{1}{3} \times \frac{22}{7} \times (21)^2 \times h = 12936$

$\Rightarrow h = \frac{12936 \times 3 \times 7}{22 \times (21)^2}$

$= \frac{588}{21} = 28$ cm

Hence, height of cone = 28 cm.

45. (D): Given, The sum of frequencies = 24

$\therefore \quad x + 5 + 6 + 1 + 2 = 24$

$\Rightarrow \quad x + 14 = 24$

$\Rightarrow \quad x = 24 - 14 = 10$

$\Rightarrow \quad x = 10.$

46. (B): The cumulative frequency table is useful in determining the median.

48. (D): Given,

$\cos(\alpha + \beta) = 0$

$\Rightarrow \cos(\alpha + \beta) = \cos 90°$

$\Rightarrow \quad \alpha + \beta = 90°$

$\Rightarrow \quad \alpha = 90° - \beta$

$\therefore \quad \sin \alpha = \sin (90° - \beta)$

$\Rightarrow \quad \sin \alpha = \cos \beta$

and $\quad \cos \alpha = \cos (90 - \beta)$

$\Rightarrow \cos \alpha = \sin \beta$

Now, $\sin (\alpha - \beta)$

$= \sin \alpha \cos \beta - \cos \alpha \sin \beta$

$= \cos \beta \,.\, \cos \beta - \sin \beta \cos \beta$

$= \cos^2\beta - \sin^2 \beta$

$= \cos 2\beta$

$\Rightarrow \quad \sin (\alpha - \beta) = \cos 2\beta.$

49. (C): $\frac{\cos 38° \operatorname{cosec} 52°}{\tan 18° \tan 35° \tan 60° \tan 72° \tan 55°}$

$= \frac{\cos(90° - 52°) \operatorname{cosec} 52°}{\tan(90° - 72°) \tan(90° - 55°) \tan 60° \tan 72° \tan 55°}$

$= \frac{\sin 52° \operatorname{cosec} 52°}{\cot 72° \cot 55° (\sqrt{3}) \tan 72° \tan 55°}$

$= \frac{\frac{1}{\operatorname{cosec} 52°} \operatorname{cosec} 52°}{\frac{1}{\tan 72°} \cdot \frac{1}{\tan 55°} (\sqrt{3}) \tan 72° \tan 55°}$

$= \frac{1}{\sqrt{3}}.$

51. (B): The surface area of a solid is observed to increase with decrease in the particle size: When particle size is reduced, the overall surface area per unit mass increases. For example, if we break down a 1 cm^3 cube into 1 mm^3 cubes, the total exposed surface grows dramatically. This principle is important in catalysis and drug formulation, where a higher surface area can accelerate reactions or dissolution. Mathematically, surface area is inversely proportional to the particle radius ($S \propto 1/r$).

52. (C): Paramecia are covered with thousands of tiny hair-like cilia that beat in coordinated waves to propel the organism forward. Each cilium typically beats at a frequency of about 40–50 times per second. These coordinated beating motions help in locomotion as well as in guiding food particles into the oral groove. In comparison, villi are found in the small intestine of higher organisms for absorption, not for locomotion in paramecia.

53. (B): Organic farming strictly avoids synthetic chemicals, emphasizing natural methods like crop rotation, green manures, and biological pest control. Chemical fertilizers supply nutrients rapidly but can harm soil microflora and contaminate water sources. Instead, organic farming prefers compost, farmyard manure, and bio-fertilizers to maintain soil fertility and ecological balance. World statistics show that organic agricultural land has increased steadily, reflecting concerns about sustainability.

54. (C): J.J. Thomson's cathode ray experiments in 1897 showed that cathode rays were made of negatively charged particles, later named electrons. He determined the charge-to-mass ratio of these particles, proving they were much smaller than atoms. This discovery revolutionized the atomic model and demonstrated that all substances (atoms) contained these fundamental negative particles.

55. (B): Linear momentum $p = mv$. If m becomes $2m$ and v becomes $v/2$, then new momentum $= (2m)(v/2) = mv$, which is the original momentum.

Numerically, if m was 1 kg and v was 2 m/s, $p = 2$ kg.m/s;

After doubling mass (2 kg) and halving velocity (1 m/s),

$p = 2 \times 1 = 2$ kg.m/s, hence remains unchanged.

56. (C): When submerged, the primary forces are buoyant force (acting upwards) and gravitational force (weight) acting downwards. The net effect determines whether the object floats or sinks. Additional minor forces like drag or lift may act if there is fluid motion, but the main forces are just two—buoyancy and weight. For an object completely immersed at rest, these are the principal opposing forces.

57. (B): Plastics do not decompose easily because microorganisms cannot break down their long polymer chains. They can persist in landfills and oceans for hundreds of years. In contrast, paper, wood, and food waste are readily broken down by microbes, turning into simpler substances that re-enter natural cycles.

58. **(C):** It contains an ionic bond between Na^+ and OH^-, a covalent bond within the OH^- ion (between O and H), and a coordinate bond formation in the hydroxyl group where the electron pair from oxygen is shared. Such bonding features make it a classic example having all three types of bonds.

59. **(B):** Human retina contains roughly 120 million rods and 6-7 million cones. Rods function better in low light (scotopic vision) but do not provide color information. Cones need brighter light and enable color vision and high acuity. Hence, rods are crucial for night vision and are more sensitive to dim light stimuli.

60. **(D):** In plants, the rigid cell wall comprises primarily cellulose microfibrils embedded in other polysaccharides. Cellulose is a polysaccharide of β-glucose units, giving structural support. It helps maintain cell shape and withstand turgor pressure. This structural carbohydrate is absent in animal cells, which instead rely on flexible plasma membranes.

61. **(B):** It refers to the inflammation of the vermiform appendix, often presenting with abdominal pain, vomiting, and fever. The condition may require surgical removal (appendectomy) if the appendix risks rupture. Statistically, about 5–10% of the population is affected by appendicitis in their lifetime.

62. **(B):** These organisms secrete digestive enzymes onto external food sources and absorb the breakdown products. This mode of nutrition is called saprophytic. For example, bread mould (Rhizopus) releases enzymes into bread, and then absorbs the nutrients from the digested material.

63. **(C):** This involves the complete removal of trees in an area, which is highly detrimental to forest conservation. It destroys habitats, reduces biodiversity, and disrupts ecological balance. Sustainable practices like selective logging or controlled lumbering are preferred to maintain forest health.

64. **(D):** They exhibit characteristics of both non-living entities (no metabolic machinery outside a host) and living organisms (ability to reproduce in a host). Viruses are essentially nucleic acid wrapped in a protein coat and become active only inside living cells. The average size of viruses ranges from about 20–300 nm.

65. **(C):** When a solid is submerged in a measuring cylinder, the increase in water level equals the object's volume. Archimedes' principle underlies this technique. For instance, if the water rises from 50 mL to 65 mL, the object's volume is 15 mL.

66. **(D):** Electric current I = Q/t, so if 10 coulombs pass in 2 seconds, then I = 10/2 = 5 amperes. The SI unit of current is ampere, defined by the rate of flow of electric charge. One ampere equals one coulomb per second.

67. **(C):** An electric bell uses an electromagnet that attracts and releases an armature repeatedly to produce a ringing sound. When current flows, it magnetizes the iron core, pulling the clapper to strike the gong. On breaking the circuit, the iron core loses magnetism, and the clapper returns, repeating the cycle.

68. **(D):** Lichens are sensitive to sulphur dioxide and other atmospheric pollutants, making them biological indicators of air quality. Epiphytic lichens growing on tree barks get nutrients mainly from the air, so if pollution is severe, they fail to thrive.

69. **(A):** Non-conventional sources of energy can be depleted over time if overused or not sustainably managed. Though often considered cleaner, these sources rely on finite infrastructures or conditions, making them exhaustible when demands exceed their regeneration rate.

70. **(A):** One of Mendeleev's notable achievements was foreseeing the possibility of inert elements fitting a distinct column in the table. When noble gases (like helium, neon, argon) were discovered later, they were placed smoothly without disturbing the periodic order.

71. **(C):** She was the daughter of Empress Maria Theresa of Austria and married Louis XVI in 1770. She became Queen of France at 19 and famously, though perhaps apocryphally, was associated with the remark, "Let them eat cake." Her lavish lifestyle and perceived aloofness contributed to her unpopularity before the French Revolution.

72. **(C):** Under colonial rule, forests were systematically exploited for timber to fuel the railway network, shipbuilding, and other industries in Britain. The British government declared large tracts of forests as "Reserved" to control timber harvest and restrict local community access.

73. **(B):** The Napoleonic wars (I) took place from 1803–1815, followed by the Treaty of Vienna (II) in 1815, the Greek struggle for independence (III) began in 1821, and Slav nationalism in the Ottoman Empire (IV) emerged prominently in the latter half of the 19th century.

74. **(B):** He played a significant role influencing the incident at Chauri Chaura that led to the burning of a police station. This violent outbreak prompted the suspension of the Non-Cooperation Movement, reflecting Mahatma Gandhi's stance against the use of violence.

75. **(B):** Invented by John Kay in 1733, the fly shuttle accelerated handloom weaving by allowing weavers to propel the shuttle through the warp yarns more efficiently.

This innovation nearly doubled weaving productivity and helped many traditional weavers briefly compete with emerging mechanized mills.

76. **(A):** It is situated at the southernmost tip of the Indian mainland in Tamil Nadu. Known also as Cape Comorin, it marks the confluence of the Arabian Sea, the Bay of Bengal, and the Indian Ocean, making it geographically prominent.

77. **(D):** Groundwater can be contaminated through septic tanks, leaky underground fuel tanks, and faulty sewage systems. These sources allow harmful chemicals and pathogens to seep into aquifers. According to WHO, about 785 million people globally still lack basic drinking water service.

78. **(B):** Natural resources: Resources like sunlight, air, water, and certain minerals can be directly used without modification. For example, we drink water from a spring, use solar energy for drying clothes, or breathe air directly from the atmosphere. Such naturally available resources form the basis of human survival.

79. **(D):** They constitute about 97% of Earth's water and are saline, hence not considered a direct source of fresh water. Groundwater, rivers, and ice sheets are primary reservoirs of fresh water. Only about 2.5–3% of the total water on Earth is fresh and suitable for drinking or irrigation.

80. **(D):** Statements A, B, and C are correct regarding mangrove forests, so the claim "All of these are wrong" is itself incorrect. Mangroves thrive in saline–freshwater mixtures, grow along coastlines or deltas, and often proliferate in soft, muddy soils with low oxygen.

81. **(A):** Firewood is a conventional (traditional) source of energy that has been used for centuries for cooking and heating, especially in rural areas. Even today, according to the World Bank, nearly 2.4 billion people worldwide rely on wood and other biomass fuels. It is one of the oldest sources of energy harnessed by humans.

82. **(C):** In 1859, the first jute mill in India was established at Rishra on the banks of the Hooghly River, close to Kolkata. This marked the beginning of India's jute industry under British colonial influence. Later, the region became a major global hub for jute processing and trade.

83. **(C):** As per the 2011 census, about 58–60% of Bihar's population is under the age of 25. This makes Bihar one of the youngest demographic states in India, which has implications for its education system, job market, and development policies focusing on youth.

84. **(B):** A colony is a territory under the direct political control of another state or government. Historically, many Asian, African, and American territories were colonized by European powers for economic

exploitation, military advantage, or strategic positioning.

85. **(B):** Dr. Rajendra Prasad was elected as the permanent president (Chairman) of the Constituent Assembly. Later, he became the first President of India, holding office from 1950 to 1962. He played a pivotal role during India's freedom struggle and in framing the Constitution.

86. **(D):** Members of the Rajya Sabha hold office for six years, with one-third retiring every two years. This system ensures continuity within the house. The Rajya Sabha is a permanent body, unlike the Lok Sabha, which is dissolved every five years or earlier.

87. **(D):** Under the Right to Information (RTI) Act, applications must be addressed to the designated PIO. The PIO has the responsibility to provide information or reject the request under the provisions of the RTI Act within the prescribed time limit (usually 30 days).

88. **(C):** Horizontal division of power or power shared among different organs of the government: This system is often termed 'checks and balances', where each organ (legislature, executive, judiciary) exercises some control over the other two, preventing any single entity from becoming too powerful.

89. **(D):** Free and fair elections, education, political freedoms, and an independent judiciary are key elements for a successful democracy in India. Periodic elections ensure accountability, education fosters informed citizenry, and judicial review protects constitutional values.

90. **(D):** Suggestions or proposals for tackling democratic challenges—such as electoral reforms, transparency laws, or accountability measures—are broadly termed 'political reform'. These initiatives aim to strengthen institutions, increase public trust, and enhance the effectiveness of democracy.

91. **(A):** The sentence "Masons gather all the building materials before they construct a house." is in the present tense. It describes a habitual action that masons perform before starting to build a house, indicating a general truth or regular occurrence.

92. **(C):** The italicized word "was reading" in the sentence "The light went out while I was reading." is in the past continuous tense. This tense is used to describe an action that was ongoing at a specific time in the past.

93. **(A):** He could not/then: In indirect speech, "I cannot take them home now" becomes "He said that he could not take them home then." The pronoun changes from "I" to "he," and "cannot" changes to "could not" to reflect the past reporting context; "now" changes to "then" to reflect the time shift from direct to indirect speech.

94. **(B):** The correct change from direct to indirect speech for the sentence "They said to Geeta,

'We are waiting for someone'" is "They said to Geeta that they were waiting for someone." The pronoun "We" changes to "they" and "are" changes to "were" to reflect the shift in perspective and tense.

95. (C): In the sentence "She is really good at confusing people," the non-finite verb is "confusing." Non-finite verbs, like gerunds or infinitives, do not change form according to the subject or tense. Here, "confusing" acts as a gerund.

96. (B): In the sentence "All the teachers have gone to the picnic together," the non-finite verb is "gone." This is the past participle form used in the perfect tense structure "have gone," which does not change with the subject or tense.

97. (B): The correct fill for the sentence "The money _________ stolen by the thieves if you leave it there." is "will be." This is a future passive form, indicating that something will happen to the money in the future if it is left unattended.

98. (B): A comma is typically used to separate short coordinate clauses in a compound sentence. This punctuation helps clarify the sentence structure and separates elements that are equally important.

99. (B): This is the correct sentence as it uses commas to set off a non-restrictive clause, "who lives in Mumbai," which adds extra information about "my aunt" that isn't essential to the meaning of the sentence.

100. (B): The correct preposition to use in the sentence "He was shocked.......... the news of his father's death." is "at." In English, "shocked at" is the standard collocation used to express surprise or distress caused by a specific event.

101. (A): The correct option is "in memory of." The Taj Mahal was built in memory of Mumtaz Mahal, the wife of Mughal Emperor Shah Jahan. This phrase is commonly used to denote that something was created or done to honor or remember someone who has passed away.

102. (B): This option effectively combines the two given sentences into one simple sentence by using apposition. "Robin, my friend, is a journalist" clearly communicates that Robin is the speaker's friend and he is also a journalist.

103. (A): This option correctly and succinctly combines the two actions of making a promise and keeping it. The phrase "and kept it too" emphasizes that not only did he make a promise, but he also followed through with it.

104. (A): The idiom "hit the nail on the head" means to do or say something exactly right or perfectly accurate. It is often used when someone has made a comment that is precisely correct or has performed an action that perfectly achieves its goal.

105. (B): The phrase "call upon" can often mean to formally ask or demand something from someone, which aligns well with the option "To order." This can involve invoking authority or expecting action, typically seen in formal requests or summonses in a more authoritative context, hence matching closely with the action of ordering someone to perform a duty or task.

106. (B): The idiom "go by" can have several meanings depending on the context, but the most common is to follow a rule, method, or example. It implies adhering to something that has been set or previously established.

107. (C): The correct phrase to complete this conditional sentence is "hadn't been." This option correctly forms a past perfect conditional, which is used to speculate about outcomes based on different past circumstances. The sentence "If he hadn't been the best player in the team, he wouldn't have earned so much" suggests he was indeed the best, which influenced his earnings.

108. (C): This is the correct option for forming a past perfect conditional sentence. "If you hadn't lied to me before, I would have believed you today" means that the action of lying in the past affects the trust level today.

109. (A): "Every one was rewarded" is grammatically correct. "Everyone" is treated as a singular subject, therefore the verb "was" is appropriate. The singular form matches the singular pronoun.

110. (A): The phrase "Hammer and sickle" refers to a single symbol, often representing communism, thus it is treated as a singular noun. Therefore, the correct verb form is "is," indicating the presence of this symbol.

111. (D):

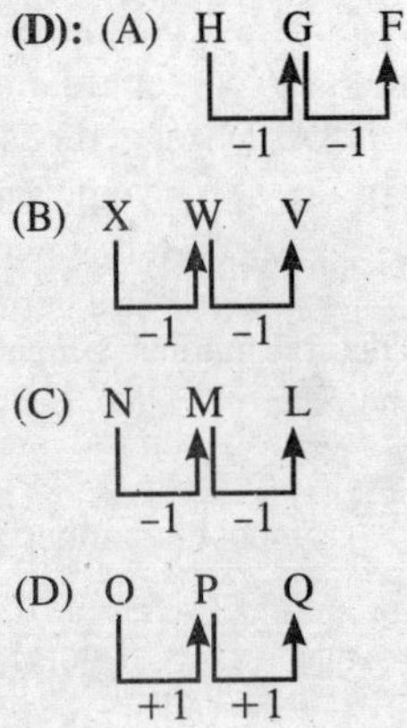

Hence, option (D) is odd element.

112. (A): Given, Police = Teacher

Teacher = Politician

Politician = Doctor

Doctor = Lawyer

Lawyer = Surgeon

∴ Politician will teach children.

113. (D): Here, Starting point = A

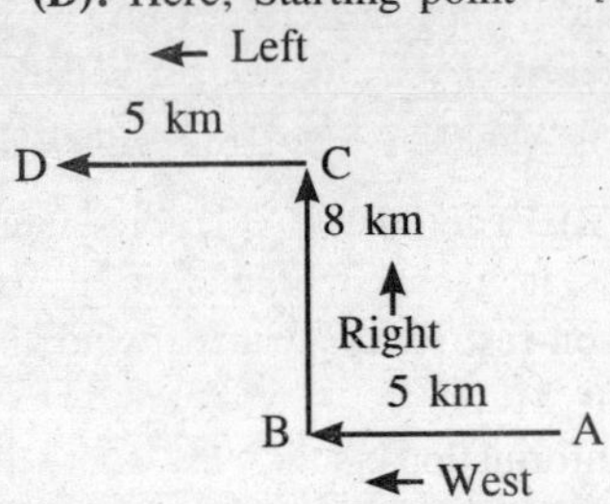

AB = 5 km

BC = 8 km

CD = 5 km

Now, He is walking in West direction.

115. **(C):** Given, there are 7students in a class (including boys and girls)

Bench:	I. FB		I. AED
	II. AED	or	II. FB
	III. GC		III. GC

Here, G sits with C.

116. **(D):** A natural number which is not prime number is called composite number.

∴ Here, Composite number = 91.

117. **(B):** cecbd

∴ b $\underline{c}$ d $\underline{e}$, e d $\underline{c}$ b, $\underline{b}$ c $\underline{d}$ e

Here, bcde in each section.

∴ Option (B) complete the series.

118. **(B):**

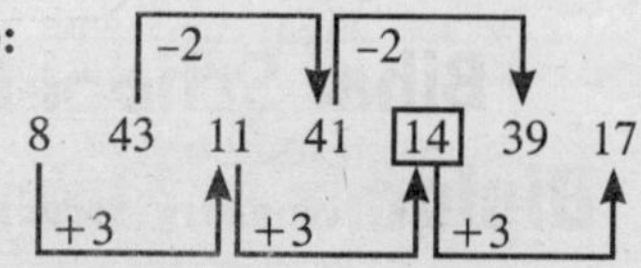

∴ ? = Missing number = 14.

119. **(D):** In the afternoon of working days + Next day + Next evening

= Friday

∴ Afternoon of working day.

= Friday – 2 days = Wednesday

Hence, application received by the inward on Wednesday.

120. **(D):**

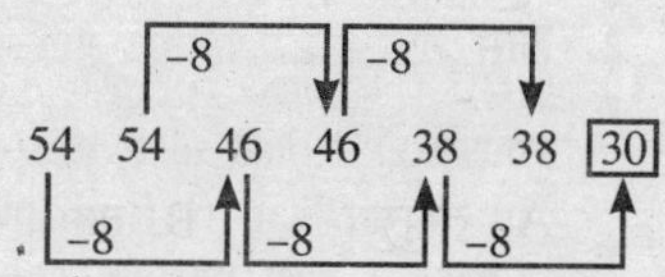

Hence, 30 will come at the place of question mark.

Previous Years' Paper

Bihar School Examination Board, Patna

Diploma in Elementary Education (D.El.Ed.)

Common Entrance Exam-2024

(Exam held on 14 April, 2024)

सामान्य हिन्दी

1. 'संस्कृत' का संधि-विच्छेद करें :

A. संस् + कृत B. सम् + कृत

C. संस्कृ + त D. सम + कृत

2. जिस शब्द का प्रथम पद प्रधान हो उसे .... समास कहते हैं।

A. तत्पुरुष B. कर्मधारय

C. द्वंद्व D. अव्ययीभाव

3. 'देव जो महान है' यह किस समास का उदाहरण है?

A. कर्मधारय B. बहुब्रीहि

C. तत्पुरुष D. अव्ययीभाव

4. निर्देश : गद्यांश को पढ़कर प्रश्न के उत्तर दें।

भारत माता को हम नमन करते हैं। उत्तर में हिमालय इसका प्रहरी है। दक्षिण में हिंद महासागर उसके चरण पखारता है। पश्चिम में कच्छ की खाड़ी और पूरब में बांग्लादेश है। गंगा-यमुना, नर्मदा-ताप्ती, कृष्णा, गोदावरी, ब्रह्मपुत्र आदि नदियाँ भारत के मैदानी क्षेत्रों की शोभा बढ़ाती हैं। खेतों में लहराती फसलें और बागों में पके फलों की बहार भारत माता का उपहार है। प्रत्येक धर्म का व्यक्ति भारत माँ का सपूत है। सबकी प्रिय है भारत माता।

भारत माता के सपूत किसे कहा गया है?

A. हिन्दू धर्म के लोगों को

B. इस्लाम धर्म के लोगों को

C. सिक्ख धर्म के लोगों को

D. सभी धर्म के लोगों को

5. 'आपकी वह किताब कहाँ है जो आप कल लाए थे?' किस वाक्य का उदाहरण है?

A. सरल वाक्य

B. मिश्र वाक्य

C. संयुक्त वाक्य

D. इनमें से कोई नहीं

1. B	2. D	3. A	4. D	5. B

6. निम्नलिखित शब्दों में से एक का अर्थ 'धन', 'मतलब', 'कारण' और 'लिए' हैं?

A. आशय B. तात्पर्य
C. अर्थ D. अभिप्राय

7. शब्द एवं उसके अर्थ की दृष्टि से निम्न में से कौन-सा युग्म सही नहीं है?

A. अनल-आग; अनु-पीछे
B. अनु-पीछे; अणु-कण
C. अपेक्षा-इच्छा; उपेक्षा-अनादर
D. अन्य-अनाज; अन्य-दूसरा

8. निम्नलिखित में एक वचन-बहुवचन का कौन-सा युग्म सही नहीं है?

A. पहिया-पहिए
B. आदत-आदतें
C. हाथी-हथिनी
D. कामना-कामनाएं

9. 'जूते चाटना' मुहावरा का अर्थ है :

A. जूता से मारना
B. जूता साफ करना
C. चापलूसी करना
D. स्वाभिमानी बनना

10. इनमें से कौन-सा वाक्य अशुद्ध है?

A. प्रातः काल घूमना चाहिए।
B. समाज में अराजकता बढ़ रही है।
C. 'जलसा' शीर्षक निबंध अच्छा है।
D. राजा अपनी ताकत के बल पर जीत गया।

11. देश के लिए शहीद हुआ सुभाष सच्चा देश भक्त था। रेखांकित शब्द कौन-सा पदबंध है।

A. संज्ञा पदबंध
B. सर्वनाम पदबंध
C. क्रिया पदबंध
D. क्रिया विशेषण पदबंध

12. कर्मवाच्य में किस क्रिया का प्रयोग होता है?

A. अकर्मक
B. सकर्मक
C. एक से अधिक विकल्प सही है
D. इनमें कोई नहीं

13. निम्न में कौन-सा वाक्य शुद्ध है :

A. अभंग एक प्रकार का छंद है।
B. आजकल वहां काफी सरगर्मी दिखाई देती है।
C. सोहन मिठाई लेकर भागता हुआ घर आया।
D. उन्होंने इस बात पर आपत्ति प्रकट की।

14. कौन-सी शब्द शक्ति में अन्य अर्थ प्रकट होता है :

A. लक्षणा B. अभिधा
C. व्यंजना D. छंद

15. किसी शब्द का छुपा हुआ अन्य अर्थ ज्ञात करना किस शब्द शक्ति की विशेषता है?

A. व्यंजना B. लक्षणा
C. अभिधा D. तीनों

6. C **7.** D **8.** C **9.** C **10.** D **11.** A **12.** B **13.** B **14.** C **15.** A

16. जो रहीम गति दीप की कुल कपूत गति सोय।

बारै उजियारे करै बढ़े अंधेरो होय।।

उक्त पंक्ति में कौन-सा अलंकार है :

A. उपमा B. श्लेष

C. यमक D. रूपक

17. जहाँ बिना कारण के कार्य का होना पाया जाए वहाँ कौन-सा अलंकार होता है?

A. विरोधाभास अलंकार

B. विशेषोक्ति अलंकार

C. विभावना अलंकार

D. भ्रांतिमान अलंकार

18. जलता है यह जीवन-पतंग में कौन-सा अलंकार है?

A. उपमा अलंकार

B. अनुप्रास अलंकार

C. रूपक अलंकार

D. मानवीकरण अलंकार

19. आवत जात कुंज की गालियन रूप सुधा नित पीजै। में अलंकार है :

A. रूपक

B. अनुप्रास

C. दोनों विकल्प सही हैं

D. इनमें से कोई नहीं

20. मुख मानो चंद्र है। इस पंक्ति में कौन-सा अलंकार है:

A. विभावना B. रूपक

C. श्लेष D. उत्प्रेक्षा

21. बैन सुन्या जब ते मधुर, तबते सुनत न बैन। इस पंक्ति में कौन-सा अलंकार है:

A. विरोधाभास B. यमक

C. रूपक D. श्लेष

22. छन्दों को पढ़ते समय विराम स्थल को क्या कहा जाता है?

A. यति B. गति

C. तुक D. लय

23. किस वर्णिक छन्द के प्रत्येक चरण में 1 नगण, 2 भगण, और 1 रगण के क्रम में कुल 12 वर्ण होते हैं।

A. कवित्त

B. सवैया

C. कवित्त और सवैया दोनों

D. दूतविलम्बित

24. "वीर तुम बढ़े चलो धीर तुम बढ़े चलो" उपर्युक्त पंक्तियों में कौन-सा काव्य गुण है?

A. ओज गुण

B. माधुर्य गुण

C. प्रसाद गुण

D. इनमें से कोई नहीं

25. रस सिद्धान्त के प्रवर्त्तक कौन है?

A. अभिनव गुप्त B. मम्मट

C. भरत मुनि D. भर्तृहरि

16. B **17.** C **18.** C **19.** C **20.** D **21.** A **22.** A **23.** D **24.** A **25.** C

Mathematics

26. 0.12112111211112 is a number which is:

A. rational B. irrational
C. not rea D. none of these

27. The HCF of the number 144 and 372 is ....

A. 60
B. 24
C. 12
D. None of these

28. For two positive integers c and $d(c>d)$, then what is its HCF if $r = 0$?

A. (c, d) B. (d)
C. (c) D. (r)

29. Which of the following is a polynomial ?

A. $x^2 + 3\sqrt{x}$
B. $2x^2 + \sqrt{3x}$
C. $x^2 + \frac{1}{x^2} = 2$
D. $3x^2 + 2\sqrt{x}$

30. If α and β are the zeroes of Polynomial $2x^2 + 5x - 10$ then the value of $\alpha \,.\, \beta$ will be:

A. $\frac{-5}{2}$ B. $\frac{2}{5}$
C. 5 D. –5

31. For which value of K the equation $x + 2y - 7 = 0$ and $2x + ky = 14$ will be coincident?

A. 4
B. 1
C. 3
D. None of these

32. If α, β are zeroes of equation $x^2 + 9x + 20 = 0$ then $\alpha^2 + \beta^2$ ....

A. 21 B. 40
C. 41 D. 39

33. If the sum of the roots of the equation $x^2 - x = p(2x - 1)$ zero then p............ .

A. –2 B. 2
C. $\frac{-1}{2}$ D. $\frac{1}{2}$

34. The graphic representation of the equation $x + 2y = 3$ and $2x + 4y + 7 = 0$ gives a pair of:

A. Parallel lines
B. Inersecting lines
C. Coincident lines
D. None of these

35. After getting a discount of 5%, purchaser got 2 kg sugar more in ₹ 608 then what will be the selling price of Sugar?

A. ₹ 20 per kg
B. ₹ 25 per kg
C. ₹ 16 per kg
D. ₹ 18 per kg

26. B **27.** C **28.** B **29.** C **30.** D **31.** A **32.** C **33.** C **34.** A **35.** C

36. A discount of 15% on one item is equal to discount of 20% on other item. What will be the ratio of cost of two items.

A. 3 : 4 B. 4 : 3
C. 4 : 5 D. 5 : 4

37. In which ratio y-axis divides the line segment which joins the points (–3, –4) and (1, 2):

A. 1 : 3
B. 2 : 3
C. 3 : 1
D. None of these

38. There is a point P lies on line segment AB such that AP = 2BP. If A = (2, –3) and B = (2, 3) then y-co-ordinates of P is equal to....

A. –2 B. –1
C. 2 D. 1

39. In angle greater than 90° but less than 180° is called:

A. A right angle
B. A straight angle
C. A reflex angle
D. An obtuse angle

40. If one angle of a parallelogram is 24° less than twice the smallest angle, then the measure of the largest angle of a parallelogram is:

A. 176° B. 68°
C. 112° D. 102°

41. If all the sides of Parallelogram touches a circle then it will be called ....

A. Parallelogram
B. Rhombus
C. Chord
D. Radius

42. The height of a cylinder whose radius is 7 cm and the total surface area is 968 cm^2:

A. 15 cm
B. 17 cm
C. 19 cm
D. 21 cm

43. Two cubes each of volume 8 cm^3 are joined end to end, then the surface area of the resulting cuboid is:

A. 80 cm^2 B. 64 cm^2
C. 40 cm^2 D. 8 cm^2

44. A shuttle cock used for playing badminton has the shape of a combination of:

A. a cylinder and a sphere
B. a cylinder and a hemisphere
C. a cone and a sphere
D. a frustum of a cone and a hemisphere

45. In the set of number mean, median, mode is equal ....

A. 2, 2, 2, 2, 4
B. 1, 3, 3, 3, 5
C. 1, 1, 2, 5, 6
D. 1, 1, 1, 2, 5

36. B **37.** C **38.** D **39.** D **40.** C **41.** A **42.** A **43.** C **44.** D **45.** B

46. In the following .... is not formula of mean.

A. $\bar{X} = \frac{\Sigma f_i x_i}{\Sigma f_i}$

B. $\bar{X} = A + \frac{\Sigma f_i d_i}{\Sigma f_i}$

C. $\bar{X} = A + \frac{\Sigma f_i u_i}{\Sigma f_i} \times h$

D. $\bar{X} = \frac{\Sigma f_i d_i}{\Sigma f_i}$

47. The mean of first fifty nine natural number is ....

A. 30 B. 40
C. 50 D. 60

48. $\cos^4 A - \sin^4 A =$ ......

A. $2\cos^2 A + 1$
B. $2\cos^2 A - 1$
C. $2\sin^2 A - 1$
D. $2\sin^2 A + 1$

49. If sin 2A = 2 sinA then A = ...

A. 0°
B. 30°
C. 45°
D. 60°

50. If $\sin\alpha + \sin\beta + \sin\gamma = 3$ then $\sin^3\alpha + \sin^3\beta + \sin^3\gamma =$ ......

A. 0 B. 2
C. 3 D. 1

Science

51. Commercially produced chemical substance which increases fertility of soil is:

A. Herbicides
B. Pesticides
C. Insecticides
D. Fertilizers

52. What is the colour of Silver chloride?

A. White B. Yellow
C. Green D. Black

53. Which of the following is an ore of mercury ?

A. Brass B. Solder
C. Amalgam D. Cinnabar

54. The number of neutrons in an atom of $11^{23}x$ is:

A. 23 B. 11
C. 34 D. 12

55. Physical basis of life is:

A. Nucleus
B. Protoplasm
C. Cell
D. Food

56. The biological processes found in living beings are:

A. Respiration
B. Nutrition
C. Reproduction
D. All of these

46. D	**47.** A	**48.** B	**49.** A	**50.** C	**51.** D
52. A	**53.** D	**54.** D	**55.** B	**56.** D	

57. The study of interactions between living and non-living components of the environment is called:

A. Ecology
B. Geology
C. Meteorology
D. Anthropology

58. Geotropism is the growth of plants in response to:

A. Sunlight B. Soil moisture
C. nutrients D. gravity

59. Which of the following is the place of origin of humans ?

A. Africa B. India
C. China D. America

60. Which one of the following graph indicates that the body is at rest.

A. 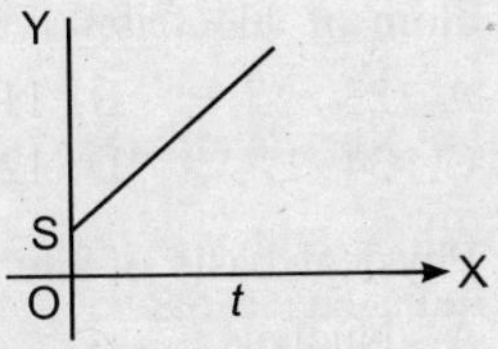

B. 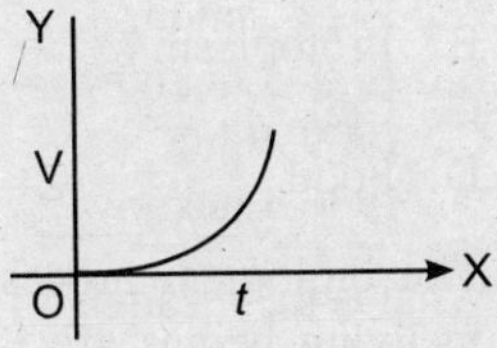

C. 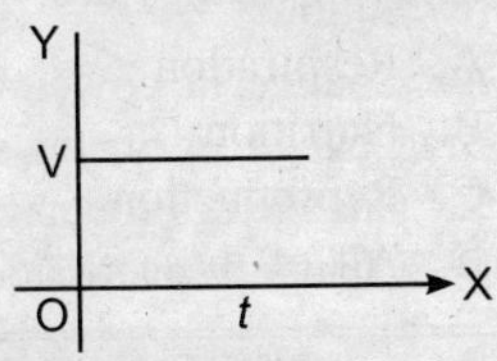

D. 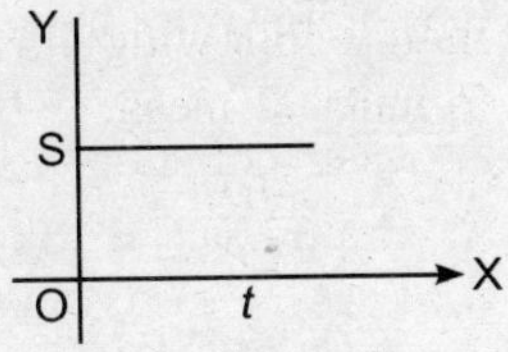

61. The mass of moon is about 0.012 times that of earth and its diameter is about 0.25 times that of earth. The value of G on the moon will be

A. More than that on the earth
B. Same as that on the earth
C. About one-sixth of that on the earth
D. Less than that on the earth.

62. Archimedes' principle helps to calculate the buoyancy of any floating object that is _____ immersed in a fluid.

A. Only partially
B. Only completely
C. Neither partially nor completely
D. Both partially and completely

63. The minimum distance to hear an echo is (taking the velocity of sound in air 330 ms^{-1})

A. 1/20 m B. 20 m
C. 16.5 m D. 330 m

64. Resources are divided in how many parts on the basis of its origin?

A. 1 B. 2
C. 3 D. 4

57. A **58.** D **59.** A **60.** D **61.** B **62.** D **63.** C **64.** B

65. Which of following parts of human body is severely affected by water pollution?

A. Brain B. Skin
C. Legs D. Liver

66. When world environmental day is held?

A. 05th June B. 10th June
C. 15th June D. 20th June

67. The power generated in a windmill ....

A. depends on the tower height
B. depends on wind velocity
C. does not depend on wind velocity
D. depends on the trees surrounding it

68. One micro ampere electric current is equal to

A. 10^{-4}A B. 10^{-5}A
C. 10^{-6}A D. 10^{-7}A

69. Magnetic needle points due to the Earth's magnetic field in:

A. North-South direction
B. East-west direction
C. In the middle of the north-east
D. In the centre of north-west

70. What type of mirror is used for beard making?

A. Concave
B. convex
C. plane
D. None of these

Social Studies

71. When was the East India Company established in India?

A. 1664 B. 1498
C. 1600 D. 1602

72. Type of farming to meet family needs is known as:

A. Subsistence
B. Mixed
C. Organic
D. None of these

73. Who was the only Secretary General of the UNO to have died while in office?

A. U Thant
B. Dag Hammarskjöld
C. Trygve Lie
D. Kurt Waldhiem

74. When and where was the All India Kisan Sabha formed?

A. 1927 Sonpur
B. 1928 Lucknow
C. 1929 Bihta
D. 1936 Lucknow

75. What is the meaning of Industrial revolution?

A. Change in power
B. Change in Social system
C. Change in Production system
D. Change in distribution system

65. D	**66.** A	**67.** B	**68.** C	**69.** A	**70.** A
71. C	**72.** A	**73.** B	**74.** D	**75.** C	

76. Which of the following rivers flows through a rift valley?

A. Krishna B. Godavari
C. Narmada D. Mahanadi

77. What is scale?

A. Ratio
B. Statement
C. Distance
D. None of these

78. About ________ of India's land area is plain, which provides facilities for agriculture and industry.

A. 0.43 B. 0.53
C. 0.34 D. 0.45

79. Which of the following is not the reason of water scarcity?

A. Over-exploitation
B. Excessive use
C. Growing population
D. None of these

80. When was Project Tiger Started?

A. 1972 B. 1973
C. 1974 D. 1975

81. Largest coal producing state in India?

A. West Bangal
B. Jharkhand
C. Odisha
D. Chattisgarh

82. Bauxite is used in which industry?

A. Jute B. Copper
C. Cement D. Aluminium

83. Which of the following place receives the highest rainfall in the world ?

A. Guwahati
B. Mawsynram
C. Cherrapunji
D. Kolkata

84. The financial capital of India is?

A. Delhi B. Bengaluru
C. Hyderabad D. Mumbai

85. How many schedules are there in the Indian Constitution?

A. 390 B. 395
C. 450 D. 495

86. Who appoints the judges of the Supreme Court in India?

A. Governor
B. President
C. Prime Minister
D. Vice President

87. What is the main cause behind origin of the social differences?

A. Caste B. Region
C. Birth D. Religion

88. In which year the establishment of states Re-organization Commission was done?

A. In 1953 B. In 1954
C. In 1955 D. In 1956

76. C	**77.** A	**78.** A	**79.** D	**80.** B	**81.** B	**82.** D
83. B	**84.** D	**85.** B	**86.** B	**87.** C	**88.** A	

89. On what basis democracy is called the best governace?

A. Delay in decision
B. Lack of National feeling.
C. Lack of political awareness.
D. On the basis of referendum.

90. Where is direct democracy in modern age?

A. in Britain
B. In france
C. In India
D. In switzerland

General English

91. Identify the tense used in the following sentence.

"When I reached the bookstore, all the copies had already been sold."

A. Past perfect tense
B. Past indefinite tense
C. Present perfect tense
D. Present indefinite tense

92. Identify the tense used in the underlined phrase.

"The weatherman forecasted that it's going to rain."

A. Present indefinite tense
B. Future indefinite tense
C. Future perfect continuous tense
D. Present continuous tense

93. Select the most appropriate option to change the sentence from direct speech to indirect speech

Ramesh said, "I like this film". Ramesh said that ....

A. he likes/this film
B. he has liked/the film
C. he has been liking/ that film
D. he liked/that film

94. Select the most appropriate option to change the sentence from direct speech to indirect speech

"I will make sure to help you", my sister said.

My sister .... that .... help me.

A. told/she will
B. assured/she would
C. said/she must
D. told/she won't

95. Pickout the Non finite verb/ verbs in the sentence given below.

Teaching English is a difficult task.

A. Teaching
B. Difficult
C. Task
D. English

89. D **90.** D **91.** A **92.** D **93.** D **94.** B **95.** A

96. Pickout the Non finite verb/ verbs in the sentence given below.

Frightened by the storm, we sought shelter.

A. Frightened B. Storm

C. Sought D. Shelter

97. A sentence has been given in Active Voice. Out of the four alternative given below, select the one which best expresses the same sentence in Passive Voice

I had written the letter.

A. The letter is written by me.

B. The letter was being written by me.

C. The letter had been written by me.

D. The letter has been written by me.

98. Please go there (......) it is getting late.

A. ! B. ?

C. . D. ;

99. Fill up the blank, with correct option:

"When my mother died it was forty years ago I was an infant." We will use in place of underlined part.

A. ! B. {}

C. [] D. ()

100. Fill up the blank, with the correct option

He has been learning piano .... two years.

A. For B. Since

C. From D. Over

101. Fill up the blank, with the correct option

The lion sprang .... the prey.

A. on B. at

C. upon D. in

102. Combine the following sentences into one simple sentence.

Bob is only a child. He is very independent.

A. Bob is the only child who is very independent.

B. Bob is only independent child.

C. Bob is independent but only child.

D. Bob is an only child and he is very independent.

103. Combine the following sentences into one simple sentence.

He saw the snake. He ran away.

A. He ran away to see the Snake.

B. On seeing the snake, he ran away.

C. He saw the snake, as he ran away.

D. To see the snake, he ran away

96. A **97.** C **98.** D **99.** D **100.** A **101.** C **102.** A **103.** B

104. Select the alternative which best express the meaning of the idioms/phrase.

Birds of the same feather

A. Birds flying together
B. People working together
C. Persons of the same height
D. Persons of the same character

105. Select the alternative which best express the meaning of the idioms/phrase.

Come across

A. Meet by chance
B. To become successful
C. Boycott someone or something
D. Struggle hard

106. Select the alternative which best express the meaning of the idioms/phrase.

Cast away

A. Reject
B. Produce
C. Go away
D. Throw aside

107. Choose the correct phrase from the given option and make a conditional sentence.

My mum would have made some cake, if my dad.......... some sugar.

A. had brought
B. have brought
C. had been brought
D. have been brought

108. Choose the correct phrase from the given option and make a conditional sentence.

We would have rented the car on condition that it........... so expensive.

A. wasn't
B. weren't
C. hadn't been
D. haven't been

109. Fill up the blank with the correct option.

Bread and butter........... her favourite food.

A. are
B. is
C. has
D. have

110. Fill up the blank with the correct option.

She is the girl who.......... helped me.

A. are
B. were
C. is
D. has

104. D	**105.** A	**106.** D	**107.** A	**108.** C	**109.** B	**110.** D

Logical & Analytical Reasoning

111. Choose the correct option instead of the question mark in the given question.

Loksabha : Speaker : : Rajyasabha : ?

A. Prime Minister
B. President
C. Vice President
D. MP

112. In the given letter series what letter will come in place of the question symbol.

CAT, ECV, HFY, ?

A. LIC B. KLP
C. LCI D. LJC

113. Ajay starts walking from a point and goes 5 km East. From the same point Ranjay starts walking and goes 5 km. Opposite him. Again Ajay turns left and Ranjay right and walks 5 km. Then what is the distance between them now ?

A. 6 km B. 8 km
C. 10 km D. 12 km

114. In English alphabet which Letter is in between the Letter S and the Letter G ?

A. N B. M
C. L D. P

115. If P means –, Q means ÷, R means × and W means + then:

48Q12R10P8W4 = ?

A. 56 B. 40
C. 36 D. 24

116. Two bus tickets from city A to B and three tickets from city A to C cost ₹ 77 but three tickets from city A to B and two tickets from city A to C cost ₹ 73. What are the fares for cities B and C from A?

A. ₹ 4, ₹ 23 B. ₹ 13, ₹ 17
C. ₹ 15, ₹ 14 D. ₹ 17, ₹ 13

117. Find the missing number from the given table:

6	15	20
8	4	5
3	5	20
51	65	?

(*a*) 12 (*b*) 51
(*c*) 56 (*d*) 120

A. Option (*a*) is correct
B. Option (*b*) is correct
C. Option (*c*) is correct
D. Option (*d*) is correct

118. Look at this series:

8, 22, 8, 28, 8, ...

What number should come next?

A. 9 B. 29
C. 32 D. 34

111. C **112.** D **113.** C **114.** B **115.** C **116.** B **117.** D **118.** D

119. Calculate the total number of boys needed to make it 50, if rank of a boy in that group is 7th from the top and 28th from the bottom.

A. 15 B. 16
C. 17 D. 18

120. Find the missing number:

41, 40, 38, 35, 31, ?

A. 24
B. 26
C. 28
D. 30

EXPLANATORY ANSWERS

1. (B): संस्कृत शब्द का संधि-विच्छेद 'सम्' और 'कृत' में होता है। 'सम्' शब्द का अर्थ है 'सम्पूर्ण' या 'पूर्ण' और 'कृत' का अर्थ है 'किया हुआ'। यहाँ 'सम्' शब्द का 'म' अक्षर 'अनुस्वार' में परिवर्तित होकर 'सं' बन जाता है जब इसके बाद वाले शब्द का प्रथम वर्ण एक स्वर होता है। अन्य विकल्प 'संस्', 'संस्कृ', और 'सम' इस संधि के लिए सही नहीं हैं क्योंकि वे शब्द संरचना के हिसाब से मेल नहीं खाते हैं।

2. (D): जिस समास में प्रथम पद प्रधान होता है उसे 'अव्ययीभाव' समास कहते हैं। यहाँ, पहला पद अव्यय (क्रिया विशेषण, संबंध सूचक अव्यय, आदि) होता है जो समास का मुख्य अर्थ प्रदान करता है। अन्य समास जैसे तत्पुरुष, कर्मधारय, और द्वंद्व में प्रथम पद प्रधान नहीं होता।

3. (A): 'देव जो महान है' यह उदाहरण कर्मधारय समास का है, जहाँ दोनों शब्द (देव और महान) विशेषण और विशेष्य का संबंध रखते हैं। यहाँ 'महान' शब्द 'देव' की विशेषता बता रहा है, जिसे एक शब्द में 'महादेव' कह सकते हैं। बहुव्रीहि और तत्पुरुष में यह व्यवस्था नहीं पाई जाती।

4. (D): गद्यांश के अनुसार, 'भारत माता के सपूत' से अभिप्राय सभी धर्मों के लोगों से है, जिसमें कोई भेदभाव नहीं दिखाया गया है। यह विशेष रूप से भारतीय एकता और विविधता को दर्शाता है। अन्य विकल्प किसी विशेष धर्म को इंगित करते हैं जो गद्यांश की भावना के अनुरूप नहीं हैं।

5. (B): 'आपकी वह किताब कहाँ है जो आप कल लाए थे?' यह वाक्य मिश्र वाक्य का उदाहरण है क्योंकि इसमें एक मुख्य वाक्य और एक आश्रित वाक्य है। मुख्य वाक्य है 'आपकी वह किताब कहाँ है?' और आश्रित वाक्य है 'जो आप कल लाए थे', जो मुख्य वाक्य की जानकारी को पूरा करता है। सरल और संयुक्त वाक्य संरचना इस उदाहरण में नहीं बैठती।

6. (C): अर्थ शब्द के विविध अर्थों में 'धन', 'मतलब', 'कारण' और 'लिए' शामिल हैं। 'अर्थ' का प्रयोग कई प्रकार के संदर्भों में होता है, जिसमें वाक्य का मुख्य उद्देश्य या किसी शब्द का मूल भाव शामिल होता है।

119. B **120.** B

अन्य विकल्प जैसे 'आशय', 'तात्पर्य', और 'अभिप्राय' भी समान अर्थ रखते हैं परन्तु उनका प्रयोग विशिष्ट संदर्भों में होता है।

7. **(D):** 'अन्य' का अर्थ 'दूसरा' होता है, जबकि 'अनाज' एक प्रकार का खाद्य पदार्थ है, इसलिए यह युग्म अर्थ की दृष्टि से असंगत है। अन्य युग्म सही संबंध दिखाते हैं, जैसे 'अनल-आग' और 'अणु-कण' जो सही अर्थों में मेल खाते हैं।

8. **(C):** 'हाथी' और 'हथिनी' वचन के बजाय लिंग का भेद दर्शाते हैं। 'हाथी' एक नर हाथी को दर्शाता है, जबकि 'हथिनी' एक मादा हाथी होती है। यह वचन युग्म के रूप में गलत है क्योंकि यह एकल और बहुवचन का सही उदाहरण नहीं है।

9. **(C):** 'जूते चाटना' मुहावरे का अर्थ 'चापलूसी करना' होता है। यह मुहावरा व्यक्ति की उस व्यवहार को दर्शाता है जो अत्यधिक आज्ञाकारिता या खुशामद करने के लिए अपमानजनक स्तर तक चला जाता है। अन्य विकल्प सही संदर्भ नहीं बताते हैं।

10. **(D):** राजा अपनी ताकत के बल पर जीत गया : यह वाक्य अशुद्ध है क्योंकि यहाँ 'बल पर' का प्रयोग अनावश्यक है, जब 'जीत गया' पहले से ही ताकत या शक्ति का संकेत दे रहा है। 'अपनी ताकत से जीत गया' अधिक सटीक होता। अन्य विकल्पों में भाषागत अशुद्धियाँ नहीं हैं।

11. **(A):** वाक्य में रेखांकित शब्द 'देश भक्त' है, जो एक संज्ञा पदबंध है क्योंकि यह एक व्यक्ति का वर्णन कर रहा है। 'देश' और 'भक्त' शब्दों को मिलाकर एक सम्मिलित अर्थ बनता है जो देश के प्रति समर्पित व्यक्ति को दर्शाता है। अन्य विकल्प क्रिया पदबंध, क्रिया विशेषण पदबंध और सर्वनाम पदबंध इस संदर्भ में सही नहीं हैं क्योंकि यहां किसी क्रिया या सर्वनाम का वर्णन नहीं हो रहा है।

12. **(B):** कर्मवाच्य में सकर्मक क्रियाओं का प्रयोग होता है जिसमें क्रिया की क्रिया पर प्रत्यक्ष प्रभाव पड़ता है। सकर्मक क्रियाएँ वे होती हैं जिनके लिए एक कर्म (ऑब्जेक्ट) की आवश्यकता होती है ताकि वाक्य पूरा हो सके। अकर्मक क्रियाएँ, जिन्हें बिना कर्म के पूरा किया जा सकता है, कर्मवाच्य में प्रयुक्त नहीं होतीं।

13. **(B):** आजकल वहां काफी सरगर्मी दिखाई देती है : यह वाक्य शुद्ध है क्योंकि यहाँ व्याकरणिक संरचना सही है और सभी शब्द सही तरीके से प्रयोग किए गए हैं। अन्य विकल्प जैसे कि 'अभंग एक प्रकार का छंद है' और 'सोहन मिठाई लेकर भागता हुआ घर आया' में व्याकरणिक या शब्द संबंधी त्रुटियाँ हैं जो उन्हें अशुद्ध बनाती हैं।

14. **(C):** व्यंजना शब्द शक्ति में शब्द का अन्य अर्थ प्रकट होता है, जिसमें मूल अभिधानिक अर्थ से अलग कोई सूक्ष्म या प्रतीकात्मक अर्थ निहित होता है। लक्षणा और अभिधा अधिक सीधे और स्पष्ट अर्थ प्रदान करते हैं, जबकि व्यंजना अधिक गहराई और परतों वाला अर्थ देती है।

15. **(A):** व्यंजना शब्द शक्ति की विशेषता यह है कि इसमें किसी शब्द का छुपा हुआ अन्य अर्थ ज्ञात किया जाता है। इस शक्ति में शब्द का उपयोग ऐसे होता है कि यह

अपने प्राथमिक या सीधे अर्थ से परे कुछ और इशारा करता है, जैसे कि कविता या वाक्यांश में गहराई या भावनात्मक प्रभाव को बढ़ाने के लिए।

16. **(B):** 'श्लेष' रहीम की उक्त पंक्ति में श्लेष अलंकार है। यहाँ 'गति दीप की' और 'कुल क़पूत गति सोय' दोनों में 'गति' शब्द का विभिन्न अर्थों का प्रयोग हुआ है—पहला 'गति' का अर्थ है गतिविधि या आचरण और दूसरा 'गति' का अर्थ है गतिमान या स्थिति। इस प्रकार श्लेष अलंकार में एक शब्द के एक से अधिक अर्थ उभरते हैं।

17. **(C):** जहाँ बिना कारण के कार्य का होना पाया जाए, वहाँ विभावना अलंकार होता है। इसमें कारण और कार्य के बीच कोई स्पष्ट संबंध न होने के बावजूद कार्य को किसी कारण से जोड़ा जाता है, जो कविता में एक अद्वितीय या अनूठी व्याख्या को प्रस्तुत करता है।

18. **(C):** 'जलता है यह जीवन-पतंग में' पंक्ति में रूपक अलंकार है, जहाँ 'जीवन' को सीधे 'पतंग' से तुलना की गई है, जीवन की उत्थान और पतन की विशेषताओं को पतंग के जलने के साथ रूपकात्मक रूप से प्रस्तुत किया गया है।

19. **(C):** दोनों विकल्प सही हैं : 'आवत जात कुंज की गालियन रूप सुधा नित पीजै' में रूपक और अनुप्रास दोनों अलंकार हैं। 'रूप सुधा' में रूपक का प्रयोग है, जहां सौंदर्य को अमृत के रूप में देखा जा रहा है, और 'आवत जात' जैसे शब्दों में अनुप्रास का प्रयोग है जो ध्वनियों की पुनरावृत्ति को दर्शाता है।

20. **(D):** 'मुख मानो चंद्र है' में उत्प्रेक्षा अलंकार है। इसमें मुख को चंद्रमा के रूप में कल्पना की गई है, जो एक अतिशयोक्ति है। यहाँ मुख की सुंदरता की तुलना चंद्रमा से की गई है, जिससे उसकी अधिक सुंदरता की कल्पना की जा सकती है।

21. **(A):** 'बैन सुन्या जब ते मधुर, तबते सुनत न बैन।' इस पंक्ति में विरोधाभास अलंकार है, जहां एक ही समय में विरोधी विचारों को प्रस्तुत किया गया है। यहाँ पंक्ति कहती है कि जब से व्यक्ति ने मधुर वाणी सुनी है, तब से वह किसी और वाणी को नहीं सुन पाता। यह एक विरोधाभासी स्थिति बताती है जो असंभव प्रतीत होती है।

22. **(A):** छंदों को पढ़ते समय विराम स्थल को 'यति' कहा जाता है। यति वह स्थान है जहां एक विशेष रूप में कविता के भीतर विराम दिया जाता है, जो कविता की लय और गति को नियंत्रित करने में मदद करता है। यह छंद की संरचना में अनुशासन और रुकावट लाकर उसकी शैली को और स्पष्ट करता है।

23. **(D):** वर्णिक छंद में प्रत्येक चरण में 1 नगण, 2 भगण, और 1 रगण के क्रम में कुल 12 वर्ण होते हैं, जो 'दूतविलम्बित' छंद की विशेषता है। यह छंद संस्कृत काव्यशास्त्र में एक महत्वपूर्ण शैली है, जिसे विशेषतः गीतात्मक और लयात्मक कविता के लिए प्रयोग किया जाता है।

24. **(A):** 'वीर तुम बढ़े चलो धीर तुम बढ़े चलो' में ओज गुण प्रमुख है। ओज गुण वह है जो कविता में शक्ति, साहस, और प्रेरणा को दर्शाता है। यह पंक्तियाँ वीरता

और दृढ़ता को प्रोत्साहित करती हैं, जो श्रोता को आत्मविश्वास और उत्साह से भर देती हैं।

25. **(C):** रस सिद्धान्त के प्रवर्तक भरत मुनि हैं, जिन्होंने 'नाट्यशास्त्र' में रसों का वर्णन किया। रस सिद्धान्त भारतीय कला और साहित्य में भावनाओं और मनोविज्ञान के अध्ययन का आधार है, जिसमें कविता और नाटक के माध्यम से विभिन्न भावों को प्रकट करने की विधि बताई गई है।

26. **(B):** 0.12112111211112...
It is a number. Which is an irrational number.

27. **(C):** $\because \quad 144 = (12)^2$

and $\quad 372 = 12 \times 31$

$\therefore$ The HCF of the number 144 and 372 will be 12.

29. **(C):** (A) $x^2 + 3\sqrt{x} = x^2 + 3(x)^{1/2}$

(B) $2x^2 + \sqrt{3x} = 2x^2 + 3(x)^{1/2}$

(C) $x^2 + \dfrac{1}{x^2} = 2$

$\Rightarrow x^4 + 1 = 2x^2$

$\Rightarrow x^4 - 2x^2 + 1 = 0$ (polynomial)

(D) $3x^2 + 2\sqrt{x} = 3x^2 + 2(x)^{1/2}$

Here option (C) is a polynomial.

30. **(D):** Given α and β are the zeroes of polynomial $2x^2 + 5x - 10$

$\because \quad 2x^2 + 5x - 10 = 0$

$\therefore \quad \alpha + \beta = \dfrac{-b}{a} = \dfrac{-5}{2}$

$\Rightarrow \quad \alpha + \beta = \dfrac{-5}{2}$

and $\quad \alpha\beta = \dfrac{c}{2} = \dfrac{-10}{2}$

$\Rightarrow \quad \alpha + \beta = -5.$

31. **(A):** Given, equation

$$x + 2y - 7 = 0$$

and $\quad 2x + ky - 14 = 0$

$\because$ Equation will be coincident (It has infinite solution)

$\therefore \quad \dfrac{a_1}{a_2} = \dfrac{b_1}{b_2} = \dfrac{c_1}{c_2}$

$\Rightarrow \quad \dfrac{1}{2} = \dfrac{2}{k} = \dfrac{7}{14}$

$\Rightarrow \quad \dfrac{1}{2} = \dfrac{2}{k} = \dfrac{1}{2}$

$\Rightarrow \quad k = 4.$

32. **(C):** Given,

$$x^2 + 9x + 20 = 0$$

$\because \quad \alpha + \beta = \dfrac{-b}{a} = \dfrac{-9}{1} = 9$

and $\quad \alpha\beta = \dfrac{c}{a} = 20$

$\therefore \quad \alpha^2 + \beta^2 = (\alpha + \beta)^2 - 2\alpha\beta$

$= (9)^2 - 2 \times 20$

$= 81 - 40 = 41$

$\Rightarrow \quad \alpha^2 + \beta^2 = 41.$

33. **(C):** Given, equation

$$x^2 - x = p(2x - 1)$$

$\Rightarrow \quad x^2 - x - 2px - p$

$\Rightarrow \quad x^2 - x - 2px + p = 0$

$\Rightarrow \quad x^2 - (1 + 2p)x + p = 0$

$\because$ The sum of the roots of equation is 0

$$\therefore \quad \alpha + \beta = 0$$

$$\Rightarrow \quad \frac{(1+2p)}{1} = 0$$

$$\Rightarrow \quad 1 + 2p = 0$$

$$\Rightarrow \quad p = \frac{-1}{2}.$$

34. (A): Given, equation

$$x + 2y = 3$$

$$\Rightarrow \quad x + 2y - 3 = 0 \qquad ...(i)$$

$$\text{and} \quad 2x + 4y + 7 = 0 \qquad ...(ii)$$

$$\frac{1}{2} = \frac{2}{4} \neq \frac{-3}{7}$$

$$\Rightarrow \quad \frac{a_1}{a_2} = \frac{b_1}{b_2} \neq \frac{c_1}{c_2}$$

$$\Rightarrow \quad \frac{1}{2} = \frac{1}{2} \neq \frac{-3}{7}$$

The graphic representation of equation is parallel line.

35. (C): The selling price of sugar is ₹ x per kg.

$$\text{Then,} \quad \frac{608}{x \times \frac{95}{100}} - \frac{608}{x} = 2$$

$$\Rightarrow \quad \frac{608}{x}\left[\frac{100}{95} - 1\right] = 2$$

$$\Rightarrow \quad \frac{608}{x}\left[\frac{20}{19} - 1\right] = 2$$

$$\Rightarrow \quad \frac{608}{x}\left[\frac{1}{19}\right] = 2$$

$$\Rightarrow \quad 2x = 32$$

$$\Rightarrow \quad x = 16$$

Hence, the selling price of sugar is ₹ 16 per kg.

37. (C): Let y-axis divides the line segment PQ in ratio $\lambda : 1$

Then, co-ordinate of division point

$$R\left(\frac{\lambda - 3}{\lambda + 1}, \frac{2\lambda - 4}{\lambda + 1}\right)$$

$\because$ Point R on y-axis and co-ordinate of every point of x-axis on y-axis is zero.

$$\therefore \quad \frac{\lambda - 3}{\lambda + 1} = 0$$

$$\Rightarrow \quad \lambda = 3$$

$$\therefore \quad \text{Required ratio} = \lambda : 1 = 3 : 1.$$

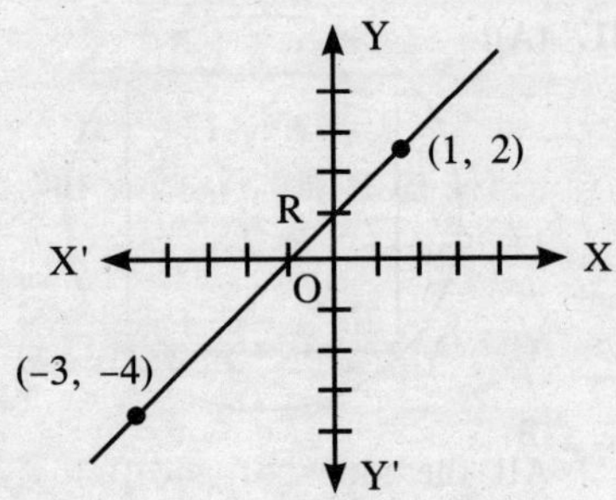

38. (D): Given, $\quad AP = 2BP$

$$\Rightarrow \quad \frac{AP}{BP} = \frac{2}{1}$$

$$\Rightarrow \quad AP : BP = 2 : 1$$

$$A = (2, -3)$$

$$\text{and} \quad B = (2, 3)$$

$\therefore p(x, y)$

$$= p\left(\frac{2 \times 2 + 1 \times 2}{2+1}, \frac{2 \times 3 + 1 \times -3}{2+1}\right)$$

$$= p\left(\frac{6}{3}, \frac{3}{3}\right) = p(2, 1)$$

$\therefore$ y co-ordinate of p = 1.

39. (D): 90° < θ < 180°

An angle greater than 90° but less than 180° is called an obtuse angle.

40. (C): Let the smallest angle of parallelogram is $x°$ and the greatest angle is $(2x° - 24°)$.

Then, $2(x + 2x - 24) = 360°$

$\Rightarrow \quad 3x - 24 = 180°$

$\Rightarrow \quad 3x = 204°$

$x = 68°$

$\therefore$ Greatest angle $= 2x - 24$

$= 2 \times 68 - 24$

$= 136 - 24$

$= 112°$.

41. (A):

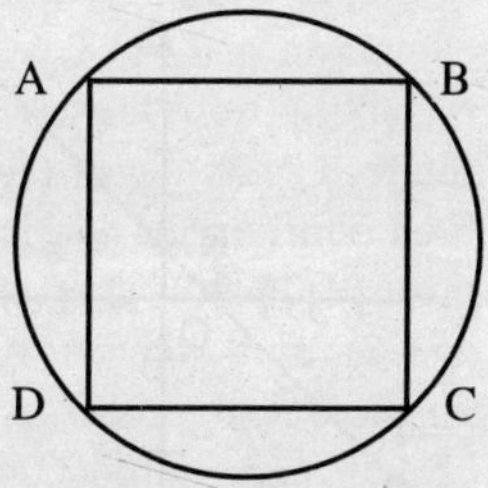

All the sides of parallelogram touches a circle than it will be called rhombus.

42. (A): Total surface area of cylinder

$= 2\pi rh + 2\pi r^2$

$968 = 2\pi \times 7 \times h + 2\pi(7)^2$

$\Rightarrow \quad 968 = 2 \times \frac{22}{7} \times 7(h+7)$

$\Rightarrow \quad 968 = 44(h + 7)$

$\Rightarrow \quad h + 7 = 22$

$\Rightarrow \quad h = 22 - 7 = 15$

$\Rightarrow \quad h = 15$ cm

Hence, height of cylinder $= h$

$= 15$ cm.

43. (C): Given, two cubes each of volume 8 cm^3

$\Rightarrow \quad (\text{Side})^3 = 2^3$

$\Rightarrow \quad \text{Side} = 2$ cm

$\because$ Two cubes are joined end to end

$\therefore$ Length of resulting cuboid

$= 2 + 2 = 4$ cm

width $= 2$ cm

and height $= 2$ cm

$\therefore$ Surface area of cuboid

$= 2(l \times b + b \times h + l \times h)$

$= 2(4 \times 2 + 2 \times 2 + 4 \times 2)$

$= 2(8 + 4 + 8)$

$= 40$ cm^2

45. (B): 1, 3, 3, 3, 5

$\therefore \quad \text{Mean} = \frac{1+3+3+3+5}{5}$

$= \frac{15}{5} = 3$

Mode = 3 (Maximum 3 times)

and Median $= \frac{5+1}{2}$ th term

= third term = 3

[n = number of data = 5]

Hence, option (B) mean, median and mode are equal.

47. (A): The sum of first fifty nine natural number is

$= \frac{59(59+1)}{2} = 59 \times 30$

$\Rightarrow$ The mean of first fifty nine natural number

$= \frac{59 \times 30}{59} = 30.$

48. (B): $\cos^4 A - \sin^4 A$

$= (\cos^2 A - \sin^2 A)(\cos^2 A + \sin^2 A)$

$= (\cos^2 A - \sin^2 A) \cdot 1$

$= \cos^2 A - (1 - \cos^2 A)$

$= \cos^2 A - 1 + \cos^2 A$

$= 2\cos^2 A - 1$

$\Rightarrow \cos^4 A - \sin^4 A = 2\cos^2 A - 1.$

49. (A): Given,

$$\sin^2 A = 2 \sin A$$

$$\Rightarrow 2 \sin A \cos A = 2 \sin A$$

$$\Rightarrow \cos A = 1 = \cos 0°$$

$$\Rightarrow A = 0°.$$

51. (D): Commercially produced chemical substances that supply essential nutrients such as nitrogen, phosphorus, and potassium to the soil, thereby enhancing its fertility and promoting higher crop yields. Globally, over 190 million tonnes of fertilizers are consumed every year to meet agricultural demands. Their excessive or imbalanced use can lead to soil degradation and environmental pollution.

52. (A): Silver chloride (AgCl) is a white crystalline solid which turns purple on exposure to sunlight due to photochemical decomposition. It is commonly utilized in photographic materials and has a molar mass of approximately 143.32 g/mol. Its low solubility in water makes it useful in various chemical applications.

53. (D): Cinnabar (HgS) is the principal ore of mercury, recognized by its bright red color. When heated, it decomposes to produce mercury vapor, which is then condensed to form liquid mercury. Historically, cinnabar was also used as a pigment called vermilion in paintings and decorations.

54. (D): An atom of sodium (symbol $11^{23}x$) has an atomic number of 11 and a mass number of 23. Neutrons are calculated by subtracting the atomic number (11) from the mass number (23), giving 12 neutrons. Sodium is an essential element in the human body, particularly for nerve impulse conduction.

55. (B): Protoplasm is the living substance within cells, composed of cytoplasm and nucleus where vital metabolic activities occur. Often referred to as the physical basis of life, it primarily consists of water (around 70–90%), proteins, lipids, and various solutes. All essential physiological processes, including growth and reproduction, proceed within this medium.

56. (D): Respiration, nutrition, and reproduction collectively characterize living organisms. Respiration provides the energy required for biological functions, nutrition ensures the intake of essential nutrients for growth and maintenance, and reproduction facilitates the survival and continuation of species. These processes distinguish living beings from non-living entities.

57. (A): Ecology is the study of interactions among organisms (biotic components) and between organisms and their physical surroundings (abiotic components). It investigates how environmental factors like temperature, water, and light affect species distribution and survival. Modern ecological research also examines the impacts of climate change on various ecosystems.

58. **(D):** Geotropism, also known as gravitropism, is the growth response of plants to gravity. Roots exhibit positive geotropism by growing downward for better anchorage and water uptake, while shoots show negative geotropism by growing upward to access sunlight. This directional growth is vital for plant stability and nutrient acquisition.

59. **(A):** Fossil records and genetic studies indicate that modern humans (Homo sapiens) originated in Africa around 200,000 to 300,000 years ago. Discoveries such as the Omo Kibish remains in Ethiopia support this African origin theory. Subsequent migrations out of Africa gave rise to the global distribution of humans seen today.

60. **(D):** The horizontal straight line of displacement with respect to time shows that there is no change in position: If S remains constant, velocity $= dS/dt = 0$, which means the body is at rest. Studies in kinematics confirm that zero velocity yields a constant displacement over time, indicating no movement.

61. **(B):** The symbol 'G' represents the universal gravitational constant, which is the same everywhere in the universe ($\approx 6.67 \times 10^{-11}$ Nm^2/kg^2). It does not depend on the mass or diameter of celestial bodies, so its value on the Moon remains the same as on Earth.

62. **(D):** Archimedes' principle states that a body wholly or partially immersed in a fluid experiences an upward thrust equal to the weight of the fluid displaced. This applies to objects floating on the surface (partial immersion) or fully submerged (complete immersion).

63. **(C):** At 330 m/s, sound takes 0.1 second to travel 33 m (to the reflecting surface and back). Hence, the minimum distance for an echo is half of that, or 16.5 m. Below this distance, the reflected sound merges with the original sound and isn't heard distinctly as an echo.

64. **(B):** Based on origin, resources are commonly split into Biotic (derived from living organisms, e.g. forests, fisheries) and Abiotic (derived from non-living elements, e.g. minerals, water). This twofold classification helps in efficient resource management strategies.

65. **(D):** Water pollution often leads to diseases like jaundice and hepatitis, which severely affect the liver (the primary organ responsible for detoxification). Contaminated water can also transmit pathogens that can harm multiple organs, but the liver is critically at risk due to its filtration function.

66. **(A):** Established by the United Nations in 1972, World Environment Day is commemorated every year on 5 June. It aims to encourage

global awareness and action for the protection of the environment through public outreach programs and policy measures.

67. **(B):** The power generated by a windmill increases significantly with wind speed (proportional to the cube of wind velocity). Although tower height can help access faster winds, ultimately the main factor in power generation is the velocity of the wind itself.

68. **(C):** One microampere is equal to one-millionth of an ampere $1\ \mu A = 10^{-6} A$. Such small currents are measured in microammeters in laboratories or delicate electronic circuits where precision is crucial.

69. **(A):** A freely suspended magnetic needle aligns with the Earth's magnetic field, pointing roughly toward the geographic North and South. This fundamental property of magnetism was historically key to navigation before modern compasses and GPS.

70. **(A):** A concave mirror (shaving mirror) magnifies the reflected image when the face is placed within its focal length. This allows for a closer, clearer view, making tasks such as beard trimming or makeup application easier.

71. **(C):** The East India Company was established on 31 December 1600 through a Royal Charter granted by Queen Elizabeth I. It began trading in India in the early 17th century and gradually expanded its influence. Eventually, it gained political control over large parts of the Indian subcontinent, marking a pivotal phase in colonial history.

72. **(A):** Subsistence farming involves growing crops and raising livestock primarily for the farmer's own family. The output is usually minimal, with little surplus for sale or trade. This type of farming relies on simple tools, limited technology, and local resources.

73. **(B):** Serving as the second Secretary-General of the United Nations (1953–1961), Dag Hammarskjöld died in a plane crash on 18 September 1961 while on a peace mission in the Congo. Posthumously awarded the Nobel Peace Prize, he remains the only Secretary-General to have died in office.

74. **(D):** The All India Kisan Sabha was formed in April 1936 at Lucknow during the Indian National Congress session. It sought to champion peasants' rights, address agrarian distress, and mobilize farmers for various socio-political causes. Prominent leaders like Swami Sahajanand Saraswati played key roles in its formation.

75. **(C):** Change in Production system: The Industrial Revolution marked a transition from manual production to machine-based manufacturing, starting in the late 18th century. It introduced mechanized processes, factory systems, and large-scale production. This led to significant socio-economic transformations across Europe and later worldwide.

76. (C): The Narmada River flows westward through a tectonic rift valley between the Vindhya and Satpura ranges. This rift formation gives the river its relatively straight course, unlike most other major Indian rivers. It eventually empties into the Arabian Sea, near the Gulf of Khambhat.

77. (A): In cartography, scale represents the ratio between a distance on a map and the corresponding distance on the ground (e.g., 1:50,000). It enables accurate understanding of geographical features and distances. A suitable scale helps in planning, navigation, and land-use management.

78. (A): About 43% of India's total land area is classified as plain, which helps support intensive agriculture and various industries. These plains, especially in the northern and coastal regions, play a crucial role in accommodating high population density and fostering economic development.

79. (D): Over-exploitation, excessive use, and growing population are all valid reasons for water scarcity. Unsustainable consumption patterns and unequal resource distribution further aggravate the crisis. Consequently, none of the listed options is incorrect, as each contributes to water shortages.

80. (B): Project Tiger was launched on 1 April 1973 to protect the Bengal tiger (Panthera tigris tigris) and its habitat. Initially covering nine tiger reserves, it has since expanded to over 50 reserves nationwide. It helped boost India's tiger population through strict habitat conservation and anti-poaching measures.

81. (B): Jharkhand produces the largest share of India's coal, with major coalfields like Jharia, Bokaro, and North Karanpura. According to government data, Jharkhand contributes around 25–30% of India's total coal production annually, making it a key resource base for the country's energy sector.

82. (D): Aluminium: Bauxite is the principal ore of aluminium, containing hydrated aluminium oxides. India has significant reserves in Odisha and Jharkhand. The extracted aluminium is widely utilized in aerospace, construction, and electrical industries due to its lightweight, corrosion-resistant properties.

83. (B): Mawsynram, located in Meghalaya, India, receives an annual rainfall of around 11,800 mm, making it the wettest place on Earth. Its unique topography and the presence of moist winds from the Bay of Bengal contribute to its extraordinarily high precipitation levels.

84. (D): Often referred to as the financial capital of India, Mumbai hosts the headquarters of major banks, financial institutions, and the Bombay Stock Exchange (BSE). The city's robust economy, large-scale industries, and international connections position it as a prominent global financial hub.

85. (B): The Constitution of India originally contained 395 Articles divided into 22 Parts and 8 Schedules. Over time, amendments have added more Articles and Schedules, but the total number of original Articles stood at 395 when the Constitution came into effect on 26 January 1950.

86. (B): In India, the President appoints the Chief Justice and other judges of the Supreme Court in consultation with the collegium system. This process includes recommendations by senior judges, ensuring judicial independence and maintaining a system of checks and balances.

87. (C): Social differences often arise based on attributes acquired by birth, such as family background or inherited status. These can intersect with factors like caste, ethnicity, and region, shaping societal hierarchies and leading to inequalities or discrimination.

88. (A): The States Reorganisation Commission (SRC) was appointed in 1953 to study and recommend the reorganization of state boundaries in India. Its recommendations ultimately led to the States Reorganisation Act of 1956, which significantly redrew state lines on linguistic grounds.

89. (D): Democracy is often hailed as the best form of governance because it empowers citizens through direct or indirect participation, such as referendums. This system upholds popular consent, accountability, and a voice for all, making governance more representative and transparent.

90. (D): Switzerland practices direct democracy through instruments like referendums and popular initiatives, allowing citizens to vote on legislative matters. This unique approach grants the Swiss populace significant influence over government decisions in the modern era.

91. (A): The sentence "When I reached the bookstore, all the copies had already been sold" uses the past perfect tense. This tense is used to describe an action that was completed before another action in the past. Here, the selling of the copies had been completed before the speaker reached the bookstore. This is indicated by the use of "had been" which is characteristic of the past perfect tense.

92. (D): The phrase "going to rain" in the sentence "The weatherman forecasted that it's going to rain" is an example of the present continuous tense, used here to express a future intention. Technically, it is a colloquial future construction but structurally, it uses the present continuous tense components of "going" combined with a base verb ("to rain").

93. (D): In the sentence "Ramesh said, 'I like this film'," when changing from direct to indirect speech, the present tense 'like' changes to the past tense 'liked' to reflect the past tense of the reporting verb 'said.' The demonstrative 'this' also changes to 'that' to indicate the shift from direct to reported speech context.

94. (B): The direct speech statement "I will make sure to help you", my sister said, when converted into indirect speech, becomes "My sister assured that she would help me." The verb "assured" is appropriate for the context of making a promise or guarantee, and "will" changes to "would" to reflect the shift in verb tense from direct to reported speech.

95. (A): In the sentence "Teaching English is a difficult task," the word "Teaching" functions as a gerund, which is a non-finite verb form. Non-finite verbs, such as gerunds, do not change according to tense or subject and often act as nouns in the sentence, here referring to the act of teaching.

96. (A): In the phrase "Frightened by the storm, we sought shelter," the word "Frightened" functions as a participle, which is a type of non-finite verb. Participles describe a condition or action related to the subject (we) and do not function as the main verb of the sentence.

97. (C): The sentence "I had written the letter" in passive voice is correctly transformed to "The letter had been written by me." This maintains the past perfect tense, switching the focus from the doer (I) to the object of the action (the letter).

98. (D): The sentence "Please go there; it is getting late" correctly uses a semicolon (;) to connect two independent clauses that are closely related in content. The semicolon here serves to balance the urgency of the request with the reasoning provided.

99. (D): The correct punctuation to replace "it was forty years ago" in the sentence "When my mother died (it was forty years ago) I was an infant" is the parentheses. Parentheses are used to include additional information that is supplementary and can be omitted without changing the fundamental meaning of the sentence.

100. (A): In the sentence "He has been learning piano for two years," the preposition "for" is used to indicate the duration of time that has passed during which the action has been continuously occurring. This is typical for expressing durations with perfect continuous tenses.

101. (C): In the sentence "The lion sprang upon the prey," the preposition "upon" correctly describes the sudden and forceful movement of the lion towards its prey. "Upon" is often used to convey a strong or assertive action, making it the best choice here compared to the other options which do not carry the same intensity or accuracy of movement.

102. (A): This option effectively combines the two original sentences into one simple sentence while maintaining the meaning of both. It identifies Bob as being an only child and also describes his quality of independence, keeping the structure straightforward and clear.

103. **(B):** This sentence accurately combines the original statements by showing causation clearly and succinctly. It establishes that the sight of the snake directly prompted him to run away, using the participle "seeing" to link the actions smoothly.

104. **(D):** The phrase "Birds of the same feather" is an idiomatic expression meaning people who are similar in character or interests. It is based on the observation that birds of a feather (type) flock together, which metaphorically applies to people.

105. **(A):** The phrase "Come across" means to encounter or meet someone or something by chance. This is the correct interpretation of the idiom, which refers to an unexpected or unplanned meeting.

106. **(D):** "Cast away" means to throw aside or dispose of something. It implies discarding something that is no longer wanted or is considered useless, aligning with the option of throwing it aside.

107. **(A):** The conditional phrase "My mum would have made some cake, if my dad had brought some sugar" correctly uses the past perfect tense "had brought" to express a condition in the past that did not occur, affecting the outcome.

108. **(C):** The sentence "We would have rented the car on condition that it hadn't been so expensive" uses the past perfect tense "hadn't been" to describe a past condition that prevented an action. This choice reflects a hypothetical past condition that influenced the decision.

109. **(B):** In English, when two nouns connected by 'and' refer to a single idea or item, they take a singular verb. "Bread and butter" is often considered a single dish or staple, thus "is" is the correct verb to use, treating the phrase as a singular subject.

110. **(D):** The correct form to complete the sentence "She is the girl who has helped me" is "has." This usage is correct because "has" follows the pronoun "who" referring back to "she," making "has" the appropriate singular third-person present perfect tense verb.

112. **(D):**

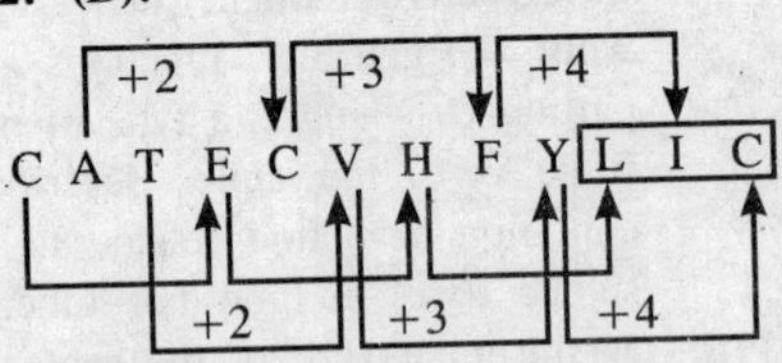

Here, ? = next term of series

= LJC.

113. **(C):** Here, starting point = A

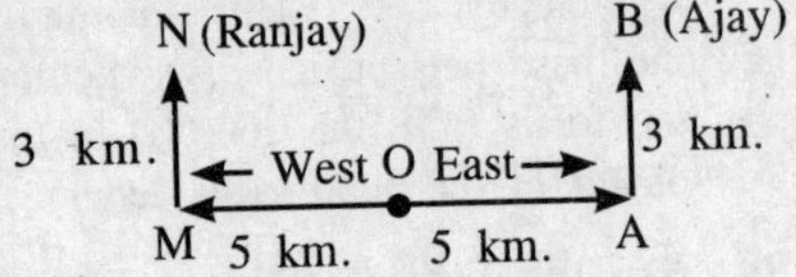

OA = 5 km.

AB = 3 km.

OM = 5 km.

MN = 3 km.

$\because \quad MN = AB = 3$ km.

$\therefore \quad NB = OM + OA$

$= 5 + 5 = 10$ km.

$\therefore$ The distance between Ajay (B) and Ranjay (N) = 10 km

Hence, distance between them = 10 km.

114. (B):

ABCDEFGHIJKLMNOPQRSTUVWXYZ

↑ (G) ↑ (M) ↑ (S)

Here, letter is in between S and G is M.

115. (C): Given,

$P = -,$

$Q = \div,$

$R = \times,$

$W = +$

$\therefore$ 48Q12R10P8W4

$= 48 \div 12 \times 10 - 8 + 4$

$= 4 \times 10 - 8 + 4$

$= 40 - 8 + 4$

$= 44 - 8 = 36.$

116. (B): Let cost of 1 ticket from city A to B be ₹ x and cost of 1 ticket from city A to C be ₹ y

Then, $2x + 3y = 77 \quad \ldots(i)$

$3x + 2y = 73 \quad \ldots(ii)$

From $(i) \times 3 - (ii) \times 2$

$$\begin{array}{r} 6x + 9y = 231 \\ 6x + 4y = 146 \\ - \quad - \quad\quad - \\ \hline 5y = 85 \end{array}$$

$\Rightarrow \quad y =$ ₹ 17

$y = 17,$

Putting the value of y in (i), we obtain $x =$ ₹ 13

Hence, the fares for cities B and C from A are ₹ 13 and ₹ 17.

117. (D): From given table

First column

$\Rightarrow 6 \times 8 + 3 = 48 + 3 = 51$

Second column

$\Rightarrow 15 \times 4 + 5 = 60 + 5 = 65$

Third column

$\Rightarrow 20 \times 5 + 20 = 100 + 20$

$= \boxed{120}$

$\therefore$? = Missing number = 120.

118. (D):

8 22 8 28 8 $\boxed{34}$

(22 → 28: +6; 28 → 34: +6)

Here, ? = next number = 34.

119. (B): Number of boys is group

$= 7 + 28 - 1 = 34$

Total number of boys needed to make it 50

$= 50 - 34 = 16.$

120. (B):

41 40 38 35 31 $\boxed{26}$

(−1, −2, −3, −4, −5)

Here, ? = missing number = 26.

YOUR SPACE

General Mental Ability

VERBAL TEST

SERIES

In questions on series, a series of four numbers is given. The numbers of the series bear some relationship among themselves. You will have to find out the relationship that obtains among the numbers. Then, on the basis of the knowledge of that relationship you can find out the next number(s) in the series.

Series questions may contain a series of letters as well as alphabets.

To begin with, we give some questions on series, eaeh with four options, of which only one is correct. You have to mark the correct answer. Then follow the *Questions for Practice* without options. Detailed answers to questions are given at the end.

Directions: *In each of the following questions on series, a series of numbers or letters is given with one space blank. Choose the correct option out of the four options given under each question.*

These questions are based on the samples of questions set for the examination.

1. 1, 3, 7, 15, ...

A. 25 B. 31
C. 33 D. 35

2. 4, 9, 16, 25, ...

A. 36 B. 38
C. 40 D. 42

3. 1, 13, 25, 37, ...

A. 41 B. 45
C. 49 D. 53

4. 64, 32, 16, 8, ...

A. 1 B. 2
C. 4 D. 6

5. AZ, DW, GT, ...

A. CX B. TG
C. JQ D. EV

6. A, D, G, ...

A. I B. K
C. H D. J

7. Z, A, Y, B, ...

A. X B. C
C. D D. W

8. If 3 + 2 = 25 and 3 + 4 = 49, then 2 + 3 = ?

A. 6 B. 15
C. 25 D. 18

9. 2, 4, 8, 16, ...

A. 20 B. 24
C. 32 D. 28

10. 20, 15, 11, 8, ...

A. 3 B. 4
C. 5 D. 6

QUESTIONS FOR PRACTICE

11. 76, 63, 50, 37, ...

12. 5, 10, 17, 26, ...

13. 2, 6, 12, 20, ...

14. 3, 6, 9, 12, ...

15. 3, 7, 11, 13, ...

16. 1, 4, 9, 16, ...

17. 0, 3, 8, 15, ...

18. 3, 6, 12, 24, ...

19. 1, 4, 8, 13, ...

20. 1, 3, 6, 10, ...

21. 1, 5, 17, 53, ...

22. 3, 8, 15, 24, ...

23. 25, 19, 14, 10, ...

24. 3, 7, 15, 31, ...

25. 80, 40, 20, 10, ...

26. 1, 6, 11, 16, ...

27. 59, 52, 45, 38, ...

28. 2, 5, 11, 23, ...

29. 13, 17, 19, 23, ...

30. 13, 23, 33, 43, ...

31. 1, 4, 10, 22, ...

32. 1, 4, 9, 16, ...

33. 96, 48, 24, 12, ...

34. 14, 10, 13, 9, 12, 8, ...

35. 4, 7, 14, 17, 34, 37, ...

36. 32, 16, 20, 10, 14, ...

37. 2, 3, 3, 5, 4, 7, ...

38. 5, 6, 8, 11, 15, 20, ...

39. 2, 9, 28, 65, ...

40. 0, 2, 6, 12, 20, ...

41. 2, 5, 10, 17, 26, ...

42. 1, 5, 11, 19, 29, ...

43. $\frac{11}{12}, \frac{10}{11}, \frac{9}{10}, \frac{8}{9}$, ...

44. 4, 5, 9, 14, 23, ...

45. 5, 10, 15, 25, 40, ...

46. 360, 180, 60, 15, ...

47. 4, 9, 16, 25, 36, ...

48. 4, 8, 3, 6, 2, 4, ...

49. 1, 8, 27, 64, ...

50. 4, 8, 16, 28, ...

51. 1, 2, 5, 10, 17, ...

52. 720, 120, 24, 6, ...

53. 1, 2, 4, 8, 16, ...

54. 1, 3, 6, 10, 15, ...

55. 0, 1, 4, 9, 16, ...

56. 810, 270, 90, 30, ...

57. 9, 16, 25, 36, ...

58. 6, 9, 12, 15, ...

59. 4, 8, 13, 19, ...

60. 3, 7, 15, 31, ...

61. 89, 79, 70, 72, ...

62. 2, 3, 4, 6, 8, ...

63. 3, 4, 9, 16, 27, ...

64. 45, 35, 26, 18, ...

65. 2, 9, 16, 23, ...

66. 40, 32, 26, 22, ...

67. 1, 3, 6, 10, ...

68. 66, 47, 28, ...

69. 5, 7, 11, 19, ...

70. 12, 6, 3, 1½, ...

71. 2, 3, 4, 6, 6, 9, ...

72. 5, 36, 10, 18, 20, ...

73. 5, 7, 11, 13, ...

74. 2, 4, 8, 16, ...

75. 45, 36, 27, ...

76. 1, 7, 13, 19, ...

77. 1, 4, 9, 16, ...

78. 54, 63, 72, ...

79. 42, 53, 63, 72, ...

80. 20, 8, 10, 4, 5, ...

81. 5, 11, 23, ...

82. 10, 22, 46, ...

83. 37, 41, 47, ...

84. 3, 2, 9, 6, 27, ...

85. 3, 6, 10, 15, ...

86. 2, 6, 12, 20, ...

87. 1, 8, 27, 64, ...

88. 125, 64, 27, 8, ...

89. 36, 49, 64, 81, ...

90. 64, 49, 36, 25, ...

91. If 3 + 4 = 25 and 4 + 5 = 41, then 5 + 6 = ?

92. If 2 + 3 = 25 and 3 + 4 = 49, then 4 + 5 = ?

93. If 6 – 4 = 20 and 5 – 3 = 16, then 4 – 3 = ?

94. If 8 – 6 = 4 and 7 – 4 = 9, then 5 – 2 = ?

95. If 7 + 9 = 32 and 3 + 6 = 18, then 5 + 4 = ?

96. If 3 + 2 = 25 and 3 + 4 = 49, then 3 + 5 = ?

97. If 9 – 5 = 2 and 25 – 15 = 5, then 12 – 6 = ?

98. If 2 x 3 = 12 and 3 x 4 = 25, then 4 x 5 = ?

99. If 2 + 3 = 13 and 3 + 4 = 25, then 2 + 5 = ?

100. If 6 – 3 = 9 and 7 – 2 = 25, then 8 – 4 = ?

101. If 5 + 2 = 19 and 2 + 3 = 13, then 3 + 5 = ?

102. If 6 – 3 = 27 and 5 – 4 = 9, then 6 – 4 = ?

103. 4 – 2 = 4 and 6 – 4 = 4, then 5 – 3 = ?

104. If 3 + 5 = 64 and 2 + 3 = 25, then 4 + 6 = ?

105. If 1 + 4 = 10 and 2 + 5 = 14, then 3 + 6 = ?

106. If 3 + 2 = 60 and 3 + 3 = 90, then 3 + 4 = ?

107. If 5 x 3 = 2 and 17 x 6 = 11, then 18 x 5 = ?

108. If 4 x 5 = 60 and 2 x 8 = 48, then 3 x 6 = ?

109. If 9 – 5 = 2 and 25 – 15 = 5, then 12 – 6 = ?

110. If 5 x 8 = 13 and 7 x 9 = 16, then 3 x 7 = ?

111. If $\frac{3}{4}+\frac{5}{6}=\frac{8}{10}$ and $\frac{6}{7}+\frac{2}{3}=\frac{8}{10}$, then $\frac{3}{4}+\frac{2}{3}=?$

112. If 4 x 7 = 11 and 11 x 4 = 15, then 7 x 9 = ?

113. If $\frac{5}{7}=12$ and $\frac{1}{10}=11$, then $\frac{3}{5}=?$

114. If 25 + 12 = 13 and 9 x 3 = 6, then 17 x 4 = ?

115. If 5 ÷ 2 = 7 and 11 ÷ 2 = 13, then 8 ÷ 3 = ?

116. BCD, CDE, DEF, ...

117. XYZ, WXY, VWX, ...

118. AZ, BY, CX, DW, ...

119. ACE, BDF, CEG, DFH, ...

120. ZX, YW, XV, WU, ...

121. AE, BF, CG, DH, ...

122. ABD, BCE, CDF, DEG, ...

123. AN, BO, CP, DQ, ...

124. ABZ, BCY, CDX, DEW, ...

125. ZA, YB, XC, WD, ...

126. A, D, G, J, ...

127. Z, W, T, Q, ...

128. AZY, BYX, CXW, ...

129. BA, DC, FE, HG, ...

130. ZYX, WVU, TSR, ...

FINDING THE WRONG OR SUPERFLUOUS NUMBER

Directions: *Below are given some series, each of which has a wrong or superfluous number. Find it out; that is your answer.*

1. 1, 4, 9, 16, 24, 36

2. 11, 12, 22, 24, 32, 36

3. 13, 17, 22, 28, 35, 41

4. 100, 81, 64, 49, 37, 25

5. 101, 110, 119, 125, 137, 146

6. 23, 33, 44, 56, 70

7. 40, 28, 19, 10, 2

8. 24, 21, 18, 15, 10, 9

9. 17, 15, 12, 13, 11, 9

10. 7, 10, 13, 17, 16, 19

11. 1, 3, 9, 25, 81

12. 2, 7, 12, 17, 19, 22

13. 4, 9, 16, 24, 25, 36, 49

14. 5, 11, 17, 23, 26, 29, 35

15. 3, 7, 8, 18, 33, 53

16. 1, 7, 27, 64, 125

17. 20, 10, 15, 11, 6, 0

18. 80, 90, 100, 111, 123, 136

19. 16, 24, 36, 49, 64, 81

20. 100, 93, 86, 76, 66

21. 11, 22, 32, 44, 55, 66

22. 216, 121, 64, 27, 8

23. 4, 9, 16, 25, 35, 49

24. 50, 39, 27, 17, 6

25. 23, 33, 44, 56, 70

26. 80, 71, 62, 52, 44

27. 4, 11, 18, 24, 32

28. 2, 4, 9, 16, 32

29. 1, 4, 8, 12, 19

30. 5, 7, 9, 13, 13, 20

31. 3, 4, 8, 16, 33, 58

32. 6, 13, 21, 27, 34

33. 6, 18, 30, 42, 48

34. 1, 8, 26, 64, 125

35. 6, 18, 28, 42, 54

36. 63, 56, 49, 43, 35

37. 91, 80, 65, 58, 47, 36

38. 2, 5, 18, 17, 26

39. 21, 25, 30, 39, 43, 51

40. 176, 88, 40, 22, 11

41. 8, 21, 34, 45, 60

42. 15, 21, 27, 34, 39

43. 17, 15, 13, 12, 9

44. 100, 90, 81, 71, 64, 52

45. 1, 4, 9, 15, 25, 36

ANALOGY

In analogy questions, three words are given. The first two words to the left of sign : : are related in some way. The same relationship holds between the third word to the right of the sign : : and one of the four responses A, B, C and D given thereunder. You have to choose the correct response, that is your answer.

Here is an example:

Student : Teacher : : Patient : ?

A. Hospital B. Medicine

C. Doctor D. Disease

In this case the correct response is C because a Doctor is related to a Patient in the same way as a Teacher is related to a Student.

QUESTIONS FOR PRACTICE

1. Milk : Curd : : Water : ?

A. River B. Thirst

C. Ice D. Vapour

2. Girl : Beautiful : : Gold : ?

A. Valuable B. Bright

C. Ornament D. Ring

3. Desert : Sand : : Sea : ?

A. Water B. Tide

C. Fish D. Crocodile

4. Beautiful : Ugly : : Healthy : ?

A. Sick B. Weak

C. Strong D. Fat

5. Cheese : Milk : : Sugar : ?

A. Molasses B. Palm

C. Sugarcane D. Syrup

6. Daughter : Mother : : Son : ?

A. Mother B. Sister

C. Father D. Brother

7. Book : Paper : : Table : ?

A. School B. Student

C. Wood D. Chair

8. Player : Team : : Ship : ?

A. Port B. Fleet

C. Ocean D. Captain

9. Kilogram : Weight : : Metre : ?

A. Journey B. Road

C. Cloth D. Length

10. Lid : Box : : Cork : ?

A. Seal B. Bottle

C. Drug D. Carton

11. Circle : Circumference Square : ?

A. Angle B. Area

C. Diagonal D. Perimeter

12. Advocate : Law : : Cook : ?

A. Cookery B. Kitchen

C. Food D. Dishes

13. Wardrobe : Clothes : : Purse : ?

A. Pocket B. Zip

C. Money D. Fare

14. Temperature : Heat : : Humidity : ?

A. Rain B. Weather

C. Night D. Moisture

15. Shakespeare : Drama : : Ghalib : ?

A. Urdu B. Literature

C. Ghazal D. Stories

16. Grass : Green : : Sky : ?

A. Endless B. Stars

C. Blue D. Bright

17. Monday : Week : : January : ?

A. Winter B. Month

C. Year D. Season

18. Thermometer : Temperature Barometer : ?

A. Atmosphere

B. Wind

C. Atmospheric Pressure
D. Velocity

19. Poverty : Riches : : Glory : ?
A. Penuary B. Happiness
C. Shame D. Suffering

20. Table : Chair : : Coat : ?
A. Pajama B. Shirt
C. Tie D. Pant

21. Hand : Elbow : : Leg : ?
A. Thigh B. Knee
C. Ankle D. Claw

22. Coal : Black : : Snow : ?
A. Water B. Mountain
C. Cold D. White

23. Precaution : Accident : : Cleanliness : ?
A. Disease B. Treatment
C. Filth D. Garbage

24. January : April : : Sunday : ?
A. Thursday B. Tuesday
C. Monday D. Wednesday

25. Soldier : Rifle : : Writer : ?
A. Book B. Paper
C. Pen D. Ink

26. Plate : Crockery : : Spoon : ?
A. Knife B. Fork
C. Chinaware D. Cultery

27. Night : Evening : : Day : ?
A. Morning B. Sun
C. Sunlight D. Daylight

28. Uncle : Aunt : : Father : ?
A. Daughter B. Mother
C. Brother D. Sister

29. Lotus : Water : : Fish : ?
A. Creature B. Food
C. Breath D. Water

30. Metre : Length : : Litre : ?
A. Weight B. Number
C. Volume D. Quantity

31. Heaven : Hell : : Drought : ?
A. Famine B. Water
C. Flood D. Crop

32. Sun : Planet : : Earth : ?
A. Satellite B. Sun
C. Moon D. Light

33. French : France : : Dutch : ?
A. Hungary B. Holland
C. Sea D. Hiroshima

34. Sri Lanka : Colombo : : Japan : ?
A. Island B. Tokyo
C. Hiroshima D. Bomb

35. Pen : Write : : Carpenter's Plane : ?
A. Tear B. Repair
C. Pierce D. Shave off

36. Thick : Thin : : Inferior : ?
A. Rough B. Spurious
C. Beautiful D. Superior

37. Table : Wood : : Book : ?
A. Pages B. Paper
C. Teach D. Student

38. Fan : Air : : Bulb : ?
A. Brightness B. Electricity
C. Switch D. Light

39. Seven : Number : : Green : ?
A. Colour B. Forest
C. Field D. Red

40. Stage : Drama : : Stadium : ?
A. Sports B. Circus
C. Wedding D. Convention

41. Fruit : Mango : : Serpent : ?

A. Cobra

B. Poison

C. Creature

D. Hood of a Cobra

42. Rain : Centimeter : : Temperature : ?

A. Celsius B. Weather

C. Sun D. Heat

43. Road : Lane : : City : ?

A. Town B. Metropolis

C. Highway D. Capital

44. Aspirin : Headache : : Quinine : ?

A. Hepatitis B. Malaria

C. Influenza D. Cough

45. Hunger : Food : : Thirst : ?

A. Tap B. River

C. Water D. Sweat

46. Cat : Kitten : : Hen : ?

A. Bird B. Cock

C. Feed D. Chicken

47. Fruit : Banana : : Mammal : ?

A. Cow B. Heron

C. Fly D. Plant

48. Radio : Listener : : Film : ?

A. Camera B. Actor

C. Viewer D. Talky

49. Money : Exchange : : Language : ?

A. Write

B. Communication

C. Knowledge

D. Book

50. Friend : Enemy : : Kind : ?

A. Diety B Demon

C. Anger D. Cruel

51. Train : Platform : : Ship : ?

A. Anchor B. Harbour

C. Ocean D. Island

52. 1st April : Fool : : 1st May : ?

A. Teacher B. Doctor

C. Labour D. Disabled

53. Time : Clock : : Rain : ?

A. Cloud B. Raingauge

C. Centimeter D. Barometer

54. Lion : Den : : Horse : ?

A. Stable B. *Tonga*

C. Chariot D. Stake

55. Book : Pages : : Flower : ?

A. Bouquet B. Buds

C. Colour D. Petals

56. Tea : Leaves : : Coffee : ?

A. Roots B. Flowers

C. Bark D. Seeds

57. Horse : Neigh : : Donkey : ?

A. Trumpet B. Roar

C. Bray D. Snarl

58. Car : Garage : : Aircraft : ?

A. Sky B. Hanger

C. Aerodrome D. Engine

59. Radius : Circle : : Spokes : ?

A. Wheel B. Table

C. Bus D. Matchbox

60. Stool : Carpenter : : Shoes : ?

A. Cobbler B. Foot

C. Leather D. Polish

61. Bus : Workshop : : Ship : ?

A. Harbour B. Yard

C. Dockyard D. Hanger

62. Ring : Finger : : Tie : ?

A. Coat B. Neck

C. Collar D. Waist

63. Sew : Needle : : Paint : ?
A. Colour B. Brush
C. Canvas D. Landscape

64. Nose : Smell : : Tongue : ?
A. Lick B. Taste
C. Speak D. Mouth

65. Pencil : Stationery : : Chair : ?
A. Carpenter B. Wood
C. Table D. Furniture

66. Cat : Dog : : Cow : ?
A. Goat B. Lion
C. Tiger D. Wolf

67. Snake : Lizard : : Fish : ?
A. Cow B. Dog
C. Cat D. Crocodile

68. Honour : Dishonour : : Fame : ?
A. Respected B. Glorious
C. Infamy D. Glory

69. Light : Rays : : Sound : ?
A. Ear B. Wave
C. Velocity D. Echo

70. Clock : Hand : : Thermometer : ?
A. Temperature B. Fever
C. Mercury D. Patient

71. Tractor : Diesel : : Scooter : ?
A. Wheel B. Petrol
C. Power D. Engine

72. Cuckoo : Cackle : : Horse : ?
A. Bray B. Neigh
C. Hiss D. Roar

73. Pitch : Cricket : : Ring : ?
A. Wrestling B. Boxing
C. Hockey D. Badminton

74. Car : Run : : Snake : ?
A. Run B. Bite
C. Creep D. Hiss

75. Urge : Deter : : Honest : ?
A. Dishonest B. *Thug*
C. Robber D. Cheat

76. Lion : Den : : Bird : ?
A. Tree B. Chrip
C. Nest D. Ruins

77. Calf : Cow : : Lamb : ?
A. Wolf B. Flesh
C. Goat D. Sheep

78. Obedience : Disobedience : Life : ?
A. Salvation B. Death
C. Heaven D. Universe

79. Tailor : Cloth : : Carpenter :
A. Machine B. Wood
C. Saw D. Table

80. Cat : Rat : : Tiger : ?
A. Lamb B. Lizard
C. Crow D. Fish

81. Bakery : Bread : : Mint : ?
A. Cheque B. Coin
C. Note D. Cake

82. Studio : Film : : Shipyard : ?
A. Ship B. Trawler
C. Boat D. Net

83. Month : Year : : Hour : ?
A. Day B. Week
C. Minute D. Second

84. Food : Hunger : : Water : ?
A. Bath B. Irrigation
C. Thirst D. Rain

85. Revolver : Bullet : : Bow : ?
A. Sword B. Club
C. Arrow D. Pistol

86. Honey : Bee : : Wool : ?
A. Goat B. Horse
C. Hare D. Sheep

FINDING THE ODD ONE OUT

In these questions four pairs of words or four words are given and one of them is odd or does not belong to the class. You have to find out that odd pair/word. Two examples are given below:

Example 1.

A. Wood-Chair
B. Water-Ice
C. Milk-Cheese
D. Teacher-Student

Solution: Chair is made of Wood, Ice is made of Water, Cheese is made of Milk. But Student is never made of Teacher. Therefore, the odd pair is D. That is your answer

Example 2.

A. Bihar
B. Gujarat
C. West Bengal
D. Calcutta

Solution: A, B and C are names of States. D is the name of a city. Therefore, D is odd. That is your answer.

QUESTIONS FOR PRACTICE

Directions: *In the following questions, find the odd one out.*

1. A. Man-Woman
B. Brother-Sister
C. Father-Son
D. Father-Mother

2. A. Fish-Water
B. Water-River
C. Coal-Mine
D. Bird-Tree

3. A. Hospital-Doctor
B. Court-Advocate
C. Thief-Robber
D. School-Teacher

4. A. Milk-Curd
B. Brick-House
C. Paper-Book
D. Horse-Stable

5. A. Milk-White
B. Leaf-Green
C. Sky-Blue
D. Blood-Red

6. A. Victory-Defeat
B. Carrot-Radish
C. North-South
D. Up-Down

7. A. Mouse-Hole
B. Bird-Nest
C. Horse-Stable
D. Tiger-Forest

8. A. Blue-Sky
B. Red-Kite
C. Blue-*Saree*
D. Black-Horse

9. A. Father-Son
B. Needle-Thread
C. Cup-Plate
D. Chair-Table

10. A. Well-Canal
B. River-Mountain
C. Lake-Sea
D. Gulf-Desert

11. A. Book-Note Book
B. Rubber-Pencil
C. Nose-Ear
D. Leg-Bone

12. A. Friend-Foe
B. Rich-Poor
C. Kind-Cruel
D. Games-Sports

13. A. Fire-Smoke
B. Sun-Heat
C. Moonlight-Cool
D. Paper-White

14. A. Mars B. Jupiter
C. Venus D. Moon

15. A. Grape B. Raisin
C. Apple D. Mango

16. A. Wolf B. Jackal
C. Goat D. Bear

17. A. *Riksha* B. Bus
C. Car D. Scooter

18. A. Tiger B. Horse
C. Elephant D. Camel

19. A. Monkey
B. Mongoose
C. Snake
D. Cat

20. A. Kanpur B. Lucknow
C. Patna D. Allahabad

21. A. Yen B. Dollar
C. Coin D. Pound

22. A. Diamond B. Mercury
C. Iron D. Copper

23. A. Legs B. Hands
C. Ankles D. Lungs

24. A. Steamer B. Boat
C. Ship D. Harbour

25. A. Rose B. Lotus
C. Dahlia D. Jasmin

26. A. Proteins
B. Carbohydrates
C. Copper
D. Vitamins

27. A. Piano B. Tabla
C. Flute D. Banjo

28. A. Metre
B. Kilometre
C. Centimetre
D. Square Kilometre

29. A. Cat B. Dog
C. Monkey D. Snake

30. A. Snake B. Lizard
C. Crocodile D. Frog

31. A. Mercury B. Earth
C. Moon D. Jupiter

32. A. Pencil
B. Rubber
C. Ink
D. Sketch Map

33. A. The Statesman
B. India Today
C. The Hindu
D. The Amrit Bazar Patrika

34. A. Ashoka
B. Chanakya
C. Chandra Gupta
D. Harsh Vardhana

35. A. Tangent
B. Arc
C. Radius
D. Hypotenuse

36. A. Delhi B. Patna
C. Mumbai D. Calcutta

37. A. Bicycle B. Scooter
C. Car D. Bus

38. A. Wheat B. Gram
C. Ragi D. Rice

39. A. Iron B. Copper
C. Steel D. Tin

40. A. Cancer B. Hepatitis
C. Bile D. Diabetes

41. A. Water B. Wind
C. Gasoline D. Soil

42. A. Cotton B. Rice
C. Tea D. Jute

43. A. Apple B. Banana
C. Sugarcane D. Mango

44. A. Dhaka B. Colombo
C. Karachi D. Rangoon

45. A. May B. March
C. April D. July

46. A. Rouble B. Diet
C. Dollar D. Taka

47. A. Libra B. Uranus
C. Pluto D. Neptune

48. A. Temple
B. Monastery
C. Mosque
D. Church

49. A. Ounce B. Shilling
C. Gram D. Pound

50. A. Shield B. Armour
C. Sword D. Helmet

51. A. Ganga B. Godavari
C. Krishna D. Narmada

52. A. Cataract B. Cornea
C. Retina D. Iris

53. A. Bigger B. Greater
C. Faster D. Larger

54. A. Fox B. Cow
C. Dog D. Horse

55. A. Jackal B. Fox
C. Stag D. Wolf

56. A. Father B. Teacher
C. Brother D. Sister

57. A. Shore B. Sea
C. River D. Pond

58. A. Moan B. Wail
C. Weep D. Sorrow

59. A. Eagle B. Crow
C. Vulture D. Cock

60. A. Dwarf B. Slender
C. Fat D. Lame

61. A. Mother B. Daughter
C. Son D. Aunt

62. A. Eye B. Ear
C. Neck D. Tooth

63. A. Tamil Nadu
B. Kerala
C. Karnataka
D. Pondicherry

64. A. Wing Commander
B. Pilot Officer
C. Colonel
D. Flight Lieutenant

65. A. Veena
B. Sitar
C. Sarod
D. Mridangam

66. A. Africa B. Asia
C. Arabia D. America

67. A. Shark B. Seal
C. Whale D. Crocodile

68. A. Square
B. Trapezium
C. Rectangle
D. Diagonal

69. A. Cat B. Dog
C. Fox D. Monkey

71. A. Potatoes
B. Tomatoes
C. Groundnuts
D. Onions

72. A. Influenza
B. Tuberculosis
C. Smallpox
D. Malaria

73. A. Bunglow B. Office
C. Hut D. House

74. A. Fly B. Sweets
C. *Kheer* D. *Gur*

75. A. Root B. Trunk
C. Stem D. Leaves

76. A. Brinjal
B. Potato
C. Beans
D. Lady Finger

77. A. Dog B. Crow
C. Cow D. Goat

78. A. C.V. Raman
B. Meghnad Saha
C. Kalidas
D. Dr. Bhabha

79. A. Pant B. Shirt
C. Shoes D. *Pajama*

80. A. Hydrogen B. Nitrogen
C. Oxygen D. Mercury

QUESTIONS RELATING TO CLOCKS AND CALENDARS

These questions are related to students' knowledge of Clock and days of week. They also involve their knowledge of directions of the hands of the clocks at various times as well as the angle between the two hands of the clock.

CLOCKS

Example: When it is 15 minutes past 12,

(i) What is the angle between the two hands of the clock?

(ii) What is the direction of the hour hand of the clock at that time?

Solution: 15 minutes past 12, is the time when the minute hand is pointing at 3 while the hour hand has just crossed 12. See the illustration below:

Therefore,

(i) The angle between the two hands of the clock is 90°.

(ii) The hour hand is pointed upwards toward 12, *i.e.*, towards north.

Remember:

(i) The sum total of all the angles at the centre of the clock is 360°.

(ii) The dial of the clock is divided into 12 equal parts.

$$\therefore \frac{360^\circ}{12} = 30^\circ$$

That the angle formed between each and every two numbers on the dial is always 30°.

(iii) The direction of the hands of the clock is indicated in the following manner:

(a) upside (where 12 is written) is always the north.

(b) down below (where 6 is written) is always the south.

(c) The right side (where 3 is written) is always the east.

(d) The left side (where 9 is written) is always west.

Another Example: When it is 5 o'clock, what is the angle between the two hands of the clock.

Solution: At 5 o'clock:

(i) the hour hand will point at 5

(ii) the minute hand will point at 12.

See the illustration below:

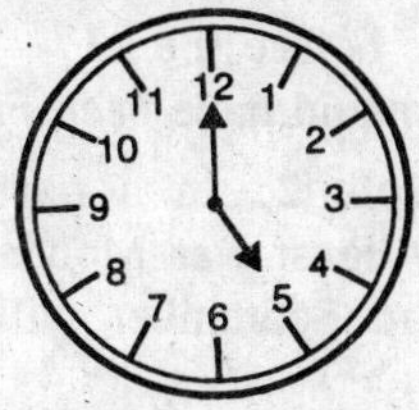

The two hands are 5 numbers apart

$\therefore$ 30° x 5 = 150°

$\therefore$ The angle between the two hands of the clock will be 150°.

Remember that in every hour:

(i) both the hands meet **once**.

(ii) The hands are straight pointing in opposite directions only **once**.

(iii) the hand make right angles **twice**.

(iv) the minute hand moves through an angle of 6° in **one minute**.

CALENDAR

Questions based on calendars are easy to solve.

Example 1: In a particular month, 17th was Friday. Then:

(i) What will be the date on the next Friday?

(ii) What was the date on the previous Friday?

Solution: We know that there are seven days in a week. If 17th of the month was Friday, then the day falling after 7 days (*i.e.*, 17 + 7 = 24), *i.e.*, the 24th will be Friday. Similarly, 17th being Friday, therefore the day falling 7 days before (*i.e.*, 17 – 7 = 10) *i.e.*, 10th should have been Friday.

Example 2: In a particular year, 20th August was Monday. On which day 3rd September will fall in that year?

Solution: August has 31 days. If 20th August was Monday, the next Monday will fall on 27th August. So, 31st August will be on Friday and accordingly, 1st September on Saturday and 3rd September will fall on Monday.

Months which have only 30 days: April, June, September and November

Months which have 31 days: January, March, May, July, August, October and December.

February has only 28 days. Every four years February has 28 + 1 = 29 days. Such a year is called Leap Year.

QUESTIONS FOR PRACTICE

1. If yesterday was Sunday, after how many days the next Sunday will come?

A. 7 B. 6
C. 5 D. 8

2. In a particular month, two days after Monday was the 5th (date), on which day will the 19th (date) of the same month fall?

A. Tuesday B. Monday
C. Sunday D. Friday

3. How many times between 4 o'clock afternoon and 10 o'clock night, the two hands of a clock are at right angles?

A. 14 B. 10
C. 12 D. 8

4. If 14th April in a particular year was Thursday. The first Thursday in May of that very year will fall on which date?

A. 3rd May B. 4th May
C. 5th May D. 6th May

5. If two days before January 11 was Monday, then the next Monday in the same month will fall on:

A. January 16 B. January 18
C. January 17 D. January 15

6. If February 28 was Tuesday in a particular year, the 5th February in that very year was on:

A. Friday B. Sunday
C. Saturday D. Monday

7. If 3 days after Monday was 11th (date) of the month, what day was there on the 22nd (date) of the same month?

A. Friday B. Monday
C. Sunday D. Saturday

8. In a particular year the 31st March was Tuesday. On which date was the first Sunday of March in that very year?

A. 1st March B. 3rd March
C. 2nd March D. 4th March

9. February 3 was Friday in a particular year. The last Sunday of February in that year will fall on?

A. February 25 B. February 26
C. February 27 D. February 28

10. If July 19 is Tuesday in a particular year, on what day will August 15 fall in that very year?

A. Friday B. Monday
C. Sunday D. Saturday

11. At 2 PM, the hands of a clock will make an angle of:

A. 60° B. 45°
C. 30° D. 80°

12. During a period of 12 hours, how many times the hands of a clock are at right angles?

A. 22 B. 24
C. 23 D. 25

13. During a day (24 hours), on how many occasions, both the hands of a clock are in a straight line?

A. 23 B. 12
C. 24 D. 22

14. At 4 AM, the hands of the clock will make an angle of:

A. 90° B. 110°
C. 120° D. 130°

15. At 25 minutes past 3, the hands of the clock will make an angle of:

A. 90° B. 60°
C. 30° D. 45°

16. At 5 minutes past 3, the hands of a clock will make an angle of:

A. 60° B. 30°
C. 90° D. 45°

17. At 9 o'clock, the hour hand of the clock will be facing towards:

A. East B. West
C. North D. South

18. At 10 minutes past 9, the hands of a clock will make an angle of:

A. 120° B. 150°
C. 180° D. 100°

19. A boy looks at the clock and tells the time as 15 minutes past 5. In doing so, he committed the mistake of treating the hour hand as minute hand and vice-versa. What was the correct time in the clock?

A. 15 minutes past 3
B. 20 minutes past 3
C. 25 minutes past 3
D. 10 minutes past 3

20. What will be the time when both the hands of the clock coincide (one over the other) and face towards the west?

A. 9 o'clock
B. 30 minutes past 8
C. 45 minutes past 8
D. 15 minutes past 8

CODING AND DECODING

In a code language the coded letters or numbers are not what they appear but they represent some other pre-determined letter or number. Coding implies use of some letter or number in a systematic way to represent another letter or number.

Decoding means resolving the system involved in a code. In other words decoding means finding out the original letter or number for which coded letters or numbers have been used.

Coding is done on a systematic way. If we are able to discover this system, we can decode.

To explain it further, we shall take some examples.

Suppose MARKET is coded as NBSLFU. In this case, for each alphabet in MARKET, certain other alphabets namely NBSLFU have been used.

Now if you are asked to find out the code for TEAM (on the basis of MARKET coded as NBSLFU), you can do it without much difficulty. You will find that all the letters in TEAM, *i.e.*, T, E, A and M occur in MARKET. To find out the code for TEAM arrange MARKET with its code in the following manner

M A R K E T
N B S L F U

You can find that N is for M, B is for A, S is for R and so on.

You also find that U is for T, F is for E, B is for A and N is for M.

∴ UFBN is for TEAM

∴ Code for TEAM is UFBN.

Similarly, you can find the code for RAT, TEA, MARK, TAKE, EAT, ARM etc. Codes for these will be as under:

RAT = SBU
TEA = UFB
MARK = NBSL
TAKE = UBLF
EAT = FBU
ARM = BSN

Now, we take another example. If EIGHT is coded as CGEFR, then SPOT will be coded as?

For finding out the code for SPOT, we shall follow the following method:

1 3 4 2
A B Ⓒ D Ⓔ Ⓕ Ⓖ H I J K L Ⓜ
5
Ⓝ O P Ⓠ Ⓡ S T U V W X Y Z
3 2 1 4

1 2 3 4 5
EIGHT are marked E I G H T, and C G E F R an marked Ⓒ Ⓖ Ⓔ Ⓕ Ⓡ.

The pattern above makes clear that one letter has been skipped anti-clockwise at each step while coding.

Therefore, now apply the same formula to find out the code for SPOT.

Mark SPOT as S P O T (1 2 3 4). Skip one letter anti-clockwise at each step to find

Ⓠ Ⓝ Ⓜ Ⓡ or Q N M R

∴ SPOT will be coded as QNMR.

In such questions, mark the expression and its code (as given in the question) in the alphabets (as shown above) to find the clue. Then apply the clue to find the code (as directed in the question).

QUESTIONS FOR PRACTICE

Directions: *In each of the following questions a coded expression is given. Then another expression is given, the code for which is to be found from*

amongst the four choices suggested below.

1. If COME is coded as BNLD, then CARE will be coded as:

A. BBQD B. BZQD
C. BZPD D. BZSD

2. If HIGH is coded as IJHI, then TURN will be coded as:

A. UVQO B. UVTO
C. UVSO D. UVSP

3. If LOAD is coded as MPBE, then PORT will be coded as:

A. QRSU B. QPRU
C. QPUS D. QPSU

4. If GOLD is coded as IQNF, then WIND will be coded as:

A. YKOF B. YLPF
C. YKPE D. YKPF

5. If SHIRT is coded as RGHQS, then ROUND will be coded as:

A. QNTMC B. QNUMC
C. QNTME D. QNTOC

6. If DEAR is coded as FGCT, then READ will be coded as:

A. FGCF B. TGFC
C. TCGF D. TGCF

7. If EASE is coded as HDVH, then SEE will be coded as:

A. DHH B. VHV
C. VHH D. VVH

8. If SERPENT is coded as TNEPRES, then PLAGUE will be coded as:

A. EUAGLP B. EUGLAP
C. EUGALP D. EULAGP

9. If DEFENCE is coded as CDEDMBD, then NEED will be coded as:

A. MCDC B. MCCD
C. MDDC D. DMMC

10. If CHAIR is coded as FKDLU, then RAID will be coded as:

A. ULGD B. ULKG
C. ULDG D. UDLG

11. If CONDEMN is coded as CNODMEN, then TEACHER will be coded as:

A. TAECHER B. TAEECHR
C. TCAEEHR D. TAECEHR

12. In a code language COME is written as 'XLNV' and ABLE as ZYOV, how would you write MOLLY in that code?

A. NLOBO B. NLBOO
C. LNOOB D. NLOOB

13. If CIGARETTE is coded as GICERAETT, then the word DEMONSTRATION is coded as:

A. MEDNSOARTOITN
B. MEDSNOATROITN
C. MEDSNOARTIOTN
D. MEDSNOARTOITN

14. If CENTURION is coded as 325791465, and RANK is coded as 18510, what will the figures 78510 represent?

A. BANK B. SANK
C. TANK D. TALK

15. In a certain code MAHESH is written as NCIGTJ. In that code NEELAM will be written as:

A. OGGNCO B. OGFNBN
C. OGFNBO D. OGHBNO

16. In a certain code FLOWER is written as SEXOMF. How will garden be written in that code?

A. OEERBH B. OFESBH
C. OEESBG D. OEERBG

17. If in a code SCRIPT is written as TCQIQT, how will DIGEST be written in that code?

A. EIGHTT B. TIHETT
C. EIFETT D. EIFERT

18. If RAM is coded as SBN, then FEW will be coded as:

A. GFX B. GHX
C. EFX D. GEX

19. If RUBBER is coded as REBBUR, then DEAD will be coded as:

A. DEAD B. DAED
C. DADE D. DDEA

20. If KANPUR is coded as LBOQVS, then NAGPUR will be coded as:

A. OHBQVS B. HBOQVS
C. OBHQVS D. BOHQVS

21. If DELHI is coded as IDHEL, then TUFAN will be coded as:

A. TNAUF B. NATUF
C. NTUAF D. NTAUF

22. If ANOTHER is coded as 7309521, then THORN will be coded as:

A. 95103 B. 95313
C. 95013 D. 95113

23. If SURENDRA is coded as DHTNPATI, then UNDER will be coded as:

A. PHANT B. HPANT
C. HPNAT D. HNPAT

24. If EFFICIENT is coded as DEEHBHDMS, then FIET will be coded as:

A. DHES B. EHSD
C. EHDS D. EDHS

25. If FACE is coded as GBDF, then BADE will be coded as:

A. CBEF B. CEBF
C. CFBE D. CBFE

26. If REST is coded as TGUV, then SETS will be coded as:

A. GUVU B. UVGU
C. UGVU D. VGUV

27. If DECADE is coded as 453145, then DEED will be coded as:

A. 5544 B. 4545
C. 4554 D. 4555

28. If BAD is coded as YZW, then MAD will be coded as:

A. MZW B. NZW
C. OZW D. LZW

29. If DIRT is coded as TDIR, then TRIM will be coded as:

A. MRTI B. MIRT
C. MTRI D. MTIR

30. If PIT is coded as QJU, then HUT will be coded as:

A. KXU B. KVU
C. IVU D. GVU

31. If DECEMBER is coded as ERMBCEDE, then NOVEMBER will be coded as:

A. ERBMVENO
B. REMBVENO
C. ERMBVENO
D. EMRBVENO

32. If ROUGH is coded as ORRJE, how will SMOOTH be coded?

A. PPLLOK B. PPLRQK

C. PJLLOK D. PPRRKK

33. If MOTHER is coded as PQWJHT, then SISTER will be coded as:

A. VKUVHT B. VKVVHU

C. VKVVHT D. VKVWHT

34. If LOFTY is coded as LPFUY, then DWARF will be coded as:

A. DXASF B. DXBSG

C. DXATF D. DWBSG

35. If PRICE is coded as SVNIL, then COST will be coded as:

A. FSXY B. FSWY

C. FTWZ D. FSXZ

36. If JAILAPPAS is coded as AIJAPLASP, then ECONOMICS will be coded as:

A. COEMONCSI

B. COEOMNCSI

C. OECMONSCI

D. COEMONCSI

37. If in a certain code CLOCK is written as KCOLC, then STEPS will be written as:

A. SPEST B. SPSET

C. SEPST D. SPETS

38. If in a certain code SPIDER is written as PSDIRE, then COMMON will be written as:

A. OCMMON B. OCMOMN

C. OCMMNO D. OCOMMO

39. In a certain code RECOMMENDATION is written as COMMENDATIONER, then REMUNERATION will be written as:

A. MUNERATION

B. MUNERATIONRE

C. MUNERATIONER

D. MUNERATIOENR

40. If in a certain code TRIPPLE is written as SQHOOKD, then DISPOSE will be written as:

A. CHRONRD B. CHROORD

C. CHROMRD D. CHROMSD

QUESTIONS BASED ON RELATIONSHIP

In these questions, one is required to find out relationship between/among persons such as whose father is A, who is A's father, or what is the relationship between A and B etc. These questions are not very difficult but somewhat involoved.

We shall take some examples to explain how to solve such questions.

Example 1. A is father of both B and C. B is not the brother of C. What relationship exists between B and C?

Solution: When both B and C are children of A, and B is not the brother of C, then only possible relationship between B and C is that one of them is the sister of the other.

Example 2. C is nephew of B. A is husband of B. How is A related to C?

Solution: C is nephew of B. A and B are husband and wife. Therefore, C must be nephew of both A and B.

∴ C is nephew of A too.

And, A is uncle of C.

QUESTIONS FOR PRACTICE

1. Ajit is brother of grandson of Mohan. What is Ajit in relation to Mohan?

A. grandfather B. grandson
C. son D. nephew

2. B is A's son. B is my son's uncle. Then A is my:

A. uncle B. grandfather
C. father D. brother

3. F is A's brother; C is A's daughter; K is F's sister and G is C's brother. Who is uncle of G?

A. A B. C
C. K D. F

4. The brother-in-law of the nephew of my wife will be my:

A. son-in-law B. nephew
C. cousin D. brother-in-law

5. Ramesh is Bihari's brother. Indira is Ramesh's wife and her son Devendra is brother of Yogendra. Bihari is Yogendra's:

A. father B. uncle
C. brother D. maternal uncle

6. Both A and B are C's children. C is A's father but B is not C's son. Then B is C's:

A. brother B. sister
C. daughter D. son

7. My maternal uncle is A and his son is B. C is B's son. Then I am C's:

A. grandfather B. uncle
C. brother D. nephew

8. Ram Bihari had three sons—Ram, Pratap and Kripa. Vijai is Ram's son and Veena is Pratap's daughter. Then Vijai is Veena's:

A. uncle B. cousin brother
C. nephew

9. K is P's sister's daughter. S is K's son. Then P is S's:

A. maternal uncle
B. maternal grandfather
C. father's sister's husband
D. grandfather

10. A is C's father. B is C's wife. Then A is B's:

A. husband's elder brother
B. husband's younger brother
C. father-in-law
D. son

QUESTIONS RELATED TO DIRECTIONS

These questions are related to directions. They are easy for solutions. Students are advised to pin-point on a piece of paper the starting-point. Then they should draw lines as directed (indicated) in the question. Thus, they will have a diagram (figure) of the movement. It will thus be easy to find the direction from the starting-point.

Example. Ramesh starts from his house and goes to the east. After covering 4 km, he turns to right and covers 2 km. Then he turns to right again and covers 4 km. In which direction now Ramesh is from his house?

Solution:

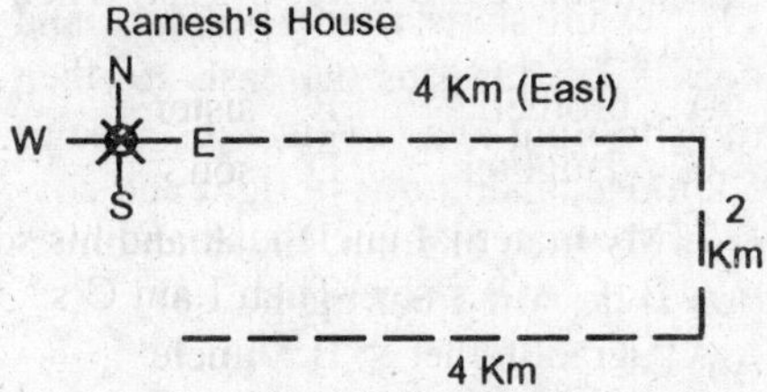

The above diagram indicates that he is now in the south from his house.

QUESTIONS FOR PRACTICE

1. Deepa starts from her house and goes 1 km towards north; then she turns to right and walks 1 km. She turns again to right and walks 1 km to reach her school. In which direction from her house is her school situated?

A. North B. East
C. South D. West

2. My house is situated to the east of your house. My friend's house is situated to the south-east of your house. To which direction should I go to reach my friend's house through the shortest route?

A. South B. South-West
C. South-East D. West

3. A person starts walking towards north. After sometime he turns to right and after walking some distance he turns to left. Then after walking the distance of 1 km, he turns again to left. To which direction is he walking now?

A. North B. Fast
C. South D. West

4. A person goes 200 m towards west from his house. Then he goes 500 m towards south. To which direction should he now walk for returning to the place from where he started his journey?

A. North-East B. North
C. South-East D. North-West

5. A person went towards west from his house and covered a distance of 5 km. Then he turned to left and covered 5 km. He, then, turned to right and covered 9 km. And finally he covered 5 km towards north. In which direction is he now from his starting-point?

A. South-West B. South
C. West D. East

6. A police van drove 5 km towards the east. Then it turned to right and travelled 3 km. After that it turned towards the west and covered a distance of 1 km. How many kms away is the van from its starting point?

A. 3 km B. 4 km
C. 5 km D. 6 km

7. Standing at the door of a room a policeman saw a wall-clock on the wall facing him, a sofa set near the wall on his right and a TV set near the wall on his left. He also saw rays on his left. He also saw rays of the setting sun falling on the wall-clock. The sofa set was near the:

A. eastern wall
B. western wall
C. northern wall
D. southern wall

8. On a straight road a police van chased a car upto 4 km towards the east. The car turned to right and was chased by the police van for 2 km. The car again turned to right and was caught by the police van after a 2 km chase. In which direction was the police van now from its starting point?

A. North-East B. North-West

C. South-East D. South-West

9. Dara is to the east of Vorli at a distance of 10 km. Towards the north is Madu situated at a distance of about 7 km from the above mentioned two places. A police van on patrol duty was proceeding towards Vorli from Dara. While on midway it was instructed to intercept a car that was speeding away from Dara to Madu. To which direction thte patrol van turn to intercept the speeding car?

A. East B. West

C. North D. South

10. A person travelled 12 km towards the north. Then he turned to left and travelled 5 km. How many kms is he away from his starting-point?

A. 14 km B. 13 km

C. 12 km D. 13.5 km

11. Shyam starts from his house and goes 5 km towards the east. He then turns to right and covers a distance of 5 km. He again turns to right and covers a distance of 5 km. In which direction is he now from his house?

A. East B. West

C. North D. South

12. A person started from his house and travelled 1 km towards the north. Then he turned to right and travelled 2 km. He again turned to right and travelled 1 km. How far is he from his house?

A. 1 km B. 2 km

C. 3 km D. 4 km

13. Ramesh starts from his house and goes 4 km towards the east. Then he turns to left and goes 3 km. He further turns to right and goes 1 km. He, then turns to left and goes 2 km and again turns to left and goes 5 km. In which direction is he now from his house?

A. East B. West

C. North D. South

ARRANGING THE LETTERS TO MAKE MEANINGFUL WORDS

In these questions, some letters are given in a haphazard manner. The students are required to rearrange those letters to make a meaningful word.

Example. Arrange the letters KOBO in such a way as to make a meaningful word.

Solution: These letters may be arranged in various forms such as KOOB, KBOO, OBOK, OKBO, BOKO and BOOK. Of these only BOOK is a meaningful word. Therefore, it is the correct answer.

In some questions, a particular direction may be included, such as arrange the letters in such a way as to make the name of an animal, fruit, vehicle, city, etc.

Example. Arrange the letters EORHS to make the name of an animal.

Solution: When arranged in right order, it will be HORSE.

QUESTIONS FOR PRACTICE

1. Arrange the letters EBUL in such a way as to make the name of a colour.

2. Arrange the letters CINHOC in such a way as to make the name of a city.

3. Arrange the letters UDUR in such a way as to make the name of an Indian language.

4. Arrange the letters NIOR in such a way as to make the name of a metal.

5. Arrange the letters CEAOCPK in such a way as to make the name of a bird.

6. Arrange the letters MANRADA in such a way as to make the name of a river.

7. Arrange the letters RHATE in such a way as to make the name of a planet.

8. Arrange the letters NIPELC in such a way as to make the name of an item of stationery.

9. Arrange the letters IRTEG in such a way as to make the name of a wild animal.

10. Arrange the letters COHYKE in such a way as to make the name of a sport.

11. Arrange the letters RISHT in such a way as to make the name of a wear.

12. Arrange the letters GNMAO in such a way as to make the name of a fruit.

13. Arrange the letters IERC in such a way as to make the name of a foodgrain.

14. Arrange the letters RAGA in such a way as to make the name of a city.

15. Arrange the letters AIRHC in such a way as to make the name of an item of furniture.

16. Arrange the letters NADH in such a way as to make the name of a part of human body.

17. Arrange the letters GIRN in such a way as to make the name of an ornament.

18. Arrange the letters LITMA in such a way as to make the name of the language of a State in India.

19. Arrange the letters MENE in such a way as to make the name of tree.

20. Arrange the letters IRATN in such a way as to make the name of a vehicle (transport).

21. Arrange the letters APUBJN in such a way as to make the name of a State in India.

22. Arrange the letters TCKEICR in such a way as to make the name of a sport.

23. Arrange the letters TERLPO in such a way as to make the name of a fuel.

24. Arrange the letters RIGOUT in such a way as to make the name of a musical instrument.

25. Arrange the letters BYBA in such a way as to make the name of a word representing infants.

26. Arrange the letters DEKYIN in such a way as to make the name of a part of body.

27. Arrange the letters UGOENT in such a way as to make the name of a part of the mouth.

28. Arrange the letters NKODYE in such a way as to make the name of an animal.

29. Arrange the letters ARINHSK in such a way as to make the name of a river.

30. Arrange the letters IDASLAK in such a way as to make the name of a classical Sanskrit poet.

31. Arrange the letters HAIKS in such a way as to make the name of a place of pilgrimage.

32. Arrange the letters RAISP in such a way as to make the name of capital of an European country.

33. Arrange the letters ROPEPC in such a way as to make the name of a metal.

34. Arrange the letters PRAEG in such a way as to make the name of a fruit.

35. Arrange the letters ARNAYMA in such a way as to make the name of an Indian epic.

36. Arrange the letters BRAAK in such a way as to make the name of a Mughal ruler of India.

37. Arrange the letters ABMUR in such a way as to make the name of a neighbour country of India.

38. Arrange the letters TACWH in such a way as to make the name of a machine that tells time.

39. Arrange the letters JNALRIB in such a way as to make the name of a vegetable.

40. Arrange the letters GOEYNX in such a way as to make the name of a gas.

ARRANGING WORDS IN THEIR NATURAL ORDER

In these questions, some words are given. They are to be arranged in their natural order. The arrangement may be, as required in the ascending order, descending order or alphabetical order (as used in dictionary). Sometimes the arrangement has to be made in such order as the things, activities happen in nature or in one's life, *i.e.*, brushing the teeth, breakfast, bath, lunch.

We shall have some examples.

Example 1. Which one of the following words will come in the first place if they are arranged in the manner as in a dictionary.

CAT, CAME, CAR, CAN

A. CAT B. CAN

C. CAME D. CAR

Solution: If arranged as required these words (given in the above example) will appear in the following order:

CAME, CAN, CAR, CAT.

Example 2. Which one of the following will come at the end in the natural order:

A. Printing B. Book
C. Binding D. Paper

In the natural order these items will appear as: Paper, Printing, Binding and Book.

QUESTIONS FOR PRACTICE

1. Which one is the smallest?

A. Lane B. Caste
C. Family D. Town

2. Which one of the followoing came into existence before others?

A. Caste B. Community
C. Family D. Clan

3. Which one of the following came into existence first?

A. Wood B. Chair
C. Seed D. Tree

4. Which one will come first in the natural order?

A. Shirt B. Stitching
C. Cloth D. Cutting

5. Which one will come first in the natural order?

A. Sugar B. *Khand*
C. Jaggery D. Sugarcane

6. Which one of the following will come last in the ascending order?

A. Adolscence B. Adulthood
C. Old age D. Childhood

7. Which will come in the third place from the top?

A. Eyes B. Waist
C. Knees D. Legs

8. Which one of the following will come first in the regular order?

A. College B. University
C. School D. Nursery

9. Which one of the following is the first vital requirement for life?

A. Food B. Water
C. Vitamins D. Air

10. The first thing while crossing the road is:

A. look around B. stop
C. go D. speed up

MISCELLANEOUS

1. Vipin is taller than Ram Lal. Ram Lal is not as tall as Ahmad. Mahendra is taller than Sheikh, but not as tall as Ram Lal. Ahmad is not as tall as Vipin is. Who is the shortest among them?

A. Vipin B. Ahmad
C. Ram Lal D. Sheikh
E. Mahendra

2. School is situated to the west of the hospital which is south to the police post. The court is to the north of the school. If the four places are at the equal distance from each other, the police post is situated to the:

A. East of the court

B. West of the court

C. North of the court

D. South of the court

3. Roads from the north, south, east and west directions meet near a police post. A constable coming on the road from the east finds that the road in front of him leads to a park and the road towards his right leads to the railway station and none of those roads lead to the police post. For reaching the police post, to which direction should the policeman turn?

A. East B. West

C. North D. South

4. While standing at the bus stop in the morning I saw a policeman riding a cycle on the other side of the road. With his left hand he was protecting his face from the sun rays and his right hand was towards me. In which direction from the policeman was I standing?

A. East B. West

C. North D. South

Directions (Qs. 5-7): *Six students A, B, C, D, E and F are sitting in a park. A and B belong to Nehru House while the rest belong to Gandhi House. D and F are tallish while the others are short-sized. A, C and D put on spectacles but others do not. On the basis of the above information, answer questions 5 to 7.*

5. Two short-sized students who do not put an spectacles are:

A. A and F B. C and E

C. B and E D. E and F

6. The tallish Gandhi House student who does not put on spectacles is:

A. B B. C

C. E D. F

7. The short-sized Gandhi House student who does not put on spectacles is:

A. B B. F

C. E D. A

8. Some boys are standing in a row. Kamal is sixth from the left and Appu is fourth from the right. When Kamal and Appu exchange their places, Appu becomes 17th from the right. What will be the position of Kamal from the left?

A. 20th B. 19th

C. 21st D. 4th

9. In the letters of English alphabet from A to Z are written in reverse order, *i.e.*, ZYX.....CBA, the 8th letter to the right of the 10th letter from the left will be:

A. Y B. I

C. J D. X

Directions: *Read carefully the following statements and then answer questions 10 to 12.*

Ramesh, Mohan and Edward play cricket.

Mohan, Rahman and Edward play hockey.

Rahman, Ramesh and Mohan play volleyball.

10. Who plays all the three sports?

A. Ramesh B. Mohan

C. Edward D. Rahman

11. Who plays cricket and volleyball but does not play hockey?

A. Ramesh B. Mohan

C. Edward D. Rahman

12. Who plays hockey and volleyball but does not play cricket?

A. Ramesh B. Mohan

C. Edward D. Rahman

Directions: *A cube is painted red on all sides and then it is cut into 64 small cubes of equal sizes.*

Based on the above given information, answer questions 13 and 14.

13. How many small cubes have only one side painted?

A. 4 B. 8

C. 16 D. 24

14. How many small cubes are such as to have none of their sides painted?

A. 8 B. 6

C. 4 D. 1

15. Five boys were climbing a hillock. Hari was ahead of all of them. Ram was ahead of Govind. Krishna was behind Hari and in between Jayant and Ram. All of them were climbing up in a column. Who was in the second position?

A. Jayant B. Hari

C. Ram D. Govind

E. Krishna

16. Of the six towns, Dhulia is bigger than Alamner and Sri Rampur is bigger than Nasik; Jalgaon is not equal to Sri Rampur but bigger than Alamner. Alamner is smaller than Nasik but bigger than Manmad. The smallest of them is:

A. Alamner B. Nasik

C. Jalgaon D. Manmad

E. Sri Rampur

17. Geeta is more beautiful than Rupa but not as beautiful as Neeta.

Choose the correct statement in the light of the above statements.

A. Rupa is more beautiful than Neeta

B. Neeta is more beautiful than Rupa

C. Neeta is not more beautiful than Geeta

D. None of the above statements is correct

18. All the faces of a cube are painted with different colours. Red and blue colours are on the opposite faces while the blue colour is in between the yellow and green colours. The colour on the face opposite the green colour is:

A. Red B. Blue

C. Yellow D. Violet

19. I was alone in the park. After a short while an old man and an old woman came there. They were followed by two couples, each of which was accompanied with a child. Now how many persons were there in the park?

A. 8 B. 9

C. 10 D. 11

20. Sitting on a bench are Girija, Ishan, Francis and Hema. Hema is to the left of Francis. Ishan is flanked by Francis and Girija. Who is at the extreme right?

A. Girija B. Hema

C. Ishan D. Francis

21. Shyam is elder than Pradip. Pravin is of same age as Anjan. Amrit is younger than Suresh and Suresh is of the same age as Anjan. Pradip is elder than Pravin. Who among them is the eldest?

A. Pradip B. Pravin

C. Suresh D. Shyam

Directions: *A toy cube has pictures of different fruits on its six faces. The top face has the picture of orange. Banana is adjacent to melon and orange. Apple is not at the bottom of the cube and melon is opposite the peace.*

Answer questions 22, 23 and 24 on the basis of the above information.

22. The neighbouring faces of the sixth fruit mango, do not have the picture of:

A. Apple B. Orange

C. Peach D. Banana

23. Which fruit is opposite the face having the picture of apple?

A. Banana B. Peach

C. Orange D. Mango

24. Which one of the following does not represent the correct pair of fruits on the opposite faces?

A. Orange-Mango

B. Apple-Banana

C. Apple-Mango

D. All the above

25. Manisha is the 11th from either end of the row of girls. How many girls are there in that row?

A. 19 B. 10

C. 21 D. 22

E. 23

26. Is it possible to make a meaningful word with the second, fourth, sixth, seventh, eighth and ninth letters of the word 'LEUTENANT'. If so, write the first letter of the word thus formed.

A. T B. E

C. N D. A

E. X

27. A is 3 years elder than B and 3 years younger than C; B and D are twins. How many years elder is C than D?

A. 3 B. 6

C. 2 D. equal in age

E. 12

DETAILED ANSWERS

SERIES

1. B: Multiply the number by 2 and add one to the product to obtain the subsequent number.

2. A: The numbers are 2^2, 3^2, 4^2 and 5^2 respectively. Therefore, the next number will be $6^2 = 36$.

3. C: Add 12 to each number to obtain the subsequent number

4. C: The numbers are divided by 2 to obtain the subsequent number.

5. C: Two letters are skipped from the beginning (A, D, G) of the alphabets in the first units and two letters are skipped from the end (Z, W, T) of the alphabet in the second units respectively.

6. D: Skip two letters respectively from the beginning of the alphabets.

7. A: The letters in the series are first letter of the alphabet from the end, first letter of the alphabet from the beginning, the second letter of the alphabet from the end and the second letter of alphabet from the beginning respectively. Proceed further on the same pattern.

8. C: $3 + 2 = 5$; $5^2 = 25$ and $3 + 4 = 7$; $7^2 = 49$. Similarly $2 + 3 = 5$; $5^2 = 25$.

9. C: Subsequent numbers are obtained by doubling the number.

10. D: Subsequent numbers are obtained by subtracting 5, 4, 3, etc. from the numbers respectively.

11. 24: Subsequent numbers have been obtained by subtracting 13 from the numbers.
$76 - 13 = 63$; $63 - 13 = 50$; $50 - 13 = 37$.
$\therefore$ Next number $= 37 - 13 = 24$.

12. 37: The numbers in the series are $2^1 + 1$, $3^2 + 1$, $4^2 + 1$ and $5^2 + 1$. Therefore, the next number will be $6^2 + 1 = 37$.

13. 30: The numbers in the series are $2^2 - 2$, $3^2 - 3$, $4^2 - 4$, $5^2 - 5$. Therefore, the next number will be $6^2 - 6 = 30$.

14. 15: The numbers in the series increase by 3 at each step. $3 + 3 = 6$; $6 + 3 = 9$; $9 + 3 = 12$. Therefore, the next number will be $12 + 3 = 15$.

15. 17: The numbers in the series are consecutive prime numbers 3, 7, 11 and 13. Therefore, the next prime number will be 17.

16. 25: The numbers in the series are 1^2, 2^2, 3^2, 4^2. Therefore, the next number will be $5^2 = 25$.

17. 24: The numbers in the series are $1^2 - 1$; $2^2 - 1$; $3^2 - 1$ and $4^2 - 1$. Therefore, the next number will be $5^2 - 1 = 24$.

18. 48: Multiply each number by 2 to find the next number. Therefore, the next number in the series will be $24 \times 2 = 48$.

19. 19: 3, 4 and 5 have been added respectively to find the next numbers in the series. Therefore, $13 + 6 = 19$ will be the next number.

20. 15: 2, 3 and 4 have been added respectively to find the next numbers in the series. Therefore, $10 + 5 = 15$ will be the next number.

21. 161: Multiply the number by 3 and then add 2 to the product to find the next number. Therefore, $53 \times 3 + 2 = 161$ will be the next number in the series.

22. 35: The numbers in the series are $2^2 - 1$, $3^2 - 1$, $4^2 - 1$ and $5^2 - 1$. Therefore, the next number will be $6^2 - 1 = 35$.

23. 7: The numbers in the series are reduced by 6, 5, 4 respectively to find the next numbers. Therefore, the next number will be $10 - 3 = 7$.

24. 63: The numbers in the series are doubled and then 1 is added to the product to obtain the next numbers. Therefore, the next number will be $31 \times 2 = 62 + 1 = 63$.

25. 5: The numbers are reduced to half to get the next numbers. Therefore, the next number will be $10 \div 2 = 5$.

26. 21: Add 5 to each number to find the subsequent number. Therefore, $16 + 5 = 21$.

27. 31: Subtract 7 from each number to find the subsequent number. Therefore, $38 - 7 = 31$.

28. 47: Double the number and then add 1 to the product to obtain the next number. Therefore, $23 \times 2 + 1 = 47$.

29. 29: The numbers in the series are consecutive prime numbers. The next prime number will be 29.

30. 53: Add 10 to obtain each subsequent number. Therefore, the next number will be $43 + 10 = 53$.

31. 46: Multiply the number by 2 and then add 2 to the product to obtain the next number. Therefore, the required number will be $22 \times 2 + 2 = 46$.

32. 25: The number in the series are 1^2, 2^2, 3^2 and 4^2.
$\therefore$ The next number will be $5^2 = 25$.

33. 6: The numbers in the series have been divided by 2 to obtain the next number. Therefore, the next number will be $12 \div 2 = 6$.

34. 11: Alternate numbers are reduced by 1.
For example 14, 13, 12 ...(*i*)
and 10, 9, 8 ...(*ii*)
The next number will be in series (*i*) above.
$\therefore$ The required number will be $12 - 1 = 11$.

35. 74: In this question, the relationship among the numbers of the series is as under:

(*i*) add 3 to get the second number.
(*ii*) double the second number to get the third number.
(*iii*) again add 3 to get the 4th number.
(*iv*) again double the 4th number to get the 5th number.
(*v*) again add 3 to get the 6th number.

$\therefore$ Double the 6th number (37) to get the 7th number, $37 \times 2 = 74$.

36. 7: In this series, divide the first number by 2 to get the second number; now add 4 to the second number to get the third number. This pattern is repeated.

$\therefore$ 32 ÷ 2 = 16; 16 + 4 = 20; 20 ÷ 2 = 10; 10 + 4 = 14;

Now divide 14 by 2. You get 7. This is your answer.

37. 5: There are two series:

(i) 2, 3, 4

(ii) 3, 5, 7

In series *(i)* numbers increase by 1 at each step.

In series *(ii)* numbers increase by 2 at each step.

The next number will be in series *(i)* add 1 to 4 to get 5. This is the required number.

38. 26: Subsequent numbers have been obtained by adding 1, 2, 3, 4 and 5 respectively to the numbers.

$\therefore$ The next number will be 20 + 6 = 26.

39. 126: The numbers in the series have been obtained by adding 1 to the cubes of 1, 2, 3 and 4 respectively such as $(1^3 + 1) = 2$; $(2^3 + 1) = 9$; $(3^3 + 1) = 28$; $(4^3 + 1) = 65$.

$\therefore$ The next number will be $5^3 + 1 = 126$.

40. 30: The numbers in the series are obtained as under:

$(1^2 - 1) = 0$; $(2^2 - 2) = 2$; $(3^2 - 3) = 6$; $(4^2 - 4) = 12$ and $(5^2 - 5) = 20$.

$\therefore$ The next number will be $(6^2 - 6) = 30$.

41. 37: Subsequent numbers in the series have been obtained by adding 3, 5, 6 and 9 to the given numbers. The numbers added, *i.e.*, 3, 5, 7, 9 are consecutive odd numbers. The next odd number will be 11. Therefore, the next number in the series will be obtained by adding 11 to 26. 26 + 11 = 37.

42. 41: Subsequent numbers in the series have been obtained by adding 4, 6, 8 and 10 to the given numbers. The numbers added, *i.e.*, 4, 6, 8 and 10 are consecutive even numbers. The next even number is 12. Therefore, the next number in the series will be 29 + 12 = 41.

43. $\frac{7}{8}$**:** The numerators and denominators of each fraction in the series have been reduced by 1 to obtain the numerators and denominators of the subsequent fractions in the series. For example, the numerators when reduced by 1 become 11 – 1 = 10, 10 – 1 = 9 and 9 – 1 = 8, and the denominators 11, 10 and 9 when reduced by 1. Now to obtain the next unknown fraction in the series, take the last fraction *i.e.* $\frac{8}{9}$ and reduc both the numerator and the denominator by 1.

$\therefore \frac{8-1}{9-1} = \frac{7}{8}.$

44. 37: In this series the third number, *i.e.*, 9 has been obtained by adding the first number (4) to the second number (5), *i.e.*, 4 + 5 = 9. The fourth number, *i.e.*, 14 has been obtained by adding the second and the third number *i.e.*, 5 + 9 = 14, and so on. Therefore the sixth number in the series may be obtained by adding together the fourth and the fifth numbers, *i.e.*, 14 + 23 = 37.

45. 65: In this question also the method is the same as applied in Q. No. 44. First number + second number = third number; second number + third number = fourth number; and third number + fourth number = fifth number. To obtain subsequent number, apply same method.
∴ Sixth number will be = fourth number (25) + fifth number (40).
∴ 25 + 40 = 65.

46. 3: In this series, subsequent numbers have been obtained by dividing the numbers by 2, 3 and 4 respectively. Therefore, to obtain the next number, divide the fifth number by 5.
∴ 15 ÷ 5 = 3.

47. 49: The numbers in the series are squares of 2, 3, 4, 5 and 6. Therefore the next number will be square of 7 = 49.

48. 1: There are two series. *(i)* 4, 3, 2 and
(ii) 8, 6, 4
The numbers in *(i)* are reduced by 1 at each step.
Similarly, the numbers in *(ii)* are reduced by 2 at each step.
On the same analogy the next number in *(i)* will be 2 – 1 = 1.

49. 125: The numbers in the series are cubes of 1, 2, 3 and 4 respectively.
∴ The next number in the series will be cube of 5 = 125.

50. 44: In this series, the numbers increase by 4, 8 and 12 respectively.
∴ Add 16 to obtain the next number: 28 + 16 = 44.

51. 26: Subsequent numbers have been obtained by adding 1, 3, 5 and 7 to the numbers. These numbers, *i.e.*, 1, 3, 5 and 7 are consecutive odd numbers. The next odd number is 9.
∴ Add 9 to 17 to obtain the next number in the series.
∴ 17 + 9 = 26.

52. 2: The numbers in the series have been divided by 6, 5 and 4 respectively to obtain the subsequent numbers.
∴ Divide the last number in the series, *i.e.*, 6 by 3 to obtain the next number. ∴ 6 ÷ 3 = 2.

53. 32: Each subsequent number is double of the previous number, as $1 \times 2 = 2$; $2 \times 2 = 4$; $4 \times 2 = 8$ and $8 \times 2 = 16$.
Now multiply 16 by 2 to obtain the next number in the series.
$\therefore 16 \times 2 = 32$.

54. 21: Subsequent numbers in the series increase by 2, 3, 4 and 5. On the same analogy add 6 to the last number to find the next number in the series.
$\therefore 15 + 6 = 21$.

55. 25: The numbers in the series are squares of 0, 1, 2, 3 and 4.
$\therefore$ The next number will be $5^2 = 25$.

56. 10: Subsequent numbers have been obtained by dividing the numbers by 3.
$\therefore$ The next number will be $30 \div 3 = 10$.

57. 49: The numbers in the series are 3^2, 4^2, 5^2 and 6^2 respectively. Therefore, the next number will be $7^2 = 49$.

58. 18: The subsequent numbers have been obtained by adding 3 to each number. Therefore, the next number will be $15 + 3 = 18$.

59. 26: The subsequent numbers are obtained by adding 4, 5, 6. Therefore, the next number will be $19 + 7 = 26$.

60. 63: Double the number and add 1 to obtain the next number. Therefore, the next number will be $31 \times 2 + 1 = 63$.

61. 65: The numbers are reduced by 10, 9, 8 etc. respectively. Therefore, the next number will be $72 - 7 = 65$.

62. 12: There are two series—*(i)* 2, 4, 8 and *(ii)* 3, 6, 12. In both the series the numbers are doubled to obtain the subsequent numbers. Therefore, the next number will be $6 \times 2 = 12$.

63. 64: There are two series—*(i)* 3, 9, 27 and *(ii)* 4, 16, ... In series *(i)* the numbers are multiplied by 3. In series *(ii)* the numbers are multiplied by 4. Therefore, the next number will be $16 \times 4 = 64$.

64. 11: The numbers in the series are reduced by 10, 9, 8 to obtain the next numbers. Therefore, the next number will be $18 - 7 = 11$.

65. 30: Add 7 to each number to obtain subsequent numbers. Therefore, the next number will be $23 + 7 = 30$.

66. 20: The numbers have been reduced by 8, 6, 4 respectively. Hence the next number will be $22 - 2 = 20$.

67. 15: Add 2, 3 and 4 to the numbers respectively to obtain the next number. The next number will be $10 + 5 = 15$.

68. 9: Reduce each number by 19 to get the subsequent number. The next number will be $28 - 19 = 9$.

69. 35: The subsequent numbers have been obtained by adding 2, 4, 8 respectively. Therefore, the next number will be $19 + 16 = 35$.

70. $\frac{3}{4}$**:** The subsequent numbers have been obtained by dividing the number by 2. $1\frac{1}{2} \div 2 = \frac{3}{4}$.

71. 8: There are two series—*(i)* 2, 4, 6 and *(ii)* 3, 6, 9. In series *(i)* the next number will be 8.

72. 9: There are two series—*(i)* 5, 10, 20 and *(ii)* 36, 18, ... In series *(ii)* the next number will be 9.

73. 17: The numbers in the series are prime numbers. The prime number after 13 will be 17.

74. 32: Each number has been doubled to obtain the next number 16 x 2 = 32.

75. 18: Subtract 9 to obtain the next number 27 – 9 = 18.

76. 25: Add 6 to obtain the next number 19 + 6 = 25.

77. 25: The numbers in the series are 1^2, 2^2, 3^2 and 4^2. The next number will be $5^2 = 25$.

78. 81: Add 9 to obtain the next number. The next number will be 72 + 9 = 81.

79. 80: The numbers in the series have been increased by 11, 10 and 9 respectively to obtain the next numbers. Therefore, the next number will be 72 + 8 = 80.

80. 2: There are two series—*(i)* 20, 10, 5 and *(ii)* 8, 4, ... The next number in series *(ii)* will be 2.

81. 47: Double the number and add 1 to the product to obtain the next number. Therefore, the next number will be 23 x 2 + 1 = 47.

82. 94: Double the number and add 2 to the product to obtain the next number. Therefore, the next number will be 46 x 2 + 2 = 94.

83. 53: The numbers in the series are prime numbers. The next prime number after 37 will be 53.

84. 18: There are two series—*(i)* 3, 9, 27 and *(ii)* 2, 6, ... In series *(ii)*, the next number will be 18.

85. 21: The next numbers in the series have been obtained by adding 3, 4, 5 etc. Therefore, the next number in the series will be 15 + 6 = 21.

86. 30: The numbers in the series are $2^2 - 2$; $3^2 - 3$; $4^2 - 4$ and $5^2 - 5$. Therefore, the next number will be $6^2 - 6 = 30$.

87. 125: The numbers in the series are 1^3, 2^3, 3^3, 4^3. Therefore, the next number will be $5^3 = 125$.

88. 1: The numbers in the series are 5^3, 4^3, 3^3, 2^3. Therefore, the next number will be $1^3 = 1$.

89. 100: The numbers in the series are 6^2, 7^2, 8^2 and 9^2. Therefore, the next number will be $10^2 = 100$.

90. 16: The numbers in the series are 8^2, 7^2, 6^2 and 5^2. Therefore, the next number will be $4^2 = 16$.

91. 61: $3^2 + 4^2 = 25$ and $4^2 + 5^2 = 41$. Therefore, $5^2 + 6^2 = 61$.

92. 81: $2 + 3 = 5$; $5^2 = 25$ and $3 + 4 = 7$; $7^2 = 49$. Therefore, $4 + 5 = 9$; $9^2 = 81$.

93. 7: $6^2 - 4^2 = 20$ and $5^2 - 3^2 = 16$. Therefore, $4^2 - 3^2 = 7$.

94. 9: $8 - 6 = 2$; $2^2 = 4$ and $7 - 4 = 3$; $3^2 = 9$. Therefore, $5 - 2 = 3$; $3^2 = 9$.

95. 18: $7 + 9 = 16$; $16 \times 2 = 32$ and $3 + 6 = 9$; $9 \times 2 = 18$. Therefore, $5 + 4 = 9$; $9 \times 2 = 18$.

96. 64: $(3 + 2)^2 = 25$ and $(3 + 4)^2 = 49$. Therefore, $(3 + 5)^2 = 64$.

97. 3: $\frac{9-5}{2} = 2$ and $\frac{25-15}{2} = 5$. Therefore, $\frac{12-6}{2} = 3$.

98. 41: $2^2 + 3^2 = 13$ and $3^2 + 4^2 = 25$. Therefore, $4^2 + 5^2 = 41$.

99. 29: $2^2 + 3^2 = 13$ and $3^2 + 4^2 = 25$. Therefore, $2^2 + 5^2 = 29$.

100. 16: $6 - 3 = 3$; $3^2 = 9$ and $7 - 2 = 5$; $5^2 = 25$. Therefore, $8 - 4 = 4$; $4^2 = 16$.

101. 34: $5^2 + 2^2 = 29$ and $2^2 + 3^2 = 13$. Therefore, $3^2 + 5^2 = 34$.

102. 20: $6^2 - 3^2 = 27$ and $5^2 - 4^2 = 9$. Therefore, $6^2 - 4^2 = 20$.

103. 4: $4 - 2 = 2$; $2^2 = 4$ and $6 - 4 = 2$; $2^2 = 4$. Therefore $5 - 3 = 2$; $2^2 = 4$.

104. 100: $3 + 5 = 8$; $8^2 = 64$ and $2 + 3 = 5$; $5^2 = 25$. Therefore $4 + 6 = 10$; $10^2 = 100$.

105. 18: $1 + 4 = 5$; $5 \times 2 = 10$ and $2 + 5 = 7$; $7 \times 2 = 14$. Therefore, $3 + 6 = 9$; $9 \times 2 = 18$.

106. 120: $3 \times 2 = 60$ and $3 \times 3 = 90$. Therefore, $3 \times 4 = 120$.

107. 13: $5 - 3 = 2$ and $17 - 6 = 11$. Therefore, $18 - 5 = 13$.

108. 54: $4 \times 5 = 20$; $20 \times 3 = 60$ and $2 \times 8 = 16$; $16 \times 3 = 48$. Therefore, $3 \times 6 = 18$; $18 \times 3 = 54$.

109. 3: $9 - 5 = 4$; $\frac{4}{2} = 2$ and $25 - 15 = 10$; $\frac{10}{2} = 5$. Therefore, $12 - 6 = 6$; $\frac{6}{2} = 3$.

110. 10: $5 + 8 = 13$ and $7 + 9 = 16$. Therefore, $3 + 7 = 10$.

111. $\frac{5}{7}$: Add the numerator and denominators:

$$\frac{3}{4} + \frac{5}{6} = \frac{8}{10} \text{ and } \frac{6}{7} + \frac{2}{3} = \frac{8}{10}$$

$$\therefore \frac{3}{4} + \frac{2}{3} = \frac{5}{7}$$

112. 16: Add the two numbers: $4 + 7 = 11$ and $11 + 4 = 15$. Therefore, $7 + 9 = 16$.

113. 8: Add the numerator to the denominator: 5 + 7 = 12; and 1 + 10 = 11. Therefore, 3 + 5 = 8.

114. 13: Subtract 25 – 12 = 13 and 9 – 3 = 6. Therefore, 17 – 4 = 13.

115. 11: Add the two numbers. 5 + 2 = 7 and 11 + 2 = 13. Therefore, 8 + 3 = 11.

116. EFG: These are two successive letters.

117. UVW: U after X, W, V; V after Y, X, W and W after Z, Y, X.

118. EV: One letter from the beginning and one letter from the end in the same order.

119. EGI: Next successive letters are taken.

120. VT: From the end, the letter just before the letter W, *i.e.*, the letter V, and the letter just before the letter U, *i.e.*, the letter T.

121. EI: Skip three continuous letters in the same order.

122. EFH: One letter is skipped after two letters in their natural sequence.

123. ER: The letters are the first letter and 14th letter; the second letter and the 15th letter; the third letter and 16th letter and so on.

124. EFV: From the beginning, the first two successive letters and one letter from the end.

125. VE: The last letter of the alphabet and the first letter of the alphabet are taken. It is repeated.

126. M: Two letters have been skipped at each step.

127. N: From the end, two letters have been skipped at each step.

128. DWV: One letter from the beginning and two letters from the end have been taken. The same process is repeated.

129. JI: Two successive letters have been transposed. Their order is second-first, fourth-third, sixth-fifth.

130. QPO: From the end, three letters in the reverse order.

FINDING THE WRONG OR SUPERFLUOUS NUMBER

1. 24: It should be 25 as the numbers in the series are 1^2, 2^2, 3^2, 4^2, 5^2 and 6^2.

2. 32: It should be 33 because there are two series—*(i)* 11, 22, 33 and *(ii)* 12, 24, 36.

3. 41: It should be 43 as the numbers increase by 4, 5, 6, 7 and 8 respectively.

4. 37: It should be 36 as the numbers in the series are 10^2, 9^2, 8^2, 7^2, 6^2 and 5^2.

5. 125: It should be 128 as the numbers increase by 9 at each step.

6. 70: It should be 69 as the subsequent numbers are obtained by adding 10, 11, 12 and 13 respectively.

7. 28: It should be 29 as the subsequent numbers are obtained by subtracting 11, 10, 9 and 8 respectively.

8. 10: It should be 12 as the subsequent numbers are obtained by subtracting 3 successively.

9. 12: 12 is superfluous as the numbers are reduced by 2 successively.

10. 17: 17 is superfluous as the numbers increase by 3 successively.

11. 25: 25 is wrong; it should be 27. The numbers are multiplied by 3 to obtain the subsequent number.

12. 19: 19 is superfluous. 5 is added to each number to obtain subsequent number.

13. 24: 24 is superfluous. The numbers in the series are 2^2, 3^2, 4^2, 5^2, 6^2 and 7^2 respectively.

14. 26: 26 is superfluous. The numbers increase by 6 at each step.

15. 7: 7 is superfluous. The numbers increase by 5, 10, 15 and 20 at each step.

16. 7: It should be 8 as the numbers are 1^3, 2^3, 3^3, 4^3 and 5^3.

17. 10: It should be 18 as the numbers decrease by 2, 3, 4, 5 and 6 at each step.

18. 80: It should be 81 as the numbers increase by 9, 10, 11, 12 and 13 respectively.

19. 24: It should be 25 as the numbers are 4^2, 5^2, 6^2, 7^2, 8^2 and 9^2 respectively.

20. 86: It should be 85 as the numbers decrease by 7, 8, 9 and 10 respectively.

21. 32: It should be 33 as the numbers increase by 11 at each step.

22. 121: It should be 125 as the numbers are 6^3, 5^3, 4^3, 3^3 and 2^3 respectively.

23. 35: It should be 36 as the numbers are 2^2, 3^2, 4^2, 5^2, 6^2 and 7^2 respectively.

24. 27: It should be 28 as the subsequent numbers are obtained by subtracting 11 at each step.

25. 70: It should be 69 as the subsequent numbers are obtained by adding 10, 11, 12 and 13 respectively.

26. 52: It should be 53 as the subsequent numbers are obtained by subtracting 9 at each step.

27. 24: It should be 25 as the subsequent numbers are obtained by adding 7 at each step.

28. 9: It should be 8 as the numbers are doubled at each step.

29. 12: It should be 13 as the subsequent numbers increase by 3, 4, 5 and 6 respectively.

30. 20: It should be 19 as there are two series—*(i)* 5, 9, 13 and *(ii)* 7, 13, 20. In series *(ii)*, the numbers increase by 6 at each step.

31. 16: It should be 17 as the subsequent numbers are obtained by adding 1^2, 2^2, 3^2, 4^2 and 5^2 respectively to them.

32. 21: It should be 20 as the numbers are increased by 7 at each step.

33. 48: It should be 54 as the numbers are increased by 12 at each step.

34. 26: It should be 27 as the numbers are 1^3, 2^3, 3^3, 4^3, 5^3 respectively.

35. 28: It should be 30 as the numbers are 6 x 1; 6 x 3; 6 x 5; 6 x 7; 6 x 9 respectively.

36. 43: It should be 42 as the subsequent numbers are obtained by subtracting 7 at each step.

37. 65: It should be 69 as the numbers decrease by 11 at each step.

38. 18: It should be 10 as the numbers are $1 + 1^2$; $1 + 2^2$; $1 + 3^2$; $1 + 4^2$ and $1 + 5^2$ respectively.

39. 39: It should be 36 as the number increase by 4, 5, 6, 7 and 8 respectively.

40. 40: It should be 44 as the numbers are reduced by half at each step.

41. 45: It should be 47 as the numbers are increased by 13 at each step.

42. 34: It should be 33 as the numbers are increased by 6 at each step.

43. 12: It should be 11 as the numbers are reduced by 2 at each step.

44. 64: It should be 62 as the numbers are reduced by 10 and 9, 10 and 9 and 10 and 9 respectively.

45. 15: It should be 16 as the numbers increase by 3, 5, 7, 9 and 11 respectively.

ANALOGY

1. C: We get curd from milk: similarly we get ice from water.

2. B: Girl is beautiful (quality): similarly gold is bright.

3. A: In desert we find sand: similarly in sea we find water.

4. A: Beautiful is to ugly (opposite): similarly healthy is to sick (opposite).

5. C: Cheese is made from milk. Similarly sugar is made from sugarcane.

6. C: Daughter is to mother as son is to father.

7. C: Book is made of paper: similarly table is made of wood.

8. B: A group of players is a team: similarly a group of ships is a fleet.

9. D: Kilogram is to weight as metre is to length.

10. B: Lid is to box as cork is to bottle.

11. D: Circle has a circumference as square has a perimeter

12. A: Advocate knows law as cook knows cookery.

13. C: Wardrobe is meant for clothes: similarly purse is meant for money.

14. D: Temperature indicates level of heat: similarly humidity indicates level of moisture.

15. C: Shakespeare is known for his dramas: similarly Ghalib is known for his *ghazals*.

16. C: Grass is green (colour): similarly sky is blue.
17. C: Monday is a day in a week: similarly January is a month in a year.
18. C: Thermometer measures temperature: similarly barometer measures atmospheric pressure.
19. C: Poverty is to riches (opposite): similarly glory is to shame (opposite).
20. D: Table is to chair (pair): similarly coat is to pant (pair).
21. B: Hand is to elbow (relation): similarly leg is to knee (relation).
22. D: Coal is to black (colour): similarly snow is to white (colour).
23. A: Precaution prevents accident: similarly cleanliness prevents disease.
24. D: January is to April (4th month): similarly Sunday is to Wednesday (4th day).
25. C: Soldier is associated with rifle: similarly writer is associated with pen.
26. D: Plate is an item of crockery: similarly spoon is an item of cultery.
27. A: Night comes after evening: similarly day comes after morning.
28. B: Uncle is to aunt: similarly father is to mother.
29. D: Lotus grows in water: similarly fish lives in water.
30. C: Metre is to length (measure): similarly litre is to volume.
31. C: Heaven is to hell (opposite): similarly drought is to flood.
32. C: Planet revolves round the sun as moon revolves round the earth.
33. B: French is the language of the people of France: similarly Dutch is the language of the people of Holland.
34. B: Colombo is capital of Sri Lanka: similarly Tokyo is capital of Japan.
35. D: Pen writes: similarly carpenters' plane shaves off.
36. D: Thick is to thin (opposite): similarly inferior is to superior.
37. B: Table is made of wood: similarly book is made of paper.
38. D: Fan gives air: similarly bulb gives light.
39. A: Seven is a number (class): similarly green is a colour (class).
40. A: Stage is associated to drama as stadium is associated to sports.
41. A: Mango is a variety of fruit: similarly cobra is a variety of serpent.
42. A: Rain is measured in centimeter: similarly temperature is measured in celsius.
43. A: Lane is a smaller road. similarly town is a smaller city.
44. B: Aspirin cures headache: similarly quinine cures malaria.
45. C: Food satisfies hunger: similarly water satisfies thirst.
46. D: Young one of a cat is kitten: similarly young one of a hen is chicken.
47. A: Banana is one of the fruits: similarly cow is one of the mammals.

48. C: One listens to radio: similarly one views film.

49. B: Money, a medium of exchange: similarly language, a medium of communication.

50. D: Friend is to enemy (opposite): similarly kind is to cruel.

51. B: Train stops at platform: similarly ship stops at harbour.

52. C: 1st April is called Fools Day: similarly 1st May is called Labour Day.

53. B: Clock measures time: similarly rainguage measures rain.

54. A: Lion lives in den: similarly horse lives in stable.

55. D: Book is made up of pages: similarly flower is made up of petals.

56. D: Tea is made from leaves: similarly coffee is made from seeds.

57. C: Horse neighs: similarly donkey brays.

58. B: Garage is the place where car is kept when not in use: similarly hanger is the place where aircraft is kept when not in use.

59. A: Radius is to a circle as spoke is to a wheel.

60. A: Carpenters mends stool: similarly cobbler mends shoes.

61. C: Bus is repaired in the workshop: similarly ship is repaired in the dockyard.

62. B: Ring is put on the finger: similarly tie is put on the neck.

63. B: Needle is used for sewing: similarly brush is used for painting.

64. B: We smell through nose: similarly we taste through tongue.

65. D: Pencil is an item of stationery: similarly chair is an item of furniture.

66. A: Both cat and dog are carnivorous: similarly both cow and goat are harbivorous.

67. D: Both snake and lizard are reptile: similarly both fish and crocodile live in water.

68. C: Honour is to dishonour (opposite) as fame is to infamy.

69. B: Light travels through rays: similarly sound travels through waves.

70. C: In a clock hands tell time: similarly in a thermometer mercury indicates temperature.

71. B: Tractor runs on diesel: similarly scooter runs on petrol.

72. B: Cuckoo cackles: similarly horse neighs.

73. B: Pitch is a term associated with cricket: similarly ring is a term associated with boxing.

74. C: Car runs: similarly snake creeps.

75. A: Urge is to deter (opposite): similarly honest is to dishonest.

76. C: Lion lives in den: similarly bird lives in nest.

77. D: Calf is young one of a cow: similarly lamb is young one of a sheep.

78. B: Obedience is to disobedience (opposite): similarly life is to death.

79. B: Tailor uses cloth to make garments: similarly carpenter uses wood to make furniture.

80. A: Cat kills rat: similarly tiger kills lamb.

81. B: Bakery is the place where bread is prepared: similarly mint is the place where coins are produced.

82. A: Studio is associated with film: similarly shipyard is associated with ship.

83. A: Months make a year: similarly hours make a day.

84. C: Food satisfies hunger: similarly water satisfies thirst.

85. C: Revolver is associated with bullet: similarly bow is associated with arrow.

86. D: Bees give honey: similarly sheep give wool.

FINDING ODD ONE OUT

1. C: In this pair both the items are males while in other pairs one item is male and the other item is female.

2. D: Bird and tree are not related in the same way as coal and mine, water and river and fishes and water.

3. C. Thief and robber are not related to each other as hospital and doctor, court and advocate, and school and teacher are.

4. D: Curd is made from milk, house is made from brick, book is made from paper, but stable is not made from horses.

5. B: Milk is always white, sky is always blue and blood is always red, but leaf may be brown and yellow as well.

6. B: Carrot and radish are not opposite to each other whereas victory and defeat, north and south, and up and down are opposite to each other.

7. D: Tiger lives in den.

8. A: Sky is always blue whereas kite, saree and horse may be of different colours.

9. A: Items in pair A are living beings, whereas items in other pairs are non-living beings.

10. A: Items in pair A are man made whereas items in all other pairs are nature-made (natural).

11. D: It is not a pair. Others are pairs.

12. D: The two items in the pair are not opposites whereas the two items in other pairs are opposite to each other.

13. D: Paper may be of other colours than white, whereas smoke, heat and cool are essential elements of fire, sun and moonlight respectively.

14. D: Moon is a satellite while others are planets.

15. B: Raisin is a dryfruit while others are fresh fruits.

16. C: Goat is a domestic cattle while others are wild animals.

17. A: Riksha is man driven while others are power driven.

18. A: Tiger is a wild animal while others are draught animals.

19. C: Snake does not have legs while all others have legs.

20. C: Patna is in Bihar while all others are in UP.

21. C: Coin is a general name while all others are names of currencies of various countries.

22. A: Diamond is not a metal while all others are names of metals (minerals).

23. D: Legs, Hands and Ankles are external parts of body, while Lungs are inside the body.

24. D: Steamer, Boat and Ship are means of transport, while Harbour is a place of shelter for ship.

25. B: Lotus is a flower that grows in water. Rose, Dahlia and Jasmin grow on land.

26. C: Protein, Carbohydrates and Vitamins are needed by human body as parts of balanced diet, while copper is not needed.

27. C: Piano, Tabla and Banjo are musical instruments that require the help of hands and fingers in playing, whereas Flute is a wind instrument.

28. D: Metre, Kilometre and Centimetre are units of linear distances whereas Square Kilometre is a unit of area.

29. D: Snake is a reptile, while others are not.

30. D: Snake, Lizard and Crocodile are reptile, whereas Frog is not a reptile.

31. C: Moon is a satellite, whereas others are planets.

32. D: Sketch Map is not an item of stationery. Others are items of stationery.

33. B: India Today is a forgnightly magazine whereas all others are daily newspapers.

34. B: Chanakya was a statesman and not a ruler or king whereas others were kings or rulers.

35. D: Tangent, Arc and Radius are associated with circle. Hypotenuse is related to right-angled triangle.

36. A: Delhi is capital of Delhi (of a country) whereas Patna (Bihar), Mumbai (Maharashtra) and Calcutta (West Bengal) are state capitals.

37. A: Scooter, Car and Bus are engine driven vehicles whereas bicycle is pedal driven.

38. B: Wheat, Ragi and Rice are cereals where Gram is a pulse.

39. C: Iron, Copper and Tin are not alloys whereas steel is an alloy.

40. C: Bile is a fluid secreted by liver and helps in the digestion, whereas Cancer, Hepatitis and Diabetes are names of diseases.

41. D: Soil cannot be used as a source of energy whereas all others can be used as a source of energy.

42. B: All other except B are commercial or cash crops.

43. C: Sugarcane is not a fruit whereas all others are fruits.

44. C: Karachi is not a capital town. All others are capital towns.

45. C: April has 30 days whereas May, March and July have 31 days each.

46. B: Diet is the name of the Japanese Parliament whereas Rouble, Dollar and Taka are currencies of different countries.

47. A: Libra is a constellation, whereas Uranus, Pluto and Neptune are planets.

48. B: Monastery is a building where monks live whereas Temple, Mosque and Church are places of worship.

49. B: Shilling is a currency whereas others are units of measurements.

50. C: Sword is a weapon of offence whereas others are defensive coverings.

51. D: Ganga, Godavari and Krishna, all flow from west to east whereas Narmada flows from east to west.

52. A: Cataract is a disease of eye whereas others are parts of eye.

53. C: Faster indicates speed, whereas all the other three words Bigger, Greater and Larger indicate size.

54. A: Cow, Dog and Horse are domesticated but not the Fox.

55. C: Jackal, Fox and Wolf, all are flesh eaters, but stag does not eat flesh.

56. B: Father, Brother and Sister are blood relations whereas Teacher is not.

57. A: Shore is the land that skirts any large body of water, whereas Sea, River and Pond are large body of water.

58. D: Sorrow is a state of sadness. Other words Moan, Wail and Weep are results of state of sadness.

59. D: Cock is a domestic or farmyard fowl, whereas others are not.

60. D: Lameness is the result of some or other accident or disease whereas Dwarfness, Slenderness and Fatness need not be associated with any accident or disease.

61. C: It is different, because son is the only male member among females.

62. C: The word Neck has only one vowel, all other words have two vowels each.

63. D: Pondicherry is a Union Territory whereas others are states of Indian Union.

64. C: Colonel is a rank in the Army whereas the other three are ranks in the Air Force.

65. D: Mridangam is a percussion instrument whereas the other three are string instruments.

66. C: Arabia is the name of a country whereas others are names of continents.

67. D: Crocodile is not a fish, whereas others are names of fish.

68. D: Diagonal is a line that connects one angle to the opposite one, whereas Square, Trapezium and Rectangle are quadrilaterals.

69. D: Monkey does not eat flesh whereas Cat, Dog and Fox eat flesh.

70. D: Penicillin is an antibiotic drug whereas the other three are analgesic (pain reliever).

71. B: The other three grow under the earth.

72. D: Malaria is not an infectious disease, whereas the other three are infectious diseases.

73. B: Office is not a place for living, whereas Bunglow, Hut and House are places for living.

74. A: Fly is an insect, all others are non-living things.

75. A: Root is not visible because it is underground; other parts of a tree are visible.

76. B: Potato grows underground; other vegetables grow under land.

77. B: Crow is a bird; all others are animals.

78. C: Kalidas was a poet; all others are scientists.

79. C: All others except shoes are items of garments.

80. D: Except Mercury all others are gases.

QUESTIONS RELATING TO CLOCKS AND CALENDARS

1	2	3	4	5	6	7	8	9	10
B	B	C	C	A	B	D	A	B	B
11	**12**	**13**	**14**	**15**	**16**	**17**	**18**	**19**	**20**
A	A	A	C	B	A	B	B	C	C

CODING AND DECODING

1. B: The letters just preceding the letters C, O, M and E are B, N, L and D. On the same pattern, the letters just preceding the letters C, A, R and E will be B, Z, Q and D.
Hence CARE will be coded as BZQD.

2. C: The letters succeeding H, I, G and H are I, J, H and I. On the same pattern the letters succeeding T, U, R and N will be U, V, S and O. Therefore, TURN will be coded as UVSO.

3. D: The letters just succeeding L, O, A and D are letters M, P, B and E. On the same pattern, the letter just succeeding P, O, R and T will be Q, P, S and U. Therefore, PORT will be coded as QPSU.

4. D: Skip one letter clockwise at each step to find the coded letters for G, O, L and D. These letters are I, Q, N and F. On the same pattern skip one letter at each step to find the codes for W, I, N and D. You will find such letters Y, K, P and F.
Hence, the code for WIND will be YKPF.

5. A: SHIRT has been coded as RGHQS. You will find that just preceding letters have been used as codes, *i.e.,* R for S, G for S, H for I; Q for R and S for T. On the same pattern, the just preceding letters R, O, U, N and D will make the code. These letters are Q, N, T, M and C.
Therefore, code for ROUND is QNTMC.

6. D: DEAR is coded as FGCT. It means one letter has been skipped at each step to find the code letters, *i.e.,* F for D, G for E, C for A and T for R. On the same pattern, skip one letter at each step to find the code for R, E, A and D. These letters will be T, G, C and F.
Therefore, code for READ will be TGCF.

7. C: You will find that two letters have been skipped to find the codes for E, A, S and E. The coded letters are H, D, V and H. On the same pattern skip two letters at each step to find the codes for S, E and E. Code for S will be V, and code for E will be H.
Therefore, code for SEE will be VHH.

8. C: The letters have been written in reverse order as is evident from SERPENT and TNEPRES. On the same pattern, letters of PLAGUE will be written in reverse order to find the code. PLAGUE written in reverse order will be EUGALP.

9. C: The letters just preceding the letters D, E, F, E, N, C and E are C, D, E, F, M, B and D. On the same pattern, the letters just preceding the letters N, E, E and D will be M, D, D and C.
Therefore, code for NEED will be MDDC.

10. D: CHAIR has been coded as FKDLU. It shows that two letters have been skipped clockwise at each step to find the code letters F for C, K for H, D for A, L for I and U for R. On the same pattern, skip two letters to find the code for R, A, I and D. These letters will be U, D, L and G.
Therefore, code for RAID will be UDLG.

11. D: A close look will reveal that letters have exchanged their places to make the coded expression. Your will find that the second and the third letters have exchanged their places; similarly the fifth and the sixth letters have exchanged their places. On the same pattern, in finding out the code for TEACHER, exchange the position of the second and the third letters, *i.e.,* make them AE instead of EA; also exchange the position of the fifth and the sixth letters, *i.e.,* make them EH instead of HE.

Thus the code for TEACHER will be TAECEHR.

12. D: COME = XLNV

[C = 3rd alphabet from the beginning
X = 3rd alphabet from the end

[O = 15th alphabet from the beginning
L = 15th alphabet from the end

[M = 13th alphabet from the beginning
N = 13th alphabet from the end

[E = 5th alphabet from the beginning
V = 5th alphabet from the end

Similarly, A, B, L and E are 1st, 2nd, 12th and 5th alphabets from the beginni..g and Z, Y, O and V are the 1st, 2nd, 12th and 15th alphabets from the end.

Therefore, on the same pattern M, O, L, L, Y will be coded as NLOOB.

13. D: CIG ARE TTE. Make groups of three alphabets each from the left. Write letters in each group in reverse order, and you will get GIC ERA ETT. On the same pattern, make groups of three alphabets each in DEM ONS TRA TION.

Write letters in each group in reverse order as under MED SNO ART OIT N.

14. C:

8		3		2				4		10		
A	B	C	D	E	F	G	H	I	J	K	L	M
5, 5	6	5		1, 1		7	9					
N	O	P	Q	R	S	T	U	V	W	X	Y	Z

CENTURION = 325791465
RANK = 18510
] Mark the position assigned in the alphabets above.

It means 7 = T
8 = A
5 = N
10 = K, ∴ 78510 = TANK

15. C: The first, third and fifth letters, *i.e.*, M, H and S are replaced by letters just following them, *i.e.*, N, I and T. Similarly, the second, fourth and sixth letters, *i.e.*, A, E and H are replaced by letters obtained by skipping one letter at each step, *i.e.*, C, G and J.
Therefore NEELAM, the first, third and fifth letters, *i.e.*, N, E and A will be replaced by letters just following them, *i.e.*, O, F and B; while the 2nd, 4th and 6th letters, *i.e.*, E, L and M will be replaced by letters obtained by skipping one letter at each step, *i.e.*, G, N and O.
Thus NEELAM will be OGFNBO.

16. D: In FLOWER and SEXOMF, you will find that the second, fourth and sixth letters in F L O W E R are replaced by letters just following these letters, *i.e.*, M, X and S written in reverse order that is S, X and M. The order of the other three letters, *i.e.*, F, O and E is also reversed to make it E, O and F.
Now in G A R D E N, the 2nd, 4th and 6th letters will be placed by letters just following these letters, *i.e.*, B, E and O, but in reverse order, *i.e.*, O, E and B. The other three letters, *i.e.*, G, R and E will also be written in the reverse order.
Thus GARDEN will be OEERBG.

17. C: Compare SCRIPT and TCQIQT. You will find that the 2nd, 4th and 6th letters remain unchanged. The other three letters, *i.e.*, 1st, 3rd and 5th (S, R and P) have changed to T, Q and Q. Here you will notice that T is the letter just following letter S in the alphabet, Q is the letter just preceding letter R in the alphabet and Q is the letter just following letter P in the alphabet.
Now in DIGEST, the 2nd, 4th and 6th letters, *i.e.*, I, E and T will remain unchanged. The first, third and fifth letters, *i.e.*, D, G and S will change to the just following letter E, just preceding letter F and just following letter T.
Thus DIGEST will be coded as EIFETT.

18. A: Compare RAM and SBN. You will find that letter just following in the alphabet have been taken in code. S for R, B for A and N for M are just on the above pattern.
Now for FEW, take the letters just following these letters in the alphabets, *i.e.*, G for F, F for E and X for W.
∴ FEW will be coded as GFX.

19. B: Compare RUBBER and REBBUR. You will find that the letters in RUBBER have been written in just reverse order as REBBUR.
On the same pattern, to find the code for DEAD, write these letters in reverse ord

20. C: You will find that the letters as coded (LBOQVS) are the letters just following the letters KANPUR.
On the same pattern, the letters just following the letters N, A, G, P, U and R will be O, B, H, Q, V and S.
Therefore NAGPUR = OBHQVS.

21. D: Compare DELHI with IDHEL. You will find that the same letters have been arranged in a different order. The order is last, first, last but one, second and then the third letter at the end.
On the same pattern, change the order of the letters in TUFAN. It will become NTAUF.

22. C: ANOTHER is coded as 7309521

	7	3	0	9	5	2	1
∴	A	N	O	T	H	E	R

∴ THORN = 95013.

23. B: Surendra is coded as DHTNPATI

	↑	↑	↑	↑	↑		
S	U	R	E	N	D	R	A
D	H	T	N	P	A	T	I

∴ UNDER = HPANT

24. C: Compare EFFICIENT with DEEHBHDMS.

E	F	F	I	C	I	E	N	T
D	E	E	H	B	H	D	M	S

∴ FIET = EHDS.

25. A: G, B, D and F are letters just following the letters FACE. On the same pattern, B, A, D, E will be coded as (just the following letters *i.e.*) C, B, E, F. Therefore, BADE will be coded as CBEF.

26. C: All the letters of SETS are contained in REST
REST = TGUV
∴ SETS = UGVU

27. D: DECADE = 453145

D	E	C	A	D	E
4	5	3	1	4	5

∴ DEED = 4554.

28. B: AD is common to BAD and MAD. So it will be coded as ZW. Now B is the 2nd alphabet from the beginning and Y is the 2nd alphabet from the end. On the same pattern, M in MAD is the 13th alphabet from the beginning; it will be coded by the 13th alphabet from the end, *i.e.*, N.
∴ MAD will be coded as NZW.

29. C: DIRT is coded as TDIR. You will find that the same alphabets appear

in the coded expression but the order of the alphabets is changed. The pattern of change in the order of the alphabets is:
The first becomes the second,
The second becomes the third,
The third becomes the fourth, and
The fourth becomes the first.
Now, change the order of alphabets in TRIM as shown above.
Thus TRIM will be MTRI.

30. C: PIT is coded as QJU. You will find that the letters just following PIT are QJU. On the same pattern the letters just following HUT will be IVU.

31. C: D E   C E   M B   E R = E R   M B   C E   D E

∴ N O   V E   M B   E R = E R   M B   V E   N O

32. B: ROUGH is coded as ORRJE. You will find that alternately 2 letters are skipped backward and forward to find the letters in the code.
R = O (2 letters skipped backward)
O = R (2 letters skipped forward)
U = R (2 letters skipped backward)
G = J (2 letters skipped forward)
H = E (2 letters skipped backward)
On the same pattern, the code for SMOOTH will be PPLRQK.

33. C: MOTHER is coded as PQWJHT. You will find that alternately 2, 1, 2, 1, 2 letters are skipped forward in writing the coded letters, as:
M = P (2 letters NO skipped)
O = Q (1 letter P skipped)
T = W (2 letters UV skipped)
H = J (1 letter I skipped), and so on.
On the same pattern
S = V (2 letters TU skipped)
I = K (1 letter J skipped)
S = V (2 letters TU skipped)
T = V (1 letter U skipped)
E = H (2 letters FG skipped)
R = T (1 letter S skipped)
SISTER = VKVVHT

34. A: LOFTY = LPFUY. You will find that the first, third and fifth letters remain unchanged, while the second and the fourth letters are replacd by the next letters in the alphabets, *i.e.*, P for O and U for T.
On the same pattern in DWARF, the first, third and fifth letters will

remain unchanged. The second and the fourth letters, *i.e.*, W and R will be replacd by the just following letters, *i.e.*, X and S.

Thus D W A R F

– X – S –

∴ DXASF.

35. D: PRICE = SVNIL.

You will find that 2, 3, 4, 5 and 6 letters are skipped in writing the code.

P = S (2 letters, *i.e.*, QR are skipped).

R = V (3 letters, *i.e.*, STU are skipped)

I = N (4 letters, *i.e.*, JKLM are skipped)

C = I (5 letters, *i.e.*, DEFGH are skipped)

E = L (6 letters, *i.e.*, FGHIJK are skipped)

On the same pattern, to find the code for COST, skip 2, 3, 4 and 5 letters.

C = F (2 letters DE skipped)

O = S (3 letters PQR skipped)

S = X (4 letters TUVWskipped)

T = Z (5 letters UVWXY skipped)

∴ COST = FSXZ

36. B: The letters in JAILAPPAS are divided into groups of three letters each as JAI, LAP and PAS. In each group the first letter is made the third letter as JAI becomes AIJ, LAP becomes APL and PAS becomes ASP. Thus JAILAPPAS becomes AIJALASP.

On the same pattern divide the expression ECONOMICS into groups of three letters each as ECO, NOM and ICS. Now, in each group make the first letter as third letter. They will becme COE, OMN and CSI.

∴ ECONOMICS will be coded as COEOMNCSI.

37. D: CLOCK is written as KCOLC. You will see that the letters have been written in reverse order beginning from the last letter

C L O C K = K C O L C

On the same pattern STEPS will be SPETS.

38. C: SPIDER is written as PSDIRE. The expression SPIDER is divided into groups of two letters each as SP, ID, ER. You will find the letters in each group exchange their place, *i.e.*, SP becomes PS, ID becomes DI and RE becomes ER. Thus SPIDER is written as PSDIRE.

On the same pattern divide the expression COMMON into groups of two letters each, *i.e.*, CO, MM and ON. When letters in each group exchange their places, the group will become OC, MM and NO. Thus COMMON will become OCMMNO.

39. C: Compare RECOMMENDATION and COMNENDATIONER

RE COMMENDATION

COMMENDATION ER

You will find that the first two letters RE exchange their position and occupy the last, position in the expression.

On the same pattern, when RENUMERATION will be written in the code, the first two letters, *i.e.*, RE will exchange their position to become ER and will occupy the last position. Thus the coded expression will become--MUNERATIONER.

40. A: TRIPPLE is coded as SQHOOKD. You will find that the coded letters are just the preceding letters of the letters in the expression. For example, S for T, Q for R, H for I, O for P again O for P, K for L and D for E.

On the same pattern use the just preceding letters to obtain the code for DISPOSE.

D = C

I = H

S = R

P = O

O = N

S = R

E = D

∴ DISPOSE will be coded as CHRONRD.

QUESTIONS BASED ON RELATIONSHIP

1. B: Ajit is brother of Mohan's son. Therefore, Mohan is father of Ajit and his brother. Therefore, Ajit is Mohan's grandson.

2. C: B is A's son.

B is my son's uncle.

∴ A is my father.

3. D: G's uncle is A's brother.

4. A: son-in-law.

5. B: Bihari is Yogendra's uncle.

6. C: C has two children A and B. A is his son while B is his daughter.

7. B: The son of my maternal uncle's son will be my nephew and I will be his uncle.

8. B: Children of Ram, Pratap and Kripa will be cousins.

9. B: The son of the daughter of P's sister will address P as maternal grandfather.

10. C: B is C's wife and A is C's father.
∴ A is father-in-law of B.

QUESTIONS RELATED TO DIRECTIONS

1	2	3	4	5	6	7	8	9	10
B	B	D	A	C	C	D	C	C	B

11	12	13
D	B	C

ARRANGING THE LETTERS TO MAKE MEANINGFUL WORDS

1. BLUE
2. COCHIN
3. URDU
4. IRON
5. PEACOCK
6. NARMADA
7. EARTH
8. PENCIL
9. TIGER
10. HOCKEY
11. SHIRT
12. MANGO
13. RICE
14. AGRA
15. CHAIR
16. HAND
17. RING
18. TAMIL
19. NEEM
20. TRAIN
21. PUNJAB
22. CRICKET
23. PETROL
24. GUITAR
25. BABY
26. KIDNEY
27. TONGUE
28. DONKEY
29. KRISHNA
30. KALIDAS
31. KASHI
32. PARIS
33. COPPER
34. GRAPE
35. RAMAYAN
36. AKBAR
37. BURMA
38. WATCH
39. BRIJNJAL
40. OXYGEN

ARRANGING WORDS IN THEIR NATURAL ORDER

1	2	3	4	5	6	7	8	9	10
C	C	D	C	D	C	C	D	D	B

MISCELLANEOUS

1. D.

2. A: School is to the west of hospital. Police post is to the north of the hospital. Court is to the north of the school. Therefore, the police post is to the each of court.

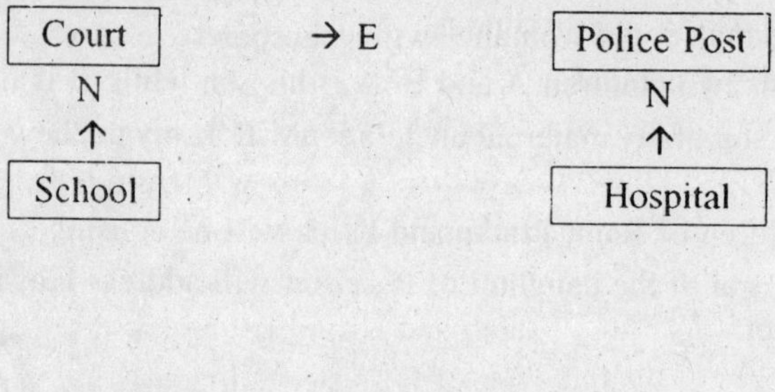

3. D.

4. B.

5. C: B and E are the two short-sized students without spectacles.

6. D: The tallish Gandhi House student without spectacles is F.

7. C:

S. sized	S. sized	S. sized	Tallish	S. sized	Tallish
A	B	C	D	E	F
Nehru	House		Gandhi	House	
↓		↓	↓		
Spectacles	X	Spectacles	Spectacles	X	X

The Gandhi House short sized student without spectacles is E.

8. B: After exchanging positions with Kamal, Appu becomes sixth from the left and seventh from the right which means that there are twenty two children in the row. After exchanging position with Appu, Kamal will be fourth from the right and nineteenth from the left.

9. B: The eighteenth letter from the left will be I.

10. B.

11. A.

12. D.

13. D.

14. C.

15. A: The position of the five boys from the top was as under—Hari, Jayant, Krishna, Ram and Govind.

16. D: Dhulia > Amalner; Sri Rampur > Nasik; Jalgaon < Sri Rampur; Jalgaon > Amalner; Amalner < Nasik; Amalner > Manmad.

Dhulia, Nasik, Sri Rampur and Jalgaon are bigger than Amalner; Manmad is smaller than Amalner.

17. B.

18. C.

19. B: I + old man + old woman + wife + husband + child + wife + husband + child = 9 persons.

20. A.

21. D.

22. B.

23. A.

24. C: Apple is not at the bottom, so it cannot be opposite orange which is at the top. Melon and peach are opposite each other. So none of these will be opposite orange. Also, banana is one of its neighbours. So, the sixth fruit mango must be opposite the orange, and at the bottom.

25. C: 10 + Manisha + 10 = 21.

26. A: The second letter is E, the fourth is T, the sixth is N, the seventh is A, the eighth is N and the ninth letter is T. The meaningful word made from these letters is TENANT.

27. B: Since B and D are twins, therefore, D is also 3 years younger to A, and A is 3 years younger to C. Therefore, C is older than D by 3 + 3, *i.e.*, 6 years.

Analogy (Non-Verbal)

Directions: *In each of the following questions, the first two figures in the Problem Figures are related in some way. The same relationship holds between the third figure of the Problem Figures and one of the Answer Figures A, B, C, D and E. Identify that figure.*

1. PROBLEM FIGURES

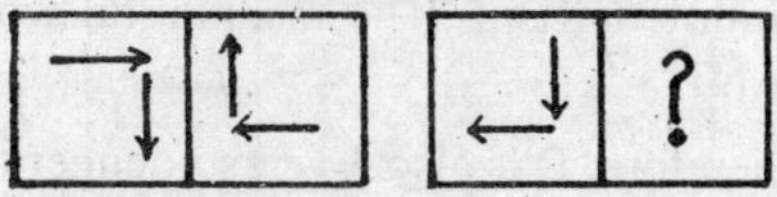

ANSWER FIGURES

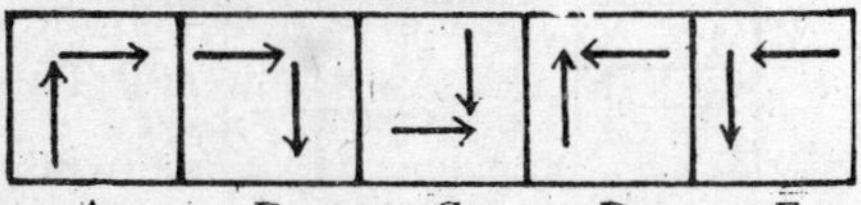

A B C D E

2. PROBLEM FIGURES

ANSWER FIGURES

A B C D E

3. PROBLEM FIGURES

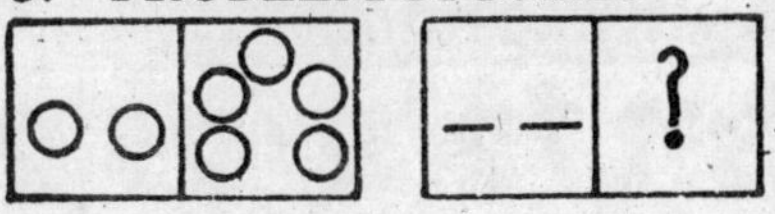

ANSWER FIGURES

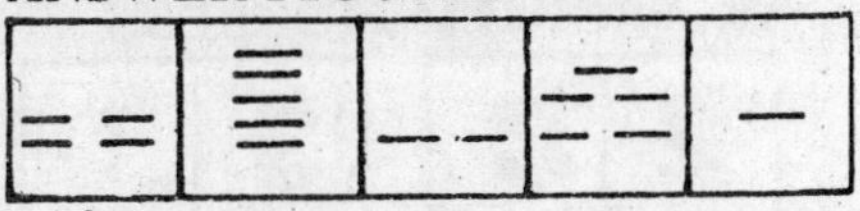

A B C D E

4. PROBLEM FIGURES

11	33	29	?

ANSWER FIGURES

44	40	99	58	87
A	B	C	D	E

5. PROBLEM FIGURES

ANSWER FIGURES

A B C D E

6. PROBLEM FIGURES

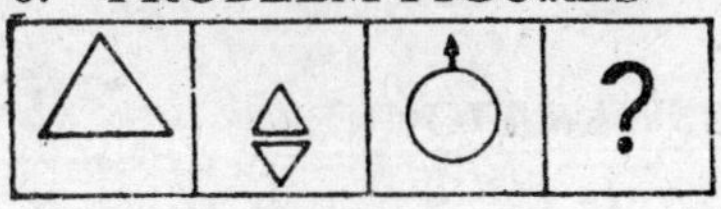

ANSWER FIGURES

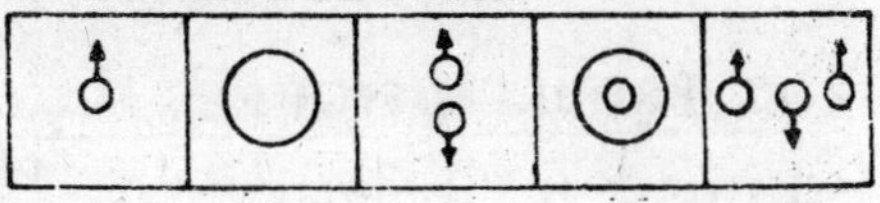

A B C D E

7. PROBLEM FIGURES **ANSWER FIGURES**

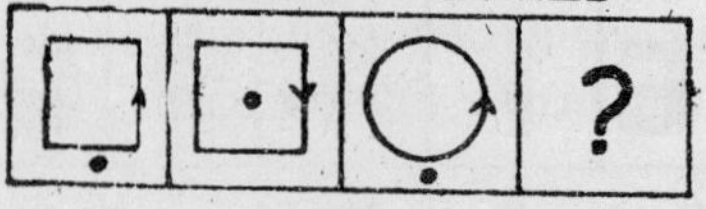

A B C D E

8. PROBLEM FIGURES **ANSWER FIGURES**

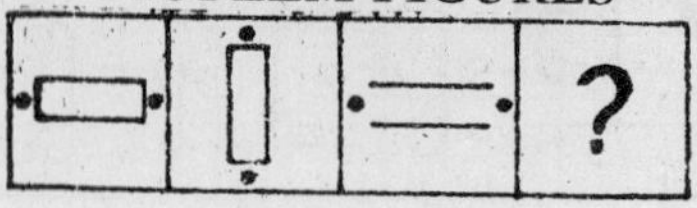

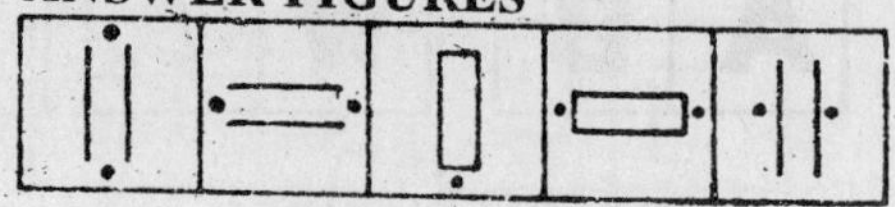

A B C D E

9. PROBLEM FIGURES **ANSWER FIGURES**

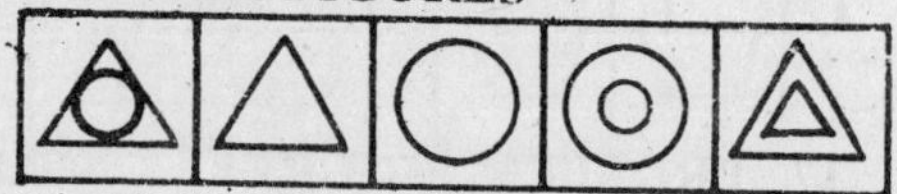

A B C D E

10. PROBLEM FIGURES **ANSWER FIGURES**

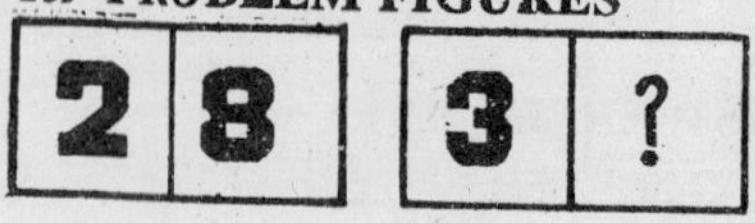

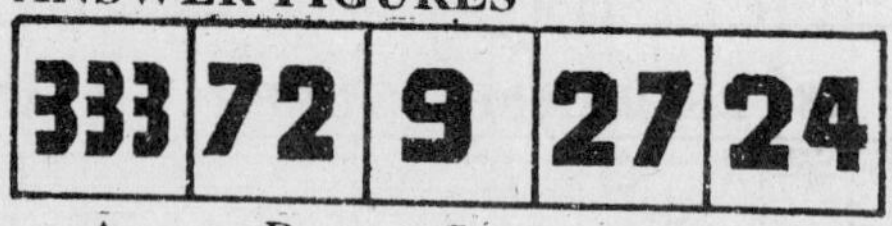

A B C D E

11. PROBLEM FIGURES **ANSWER FIGURES**

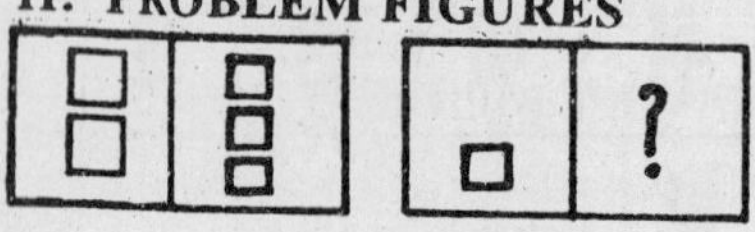

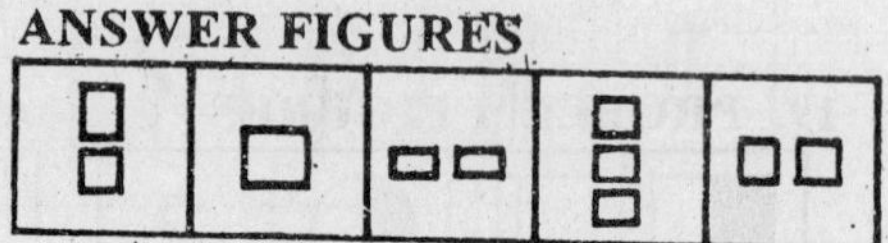

A B C D E

12. PROBLEM FIGURES **ANSWER FIGURES**

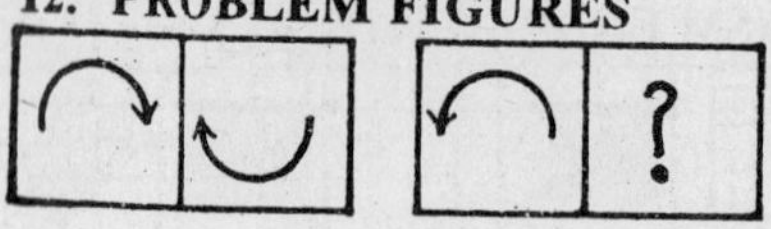

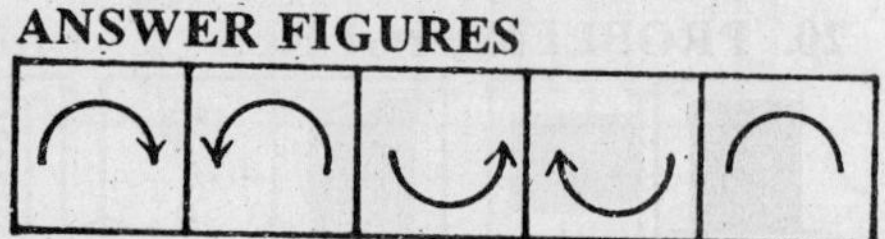

A B C D E

13. PROBLEM FIGURES **ANSWER FIGURES**

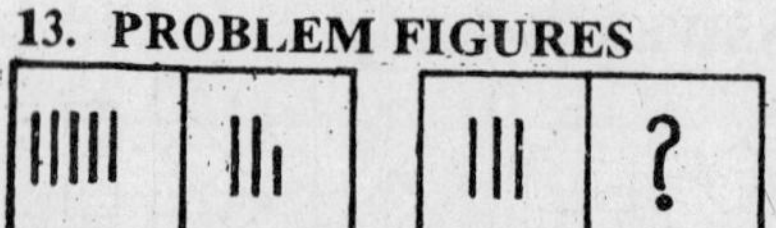

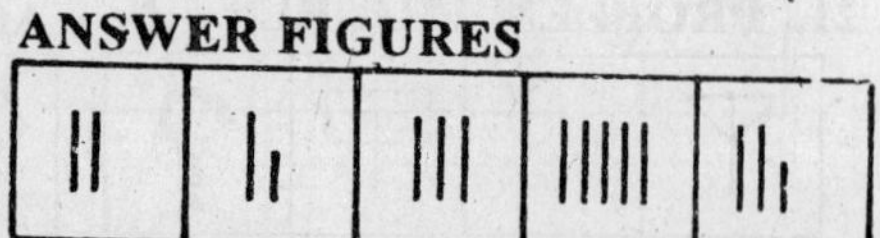

A B C D E

14. PROBLEM FIGURES | **ANSWER FIGURES**

1	4	2	?

16	1	4	8	2
A	B	C	D	E

15. PROBLEM FIGURES | **ANSWER FIGURES**

A	B	W	?

Y	Z	X	V	A
A	B	C	D	E

16. PROBLEM FIGURES | **ANSWER FIGURES**

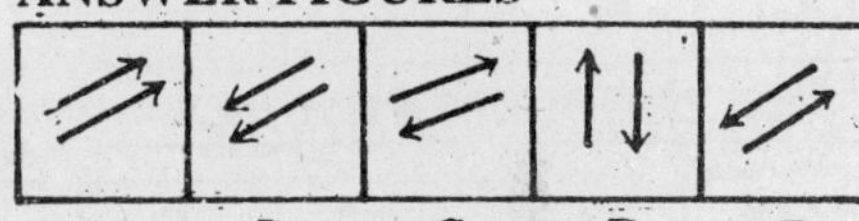

A B C D F

17. PROBLEM FIGURES | **ANSWER FIGURES**

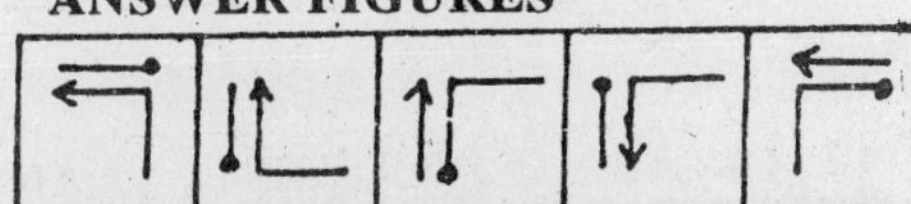

A B C D E

18. PROBLEM FIGURES | **ANSWER FIGURES**

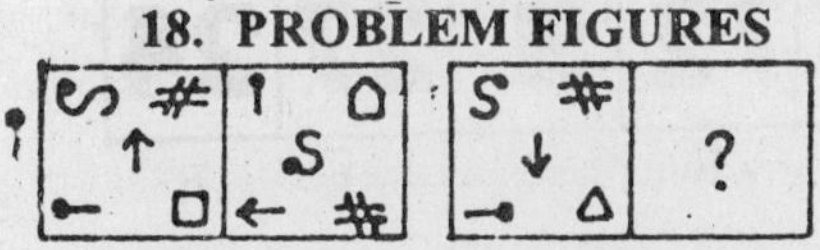

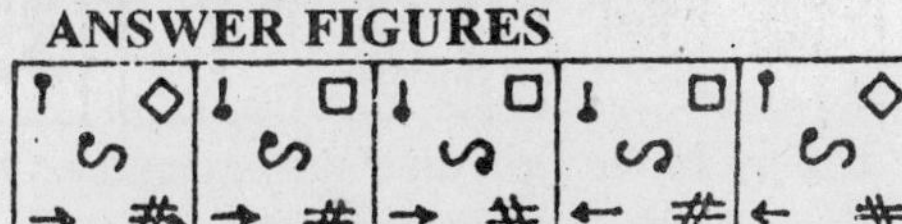

A B C D E

19. PROBLEM FIGURES | **ANSWER FIGURES**

A B C D E

20. PROBLEM FIGURES | **ANSWER FIGURES**

A B C D E

21. PROBLEM FIGURES | **ANSWER FIGURES**

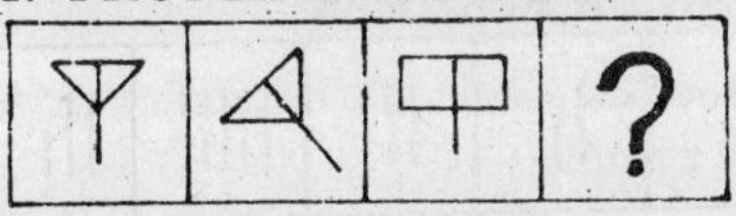

A B C D E

22. PROBLEM FIGURES **ANSWER FIGURES**

A B C D E

23. PROBLEM FIGURES **ANSWER FIGURES**

A B C D F

24. PROBLEM FIGURES **ANSWER FIGURES**

25. PROBLEM FIGURES **ANSWER FIGURES**

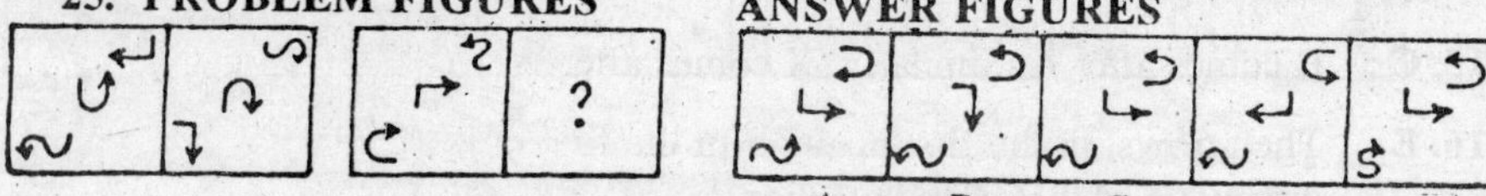

A B C D E

Explanatory Answers

1. A : The vertical and horizontal arrows point just to the opposite direction in the second position in the first unit in a particular style. Choice 'A' completes the pattern.

2. C : In the first unit, the contents of the bowl increases at the second stage. Same applies to the second unit.

3. D : The number of circles, in the first unit, increases by three in the second position and they indicate a particular pattern of distribution.

4. E : In the problem figure, the figure 11 in the first position has been trebled in the second position.

5. A : Four equal lines have replaced a square; the triangle should be replaced by three lines.

6. C : One triangle followed by two small triangles facing opposite directions in the second position. Choice 'C' completes the analogy.

7. B : In the problem figure, the dot comes within the square in the second position and the arrow, on the line, is turned upside down.

8. A : The figure moves from horizontal to vertical position.

9. C : Since the second triangle is without the circle, the second circle in the second unit, should be without the triangle.

10. D : In the first unit, 8 is obtained by multiplying 2 by its square 4. Similarly, 3, multiplied by its square 9, should give the figure in response 'D'.

11. A : The number of squares increases by one in the second position in the first unit.

12. C : The figure, in the first unit, has inverted shape in the second position with the arrow mark changing its position from right to left. 'C' is the only response which is in keeping with the order.

13. B : The last vertical line, in the second position of the first unit, is shorter in length than the rest and also the number of lines has decreased by two.

14. D : In the first unit, the ratio is 1 is to 4. Applying the same logic, answer should be 2 is to 8.

15. C : B comes after A. Similarly, X comes after W.

16. E : The arrows, in the first position in the first unit, change their respective directions, in the second position.

17. D : In alternate figures, the units are rotated at an angle of 90°

18. B : The left upper corner figure comes in the centre, the left lower corner figure rotates by 90° and moves to the upper left corner. The centre figure turns by 90° and moves to lower left corner, the top right corner figure comes to the lower right corner. The lower right corner figure moves to the upper right corner and changes the shape.

19. D : The half blackened square, in the second portion, has only 3 vertical lines to the right of its centre.

20. B : The figure turns clockwise 90°.

21. C : The first figure is placed diagonally in the second position with its tail pointing towards the bottom right hand corner.

22. E : The incomplete figure is completed in the second position and the smaller figure, inside it, is omitted.

23. A : The figure is turned clockwise 45°. The unit in the right upper corner changes shape, while the other three are inverted and interchange place clockwise.

24. E : The upper figure loses its left half and the colour while the lower figure loses its right half and is blackened.

25. C : All the three units are inverted and the two corner units exchange places.

Classification (Non-Verbal)

Directions : *In each of the following questions there are five figures. Four of them have common characteristics and belong to a class in some respect. Select the figure which is different.*

1. PROBLEM FIGURES

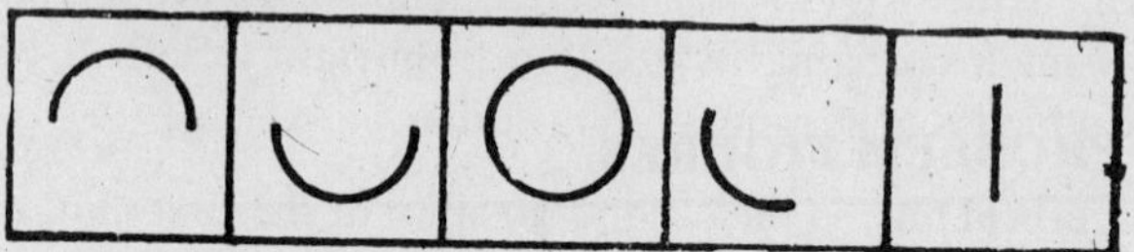

A B C D E

2. PROBLEM FIGURES

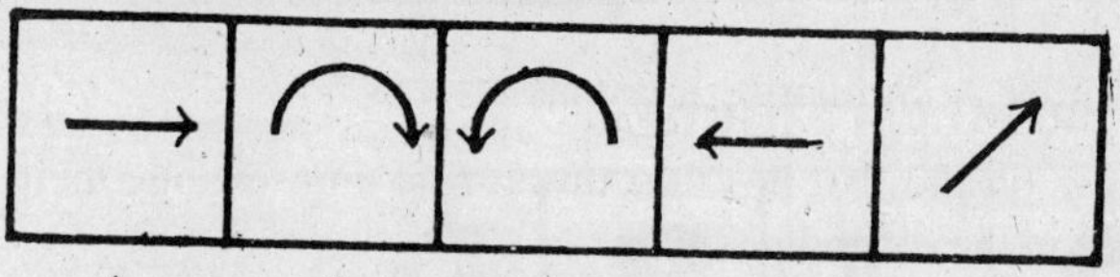

A B C D E

3. PROBLEM FIGURES

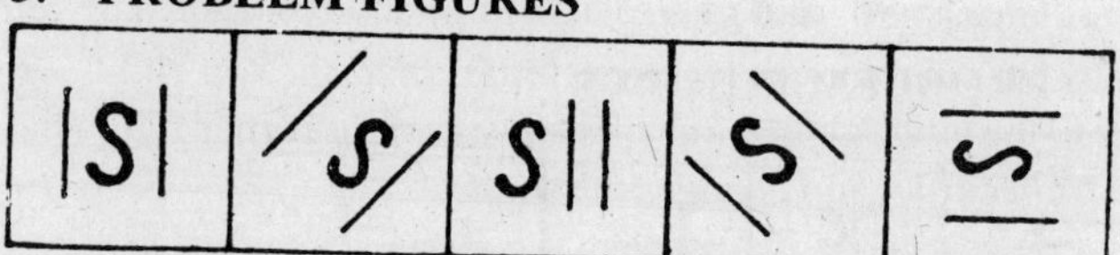

A B C D E

4. PROBLEM FIGURES

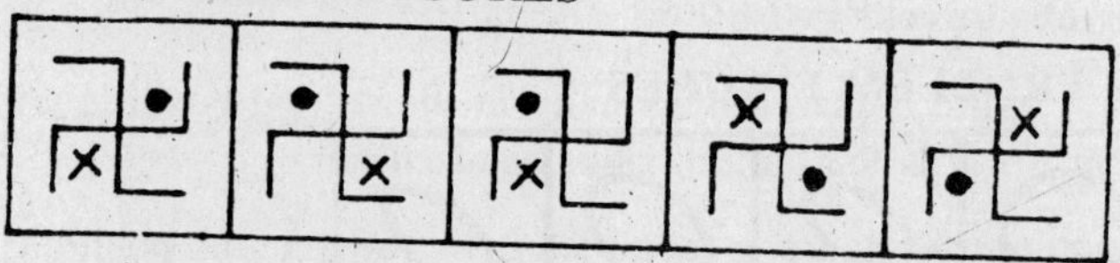

A B C D E

5. PROBLEM FIGURES

A B C D E

6. **PROBLEM FIGURES**

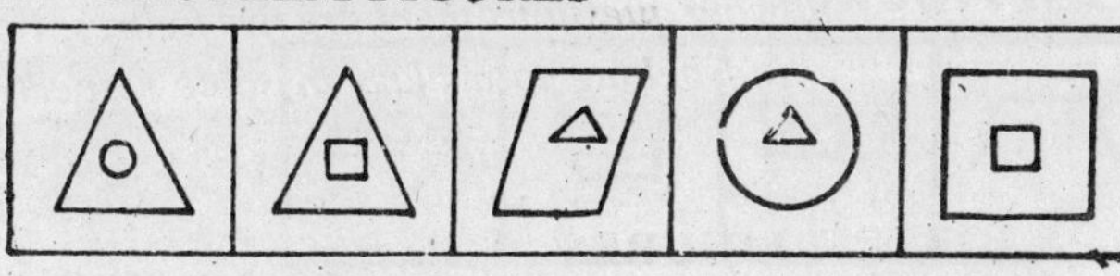

A B C D E

7. **PROBLEM FIGURES**

A B C D E

8. **PROBLEM FIGURES**

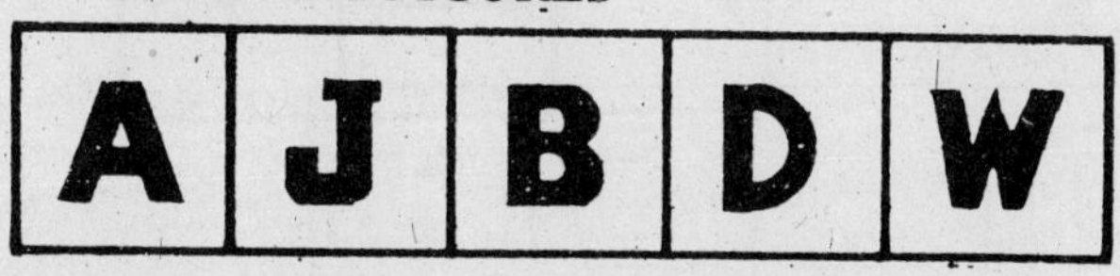

A B C D E

9. **PROBLEM FIGURES**

A B C D E

10. **PROBLEM FIGURES**

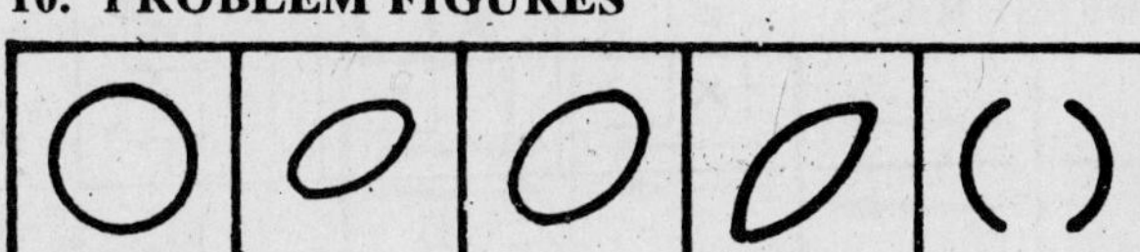

A B C D E

11. **PROBLEM FIGURES**

A B C D E

12. PROBLEM FIGURES

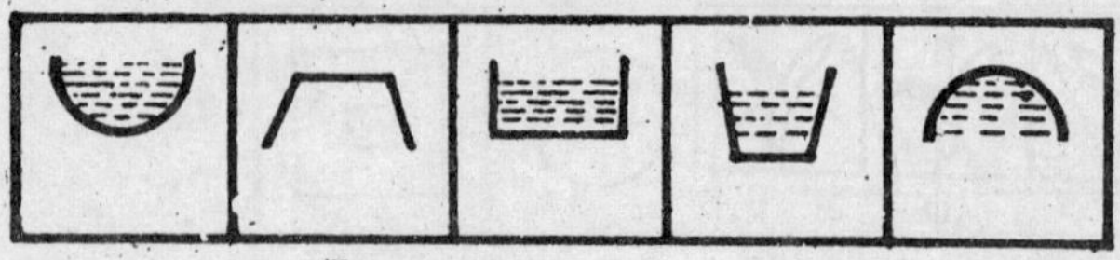

A B C D E

13. PROBLEM FIGURES

A B C D E

14. PROBLEM FIGURES

A B C D E

15. PROBLEM FIGURES

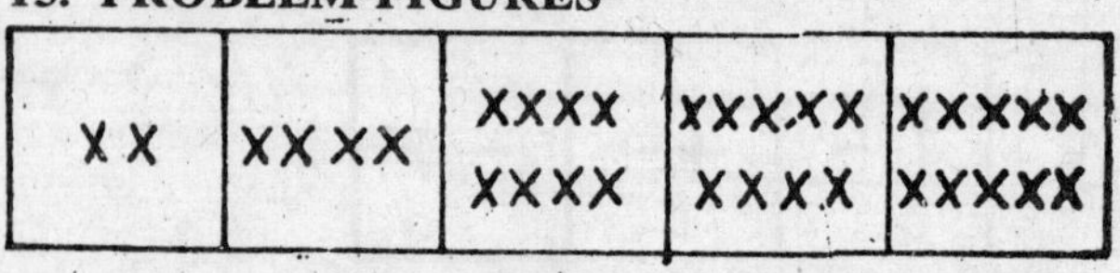

A B C D E

16. PROBLEM FIGURES

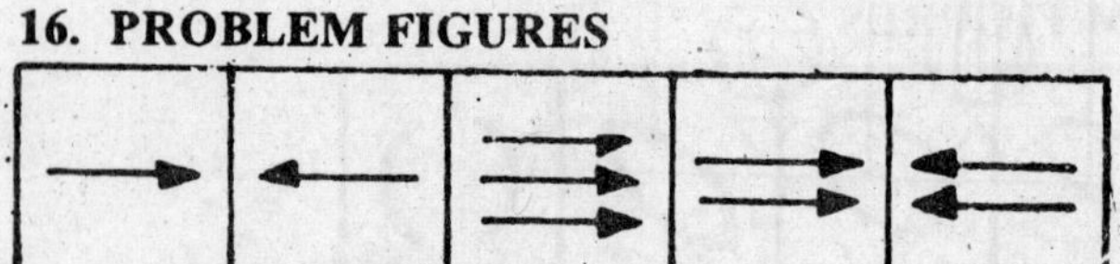

A B C D E

17. PROBLEM FIGURES

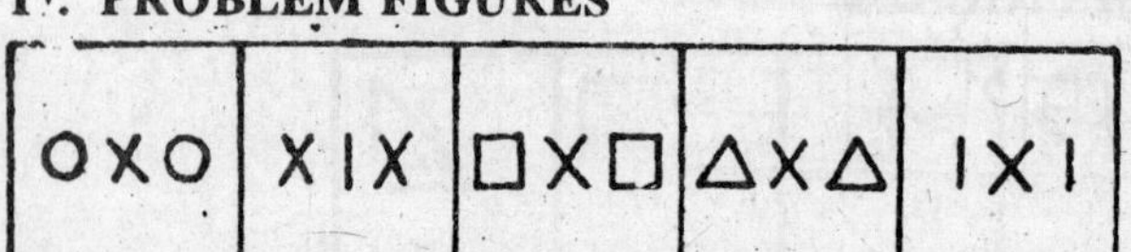

A B C D E

18. PROBLEM FIGURES

A B C D E

19. PROBLEM FIGURES

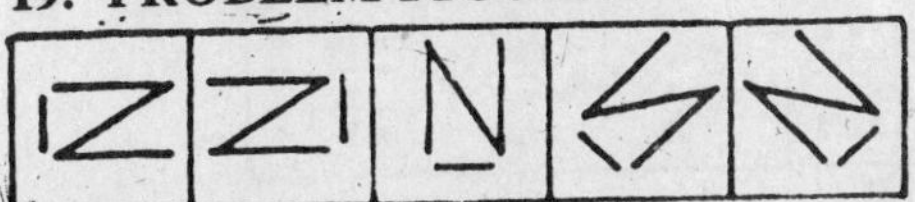

A B C D E

20. PROBLEM FIGURES

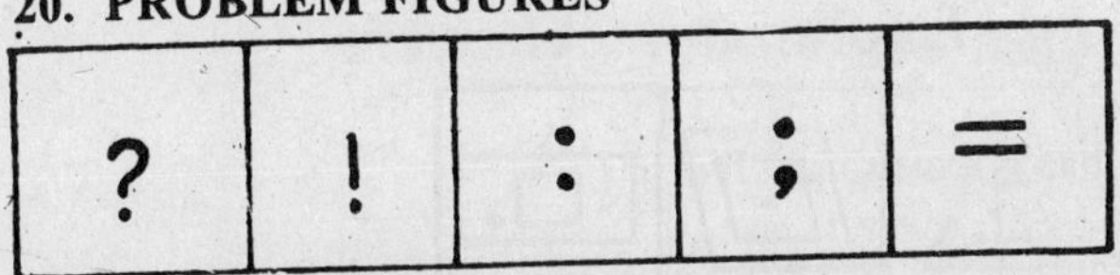

A B C D E

21. PROBLEM FIGURES

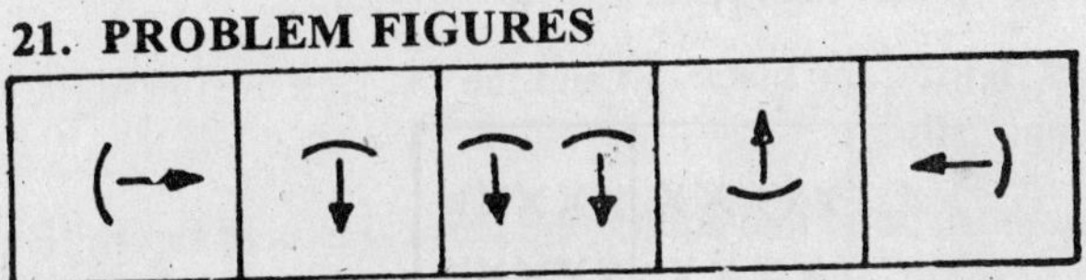

A B C D E

22. PROBLEM FIGURES

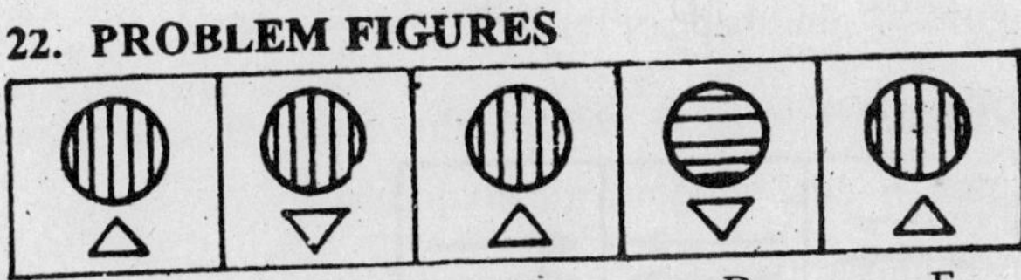

A B C D E

23. PROBLEM FIGURES

A B C D E

24. PROBLEM FIGURES

A B C D E

25. PROBLEM FIGURES

A B C D E

Explanatory Answers

1. E : Only 'E' has got a straight line.

2. E : Figure 'E' is without a matching one (in its direction).

3. C : 'S' is placed outside the two lines.

4. C : In all other figures, the black dot and the 'X' sign occurs in the segments placed diagonally.

5. E : There is no horizontal line cutting the vertical axis in figure 'E'.

6. E: Unlike other figures, both figures are identical in 'E'.

7. C : Only in figure 'C' the shape of the two figures is same.

8. A : All others are consonants. 'A' is a vowel.

9. C : Only in figure 'C', the two lines are not joined.

10. E : All others are closed figures.

11. E : All others have just two lines each.

12. B : The figure has no dotted lines inside.

13. E : The triangle is divided into more than three sections.

14. D : The dot has been put in the middle of the inset figure.

15. D : The total number of 'X' signs, in all other boxes, are divisible by two.

16. C : Choices A and B are facing each other; same is the case with choices D and E. Choice 'C' is the odd man out.

17. B : Inbetween the two figures, comes the 'X' sign in each case except in 'B'.

18. E : In all others, the shaded leaf is on the left of the straight line.

19. D : The small line segment should be in the opposite direction.

20. E : All others are punctuation marks, while '=' is a mathematical sign.

21. C : All other figures have one curve and one arrow.

22. D : The circle has horizontal lines instead of vertical ones.

23. C : In all others, three identicai curves are occurring together.

24. A : In all others the two arrows point or originate from the left side of the base of the figure.

25. A : The three dots, on the right segments of the square, are on the left side in figure 'A'.

Diagrammatic Problems

1. How many triangles are hidden in the figure given below ?

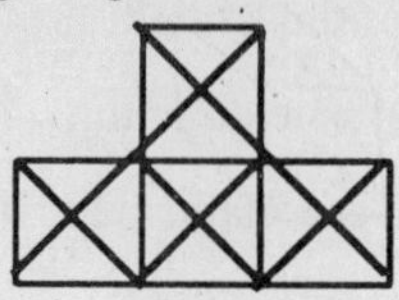

A. 38 B. 40

C. 42 D. 46

2. How many circles are there in the given figure ?

A. 9 B. 7

C. 10 D. 8

3. How many right angle triangles are there in the given figure ?

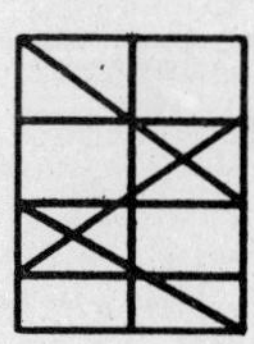

A. 12 B. 15

C. 9 D. 11

4. How many different geometrical figures are hidden in this figure ?

A. 7 B. 8

C. 9 D. 10

5. Count the number of squares hidden in the simple figure given below.

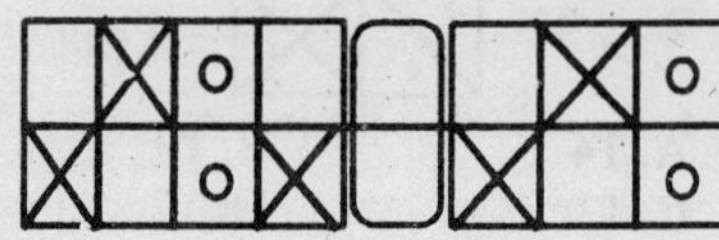

A. 13 B. 15

C. 17 D. 19

6. How many cubes are there in the figure given below ?

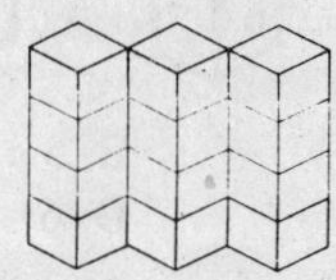

A. 12 B. 15

C. 19 D. 23

7. How many rectangles are there in the figure given below ?

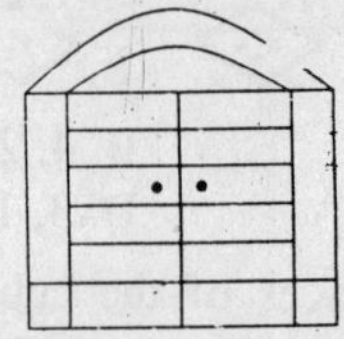

A. 16 B. 48

C. 60 D. 82

8. How many straight lines are there in the figure given below ?

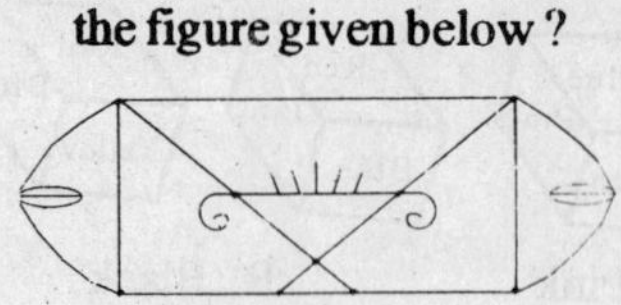

A. 9 B. 26
C. 15 D. 20

9. How many triangles are there in the simple figure given below ?

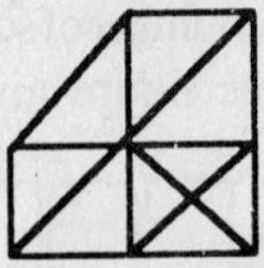

A. 14 B. 10
C. 13 D. 17

10. Study the dices given below. What number will be on the face opposite to 4 ?

A. 2 B. 5
C. 3 D. 6

11. Which of the following two numbers are on the opposite faces of the given dice ?

A. 4, 5 B. 4, 2
C. 2, 6 D. 3, 1

12. The six faces of the cube are of different colours – Blue, Pink, Red, Green, Black and Yellow. Which colour will be on the face opposite to Blue ?

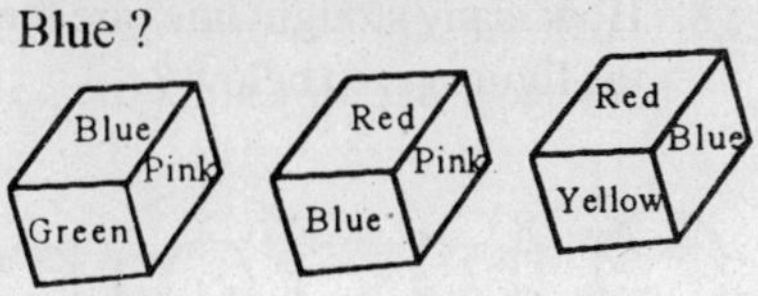

A. Pink B. Black
C. Green D. Red

13. If the numbers, on the opposite sides of the cube, total as 7, which one of the following dices is defective ?

A.

B.

C.

D.

14. What letter will be on the face opposite to C in the given dice ?

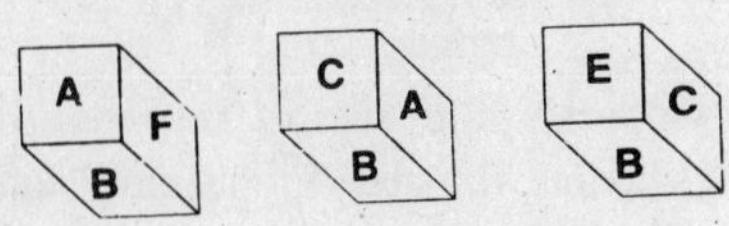

A. D B. F
C. A D. E

Directions : *Study the following diagrammatic information and answer questions 15 and 16.*

15. Which region represents children who are naughty as well as studious?

A. 2 and 4 B. 3 and 6
C. 3 only D. 4 only

16. The region(s) representing those who are not children but, are both naughty and studious is/are :

A. 5 only B. 7 only
C. 2 and 4 D. 6 only

Directions : *Study the following diagrammatic information and answer the questions 17 and 18.*

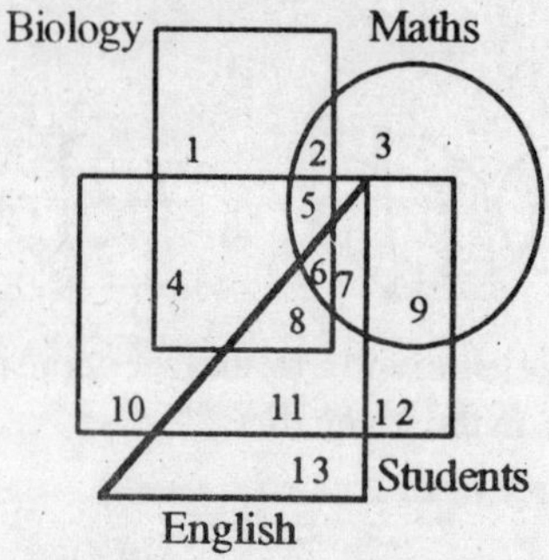

17. Identify the region representing students who study English and Maths, but not Biology.

A. 5 B. 7
C. 8 D. 6

18. Identify the region representing students who study Biology and Maths, but not English.

A. 4 B. 2
C. 5 D. 8

Directions : *Based on the diagrammatic information given below, the answer questions 19 to 22.*

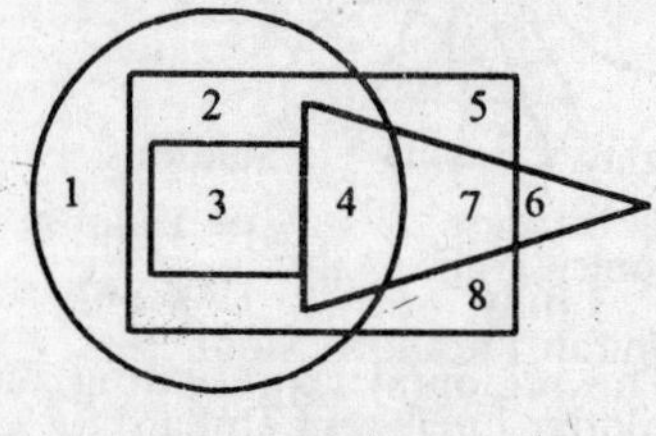

The circle represents rich persons.

The rectangle represents surgeons.

The square represents researchers and

The triangle represents engineers.

19. Which of the following statements is not true ?

A. Some surgeons are rich persons and all are researchers.

B. All researchers are surgeons.

C. Some of the rich persons are engineers.

D. None of the above.

20. Which of the following statements is true ?

A. All surgeons are rich persons.

B. All engineers are researchers.

C. There are surgeons who are engineers, but not rich persons.

D. None of the above.

21. Some of the surgeons, are neither engineers nor researchers, but they are rich persons. Which section represents them ?

A. 4 B. 7
C. 2 D. 1

22. Which section represents rich persons who are not researchers, but engineers ?

A. 5 B. 8
C. 6 D. 4

23. The figure representing relationship between horse, dog and bird is :

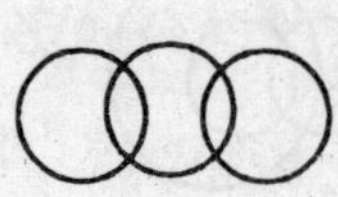

A.

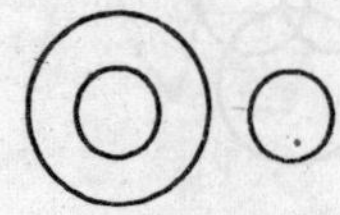

B.

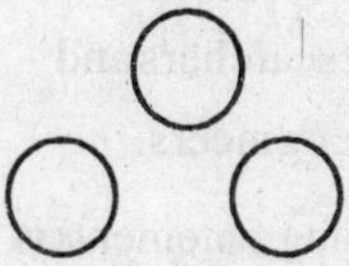
C.

D.

24. Which figure best represents the relationship between scent, flower and rose ?

A.

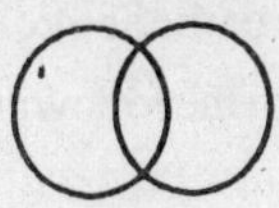
B.

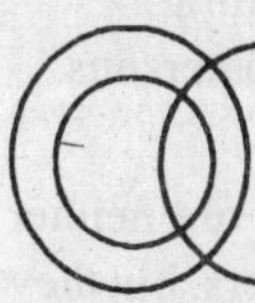
C.

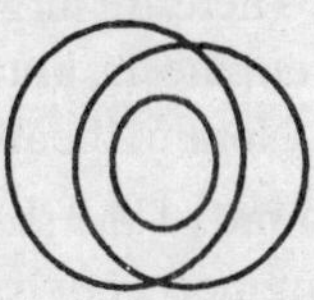
D.

25. Which figure best represents the relationship between Month, Day and Minute

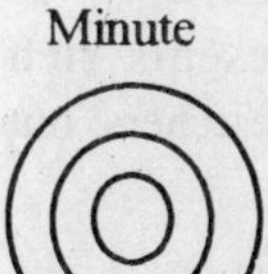
A.

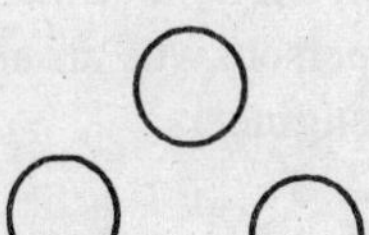
B.

C.

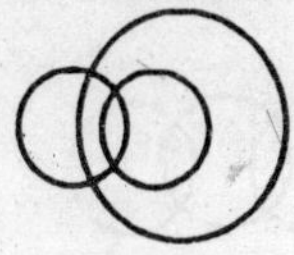
D.

26. Which of the following figures represents the relationship between Women, Architects and Doctors ?

A.

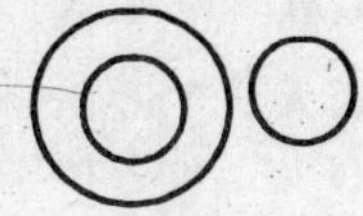
B.

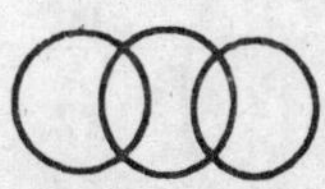
C.

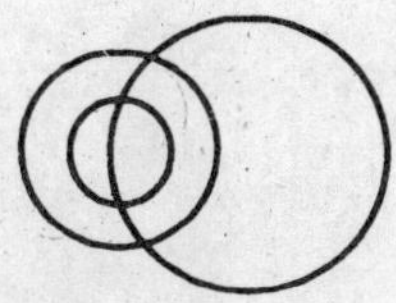
D.

Directions : *Given below are four logical diagrammatic representations. In questions 27 to 30, a set of three words are given. Select the figure which best represent the relationship between the given set of three words.*

A.

B.

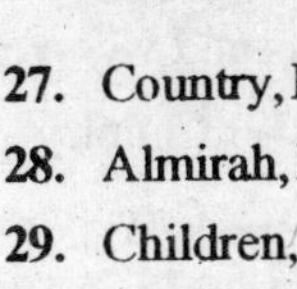
C.

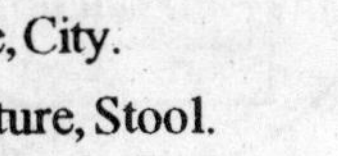
D.

27. Country, House, City.

28. Almirah, Furniture, Stool.

29. Children, Intelligent, Dullard.

30. Scarf, Perfume, Garment.

Answers with Some Selected Explanations

1. B ; **2. A ;** **3. A ;**

4. A : The figures are : circle, square, hexagon, rhombus, pentagon, triangle and rectangle.

5	6	7	8	9
D	A	B	D	A
10	**11**	**12**	**13**	**14**
D	C	B	A	B
15	**16**	**17**	**18**	**19**
C	D	B	C	A
20	**21**	**22**		
C	C	D		

23. C : Horse, Dog and Bird are three separate identities.

24. D : All roses are flowers. All roses are scented, but not all flowers have scent.

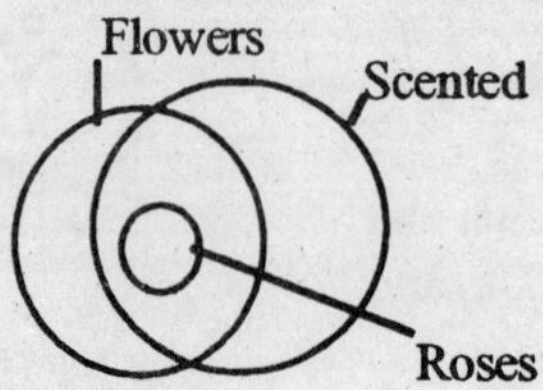

25. A :

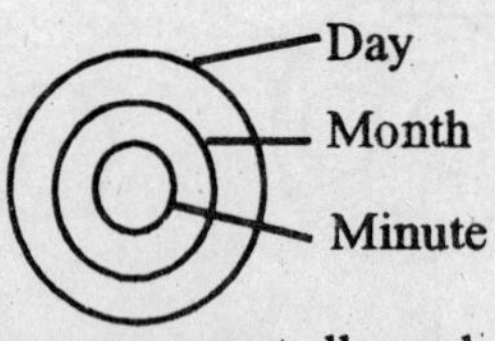

26. C : Some women, not all, can be architects and vice-verca. Some women, not all, can be doctors and vice-verca.

27. B :

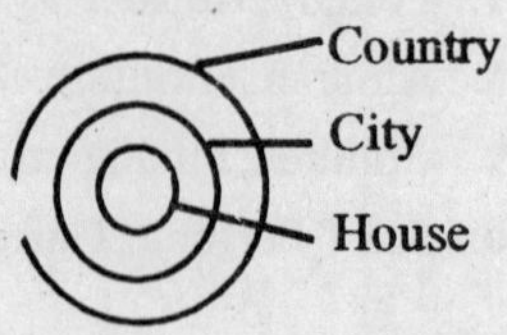

28. C :

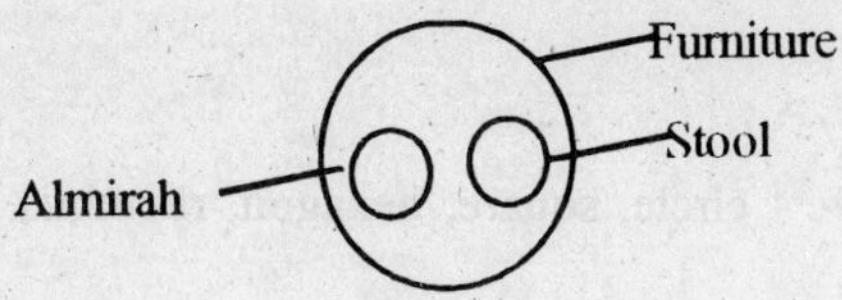
Furniture
Stool
Almirah

29. D :

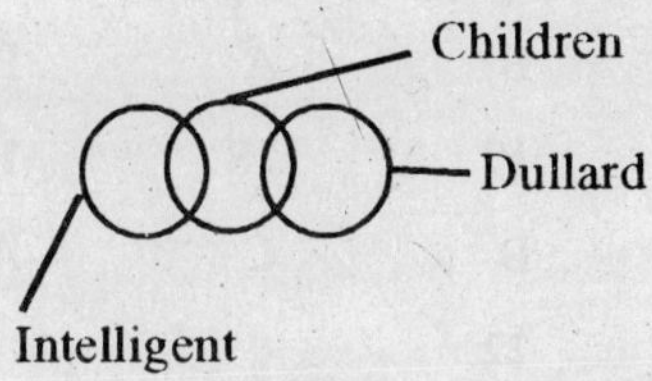
Children
Dullard
Intelligent

30. A :

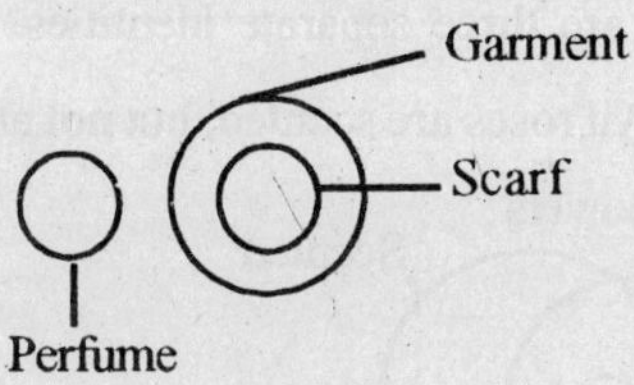
Garment
Scarf
Perfume

Tables and Graphs

1. The temperature of the patient at 12 Noon is :

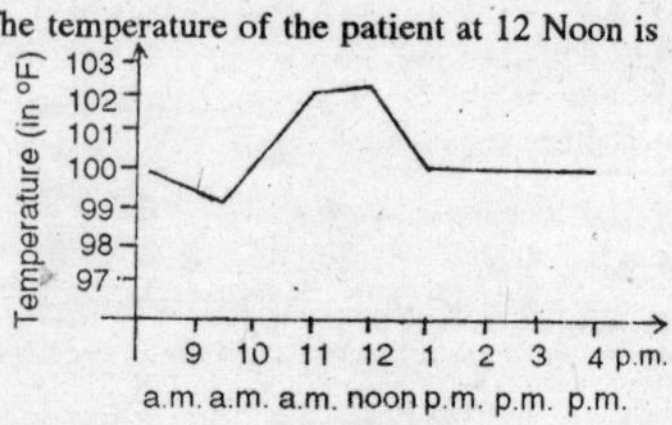

A. 100°F   B. 101°F
C. 102°F   D. 103°F

2. The following bar chart shows the enrolment of a school over different years. The per cent decrease in enrolment of the school from 1985 to 1990 is :

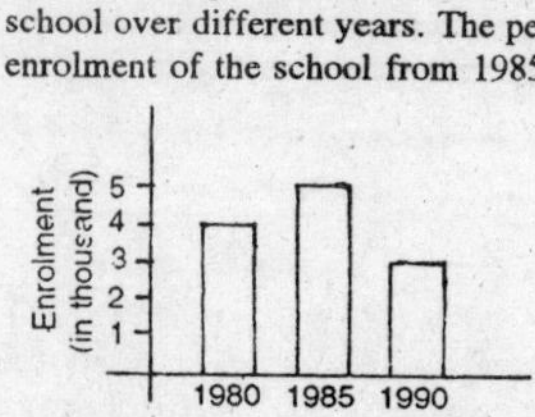

A. 20%   B. 25%
C. 40%   D. 50%

3. In the following figure, if the distance between two villages *A* and *B* is 25 km, then the distance between *C* and *D* is :

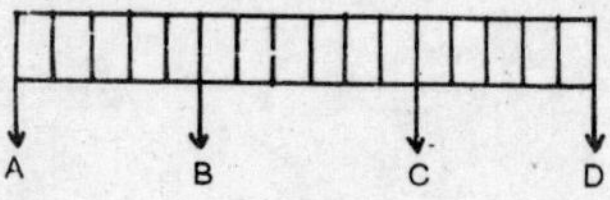

A. 20 km   B. 25 km
C. 30 km   D. 55 km

4. The cashier of a store has only 10 paise and 25 paise coins in his cash box. The total number of these coins is 55 and their total value Rs. 7.15. By drawing suitable graphs of the possible values of the two unknowns *x* and *y*, find how many coins of each kind does he have in the box.

A. 45, 10   B. 10, 45
C. 44, 11   D. 33, 22

5.

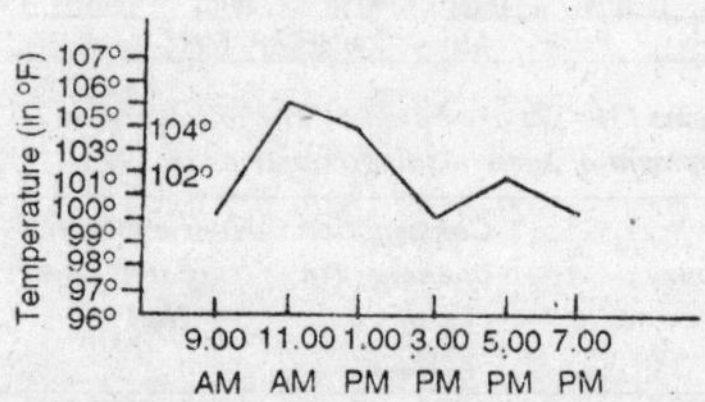

In the above figure the temperature of the patient at 11AM and 3 PM respectively are:

A. 100°F, 105°F   B. 100°F, 103°F
C. 104°F, 100°F   D. 105°F, 100°F

6. Study the following table and answer the question given below :

States	Student Enrolment (1980-84)				
	1980	*1981*	*1982*	*1983*	*1984*
Maharashtra	723	840	900	920	925
Kerala	1035	940	1200	1400	1500
Karnataka	750	600	830	575	900
West Bengal	500	550	450	600	525
Andhra Pradesh	800	840	875	925	785

Which of the following statements is not correct?

A. In the year 1981, Maharashtra and Andhra Pradesh had same number of students.

B. In Andhra Pradesh, there was a continuous increase in the number of students except in the year 1984.

C. In West Bengal, the number of students was the lowest in all the years as compared to the other States.

D. In Kerala, the number of students was higher in all the years as compared to the other States

7. Given below straight line graphs for : $y = mx + c$, what are the values of m and c for the lines A and B ?

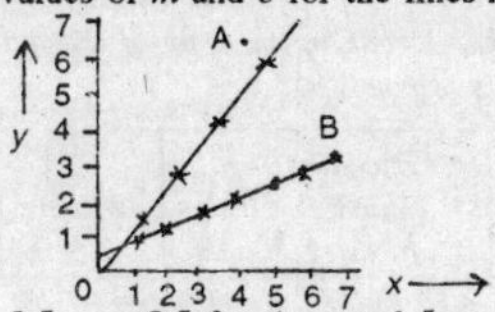

A. $m = 0.5$, $c = 0.5$ for A; $m = 1.5$, $c = 0$ for B
B. $m = 0.5$, $c = 0$ for A, $m = 1.5$, $c = 0.5$ for B
C. $m = 1.5$, $c = 0.5$ for A; $m = 0.5$, $c = 0$ for B
D. $m = 1.5$, $c = 0$ for A; $m = 0.5$, $c = 0.5$ for B

Study the following graph carefully and answer the questions (8-12) :

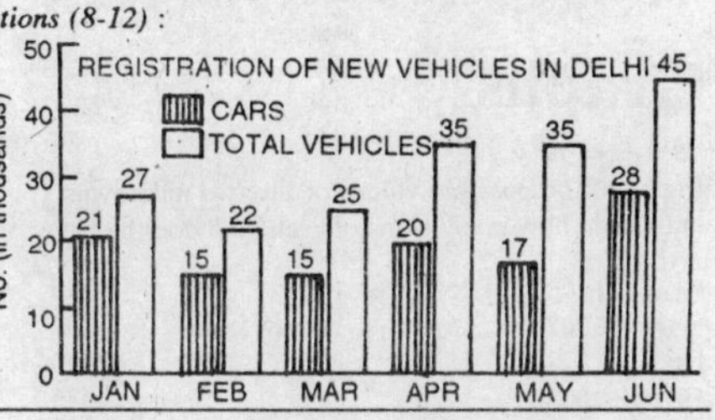

8. What was the difference between the numbers of cars registered in January and those registered in June ?
A. 2000 B. 6000
C. 5000 D. No difference
E. None of these

9. What was the number of vehicles other than cars registered in March?
A. 5000 B. 10000
C. 40000 D. 37000
E. None of these

10. What was the percentage increase in registration of cars from February to March?
A. 0% B. 1%
C. 2% D. 2.5%
E. None of these

11. What was the increase in registration of vehicles other than cars from January to April?
A. 5000 B. 10000
C. 15000 D. No increase
E. None of these

12. In which of the following months was the registration of vehicles other than cars maximum?
A. April B. June
C. May D. February
E. January

Questions (13–17) are based on the following .able. The table shows the per capita figures relating to economic development of some leading countries in 1973.

Country	*Consumption of energy (in kg of coal equivalent)*	*Consumption of steel (kg)*	*Production of coal (kg)*	*Production of cement (kg)*	*Production of sulphuric acid (kg)*	*Vehicles**
Australia	5956	537	4159	383	171	425
Brazil	566	94	22	131	–	–
Canada	11237	640	760	454	133	455
China	594	36	524	28	–	–
Egypt	294	22	–	101	3	6
Germany	5792	652	1662	661	81	285
France	4389	495	505	589	84	–
India	188	14	134	26	2	–
Israel	2868	279	–	395	60	110
Japan	3601	805	206	721	65	227
New Zealand	3225	326	142	357	–	423
S. Africa	2815	213	2628	289	–	99
Swiss	3752	491	–	895	–	283
U.K.	5778	441	2362	357	69	277
U.S.A.	11960	711	2519	368	135	586
U.S.S.R.	5792	518	1846	438	59	–

* per thousand persons

13. Largest consumer of energy is :
A. Japan B. UK
C. USA D. USSR

14. In New Zealand, the ratio of consumption of energy to that of steel is about :
A. 0.1 B. 10
C. 0.25 D. 2.5

15. Chemical industry is most developed in :
A. Canada B. Japan
C. USSR D. Australia

16. Most developed country is :
A. USA
B. USSR
C. UK
D. Cannot be calculated from the table

17. Most developed country in the production of coal is
A. USA B. Japan
C. Australia D. S. Africa

Questions (18-21) are based on the following table which shows the profits of major US Oil Companies in million dollars from 1975 to 1978.

Profits of Major Oil Companies (Million Dollars)

Company	*1975*	*1976*	*1977*	*1978*
Exxon	1503.0	2640.0	2443	2716
Texaco	830.6	869.7	890	852
Mobil	809.9	942.0	999	1124
Gulf	700.0	716.0	752	792
SOCAL	772.5	880.0	1004	1106
Total	4616.0	6047.7	6088	6590

Sources : Fortune, May 1976, Petroleum Economist, March 1971.

18. In 1977, profit earned by "Gulf" was x% of the total profit earned by all oil companies. The value of x is:
A. 7.8 B. 6.9
C. 12.3 D. 13.7

19. There is a decline in the profit of companies from 1976 to 1977. The percentage decline in total profit was about :
A. 0.97% B. 0.38%
C. 0.87% D. 0.12%

20. The decline in the total profits in the year 1977 was mainly due to the decline in profit of the company :
A. 'Exxon' B. 'Texaco'
C. 'Mobil' D. 'Gulf'

21. Considering 1975 as the base year, the index number of 'Exxon' in 1978 would be :
A. 107.8 B. 108.8
C. 177.6 D. 180.7

Questions (22-25) are based on following table which shows the number of persons employed by industry alongwith their break up in some of the industries as a whole in Japan from 1955 to 1972.

Year	*Total*	*Agriculture and forestry*	*Fisheries*	*Mining*	*Construction*
			Both sexes		
1955	40900	14780	580	450	1950
1960	44360	12730	670	430	2530
1965	47300	10460	670	290	3280
1970	50940	8420	440	200	3940
1972	51090	7050	490	160	4310
			Males		
1955	23900	7290	450	380	1720
1960	26290	6120	490	390	2200
1965	28520	4930	470	260	2830
1970	30910	4010	350	170	3410
1972	31530	3380	390	140	3750
			Females		
1955	17000	7490	130	70	230
1960	18070	6610	180	40	330
1965	18780	5530	200	30	450
1970	20030	4420	90	30	530
1972	19560	3670	100	20	560

Total Population in 1972 was about 100 millions.

Source : Bureau of Statistics, Office of the Prime Minister, Japan.

22. In 1970, maximum number of persons were employed in :
A. Construction
B. Mining
C. Fisheries
D. Agriculture and forestry

23. From 1955 to 1972, employment rate had increased in:
A. Construction
B. Mining
C. Agriculture and forestry
D. Fisheries

24. In Japan, male to female ratio is minimum in :
A. Construction B. Mining
C. Agriculture & forestry D. Fisheries

25. In Japan females prefer to work in :
A. Fisheries industry
B. Agriculture and forestry
C. Mining industry
D. Construction industry

Questions (26-29) are based on following table which shows the production of gold by various countries from 1960 to 1967.

Gold : Production *(in thousand kilograms)*

Countries	1960	1961	1962	1963	1967
World	1047	1080	1080	1080	1084
S.Africa	665.1	713.6	689	701	702
Canada	144	138.2	141	142	141
Australia	33.8	33.3	33.6	33.7	34
U.S.A.	52.2	48.7	49.5	50.1	50
Ghana	27.3	25.9	26.3	26.3	26
India	5.0	4.8	4.9	5.0	5

26. During 1960–67 largest producer of gold was:
A. America B. S.Africa
C. Canada D. Australia
E. None of the above

27. In 1967, percentage of gold produced in S.Africa of the world's total gold production was about :
A. 25% B. 42.4%
C. 63.7% D. 68.0%

28. In 1963, percentage of gold production in India of the world's total gold production was about :
A. 0.5% B. 5.0%
C. 2.0% D. Negligible

29. In 1961, the world gold production increased as compared to preceding year by about :
A. 350 kg B. 330 quintals
C. 310 quintals D. 33 quintals

Motion picture business in Japan has declined owing to television and the number of cinemas has been gradually decreasing. Questions (30-34) are based on the following table which shows data of Japan motion pictures, their annual attendance and income from film exports.

Movies

Year	Feature films	Imported feature films	Educational films	Cinemas	Annual attendance: Total (millions)	Annual attendance: Per inhabitant	Income from film export (1000 dollars)
1955	423	193	571	5184	869	9.7	
1960	547	216	970	7457	1014	10.9	3305
1965	487	264	995	4649	373	3.8	4872
1969	494	253	1304	3602	284	2.8	4545
1970	423	236	1502	3246	255	2.5	4027
1971	421	243	1375	2974	217	2.1	4024
1972	400	283	–	2673	187	1.8	4000

Source : Motion Picture Producers' Association of Japan.

30. Which of the following statements is correct?
A. People of Japan are more interested in viewing TV
B. Economy of Japan is balanced because of export of films
C. The production of movies in Japan is decreasing day by day
D. Imported feature films are more impressive

31. The maximum interest towards movies was shown in the year :
A. 1955 B. 1960
C. 1970 D. 1972

32. The imported feature films were most popular in the year:
A. 1960 B. 1965
C. 1970 D. 1972

33. The class of moves which had improved its image in 1970 over its preceding year was :
A. Feature films B. Imported feature films
C. Educational films D. Cinemas

34. Maximum amount was earned by exporting films from Japan in the year:
A. 1960 B. 1965
C. 1970 D. 1972

ANSWERS

1	2	3	4	5	6	7	8	9	10
C	C	B	C	D	C	D	E	B	A
11	**12**	**13**	**14**	**15**	**16**	**17**	**18**	**19**	**20**
E	C	C	B	D	D	C	C	A	A
21	**22**	**23**	**24**	**25**	**26**	**27**	**28**	**29**	**30**
D	D	A	C	B	B	C	A	B	C
31	**32**	**33**	**34**						
B	D	C	B						

Explanations of Difficult Sums

1. From the figure, the temperature of the patient at 12 Noon = 102°F

2. Enrolment in 1985 = 5000

Then from the figure,

Enrolment in 1990 $= \frac{3}{5} \times 5000 = 3000$

Decrease in enrolment = 5000 – 3000 = 2000

% decrease in enrolment $= \frac{2000}{5000} \times 100 = 40\%$

3. From the figure,

Distance between *C* and *D* = Distance between *A* and *B*

Hence distance between *C* and *D* = 25 km

4.

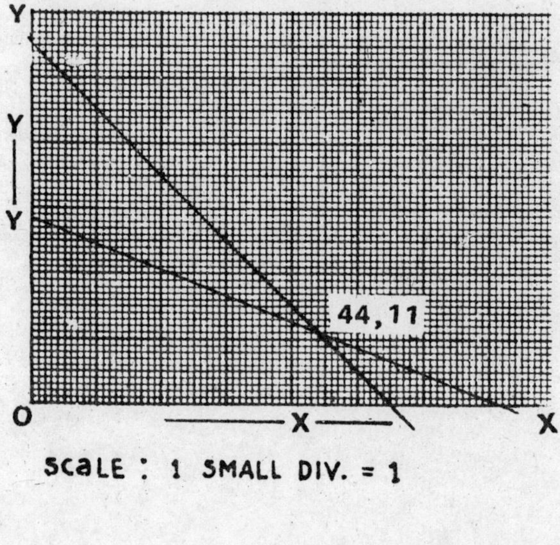

Let the No. of 10 paise coins = x
and the No. of 25 paise coins = y

$\therefore \quad 10x + 25y = 715$

and $\quad x + y = 55$

or $\quad 10x + 25y = + 715$

$\quad \underline{\underset{-}{+} 10x \underset{-}{+} 10y = \underset{-}{+} 550}$

$\quad 15y = 165$

$\therefore \quad y = \dfrac{165}{15} = 11$

$\therefore \quad x = 55 - 11 = 44$

Hence 10 paise coins = 44
25 paise coins = 11

7. For straight line A, if we put
$m = 1.5$, $c = 0$, then
$y = mx + c$
$3 = 2 \times 1.5 + 0$ which is correct.
For straight line B, if we put
$m = 0.5$, $c = 0.5$ then
$y = mx + c$
$1.5 = 0.5 \times 2 + 0.5$ which is correct.
Hence $m = 1.5$, $c = 0$ for A; $m = 0.5$, $c = 0.5$ for B is correct answer.

GENERAL ENGLISH

NOUN

		Answer
1.	She had no **rupees**.	*money*
2.	It is a nice **poetry** written by William Wordsworth.	*poem*
3.	The **sceneries** of Kashmir is beautiful.	*scenery*
4.	Four **dozens** eggs have been sold today.	*dozen*
5.	**Polices** are interrogating the thives.	*The police*
6.	My **son-in-laws** are leaving for Mumbai tomorrow.	*sons-in-law*
7.	She has got ten **rupees** note.	*a ten-Rupee*
8.	This is one of the **photograph** I like the most.	*photographs*
9.	The **spectacle** I brought yesterday is not mine.	*spectacles*
10.	He has ordered **bricks** for the proposed hotel and bar.	*for bricks*
11.	She uses a fine quality of shampoo and so, her **hairs** are black.	*hair*
12.	Your **advise** is a proof of your discriminating mind and pragmative approach.	*advice*

SUBJECT AND PREDICATE

The use of mathematical instruments **are** allowed now. *(is)*

The members of the committee **has** resigned. *(have)*

Ram **as well as** Shyam **were** present. *(was)*

'Travels with a Donkey' **were** written by stevenson. *(was)*

Many a man **have** acted so. *(has)*

Rice and curry **form** our staple diet. *(forms)*

The ship, with all its passengers, **were** sunk *(was)*

This is one of the cars that **was** damaged. *(were)*

These news **have** gladdened us. *(This news has)*

The Secretary and Treasurer **were** absent. *(was)*

Note: *Only **one** person is implied by "**the** Secretary and Treasurer." **Two** persons are implied by "**the** Secretary and **the** Treasurer."*

Neither of the applicants **are** eligible. *(is)*

N.B.: *If two singular subjects are separated by **or** or **nor,** the verb agrees with the nearer subject:*

*(1) Either you or **he has** done this.*

*(2) Neither Raju nor **I know** you.*

You as well as **I are** in the wrong. *(am, or You are in the wrong as well as **I**)*

Everyone of you **have** to pay the fine. *(has)*

Each of the children **were** given a packet of sweets. *(was)*

Each hour and each minute **draw** us nearer the grave. *(draws)*

Every boy and every girl **have** to write these lines. *(has)*

Note: *A singular verb is used with two singular nouns qualified by* ***each*** *and* ***every*** *even though connected by* ***and****.*

Everybody **seem** satisfied with the award. *(seems)*

Our greatest need at the present moment **are** funds. *(is)*

Politics **are** not meant for you. *(is)*

Your data **is** incorrect. *(are)*

Fifty rupees **were** given to him. *(was)*

His poultry **has** been sold out. *(have)*

The jury **were** unanimous in its decision. *(was)*

Nothing but mischief and pranks **please** him. *(pleases)*

One or the other of you **have** to answer for this. *(has)*

Here is a list of what **is** considered to be offences against the law. *(are)*

Her happiness was only short-lived, her **suffering** long and pitiful. *(sufferings)*

He has been given three books and **two** lost. *(two have been)*

I have always **been** and shall ever continue to, help the needy. *(been helping)*

I am no stranger to you; **isn't it**? *(am I?)*

He looks after you well, **isn't it?** *(doesn't he?)*

NUMBER

Many **poetries** describe beautiful sceneries. *(poems; scenery)*

We can do your **works** without your **advices.** *(work; advice)*

N.B.: ***Furniture, folk, gram, mischief, cannon*** *are similarly misused.*

I have four **dozens** pencils. *(dozen)*

This car has cost me three **thousands** rupees. *(thousand)*

N.B.: **Gross, hundred weight, pair, hundred, score,** *etc., should be used in the singular after numeral adjectives.*

There were many people on either **sides** of the road. *(side)*

CASE

I am stronger than **him**. *(he)*

There is no disagreement between you and **I**. *(me)*

Whom, do you think, has taken my pen? *(who)*

Ram's dog is better than **Shyam.** *(Shyam's)*

It was **him** that broke the glass not **me.** *(he; I)*

I took it to be **him.** *(he)*

No one knew the answer but **I.** *(me)*

He bought some toys for you and **myself.** *(me)*

We scored as many runs as **them.** *(they)*

Is it my friend **who** you are talking of? *(of whom)*

Let Mahesh and **I** do this for you. *(who)*
Somebody gave me this note, I forgot **whom.** *(who)*
I gave it to somebody, I forgot **who**. *(whom)*
It is yet a matter of speculation as to **whom** will be our Prime Minister. *(who)*
I never knew so clever a singer as **she.** *(her)*
He is a relative of my **father's.** *(father)*

PRONOUNS

Each of the actors did **their** part well. *(his)*
Every soldier and every sailor must be given **their** just reward. *(his)*
Either Rajbir or Ranjeet has not paid **their** money. *(his)*
Prem and **myself** have paid the money. *(I)*
Both my father and **self** are keeping well. *(I)*
He went to Kolkata with his brother and **myself.** *(me)*
Two brothers quarrelled with **one another.** *(each other)*
They who are meek shall be exalted. *(Those)*
I am one of **them** that attended the meeting. *(those)*
I am shorter than **either** of my three sisters. *(any)*
He ruined himself and **family** by drinking. *(his family)*
One must do **his** work **himself.** *(one's; oneself)*

RELATIVE PRONOUNS

What is it **which** you want? *(that)*
Do you know my mother **that** lives at Kanpur? *(who)*
Solomon was one of the wisest men **who** ever lived. *(that)*
It is only the blind **who** will not see this. *(that)*
This is the same person **who** came to see you yesterday. *(that)*
I am not one of those who **is** interested in matters that do not concern **me.** *(are; them)*
This is the house built by my brother during the war **and** which cost him a tidy sum. (omit *and)*
He offered me a job on his estate **but** which I declined. (omit *but)*
Hitler prepared for such a war **which** he thought would make him master of the world. *(as)*
This is a fine place **in which to live.** *(to live in)*
We have no rice **with which** to feed so many. (omit *with which)*
He was not allowed to put up any building on **that** land reserved for the military. *(the; or that land which is)*

ADJECTIVES

I have **fewer** money than you. *(less)*
I have **less** marbles than you. *(fewer)*
How **much** goals did you score? *(many)*
We have **many works** today. *(much work)*

N.B.: ***Much** and **less** refer to Quantity or Degree; **Many** and **fewer** to number.*

Of the three boys Ram, Shyam and Dinesh, the **latter** is the smallest. *(last)*
Gopal and Raju are here; the **later** has a hat. *(latter)*

N.B.: ***Later** and **latest** refer to time; **latter** and **last** to position.*

I gave him **a verbal** message. *(an oral)*
If you do not work you are **liable** (or **apt**) to fail. *(likely)*
I was not interested in the **future** developments. *(subsequent)*
Our **mutual** friend is in difficulties. *(common)*

N.B.: ***Our mutual friendship** means the friendship we both feel for each other, **our common friendship** means the friendship we both feel for another.*

He looks very **smartly** in this new dress. *(smart)*
I like these **kind of biscuits.** *(biscuits of this kind; this kind of biscuits)*
Quinine was rushed to **such** places where malaria was raging. *(the* or *those)*
A **comparatively** few know the principle of the atomic bomb.
(comparative or *comparatively few people know)*
No further threats, economic or **otherwise** were held out. *(other threats)*

Note: *Otherwise is an **adverb** and cannot do the work of a **noun** or an **adjective.***

There was **quite** a crowd at the fair. *(big* or *large)*
He gave us **farther** proofs of his innocence. *(further)*
Amritsar is **further** from Delhi than Aligarh. *(farther)*
The boys **each** have ten oranges. *(have ten oranges each)*
Only the **two first** boys were given prizes. *(first two)*

COMPARISON OF ADJECTIVES

Ram is a **cleverest** boy. *(very clever)*
Of the two brothers the **eldest** runs **fastest.** *(elder; faster)*
Iron is the most useful of all **other** metals. (omit *other)*
The lion is more ferocious than **any** animal. *(any other)*
I am **taller than all the boys.**
(taller than any other boy; taller than all the other boys; or *the tallest of all the boys)*
Hitler was **bolder** than prudent. *(more bold)*
The fox is **cunning** than the bear. *(more cunning)*
Gulmarg is a far **more** better place than Srinagar. (omit *more)*
Peace is **more preferable than** war. *(preferable to)*

I am **senior than** you in service. *(senior to)*

Dr Ray has **the best practice of any** medical practitioner here.

(a better practice than any other)

The speed of a motor car is greater **than** a bicycle. *(than that of)*

THE ARTICLES

A elephant is bigger than **an** ewe. (Interchange *a* and *an*)

An European visits us once **an** year. (*a* in both places)

The bulls eat **the** grass. (omit *the* in both places)

Does your son attend **the** school? (omit *the*)

Lion is king of the beasts. *(The lion is the king of beats)*

The man is mortal. (Omit *The*)

The virtue is better than the wealth (Omit both *The's*)

The boys are fond of **the games** (Omit *the* in both places)

Krishan is **a best** runner in our school. *(the best)*

I read **the** most interesting book. *(a)*

The iron is more useful than **the** gold. (omit both *the's*)

Ganges rises in **Himalayas.** *(The Ganges; the Himalayas)*

Sun is bigger than **earth.** *(The sun; the earth)*

He gave me **few** paise he had. *(the few)*

Rich must help poor. *(The rich; the poor)*

Yours is **more pressing a need** than mine. *(a more pressing need)*

I sent him **the** word that you were sent to **the** prison.

(omit *the* in both places)

What kind of **a** person is he? (omit *a*)

The patient is **little** better now. *(a little)*

The black and **brown** pup were sold. *(the brown)*

Churchill was a greater war leader than **a** statesman. (omit *a*)

A teacher and **student** are involved in this matter. *(a student)*

I drink **half** bottle of milk every morning. *(half a)*

N.B.:

1. *A is used as **an** before a word beginning with a **vowel** sound.*
2. ***The** is used (a) to particularise a person or thing (**the** man); (b) before geographical names excepting names of towns. (**the** Ganges); (c) before an adjective used as a noun (**the** wicked); (d) before a superlative (**the** best place); (e) before a noun, to give it emphasis, (**the** man of the day); (f) as an adverb before a comparative (**The** more, **the** merrier); (g) before a singular noun representing a whole class (**the** lion is a carnivoroys animal.)*
3. ***The** is omitted (a) before proper nouns (Ram); (b) before abstract nouns used in a general sense (Truth conquers); (c) before material nouns (Gold is*

precious); (d) before a noun used in its widest sense (Man is mortal; tigers eat flesh); (e) before a noun following 'kind of' (What kind of man is he?); (f) in some phrases having a transitive verb followed by its object (to give ear); (g) in certain phrases having a preposition followed by its object (in bed).

4. *The **Indefinite Article** is used (a) in its original numeral sense of **one** (**a** pen, **an** egg); (b) in a sense of indefiniteness (One day **a** man came to a house); (c) in the sense of **any** (A cow will give milk); (d) to make a common noun of a proper noun (A Shakespeare).*

VERBS

You must **lay** quietly on bed. *(lie)*
I **laid** unconscious for more than an hour. *(lay)*
I shall **go** to see you next week. *(come)*
My father **took** me to this hospital a week ago. *(brought)*
I was **drowned** but a man saved me. *(about to drown)*
The man who **committed suicide** was charged by the Police.
(attempted to commit suicide)
The picture was **hanged** on the wall. *(hung)*

TENSES

He said that he **is** not well. *(was)*
I **have** posted your letter yesterday. (omit *have*)
They **had gone** to Kolkata last month. *(went)*
No sooner **the bell was rung** than we came to school.
(had the bell been rung or *As soon as the bell was rung we came to school)*
I hope that you **would** succeed. *(will)*
I shall have been the first **to have greeted** you. *(to greet)*
I met him while **I came** home. *(was coming)*
He said that the earth **went** round the Sun. *(goes)*
The man, who **had been** arrested, **has admitted** the charge.
(...who was arrested etc., or *omit has)*
We eat so that we **might** live. *(may)*
I sent him word that I **can** attend the meeting. *(could)*
Although he **is** away from home for two months, yet he has not written to us.
(smart)
I told him that many had failed in their duty; he **seemed** to have misunderstood me. *(seems)*
My father **did not come** home yet. *(has not come)*
I **did not see** you since Monday. *(have not seen)*

I **am** suffering from fever since Monday. *(have been)*
I was ill since two days. *(have been ill for; or was ill for)*
I **did not see** you for the last five days. *(have not seen)*

VOICE

This war **will not be ended** this year. *(will not end)*
The universe **is consisted of** several planets. *(consists of)*
The earth **is rotated** round the Sun. *(rotates)*
The **Sun is set** in the evening. *(Sun sets)*
This **was happened** long ago. (Omit *was)*
I know what **to say.** *(is to be said)*
The ship **wrecked** near London. *(was wrecked)*
This match is hard **to be won**. *(to win)*
This is claimed to be the best pen in the market. *(They claim that this is)*

ADVERBS

I am **much** grateful to you. *(very)*
He was **very** interested in the game. *(much)*
The weather is **too** warm today. *(very)*
I am **quite** sorry for you. *(very)*
He **fell down** on the ground. (Omit *down)*
We shall **likely** meet again. *(probably)*
He hit me **hardly** on the face. *(hard)*
At once the car stopped. *(suddenly)*
I brought the doctor **suddenly.** *(at once)*
Read the lesson **loud.** *(aloud)*
On seeing him we **literally** laughed. *(actually)*
He **scarcely** did not see me. (Omit *scarcely* or say *scarcely saw me)*
Presently, there is a war in Europe. *(At present)*
Please take **out** your coat. *(off)*
Please kindly give me a Rupee. (Omit *please* or *kindly)*
I knew this long **before.** *(ago)*
We did the work **quicker** than usual. *(more quickly)*
My friend's death made me **so** sad. *(very)*
The weather was **exceeding** cold at the time. *(exceedingly)*
We are **too** occupied now to undertake fresh work. *(too much)*
From thence we went to the museum. (Omit *From;* or *From there)*

MISCELLANEOUS

Have you **a match-box**, please? *(a box of matches)*
At **his sight** the thief ran away. *(sight of him)*
I refrained **myself** from expressing my views. (Omit *myself*)
Due to the long drought the crop has failed. *(Owing to)*

Note: *Owing to can be either adjectival or* ***adverbial*** *in force;* ***due to*** *can only be adjectival.*

I shall try **and** help you this time too. *(to)*
I am not certain **as to** whether he will agree. (Omit *as to*)
As far as the funds needed for putting up this building there will be no difficulty. (Read *are concerned after building*)
While **being** in full agreement with what you say, I confess I cannot assist you. *(I am)*
This is worth **while** saying. (Omit *while*) - Fowler
Tell me how **did you go** home. *(you went)*
Do you know **to swim**? *(how to swim)*
He went to India **on** his own accord. *(of)*

(i) PARTICIPLES

The stream has **overflown** its banks. *(overflowed)*
I was **awoke** by the report of a gun. *(awakened)*
We could have **laid** there all day. *(lain)*
The table has been **laid** for two. (laid)

(ii) UNRELATED PARTICIPLES

Entering the room, a dog sprang at me.
(While I was entering or *When I entered)*
Having caught the thieves, **the headman was sent for.**
(... *we sent for the headman*)
While going to the market, **my purse was lost.** (... *I lost my purse*)
Being my birthday, I received many presents. *(It being)*
Encouraged by recent successes, **several new industrial schemes are under contemplation.** (...*we are contemplating several... schemes*)
My father left for Singapore on Monday, **arriving** there on Friday.
(and arrived)
Since writing this, **your parcel has been delivered to me.**
(... *I have received your parcel*)
Whilst admitting that this is an ideal scheme, it is absurd to suggest that it can be put into immediate operation. *(Whilst we admit)*

(iii) GERUNDS

I do not object to **you** joining the army. *(your)*
He has no objection to his **brother** taking part in the concert. *(brother's)*

Do you remember **Ram** writing me a letter? (*Ram's*)
There is little danger of this **rule** being broken. (*rule's*)
The State Council approved of the **Board of Ministers** levying this tax. (*Board of Ministers'*)

(iv) **GERUNDS AND INFINITIVE CONFUSED**

Please assist me **to do** this work. (*in doing*)
You have no excuse **to be** late. (*for being*)
You may now commence **to write.** (*writing*)
You are prohibited **to ask** favours. (*from asking*)
I have thought **to buy** a new car. (*of buying*)
All right thinking people will condemn school children's habit **to go** on strikes. (*of going*)
We look forward **to meet** old friends at the rally. (*to meeting*)
I reminded the Scouts of their chief duty **to do** a good turn every day. (*of doing*)
The income tax payers object **to pay** the new tax. (*to paying*)
This land was bought with a view **to build** a school. (*to building*)
Our efforts are aimed **to bring** about a reconciliation. (*to bringing*)

(v) **SPLIT INFINITIVE**

I shall try **to once again help** you. (*to help you once again*)
It is difficult **to amicably settle** their grievances. (*to settle their grievances amicably*)

N.B.: *Sometimes the split position is preferable; e.g., (1) "The object of this measure is to partly keep out foreign trade." (2) "Such men are powerless to correctly analyse agricultural conditions."*

(vi) **SHALL AND WILL: SHOULD AND WOULD**

I hope I **will** be able to see you. (*shall*)
Shall he also be present? (*will*)
The judge said to the prisoner, "You **will** be punished for your atrocious crime!" (*shall*)
I **will** be drowned; no one **shall** save me. (*shall; will*)
We **shall** win, or die in the attempt! (*will*)

N.B.: *(a)* ***SHALL** in the **First Person** and **WILL** in the **Second** and **Third Persons** express **simple futurity**.*

(b) ***WILL** in the **First Person** and **SHALL** in the **Second** and **Third Persons** express **determination, desire** or **promise**.*

I think this **would** suit you. (*will*)
I **would** like to meet old friends. (*should*)
If I were you, I **should** not do that. (*would*)
You **would** obey your elders at all times. (*should*)
My friend **should** sit and dream all the day. (*would*)

I intervened lest you **might** be punished. (*should*)

If it **would** rain, the match will not come off. (*should*)

I **would** certainly prefer the train to the bus. (*should*)

Note: ***Should, not would**, is the right form before the verbs **prefer, like, be glad, be inclined** etc., in first person conditional statements. — Fowler*

It looks (or seems) as if the Labour Party **will** come to power (*would*)

The ministers are anxious that there **will** be no unemployment after the war. (*shall*)

Note: ***That** clauses after **intend** or **intention, desire, demand, be anxious** etc. have **shall** and **should** for all persons. — Fowler*

(vii) CONJUCTIONS

I **neither** know you nor him. (*know neither you nor him*)

He had scarcely (or hardly) finished eating **than** he collapsed. (*when*)

He says **that,** if you promise to help him, **that** he will continue his studies. (Omit the second *that*)

He was no other person **but** our friend (*than*)

I did nothing else *than* rat. (*but*)

He was not only a good general, but a firm ruler. (*but also*)

Although he wrongs me, I love him (*yet* I love him)

Do this **like** I do. (*as*)

I shall not speak to you **except** you apologise to me. (*unless*)

Your essay is as **good,** if not better than, mine. (*as good as*)

It was not long **until** the good news came. (*when*)

Directly the bell rang, we went to the play ground. (*As soon as*)

The reason for his sudden departure is **because** his brother is very ill. (*that*)

Was it ten years ago **since** you visited Delhi. (*that*)

There is nothing praiseworthy **or** nothing blameworthy in his conduct. (*and*)

(viii) MISPLACEMENT

He **both gave me** food and clothes. (*gave me both*)

The boys were **given an apple each**. (*each given an apple*)

The boy was caned by the Principal who was absent yesterday. (*The boy who was absent...*)

He only caned me once. (*He caned me only once*)

He will succeed in his attempt **certainly.** (*will certainly*)

Haven't you any **other suggestion than this.** (*suggestion other than*)

(ix) REDUNDANCY

We returned **back** the same day. (Omit *back*)

This is a **universal** fact, **which all people know.** (Omit either *universal* or *which all people know*)

We restored him to life **again.** (Omit *again*)

As a rule, I **often** go for a change. (Omit *often*)

He stamped **with his foot** on the ground. (Omit *with his foot*)

It is **quite all** right. (Omit *quite* or *all*)

Most of our councillors are not sure of being returned **if and** when a general election is held. (Omit *if and*)

We shall not help you **unless and** until you reform your ways. (Omit *unless and*)

As you have neither paid the money nor have made any effort to do so, **therefore** the land will not be given to you. (Omit *therefore*)

We are **equally** as guilty as you. (Omit *equally*)

Our friends **continue to remain** optimistic. (Say *continue to be*)

He disobeys **both** his father **as well as** his mother. (Omit *both* or say *both his father and his mother*)

This happened **just exactly** ten years ago. (Omit either *just* or *exactly*)

Most men think that money **alone** is the **only** thing that matters. (Omit either *alone* or *only*)

We came back at 8 A.M. time this morning. (Omit time)

This behaviour is **somewhat** extraordinary. (Omit *somewhat*)

The effect of this drought is likely to be **productive of** a famine. (Omit *either 'the effect of'* or *'productive of'*)

This is a **most** unique event in our history. (Omit *most*)

Note: *Perfect, universal, round, ideal, wooden, square, right, etc., admit of no comparison.*

CORRECT USE OF VERBS

Under each sentence, four forms of verbs have been suggested. Choose and mark the one that will most suitably fill in the blank in the sentence.

1. The opening sentence of the passage ..... that a city provides better opportunities for good life.

A. has implied B. has been implying
C. is implied D. implies

2. I ..... a dream and there is none that can interpret it.

A. have dreamed B. am dreaming
C. have been dreaming D. am dreamed

3. I searched the village for a carpenter, but not a single one ..... .

A. found B. is to be found
C. was to be found D. was found

4. Many years ..... since I last ate mangoes.

A. passed B. had passed
C. have passed D. have been passed

5. Someone must ..... this message with a very scratchy pen.
A. write B. have written
C. had written D. had been written
6. The two gunmen ..... by the police at the airport.
A. were caught B. are caught
C. have caught D. had caught
7. Someone or the other must ..... it.
A. had stolen B. steal
C. have stolen D. be stolen
8. How would that situation ..... us?
A. helps B. had helped
C. have helped D. did help
9. He ..... in this town for many years, so he is likely to know it well.
A. has lived B. had lived
C. lived D. has been living
10. These letters ..... already.
A. have signed B. are signed
C. had signed D. have been signed
11. If I ..... to sell my house, I will depart next month.
A. managed B. have managed
C. will manage D. manage
12. The two boys ..... the weather will be all right tomorrow.
A. had hoped B. hope
C. hoped D. have hoped
13. They ..... you next month.
A. will pay B. pay
C. have paid D. paid
14. I must have your agreement before I ..... this document.
A. am signing B. sign
C. signed D. have signed
15. You must buy a ticket if you ..... to enter the theatre.
A. wanted B. are wanting
C. want D. have wanted
16. If Ram ..... them, he would have told them the news.
A. saw B. had seen
C. have seen D. see
17. If the examination is cancelled, I will let you .....
A. know B. known
C. knew D. have known
18. I will let you have this money. But you must ..... to sign this paper.
A. agree B. have agreed
C. agreed D. had agreed

19. His eyesight ..... . A small object got into his eye while he was swimming.
A. damaged B. was damaged
C. had damaged D. is damaged

20. Although the price was very high, she ..... to buy it.
A. agrees B. had agreed
C. agreed D. has agreed

21. It started raining heavily while we ..... tennis.
A. are playing B. were playing
C. had played D. play

22. My brother ..... here for the last five years.
A. has been working B. works
C. is working D. worked

23. If Charu appears in this paper, she ..... through the examinations.
A. gets B. will get
C. is getting D. has got

24. If I were a bird, I ..... in the sky.
A. would fly B. will fly
C. was flying D. had flied

25. If I had received the parcel, I ..... immediately.
A. would reply B. would have been replied
C. would have replied D. were replied

26. No sooner had she completed her work than she ..... for shopping.
A. gets prepared B. get prepared
C. prepared D. got prepared

27. As soon as India got freedom, she ..... to strengthen her power.
A. has started B. had started
C. started D. starts

28. Until the examination comes to an end, we ..... no time for starting any fresh work.
A. will spare B. spare
C. will be sparing D. will have spared

29. The old man, who is sitting here, ... in this room for more than a month.
A. lived B. was living
C. has lived D. is living

30. I ..... him for ten years but I do not know where he lives.
A. have been knowing B. have known
C. was knowing D. knew

31. It is time you ..... your children to school.
A. took B. have taken
C. had taken D. were taking

32. He informed me about the accident, which ..... two days before.
A. has occured B. had occured
C. was occured D. occured

33. Did you think you ..... me somewhere before?
A. have seen B. had seen
C. were seeing D. see

34. Many observations indicate that the number of drug addicts ..... day by day.
A. is grew B. is growing
C. has grown D. have growing

35. I have come to know that your father ..... last week.
A. has died B. had died
C. died D. dies

ANSWERS

1	2	3	4	5	6	7	8	9	10
D	A	C	C	B	A	C	C	D	D
11	**12**	**13**	**14**	**15**	**16**	**17**	**18**	**19**	**20**
D	B	A	B	C	B	A	A	B	C
21	**22**	**23**	**24**	**25**	**26**	**27**	**28**	**29**	**30**
B	A	B	A	C	D	C	A	C	B
31	**32**	**33**	**34**	**35**					
A	B	B	B	C					

PREPOSITION

The Preposition is the most important part of English Language Test in various Competitive Examination. The questions based on prepositions primarily test a candidate's understanding of the correct usage of Prepositions. The questions asked in examinations are always followed by four options as answers in which, at times, two answers may seem to be correct. Hence, it becomes very difficult to select a right answer. Therefore, a candidate is required to get acquainted with the maximum number of preposition and phrases to avoid any confusion.

A preposition is a word placed before a noun or a pronoun to show in what relation the person or thing denoted by it stands in regard to something else.

For Example:

1. There is a book **on** the table.
   Explanation: Here the word 'on' shows the relationship between two things – **book** or **table**.
2. She is fond **of** flowers.
   Explanation: Here the word **of** shows the relationship between the attribute

expressed by the objective **fond** and the noun a **flower**.

3. The fox jumped **off** the table.

Explanation: Here the word **off** shows the relationship between the action expressed by the verb **jumped** and noun **table.**

Now, let us discuss some commonly used prepositions. These examples would give you a fair idea about the types of prepositions being asked in the ETE examination.

Examples:

1. **Agree with a person:** I entirely agree with him.
2. **Agree to a proposal:** She is not agreeing to my proposal.
3. **Apologise for:** She must apologise for offending you.
4. Bad **at:** I am bad at cricket.
5. Congratulate **on** something: I congratulate you on your success in the ETE entrance examination.
6. Depend **on:** I depend on my parents.
7. Disappointed **with** somebody: My mother never showed as if she were disappointed with me.
8. Explain something **to** somebody: Could you explain this sentence to me?
9. **Good at:** She is good at tennis.
10. Impress **with/by:** I am very much impressed with/by her work.
11. Interest **in:** I have no interest in fine arts.
12. Kind **to:** People have always been very kind to me.
13. Look **after:** His mother always looks after her son.
14. Look **for:** Can you help me look for my spectacles?
15. Get married **to:** I still hope to get married to Anjali.
16. Popular **with:** Saurabh is popular with his friends.
17. Responsible/responsiblity **for:** Who should be made responsible for this mishap?
18. Shocked **by/at:** I was terribly shocked at/by the news of Sonu's accident.
19. Suffer **from:** She is suffering from cold.
20. Take part **in:** I don't want to take part in any more conferences.
21. Typical **of:** The food was typical of the region.
22. Wrong **with:** What is wrong with Geetika today?

In the exercise that follows, forty questions have been appended for practice. Read each sentence carefully and identify the preposition, from amongst the options given, which would be suitable at the blank space in the sentence. Such a preposition would make the "right sense," though you may find other suitable prepositions as well that could be placed in the blank space.

Read the sentences *carefully* and choose suitable *prepositions* for the purpose.

1. She is proud ..... her beauty.
   A. at B. on C. of D. about
2. Mohan belongs ..... the upper strata of the society.
   A. from B. for C. to D. of
3. We offer heartiest congratulation ..... your success.
   A. at B. on C. upon D. for
4. M/s Ram Avtar & Sons are the famous dealers ..... sugar and wheat.
   A. of B. in C. at D. for
5. So far that case is concerned I have not dealt ..... it.
   A. No preposition is required B. in
   C. into D. with
6. The man killed ..... road accident was a stranger.
   A. of B. by C. in D. on
7. He did not go ..... the right direction.
   A. to B. by C into D. in
8. The train reached ..... the station right time.
   A. to B. by
   C. on D. No preposition is required
9. He slipped away ..... the crowd to avoid arrest.
   A. of B. from C. by D. with
10. The man died ..... heart attack without receiving any treatment.
    A. of B. with C. in D. by
11. This remark is not ..... your favour.
    A. to B. for C. in D. of
12. Parole can be granted ..... any convict under the provisions of law.
    A. for B. to C. unto D. upon
13. An appeal has been admitted ..... the Supreme Court.
    A. by B. into C. with D. in
14. When I entered the room he was lying ..... bed.
    A. over B. at C. on D. in
15. Please accompany me ..... my room to collect the material.
    A. for B. to C. upto D. into
16. This item has been included ..... the agenda of the meeting.
    A. into B. in C. on D. with
17. Indian team had played ..... the MCC last year.
    A. with B. upon C. against D. of
18. The fare to Mumbai has been increased ..... six rupees from here recently.
    A. to B. by C. with D. upto
19. He is good ..... chess.
    A. for B. at C. on D. with

20. Payments were made ..... cash at the Head Office.
A. in B. by
C. through D. No preposition required

21. He entrusted me ..... some work.
A. from B. at C. of D. with

22. The girl said that she preferred the blue gown ..... the red one.
A. to B. than C. from D. in

23. The article deals ..... the burning problems of the society.
A. in B. of C. with D. against

24. Her mother is sick but he does not look ..... her.
A. into B. after C. at D. to

25. The teacher distributed sweets ..... his students.
A. from B. among C. between D. in

26. The poet describes the beauty of the nature ..... students.
A. of B. in C. to D. among

27. The villagers saved me ..... being drowned in the river.
A. to B. from C. with D. of

28. My father was angry ..... the servant due to his rude behaviour.
A. of B. into C. at D. with

29. Mohan is also sick because he does not take care ..... his health.
A. of B. to C. from D. off

30. Thousands of patriots died ..... the sake of their country.
A. for B. of C. from D. in

31. This is a secret plan ..... you and me.
A. among B. of C. between D. to

32. Some animals became extinct because they could not adapt ..... new surroundings.
A. of B. to C. from D. than

33. My mother always prays to God ..... my success.
A. of B. for C. from D. to

34. The English nation ruled ..... many countries of the world.
A. of B. over C. on D. into

35. The Principal was ashamed ..... his students' misconduct.
A. of B. to C. from D. with

36. The meeting was adjourned ..... 5 o'clock in the evening.
A. by B. at C. for D. [illegible]

37. The train was running ..... a speed of sixty kilometres per hour.
A. by B. of C. into D. at

38. She looked very different ..... the photograph I had of her.
A. of B. than C. from D. to

39. The health conscious people should take precaution ..... infection.
A. against B. with C. at D. from

40. The employee got an opportunity ..... going abroad.
A. from B. of C. for D. to

ANSWERS

1	2	3	4	5	6	7	8	9	10
C	C	B	B	D	E	D	D	B	A
11	12	13	14	15	16	17	18	19	20
C	B	A	D	B	A	C	B	B	A
21	22	23	24	25	26	27	28	29	30
D	A	C	B	B	C	B	D	A	A
31	32	33	34	35	36	37	38	39	40
C	B	B	B	A	B	D	C	A	C

FILL IN APPROPRIATE WORDS

Pick out the most effective word from the given words to fill in the blanks to make the sentence meaningfully complete in the context of the sentence.

1. The government in our state has been from the beginning ineffective, if not ..... in combating the lawlessness.
A. deficient B. depressing
C. reluctant D. proficient
E. dishonest

2. Environmental pollution has assumed ..... proportion of late.
A. alarming B. depressing
C. critical D. enlarged
E. disappointing

3. Now that you have ..... me, I shall have nothing to do with you in future.
A. prohibited B. deprived
C. retaliated D. abdicated
E. deserted

4. My ten-year-old son was talking in such an impudent manner that I lost patience and ..... him soundly.
A. warned B. thrashed
C. admonished D. reprimanded
E. scolded

5. The plea for a separate State is too serious a matter to be treated .....
A. rationally B. cavalierly
C. professionally D. quickly
E. politically

6. We witness a sad ..... of terrorism in the State taking the lives of innocent people.
   A. danger
   B. calamity
   C. spectacle
   D. encounter
   E. fortitude
7. Your education has been in vain if it has not ..... in you the habit of clear and independent thinking.
   A. established
   B. involved
   C. indulged
   D. practised
   E. fostered
8. Since the unity of the country is regarded as ..... the States are vested only with limited powers.
   A. categorical
   B. durable
   C. inalienable
   D. paramount
   E. inexorable
9. Which of the following is most nearly the same in meaning as the word despised?
   A. appreciated
   B. criticized
   C. regarded as laudable
   D. regarded as worthless
   E. regarded as objectionable
10. The facts ..... to my report in your newspaper are wrong.
   A. contributed
   B. attributed
   C. alleged
   D. affirmed
   E. attached
11. It has been observed that income ..... has widened between urban and rural areas.
   A. accretion
   B. tax
   C. disparity
   D. deviation
   E. disbursement
12. Government might ..... whether it will be safe to make a completely dependent organisation suddenly wholly independent.
   A. think
   B. report
   C. ignore
   D. consult
   E. consider
13. He was visibly unnerved when he was ..... with the documents bearing his own signature.
   A. shown
   B. challenged
   C. confronted
   D. questioned
   E. produced
14. I recommend a severe punishment so that he ..... from drinking in future.
   A. desists
   B. avoids
   C. withdraws
   D. recoils

E. retracts

15. This investigation revealed ..... evidence, all pointing to murder.

A. dangerous
B. intimidatory
C. doubtful
D. frivolous
E. incriminating

16. Because of the poor ..... in the hall, the singers were barely audible.

A. acoustics
B. visibility
C. quality
D. tone
E. lighting

17. His ..... handling of the situation landed his own party into trouble.

A. inept
B. inspired
C. skillful
D. sophisticated
E. uncouth

18. Even after hearing for a fairly long time, we were at a loss to know what he was driving .....

A. to
B. on
C. in
D. at
E. after

19. Chitra looks ..... the sapling as if it were her own child.

A. upon
B. over
C. for
D. at
E. after

20. Barring last minute surprises, he is ..... to become the President.

A. designated
B. poised
C. endorsed
D. elected
E. selected

21. The accused persons were ..... from the jail in the dark of night.

A. escaped
B. released
C. bailed
D. freed

22. The President of our country ..... an excellent speech yesterday.

A. gave
B. said
C. delivered
D. produced

23. There are many ..... spaces in the passage with answers below it.

A. vacant
B. blank
C. hollow
D. gap

24. We have to ..... old considerations if we want to survive in modern age.

A. forswear
B. renounce
C. recant
D. leave out

25. The people took the step of ..... against the misrule of the administration in my district.

A. insurrection
B. hatred

C. hostility D. revolution

26. There is ..... interpretation in most of the romantic poems.

A. sensual B. sensuous

C. sensational D. rational

27. There is ..... attitude of various writers upon me.

A. rancour B. hostility

C. animosity D. antagonist

28. We paid our sympathetic ..... to the family of deceased.

A. mercy B. grace

C. charity D. homage

29. A beautiful morning ..... and the young boys left their beds.

A. came B. happened

C. occured D. appeared

30. Own your wagon, own your container is another new scheme ..... by the railways this year.

A. launched B. devised

C. broadcasted D. moved

E. manipulated

31. Instances of security ..... over the past few years are too familiar.

A. lapse B. actions

C. acts D. steps

32. We ..... the family members after expressing our grief at the tragedy.

A. mourned B. condoled

C. satisfied D. consoled

33. The country needs ..... government to tackle the challenges it faces today.

A. stable B. stationary

C. stagnant D. sustained

34. The General said that the position must be ..... at all costs.

A. arrested B. caught

C. captured D. possessed

35. The nation decided to erect a fire ..... in honour of the martyrs.

A. museum B. monument

C. momentum D. monastery

36. He returned the lost bag to its rightful owner and we handsomely rewarded for his ..... .

A. foresight B. wisdom

C. honesty D. intelligence

37. The payment was ..... delayed this time because some of the supporting documents for the claim were missing.

A. unjustifiably B. undeseruedly

C. untoreseemly D. unduly

38. A glue produced by bees to ..... their hives appears to contain antibiotic substances.

A. decorate B. structure
C. design D. build

39. Automobile manufacturers are reviving upto launch a compaign designed to increase consumer ..... about the new emission control.

A. education B. awareness
C. capacity D. production

40. Some illegal organizations have ..... practices which are known only to members.

A. esoteric B. serctive
C. exotic D. subservient

41. Sonali had a dreadful night caused by an ..... while she was sleeping.

A. euthanasia B. inclubus
C. insonciance D. insipidity

42. The experts group would .... the issue relating to redevelopment of forces.

A. tackle B. handle
C. manipulate D. administer

43. Two nations have decided to sign a new trade ..... to be affected from next month.

A. paper B. business
C. proposal D. agreement

44. Sita was badly ..... by the information which she got in the letter.

A. shaken B. petrified
C. revamped D. evaded

45. We are not ..... with this area so we cannot say more about it.

A. familiar B. attached
C. introduced D. related

ANSWERS

1	2	3	4	5	6	7	8	9	10
C	A	E	B	B	C	E	C	D	B
11	**12**	**13**	**14**	**15**	**16**	**17**	**18**	**19**	**20**
C	E	C	A	E	A	A	D	E	B
21	**22**	**23**	**24**	**25**	**26**	**27**	**28**	**29**	**30**
A	C	B	C	A	B	A	D	A	A
31	**32**	**33**	**34**	**35**	**36**	**37**	**38**	**39**	**40**
A	D	A	C	B	C	C	D	B	B
41	**42**	**43**	**44**	**45**					
A	A	D	A	C					

TEST OF ANTONYMS

An Antonym is also a common test in the English Language Tests. In this test, a candidate is asked to select an appropriate opposite word of a particular word, printed in bold letter in the question, from among the given four alternatives. Among those alternatives, one will find some relatively opposite and some relatively similar words of the particular word. There can also be some unrelated words. Therefore, a candidate is required to consider each one of the words carefully and choose that word, which is most nearly the opposite of the particular word, thus ignoring those unnecessary words.

For Example:

Old and new are antonyms of each other.

For Example:

Choose the right antonym of ABUNDANCE.

A. scarcity B. respect

C. reject D. fullness

Answer: A

Explanation: 'Abundance' means plenty or enough. Since option (A) 'scarcity' means shortage which is the most nearest antonym of the particular word. Option (B) 'respect' stands for admire somebody. Option (C) 'reject' means refuse to accept and lastly, option (D) 'fullness' expresses the nearest synonym of the given word. Hence, all other options except (A) are incorrect. Therefore option (A) 'scarcity' is the appropriate antonym of 'abundance'.

In the following exercise you are given *words* and below each one of them, there is a set of four words. You are required to choose one word from each set, which is an *antonym* of the word given in question. Remember that an antonym means the word that is opposite to the given word. There may not exist exact antonyms of certain words or certain words may not be antonyms of the given words in the absolute term. The term is *relative* and a choice has to be made from the given set of words.

1. Abandon

A. Give up B. Abdicate

C. Desert D. Uphold

2. Abate

A. Dwindle B. Aggravate

C. Mitigate D. Ebb

3. Abbreviate

A. Enlarge B. Reduce

C. Abridge D. Contract

4. Abeyance

A. Expectancy

B. Suspension

C. Dormancy

D. Action

5. Baffle

A. Balk B. Foil

C. Outwit D. Abet

6. Becoming

A. Congruous

B. Seemly

C. Awkward

D. Decent

7. Bleak

A. Exposed B. Bright

C. Dull D. Cold

8. Candid

A. Frank

B. Transparent

C. Straight forward

D. Crafty

9. Deception

A. Equivocation

B. Honesty

C. Dissimulation

D. Falsehood

10. Defile

A. Contaminate B. Disinfect

C. Pollute D. Spoil

11. Eager

A. Earnest B. Cool

C. Animated D. Anxious

12. Enmity

A. Harmony B. Animosity

C. Acrimony D. Bitterness

13. Fallacy

A. Refinement B. Sophism

C. Sureness D. Subterfuge

14. Fickle

A. Capricious

B. Firm

C. Ever changing

D. Fluctuating

15. Formidable

A. Dangerous

B. Impregnable

C. Powerless

D. Invincible

16. Frugality

A. Miserliness

B. Extravagance

C. Percimony

D. Providence

17. Heterogeneous

A. Mingled

B. Unhomogeneous

C. Identical

D Conglomerate

18. Incongruous

A. Conflicting

B. Contradictor

C. Ill-matched

D. Compatible

19. Inherent

A. Congenital

B. Indispensable

C. Innate

D. Accidental

20. Inquisitive

A. Careless B. Intrusive

C. Meddling D. Peeping

21. Latent

A. Undeveloped B. Apparent

C. Hidden D. Implied

22. Pity

A. Compassion

B. Ferocity

C. Sympathy

D. Tenderness

23. Prejudice

A. Reasoning

B. Preconception

C. Prepossession
D. Presumption

24. Reproof
A. Approbation
B. Comment
C. Condemnation
D. Criticism

25. Vigilant
A. Cautious B. Heedless
C. Awake D. Careful

26. Acquaint
A. Compel B. Deceive
C. Accustom D. Coincide

27. Brevity
A. Conciseness
B. Elongation
C. Terseness
D. Accuracy

28. Celestial
A. Arraign B. Private
C. Terrestrial D. Divine

29. Disdain
A. Honour B. Judgement
C. Scorn D. Dogma

30. Eccentric
A. Regular B. Effective
C. Anomalous D. Particular

31. Epitome
A. Amplification
B. Undervalue
C. Superfluous
D. Summary

32. Gracious
A. Lofty
B. Benevolent
C. Arrogant
D. Courteous

33. Hypocrisy
A. Despise
B. Optimistic
C. Deception
D. Candour

34. Ignominious
A. Honourable
B. Infamous
C. Disgraceful
D. Impressive

35. Lascivious
A. Slay
B. Blithe
C. Chaste
D. Libidinous

36. Magnanimous
A. Condour B. Assuage
C. Selfish D. Lofty

37. Obsolete
A. Inadvertence
B. Modern
C. Disregard
D. Old-fashioned

38. Prelude
A. Epilogue B. Subvert
C. Conclusion D. Preface

39. Recess
A. Refresh B. Restore
C. Projection D. Vacation

40. Solitary
A. Decipher B. Implicit
C. Accompanied D. Lonely

41. Transcend
A. Proxy
B. Incredulity
C. Fail
D. Overstep

42. Unanimous
A. Auspicious
B. Proficiency
C. Disagreeing
D. Like-minded

43. Vigorous
A. Passion B. Denounce
C. Weak D. Powerful

44. Vivacious
A. Dusky B. Somber
C. Brisk D. Languid

45. Worthy
A. Erroneous B. Equity
C. Worthless D. Deserving

ANSWERS

1	2	3	4	5	6	7	8	9	10
D	B	A	D	D	C	B	D	B	B
11	12	13	14	15	16	17	18	19	20
B	A	C	B	C	B	C	D	D	A
21	22	23	24	25	26	27	28	29	30
B	B	A	A	B	B	B	C	A	A
31	32	33	34	35	36	37	38	39	40
A	C	D	A	C	C	B	A	C	C
41	42	43	44	45					
C	C	C	D	C					

TEST OF SYNONYMS

Test of Synonyms is the most common test in the English language. In this test, a candidate is asked to choose a suitable word that is most nearly similar to the word given in the question. There are four alternatives. From amongst those alternatives, a relative/a similar word, an opposite word of the particular word and sometimes, even unrelated words in the set of alternatives. Therefore, a candidate is required to consider each alternative very carefully and select the most Apposite (similar) word of that particular word ignoring all other words.

For Example:

Slay and kill are synonyms of each other.

Explanation:

'Slay' means to kill in a violent manner. Therefore, 'kill' is the appropriate synonym of 'slay'.

For Example:

Choose the synonym of **ADIEU** from the options given below:

A. Farewell B. Kind C. Welcome D. Divert

Answer: A

Explanation: 'ADIEU' means good-bye. Option (A) 'Farewell' expresses nearly the same meaning of the particular word. Farewell is a term applied for someone's departure. Option (B) 'Kind' means friendly towards and thoughtful for others. Option (C) 'Welcome' stands for receiving with warmth and pleasure. Hence, it is nearest to the apposite of the particular word. And lastly, option (D) 'Divert' means turn somebody or something from one course to another or change. Therefore option (A) 'Farewell' is the most appropriate synonym of 'ADIEU.'

In this exercise you are given words and below each one of them is a set of four words. You are required to choose one word from each set, which is the synonym of the word given in question. Remember that exact synonym of any word can be rarely located. What we mean by synonym here is the word that is most near to the meaning or sense of the word in question.

1. Adapt
   A. Confound B. Confuse
   C. Disjoint D. Adjust
2. Allure
   A. Deter
   B. Drive away
   C. Captivate
   D. Dissuade
3. Amiable
   A. Acrimonious
   B. Churlish
   C. Attractive
   D. Disagreeable
4. Anticipation
   A. Expectation
   B. Doubt
   C. Despair
   D. Confidence
5. Anxiety
   A. Apathy B. Calmness
   C. Assurance D. Concern
6. Augur
   A. Assure B. Predict
   C. Determine D. Insure
7. Brutish
   A. Elevated B. Base
   C. Exalted D. Grand
8. Catastrophe
   A. Disaster B. Boon
   C. Favour D. Blessing
9. Clear
   A. Ambiguous B. Dubiuous
   C. Mysterious D. Explicit
10. Deception
    A. Candour B. Duplicity
    B. Frankness D. Honesty
11. Difference
    A. Agreement B. Identity
    C. Uniformity D. Variation
12. Docile
    A. Determined B. Submissive
    C. Inflexible D. Obstinate
13. Endure
    A. Give up B. Succumb
    C. Sustain D. Break
14. Enthusiasm
    A. Fervency B. Passion
    C. Intensity D. Ardour
15. Equivocal
    A. Indisputable
    B. Manifest
    C. Indeterminate
    D Unquestionable
16. Abroad
    A. Inaccessible
    B. Away
    C. Inattentive
    D. Nearby
17. Absolute
    A. Sudden
    B. Immediate
    C. Imperative
    D. Relative
18. Adjacent
    A. Neighbouring
    B. Separate
    C. Remote
    D. Indoors

19. Compassionate
A. Cruel
B. Benevolent
C. Remunerate
D. Compensate

20. Destitute
A. Poor
B. Wretched
C. Prosperous
D. Lewd

21. Eclipse
A. Solistice
B. Eventual
C. Shade
D. Enhancement

22. Embrace
A. Leisure
B. Except
C. Clasp
D. Prescribe

23. Frivolous
A. Soothe B. Meagre
C. Trivial D. Generous

24. Gorgeous
A. Superb B. Shabby
C. Impious D. Infinite

25. Hazard
A. Obstacle B. Gravity
C. Guard D. Tedious

26. Imperious
A. Jealousy
B. Solemnity
C. Authoritative
D. Confluence

27. Juvenile
A. Adolescent B. Matured
C. Affection D. Adulthood

28. Lassitude
A. Ephemeral B. Emotion
C. Weariness D. Activity

29. Mutual
A. Independent
B. Interchangeable
C. Disciplined
D. Divided

30. Pacific
A. Agonise
B. Agonising
C. Peaceful
D. Turbulent

31. Plea
A. Excuse
B. Exonerate
C. Vindicate
D. Impiety

32. Reluctant
A. Exquisite
B. Restore
C. Unwilling
D. Willing

33. Scorn
A. Contempt
B. Penetrate
C. Impregnate
D. Honour

34. Tangible
A. Savoury
B. Eudlogy
C. Substantial
D. Impalpable

35. Treaty
A. Negotiation
B. Neutrality
C. Negligible
D. Auspicious

36. Utmost
A. Farthest
B. Megnanimous
C. Distinct
D. Approximate

37. Vague
A. Specific B. Prodigious
C. Undetermind D. Definite

38. Vindictive
A. Assert B. Vicious
C. Unforgiving D. Wilderness

39. Vouch
A. Pivot B. Pounce
C. Asssure D. Smack

40. Withstand
A. Involute B. Submit
C. Endure D. Abandon

ANSWERS

1	2	3	4	5	6	7	8	9	10
D	C	C	A	D	B	B	A	D	B
11	**12**	**13**	**14**	**15**	**16**	**17**	**18**	**19**	**20**
D	C	C	D	C	B	C	A	B	B
21	**22**	**23**	**24**	**25**	**26**	**27**	**28**	**29**	**30**
C	C	C	A	A	C	A	C	B	C
31	**32**	**33**	**34**	**35**	**36**	**37**	**38**	**39**	**40**
A	C	A	C	A	A	C	C	C	C

ONE WORD SUBSTITUTION

In each one of the following questions, there is a definition / expression followed by five words. Select the word that fits the definition/expression most closely.

1. Ask too much money for something
A. Bargain B. Cheap
C. Overcharge D. Price
E. Prize

2. Border made up of wood or other material
A. Boundary B. Frame
C. Outline D. Ring
E. Room

3. Children, grandchildren, great-grand-children, etc.
A. Descendants B. Family
C. Followers D. Outcome
E. Youth

4. Coming at the right time
A. Early B. Lucky
C. Occasion D. Often
E. Punctuality

5. Demand as a right
A. Borrow B. Claim
C. Earn D. Insure
E. Owe

6. Doing what one is told
A. Citizen
B. Commanding
C. Lawful
D. Listen
E. Obedience

7. Larger to make progress
A. Advanced B. Ambitious
C. Anxious D. Forward
E. Greedy

8. Easily hurt
A. Bad of tempered
B. Damaged
C. Painful
D. Sensible

E. Sensitive

9. An inner feeling that tells one what is right or wrong
A. Cleverness
B. Conscience
C. Consciousness
D. Fear
E. Virtue

10 Get one thing for another
A. Bargain B. Borrow
C. Change D. Exchange
E. Owe

11. A group of people who meet together to discuss and take decisions
A. Class B. Club
C. Committee D. Rat
E. Seat

12. To have enough money to be able to buy
A. Afford B. Borrow
C. Last D. Offer
E. Owe

13. A line/boundary that cannot be crossed
A. Border B. Edge
C. Limit D. Mark
E. Stop

14. A person who receives guests
A. Fellow B. Friend
C. Gentleman D. Host
E. Inviting

15. The name of a book
A. Headline B. Printed
C. Style D. Text
E. Title

16. Not in one's own country
A. Aboard B. Abroad
C. At sea D. Foreign
E. Strange

17. One of the bones in which, the teeth are set
A. Ankle B. Chew
C. Jaw D. Muscle
E. Throat

18. A person who is accused of something and brought before a judge
A. Accuser B. Criminal
C. Defendant C. Justice
E. Lawyer

19. A person who saw an event
A. Eye-sight B. Report
C. Scene D. Theatre
E. Witness

20. A piece of wood supporting a roof
A. Bar B. Beam
C. Mast D. Stock
E. Strip

21. A person who never tires of doing something
A. Magnanimous
B. Obdurate
C. Indefatigable
D. Compunctious

22. Excessive fear of the night time or darkness
A. Bibliomania
B. Agromania
C. Dipsomania
D. Nyctophobia

23. A person who advocates extreme patriotism believes in
A. Chauvinism B. Fascism
C. Communism D. Egoism

24. A person who is indifferent to pains and pleasures follows
A. Stoicism

B. Polytheism
C. Nepoticm
D. Liberation

25. A summary giving a general view of the whole
A. Tacit B. Synopsis
C. Taciturnity D. Syllabus

26. Suitable for daily conversation
A. Synod B. Synthesis
C. Colloquial D. Tacit

27. The one that is outdated or out of use of fashion
A. Modern
B. Obsolete
C. Typical
D. Homogeneous

28. A government where the powers are concentrated in the hands of one person
A. Plutocracy B. Democracy
C. Oligarchy D. Autocracy

29. A letter or a document which does not bear the name of its writer
A. Pseudonym
B. Anonymous
C. Acknowledge
D. Elite

30. Murder of one man by another man.
A. Suicide B. Homicide
C. Genocide D. Insecticide

ANSWERS

1	2	3	4	5	6	7	8	9	10
C	B	A	E	B	E	B	E	B	D
11	**12**	**13**	**14**	**15**	**16**	**17**	**18**	**19**	**20**
C	A	C	D	E	B	C	C	E	B
21	**22**	**23**	**24**	**25**	**26**	**27**	**28**	**29**	**30**
C	D	A	A	B	C	B	D	B	B

COMMON ERRORS IN SENTENCES

Identifying common errors is the most important feature of English Language Tests of various competitive examinations. The questions based on common errors are always expected in the entrance test of the JBT Examination. The common error test is designed to test whether a candidate is capable of sorting out an error related to the rules of grammar,. The errors or related to subject-verb-agreement, numbers, cases, nouns, pronouns, adjectives, verbs, adverbs, prepositions, tenses etc., are generally embedded. These have to be identified within the limited hours. Therefore, a candidate is required to know the basic rules of English grammar. Keeping fact view, this guide common errors related to all the aforesaid parts or speech. There are forty questions related to common errors, with short answers have also been incorporated to guide the student.

In this exercise each sentence has been divided into four parts — A, B, C, D. Out of these four parts, one has a mistake. While answering the question, you will quote that part A, B, C or D (as the case may be) that contains the mistake. In case you find the whole sentence to be completely correct, your answer will be "E". The following examples will make you understand it practically :

(i) (A) We/(B) availed to/(C) the services of /(D) a lawyer for appeal. (E) All correct.

Answer with reasoning : (B) contains the mistake. It should be 'availed ourselves of' and not availed to; 'availed of' means benefited from or utilised.

(ii) (A) the parties/(B) agreed to/(C) the terms/(D) of the draft. (E) All correct

Answer with reasoning : A careful examination of the sentence leads us to the conclusion that there is no mistake in any part of this sentence.

Now answer the following questions:

1. (A) She was conscious to/(B) all that/(C) was going on/(D) around her./ (E) All correct

2. (A) The soldier aimed at/(B) the target and went on firing shots/(C) till it was hit rightly/(D) in the centre./(E) All correct

3. (A) Our mother told us fairy tales/(B) before we go to sleep/(C) in bed/ (D) and we do not miss to listen it any day./(E) All correct

4. (A) Mohan is ungrateful of/(B) his uncle for the moral/(C) and material support on his part/(D) to enable him continue higher studies./(E) All correct

5. (A) Early in the morning/(B) one enemy vessel had sunk in the sea/(C) off Bombay port/(D) in an encounter./(E) All correct

6. (A) The court awarded/(B) death sentence for/(C) all the three accused/ (D) in the triple murder case./(E) All correct

7. (A) We use to go/(B) to play hockey/(C) in the college ground/(D) every evening./(E) All correct

8. (A) This pen is better/(B) from your pen/(C) as it writes/(D) quite fluently./ (E) All correct

9. (A) I am interested/(B) to any subject which/(C) is dry and requires/ (D) hard labour to prepare for examination./(E) All correct

10. (A) The teacher entered the class room/(B) and asked the boys to/(C) do dictation/(D) at a higher speed./(E) All correct

11. (A) We do not want/(B) to go for/(C) participating into the rally on the/ (D) boat club./(E) All correct

12. (A) Floods has taken/(B) a toll of fifty lives/(C) in Uttar Pradesh and/ (D) have made much havoc in the state./(E) All correct

13. (A) There were long queues/(B) on the booking windows/(C) of cinema halls/(D) on the eve of Holi./(E) All correct

14. (A) Mohan was suffering with fever/(B) for the last three days/(C) and had not come/(D) to school./(E) All correct

15. (A) He was taken/(B) with surprise/(C) to see me wearing/(D) a new uniform./ (E) All correct

16. (A) The proceedings of the case/(B) were stalled with an order/(C) of the High Court, admitting/(D) a writ petition of the accused./(E) All correct

17. (A) If you are not conversant/(B) with the job/(C) how can you do your routine/(D) office work in that department./(E) All correct

18. (A) He got tired/(B) walking over/(C) a distance of ten kilometers and/ (D) avoided seeing people of talking to them./(E) All correct

19. (A) As soon as the captain/(B) alighted by the coach,/(C) the syce drove it away/(D) from the portico./(E) All correct

20. (A) He cannot distinguish/(B) in wrong and right/(C) and therefore he is very simple person,/(D) not a dishonest one./(E) All correct

21. (A) What do you think/(B) for the person/(C) I had recommended for a job/ (D) in your office./(E) All correct

22. (A) Make good preparation/(B) by studying hard/(C) to get from the university examination/(D) in first attempt./(E) All correct

23. (A) He was stabbed on the back/(B) and was removed to/(C) the hospital by the police/(D) in an ambulance./(E) All correct

24. (A) The thieves broke up the house/(B) while he had gone/(C) out of station/ (D) on a business tour./(E) All correct

25. (A) He was in need of money and/(B) sold his pen/(C) for Rs. 10/(D) to one of his friends./(E) All correct

26. (A) I am obliged with you/(B) and your entire family/(C) for showing kindness/ (D) and generosity towards us./(E) All correct

27. (A) Not only he, but/(B) also his sons were/(C) blamed for the./ (D) act and rightly so./(E) All correct

28. (A) The economical condition/(B) of our country is bad/(C) and unlikely to improve/(D) in the near future./ (E) All correct

29. (A) I and he will/(B) proceed on journey tomorrow/(C) as it is an auspicious day/(D) according to my father.(E) All correct

30. (A) He will certainly/(B) help you if/(C) you will ask him/(D) in a pleasant manner/(E) All correct

31. (A) The defence minister has said that/(B) India would not have spent so much on defence/(C) if some of the neighbouring countries./(D) adopted the policy of restricting defence expenditure./(E) All correct

32. (A) Being a nice day/(B) we visited the/(C) zoo where we found/(D) the spectacle of nature/(E) All correct

33. (A) He is well-known for both/(B) his kindness/(C) as well as./(D) his understanding./(E) All correct

34. (A) The waitor came to us/(B) and inform that no snacks/(C) were available but/(D) he could give us some cold drinks./(E) All correct

35. (A) It is necessary to check every passenger for security/(B) and do not load his luggage/(C) on to the aircraft/(D) unless he identifies it/(E) All correct

36. (A) In case you apologize/(B) for having /(C) broke your promise,/(D) I shall forgive you./(E) All correct

37. (A) His elder brother/(B) is afraid from /(C) of dogs though he./(D) is twenty years old./(E) All correct

38. (A) No sooner had he reached home/(B) than all the villagers/(C) gathered at his house/(D) to listen to his story./(E) All correct

39. (A) The instructor told me/(B) that if I/(C) took lessons regularly, I would/ (D) certainly get good marks./(E) All correct

40. (A) A cousin sister/(B) of the manager said that she would/(C) like to succeed him/(D) when his term expired./(E) All correct

EXPLANATORY ANSWERS

1. (B) It should be "conscious of" and not "conscious to".
2. (C) After "till", simple past tense is required.
3. (A) 'Told' should he replaced by 'tells'.
4. (A) It should be "ungrateful to" and not "ungrateful of".
5. (B) Simple part tense is required here.
6. (B) "for" should be replaced by 'of'.
7. (C) "used to" should be used in place of "use to."
8. (B) "from" should be replaced by "than".
9. (B) "interested in" is the correct prepositional phrase.
10. (C) Use "write" in place of "do".
11. (C) "participate in" is the correct prepositional phrase
12. (D) "has" is inappropriate here.
13. (B) "on" should be replaced by "at".
14. (A) "with" should be replaced by "from".
15. (B) "with" should be replaced by "by".
16. (B) "with" should be replaced by "by".
17. (E) The sentence is correct.
18. (B) "tired of" is the correct prepositional phrase.
19. (B) "by" should be replaced by "from".
20. (B) "in" should be replaced by "between".
21. (B) "think about (somebody)" should be the correct prepositional phrase.
22. (C) "by/through" should be used in place of "from".
23. (A) "on" should be replaced by "in".
24. (A) It should be "broke into" and not broke up.
25. (E) The sentence is correct.
26. (A) "obliged with" should be replaced by "obliged to".
27. (E) The sentence is correct.
28. (A) "economical" should be replaced by economic.
29. (A) "I and he" should be replaced by "he and I".
30. (C) Delete "will", because present tense is required here.
31. (D) "adopted" should be preceded by "had".

32. (C) "being a nice day" should be replaced by "it being a nice day".
33. (C) "as well as" should be replaced by "and".
34. (B) "inform" should be replaced by "informed".
35. (B) It should be "not to load."
36. (C) It should be "for having broken".
37. (B) "afraid of" should be used in place of "afraid form".
38. (A) No sooner + had + V_3 .... structure should be followed.
39. (C) "do" should be replaced by "died".
40. (A) "sister" is superfluous here.

SENTENCE ARRANGEMENT

Sentence arrangement is an important test of English language. The questions based on sentence arrangement consist of four parts 1, 2, 3, 4 of each of the sentence. These four parts of the sentence from four combinations out of which, one is correct. Therefore, the candidate is required to read each one of the fragments of the sentence very carefully and try to understand its meaning to reorganise them rightly in order to make a meaningful sentence. After that the candidate is expected to find out, which one of the four combinations is suitable. One should always keep it in mind that he or she will require adequate practices in order to be perfect in the skill of arranging the sentence. For example, a question of this kind has been illustrated here as :

1. From a distance 1/ of the Taj Mahal 2/ the beautiful dome 3/ can be seen 4/
(A) 3, 4, 2, 1 (B) 3, 1, 2, 4
(C) 3, 2, 4, 1 (D) 3, 4, 1, 2
Answer - (C)

Only option (C) makes a meaningful and systematic sentence, for it follows all the grammatical rules, which are as follows :
Adj. noun + of + noun + verb + complement. However other option do not follow any rule. Therefore, option(C) is appropriate.

Direction : *In the following questions, a disarranged sentence is given in which, words or phrases are given as 1, 2, 3 and 4. Arrange these parts to form meaningful sentences. Then, point out the correct combinations from amongst the options.*

1. In sports 1/ a killing 2/if you have the talent 3/you can make 4/
(A) 1, 2, 4,3 (B) 2, 4, 3, 1
(C) 4, 3, 2, 1 (D) 1, 3, 4, 2

2. In Kutch 1/ that law and order 2/ first hand reports suggest 3/ has completely broken down 4/
(A) 2, 1, 3, 4 (B) 4, 2, 1, 3
(C) 3, 2, 4, 1 (D) 3, 2, 1, 4

3. Defence Minister on Tuesday said 1/ could exceed one lakh 2/ that devastated Gujart 3/ the final toll in Friday's killer quake 4/
(A) 1, 4, 3, 2 (B) 4, 1, 2, 3
(C) 1, 3, 4, 2 (D) 4, 3, 2, 1

4. To keep awake 1/the city has not slept 2/and everyone has his own reason 3/ since Black Friday 4/

(A) 2, 3, 1, 4 (B) 4, 2, 1, 3
(C) 2, 4, 3, 1 (D) 1, 3, 2, 4

5. Who should be involved in the selection process 1/ and I think experienced players are the ones /2 out into the arean /3 the indian selectors have not been able to bring the best played /4

(A) 2, 1, 3, 4 (B) 4, 3, 2, 1
(C) 4, 2, 1, 3 (D) 2, 3, 4, 1

6. Indian skipper 1/ to promote himself 2/ would do well 3/ in batting order in Test Matches 4/

(A) 1, 3, 2, 4 (B) 1, 2, 3, 4
(C) 1, 2, 4, 3 (D) 4, 1, 2, 3

7. It would develop 1/ by the end of the year 2/ Japanese Video game maker on Wednesday said 3/ games for Palm Inc's handheld computers 4/

(A) 3, 2, 4, 1 (B) 1, 2, 4, 3
(C) 3, 1, 4, 2 (D) 3, 4, 2, 1

8. Of News and Events 1/ which is a popular magazine 2/ a dozen copies 3/ he has bought 4/

(A) 3, 4, 2, 1 (B) 1, 3, 4, 2
(C) 2, 4, 1, 3 (D) 4, 3, 1, 2

9. Why did you not deem fit 1/ while you were in power 2/ as a popularly elected leader 3/ to share this information with the people of the nation?/4

(A) 3, 1, 4, 2 (B) 1, 4, 2, 3
(C) 2, 4, 1, 3 (D) 3, 4, 2, 1

10. During your first tenure 1/ can you provide more examples of 2/ operated to destabilise democracy 3/ how the military establishment and the intelligence agencies 4/

(A) 2, 1, 3, 4 (B) 2, 3, 4, 1
(C) 4, 3, 1, 2 (D) 2, 4, 3, 1

11. Healthy and fresh 1/ a two-mile walk 2/ he says that 3/ always keeps him 4/

(A) 4, 2, 1, 3 (B) 3, 2, 4, 1
(C) 3, 2, 1, 4 (D) 1, 2, 4, 3

12. Medical treatment for a long time 1/ the doctor declared that 2/ the patient's intestine was 3/ not working properly and so he needed 4/

(A) 2, 3, 4, 1 (B) 1, 3, 4, 2
(C) 2, 4, 3, 1 (D) 3, 4, 2, 1

13. The beautiful surroundings I/ of the palace 2/ attracted a large number of tourists 3/ coming from abroad /4

(A) 3, 2, 1, 4 (B) 4, 2, 3, 1
(C) 1, 2, 3, 4 (D) 1, 2, 4, 3

14. The wall of this magnificent 1/ building is 2/ are very striking 3/ fifty feet high and its painting 4/

(A) 4, 3, 1, 2 (B) 1, 2, 4, 3

(C) 2, 1, 3, 4 (D) 4, 3, 1, 2

15. Not even 1/ to take drugs and drive 2/ basketball legends 3/ nobody has the licence 4/

(A) 1, 3, 2, 4 (B) 3, 2, 4, 1

(C) 4, 2, 1, 3 (D) 1, 2, 3, 4

16. At Lord's in 1932 was inevitable 1/ were so sublime that 2/ Amar Singh's performances in domestic cricket 3/ his selection and inclusion for India's debut Test 4/

(A) 3, 2, 4, 1 (B) 1, 2, 3, 4

(C) 4, 1, 2, 3 (D) 3, 4, 2, 1

17. Situation towards the end of the eighteenth century 1/ that woman's life was almost like that of a beast 2/ was so bad 3/ be used and beaten up like any other farm animals 4/

(A) 2, 3, 1, 4 (B) 1, 3, 4, 2

(C) 1, 4, 3, 2 (D) 1, 3, 2, 4

18. A young person Saurabh 1/ one day 2/ along with his friend Anjali 3/ come to his dispensary 4/

(A) 1, 3, 2, 4 (B) 1, 2, 4, 3

(C) 2, 1, 3, 4 (D) 1, 2, 3, 4

19. As soon as 1/ Amitabh and Rahul rushed in 2/ the patient came out 3/ from the doctor's cabin 4/

(A) 1, 3, 4, 2 (B) 2, 1, 4, 3

(C) 1, 2, 3, 4 (D) 4, 3, 1, 2

20. The limitation of western allopathic medicine 1/ during the last two decades 2/ have begun to discover 3/ physician and mental health professionals 4/

(A) 1, 2, 3, 4 (B) 4, 3, 2, 1

(C) 2, 3, 4, 1 (D) 2, 4, 3, 1

ANSWERS

1	2	3	4	5	6	7	8	9	10
D	C	A	C	B	A	C	D	A	D
11	**12**	**13**	**14**	**15**	**16**	**17**	**18**	**19**	**20**
B	A	C	B	C	A	D	C	A	D

COMPREHENSION

Read the following passages carefully and choose the best answer to each of the questions out of the four alternatives.

I

A British survey found that 44 per cent of firms, which started using robots, met with initial failure and 22 per cent abandoned them altogether, mainly because of inadequate technological know-how and skills at all plant levels.

Robotisation is by and large a viable proposition. These machines can work round the clock, raise output, protect quality and enhance industrial competitiveness.

One robot can replace between two and five production workers, while providing cheaper labour. In the US car industry, a man-hour costs around $ 23 but a robot-hour costs only $ 6.

Certain jobs, mostly simple or hazardous ones, are irretrievably lost to robotics. Thus spot welders, press operators, spray painters, cleaners, machine leaders and operator of grinding and polishing machines are endangered species.

QUESTIONS

1. In the first para the writer says that in view of initial failure :

(A) 50 per cent of the firms, which started using robots, abandoned them

(B) half of the 44 per cent of firms, which started using robots, stopped the practice

(C) 22 per cent of the total number of firms, which had used robots, abandoned their use

(D) British companies stopped the use of robots

2. In the second para, the word 'robotisation' is used in the sense of:

(A) making robots

(B) marketing robots

(C) introducing the use of robots

(D) total replacement of human workers with robots

3. 'A viable proposition' is :

(A) a workable idea

(B) a fanciful idea

(C) an imaginative idea

(D) an unworkable idea

4. Robots are a substitute for :

(A) planners

(B) production workers

(C) motor / cars

(D) any kind of labour

5. In the context of the passage, the expression "endangered species" means that :

(A) workers like spot welders are in danger

(B) robots might destroy the workers mentioned

(C) robots may replace the workers in future

(D) we may not get workers after a few years

II

The report that the union cabinet considered the draft of a Bill to prohibit the denigration of women in photographs, advertisement and films, is welcome. There has been for sometime, growing criticism of projection of women in these three media. Advertisement in the print media, as well as in films and television, frequently rely on feminine sex appeal to attract attention to products or to suggest that these products make Casanovas of ordinary mortals. Things are even worse in films. Some of these unabashedly rely on sex for box office success, showing scantily-attired women in provocative postures. In these, as well as in many advertisement, women clearly appear as objects of erotic stimulation. By showing heroes misbehaving with heroines and getting away with it, films invite emulation in real life and this results in the molestation of women in public places.

QUESTIONS

1. The passage says that the bill to prohibit media exploitation of women :

(A) has been made a law

(B) has been discussed in the Union Cabinet

(C) is being drafted

(D) is going to create a lot of controversy

2. 'Denigration' in the phrase 'denigration of women' means :

(A) abuse

(B) ill-treatment

(C) scandalizing

(D) tarnishing the good image

3. Feminine sex appeal is used in advertisement

(A) entertain the customers

(B) distract the customers' attention

(C) get the attention of prospective customers

(D) show how women at home would like the product

4. 'Unabashedly' means :

(A) with great shyness

(B) openly

(C) indifferently

(D) with no sign of being ashamed

5. The last sentence of the passage underlines :

(A) the healthy influence of films

(B) harmful effect of bad films

(C) the fact that films have nothing to do with a society's morals

(D) the need to teach morals through films

ANSWERS

Passage I

1	2	3	4	5
C	D	A	B	D

Passage II

1	2	3	4	5
C	D	C	B	B

IDIOMS & PHRASES

Directions: *In the following questions, four alternatives have been given for the bold idiom/phrase, choose the alternative, which best expresses the meaning of the bold idiom/phrase.*

1. I don't believe him, he has always **an axe to grind.**

(A) an intention of killing a man (B) a plan to work diligently

(C) an evil intention (D) a private end to serve

2. He left the town **under a cloud.**

(A) of his own accord (B) in disgrace

(C) with a heavy heart (D) when it wasy raining

3. He is an indifferent student. He is often **all at sea.**

(A) very knowledgeable (B) completely confused

(C) in a state of ignorance (D) in a state of shock

4. Biased umpiring can create **bad blood** between the two competing teams.

(A) violence (B) mischief

(C) suspicion (D) hostility

5. Through he challenged him for a match, he had to **eat a humble pie.**

(A) to starve (B) to carry on the battle

(C) to humiliate himself (D) be friendly

6. He sold his house **for a song.**

(A) at a reasonable price (B) at a discount

(C) very cheaply (D) at a premium

7. He went to his friend's house in the evening as **was his want.**

(A) as usual (B) as he wanted

(C) as his want was (D) as he wanted that day.

8. As a politician, he is used to being in the **limelight all the time.**

(A) giving speeches (B) the object of administration

(C) the centre of attraction (D) an object of public notice

9. Why must you look **a gift horse in the mouth ?**

(A) welcome a gift (B) find fault with a gift

(C) be fastidious (D) examine a gift carefully

10. Companies producing goods **play to the gallery to boost their sales.**

(A) advertise

(B) cater to the public taste

(C) attempt to appeal to the popular caste

(D) depend on the public for approval

11. The thief **took to heels** as he saw the police.

(A) ran away (B) moved back

(C) put on the shoes (D) put off the shoes

12. **In the long run**, honesty is the best policy.

(A) occasionally (B) usually

(C) ultimately (D) casually

13. After forty years of age, many ladies tent to **put on flesh.**

(A) wear bright clothes (B) be angry

(C) become light (D) grow fat

14. It is difficult for me to believe you, please put down everything in **black-and-white**

(A) simple expression (B) colourless way

(C) pictorial shape (D) written form

15. Very often, the ancestral property becomes a **bone of contention** among brothers.

(A) source of income (B) cause of quarrel

(C) back-bone of unity (D) pitfall for corruption

16. *Sodhus* are not interested in the question of **bailing out** one political party or another.

(A) pleasing (B) protecting

(C) promoiling (D) helping

17. Ram has **made amends** for insolance of his past.

(A) suffered (B) felt

(C) regretted (D) compensated for wrong or damage

18. Nobody prepared then for **winds of change.**

(A) changing conditions (B) different weather

(C) the hurricane (D) deteriorating state

19. The opposition will not **fight shy of** rejecting any economic policy that makes life difficult for the poorest of the poor.

(A) avoid (B) feel ashamed of

(C) be afraid of (D) hesitate

20. I told him that I was prepared to **show my hand** provided he also agreed to do the same.

(A) forget and forgive (B) fight it out

(C) agree to a settlement (D) reveal my plan of action

21. **"Too clever by half"** is what the director thought when Ram gave him some advice.

(A) deeply intelligent (B) superficial show of knowledge

(C) knows half the facts (D) party knowledgeable

22. It is not surprising to see a teacher in India living **from hand to mouth.**

(A) in miserly conditions

(B) in an independent way

(C) without any provision for the future

(D) without any regard for ideals

23. The escaped prisoner **was making for** the railway station.

(A) running towards (B) thinking of going to

(C) asking the way to (D) travelling towards

24. The detective went abroad in search of a culprit but his journey proved to be **a wild goose chase.**

(A) expensive (B) unprofitable adventure

(C) full of difficulties (D) ill-advised

25. He worked hard in his attempt to **keep the wolf from the door.**

(A) avert danger (B) remain happy

(C) protect himself (D) avoid starvation

ANSWERS

1	2	3	4	5	6	7	8	9	10
D	B	B	D	C	C	A	D	B	B
11	**12**	**13**	**14**	**15**	**16**	**17**	**18**	**19**	**20**
A	C	D	D	B	C	D	A	A	D
21	**22**	**23**	**24**	**25**					
B	A	A	D	D					

WORD POWER

Against each word (key word printed in CAPITAL letters) four meanings have been given in four options. Select and mark the one, which means almost nearly the same as the key word.

1. ARGUE
   (A) to talk loudly
   (B) to disobey
   (C) to dispute
   (D) to agree
2. BASIC
   (A) serious
   (B) deep
   (C) rough
   (D) fundamental
3. COLLUDE
   (A) to conspire
   (B) to conceal
   (C) to strike
   (D) to allege
4. DECEIVE
   (A) to falsify
   (B) to decline
   (C) to cheat
   (D) to entice
5. ENORMOUS
   (A) deadly
   (B) immense
   (C) hostile
   (D) definite
6. FIRMLY
   (A) permanently
   (B) forcefully
   (C) fondly
   (D) steadfastly
7. GAOL
   (A) destination
   (B) jail
   (C) garden
   (D) a sea-bird
8. HANDY
   (A) small
   (B) popular
   (C) portable
   (D) convenient
9. INDELIBLE
   (A) that cannot be effaced
   (B) that cannot be expanded
   (C) that cannot be delayed
   (D) that cannot be rectified
10. JOLLY
   (A) gay
   (B) peusive
   (C) talkative
   (D) buffoon
11. KIDNAP
   (A) to steal
   (B) to waylay
   (C) to ambush
   (D) to abduct
12. LEAST
   (A) meanest
   (B) smallest

(C) last
(D) farthest

13. MILD
(A) soft
(B) sharp
(C) cowardly
(D) docile

14. NAIVE
(A) unfurnished
(B) clever
(C) simple
(D) skilful

15. ONCE FOR ALL
(A) seldom
(B) immediately
(C) at one time
(D) finally

16. PERFUNCTORILY
(A) in a careless manner
(B) in a ceremonious fashion
(C) in a professional manner
(D) in a laborious manner

17. REDRESS
(A) to make reparation for
(B) to dress again
(C) to subdue again
(D) to describe again

18. SCANT
(A) not enough
(B) malicious
(C) progressive
(D) unplanned

19. TIMID
(A) shy
(B) boastful
(C) courageous
(D) fierce

20. VEX
(A) to implicate
(B) to exclude
(C) to appease
(D) to irritate

21. ACQUAINTANCE
(A) knowledge
(B) preference
(C) danger
(D) pretext

22. ANIMOSITY
(A) similarity
(B) honesty
(C) chastity
(D) hostility

23. ARID
(A) acrid
(B) fertile
(C) uninteresting
(D) unlawful

24. ACUMEN
(A) prudence
(B) accuracy
(C) a man with acute vision
(D) sharpness of mind

25. CATASTROPHE
(A) fierce battle
(B) ruin
(C) boom
(D) adversity

26. ESCHEW
(A) chew
(B) crumble

(C) to keep a secret

(D) abstain

27. ENIGMA

(A) openness

(B) mystery

(C) problem

(D) hard days

28. IMPUNITY

(A) free from any punishment

(B) purity

(C) frankness

(D) fallacy

29. LANGUOR

(A) wickedness

(B) fatigue

(C) length

(D) outery

30. MERETRICIOUS

(A) false

(B) deserving praise

(C) stern

(D) falsely attractive

31. MEAGRE

(A) much

(B) ordinary

(C) a bit

(D) sharp

32. NAUSEA

(A) cheerfulness

(B) calmness

(C) sickness

(D) sleepiness

33. OSCILLATE

(A) swing to and fro

(B) escalate

(C) erase

(D) fear

34. PAMORAMA

(A) constantly changing

(B) scene

(C) preference

(D) pungency

35. QUIESCENT

(A) motionless

(B) happy

(C) dreadful

(D) empty

36. QUINTESSENCE

(A) quotable example

(B) perfection

(C) move

(D) material

37. RAPPORT

(A) discord

(B) conflict

(C) dympathetic relationship

(D) noise

38. RETRIBUTION

(A) fluster

(B) vengeance

(C) condiment

(D) alacrity

39. SANGUINE

(A) severe

(B) hatred

(C) hopeful
(D) tolerant

40. STOICISM
(A) fearlessness
(B) great courage
(C) unemotionality
(D) rationality

ANSWERS

1	2	3	4	5	6	7	8	9	10
C	D	A	C	B	D	B	D	A	A
11	12	13	14	15	16	17	18	19	20
D	B	A	C	D	A	A	A	A	D
21	22	23	24	25	26	27	28	29	30
A	D	C	D	B	D	B	A	B	D
31	32	33	34	35	36	37	38	39	40
C	C	A	A	A	A	C	B	C	C

खण्ड I- अध्ययन सामग्री

अध्याय 1

हिन्दी भाषा और व्याकरण

भाषा

भाषा अभिव्यक्ति का समर्थ साधन है। इसका विकास कालान्तर में आवश्यकतानुसार हुआ है। संसार की सभी भाषाओं के बारे में यह तथ्य लागू होता है। आदिकाल से लेकर अब तक भाषा के अनेक रूप रहे हैं।

भाषा का नाम उसे दिया जाता है, जो आम जनता के व्यवहार में आती हो। इसमें लोक व्यवहार के शब्दों का बाहुल्य होता है। लिखने-पढ़ने और बोलने की भाषा में सामान्यतया अन्तर पाया जाता है। लिखने-पढ़ने की भाषा व्याकरण के नियमों से बँधी होती है और उसमें शुद्धाशुद्ध का ध्यान रखा जाता है। बोलने की भाषा में व्याकरण के नियमों का बन्धन अधिक कठोर नहीं होता।

हिन्दी भाषा के विकासक्रम में आरम्भ में अर्थात् आदि काल में हिन्दी भाषा पर अपभ्रंश का अधिक प्रभाव था। साथ ही देशज शब्दों के प्रयोग की भी भरमार थी। मध्यकाल में अपभ्रंश के स्थान पर संस्कृत का प्रयोग बढ़ने लगा और देशज शब्दों के स्थान पर तत्सम शब्दों का प्रयोग अधिक होने लगा। इस काल में ब्रज और अवधी का खूब विकास हुआ। 'खड़ी बोली' कही जाने वाली भाषा का विकास आधुनिक युग में हुआ। इस काल में गद्य-पद्य दोनों के लिए खड़ी बोली का प्रयोग हुआ।

आज हिन्दी–भाषी क्षेत्र में बोली जाने वाली प्रमुख बोलियाँ हैं– बाँगरू, खड़ी बोली, ब्रजभाषा, बुन्देली, कन्नौजी, अवधी, बघेली, छत्तीसगढ़ी और भोजपुरी।

मानव-व्यवहार विचारों के आदान-प्रदान के बिना नहीं चल सकता। संकेत कुछ हद तक ही विचारों के आदान-प्रदान का माध्यम बन सकते हैं। गूँगा आदमी लाख प्रयत्नों के बावजूद अपने मन की बात या भाव को पूरी तरह समझा सकने में असमर्थ होता है। अतः दूसरों की बात समझने और अपनी बात समझाने का समर्थ साधन भाषा ही है। भाषा का प्रयोग दो प्रकार से होता है– बोलकर और लिखकर। बोलने में ध्वनियों का सहारा लिया जाता है और लिखने में लिपि का व्यवहार होता है।

व्याकरण

व्याकरण वह विद्या है, जिससे भाषा का प्रयोग करना सीखा जाता है। यह विद्या हमें शुद्ध उच्चारण, शुद्ध लिखने, शुद्ध बोलने और शुद्ध पढ़ने का ज्ञान प्रदान करती है। व्याकरण में भाषा का वैज्ञानिक अध्ययन होता है। इसमें भाषा से जुड़े हुए नियम आदि होते हैं। व्याकरण के नियमों से भाषा का सर्वमान्य रूप निर्धारित होता है।

वर्ण–वर्ण का अर्थ है अक्षर। वर्ण या अक्षर वह मूल ध्वनि है जिसके खण्ड या टुकड़े नहीं किए जा सकते, जैसे अ, इ, उ आदि। वर्णों के समूह को वर्णमाला कहते हैं।

हिन्दी वर्णमाला में 46 वर्ण या अक्षर हैं–

स्वर–	अ आ इ ई उ ऊ ऋ ए ऐ ओ औ	(11 स्वर)
व्यंजन–	क ख ग घ ङ कवर्ग	
	च छ ज झ ञ चवर्ग	
	ट ठ ड ढ ण टवर्ग	(33 व्यंजन)
	त थ द ध न तवर्ग	
	प फ ब भ म पवर्ग	
	य र ल व श ष स ह	
अयोगवाह–	अं (अनुस्वार)	
	अः (विसर्ग)	

अनुस्वार और विसर्ग– अनुस्वार का चिन्ह (ं) है और विसर्ग का चिन्ह (:) है। ये दोनों व्यंजन हैं; क्योंकि इनका प्रयोग (उच्चारण) स्वर की सहायता के बिना नहीं किया जा सकता। ध्यान रहे कि चन्द्रबिन्दु (ँ) और अनुस्वार दोनों अलग-अलग हैं। चन्द्रबिन्दु (ँ) का उच्चारण मुँह और नासिका दोनों की मदद से होता है, जैसे हँसना। अनुस्वार का उच्चारण केवल नासिका से किया जाता है, जैसे हंस।

वर्ण दो प्रकार के होते हैं– स्वर और व्यंजन।

स्वर– स्वर मूल ध्वनि हैं। इन्हें किसी अन्य ध्वनि की सहायता के बिना उच्चरित किया जा सकता है, जैसे–अ, इ, उ। स्वरों की संख्या 11 है– अ, आ, इ, ई, उ, ऊ, ऋ, ए, ऐ, ओ और औ। उच्चारण में लगने वाले समय के अनुसार स्वरों को तीन भागों में बाँटा जा सकता है– (i) ह्रस्व स्वर, (ii) दीर्घ स्वर, और (iii) प्लुत स्वर। जिन स्वरों के उच्चारण में 'अ' के उच्चारण के बराबर समय लगता है, उन्हें ह्रस्व स्वर कहा जाता है। अ, इ, उ, ऋ ह्रस्व स्वर हैं। जिन स्वरों के उच्चारण में 'आ' के उच्चारण के बराबर समय लगता है, उन्हें दीर्घ स्वर कहा जाता है। आ, ई, ऊ, ओ और औ दीर्घ स्वर हैं। प्लुत स्वरों के उच्चारण में तीन मात्राओं के उच्चारण के बराबर समय लगता है। सतीश में 'ती' के उच्चारण और ओम में 'ओ' के उच्चारण में तीन मात्राओं के उच्चारण के बराबर समय लगता है।

रचना के आधार पर स्वरों को दो भागों में बाँटा जा सकता है– (i) मूल स्वर और (ii)

संयुक्त स्वर। मूल स्वर हैं– अ, इ, उ, ऋ और संयुक्त स्वर हैं– अ + अ = आ, अ + इ = ए, अ + ए = ऐ, अ + उ = ओ आदि।

व्यंजन– व्यंजन उन वर्णों को कहते हैं, जिनके उच्चारण में स्वरों की सहायता ली जाती हैं। क् + अ = क, च् + अ = च, त् + अ = त– ये सब व्यंजन के उदाहरण हैं। यहाँ क, च और त के उच्चारण में 'अ' की सहायता ली गई है।

हिन्दी में तीन संयुक्त व्यंजन हैं– क्ष, त्र, और ज्ञ। इनका निर्माण इस प्रकार होता है– क् + ष = क्ष; त् + र = त्र और ज् + ञ = ज्ञ।

व्यंजन तीन प्रकार के होते हैं– (i) स्पर्श, (ii) अन्तस्थ और (iii) ऊष्म। क से म तक 25 वर्ण स्पर्श कहलाते हैं; य, र, ल, व अन्तस्थ कहे जाते हैं और श, ष, स, ह ऊष्म कहे जाते हैं।

उच्चारण स्थान के आधार पर वर्णों का वर्गीकरण इस प्रकार होता है–

(1) **कण्ठ्य**– अ, आ, कवर्ग (क, ख, ग, घ, ङ), ह और विसर्ग के उच्चारण में जिह्वा कण्ठ छूती है।
क, ख, ग–इनका उच्चारण कण्ठ और जिह्वा मूल से होता है।

(2) **तालव्य**– इ, ई, चवर्ग (च, छ, ज, झ, ञ), य और श केवल तालु से बोले जाते हैं।

(3) **मूर्द्धन्य**– ऋ, टवर्ग (ट, ठ, ड, ढ ण), र, ष तथा ड़ और ढ़ का उच्चारण मूर्द्धा से होता है।

(4) **दन्त्य**– तवर्ग (त, थ, द, ध, न), ल और स का उच्चारण दाँतों के साथ जिह्वा के मेल से होता है।

(5) **ओष्ठ्य**– उ, ऊ (प, फ, ब, भ, म) का उच्चारण ओठों से होता है।

(6) **कण्ठन्तालु**– ए, ऐ का उच्चारण कण्ठ और तालु के मेल से होता है।

(7) **कण्ठोष्ठ**– ओ, औ का उच्चारण कण्ठ और ओठों के मेल से होता है।

(8) **दन्तोष्ठ**– व (फ) का उच्चारण दाँत और ओठों से होता है।

(9) **अनुनासिक**– ङ, ञ, ण, न, म का उच्चारण मुँह और नाक से होता है।

(10) **नासिका**– सभी अनुस्वार नाक से बोले जाते हैं।

शब्द

उन ध्वनियों को शब्द कहते हैं, जो एक या एक से अधिक वर्णों से मिलकर बनी हों और जिनका कुछ अर्थ निकलता हो।

अर्थ की दृष्टि से शब्द दो प्रकार के होते हैं– (1) सार्थक और (2) निरर्थक। सार्थक शब्द वे हैं, जिनसे किसी अर्थ का बोध होता हो, जैसे, कुत्ता, गाय, जंगल, कमीज, पुस्तक आदि। निरर्थक शब्द वे हैं, जिनसे किसी अर्थ का बोध नहीं होता, जैसे पशुओं और पक्षियों की आवाजें।

व्युत्पत्ति के आधार पर शब्दों के तीन भेद हैं– (i) रूढ़, (ii) यौगिक और (iii) योगरूढ़। रूढ़ शब्द उन्हें कहते हैं जो दूसरे शब्दों के मिलने से नहीं बनते; जिनकी अपनी स्वतंत्र स्थिति होती है और जिनके सार्थक खण्ड नहीं हो सकते। रूढ़ शब्दों के उदाहरण हैं–घर, जल, मोर, घोड़ा आदि। यौगिक शब्द उन्हें कहते हैं जो दो या दो से अधिक शब्दों के योग से बनते हैं और जिनके सार्थक खण्ड हो सकते हैं। यौगिक शब्दों के उदाहरण हैं– पाठशाला (पाठ + शाला), हिमालय (हिम + आलय) आदि। योगरूढ़शब्द उन्हें कहते हैं जो यौगिक हों और जिनका विशेष अर्थ निकलता हो। नीलकंठ योगरूढ़ है। इसमें नील + कंठ का योग है और इसका अर्थ है 'शिव'।

उत्पत्ति के आधार पर शब्दों के चार भेद किये जाते हैं– (i) तत्सम, (ii) तद्भव, (iii) देशज और (iv) विदेशी। तत्सम शब्द वे हैं, जो संस्कृत के हैं और हिन्दी में उन्हें ज्यों-का-त्यों प्रयोग किया जाता है, जैसे – मित्र, अग्नि आदि। तद्भव शब्द संस्कृत मूल के हैं, लेकिन हिन्दी में उन्हें कुछ बदल कर इस्तेमाल किया जाता है, जेसे – 'क्षेत्र' का 'खेत', 'दुग्ध' को 'दूध', 'चूर्ण' का 'चूरन' आदि। देशज शब्द संस्कृत मूल के नहीं हैं, जैसे – पेट, जिन्दगी आदि। विदेशी शब्द विदेशी भाषाओं के हैं, जिन्हें हिन्दी में स्वीकार कर लिया गया है, जैसे कोट, डॉक्टर, प्लेटफार्म आदि।

अर्थ के आधार पर शब्दों का वर्गीकरण इस प्रकार किया गया है– (i) वाचक, (ii) लाक्षणिक, (iii) व्यंजक। साधारण, लोक-प्रसिद्ध अर्थ देने वाले शब्दों को वाचक शब्द कहते हैं, जैसे– गौ भारत का पवित्र पशु है। यहाँ 'गौ' का जो सामान्य लोक-प्रसिद्ध अर्थ है, वह हम सभी समझते हैं। लाक्षणिक शब्द लोक-प्रसिद्ध अर्थ से हटकर लक्षण बोध कराता है, जैसे गोविन्द गधा है। यहाँ 'गधा' शब्द बुद्धिहीनता का द्योतक है। ऐसे शब्दों को व्यंजक कहते हैं, जो वाचक और लाक्षणिक अर्थ से हटकर व्यंजक अर्थ प्रकट करें, जैसे घंटी बज गई। इसका व्यंजक अर्थ है 'छुट्टी हो गई'।

वाक्य में प्रयोग के अनुसार शब्दों के आठ भेद हैं–

(1) संज्ञा, (2) सर्वनाम, (3) विशेषण, (4) क्रिया, (5) क्रिया-विशेषण, (6) संबंधबोधक, (7) योजक और (8) विस्मयादिबोधक।

इनके संबंध में अध्ययन करने से पूर्व हम संक्षेप में लिंग और वचन के बारे में पढ़ेंगे।

लिंग

हिन्दी में दो लिंग होते हैं– स्त्रीलिंग और पुल्लिंग। जो शब्द स्त्री जाति का बोध कराते हें, उन्हें स्त्रीलिंग कहा जाता है जैसे– राधा, लड़की, पुत्री, पुस्तक, शेरनी, चिड़िया आदि। इसके विपरीत जो शब्द पुरुष जाति का बोध कराते हैं, उन्हें पुल्लिंग कहा जाता है, जैसे– कृष्ण, शेर, बैल, गीदड़, पुत्र, लड़का। ध्यान रहे कि नपुंसक लिंग का प्रयोग संस्कृत में होता है, हिन्दी में नहीं होता।

कुछ शब्द जो प्रायः स्त्रीलिंग ही होते हैं–

(1) ईकारान्त शब्द। जैसे– चिट्ठी, पत्री, लेखनी, पोथी, बोली, गोली, चोली, डोली इत्यादि।

अपवाद– मोती, घी, जी, पानी आदि शब्द पुल्लिंग हैं।

(2) नदियों के नाम। जैसे– गंगा, यमुना, सरस्वती, रावी इत्यादि। प्रायः सभी नदियों के साथ नदी शब्द का प्रयोग किया जा सकता है।

(3) संस्कृत के स्त्रीलिंग और नपुंसक लिंग। जैसे– आशा, माता, दिशा इत्यादि।

(4) राशियों, तिथियों और नक्षत्रों के नाम। जैसे– मेष, वृष, मिथुन, कन्या, तीज, प्रतिपदा, आश्विन, रोहिणी आदि।

(5) **धातुओं के नाम जैसे– चाँदी, मिट्टी, धातु आदि।**

(6) **कुछ समुदायवाचक** संज्ञाएँ। जैसे– सेना, शाला, फौज, टोली, सभा, श्रेणी, कक्षा **इत्यादि।**

(7) **अनाज,** दालें इत्यादि। जैसे– अरहर, **मकई आदि।**

(8) कुछ प्राणीवाचक शब्द। जैसे– भगिनी, गाय, कोयल, चील, मैना, बिल्ली आदि।

कुछ शब्द जो प्रायः पुल्लिंग ही होते हैं-

(1) पर्वतों आदि के नाम। जैसे– हिमालय, शिवालिक, विंध्याचल आदि।

(2) भाववाचक संज्ञाएँ– जिनके अन्त में आव, पन, पा, त्व हों। जैसे– चढ़ावा, बहाव, बड़प्पन, बचपन, रंडापा, बुढ़ापा, महत्व, पुरुषत्व।

(3) महीने और दिनों के नाम। जैसे– ज्येष्ठ, बैसाख, चैत्र, मंगलवार, रविवार।

(4) ग्रहों के नाम। जैसे– मंगल, बुध, राहु, केतु आदि।

(5) वर्णमाला के सभी अक्षर – केवल इ, ई और ऋ को छोड़कर।

(6) संस्कृत के नपुंसक लिंग। जैसे– दही, मधु आदि।

(7) पेड़, अनाज सम्बन्धी शब्द। जैसे– बड़, पीपल, आम, चावल, गेहूँ, बाजरा उड़द।

(8) द्रव्यवाचक शब्द। जैसे– सोना, ताँबा, लोहा, मोती, माणिक आदि।

पुल्लिंग से स्त्रीलिंग बनाने के नियम–

(1) अकारान्त और आकारान्त शब्दों के अन्त में ई जोड़ देने से स्त्रीलिंग बन जाता है, जैसे–

नाना–नानी	लड़का–लड़की	दादा–दादी
चाचा–चाची	पुत्र–पुत्री	देव–देवी
गीदड़–गीदड़ी	कबूतर–कबूतरी	नट–नटी

(2) कुछ आकारान्त शब्दों के अन्त का 'आ' हटा कर 'इया' जोड़ दिया जाता है, जैसे–

चिड़ा–चिड़िया	चूहा–चुहिया	डिब्बा–डिबिया
कुत्ता–कुतिया	बेटा–बिटिया	बूढ़ा–बुढ़िया

(3) कुछ व्यवसाय-सूचक (अकारान्त, आकारान्त, इकारान्त) शब्दों के पीछे 'इन' प्रत्यय लगाकर स्त्रीलिंग बनाते हैं, जैसे–

जुलाहा–जुलाहिन धोबी–धोबिन कहार–कहारिन
माली–मालिन ठठेरा–ठठेरिन ग्वाला–ग्वालिन

(4) कुछ प्राणीवाचक शब्दों के पीछे 'नी' या 'इनी' प्रत्यय लगाया जाता है, जैसे–

हंस–हंसिनी जाट–जाटिनी हाथी–हथिनी
शेर–शेरनी

(5) कुछ प्राणीवाचक शब्दों के पीछे 'आनी' प्रत्यय भी लगाया जाता है, जैसे–

नौकर–नौकरानी जेठ–जेठानी देवर–देवरानी
चौधरी–चौधरानी सेठ–सेठानी मेहतर–मेहतरानी

(6) कुछ अकारान्त शब्दों के अन्त में 'आ' प्रत्यय लगाया जाता है, जैसे–

शिव–शिवा शूद्र–शूद्रा प्रिय–प्रिया
बाल–बाला सुत–सुता

(7) कुछ शब्दों के अन्त में 'वती' या 'मती' लगाया जाता है, जैसे–

भगवान्–भगवती गुणवान्–गुणवती श्रीमान्–श्रीमती
रूपवान्–रूपवती बुद्धिमान–बुद्धिमती धनवान्–धनवती

(8) कुछ उपनाम सम्बन्धी शब्दों के अन्त में 'आइन' प्रत्यय लगाया जाता है,

लाला–ललाइन ठाकुर–ठकुराइन बाबू–बबुआइन
दुबे–दुबाइन पण्डित–पण्डिताइन

(9) कुछ शब्दों के अन्त में 'अक' आता है। उनको स्त्रीलिंग बनाने के लिए 'अक' प्रत्यय का 'इका' कर लिया जाता है, जैसे–

अध्यापक–अध्यापिका सेवक–सेविका नायक–नायिका
बालक–बालिका प्रेषक–प्रेषिका लेखक–लेखिका

(10) कुछ शब्दों के अन्त में 'त्री' लगाने से स्त्रीलिंग बन जाता है। जैसे–

कवि–कवयित्री कर्ता–कर्त्री

(11) कुछ इकारान्त शब्दों के अन्त में 'ई' प्रत्यय को 'इ' करके और उसके बाद 'णी' जोड़कर स्त्रीलिंग बना लिया जाता है, जैसे–

परोपकारी–परोपकारिणी अधिकारी–अधिकारिणी
सहधर्मी–सहधर्मिणी कल्याणकारी–कल्याणकारिणी

(12) कुछ पुल्लिंग शब्दों के स्त्रीलिंग सर्वथा भिन्न होते हैं, जैसे–

पिता–माता वर–वधू राजा–रानी
विद्वान–विदुषी बेटा–बेटी पुत्र–पुत्री
भाई–बहन पति–पत्नी

वचन

वचन शब्द संख्या-द्योतक है। वचन दो होते हैं– (1) एकवचन और (2) बहुवचन।

जिस शब्द से एक संख्या का बोध हो, उसे एक वचन कहते हैं, जैसे– पुस्तक, लड़का, कुत्ता, घोड़ा, कमीज, सड़क आदि।

जिस शब्द से एक से अधिक संख्या को बोध हो, उसे बहुवचन कहते हैं, जैसे– पुस्तकें, लड़के, कुत्ते, घोड़े, कमीजें, सड़कें आदि।

बहुवचन बनाने के नियम–

(1) आकारान्त पुल्लिंग शब्दों में 'ए' जोड़ देने से वे बहुवचन बन जाते हैं, जैसे–
कपड़ा–कपड़े, घोड़ा–घोड़े, बेटा–बेटे

(2) आकारान्त स्त्रीलिंग शब्दों के अन्त में 'अ' को 'ए' कर देने से वे बहुवचन बन जाते हैं, जैसे–
आँख–आँखें, बहिन–बहिनें, सड़क–सड़कें

(3) आकारान्त स्त्रीलिंग शब्दों के अन्त में 'आ' के बाद 'ए' कर देने से वे बहुवचन बन जाते हैं, जैसे–
सूचना–सूचनायें कन्या–कन्याएँ माता–माताएँ

(4) इकारान्त और ईकारान्त शब्दों के अन्त में 'याँ' जोड़ देने से वे बहुवचन बन जाते हैं। ऐसा करते समय दीर्घ ई का इ हो जाता है, जैसे–
रीति–रीतियाँ पुत्री–पुत्रियाँ टोपी–टोपियाँ स्त्री–स्त्रियाँ

(5) जिन शब्दों के अन्त में 'या' हो, उनमें 'या' को याँ कर देने से बहुवचन बन जाता है, जैसे–
डिबिया–डिबियाँ गुड़िया–गुड़ियाँ

(6) उकारान्त, ऊकारान्त और ओकारान्त शब्दों के अन्त में 'एं' जोड़ देने से वे बहुवचन बन जाते हैं, जैसे–
बहू–बहुएँ गौ–गौएँ

(7) कुछ अकारान्त, आकारान्त और एकारान्त शब्दों को बहुवचन बनाने के लिए उनके अन्त में 'ओ' लगा देते हैं, जैसे–
लड़का–लड़कों चोर–चोरों
कुछ विदेशी शब्दों के बहुवचन इस प्रकार होते हैं:–
स्टेशन–स्टेशनों लालटेन–लालटेनों

कुछ विशेष नियम–

(1) बहुवचन बनाने के लिए गण, जन, लोग आदि जोड़ लिए जाते हैं। जैसे– पाठक से पाठकगण। आर्य से आर्यजन। क्षत्रिय से क्षत्रिय लोग।

(2) आदर प्रकट करने के लिए एकवचन को बहवचन की भाँति प्रयक्त करते हैं। **जैसे– दादाजी आये हैं। भगवान शकर जग क कल्याणकारा थ। ऋाष दयानन्द संसार का उद्धार करने के लिए आए थे।**

(3) केवल क्रिया को एकवचन से बहुवचन बनाने पर कत्ता और कर्म आदि शब्द

बहुवचन बन जाते हैं। जैसे मनुष्य (एकवचन) जाता है। मनुष्य (बहुवचन) जाते हैं। सतीश ने आम (एकवचन) खाया। सतीश ने आम (बहुवचन) खाये।

संज्ञा

जो शब्द किसी व्यक्ति, वस्तु स्थान आदि का बोध कराते हैं, उन्हें संज्ञा कहते हैं, जैसे– शुभा, मनुष्य, कुर्सी, बाजार, पाठशाला, रंगमंच, पुस्तक आदि।

संज्ञा के पाँच भेद होते हैं– (1) व्यक्तिवाचक संज्ञा, (2) जातिवाचक संज्ञा, (3) समुदायवाचक संज्ञा, (4) द्रव्यवाचक संज्ञा और (5) भाववाचक संज्ञा।

व्यक्तिवाचक संज्ञा– उस संज्ञा को कहते हैं, जो किसी विशेष स्त्री, पुरुष अथवा स्थान का बोध कराये, जैसे– मालिनी, सतीश, बनारस आदि।

जातिवाचक संज्ञा– उस संज्ञा को कहते हैं जो किसी एक जाति की वस्तुओं, मनुष्यों आदि का बोध कराये, जैसे– स्त्री, पुरुष, जानवर, नदी, पुस्तक, पर्वत, मकान आदि।

समुदायवाचक संज्ञा– उस संज्ञा को कहते हैं जो किसी समुदाय या समूह का बोध कराये, जैसे– सेना, कक्षा, संघ आदि।

द्रव्यवाचक संज्ञा- उस संज्ञा को कहते हैं, जो किसी द्रव्य (धातु) का बोध कराये, जैसे– सोना, लोहा, ताँबा, तेल, पानी आदि।

भाववाचक संज्ञा– उस संज्ञा को कहते हैं, जो किसी पदार्थ के गुण, दोष, अवस्था, कार्य-व्यापार आदि का बोध कराये, जैसे– दया, चोरी, दुबे, सुख, दुख, यौवन, बचपन आदि।

जातिवाचक संज्ञा, सर्वनाम, विशेषण और क्रिया से भाववाचक संज्ञा बना सकते हैं, जैसे– पशु से पशुता, शत्रु से शत्रुता, लड़का से लड़कपन, मनुष्य से मनुष्यता, अपना से अपनापन, निज से निजत्व, मीठा से मिठास, मूर्ख से मूर्खता, चढ़ना से चढ़ाई, पढ़ना से पढ़ाई, सजाना से सजावट आदि।

कारक– संज्ञा या सर्वनाम के जिस रूप से वाक्य के दूसरे शब्दों के साथ सम्बन्ध जाना जाये, उसे कारक कहते हैं। संज्ञा या सर्वनाम के साथ जो शब्द लगाये जाते हैं, उन्हें विभक्ति कहते हैं, जैसे– राम ने फल खाया। गोविन्द को पाठशाला जाना है।

हिन्दी में आठ कारक हैं–

	कारक	**विभक्ति (चिन्ह)**
1.	कर्त्ता	ने (राम ने खाया)
2.	कर्म	को (हरी ने कुत्ते को बचाया)
3.	करण	से, के द्वारा (माध्यम से) (बाण से मारा; पेन से लिखा)
4.	सम्प्रदान	को, के लिए, के वास्ते (सुधा के लिए फल खरीदो)
5.	अपादान	से (पृथक करने के लिए) (आसमान से गिरा; पेंड़ से पत्ता गिरा।)
6.	सम्बन्ध	का, के, की : ना, ने, नी (लड़के का भाई; लड़के के दोस्त)
7.	अधिकरण	में, पर (कमरे में, सड़क पर, टेबुल पर)
8.	सम्बोधन	हे!, हो!, अरे!, हा!, ओ! (हे राम! रक्षा करो।)

सर्वनाम

सर्वनाम उन शब्दों को कहते हैं, जिनका प्रयोग संज्ञा के स्थाान पर किया जाता है, जैसे– राम परिश्रम करेगा, तो वह अवश्य सफल होगा। इसी प्रकार मैं, हम, आप, तुम, वे आदि भी सर्वनाम हैं।

सर्वनाम छः प्रकार के होते हैं– 1. पुरुषवाचक सर्वनाम, 2. निजवाचक सर्वनाम 3. निश्चयवाचक सर्वनाम, 4. अनिश्चयवाचक सर्वनाम, 5. सम्बन्धवाचक सर्वनाम और 6. प्रश्नवाचक सर्वनाम।

पुरुषवाचक सर्वनाम उन्हें कहते हैं, जिनसे वक्ता, श्रोता या प्रसंगाधीन व्यक्ति का बोध होता है। पुरुषवाचक सर्वनाम तीन प्रकार के होते हैं– (i) उत्तम पुरुष (ii) मध्यम पुरुष (iii) अन्य पुरुष। उत्तम पुरुष के उदाहरण हैं– मैं, हम; मध्यम पुरुष के उदाहरण हैं– आप, तुम; और अन्य पुरुष के उदाहरण हैं– वह, वे आदि।

निजवाचक सर्वनाम उन्हें कहते हैं। जिससे स्वयं अर्थ का बोध हो जाता है, जैसे– आप, स्वयं, खुद।

निश्चयवाचक सर्वनाम उन्हें कहते हैं, जो किसी वस्तु विशेष का निश्चय करते हैं, जैसे– यह, वह, ये, वे आदि।

अनिश्चयवाचक सर्वनाम उन्हें कहते हैं, जो किसी वस्तु का निश्चय न करें, जैसे– सब, कुछ और कोई।

सम्बन्धवाचक सर्वनाम उन्हें कहते हैं, जो पहले या बाद के उपवाक्य में आये संज्ञा या सर्वनाम से सम्बन्ध बताये और दोनों उपवाक्यों को जोड़ें, जैसे– जो जैसा करेगा, वह वैसा भरेगा।

प्रश्नवाचक सर्वनाम उन्हें कहते हैं, जिनका प्रयोग किसी बारे में प्रश्न करने के लिए किया जाए, जैसे– क्या, कौन।

विशेषण

जो शब्द संज्ञा या सर्वनाम की विशेषता प्रकट करत हैं, उन्हें विशेषण कहते हैं, जैसे– सुन्दर, मोटा, काला, ऊँचा, भव्य आदि। विशेषण जिस संज्ञा या सर्वनाम की विशेषता बताते हैं, उसे विशेष्य कहते हैं। 'सुन्दर बाग' में सुन्दर विशेषण है और बाग विशेष्य है।

विशेषण चार प्रकार के होते हैं–

1. गुणवाचक विशेषण, 2. संख्यावाचक विशेषण, 3. परिमाणवाचक विशेषण और 4. संकेतवाचक विशेषण।

गुणवाचक विशेषण उसे कहते हैं जो किसी संज्ञा या सर्वनाम के गुण, रंग, आकार, अवस्था आदि का बोध कराये, जैसे– लाल, पीला, दुबला, मोटा, सुशील, दुष्ट, भारतीय, जापानी, ऊँचा, नीचा आदि।

संख्यावाचक विशेषण उसे कहते हैं, जो संज्ञा या सर्वनाम की संख्या, गणनाक्रम, समूह आदि का बोध करते हैं, जैसे– **चार** कि॰ग्रा॰, **दो** हाथी, **तीसरा** मकान।

संख्यावाचक विशेषण तीन प्रकार के होते हैं–

(i) निश्चित सख्यावाचक विशेषण, (ii) अनिश्चित संख्यावाचक विशेषण, (iii) विभाग वाचक विशेषण।

(i) निश्चित संख्यावाचक, जैसे– एक, दो, तीन, पहला, दूसरा, तीसरा, दोगुना, चौगुना, दोनों, तीनों आदि।

(ii) अनिश्चित संख्यावाचक, जैसे– बहुत, कुछ, थोड़ा आदि।

(iii) विभाग वाचक, जैसे– प्रत्येक, हर एक आदि।

परिमाणवाचक विशेषण उसे कहते हैं, जो किसी संज्ञा या सर्वनाम का **परिमाण** बताये, जैसे– **थोड़ा** दूध, **अधिक** वर्षा आदि।

संकेतवाचक विशेषण उसे कहते हैं, जो संज्ञा या सर्वनाम की ओर संकेत करे, जैसे– ऐसा, उस, यह, वैसा, उतना, जो, जिस, आदि।

विशेषण बनाने की रीति–संज्ञा के अन्त में ई, भर, भरा, युक्त, मान्, रूपी, शाली, रहित, वाला, पूर्वक, हरी, हरा, हीन, सा आदि लगा देने से विशेषण बन जाता है। जैसे–बुद्धिहीन, शक्तिशाली, स्नेहपूर्वक, ज्ञानरहित, घोड़ेवाला, गुणवान्, गुणी, बुद्धिमान, कटोराभर, रसभरा, पशुरूपी, स्नेहयुक्त, सुनहरी, सुनहरा आदि।

विशेषणों के रूप में परिवर्तन–हिन्दी में लिंग और वचन के कारण विशेषण के रूप में परिवर्तन आ जाता है। जैसे–छोटा लड़का, छोटे लड़के, छोटी लड़की। परिवर्तन के नियम निम्न हैं:

(क) अकारान्त और उकारान्त शब्दों में कोई अन्तर नहीं होता। जैसे–सुशील लड़का, सुशील लड़की, भीरु स्त्री, भीरु स्त्रियाँ, भीरु आदमी आदि।

(ख) अकारान्त शब्द का 'आ' स्त्रीलिंग में 'ई' और पुल्लिंग में 'ए' हो जाता है। जैसे–काला कुत्ता, काले कुत्ते; काली घोड़ी, काली घोड़ियाँ आदि।

क्रिया

जिस शब्द से किसी कार्य के होने का बोध हो, उसे क्रिया कहते हैं। जैसे– वह लिखता है। इसमें *लिखना* शब्द क्रिया का द्योतक है।

(हर वाक्य में क्रिया का होना अनिवार्य होता है।)

क्रियाएँ दो प्रकार की होती हैं– (i) अकर्मक और (ii) सकर्मक।

(i) अकर्मक क्रिया–उसे कहते हैं जिसका कर्म नहीं होता और जिसका फल व प्रभाव कर्त्ता पर ही पड़ता है, जैसे– वह जाता है, वे खेलते हैं, तुम रोते हो, लड़कियाँ खेलती हैं, राम सोता है, पूर्णिमा हँसती है।

(ii) सकमर्क क्रिया–उसे कहते हैं, जिसका प्रभाव या फल कर्म पर पड़े; अर्थात् सकर्मक क्रिया के साथ कर्म होता है, जैसे–राम पुस्तकें पढ़ता है, राम ने रावण को मारा।

कुछ अकर्मक क्रियाओं को सकर्मक बनाया जा सकता है, जैसे–पिसना से पिसाना और गड़ना से गाड़ना आदि।

क्रिया के सम्बन्ध में जानने के साथ ही हम काल के सम्बन्ध में भी कुछ जान लें।

काल– काल क्रिया का समय काल बताता है। काल तीन होते हैं– (i) भूतकाल, (ii) वर्तमान काल और (iii) भविष्यत् काल।

यदि क्रिया पहले हो चुकी हो, तो वह भूतकाल होता है, जैसे उसने पत्र लिख लिया; वह

दिल्ली गया था; वे सो रहे थे।

यदि क्रिया इस समय हो रही हे तो वह वर्तमान काल होता है, जैसे– बच्चे खेलते हैं, मैं पढ़ रहा हूँ।

यदि क्रिया आगे आने वाले समय में होने वाली हो, तो वह भविष्यत् काल होता है, जैसे– मैं जाऊँगा, वह खेलेगा।

क्रिया के लिंग, वचन और पुरुष– क्रिया के लिंग, वचन और पुरुष कहीं कर्त्ता के अनुसार, कहीं कर्म के अनुसार और कहीं अपने स्वाधीन ढंग से होते हैं।

क्रिया-विशेषण

क्रिया-विशेषण ऐसे शब्द होते हैं, जिनसे क्रिया की विशेषता विदित हो। इन शब्दों (क्रिया-विशेषणों) का रूप बदलता नहीं, अतः इन्हें अविकारी और अव्यय भी कहते हैं। जोर से, कल, धीरे-से, वैसा, जैसा, सचमुच, ऊपर, नीचे, भीतर, बाहर, अवश्य, ठीक, नहीं, अतः अतएव, किसलिए, अचानक, निकट, क्रमश, ज्यों, त्यों, बहुधा, सुबह, शाम, एकदम आदि क्रिया-विशेषण के उदाहरण हैं।

क्रिया-विशेषण स्थानवाचक, कालवाचक, रीतिवाचक और परिमाणवाचक होते हैं। स्थान वाचक क्रिया विशेषण स्थान या स्थिति का बोध कराते हैं, जैसे पास, दूर, यहाँ, वहाँ, सामने, नीचे, दायें, बायें, इधर, उधर आदि।

कालवाचक क्रिया-विशेषण काल (समय) का बोध कराते हैं, जैसे आज, कल, सदा, शीघ्र, प्रायः, दिन भर, सबेरे, अब, कब, तभी आदि। रीतिवाचक क्रिया-विशेष्ण क्रिया की अवस्था (स्थिति) का बोध कराते हैं, जैसे धीरे-धीरे, अचानक, अच्छी तरह आदि। परिमाणवाचक क्रिया-विशेषण परिमाण या मात्रा का बोध कराते हैं, जैसे मात्र, थोड़ा, बहुत, तनिक, इतना, उतना आदि।

संबंधबोधक

संज्ञा या सर्वनाम के साथ संबंध स्थापित करने हेतु उनके ठीक बाद में जोड़े जाने वाले शब्द संबंधबोधक कहलाते हैं, जैसे ने, को, से, के लिए, का, के, की आदि

योजक

संज्ञा या सर्वनाम का दूसरे शब्दों के साथ संबंध स्थापित करने हेतु उनके बाद में इस्तेमाल किए जाने वाले शब्द योजक कहे जाते हैं, जैसे और, एवं, तथा, जो आदि।

विस्मयादि बोधक

हर्ष, शोक आश्चर्य, घृणा आदि भावों को व्यक्त करने वाले शब्द विस्मयादि बोधक कहलाते हैं, जैसे अहा, वाह-वाह (हर्ष), अरे! हैं! क्या (आश्चर्य), हाय, आह, उफ (शोक), छिः, थू, धिक्कार (घृणा)।

अध्याय 2

वर्तनी

लिखने में वर्तनी का बड़ा महत्व है। विद्यार्थी लिखने में प्रायः वर्तनी की अशुद्धियाँ करते हैं। इन अशुद्धियों से बचने का यही उपाय है कि शुद्ध वर्तनी का ज्ञान हो। नीचे कुछ शब्दों की शुद्ध और अशुद्ध वर्तनियाँ दी जा रही हैं। इन्हें पढ़कर सही वर्तनी समझ लें और इसका अभ्यास करें। बाद में शुद्ध वर्तनी के सम्बन्ध में प्रश्न दिए गए हैं।

साधारण अशुद्धियाँ

अशुद्ध	**शुद्ध**	**अशुद्ध**	**शुद्ध**
मुनी	मुनि	ह्विदय	हृदय
साधू	साधु	क्रितज्ञ	कृतज्ञ
दुध	दूध	ऋन	ऋण
निरिप	नृप	प्रिथ्वी	पृथ्वी
बहूत	बहुत	त्रण	तृण
हिन्दु	हिन्दू	म्रिग	मृग
क्रषि	कृषि	श्रृष्टि	सृष्टि
विधी	विधि	उक्ती	उक्ति
उत्पती	उत्पत्ति	शुद्धी	शुद्धि
रवी	रवि	वृद्धी	वृद्धि
छवी	छवि	ऋिषि	ऋषि
आदी	आदि	कवी	कवि
अधिन	अधीन	विपत्ती	विपत्ति
अती	अति	योज्ञ	योग्य
मनू	मनु	घनिष्ट	घनिष्ठ
रूचि	रुचि	अत्याधिक	अत्यधिक
घ्रित	घृत	पौत्रिक	पैतृक
क्रिपा	कृपा	रुग्न	रुग्ण
किर्या	क्रिया	शिक्क्षा	शिक्षा
आपत्ती	आपत्ति	दीक्क्षा	दीक्षा
पुत्रि	पुत्री	व्योहार	व्यवहार

अशुद्ध	शुद्ध
आचर्य	आचार्य
प्रन्तु	परन्तु
प्रांगन	प्रांगण
विशाद	विषाद
बृजभाषा	ब्रजभाषा
प्रतयुत	प्रत्युत
पर्गट	प्रकट
धियान	ध्यान
पक्क्ष	पक्ष
नमश्कार	नमस्कार
तिरष्कार	तिरस्कार
निश्फल	निष्फल
महतव	महत्त्व
भग्त	भक्त
पुरश्कार	पुरस्कार
रामायन	रामायण
भगीरथी	भागीरथी
अभिशेक	अभिषेक
लक्क्षमन	लक्ष्मण
आरोज्ञ	आरोग्य
प्रत्यन	प्रयत्न
संष्कृत	संस्कृत
पछ्छी	पक्षी

त्र की अशुद्धियाँ

पवितृ	पवित्र
पतृ	पत्र
पतृका	पत्रिका
विचितृ	विचित्र

ण की अशुद्धियाँ

हरन	हरण
शरन	शरण
आचरन	आचरण

अशुद्ध	शुद्ध
ग्रामीन	ग्रामीण
अपर्न	अर्पण
गृहण	ग्रहण

र की अशुद्धियाँ

करम	कर्म
धरम	धर्म
परव	पर्व
विकर्म	विक्रम
दरशन	दर्शन
पर्भाव	प्रभाव
अरक	अर्क
परवत	पर्वत

श, ष, स की अशुद्धियाँ

शेश	शेष
दोश	दोष
समरपण	समर्पण
हर्श	हर्ष
श्नेह	स्नेह
शश्त्र	शस्त्र
श्नान	स्नान
कुषल	कुशल
पुरुश	पुरुष

अन्य सामान्य अशुद्धियाँ

अस्नान	स्नान
ग्यानी	ज्ञानी
द्रष्टि	दृष्टि
पुश्टि	पुष्टि
संग्या	संज्ञा
विग्य	विज्ञ
विग्यापन	विज्ञापन
अनुवादित	अनूदित
अकस्मात्	आकस्मात

अशुद्ध	शुद्ध	अशुद्ध	शुद्ध
अन्तेष्टि	अन्त्येष्टि	प्रतीकार	प्रतिकार
उषा	ऊषा	प्रशाद	प्रसाद
क्षत्र	छत्र	दंपति	दम्पत्ति
क्षात	छात्र	दवक्ष	दक्ष
तृकाल	त्रिकाल	धनुस	धनुष
छमा	क्षमा	मध्यान्ह	मध्याह्न
छमिय	क्षमिय	यसस्वी	यशस्वी
निकलंक	निष्कलंक	रिण	ऋण
निर्वान	निर्वाण	रिशि	ऋषि
निसन्देह	निस्संदेह	विषेश	विशेष
निष्चेष्ठ	निश्चेष्ट	व्रिद्धि	वृद्धि
परिक्षा	परीक्षा	समवेदना	सम्वेदना
प्रक्रिति	प्रकृति	सन्सकार	संस्कार
प्रतिद्वन्दी	प्रतिद्वन्द्वी	सौहाद्र	सौहार्द

अध्याय 3

उपसर्ग और प्रत्यय

उपसर्ग

उपसर्ग (prefix) शब्दांश होते हैं। इनका प्रयोग स्वतंत्र रूप से नहीं किया जा सकता। किसी शब्द के प्रारंभ में उपसर्ग जोड़ने से उस शब्द का अर्थ बदल जाता है। हिन्दी का शब्द **अज्ञान** है। इसमें अ उपसर्ग है। ज्ञान शब्द में अ उपसर्ग जोड़ कर अज्ञान बना है। अ उपसर्ग जोड़ने से ज्ञान शब्द का अर्थ उल्टा हो गया है। इसी प्रकार कर्म शब्द में कु उपसर्ग जोड़ने से कुकर्म शब्द बन जाता है, जिसका अर्थ कर्म से भिन्न हो गया है। गुण शब्द में अव उपसर्ग जोड़ने से अवगुण शब्द बनता है। उपसर्ग लगाकर नए-नए शब्द बनाये जाते हैं। अतः इसका अध्ययन महत्त्वपूर्ण है।

चूंकि हिन्दी में संस्कृत और अरबी-फारसी के शब्दों का भी प्रयोग होता है, अतः इनके उपसर्गों के बारे में भी जानना आवश्यक है।

1. संस्कृत उपसर्ग

यहाँ संस्कृत के केवल उन्हीं उपसर्गों को दिया जा रहा है, जिनका प्रयोग हिन्दी में बिना झिझक होता है।

अति (अर्थ = अधिक या परे)– अतिवृष्टि, अतिक्रमण, अतिमानव, अतिशय

अधिक (अर्थ = ऊपर या अधिक)– अधिराज, अधिनायक, अधिकरण, अधिमास

अनु (अर्थ = पीछे या समान)– अनुताप, अनुकरण, अनुज, अनुकूल, अनुचर

अप (अर्थ = बुरा, उल्टा)– अपयश, अपशकुन, अपव्यय अपकर्ष, अपशब्द

अभि (अर्थ = विशेष, पास)– अभिवादन, अभिभाषण, अभिमुख, अभीष्ट, अभिशंसा, अभिराम

अव (अर्थ = बुरा, उल्टा)– अवगुण, अवरोध, अवलोकन अवनति, अवसाद, अवज्ञा

आ (अर्थ = तक, से)– आजन्म, आमरण, आरंभ, आकर्षण, आमोद

उत् (अर्थ = ऊपर, श्रेष्ठ)– उत्कर्ष, उन्माद, उल्लास, उत्थान, उत्कृष्ट, उत्सर्ग, उन्नति

उप (अर्थ = पास (निकट), सहायक (छोटा)– उपनिषद, उपन्यास, उपमंत्री, उप-समिति, उपभेद

दुः (अर्थ = कठिन, बुरा, विपरीत)– दुर्गम, दुर्जेय दुर्लभ दुर्जन, दुर्गुण, दुर्गति, दुस्साहस, दुर्दशा, दुराशा

नि (अर्थ = विशेष, निषेध)– निपुण, निवास, नियोजन, निषेध, निरोध, निलम्बन

निः (अर्थ = बिना)– निरादर, निर्दोष, निराकार, निरुपाय, निर्बल, नीरव, निर्विरोध, निष्फल

परि (अर्थ = चारों ओर)– परिक्रमा, परिधान, परिधि, पर्यावरण

प्र (अर्थ = आगे, अधिक)– प्रगति, प्रचार, प्रचुर, प्रगाढ़, प्रबल

प्रति (अर्थ = विपरीत, प्रत्येक)– प्रतिवादी, प्रतिकूल, प्रतिवाद, प्रतिदिन, प्रत्येक, प्रतिशत

वि (अर्थ = विशेष)– विख्यात, विज्ञान, विनय, विभेद, विकृत

सम् (अर्थ = पूर्ण, शुद्ध, साथ)– सम्पूर्ण, सन्तोष, सन्लग्न, सम्पर्क, समन्वय

सु (अर्थ = अच्छा, विशद)– सुमार्ग, सुगन्ध, सुजन, सुगति, सुलभ, सुशील, सुपरिचित

2. अरबी-फारसी के उपसर्ग

अल – अलमस्त

ऐन (अर्थ = ठीक) – ऐनवक्त, ऐनमौका

कम (अर्थ = न्यून) – कमअक्ल, कमसिन

खुश (अर्थ = अच्छा) – खुशखबरी, खुशबू, खुशकिस्मत

गैर (अर्थ = बिना) – गैर-कानूनी, गैर-जिम्मेदार

ब (अर्थ = साथ) – बमुश्किल, बदस्तूर, बतौर, बखूबी

बद (अर्थ = बुरा) – बदचलन, बदनाम, बदबू, बदकिस्मत

बा (अर्थ = के साथ) – बाकायदा, आअदब, बाइज्ज़त

बे (अर्थ = बिना) – बेहद, बेदर्द, बेचारा, बेलाग, बेवफा

ला (अर्थ = बिना) – लापता, लावारिस, लाइलाज

ना (अर्थ = बिना) – नाखुश, नापाक, नापसन्द, नालायक

हम (अर्थ = समान) – हमदर्द, हमवतन, हमसफर

3. हिन्दी उपसर्ग

अ (अर्थ = नहीं, बिना, विहीन) – अचेत, अपच, अचल, अटल

अन (अर्थ = बिना) – अनहित, अनमेल, अनपढ़, अनहोनी

अध (अर्थ = आधा) – अधपका, अधमरा, अधजला

कु (अर्थ = बुरा) – कुपूत, कुठौर

नि (अर्थ = बिना) – निडर, निकम्मा

सु (अर्थ = अच्छा) – सुजन, सुघड़, सुडौल

भर (अर्थ = पूरा, भरके) – भरपूर, भरपेट, भरसक

प्रत्यय

उपसर्ग (prefix) की ही भाँति प्रत्यय (suffix) भी स्वतंत्र रूप से प्रयोग में नहीं आते, पर शब्द के बाद में इनको जोड़ देने से शब्द के अर्थ में परिवर्तन आ जाता है। उपसर्गों की भाँति ही प्रत्यय लगाकर नए-नए शब्द बनाये जाते हैं। अतः इनका अध्ययन महत्त्वपूर्ण है।

प्रत्यय दो प्रकार के होते हैं– **कृत् प्रत्यय** और **तद्धित प्रत्यय।** कृत प्रत्यय धातु के अन्त में लगते हैं और उनसे निर्मित शब्दों को कृदन्त कहा जाता है। तद्धति प्रत्यय संज्ञा, सर्वनाम और विशेषण के अन्त में लगते हैं और उनसे बनने वाले शब्द तद्धितान्त कहलाते हैं।

कृत प्रत्यय

हिन्दी में 5 प्रकार के कृत प्रत्यय हैं–(i) कर्तृवाचक, (2) कर्मवाचक, (3) कारकवाचक, (4) भाववाचक, (5) क्रियावाचक।

1. कर्तृवाचक

अक = जात से जातक
लिख से लेखक
पाठ से पाठक

आऊ = चल से चलाऊ
टिक से टिकाऊ
दिख से दिखाऊ

आकू = लड़ से लड़ाकू
पढ़ से पढ़ाकू

ई = हँस से हँसी
बोल से बोली

ता = दा से दाता
भा से भाता
ज्ञा से ज्ञाता
श्रु से श्रोता

2. कर्मवाचक

औना = खेल से खिलौना
बिछ से बिछौना

ना = गा से गाना
दा से दाना

नी = चल से चलनी
ओढ़ से ओढ़नी

3. करणवाचक

आ = झूल से झूला
मेल से मेला
ठेल से ठेला

ई = गागर से गगरी
रेत से रेती

ऊ = झाड़ से झाड़ू
बाजार से बाजारू

न = चुभ से चुभन
झाड़ से झाड़न

नी = लेख से लेखनी
छल से छलनी

4. भाववाचक

अत = बच से बचत
पढ़ से पढ़त

अन = चल से चलन
घुट से घुटन

आऊ बिक से बिकाऊ
टिक से टिकाऊ

आई = लिख से लिखाई
चढ़ से चढ़ाई
सच से सचाई
लड़ से लड़ाई

5. क्रियावाचक

हुआ = पढ़ से पढ़ता हुआ
सुन से सुनता हुआ

तद्धित प्रत्यय

तद्धित प्रत्यय छह प्रकार के हैं– (1) कर्त्तावाचक (2) भाववाचक (3) गुणवाचक, (4) अपत्यवाचक, (5) ऊनतावाचक, (6) स्त्रीवाचक

1. कर्त्तावाचक

आर = लोहा से लुहार
सोना से सुनार
कह से कहार

ई = तेल से तेली
भेद से भेदी

ची = खजान से खजानची
नकल से नकलची

वाला = घर से घरवाला
दूध से दूधवाला

2. भाववाचक

आई = भला से भलाई
बुरा से बुराई
चौड़ा से चौड़ाई

आपा = बूढ़ा से बुढ़ापा
मोटा से मुटापा

आस = खट्टा से खटास
मीठा से मिठास

इमा = लाल से लालिमा
अरुण से अरुणिमा
हरित से हरीतिमा

ई = खुश से खुशी
लाल से लाली
चोर से चोरी

त = बढ़ से बढ़त
रंग से रंगत
संग से संगत

ता = लघु से लघुता
मित्र से मित्रता
शत्रु से शत्रुता

त्व = बन्धु से बन्धुत्व
गुरु से गुरुत्व

पन = भोला से भोलापन
पागल से पागलपन

गुणवाचक

आ = भूख से भूखा
प्यास से प्यासा

इन = कठ से कठिन
मल से मिलन

आलु = दया से दयालु
कृपा से कृपालु

इक = देव से दैविक
पशु से पाशविक
मूल से मौलिक
देह से दैहिक
वेद से वैदिक
विकल्प से वैकल्पिक

इत = द्रव से द्रवित
फल से फलित

इष्णु = सह से सहिष्णु
प्रभाव से प्रभविष्णु

ई = हठ से हठी
ध्यान से ध्यानी
दुख से दुखी

ईला = रस से रसीला
हठ से हठीला
रंग से रंगीला

ईय = मानव से मानवीय
राष्ट्र से राष्ट्रीय

उक = भाव से भावुक
भिक्षु से भिक्षुक

मान = बुद्धि से बुद्धिमान
मूर्ति से मूर्तिमान

वान = धन से धनवान
गुण से गुणवान

4. अपत्यवाचक

अ = वसुदेव से वासुदेव
पाण्डु से पाण्डव
यदु से यादव

इ = दशरथ से दाशरथि
मारुत से मारुति

एय = गंगा से गांगेय
कुन्ती से कौन्तेय

5. ऊनतावाचक

आ = बाबू से बबुआ

इया = बेटी से बिटिया

लाठी से लठिया
डिब्बा से डिबिया

ड़ा, ड़ी = दुख से दुखड़ा
आँत से अँतड़ी

6. स्त्रीवाचक

आ = प्रिय से प्रिया
सुत से सुता

आइन = पंडित से पंडिताइन
ठाकुर से ठकुराइन

आनी = नौकर से नौकरानी
इन्द्र से इन्द्राणी

इका = लेखक से लेखिका
अध्यापक से अध्यापिका

इया = कुत्ता से कुतिया
बन्दर से बन्दरिया

ई = देव से देवी
घोड़ा से घोड़ी

नी = नट से नटनी
शेर से शेरनी

अन्य महत्त्वपूर्ण प्रत्यय

कर = दिन से दिनकर
रुचि से रुचिकर

चर = जल से जलचर
थल से थलचर
गो से गोचर

चित = कदा से कदाचित
कः से कश्चित

ज = अम्बु से अम्बुज
पयः से पयोज
वारि से वारिज
नीर से नीरज

जा = गिरि से गिरिजा
शैल से शैलजा

ज्ञ = सर्व से सर्वज्ञ
मर्म से मर्मज्ञ

तः = मूल से मूलतः
अन्त से अन्ततः

द = जल से जलद
नीर से नीरद
वारि से वारिद
मान से मानद

इ, ई, ए, ऐ = विराग से वैराग्य
विधव से वैधव्य

उ, ऊ, ओ, औ = सुन्दर से सौन्दर्य
उदार से औदार्य

ल = मंजु से मंजुल
उर्मि से उर्मिल

स्थ = तट से तटस्थ
कण्ठ से कण्ठस्थ

अध्याय 4

संधियाँ और समास

संधियाँ

दो वर्णों के मेल को संधि कहते हैं। संधि तीन प्रकार की होती हैं–

स्वर संधि : जिसमें दो स्वरों का मेल होता है।

व्यंजन संधि : जिसमें दो व्यंजनों का मेल होता है।

विसर्ग संधि : विसर्ग के साथ स्वर या व्यंजन के मेल को विसर्ग संधि कहते हैं।

इन उपर्युक्त तीनों प्रकार की संधियों की संक्षिप्त व्याख्या नीचे दी जा रही है–

I. स्वर संधि

अ से औ तक जिसमें ऋ तथा लृ भी सम्मिलित है, स्वर कहलाते हैं। इनके परस्पर मेल को स्वर संधि कहते हैं। इसके सात भेद हैं– दीर्घ, गुण, वृद्धि, परस्पर, पूर्वरूप, यण, अयादि।

दीर्घ संधि : जब अ + अ का योग हो, तो 'आ' हो जाता है; जब अ + आ का योग हो, तो 'आ' हो जाता है; जब आ + आ का योग हो तो 'आ' हो जाता है; जब आ + अ का योग हो तो 'आ' हो जाता है। इसी प्रकार, जब इ + इ का योग हो, तो 'ई' हो जाता है; जब इ + ई का योग हो, तो 'ई' हो जाता है; जब ई + ई का योग हो, तो 'ई' हो जाता है; जब ई + इ का योग हो, तो 'ई' हो जाता है। जब उ + उ को योग हो, तो 'ऊ' हो जाता है जब उ + ऊ का योग हो तो ऊ हो जाता है; जब ऊ + ऊ का योग हो, तो 'ऊ' हो जाता है; जब ऊ + उ का योग हो तो 'ऊ' हो जाता है। नीचे इनके उदाहरण देकर समझाया गया है। जैसे–

अ + अ = आ → धर्म + अर्थ = धर्मार्थ
अ + आ = आ → परम + आनन्द = परमानन्द
आ + आ = आ → नाना + आकार = नानाकार
आ + अ = आ → महा + अर्णव = महार्णव
इ + इ = ई → रवि + इन्द्र = रवीन्द्र
इ + ई = ई → कपि + ईश = कपीश
ई + ई = ई → मही + ईश = महीश
ई + इ = ई → मही + इन्द्र = महीन्द्र
उ + उ = ऊ → लघु + उत्तम = लघूत्तम
उ + ऊ = ऊ → सिंधु + ऊर्मि = सिंधूर्मि
ऊ + ऊ = ऊ → भू + ऊर्जा = भूर्जा

ऊ + उ = ऊ → वधू + उत्सव = वधूत्सव

गुण संधि : जब अ + इ का योग हो, तो 'ए' हो जाता है; जब अ + ई का योग हो, तो 'ए' हो जाता है; जब आ + इ का योग हो, तो 'ए' हो जाता है; जब आ + ई का योग हो, तो 'ए' हो जाता है; जब अ + उ को योग हो, तो 'ओ' हो जाता है; जब अ + ऊ का योग हो, तो 'ओ' हो जाता है; जब आ + उ का योग हो, तो 'औ' हो जाता है, जब अ + ऋ का योग हो, तो 'अर्' हो जाता है, जब आ + ऋ को योग हो तो 'अर' ह्रो जाता है। नीचे इनके उदाहरण देकर समझाया गया है, जैसे–

अ + इ = ए → देव + इन्द्र = देवेन्द्र
अ + ई = ए → सुर + ईश = सुरेश
आ + इ = ए → महा + इन्द्र = महेन्द्र
आ + ई = ए → उमा + ईश = उमेश
अ + उ = ओ → देव + उत्सव = देवोत्सव
अ + ऊ = ओ → सागर + ऊर्मि = सागरोर्मि
आ + उ = ओ → महा + उत्सव = महोत्सव
आ + ऊ = ओ → महा + ऊर्जा = महोर्जा
अ + ऋ = अर् → देव + ऋषि = देवर्षि
आ + ऋ = अर् → महा + ऋषि = महर्षि

वृद्धि संधि : जब अ + ए का योग हो, तो 'ऐ' हो जाता है; जब आ + ए का योग हो, तो 'ऐ' हो जाता है; जब आ + ऐ का योग हो तो 'ऐ' हो जाता है; जब अ + ओ का योग हो, तो 'औ' हो जाता है; जब आ + औ का योग हो, तो 'औ' हो जाता है। नीचे इनके उदाहरण देकर समझाया गया है, जैसे–

अ + ए = ऐ → एक + एक = एकैक
आ + ए = ऐ → सदा + एव = सदैव
आ + ऐ = ऐ → महा + ऐश्वर्य = महैश्वर्य
अ + ओ = औ → पक्व + ओदन = पक्वौदन
आ + औ = औ → महा + औषधि = महौषधि

पररूप संधि : जब अ + ए का योग हो, तो 'ए' हो जाता है, और जब अ + ओ का योग हो, तो 'ओ' हो जाता है। नीचे इनके उदाहरण देकर समझाया गया है, जैसे–

अ + ए = ए → सप + एरा = सपेरा
अ + ओ = ओ → दन्त + ओष्ठ = दन्तोष्ठ

पूर्वरूप संधि : जब ए + अ का योग हो, तो 'एऽ' हो जाता है; जब इ + अ का योग हो, तो 'ओंऽ' हो जाता है, जैसे–

ए + अ = एऽ → ते + अपि = तेऽपि
ओ + अ = ओऽ → सो + अनुमानै = सोऽनुमानै

जब इ + उ का योग हो, तो 'य' हो जाता है; जब इ + अ का योग हो, तो 'ये' हो जाता है; जब उ + अ का योग हो, तो 'व' हो जाता है; जब उ + आ का योग हो, तो 'वा' हो जाता है; जब उ + ए का योग हो, तो 'वे' हो जाता है; और जब ऋ + आ का योग हो, तो 'रा' हो जाता है। नीचे इनके उदाहरण देकर समझाया गया है,

इ + अ = य → यदि + अपि = यद्यपि

इ + आ = या → इति + आदि = इत्यादि

इ + उ = यु → प्रति + उपकार = प्रत्युपकार

इ + ए = ये → प्रति + एक = प्रत्येक

उ + अ = व → अनु + अर्थ = अन्वर्थ

उ + आ = वा → सु + आगत = स्वागत

उ + ए = वे → अनु + एषण = अन्वेषण

ऋ + आ = रा → मातृ + आनन्द = मात्रानन्द

नोट : हिन्दी में पररूप सन्धि और पूर्वरूप सन्धि से निर्मित शब्दों का प्रयोग नहीं के बराबर होता है।

अयादि सन्धि : जब ए + अ का योग हो, तो 'अय' हो जाता है; जब ऐ + अ का योग हो, तो 'आय' हो जाता है; जब ऐ + इ का योग हो, तो 'आयि' हो जाता है; जब ओ + अ का योग हो, तो 'अव' हो जाता है; जब ओ + इ का योग हो, तो 'अवि' हो जाता है; जब ओ + ई का योग हो, तो 'अवी' हो जाता है, जब औ + अ का योग हो, तो 'आव' हो जाता है; जब औ + इ का योग हो, तो 'आउ' हो जाता है। नीचे इनके उदाहरण देकर समझाया गया है, जैसे–

ए + अ = अय → ने + अन = नयन

ऐ + अ = आय → नै + [illegible]क = नायक

ऐ + इ = आयि → नै [illegible] इका = नायिका

ओ + अ = अव → पो + अन = पवन

ओ + इ = अवि → पो + इत्र = पवित्र

ओ + ई = अवी → गो + गवीश = गवीश

औ + अ = आव → पौ + अक = पावक

औ + ई = आवि → नौ + इक = नाविक

औ + उ = आउ → भौ + उक = भावुक

II. व्यंजन संधि

व्यंजन के साथ किसी व्यंजन अथवा स्वर के मेल (योग) को व्यंजन संधि कहते हैं। इसके उदाहरण निम्नलिखित हैं–

यदि क्, च्, ट्, प् के साथ अनुनासिक के अतिरिक्त कोई स्वर अथवा वर्ग का तीसरा,

चौथा अथवा पाँचवाँ अक्षर आता हैं तो उसके स्थान पर वर्ग का तीसरा अक्षर हो जाता है, जैसे–

वाक् + मय = वाङ्मय षट् + मास = षण्मास

जगत् + नाथ = जगन्नाथ

त्, व्, द्, के आगे च, व, छ हो तो त्, व्, द् के स्थान में 'च' होता है; ज अथवा झ आए तो 'ज' होता है; ट, व, ठ हो तो 'ट्'; ड, व, ढ हो तो 'ड्' तथा 'ल' आए तो ल् हो जाता है, यथा–

उत् + चरण = उच्चारण बृहत् + टीका = बृहट्टीका

शरद् + चन्द्र = शरच्चन्द्र उत् + डयन = उड्डयन

विपद् + जाल = विपज्जाल उत् + लास = उल्लास

त्, वा, द् के आगे यदि 'श' आवे तो त् व द् के स्थान पर 'च्' और श की जगह 'छ' हो जाता है और ह हो तो त्, व, द् की जगह 'द्' तथा ह की जगह 'ध' हो जाता है, यथा–

उत् + शिष्ट = उच्छिष्ट तत् + हित = तद्धित

छ के पूर्व यदि स्वर हो तो छ के स्थान पर 'च्छ' हो जाता है, जैसे–

परि + छेद = परिच्छेद स्व + छन्द = स्वच्छन्द

म् के आगे यदि व्यंजन हो तो म के बदले अनुस्वार अथवा उसी वर्ग का अनुनासिक व्यंजन हो जाता है, यथा–

अलम् + कार = अलङ्कार (अलंकार); किम् + चित् = किञ्चित (किंचित)

'म' के आगे यदि ऊष्म वर्ण, श, ष, स, ह अथवा अन्तस्थ वर्ण य, र, ल, व आवें तो 'म' अनुस्वार में बदल जाता है, जैसे-

सम् + शय = संशय सम् + सार = संसार

सम् + हार = संहार सम् + योग = संयोग

सम् + रक्षक = संरक्षक सम् + लग्न = संलग्न

सम् + वाद = संवाद

यदि ऋ, र अथवा ष के आगे 'न' आवे तो स्वर, कवर्ग एवं अन्तरस्थ य र ल व ऊष्म 'ह' के बीच में रुकावट होने पर भी र्, या ष् से परे न् का ण् हो जाता है, यथा–

परि + नाम = परिणाम ऋ + न = ऋण

'स' से प्रारम्भ होने वाले शब्दों से पूर्व 'अ' व 'आ' को छोड़कर यदि कोई स्वर आता है तो 'स' के स्थान पर साधारणतया 'ष' हो जाता है, जैसे–

वि + सम = विषम सु + सुप्ति = सुषुप्ति

इस नियम के अपवाद भी हैं, जैसे–

अनु + स्वार = अनुस्वार वि + स्मरण = विस्मरण

ष के बाद 'त' व 'थ' वर्ण आने पर उनके स्थान में क्रमशः ट व ठ हो जाता है, जैसे–

पुष् + त = पुष्ट पृष + थ = पृष्ठ

ह्रस्व के बाद र् से परे यदि र् हो तो पहले र् का लोप हो जाता है और पहला ह्रस्व स्वर दीर्घ हो जाता है, जैसे–

निर् + रस = नीरस निर् + रोग = नीरोग

III. विसर्ग संधि

विसर्ग के साथ स्वर या व्यंजन के मेल को विसर्ग संधि कहते हैं। विसर्ग के सामनेयदि च या छ से प्रारम्भ होने वाले शब्द आवें तो विसर्ग 'श' में बदल जाता है, सामने ट व ठ आवें तो विसर्ग 'ष' में बदलते हैं तथा सामने त व थ वर्ण हों तो विसर्ग का 'स' हो जाता है, यथा–

निः + चिन्त = निश्चिन्त निः + छल = निश्छल

धनु + टंकार = धनुष्टंकार निः + ठुर = निष्ठुर

दुः + तर = दुस्तर प्रियः + थल = प्रियस्थल

विसर्ग के बाद यदि श, ष, स वर्ण हों तो विसर्ग यथावत् बना रहता है अथवा उसके स्थान पर उक्त तीनों वर्ण अपने-अपने स्थान पर ड्योढ़े हो जाते हैं, जैसे–

दुः + शासन = (दुःशासन) अथवा दुश्शासन

निः + संशय = (निःसंशय) अथवा निस्संशय

दुः + षण्ड = (दुःषण्ड) अथवा दुष्षंड

यदि विसर्ग के पूर्व अ हो तथा उसके आगे क, ख और प, फ हों तो विसर्ग में परिवर्तन नहीं होता; जैसे–

रजः + कण = रजःकण पयः + पान = पयःपान

विसर्ग से पहले ई अथवा उ हो और उसके आगे क, ख अथवा प, फ हो तो विसर्ग 'ष' में बदल जाता है, जैसे–

निः + कलंक = निष्कलंक निः + फल = निष्फल

निः + पाप = निष्पाप

विसर्ग से पूर्व अ और उसके आगे घोष व्यंजन (वर्ग का 3रा, 4था तथा 5वां वर्ण तथा य र ल व ह) होने पर विसर्ग की जगह 'ओ' हो जाता है, जैसे–

अधः + गति = अधोगति तमः + गुण = तमोगुण

मनः + रथ = मनोरथ तपः + वन = तपोवन

विसर्ग से पहले अ, आ को छोड़कर कोई अन्य स्वर होने पर विसर्ग 'र' में बदल जाता है, जैसे–

निः + गुण = निर्गुण दुः + दशा = दुर्दशा

अन्त का अक्षर 'र' होने पर आगे अघोष व्यंजन आवे तो र् के बदले विसर्ग हो जाता है; जैसे–

अन्तर् + करण = अन्तःकरण पुनर् + संस्कार = पुनःसंस्कार

अन्तर् + पुर = अन्तःपुर

समास

जब दो या दो से अधिक शब्द मिलकर किसी नए शब्द की रचना करते हैं तो इस क्रिया को समास कहा जाता है। इस प्रकार मिले हुए शब्दों को 'समस्त पद' भी कहा जाता है। समास में विभक्तियों, अथवा और, आदि का लोप हो जाता है, जैसे–शिवालय = शिव का आलय, इसमें 'का' विभक्ति का लोप होकर शिवालय बना, अतएव इसे सम्बन्ध तत्पुरुष समास कहा जाएगा।

संधि तथा समास में अंतरः संधि होने पर किसी एक या दो वर्णों में विकार होता है। समास होने पर अनेक शब्द मिलकर एक शब्द बन जाता है और बीच की विभक्ति का लोप हो जाता है।

समस्त पद जिन शब्दों से बनता है वे शब्द खण्ड कहे जाते हैं। समस्त पद के खण्ड करके उनका परस्पर सम्बन्ध दिखाने की रीति को 'विग्रह' कहते हैं, जैसे–राजकुमार; इस समस्त पद का विग्रह होगा 'राजा का कुमार'।

समासों के मुख्यतया चार भेद माने जाते हैं, यथा–

(1) अव्ययीभाव (2) तत्पुरुष
(4) बहुब्रीहि (4) द्वन्द्व

कर्मधारय तथा द्विगु को भी समास माना गया है। इससे समासों की संख्या छह हो जाती है किन्तु ये समास वस्तुतः तत्पुरुष के ही भेद हैं।

अव्ययीभाव समास : जिस समास में अर्थ की दृष्टि से पहला पद प्रधान होता है है उसे अव्ययी भाव समास कहा जाता है। इसका पहला पद अव्यय होता है जिसमें लिंग, वचन आदि के कारण कोई परिवर्तन नहीं होता, जैसे–

प्रतिदिन – (दिन-दिन)
यथाशक्ति – (शक्ति के अनुसार)
आजन्म – (जीवन पर्यन्त, जीवन भर)
सर्वप्रथम – (सबसे पहले)
प्रतिदिन – (हर (प्रति) दिन)
प्रत्येक – (हर (प्रति) एक)
साफ-साफ – (बिल्कुल साफ)
एकाएक – (एक के तुरन्त बाद एक)
रातोंरात – (रात ही रात में)
घर-घर – (हर घर में)
हाथों हाथ – (हाथ ही हाथ में)
लाजवाब – (जिसका कोई जवाब न हो)
अकारण – (बिना कारण के)

घड़ी-घड़ी	–	(हर समय)
पहले-पहल	–	(सबसे पहले)
पल-पल	–	(हर पल)
बेखटके	–	(खटके के बिना)
निःशंक	–	(शंका से रहित)

उक्त उद्धरणों में पहला पद प्रधान है और दूसरा पद संज्ञा है। समस्त पद अव्यय हो जाने पर इसमें कोई परिवर्तन नहीं हो सकता इसलिए उक्त मेल को अव्ययीभाव समास कहा जाता है।

तत्पुरुष समास : जिस समास में दूसरा पद प्रधान होता है तथा पहले खण्ड के विभक्ति चिन्ह का लोप कर दिया जाता है उसे तत्पुरुष समास कहा जाता है, जैसे–हिमालय अर्थात् हिम (बर्फ) का आलय (घर), शरणागत् अर्थात् शरण में आया हुआ। उक्त एक में 'का' विभवित तथा दूसरे 'में' विभक्ति का लोप हुआ है।

तत्पुरुष समास के दो प्रमुख भेद हैं:–

(क) व्यधिकरण तत्पुरुष

(ख) समानाधिकरण तत्पुरुष

(क) व्यधिकरण तत्पुरुष : इसमें समस्त पदों का विग्रह करके अलग-अलग विभक्तियाँ (कारक चिन्ह) लगाई जाती हैं, जैसे–

पुस्तकालय–पुस्तकों का घर (भवन), इसमें सम्बन्ध कारक की छठी विभक्ति है जिसका लोप किया गया।

आनन्दमग्न–आनन्द में मग्न, इसमें अधिकरण तत्पुरुष सूचक 'में' शब्द का लोप किया गया है।

(ख) समानाधिकरण तत्पुरुष : जिसमें समस्त पदों के विग्रह करने पर दोनों खण्डों में कर्त्ता कारक प्रथम विभक्ति ही रहे, जैसे–

अरुण कमल अर्थात् अरुण जो है कमल। इन दोनों शब्दों में विभक्ति एक ही है। व्यधिकरण तत्पुरुष ही सामान्यतया तत्पुरुष समास कहा जाता है और समानाधिकरण तत्पुरुष को कर्मधारय कहते हैं।

व्यधिकरण तत्पुरुष : इस समास के पहले खण्ड में जिस कारक की विभक्ति का लोप हुआ हो, उस कारक या विभक्ति के नाम से इस समास का नाम होता है। इस प्रकार की विभक्तियों के अनुसार इसके छह भेद किए गए हैं :

1. कर्म तत्पुरुष, 2. करण तत्पुरुष, 3. सम्प्रदान तत्पुरुष, 4. अपादान तत्पुरुष, 5. सम्बन्ध तत्पुरुष, 6. अधिकरण तत्पुरुष।

1. कर्म तत्पुरुष–इसमें कर्म के कारक चिन्ह 'को' का लोप होता है, जैसे–

गिरहकट	–	गिरह (गांठ) को काटने वाला
नरभक्षी	–	नर को भक्षण करने वाला
जलपिपासु	–	जल को पीने की इच्छा वाला
मुँहतोड़	–	मुँह को तोड़ने वाला
सर्वज्ञ	–	सब को जानने वाला

2. करण तत्पुरुष– इसमें करण कारक के चिन्ह 'से', 'के द्वारा' का लोप होता है, जैसे–

तुलसीकृत – तुलसी द्वारा लिखा गया
रससिक्त – रस से सिक्त
शोकाकुल – शोक से आकुल
कष्टसाध्य – कष्ट से साध्य
ईश्वरदत्त – ईश्वर द्वारा दिया गया

3. सम्प्रदान तत्पुरुष–इसमें सम्प्रदान कारक के चिन्ह 'के लिए' का लोप होता है, जैसे–

गोशाला – गाय के लिए शाला
देशभक्ति – देश के लिए भक्ति
सभामंडप – सभा के लिए मंडप
रसोईघर – रसोई के लिए घर
बालामृत – बालकों के लिए अमृत

4. अपादान तत्पुरुष– इसमें अपादान कारक के चिन्ह 'से' (अलग होने के अर्थ में) का लोप होता है, जैसे–

धनहीन – धन से हीन
गुणरहित – गुण से रहित
दोषमुक्त – दोष से मुक्त
जन्मान्ध – जन्म से अन्धा
सेवानिवृत्त – सेवा से निवृत्त

5. संबंध तत्पुरुष– इसमें संबंध कारक के चिन्हों 'का', 'के', 'की' का लोप होता है, जैसे–

हरिजन – हरि का जन
राष्ट्रपति – राष्ट्र का पति
मंत्रिपरिषद – मंत्रियों की परिषद
परधन – दूसरे का धन
गंगाजल – गंगा का जल

6. अधिकरण तत्पुरुष– इसमें अधिकरण कारक के चिन्हों 'में', 'पर' का लोप होता है, जैसे–

निशाचर – निशा में विचरण करने वाला
ईश्वराधीन – ईश्वर पर आधीन
नराधम – नरों में अधम
आपबीती – अपने पर बीती
युद्धरत – युद्ध में रत

7. कर्मधारय या समानाधिकरण तत्पुरुष– इसमें दूसरे पद का अर्थ प्रधान होता है। पहला पद विशेषण अथवा उपमान और दूसरा पद विशेष्य अथवा उपमेय होता है। जैसे

मुखचन्द्र – चन्द्रमा के समान मुख
चरणकमल – कमल के समान चरण

मुखारविन्द	–	अरविन्द के समान मुख
नरशार्दूल	–	नरों में सिंह के समान

विशेषण-विशेष्य–नीलकमल–नील विशेषण कमल विशेष्य (संज्ञा); पीताम्बर–पीत विशेषण, अम्बर विशेष्य (संज्ञा)।

उपमेय और उपमान– जिस शब्द की किसी से समता बताई जाए उसे उपमेय और जिससे समता बताई जाए उसे उपमान कहते हैं। वारिजनयन अर्थात् कमल के समान नेत्र इसमें उपमेय नयन तथा उपमान कमल है। इसी प्रकार अन्य शब्द हो सकते हैं–मृगनयनी, चन्द्रमुखी आदि।

द्विगु समास– जिस समास का पहला पद संख्यावाची हो और जिससे किसी समुदाय का बोध होता हो उसे द्विगु समास कहा जाता है, जैसे–त्रलोक्य (तीन लोकों का समूह), सतसई (सात सौ का समूह), इस प्रकार के शब्द हैं–पंचानन, अधमरा, नवग्रह, पंचवटी, अष्टाध्यायी आदि। ये सभी द्विगु समास का बोध कराते हैं। अन्य उदाहरण हैं–चौराहा, अठन्नी, षडऋतु, तिमंजिला, दुभाषिया, तिपहिया, त्रिवेणी, चतुर्वेदी, चौपाई, नौलखा, पंचतत्व, नवरत्न, सप्तसिन्ध, छप्पय, शतांश आदि।

बहुब्रीहि समास– जिस सयुक्त शब्द का कोई खण्ड प्रधान न होकर समान रूप से महत्त्व के होते हुए किसी अन्य शब्द, पदार्थ अथवा वस्तु का बोध कराते हैं, उसे बहुब्रीहि समास कहा जाता है। जैसे–

चतुर्भुज–चार भुजाएँ हैं जिनके अथवा चार भुजा धारी–विष्णु।

चन्द्रमौलि–चन्द्रमा है सिर पर जिनके अर्थात् 'शिव'।

दुष्टात्मा–दुष्ट है आत्मा जिसकी।

बारहसिंगा–बारह हैं सींग जिसके अर्थात् एक प्रकार का हिरण।

अन्य उदाहरण हैः–एकदन्त (गणेश), दशमुख (रावण), गिरधर, (कृष्ण), धनञ्जय (अर्जुन), लम्बोदर, (गणेश), नीलकंठ (शिव), घनश्याम (कृष्ण), पंचशर (कामदेव),

द्वन्द्व समास– जिस समास के दोनों खण्ड समान महत्त्व के होते हैं, उसे द्वन्द्व समास कहते हैं, जैसे– रोटी–दाल, माता–पिता, लोक–परलोक, दिन–रात

अन्य उदाहरण हैं–आजकल, अन्न-जल, बाप-दादा, खान-पान, घास-फूस, दाना-पानी, राग-द्वेष, धनी-मानी, हार-जीत, उछल-कूद, लेन-देन, हानि-लाभ, यश-अपयश, चढ़ाव-उतार, घट-बढ़ आदि।

बहुब्रीहि और कर्मधारयः बहुब्रीहि और कर्मधारय समास में मुख्य अंतर यह है कि कर्मधारय में समस्त पद का एक खण्ड दूसरे का विशेषण होता है जबकि बहुब्रीहि में समास के दोनों खण्ड अपने से भिन्न किसी अन्य अर्थ का संकेत देते हैं। जैसे अरुण कमल में अरुण शब्द कमल का विशेषण है, इसलिए यह कर्मधारय समास है; किन्तु जब हम पीताम्बर कहते हैं और यदि हमारा अभिप्राय केवल पीले कपड़े से है तो यह कर्मधारय होगा; लेकिन जब इसका अर्थ होगा पीला है अम्बर जिसका (पीत + अम्बर वाला है जो श्रीकृष्ण) अर्थात् श्रीकृष्ण तो यह बहुब्रीहि समास बन जाएगा। इसलिए इन दोनों समासों– कर्मधारय एवं बहुब्रीहि के मध्य ज्यादा अन्तर नहीं है।

अध्याय 5

अलंकार

अलंकार विभूषित करते हैं। अलंकार से उक्ति की शोभा बढ़ जाती है। सुन्दर उक्ति सबको मनभाती है। अलंकार काव्य का वह गुण-धर्म है, जिससे काव्य की शोभा बढ़ती है। आचार्य मम्मट ने अलंकारों के सम्बन्ध में कहा है कि जैसे हार आदि आभूषण से कंठ की शोभा बढ़ जाती है वैसे ही उपमा और अनुप्रास आदि अलंकारों से काव्य के सौन्दर्य में वृद्धि हो जाती है। काव्य की आत्मा रस है, किन्तु उसका भूषण अलंकार है। इसीलिए अलंकार को काव्य का अस्थिर धर्म-गुण माना जाता है। अतः अलंकार साध्य नहीं, साधन है।

अलंकारों के दो भेद हैं– (1) शब्दालंकार और (2) अर्थालंकार। शब्दालंकार काव्य में शब्दों में चमत्कार पैदा करते हैं, जबकि अर्थालंकार काव्य में अर्थ सम्बन्धी विशेषता उत्पन्न करते हैं। कुछ अलंकार शब्द और अर्थ दोनों विशेषता उत्पन्न करते हैं। ऐसे अलंकारों को उभयालंकार कहा जाता है।

अलंकार असंख्य हैं। यहाँ केवल थोड़े-से विशिष्ट अलंकारों का वर्णन किया जायेगा।

शब्दालंकार

जहाँ शब्दों के कारण काव्य में सौन्दर्य उत्पन्न हो, वहाँ शब्दालंकार होता है। मुख्य-मुख्य शब्दालंकारों का वर्णन नीचे दिया गया है।

अनुप्रास– जब किसी पद में एक व्यंजन या कई व्यंजन एक ही क्रम में एक से अधिक बार आयें अर्थात् उसकी आवृत्ति हो, तो वह अनुप्रास कहा जाता है। यदि व्यंजन के अतिरिक्त शब्द या वाक्यांश की आवृत्ति हो, तो वहाँ भी अनुप्रास होता है।

जैसे, केलिन के कूलन कछारन में, कुंजन में

यहाँ 'क' और 'न' की पाँच और तीन आवृत्तियाँ हैं

एक अन्य उदाहरण–

'काली लहर कल्पना काली
मेरी काल कोठरी काली'

इसमें 'क' की 6 बार आवृत्ति हुई है।

कभी-कभी पूरे वाक्य की पुनरावृत्ति होती है, जैसे–

पूत संपूत तो क्या धन संचय।
पूत कपूत तो क्या धन संचय।।

अनुप्रास के कई भेद हैं–छेकानुप्रास, वृत्यानुप्रास, लाटानुप्रास, श्रुत्यानुप्रास और अन्त्यानुप्रास।

इसमें लाटानुप्रास में शब्दों अथवा वाक्यों की पुनरावृत्ति होती है, जैसे कि ऊपर के "पूत सपूत सो क्या धन संचय। पूत कपूत तो क्या धन संचय" ।। उदाहरण में है।

यमक–ऊपर हमने देखा कि लाटानुप्रास में शब्दों अथवा वाक्यों की पुनरावृत्ति होती है किन्तु शब्द का अर्थ वही रहता है; अर्थात् शब्दों के अर्थ में भेद या अन्तर नहीं होता। किन्तु यमक में जो शब्द दोबारा आते हैं, उनके अर्थ बदल जाते हैं। जैसे–

कनक कनक ते सौ गुनी मादकता अधिकाय।
वा खाये बौराय जग या पाये बौराय ।।

यहाँ कनक शब्द दो बार आया है। दोनों स्थानों पर कनक शब्द का अर्थ अलग-अलग है। पहले स्थान पर इसका अर्थ है 'स्वर्ण' और दूसरे स्थान पर इसका अर्थ है 'धतूरा'। इसी प्रकार 'बौराय' शब्द भी दो बार आया है और दोनों स्थानों पर इस शब्द का अर्थ अलग-अलग है। पहले स्थान पर इसका अर्थ है–सम्पन्न होना और दूसरे स्थान पर इसका अर्थ है 'पागल होना'।

श्लेष–यमक अलंकार में एक ही शब्द एक से अधिक बार प्रयुक्त होता है, परन्तु अलग-अलग स्थान पर इसका अर्थ भी अलग-अलग होता है, जैसा कि आप पढ़ चुके हैं। इसके विपरीत श्लेष में एक शब्द एक ही बार प्रयुक्त होता है, लेकिन उसके दो या अधिक अर्थ निकलते हैं। जैसे–

"चिर जीवै जोड़ी युगल, क्यों न सनेह गंभीर।
को घटि ये वृषभानुजा, वे हलधर के बीर।।"

उक्त पंक्तियों में 'वृषभानुजा' और 'हलधर' में श्लेष अलंकार है। 'वृषभानुजा' का अर्थ है 'राधा' और यदि 'वृषभानुजा' शब्द को तोड़कर इसका अर्थ निकाला जाये, तो अर्थ होगा 'वृषभ + अनुजा' अर्थात् 'बैल की बहन'। इसी प्रकार हलधर के दो अर्थ 'बैल' और 'बलराम' हैं। इस प्रकार एक अर्थ के अनुसार राधा वृषभानु की पुत्री है और दूसरे अर्थ के अनुसार बैल की बहन। दूसरी ओर कृष्ण एक ओर बलराम के भाई हैं, तो दूसरी ओर बैल के भाई।

अर्थालंकार

जब भाषा के प्रयोग से अर्थ में चमत्कार पैदा हो, तो वहाँ अर्थालंकार होता है। नीचे प्रमुख अर्थालंकारों का वर्णन किया जाता है–

उपमा–जहाँ दो वस्तुओं के बीच साम्य अथवा समानता का भाव व्यक्त किया जाये, वहाँ उपमा अलंकार होता है। जैसे, "सीता का मुख चन्द्रमा के समान सुन्दर है।"

यहाँ सीता के मुख की सुन्दरता की तुलना चन्द्रमा की सुन्दरता से की गई है।

सामान्यतया उपमा के चार अंग होते हैं– (1) उपमेय, (2) उपमान, (3) धर्म, और (4) वाचक। अब इन चारों को समझिए। जिसकी तुलना की जाये, उसे **उपमेय** कहते हैं। यहाँ सीता का **मुख** उपमेय है। जिससे तुलना की जाये, उसे **उपमान** कहते हैं। यहाँ चन्द्रमा उपमान (अप्रस्तुत) है। जिस बात में तुलना की जाये, उसे **धर्म** कहते हैं। यहां

सुन्दर धर्म है। जिस शब्द से तुलना की जाये, उसे **वाचक** कहते हैं। यहाँ 'के समान' वाचक है।

जहाँ काव्य में उपमा के चारों अंगों की उपस्थिति हो, उसे पूर्णोपमा कहते हैं।

जहाँ उपमा के इन चारों अंगों में से कोई अंग लुप्त होता है, उसे लुप्तोपमा कहते हैं। जो अंग लुप्त होता है, उसी के आधार पर इसका नामकरण हो जाता है, जैसे, **उपमेय लुप्तोपमा**–इसमें उपमेय लुप्त होता है, **उपमान लुप्तोपमा**–इसमें उपमान लुप्त होता है, **धर्म लुप्तोपमा**–इसमें धर्म लुप्त होता है, और **वाचक लुप्तोपमा**–इसमें वाचक लुप्त होता है। **मालोपमा** वहाँ होती है, जहाँ कई-कई उपमान हों, जैसे,

क्या कहें कि कैसी है उसकी कमनीय कान्ति।
कुन्दन-सी, कुंद-सी या कंज सी निकाई है।

रूपक–इस अलंकार में लक्षण से चमत्कार प्रकट होता है। इसमें उपमेय पर उपमान का आरोप होता है। इसमें उपमेय और उपमान दोनों को एक रूप में प्रदर्शित किया जाता है। इसका एक उदाहरण देखिए–

अम्बर पनघट में डुबो रही, तारा घट ऊपा नागरी।

यहाँ अम्बर में पनघट का आरोप है; तारा में घट का आरोप है और ऊपा में नागरी का आरोप है।

अनन्वय–जब उपमेय की तुलना के लिए कोई उपमान होता ही नहीं और उपमेय के समान उपमेय ही कहा जाता है, तो अनन्वय अलंकार होता है। जैसे–

'राम से राम सिया सी सिया सिर मौर विरचि विचारि सँवारे'

यहाँ राम की उपमा देने के लिए कोई शब्द नहीं था, अतः राम की तुलना राम से की गई है। इसी प्रकार सीता की तुलना सीता से की गई है।

प्रतीप–इस अलंकार में प्रसिद्ध उपमानों को उपमेय का स्थान दे दिया जाता है। जैसे–

'दोनों का तन-तेज एक-से-एक प्रखर था।
उनके आगे पड़ा हुआ दिनकर फीका था।।'

सूर्य का तेज प्रसिद्ध उपमान है। लेकिन उपरोक्त पंक्तियों में 'तन-तेज' के सामने 'सूर्य का तेज' फीका पड़ गया है।

व्यतिरेक–जहाँ उपमेय को उपमान से बढ़ाकर अथवा उपमान को उपमेय से घटाकर वर्णन किया जाये, वहाँ व्यतिरेक अलंकार होता है। जैसे–

स्वर्ग की तुलना उचित ही है यहाँ
किन्तु सुरसरिता कहाँ, सरयू कहाँ?
यह मरों को मात्र पार उतारती
यह यहीं से जीवितों को तारती।

इन पंक्तियों में अयोध्या की तुलना स्वर्ग से की गई है। स्वर्ग में सुरसरिता (देव गंगा) केवल मृतकों को पार उतारती है। जबकि अयोध्या में सरयू जीवितों का ही उद्धार (मुक्ति प्रदान) कर देती है। यहाँ सरयू (उपमेय) को सुरसरिता से बढ़ाकर दिखाया गया है; या यूँ कहे कि सुरसरिता को हलका करके दिखाया गया है।

भ्रान्तिमान–जब किसी वस्तु को देखकर वैसी ही किसी अन्य वस्तु का भ्रम हो, तो वहाँ भ्रान्तिमान अलंकार होता है। जैसे–

नाक का मोती अधर की कान्ति से
बीज दाड़िम का समझकर भ्रान्ति से
देखकर सहसा हुआ शुक मौन है
सोचता है अन्य शुक यह कौन है?

यहाँ नाक के मोती पर ओठों की लालिमा पड़ने से मोती अनार के दाने जैसा दिखाई पड़ता है। इसे देखकर एक तोता नाक को (लाल चोंच देखकर) भ्रमवश दूसरा तोता मान बैठता है। इसलिए उक्त पंक्तियों में भ्रान्तिमान अलंकार है।

उत्प्रेक्षा–इस अलंकार में उपमेय में उपमान की सम्भावना की कल्पना की जाती है। इसमें प्रायः जनु, मनु, मानो, जानो जैसे शब्दों का प्रयोग किया जाता है। जैसे–

"सोहत ओढ़े पीत पट श्याम सलोने गात
मनो नील मनि शैल पर आतप पर्यो प्रभात !"

श्री कृष्ण पीताम्बर पहने हुए हैं। उनके शरीर को देखकर ऐसा लगता है (मानो) नील पर्वत पर प्रभात के सूर्य का प्रकाश (पीले रंग का) पड़ रहा हो। यहाँ उपमेय (श्रीकृष्ण) में उपमान (नील पर्वत पर सूर्य का प्रकाश) की सम्भावना है।

उत्प्रेक्षा तीन प्रकार की होती है–(1) वस्तु उत्प्रेक्षा, (2) हेतु उत्प्रेक्षा और (3) फल उत्प्रेक्षा।

अतिशयोक्ति–वर्ण्य विषय का अतिरंजित चित्रण अतिशयोक्ति कहलाता है। इसमें वर्णन बहुत बढ़ा-चढ़ाकर किया जाता है। जैसे–

'हनुमान की पूँछ में, लगन न पाई आग।
लंका सारी जल गई, गए निशाचर भाग।।

अतिशयोक्ति के कई भेद हैं– (1) रूपकातिशयोक्ति, (2) भेदकाशयोक्ति (3) सम्बन्धाशयोक्ति, (4) असम्बन्धाशयोक्ति, (5) अक्रमातिशयोक्ति, (6) चपलातिशयोक्ति, (7) अत्यन्तातिशयोक्ति।

यहाँ एक उदाहरण देकर कुछ अलंकारों के बीच का सूक्ष्म अन्तर समझाया गया है। जैसे–

(1) सीता का मुख चन्द्रमा के समान सुन्दर है (उपमा अलंकार)
(2) चन्द्रमा सीता के मुख के समान सुन्दर है (प्रतीप)
(3) सीता के मुख के सामने चाँद फीका है (व्यतिरेक)
(4) सीता का मुख चन्द्रमा है (रूपक)
(5) सीता का मुख मानों चन्द्रमा है (उत्प्रेक्षा)
(6) सीता के मुख को चकोर ने चन्द्रमा समझा और एकटक देखता रहा (भ्रान्तिमान)

व्याज स्तुति–जहाँ देखने में प्रशंसा लगे पर वास्तव में निंदा हो या देखने में निंदा लगे पर वास्तव में प्रशंसा हो, वहाँ ब्याज स्तुति अलंकार होता है। जैसे–

"काशी पुरी की कुरीति बुरी, जह देह दिये पुनि देह न पाइये"

काशी नगर की सबसे बुरी बात यह है कि यहाँ शरीर त्याग करने वाला पुनः शरीर धारण नहीं करता (जन्म-मरण के बन्धन से मुक्त हो जाता है)।

लगता है कि यह काशी नगरी की निन्दा है, किन्तु वास्तव में यह इस पवित्र नगरी की महान प्रशंसा (स्तुति) है।

विरोधाभास–जब दो परस्पर विरोधी क्रियांओं से उल्टी क्रिया या परिणाम हो, तो विरोधाभास अलंकार होता है। जैसे–

"या अनुरागी चित्त की, गति समुझै नहिं कोई।
ज्यों-ज्यों बूड़े श्याम रंग, त्यों-त्यों उज्जवल होई।।"

यहाँ कहा गया है कि श्याम रंग (काले रंग) में मन जितना अधिक डूबता है, उतना ही अधिक उज्जवल होता जाता है (जबकि काले रंग में डूबने पर काला होना चाहिए)।

खण्ड-II वस्तुनिष्ठ प्रश्न

भाषा और व्याकरण

1. हिन्दी वर्णमाला में कुल कितने अक्षर होते हैं?
(क) 44 (ख) 33
(ग) 46 (घ) 43

2. वर्तमान समय में हिन्दी का कौनसा रूप प्रचलित है?
(क) अवधी (ख) ब्रज
(ग) खड़ी बोली (घ) देवनागरी

3. हिन्दी निम्नलिखित में से किस लिपि में लिखी जाती है?
(क) गुरुमुखी (ख) ब्राह्मी
(ग) देवनागरी (घ) खरोष्ठी

4. हिन्दी में कुल कितने स्वर होते हैं?
(क) दस (ख) आठ
(ग) ग्यारह (घ) बारह

5. वर्ण को कहते हैं :
(क) मौखिक ध्वनि
(ख) लघुत्तम अक्षर
(ग) मूल ध्वनियाँ
(घ) बृहत्तम अक्षर

6. निम्नलिखित में अन्तःस्थ व्यंजन कौनसा है?
(क) य र ल व
(ख) आ ई ऊ ऋ
(ग) प फ ब भ म
(घ) ट ठ ड ढ ण

7. अयोगवाह के अन्तर्गत अनुस्वार का चिन्ह है :
(क) (:)
(ख) (∴)
(ग) (˙)
(घ) इनमें से कोई नहीं

8. उ, इ, उ, ऋ कौनसा स्वर है :
(क) ह्रस्व स्वर
(ख) प्लुत स्वर
(ग) दीर्घ स्वर
(घ) इनमें से कोई नहीं

9. श ष स ह कहलाते हैं :
(क) ऊष्म व्यंजन
(ख) संयुक्त व्यंजन
(ग) प्लुत स्वर
(घ) दीर्घ स्वर

10. निम्नलिखित में से किस अक्षर का उच्चारण मुँह और नाक से नहीं होता है?
(क) ङ (ख) ञ
(ग) म (घ) ब

11. उत्पत्ति के आधार पर शब्दों के कितने भेद होते हैं?
(क) पाँच (ख) छह
(ग) चार (घ) तीन

12. निम्नलिखित में से किस अक्षर का उच्चारण होठों से नहीं होता है?
(क) उ (ख) फ
(ग) ऊ (घ) त

13. आ, ई, ऊ, ओ और औ निम्नलिखित

में से कौनसा स्वर है?
(क) प्लुत स्वर
(ख) ह्रस्व स्वर
(ग) दीर्घ स्वर
(घ) इनमें से कोई नहीं

14. प्रयोग के अनुसार शब्दों के कितने भेद होते हैं?
(क) चार (ख) 8
(ग) तीन (घ) छह

15. भाषा किसका साधन है?
(क) बोलने का
(ख) अध्ययन का
(ग) लिखने का
(घ) अभिव्यक्ति का

16. जिन स्वरों के उच्चारण में 'अ' के उच्चारण के बराबर समय लगता है, उन्हें कहते हैं :
(क) प्लुत स्वर (ख) पूर्ण स्वर
(ग) ह्रस्व स्वर (घ) दीर्घ स्वर

17. व्यंजन तीन प्रकार के होते हैं : पहला स्पर्श, दूसरा अन्तस्थ और तीसरा :
(क) नासिका (ख) कण्ठ्य
(ग) ऊष्म (घ) दन्तोष्ठ

18. संयुक्त स्वर का एक उदाहरण है :
(क) इ (ख) उ
(ग) अ (घ) आ

19. एक या एक से अधिक वर्णों के संयोग से बनी ध्वनियों को क्या कहते हैं?
(क) शब्द (ख) व्यंजन
(ग) रूढ़ (घ) स्वर

20. 'पाठशाला' शब्द किस वर्ग का है?
(क) रूढ़ि
(ख) योगरूढ़ि
(ग) यौगिक
(घ) इनमें से कोई नहीं

21. त, थ, द, ध का उच्चारण :
(क) केवल ओठों से होता है
(ख) दाँतों के साथ जिह्वा के मेल से होता है
(ग) जीभ के प्रयोग के बिना होता है
(घ) कंठ व ओठों के मेल से होता है

22. महेश 'गधा' है। यहाँ गधा शब्द है:
(क) वाचक
(ख) लाक्षणिक
(ग) व्यंजक
(घ) इनमें से कोई नहीं

23. 'नीलकंठ' शब्द किस वर्ग का है?
(क) रूढ़ि
(ख) योगरूढ़
(ग) यौगिक
(घ) इनमें से कोई नहीं

24. "गौ" शब्द किस कोटि का है?
(क) लाक्षणिक
(ख) व्यंजक
(ग) वाचक
(घ) इनमें से कोई नहीं

25. हिन्दी में कितने 'कारक' होते हैं?
(क) पाँच (ख) दस
(ग) छह (घ) आठ

26. व्याकरण की दृष्टि से 'बुढ़ापा' क्या है?
(क) भाववाचक संज्ञा
(ख) व्यक्तिवाचक संज्ञा
(ग) क्रिया-विशेषण
(घ) जातिवाचक संज्ञा

27. 'हम' छात्र हैं। इसमें 'हम' पुरुषवाचक सर्वनाम है। यह है
(क) उत्तम पुरुष
(ख) प्रथम पुरुष
(ग) मध्यम पुरुष
(घ) इनमें से कोई नहीं

28. सीमा दौड़ती है। यहाँ 'दौड़ती है' कैसी क्रिया है?
(क) द्विकर्मक
(ख) सकर्मक
(ग) अकर्मक
(घ) इनमें से कोई नहीं

29. व्याकरण की द्रृष्टि से 'सौन्दर्य' क्या है?
(क) संज्ञा
(ख) सर्वनाम
(ग) विशेषण
(घ) क्रिया-विशेषण

30. 'पुरुष' कितने प्रकार के होते हैं?
(क) तीन (ख) पाँच
(ग) दो (घ) चार

31. विशेषण उन शब्दों को कहते हैं, जो:
(क) क्रिया की विशेषता प्रकट करें
(ख) संज्ञा के स्थान पर प्रयोग किये जायें
(ग) संज्ञा की विशेषता प्रकट करें
(घ) सर्वनाम की विशेषता बताएँ

32. संज्ञा के कितने भेद होते हैं? हैं?
(क) तीन (ख) पाँच
(ग) चार (घ) दो

33. जिन शब्दों में किसी प्रकार का विकार या परिवर्तन नहीं होता उन्हें क्या कहते हैं?
(क) धातु (ख) **मूल शब्द**
(ग) तत्सम (घ) अव्यय

34. निम्नलिखित में से कौनसा शब्द विशेषण है?
(क) चातुर्य (ख) पशुता
(ग) दुष्ट (घ) यौवन

35. 'ने' किस कारक की विभक्ति है?
(क) कर्त्ता (ख) करण
(ग) सम्प्रदाय (घ) कर्म

36. हिन्दी भाषा में कितने लिंग माने जाते हैं?
(क) तीन (ख) चार
(ग) पाँच (घ) दो

37. निम्नलिखित वाक्यों में किस वाक्य में अकर्मक क्रिया है?
(क) श्याम आम खाता है
(ख) ज्योति रोती है
(ग) मैंने उसे पुस्तक दी
(घ) उसने कमीज पहनी

38. मुख्यतः काल कितने हैं?
(क) तीन (ख) दो
(ग) चार (घ) पाँच

39. जिस शब्द के कई सार्थक खण्ड हो सकें, उन्हें क्या कहते हैं?
(क) रूढ़ (ख) संयुक्त
(ग) मिश्रित (घ) यौगिक

40. मूल क्रिया के अतिरिक्त वाक्य में जितनी भी क्रियाएँ आती हैं, उन्हें क्या कहते हैं?
(क) गौण क्रिया
(ख) रंजक क्रिया
(ग) अकर्मक क्रिया

(घ) सहायक क्रिया

41. निम्नलिखित शब्दों में से कौनसा शब्द अविकारी है?

(क) आजकल (ख) घोड़ा

(ग) नदी (घ) संकेत

42. 'कक्षा' कौनसी संज्ञा है?

(क) समुदायवाचक

(ख) भाववाचक

(ग) व्यक्तिवाचक

(घ) जातिवाचक

43. 'सीता तेज दौड़ती है'। इसमें तेज शब्द क्या है?

(क) विशेषण

(ख) क्रिया

(ग) क्रिया-विशेषण

(घ) इनमें से कोई नहीं

44. निम्न में से कौनसा शब्द सर्वनाम है?

(क) हमारे

(ख) मेरी

(ग) उन्होंने

(घ) उपरोक्त तीनों

45. निम्नलिखित में से कौनसी अकर्मक क्रिया है?

(क) हँसना (ख) चुराना

(ग) माँगना (घ) लेना

46. व्याकरण की दृष्टि से 'प्रेम' शब्द क्या है?

(क) अव्यय

(ख) भाववाचक संज्ञा

(ग) क्रिया

(घ) विशेषण

47. सर्वनाम का प्रयोग किसके बदले में किया जाता है?

(क) क्रिया

(ख) क्रिया-विशेषण

(ग) संज्ञा

(घ) विशेषण

48. विशेषण किसकी विशेषता बताता है?

(क) सर्वनाम की

(ख) क्रिया की

(ग) संज्ञा की

(घ) संज्ञा एवं सर्वनाम दोनों की

लिंग

निर्देश: *नीचे दिए गए चार शब्दों में से विपरीत लिंग ज्ञात करो।*

49. गीदड़

(क) गीदड़

(ख) गीदड़ी

(ग) गीदड़ीन

(घ) इनमें से कोई नहीं

50. कहार

(क) कहारिन (ख) कहारी

(ग) कहार (घ) कहरियाँ

51. नट

(क) नटिया

(ख) नटी

(ग) नटाईन

(घ) इनमें से कोई नहीं

52. जुलाहा

(क) जुलाही

(ख) जुलाहिन

(ग) जुलहनिया

(घ) इनमें से कोई नहीं

53. ठठेरा

(क) ठठेरिन (ख) ठठेरी

(ग) ठठेराइन (घ) ठठेरन

54. जाट
(क) जटाइन (ख) जाटिनी
(ग) जाटी (घ) जाटेरन

55. चौधरी
(क) चौधरानी
(ख) चौधराइन
(ग) चौधरिन
(घ) इनमें से कोई नहीं

56. जेठ
(क) जेठानी (ख) जेठी
(ग) जेठरानी (घ) जेठाइन

57. देवर
(क) देवरी (ख) देवरानी
(ग) देवराइन (घ) देवरिन

58. प्रिय
(क) प्रियसी (ख) प्रियतम
(ग) प्रिया (घ) प्रिये

59. बाल
(क) बाली (ख) बाला
(ग) बालीन (घ) बालिके

60. रूपवान
(क) रूपमती (ख) रूपवानी
(ग) रूपवाइन (घ) रूपवती

61. धनवान
(क) धनवाइन (ख) धनवानी
(ग) धनवती (घ) धनमती

62. बाबू
(क) बाबूनी (ख) बाबूरानी
(ग) बबुआइन (घ) बाबूरिन

63. दुबे
(क) दुबी (ख) दुबाइन
(ग) दुबीन (घ) दुबिआइन

64. प्रेषक
(क) प्रेषकी (ख) प्रेषिका
(ग) प्रेषिकाइन (घ) प्रेषिकिन

65. विद्वान
(क) विद्वानी (ख) विद्वनी
(ग) विदुषी (घ) विद्ववाइन

वचन

निर्देश: *निम्नलिखित शब्दों का बहुवचन ज्ञात करो।*

66. शक्ति
(क) शक्तियाँ (ख) शक्ती
(ग) शक्ते (घ) शक्तियें

67. डिबिया
(क) डिबियाँ (ख) डिबियाएँ
(ग) डिबियों (घ) डिबियाओं

68. खूंटी
(क) खूंटे (ख) खूंटियाँ
(ग) खूंटियाएँ (घ) खूंटियाओं

69. गुड़िया
(क) गुड़ियाँ (ख) गुड़ियें
(ग) गुड़ियों (घ) गुड़ियाएँ

70. बहू
(क) बहुओं (ख) बहुएँ
(ग) बहू (घ) बहुआएँ

71. रीति
(क) रीते (ख) रीतियें
(ग) रीतियाँ (घ) रीतियों

72. श्रीमती
(क) श्रीमते (ख) श्रीमतिएँ
(ग) श्रीमतियाँ (घ) श्रीमतीने

73. लालटेन
(क) लालटेनों
(ख) लालटेनें
(ग) लालटेन
(घ) इनमें से कोई नहीं

74. चोर
(क) चोरें (ख) चोरों
(ग) चोरियाँ (घ) चोर

75. गौ
(क) गौवाँ (ख) गौएँ
(ग) गौवन (घ) गौवें

76. आँख
(क) अंखियाँ (ख) आँखें
(ग) आँखों (घ) अँखियाएँ

77. भाई
(क) भाइया (ख) भाइयाँ
(ग) भाइयों (घ) भाइएँ

78. सिपाही
(क) सिपाहियों (ख) सिपाहियाँ
(ग) सिपहिये (घ) सिपाहें

79. घर
(क) घरों (ख) घरें
(ग) घराएँ (घ) घरे

80. कन्या
(क) कन्याएँ (ख) कन्याओं
(ग) कन्याइयाँ (घ) कन्ये

81. लड़का
(क) लड़के (ख) लड़काओं
(ग) लड़कों (घ) लड़काएँ

82. मैं
(क) हम (ख) मैंने
(ग) हमारा (घ) मेरा

83. चुहिया
(क) चुहियों (ख) चुहिए
(ग) चुहियाओं (घ) चुहियाँ

84. भेड़िया
(क) भेड़ियों (ख) भेड़ियाँ
(ग) भेड़ियाएँ (घ) भेड़िए

85. आत्मा
(क) आत्माओं (ख) आत्माएँ
(ग) आत्में (घ) आत्माँ

भाववाचक शब्द

निर्देश: *निम्नलिखित शब्दों में से भाववाचक शब्द छाँटो।*

86. भ्राता
(क) भ्रातृ
(ख) भ्रातृत्व
(ग) भ्राताश्री
(घ) इनमें से कोई नहीं

87. तपस्वी
(क) तपस्या (ख) तप
(ग) तपस्वरी (घ) तपस्वीया

88. भारत
(क) भरत (ख) भारतीय
(ग) भारतीयता (घ) भारतीए

89. अहम्
(क) मैं (ख) अहंकार
(ग) अहंकर (घ) अहंकारे

90. उचित
(क) औचित्य (ख) जायज
(ग) उपयुक्त (घ) उचितया

91. कठिन
(क) कठिनतम (ख) कठिनता
(ग) कठिनाइयाँ (घ) कठिनाई

92. चतुर
(क) चतुराई (ख) चालाक
(ग) चतुरे (घ) चतुर

93. बूढ़ा
(क) बुढ़ापा (ख) वृद्धा
(ग) बुढ़ावी (घ) बुढ़ौती

94. बड़ा
(क) बड़प्पन (ख) युवा
(ग) बड़े (घ) बुजुर्ग

95. कृपण
(क) कृपाण (ख) कृपालु
(ग) कृपणता (घ) कृपणे

96. युवा
(क) युवक (ख) यौवन
(ग) युथ (घ) नवयुवक

97. व्यक्ति
(क) व्यक्तित्त्व (ख) प्राणी
(ग) व्यक्तित्त्वता (घ) व्यक्तिगत

98. मरना
(क) मृत्यु (ख) मिथ्या
(ग) मरण (घ) परलोक

99. शूर
(क) शूरत्व (ख) शूरवीर
(ग) शौर्य (घ) शूरमा

100. अपना
(क) अपनत्व (ख) अपनापन
(ग) अर्पण (घ) अर्पित

101. महान
(क) महन्ता (ख) महानता
(ग) महामना (घ) महन्त

102. आलसी
(क) अलसस्य (ख) आलस्य
(ग) अलसे (घ) आलसीया

103. कंजूस
(क) कंजूसी
(ख) कंजूसता
(ग) कंजूसई
(घ) इनमें से कोई नहीं

104. कहना
(क) कथन (ख) कथनीय
(ग) कहावत (घ) कथानक

105. ईश्वर
(क) ऐश्वर्य (ख) ईश्वरीय
(ग) दैवी (घ) ईश्वरता

विशेषण

निर्देशः *निम्नलिखित शब्दों के विशेषण छांटोः*

106. उत्कर्ष
(क) उत्कर्षी (ख) उत्कृष्ट
(ग) उत्कर्षे (घ) अत्कर्षा

107. घना
(क) घनाकार (ख) घनी
(ग) घनघोर (घ) घनयुक्त

108. अग्नि
(क) अग्निकार (ख) आग्नेय
(ग) अग्निकृत (घ) अग्निवेष

109. ऐश्वर्य
(क) ऐश्वर्यरे (ख) ऐश्वर्यवान
(ग) एकेश्वर (घ) ईश्वरीय

110. हृदय
(क) हृदयता (ख) हार्दिक
(ग) हृदयी (घ) हृदया

111. कुल
(क) कुलीन (ख) कुले
(ग) कुलता (घ) कुलरूपी

112. अभ्यास
(क) अभ्यस्थ (ख) अभ्यस्थता
(ग) अभ्यस्त (घ) अभासी

113. कृतघ्नता
(क) कृतज्ञ (ख) कृतघन
(ग) कृपालु (घ) कृतघ्न

114. चिन्ता
(क) चिन्तनीय (ख) चिन्तित
(ग) चिन्तामणि (घ) चिन्ताहरी

115. जिज्ञासा
(क) जिज्ञासु (ख) जिज्ञास
(ग) जिज्ञासपूर्ण (घ) जिज्ञासी

116. अर्थ
(क) अर्थे (ख) अनर्थ
(ग) आर्थिक (घ) अर्थक

117. धर्म
(क) धर्मज्ञ (ख) धर्मस्थ
(ग) धर्मात्मा (घ) धार्मिक

118. ज्योति
(क) ज्योतिष (ख) ज्योतिका
(ग) ज्यातिर्गमय (घ) ज्योतिके

119. दूर
(क) दुरता (ख) दूरियाँ
(ग) दूरस्थ (घ) दूरतम

120. प्रकृति
(क) प्राकृतिक (ख) प्रकृति
(ग) प्राकृत (घ) प्रकृतम

121. राष्ट्र
(क) राष्ट्रीयता (ख) राष्ट्रीय
(ग) राष्ट्रे (घ) राष्ट्रतम

122. प्रशंसा
(क) प्रशंसनीय (ख) प्रशंसे
(ग) प्रशंसा (घ) प्रसन्नतम

123. यश
(क) यशस्वी (ख) तेजस्वी
(ग) यश (घ) ओजस्वी

124. सूर्य
(क) सूर्या (ख) सूरज
(ग) सौर (घ) सूरय

125. प्यास
(क) प्यासा (ख) प्यासी
(ग) प्याश (घ) प्यासम

126. गृह
(क) गृहणी (ख) गृहस्थी
(ग) गृहीनी (घ) गृहस्थ

127. प्रयत्न
(क) प्रयत्नशील (ख) प्रयत्नी
(ग) प्रयास (घ) चेष्टा

128. निन्दा
(क) निन्दनीय (ख) नृद्रा
(ग) निन्दगीय (घ) निन्दा

129. विपत्ति
(क) विपरीत (ख) विपत्ति
(ग) विपदा (घ) विपन्न

130. भीख
(क) भिक्षा (ख) भिखारी
(ग) भिक्षावृत्ति (घ) भिखमंगा

क्रिया-विशेषण

131. क्रिया-विशेषण उन शब्दों को कहते हैं, जो–
(क) क्रिया की विशेष्रता बतायें
(ख) क्रिया का काल बतायें
(ग) क्रिया और विशेषण का काम करें
(घ) क्रिया से बने हों

132. 'जोर से बोलिए'। इसमें क्रिया-विशेषण क्या है?
(क) जोर (ख) से
(ग) जोर से (घ) बोलिये

133. 'वह कल अवश्य आयेगा'। इसमें क्रिया-विशेषण क्या है?
(क) आयेगा (ख) वह
(ग) कल (घ) अवश्य

134. 'उसे इधर आना है।' इसमें क्रिया-

विशेषण क्या है?

(क) उसे (ख) आना है

(ग) इधर (घ) उसे इधर

135. 'चोर धीरे-से खिसक गया' इसमें क्रिया-विशेषण क्या है?

(क) खिसक गया

(ख) धीरे-से खिसक गया

(ग) धीरे-से

(घ) चोर धीरे-से खिसक गया

136. कर्त्ता कारक की विभक्ति कौन-सी है?

(क) को (ख) ने

(ग) से (घ) में

137. टेबुल पर पुस्तकें रखी हैं? इस वाक्य में 'पर' किस कारक का चिन्ह है?

(क) कर्त्ता कारक

(ख) अधिकरण कारक

(ग) सम्प्रदान कारक

(घ) करण कारक

138. मुन्ना के लिए फल खरीद लो। इसमें 'के लिए' किस कारक का चिन्ह है?

(क) करण कारक

(ख) अपादान कारक

(ग) कर्म कारक

(घ) सम्प्रदान कारक

139. संबंध कारक की विभक्ति कौन-सी है?

(क) का, के, की

(ख) को

(ग) हे

(घ) उपरोक्त सभी

140. हरी ने कुत्ते को बचाया। इसमें 'को' किस कारक की विभक्ति है?

(क) संबंध कारक

(ख) कर्मकारक

(ग) अपादान कारक

(घ) सम्प्रदान कारक

141. हिन्दी की लिपि कौनसी है?

(क) देवनागरी (ख) गुरुमुखी

(ग) रोमन (घ) फारसी

142. 'च, छ, ज, झ' के उच्चारण को मुखांगों के व्यवहार के आधार पर क्या नाम दिया जाता है?

(क) तालव्य (ख) मूर्धन्य

(ग) दन्त्य (घ) ओष्ठ्य

143. 'प, फ, ब, भ' के उच्चारण को मुखांगों के व्यवहार के आधार पर क्या नाम दिया जाता है?

(क) कण्ठ्य (ख) तालव्य

(ग) दन्त्य (घ) ओष्ठ्य

144. मौखिक ध्वनियों को प्रकट करने वाले अथवा प्रकट करने के लिए निश्चित किए गए चिन्हों को क्या कहते हैं?

(क) व्याकरण

(ख) भाषा

(ग) लिपि

(घ) उपरोक्त सभी

145. 'बुढ़ापा' कौनसी संज्ञा को प्रकट करता है?

(क) द्रव्यवाचक

(ख) व्यक्तिवाचक

(ग) भाववाचक

(घ) जातिनाचक

146. 'प्रेम' कौनसी संज्ञा है?

(क) द्रव्यवाचक

(ख) जातिवाचक

(ग) भाववाचक

(घ) व्यक्तिवाचक

147. 'कक्षा' संज्ञा है :
(क) समूहवाचक
(ख) जातिवाचक
(ग) व्यक्तिवाचक
(घ) उपरोक्त सभी

148. कारक के कितने भेद हैं?
(क) चार (ख) सात
(ग) आठ (घ) तीन

149. 'छत के ऊपर मत जाओ' वाक्य में कौनसा कारक है?
(क) कर्त्ता (ख) करण
(ग) अधिकरण (घ) सम्बोधन

150. 'अजी भाई साहब, बात सुनना', वाक्य में कारक बताएँ।
(क) कर्म (ख) अपादान
(ग) अधिकरण (घ) सम्बोधन

151. सर्वनाम के कितने भेद हैं?
(क) चार (ख) आठ
(ग) छः (घ) नौ

152. 'जो प्रयत्न करता है, वह फल भी पाता है'। इस वाक्य में कौनसा सर्वनाम है?
(क) प्रश्नवाचक सर्वनाम
(ख) सम्बन्धवाचक सर्वनाम
(ग) पुरुषवाचक सर्वनाम
(घ) निजवाचक सर्वनाम

153. 'आप भला तो जग भला'—उक्त वाक्य में कौनसा सर्वनाम है?
(क) प्रश्नवाचक
(ख) सम्बन्धवाचक
(ग) निजवाचक
(घ) पुरुषवाचक

154. जो शब्द संज्ञा अथवा सर्वनाम की विशेषता प्रकट करे, उसे कहते हैं:
(क) संज्ञा (ख) विशेषण
(ग) प्रत्यय (घ) लिंग

155. 'राम आम खाता है'—उक्त वाक्य में कौनसी क्रिया है?
(क) अकर्मक
(ख) सकर्मक
(ग) संयुक्त
(घ) उपरोक्त सभी

वर्तनी

निर्देशः *नीचे के प्रश्नों में एक शब्द की चार अलग-अलग वर्तनियां दी हुई हैं। इनमें से सही वर्तनी छाँटकर उस पर निशान लगाइयेः*

1. (क) अधम्र (ख) अध्रम
(ग) अधर्म (घ) अधृम

2. (क) अधिकृत (ख) अधिक्रित
(ग) अधिक्रित्त (घ) अधिर्कित

3. (क) अनुकृम (ख) अनुक्रम
(ग) अनुकर्म (घ) अनुकम्र

4. (क) अनवेषण (ख) अन्वेषण
(ग) अन्वेछण (घ) अन्वेशण

5. (क) अभिशेक (ख) अभिषेख
(ग) अभिषेक (घ) अभीषेक

6. (क) इच्छुक (ख) इक्षुक
(ग) इक्छुक (घ) इच्छिक

7. (क) इन्र्दिय (ख) इन्दिय
(ग) इन्दिय (घ) इन्द्रिय

8. (क) ईष्या (ख) ईर्श्या
(ग) इर्ष्या (घ) ईर्ष्या

9. (क) उतकण्ठा (ख) उत्कण्ठा
(ग) उत्क्णठा (घ) उत्त्कन्ठा

10. (क) उमृिला (ख) उम्रिला
(ग) उर्मिर्ला (घ) उर्मिला

11. (क) रिषि (ख) ऋषि
(ग) त्रिषि (घ) ऋशि

12. (क) एकागृ (ख) एकाग्र
(ग) एकार्ग (घ) एक्राग्र

13. (क) ओजश्वि (ख) ओजस्वी
(ग) ओजश्वी (घ) ओजष्वी

14. (क) औशधी (ख) औषधी
(ग) औषधि (घ) औध्षि

15. (क) करम (ख) क्राम
(ग) कम्र (घ) कर्म

16. (क) ग्रिहीत (ख) ग्रहीत
(ग) गृहीत (घ) गर्हित

17. (क) कृतज्ञ (ख) क्रतज्ञ
(ग) क्रितज्ञ (घ) क्रितग्य

18. (क) चतुदर्श (ख) चर्तुदश
(ग) चतुर्दश (घ) चतुद्रश

19. (क) जर्जर (ख) जरर्जर
(ग) जज्रर (घ) जरजर

20. (क) जघ्नय (ख) जघ्रय
(ग) जघ्न्य (घ) जघन्य

21. (क) जेष्ठ (ख) ज्येश्ठ
(ग) ज्येष्ठ (घ) ज्येस्ठ

22. (क) ज्योतस्ना (ख) ज्योत्शना
(ग) ज्योस्तना (घ) ज्योत्स्ना

23. (क) तपस्वनी (ख) तपस्विनी
(ग) तपिस्वनी (घ) तपिस्विनी

24. (क) तादातमय (ख) तदात्म्य
(ग) तादात्म्य (घ) तादात्यम

25. (क) तृष्णा (ख) तिृष्णा
(ग) त्रिष्णा (घ) तृशणा

26. (क) त्रिमूर्ती (ख) त्रिमुर्ति
(ग) त्रिमूर्ति (घ) त्रमूर्ति

27. (क) दक्छ (ख) दक्च्छ
(ग) दक्ष (घ) दज्ञ

28. (क) द्रर्पन (ख) दर्पन
(ग) दपर्ण (घ) दर्पण

29. (क) दामपत्य (ख) दम्पत्य
(ग) दाम्पत्य (घ) दाम्पत

30. (क) दीप्पित (ख) दीपति
(ग) दीप्ति (घ) दीप्ती

31. (क) दीर्घायु (ख) दीरघायु
(ग) दीघार्यु (घ) दीर्घियु

32. (क) दुर्निती (ख) दुनीर्ति
(ग) दुरनीति (घ) दुर्नीति

33. (क) दुर्दषा (ख) दुहशा
(ग) दुर्दशा (घ) दुद्रशा

34. (क) दुर्योधन (ख) दुयोधन
(ग) द्ररयोधन (घ) द्रुयोधन

35. (क) दुरबुद्धि (ख) दुर्बुधि
(ग) दुबुद्धि (घ) दुर्बुद्धि

36. (क) धनुष्विद्या (ख) धनुर्विद्या
(ग) धर्नुविद्या (घ) धनुर्वेद्या

37. (क) इकट्ठा (ख) एकट्ठा
(ग) एकठा (घ) एकाट्ठा

38. (क) गायकी (ख) गोयिका
(ग) गायिका (घ) गायीका

39. (क) नर्म्रदेश्वर (ख) नम्रदेश्वर
(ग) नमर्देश्वर (घ) नर्मदेश्वर

40. (क) निश्क्षेप (ख) निक्क्षेप
(ग) निक्षेप (घ) निक्छेप

41. (क) निर्गह (ख) नृग्रह
(ग) निग्रह (घ) निगर्ह

42. (क) निरजीव (ख) निर्जीव
(ग) निृजीव (घ) निज्रीव

43. (क) निम्रूल (ख) निर्मूल
(ग) निरमूल (घ) नृर्मूल

44. (क) निवृत्त (ख) निव्रत्त
(ग) निवृत (घ) निृवत्त

45. (क) प्रिक्रमा (ख) परीक्रमा
(ग) परिकृमा (घ) परिक्रमा

46. (क) प्रयटन (ख) पृयटन
(ग) पर्यटन (घ) प्रर्यटन

47. (क) प्रक्रिति (ख) प्रकृति
(ग) प्रक्रति (घ) पृक्रति

48. (क) बर्हिमुख (ख) बहिर्मुख
(ग) बहिम्रुख (घ) बहिमुर्ख

49. (क) भरतस्ना (ख) भर्त्सना
(ग) भर्तसना (घ) भर्तृसना

50. (क) मूर्ती (ख) मूर्ति
(ग) मूर्तृ (घ) मूरती

51. (क) इकतारा (ख) एकतारा
(ग) इकेतारा (घ) एकातारा

52. (क) र्निजीव (ख) निरजीव
(ग) निर्जीव (घ) निज्रीव

53. (क) निर्मूल (ख) नृमूल
(ग) निम्रूल (घ) नृम्रूल

54. (क) पार्थिव (ख) पार्थिव
(ग) पार्थीव (घ) पाथिर्व

55. (क) विदूश्क (ख) विदूष्क
(ग) विदूशक (घ) विदूषक

56. (क) फुर्तीला (ख) फुर्तीला
(ग) फुर्तिला (घ) फुर्तला

57. (क) वर्ज (ख) वज्र
(ग) वजृ (घ) वज्रृ

58. (क) सीन्दूर (ख) सिन्दुर
(ग) सिन्दूर (घ) सीनदूर

59. (क) ब्रम्हचर्य (ख) ब्रह्मचर्य
(ग) बृह्मचर्य (घ) ब्रह्मर्चय

60. (क) भ्रर्तस्ना (ख) भर्तस्ना
(ग) भर्त्सना (घ) भ्र्त्सना

61. (क) मत्स्य (ख) मतस्य
(ग) मत्सत्य (घ) मत्श्य

62. (क) भ्रित्य (ख) भर्त्य
(ग) भृत्य (घ) भ्रत्य

63. (क) निग्रंध (ख) निर्गंध
(ग) र्निगंध (घ) नृगंध

64. (क) प्रक्रिति (ख) प्रक्रिति
(ग) पृकृति (घ) प्रकृति

65. (क) प्रकर्श (ख) प्रकर्ष
(ग) पृकर्श (घ) पृकर्ष

66. (क) भद्र (ख) भदृ
(ग) भृद्र (घ) भर्द

67. (क) मंजूशा (ख) मंजूषा
(ग) मंजुषा (घ) मंजुशा

68. (क) मुर्मूषु (ख) मुमुर्षू
(ग) मुमुर्षु (घ) मुमूर्षु

69. (क) ब्राह्मण (ख) ब्राह्मण
(ग) ब्राम्हण (घ) बृाहम्ण

70. (क) चतुदर्शी (ख) चर्तुदशी
(ग) चतुर्दशी (घ) चर्तुदशी

71. (क) तिर्स्कृत (ख) तिरस्कृत
(ग) तिरस्क्रत (घ) तिरिस्क्रित

72. (क) तरंगिणि (ख) तरंगणी
(ग) तरंगिणी (घ) तरंग्णी

73. (क) तार्क्रिक (ख) तार्किक
(ग) ताकृिक (घ) ताक्रिक

74. (क) दरपन (ख) दप्रण
(ग) दपर्ण (घ) दर्पण

75. (क) दर्रिद्र (ख) दरिद्र
(ग) दरिर्द्र (घ) दरिद्य

76. (क) ज्योत्स्ना (ख) ज्योत्सना
(ग) जयोत्स्ना (घ) ज्योस्त्ना

77. (क) प्रर्दशनी (ख) पृदर्श्नी
(ग) पृदर्शनी (घ) प्रदर्शनी

78. (क) परिकर्म्रा (ख) परिक्रमा
(ग) परिकृमा (घ) प्ररिक्रमा

79. (क) निषृद्ध (ख) निषिद्ध
(ग) निशिद्ध (घ) निषिद्द

80. (क) प्रभृति (ख) पृभृति
(ग) पृभ्रति (घ) प्रभिृति

81. (क) परवीण (ख) प्रवीण
(ग) प्रवीर्ण (घ) परविण

82. (क) पृथिवी (ख) पृथ्वी
(ग) पृथ्वी (घ) प्रिथ्वी

83. (क) धम्र (ख) धरम
(ग) धर्म (घ) धृर्म

84. (क) ध्रुव (ख) ध्रृव
(ग) ध्रुर्व (घ) धुर्व

85. (क) ध्रिष्ट (ख) धृश्ट
(ग) धृष्ट (घ) ध्रिस्ट

86. (क) नक्छत्र (ख) नक्क्षत्र
(ग) नछत्र (घ) नक्षत्र

87. (क) निर्मल (ख) निरमल
(ग) निमर्ल (घ) निम्रल

88. (क) पैतृर्क (ख) पैत्रिक
(ग) पैत्रक (घ) पैतृक

89. (क) न्रतक (ख) नृतक
(ग) नर्तक (घ) नतर्क

90. (क) निर्विघ्न (ख) निरविघ्न
(ग) निर्व्रिघ्न (घ) निरविघ्न

91. (क) निश्क्रिय (ख) निष्क्रिय
(ग) निस्क्रिय (घ) निष्कृय

92. (क) ध्रूर्त (ख) धूर्त
(ग) ध्रुर्त (घ) धूतृ

93. (क) आगृह (ख) आग्रह
(ग) आर्गह (घ) आगहर्य

94. (क) सत्क्रम (ख) सतक्रम
(ग) सत्कर्म (घ) सत्कम्र

95. (क) विस्तृित (ख) वृस्तृत
(ग) विस्त्रित (घ) विस्तृत

96. (क) वृशभ (ख) व्रशभ
(ग) वृषभ (घ) व्रषभ

97. (क) यशश्वी (ख) यशस्वी
(ग) यशष्वी (घ) यशस्वि

98. (क) रोद्दर (ख) रोद्र
(ग) रौद् (घ) रौद्र

99. (क) स्म्रति (ख) स्मृति
(ग) सृमिति (घ) स्रमिति

100. (क) पारंभ (ख) प्रारम्भ
(ग) पारम्भ (घ) प्रार्म्भ

101. (क) श्रींग (ख) शृंग
(ग) श्रिंग (घ) श्रंग

102. (क) विभ्रम्म (ख) विभर्म
(ग) विभृम (घ) विभ्रम

103. (क) वक्रृ (ख) वकृ
(ग) वक्र (घ) व्रक्र

104. (क) वर्तलु (ख) ब्रर्तुल
(ग) व्रतुल (घ) वर्तुल

105. (क) द्रश्य (ख) दृश्य
(ग) दृष्य (घ) द्रिश्य

106. (क) सन्धिग्द (ख) संदिग्द
(ग) संदिग्ध (घ) सदिग्द्व

107. (क) यथेश्ठ (ख) यथेष्ट
(ग) यथेष्ठ (घ) यथेस्ठ

108. (क) शार्दलू (ख) शाद्रूल
(ग) शार्दूल (घ) शार्द्रूल

109. (क) व्यज्ञर (ख) व्यगर
(ग) व्यगृ (घ) व्यग्र

110. (क) सुकृर्म (ख) सुक्रर्म
(ग) सुकर्म (घ) सुक्रम

111. (क) स्निग्ध (ख) स्निज्ध
(ग) श्निग्ध (घ) षिनिग्ध

112. (क) स्पिृहा (ख) स्प्रिहा
(ग) स्पृहा (घ) स्प्रीहा

113. (क) परीशिष्ट (ख) परिशिष्ट
(ग) प्रीशिष्ट (घ) परशिष्ट

114. (क) आशीवादं (ख) आशीर्वाद
(ग) आशिर्वाद (घ) आर्शीवाद

115. (क) यज्य (ख) यग्य
(ग) यज्ञ (घ) यज्ञय

116. (क) शुर्श्रुषा (ख) शुशूषा
(ग) श्रूशुषा (घ) शुश्रूषा

117. (क) प्रत्यक्ष (ख) प्रत्यक्ष्य
(ग) पृत्यक्ष (घ) प्रत्यक्छ

118. (क) अन्ताछरी (ख) अन्ताक्षरी
(ग) अन्त्याछरी (घ) अन्त्याक्षरी

119. (क) रचइता (ख) रचयिता
(ग) रचियता (घ) रचियिता

120. (क) वैयक्तिक (ख) वयक्तिक
(ग) वैयकतिक (घ) व्यक्तिक

121. (क) द्वन्ध्व (ख) द्वन्द
(ग) द्वन्द्व (घ) दन्द्व

122. (क) यथाशक्ती (ख) यथाशक्ति
(ग) यथाषक्ति (घ) यथासक्ति

123. (क) क्षत्रीय (ख) क्षत्रिय
(ग) छत्रिय (घ) क्षतृय

124. (क) राशी (ख) राषि
(ग) राशि (घ) रासि

125. (क) लक्ष्मी (ख) लक्ष्मि
(ग) लक्छमी (घ) लक्ष्मी

126. (क) रोस (ख) रोश
(ग) रोष (घ) रूष

127. (क) ग्यानशुन्य (ख) ग्यानशून्य
(ग) ज्ञानशून्य (घ) ज्ञानशुन्य

128. (क) मोहनि (ख) मोहिनि
(ग) मोहिनी (घ) मोहनी

129. (क) धनूष (ख) धनुस
(ग) धनुश (घ) धनुष

130. (क) अश्यर्च (ख) आर्श्चाय
(ग) आर्श्चय (घ) आश्चर्य

131. (क) क्रोध (ख) कृोध्
(ग) क्रोध (घ) कौध

132. (क) स्फर्ति (ख) श्फूर्ति
(ग) स्फूर्ती (घ) स्फूर्ति

133. (क) विकृत् (ख) विकर्त
(ग) विक्रत (घ) विकृत

134. (क) राश्ट्रिय (ख) राष्ट्रिय
(ग) राष्ट्रीय (घ) राश्ट्रीय

135. (क) सव्रज्ञ (ख) सर्वज्ञ
(ग) सर्वग्य (घ) सर्वग

136. (क) निष्पक्छ (ख) निस्पक्ष
(ग) निश्पक्ष (घ) निष्पक्ष

137. (क) शाष्वत (ख) शास्वात
(ग) शास्वत (घ) शाश्वत

138. (क) निरदोश (ख) निद्रोस
(ग) निर्दोष (घ) निद्रोश

139. (क) तिरभुवन (ख) त्रिभुवान
(ग) तृभुवन (घ) त्रिभुवन

140. (क) नीष्काम (ख) निश्काम
(ग) निष्काम (घ) निस्काम

प्रत्यय और उपसर्ग

1. उपसर्ग लग जाने से मूल शब्द :
(क) का अर्थ नहीं बदलता
(ख) का अर्थ बदल जाता है
(ग) सदैव उल्टा अर्थ देता है
(घ) सदैव नाकारात्मक बन जाता है

2. उपसर्ग शब्द के :
(क) आरम्भ में जोड़े जाते हैं
(ख) अन्त में जोड़े जाते हैं
(ग) बीच में जोड़े जाते हैं
(घ) कभी आरम्भ में और कभी अन्त में जोड़े जाते हैं

उपसर्ग कितने प्रकार के माने गए हैं?
(क) एक (ख) दो
(ग) तीन (घ) चार

4. उपसर्ग :
(क) शब्दों को शुद्ध बनाते हैं
(ख) शब्दों का रूप बिगाड़ देते हैं
(ग) शब्द की व्याख्या करते हैं
(घ) उपरोक्त में से कोई भी नहीं

5. 'नि' उपसर्ग लगाने से शब्द का अर्थ :
(क) स्पष्ट हो जाता है
(ख) उल्टा हो जाता है
(ग) विशिष्ट हो जाता है
(घ) असामान्य हो जाता है

6. प्रत्यक्ष में कौन-सा उपसर्ग है?
(क) प्रति
(ख) प्र
(ग) प्रत्य
(घ) उपरोक्त में से कोई नहीं

7. 'दुर्गम' कैसा उपसर्ग है?
(क) तत्सम (ख) तद्भव
(ग) विदेशी

8. 'सरस' कैसा उपसर्ग है?
(क) तद्भव (ख) तत्सम
(ग) विदेशी

9. 'बेखबर' कैसा उपसर्ग है?
(क) तत्सम (ख) तद्भव
(ग) विदेशी

10. 'चतुराई' में क्या प्रत्यय जोड़ा गया है?
(क) राई (ख) ई
(ग) आई

11. 'अधिकार' में उपसर्ग क्या है?
(क) अ (ख) अधिक
(ग) अधि

12. 'अपशकुन' कैसा उपसर्ग है?
(क) तत्सम (ख) तद्भव
(ग) विदेशी

13. 'चौपाया' कैसा उपसर्ग है?
(क) तत्सम (ख) तद्भव
(ग) विदेशी

14. 'स्वदेश' कैसा उपसर्ग है?
(क) तत्सम (ख) तद्भव
(ग) विदेशी

15. 'बेईमान' कैसा उपसर्ग है?
(क) तद्भव (ख) तत्सम
(ग) विदेशी

16. 'विज्ञान' में कौन-सा उपसर्ग जोड़ा गया है?
(क) विज्ञ (ख) ज्ञान
(ग) वि (घ) अन

17. 'चिरायु' में कौन-सा उपसर्ग जोड़ा गया है?
(क) चि (ख) चिर
(ग) यु (घ) आयु

18. 'अवनत' में कौन-सा उपसर्ग जोड़ा गया है?
(क) नत (ख) अ
(ग) अव (घ) अवन

19. 'कुसंगी' कैसा उपसर्ग है?
(क) तत्सम (ख) तद्भव
(ग) विदेशी

20. 'बेपर्दा' कैसा उपसर्ग है?
(क) तद्भव (ख) विदेशी
(ग) तत्सम

21. 'अपकर्ष' में कौन-सा उपसर्ग जोड़ा गया है?
(क) अ (ख) अप
(ग) कर्ष

22. 'होनी' में कौन-सा उपसर्ग जोड़ा जाएगा?
(क) अ (ख) अनु
(ग) अन (घ) अप

23. 'जीवन' में आ उपसर्ग जोड़कर आजीवन बना है। इसका अर्थ है:
(क) जीवन-भर
(ख) जीवन के लिए
(ग) सुखी जीवन
(घ) उद्धार

24. 'दरअसल' कैसा उपसर्ग है?
(क) तत्सम
(ख) तद्भव
(ग) विदेशी

25. 'निरपराध' में कौन-सा उपसर्ग जोड़ा गया है?
(क) नि (ख) निः
(ग) निर

26. 'सदाचारी' कैसा उपसर्ग है?
(क) तत्सम
(ख) विदेशी
(ग) तद्भव

27. कुशासन में कु उपसर्ग जोड़ा गया है। इसका अर्थ है – बुरा शासन। शासन में कौन-सा उपसर्ग जोड़कर हम उसे अच्छा शासन बना सकते हैं?
(क) वि (ख) सु
(ग) अन (घ) अभि

28. 'अनपढ़' कैसा उपसर्ग है?
(क) तत्सम (ख) तद्भव
(ग) दिदेशी

29. 'अनजान' में कैसा उपसर्ग है?
(क) विदेशी (ख) तत्सम
(ग) तद्भव

30. 'अधमरा' कैसा उपसर्ग है?
(क) तत्सम (ख) तद्भव
(ग) विदेशी

31. 'रस' में कौन-सा उपसर्ग लगाने से इसका अर्थ उल्टा हो जायेगा?
(क) अन (ख) अ
(ग) वि (घ) नि

32. 'अनमोल' में कैसा उपसर्ग है?
(क) विदेशी (ख) तत्सम
(ग) तद्भव

33. अदब में 'बे' उपसर्ग लगाकर बेअदब बना है। इसका उल्टा अर्थ देने के लिए कौन-सा उपसर्ग जोड़ेंगे?
(क) दर (ख) बा
(ग) अन (घ) बद

34. नीचे दिए गए शब्दों में किस शब्द में तत्सम उपसर्ग जुड़ा है?
(क) बिलावजह (ख) अनकही
(ग) अज्ञात (घ) निपूता

35. 'निरंकुश' में कैसा उपसर्ग है?
(क) तत्सम (ख) तद्भव
(ग) विदेशी

36. 'बेडौल' में कैसा उपसर्ग है?
(क) तत्सम (ख) विदेशी
(ग) तद्भव

37. नीचे दिए गए शब्दों में से किस शब्द में तद्भव उपसर्ग जुड़ा है?
(क) अखाद्य (ख) बेरहम
(ग) अनमोल (घ) विशुद्ध

38. 'नादान' में कैसा उपसर्ग है?
(क) तत्सम (ख) तद्भव

(ग) विदेशी

39. 'अनिष्ट' में कौन-सा उपसर्ग जुड़ा है?

(क) अ (ख) अनि

(ग) अन

40. नीचे दिए गए शब्दों में किस शब्द में उपसर्ग नहीं है?

(क) आलोक (ख) आरोहण

(ग) आमरण (घ) आपूर्ति

41. 'रोग' शब्द में कौन-सा उपसर्ग लगेगा?

(क) ई (ख) वि

(ग) त्रि (घ) अ

42. 'परवाह' में कौन-सा उपसर्ग जोड़ा जायेगा?

(क) ना (ख) ला

(ग) बा (घ) अव

43. 'निहत्था' में कैसा उपसर्ग है?

(क) तत्सम (ख) तद्भव

(ग) विदेशी

44. 'अनुज' में क्या उपसर्ग जोड़ा गया है?

(क) अ (ख) अनु

(ग) ज (घ) अन

45. 'निस्वार्थ' में कैसा उपसर्ग है?

(क) तत्सम (ख) तद्भव

(ग) विदेशी

46. 'वियोग' में कैसा उपसर्ग है?

(क) तद्भव (ख) विदेशी

(ग) तत्सम

'7. 'प्रत्युपकार' में कैसा उपसर्ग है?

(क) विदेशी (ख) तत्सम

(ग) तद्भव

48. 'गुण' का अर्थ उलटने के लिए क्या उपसर्ग जोड़ा जायेगा?

(क) अ (ख) अन

(ग) अप (घ) अव

49. अधिग्रहण में क्या उपसर्ग जोड़ा गया है?

(क) अ (ख) अधि

(ग) अध्य (घ) अधिग्र

50. 'दुर्दिन' में क्या उपसर्ग जोड़ा गया है?

(क) दु (ख) दुर्

(ग) दुः (घ) दुरः

51. प्रत्यय लगाने से मूल शब्द का अर्थ :

(क) उलट जाता है

(ख) हल्का पड़ जाता है

(ग) विशिष्ट हो जाता है

(घ) संज्ञा, विशेषण या क्रिया-विशेषण आदि का रूप धारण कर लेता है

52. प्रत्यय कहाँ जोड़े जाते हैं?

(क) शब्द के आरम्भ में

(ख) शब्द के अन्त में

(ग) शब्द के बीच में

(घ) शब्द के उस भाग में, जहाँ उपयुक्त लगे

53. 'कद्रदान' में कौन-सा प्रत्यय है?

(क) तत्सम (ख) तद्भव

(ग) देशज (घ) विदेशी

54. 'पागलपन' शब्द में क्या प्रत्यय जोड़ा गया है?

(क) पागल

(ख) पन

(ग) पा

(घ) उपरोक्त में से कोई नहीं

55. निम्नलिखित में से कौन-सा प्रत्यय संज्ञा बनाने के लिए प्रयुक्त होता है?

(क) आवट (ख) इक

(ग) पूर्वक (घ) वाला

56. 'पेटू' में कैसा प्रत्यय जोड़ा गया है?

(क) तत्सम (ख) विदेशी

(ग) देशज (घ) तद्भव

57. 'मोटा' में 'पा' प्रत्यय जोड़ने से मोटापा कैसा शब्द बन गया?

(क) विशेषण

(ख) क्रिया-विशेषण

(ग) संज्ञा

(घ) लघुताबोधक

58. 'पन' प्रत्यय लगाकर कौन-सा शब्द बना है?

(क) असलीपन (ख) मोटापन

(ग) बचपन (घ) मीठापन

59. 'ता' प्रत्यय लगाकर कौन-सा शब्द बना है?

(क) सरलता (ख) कर्ता

(ग) कुरता (घ) धीरता

60. निम्नलिखित में कौन लघुताबोधन प्रत्यय का परिणाम है?

(क) डिबिया (ख) माया

(ग) घटिया (घ) आदरणीया

61. नीचे के किस शब्द में 'ई' प्रत्यय लगा है?

(क) रानी (ख) राजधानी

(ग) सावधानी (घ) मेहरबानी

62. पुष्पित शब्द में लगा प्रत्यय कैसा है?

(क) तद्भव (ख) देशज

(ग) विदेशी (घ) तत्सम

63. 'धुँधला' में क्या प्रत्यय जोड़ा गया है?

(क) धुँध

(ख) ला

(ग) धुँ

(घ) उपरोक्त में से कोई नहीं

64. गौरव को विशेषण बनाने हेतु क्या प्रत्यय जोड़ेंगे?

(क) त्व (ख) शाली

(ग) पूर्वक (घ) ता

65. माया को विशेषण बनाने हेतु क्या प्रत्यय जोड़ेंगे?

(क) पन (ख) वाला

(ग) वी (घ) वा

66. 'बतियाना' में लगा प्रत्यय कैसा है?

(क) देशज (ख) विदेशी

(ग) तत्सम (घ) तद्भव

67. 'साधारण' में तः प्रत्यय लगाने से 'साधारणतः' क्या बन गया?

(क) संज्ञा

(ख) विशेषण

(ग) क्रिया-विशेषण

(घ) क्रिया

68. 'सालाना' और 'फकीराना' में कौन-सा प्रत्यय जोड़ा गया है?

(क) ना

(ख) आना

(ग) अना

(घ) उपरोक्त में से कोई नहीं

69. 'मूलतः' में जुड़ा प्रत्यय कैसा है?

(क) विदेशी (ख) देशज

(ग) तत्सम (घ) तद्भव

70. निम्नलिखित में कौनसा शब्द 'अ' प्रत्यय लगाकर नहीं बना है?

(क) भूखा (ख) मैला

(ग) प्यारा (घ) सरलता

71. 'धार्मिक' में कौन-सा प्रत्यय जुड़ा है?
(क) ध (ख) क
(ग) इक (घ) ईक

72. 'पुराण' शब्द संज्ञा है। इसमें 'इक' प्रत्यय लगाने से यह शब्द क्या बन जायेगा?
(क) संज्ञा ही रहेगा
(ख) क्रिया-विशेषण बन जायेगा
(ग) विशेषण बन जायेगा

73. 'चतुराई' में कैसा प्रत्यय जोड़ा गया है?
(क) देशज (ख) तद्भव
(ग) तत्सम (घ) विदेशी

74. 'शिशुता' में क्या प्रत्यय जोड़ा गया है?
(क) अ (ख) आ
(ग) ता (घ) उता

75. 'सुन्दरता' में कौन-सा प्रत्यय जोड़ा गया है?
(क) तत्सम (ख) देशज
(ग) विदेशी (घ) तद्भव

76. हर्ष में 'इत' प्रत्यय जोड़ने से क्या शब्द बनेगा?
(क) हर्षीत (ख) हर्षित
(ग) हर्षइत

77. 'तपस्वी' में क्या प्रत्यय जोड़ा गया है?
(क) ई
(ख) वी
(ग) स्वी
(घ) उपरोक्त में से कोई नहीं

78. 'राष्ट्रीय' में क्या प्रत्यय जोड़ा गया है?
(क) य (ख) ट्रीय
(ग) ईय (घ) इय

79. 'नैतिक' में क्या प्रत्यय जोड़ा गया है?
(क) क (ख) तिक
(ग) इक (घ) नै

80. 'बाजार' में किस प्रकार का प्रत्यय जोड़ा गया है?
(क) तत्सम (ख) तद्भव
(ग) देशज (घ) विदेशी

81. 'नकल' में प्रत्यय लगाकर क्या शब्द बनेगा?
(क) नकलची (ख) नकली
(ग) नकलत्व (घ) नकलता

82. निम्नलिखित में से विदेशी प्रत्यय वाले शब्द को छाँटिये :
(क) दयावान (ख) बाजीगर
(ग) पंडिताइन (घ) मुख्यतया

83. निम्नलिखित में से तद्भव प्रत्यय वाले शब्द को छाँटिये :
(क) झगड़ालू (ख) कुपित
(ग) फूलदान (घ) बुढ़िया

84. 'बबुआइन' शब्द में कैसा प्रत्यय जोड़ा गया है?
(क) विदेशी (ख) तत्सम
(ग) तद्भव (घ) देशज

85. 'घबराहट' में क्या प्रत्यय जोड़ा गया है?
(क) हट (ख) राहट
(ग) आहट (घ) अहट

86. 'रसीला' में क्या प्रत्यय जोड़ा गया है?
(क) आ (ख) ला
(ग) सीला (घ) ईला

87. निम्नलिखित में से किसमें 'क' प्रत्यय नहीं लगा है?
(क) सड़क (ख) गायक
(ग) लेखक (घ) पालक

88. 'बिटिया' में कैसा प्रत्यय जोड़ा गया है?
(क) देशज (ख) तत्सम
(ग) तद्भव (घ) विदेशी

89. 'जुआड़ी' में कैसा प्रत्यय जोड़ा गया है?
(क) देशज (ख) विदेशी
(ग) तत्सम (घ) तद्भव

90. 'धैर्य' से क्रिया-विशेषण बनाने हेतु क्या प्रत्यय जोड़ा जायेगा?
(क) वान (ख) ता
(ग) पूर्वक (घ) मान

91. 'कवित्व' में क्या प्रत्यय जोड़ा गया है?
(क) व (ख) त्व
(ग) इत्व (घ) यत्व

92. 'दर्शनीय' में क्या प्रत्यय जोड़ा गया है?
(क) य (ख) नीय
(ग) ईय

93. 'चालू' में क्या प्रत्यय जोड़ा गया है?
(क) उ (ख) ऊ
(ग) लू (घ) लऊ

94. निम्नलिखित शब्दों में से कौन-सा शब्द देशज प्रत्यय से बना है?
(क) महिमा (ख) मिलावट
(ग) मरियल (घ) महकदार

95. 'पढ़ाई-लिखाई' में कैसा प्रत्यय जुड़ा हुआ है?
(क) देशज (ख) विदेशी
(ग) तत्सम (घ) तद्भव

96. 'क्रोधी' शब्द में कौन-सा प्रत्यय जोड़ा गया है?
(क) इ (ख) धी
(ग) ई

97. 'डिबिया' में क्या प्रत्यय जोड़ा गया है?
(क) या (ख) इया
(ग) ईया (घ) बिया

98. 'मासिक' में क्या प्रत्यय जोड़ा गया है?
(क) क (ख) सिक
(ग) इक

99. निम्नलिखित में से कौन-सा शब्द विदेशी प्रत्यय जोड़कर बना है?
(क) कोटिशः (ख) लाडला
(ग) पेटू (घ) अकलमंद

100. निम्नलिखित में से कौन-सा शब्द तद्भव प्रत्यय जोड़कर बना है?
(क) मनुष्यता (ख) अड़ियल
(ग) कंटीला (घ) कष्टप्रद

संधि विचार

1. 'महोत्सव' में कौन-सी संधि है?
(क) स्वर संधि (ख) व्यंजन संधि
(ग) विसर्ग संधि

2. 'तपोवन' में कौन-सी संधि है?
(क) स्वर संधि (ख) व्यंजन संधि
(ग) विसर्ग संधि

3. 'निष्फल' में कौन-सी संधि है?
(क) विसर्ग संधि
(ख) व्यंजन संधि
(ग) स्वर संधि

4. 'नमस्ते' में कौन-सी संधि है?
(क) व्यंजन संधि (ख) स्वर संधि
(ग) विसर्ग संधि

5. उच्छवास का संधि-विग्रह है :
(क) उच + श्वास
(ख) उत् + श्वास
(ग) उद् + श्वास
(घ) उछ् + श्वास

6. 'रामावतार' में कौन-सी संधि है?
(क) स्वर संधि
(ख) व्यंजन संधि
(ग) विसर्ग संधि

7. 'कपीश' का संधि-विग्रह है :
(क) कप + ईश
(ख) कपि + इश
(ग) कपि + ईश
(घ) उपरोक्त में से कोई नहीं

8. 'दिगम्बर' में कौन-सी संधि है?
(क) व्यंजन संधि
(ख) विसर्ग संधि
(ग) स्वर संधि

9. 'अन्वेषण' का संधि-विग्रह है:
(क) अन् + वेषण
(ख) अन्व + एषण
(ग) अनु + ऐषण
(घ) अनु + एषण

10. संचय का संधि-विग्रह है:
(क) सत् + चय
(ख) सम् + चय
(ग) सं + चय
(घ) सः + चय

11. महा + ईश की संधि से क्या बनेगा?
(क) महीश (ख) महेश
(ग) महिष (घ) महाईश

12. प्रत्युत्तर का संधि-विग्रह है :
(क) प्र + त्युत्तर
(ख) प्रति + युत्तर
(ग) प्रति + उत्तर
(घ) प्रत्यु + उत्तर

13. 'नीलाम्बर' में कौन-सी संधि है?
(क) स्वर संधि
(ख) व्यंजन संधि
(ग) विसर्ग संधि

14. अभीष्ट का संधि-विग्रह है :
(क) अभी + ईष्ट
(ख) अभी + इस्ट
(ग) अभि + ईस्ट
(घ) अभि + इस्ट

15. अति + अंत की संधि से बनेगा :
(क) अतीन्त
(ख) अत्यन्त
(ग) अतिन्त
(घ) अत्येन्त

16. मनः + हर की संधि से बनेगा :
(क) मनहर (ख) मनोहर
(ग) मनःहर (घ) मन्हर

17. मतैक्य का संधि-विग्रह है :
(क) मत + एक्य
(ख) मत + ऐक्य
(ग) मतः + एक्य
(घ) मत + इक्य

18. 'पुनर्जन्म' में कौन-सी संधि है?
(क) स्वर संधि
(ख) व्यंजन संधि
(ग) विसर्ग संधि

19. स्वागत का संधि-विग्रह है :
(क) स्वा + गत
(ख) स्व + आगत
(ग) स्वा + आगत
(घ) सु + आगत

20. 'हिमालय' में कौन-सी संधि है?
(क) स्वर संधि
(ख) व्यंजन संधि
(ग) विसर्ग संधि

21. तथा + एव की संधि से बनेगा :
(क) तदैव (ख) तथेव
(ग) तथैव (घ) तदेव

22. 'मुनीश' का संधि विग्रह है :
(क) मुनी + ईश
(ख) मुनि + इश

(ग) मुनि + ईश
(घ) मुनः + ईश

23. 'भावार्थ' का संधि-विग्रह है :
(क) भाव + अर्थ
(ख) भावः + अर्थ
(ग) भावा + अर्थ
(घ) भावा + र्थ

24. 'गणेश' में कौन-सी संधि है?
(क) स्वर संधि (ख) व्यंजन संधि
(ग) विसर्ग संधि

25. 'उल्लास' का संधि-विग्रह है :
(क) उद् + लास
(ख) उत् + लास
(ग) उल् + लास
(घ) उल्ल + लास

26. भारतेन्दु का संधि-विग्रह है :
(क) भार + तेन्दु
(ख) भारत + इन्दु
(ग) भरत + इन्दु
(घ) भारतः + इन्दु

27. चन्द्रोदय का संधि-विग्रह है :
(क) चन्द्रो + दय
(ख) चन्द्रो + उदय
(ग) चन्द्रः + उदय
(घ) चन्द्र + उदय

28. नीरोग का संधि विग्रह है :
(क) निः + रोग
(ख) नी + रोग
(ग) निर् + रोग
(घ) नि +रोग

29. 'सम्राट' में कौन-सी संधि है?
(क) स्वर संधि (ख) व्यंजन संधि
(ग) विसर्ग संधि

30. संरक्षक का संधि-विग्रह है :
(क) सत् + रक्षक
(ख) सं + रक्षक
(ग) सम् + रक्षक
(घ) सन् + रक्षक

31. सूर्योदय का संधि-विग्रह है :
(क) सूर्यो + योदय
(ख) सूर्य + दय
(ग) सूर्यः + उदय
(घ) सूर्य + उदय

32. इति + आदि की संधि से बनेगा :
(क) इत्यादि (ख) इत्यदि
(ग) इतिआदि (घ) इत्यादी

33. 'निराश' का संधि-विग्रह है :
(क) निः + आश
(ख) नि + राश
(ग) निर + आश
(घ) निरा + श

34. 'नीरव' में कौन-सी संधि है?
(क) स्वर संधि (ख) व्यंजन संधि
(ग) विसर्ग संधि

35. धर्मार्थ का संधि-विग्रह है :
(क) धर्मा + र्थ
(ख) धर्मा + अर्थ
(ग) धम्र + अर्थ
(घ) धर + मार्थ

36. 'दुष्कर' में कौन-सी संधि है?
(क) स्वर संधि
(ख) व्यंजन संधि
(ग) विसर्ग संधि

37. विद्यार्थी का संधि-विग्रह है :
(क) विद्या + रथी
(ख) विद्य + अर्थी
(ग) विद्य + रथी
(घ) विद्या + अर्थी

38. 'संतोष' का संधि-विग्रह है :
(क) सं + तोष
(ख) सन् + तोष
(ग) सम् + तोष
(घ) सन + तोष

39. 'जगन्नाथ' में कौन-सी संधि है?
(क) स्वर संधि (ख) व्यंजन संधि
(ग) विसर्ग संधि

40. उल्लेख का संधि-विग्रह है :
(क) उः + लेख
(ख) उत् + लेख
(ग) उल + लेख
(घ) उद् + लेख

41. पवन का संधि-विग्रह है :
(क) पव + न
(ख) प + वन
(ग) पव + अन
(घ) पो + अन

42. भानु + उदय की संधि से बनेगा :
(क) भानुदय (ख) भानूदय
(ग) भान्योदय (घ) भानुउदय

43. अति + इव की संधि से बनेगा :
(क) अतएव (ख) अतैव
(ग) अतीव (घ) अतेव

44. 'सच्चरित्र' में कौन-सी संधि है?
(क) स्वर संधि (ख) व्यंजन संधि
(ग) विसर्ग संधि

45. 'नमस्ते' का संधि-विग्रह है :
(क) नम + स्ते (ख) नम् + स्ते
(ग) नमः + ते (घ) नमः + स्ते

46. 'निर्जन' में कौन-सी संधि है?
(क) स्वर संधि
(ख) व्यंजन संधि
(ग) विसर्ग संधि

47. 'सज्जन' का संधि-विग्रह है :
(क) सज् + जन
(ख) सद् + जन
(ग) सत् + जन
(घ) सत + जन

48. यद्यपि का संधि-विग्रह है :
(क) यद्य + अपि
(ख) यद्य + पि
(ग) यदि + अपि
(घ) यद् + अपि

49. 'दुर्गुण' का संधि-विग्रह है:
(क) दुर + गुण
(ख) दुः + गुण
(ग) दुर् + गुण
(घ) दुप् + गुण

50. 'उल्लास' में कौन-सी संधि है?
(क) स्वर संधि
(ख) व्यंजन संधि
(ग) विसर्ग संधि

51. परम + अर्थ की संधि से बनेगा :
(क) परमार्थ (ख) परामार्थ
(ग) परमअर्थ (घ) परमोर्थ

52. यथा + अर्थ की संधि से बनेगा :
(क) यथाअर्थ (ख) यथार्थ
(ग) यदार्थ (घ) यथारथ

53. आच्छादनका संधि-विग्रह है :
(क) आ + छादन
(ख) आच + छादन
(ग) आच् + छादन
(घ) आच्छा + आदन

54. 'कपीश' में कौन-सी संधि है?
(क) स्वर संधि
(ख) व्यंजन संधि
(ग) विसर्ग संधि

55. निर्विकार का संधि-विग्रह है :
(क) निर + विकार
(ख) निर + अविकार
(ग) निः + विकार
(घ) निः + अविकार

56. 'निष्कलंक' का संधि-विग्रह है:
(क) नि + कलंक
(ख) निः + कलंक
(ग) निप् + कलंक
(घ) निष + कलंक

57. निश्छल में कौन-सी संधि है?
(क) स्वर संधि (ख) व्यंजन संधि
(ग) विसर्ग संधि

58. 'संहार' का संधि-विग्रह है :
(क) सं + हार
(ख) सम् + हार
(ग) सम + हार
(घ) सन् + हार

59. 'वयोवृद्ध' में कौन-सी संधि है?
(क) स्वर संधि (ख) व्यंजन संधि
(ग) विसर्ग संधि

60. 'हरिश्चन्द्र' का संधि-विग्रह है :
(क) हरि + चन्द्र
(ख) हरी + चन्द्र
(ग) हरिः + चन्द्र
(घ) हरिश + चन्द्र

61. 'सन्मार्ग' में कौन-सी संधि है?
(क) स्वर संधि (ख) व्यंजन संधि
(ग) विसर्ग संधि

62. 'महर्षि' में कौन-सी संधि है?
(क) स्वर संधि (ख) व्यंजन संधि
(ग) विसर्ग संधि

63. 'पावक' का संधि-विग्रह है :
(क) पा + वक (ख) पो + वक
(ग) पौ + वक (घ) पाव + क

64. 'स्वल्प' का संधि-विग्रह है :
(क) स्व + अल्प
(ख) स्वा + अल्प
(ग) सु + अल्प
(घ) सः + अल्प

65. 'सन्ध्या' का संधि-विग्रह है :
(क) सन् + ध्या
(ख) सम + ध्या
(ग) सं + ध्या
(घ) सन + ध्या

66. 'दुरुपयोग' में कौन-सी संधि है?
(क) स्वर संधि (ख) व्यंजन संधि
(ग) विसर्ग संधि

67. 'मनोरथ' में कौन-सी संधि है?
(क) व्यंजन संधि
(ख) स्वर संधि
(ग) विसर्ग संधि

68. 'दुष्कर' में कौन-सी संधि है?
(क) विसर्ग संधि
(ख) व्यंजन संधि
(ग) स्वर संधि

69. 'यशोदा' में कौन-सी संधि है?
(क) स्वर संधि
(ख) विसर्ग संधि
(ग) व्यंजन संधि

70. 'निश्चल' में कौन-सी संधि है?
(क) विसर्ग संधि
(ख) स्वर संधि
(ग) व्यंजन संधि

समास विचार

71. समास मुख्यतः कितने प्रकार के होते हैं?
(क) पाँच (ख) आठ
(ग) चार (घ) सात

72. किस समास में पूर्व पद प्रधान होता है?
(क) द्वन्द्व (ख) बहुब्रीहि

(ग) अव्ययीभाव (घ) तत्पुरुष

73. तत्पुरुष समास में कौन-सा पद पद प्रधान होता है?
(क) पूर्व पद
(ख) उत्तर पद
(ग) दोनों पद
(घ) कोई अन्य पद

74. 'नीलकमल' कौन-सा समास है?
(क) बहुब्रीहि (ख) तत्पुरुष
(ग) कर्मधारय (घ) द्विगु

75. 'चतुर्भुज' कौन-सा समास है?
(क) द्वन्द्व (ख) द्विगु
(ग) तत्पुरुष (घ) बहुब्रीहि

76. जिस समास का पहला पद संख्यावाचक विशेषण होता है, वह कौन-सा समास है?
(क) द्विगु (ख) तत्पुरुष
(ग) द्वन्द्व (घ) बहुब्रीहि

77. 'चौराहा' कौन-सा समास है?
(क) बहुब्रीहि (ख) तत्पुरुष
(ग) द्विगु (घ) कर्मधारय

78. 'भाई-बहिन' कौन-सा समास है?
(क) द्वन्द्व (ख) बहुब्रीहि
(ग) द्विगु (घ) तत्पुरुष

79. 'जन्मान्ध' कौन-सा समास है?
(क) तत्पुरुष (ख) द्वन्द्व
(ग) बहुब्रीहि (घ) अव्ययीभाव

80. अव्ययीभाव समास में :
(क) पूर्व पद प्रधान होता है
(ख) उत्तर पद प्रधान होता है
(ग) दोनों पद प्रधान होते हैं
(घ) उपरोक्त में से कोई भी नहीं

81. 'प्रतिदिन' कौन-सा समास है?
(क) द्विगु (ख) द्वन्द्व
(ग) अव्ययीभाव (घ) तत्पुरुष

82. किस समास में दोनों पद प्रधान होते हैं?
(क) द्विगु (ख) द्वन्द्व
(ग) अव्ययीभाव (घ) कर्मधारय

83. कौन-से दो समास तत्पुरुष के अन्तर्गत माने जाते हैं?
(क) द्विगु और द्वन्द्व
(ख) द्विगु और बहुब्रीहि
(ग) द्विगु और कर्मधारय
(घ) द्विगु और अव्ययीभाव

84. 'रातों-रात' कौन-सा समास है?
(क) तत्पुरुष (ख) अव्ययीभाव
(ग) द्वन्द्व (घ) द्विगु

85. निम्नलिखित में से कौन-सा बहुब्रीहि समास है?
(क) देशाटन (ख) दशानन
(ग) धर्माचार्य (घ) अनिद्रा

86. अव्ययीभाव समास का एक उदाहरण है :
(क) प्रतिदिन (ख) रेखांकित
(ग) धर्माचार्य (घ) अनिद्रा

87. 'पंचवटी' कौन-समास है?
(क) अव्ययीभाव (ख) द्विगु
(ग) कर्मधारय (घ) बहुब्रीहि

88. 'शरतचन्द्र' कौन-सा समास है?
(क) कर्मधारय (ख) बहुब्रीहि
(ग) तत्पुरुष (घ) द्विगु

89. 'दुनाली' कौन-सा समास है?
(क) बहुब्रीहि (ख) द्विगु
(ग) तत्पुरुष (घ) द्वन्द्व

90. 'भयभीत' कौन-सा समास है?
(क) द्विगु (ख) अव्ययीभाव
(ग) कर्मधारय (घ) तत्पुरुष

91. 'तुलसीकृत' कौन-सा समास है?
(क) बहुब्रीहि (ख) अव्ययीभाव
(ग) कर्मधारय (घ) तत्पुरुष

92. 'त्रिवेणी' कौन-सा समास है?
(क) द्वन्द्व (ख) अव्ययीभाव
(ग) द्विगु (घ) कर्मधारय

93. 'जातिभ्रष्ट' कौन-सा समास है?
(क) तत्पुरुष (ख) बहुब्रीहि
(ग) द्विगु (घ) अव्ययीभाव

94. निम्नलिखित में से कौन-सा द्वन्द्व समास है?
(क) नौचंदी (ख) राजपुत्र
(ग) प्रतिदिन (घ) सीताराम

95. 'पदच्युत' कौन-सा समास है?
(क) द्वन्द्व (ख) तत्पुरुष
(ग) कर्मधारय (घ) बहुब्रीहि

96. किस समास में दोनों पद प्रधान होते हैं?
(क) द्वन्द्व (ख) बहुब्रीहि
(ग) तत्पुरुष (घ) अव्ययीभाव

97. 'भला-बुरा' कौन-सा समास है?
(क) द्विगु (ख) द्वन्द्व
(ग) अव्ययीभाव (घ) बहुब्रीहि

98. 'महात्मा' कौन-सा समास है?
(क) अव्ययीभाव (ख) बहुब्रीहि
(ग) द्वन्द्व (घ) कर्मधारय

99. 'लम्बोदर' कौन-सा समास है?
(क) तत्पुरुष (ख) द्वन्द्व
(ग) बहुब्रीहि (घ) अव्ययीभाव

100. किस समास में दोनों पदों से भिन्न कोई अन्य पद प्रधान होता है?
(क) तत्पुरुष (ख) द्वन्द्व
(ग) अव्ययीभाव (घ) बहुब्रीहि

101. जिस समास में दोनों पद प्रधान होते हैं, उसे क्या कहते हैं?
(क) तत्पुरुष (ख) द्विगु
(ग) द्वन्द्व (घ) कर्मधारय

102. 'विद्यालय' कौन-सा समास है?
(क) तत्पुरुष (ख) बहुब्रीहि
(ग) कर्मधारय (घ) द्विगु

103. 'पशुपति' कौन-सा समास है?
(क) तत्पुरुष (ख) बहुब्रीहि
(ग) कर्मधारय (घ) अव्ययीभाव

104. 'राष्ट्रपति' कौन-सा समास है?
(क) बहुब्रीहि (ख) कर्मधारय
(ग) तत्पुरुष (घ) अव्ययीभाव

105. 'पीताम्बर' कौन-सा समास है?
(क) द्वन्द्व (ख) अव्ययीभाव
(ग) द्विगु (घ) बहुब्रीहि

106. 'पंचतत्व' कौन-सा समास है?
(क) तत्पुरुष (ख) अव्ययीभाव
(ग) द्वन्द्व (घ) द्विगु

107. 'सप्तऋषि' कौन-सा समास है?
(क) द्विगु (ख) द्वन्द्व
(ग) अव्ययीभाव (घ) बहुब्रीहि

108. 'क्षण-क्षण' कौन-सा समास है?
(क) तत्पुरुष (ख) अव्ययीभाव
(ग) बहुब्रीहि (घ) द्वन्द्व

109. 'चतुर्भुज' बहुब्रीहि समास है, क्योंकि इसमें :
(क) पूर्व पद प्रधान है
(ख) उत्तर पद प्रधान है
(ग) दोनों पद प्रधान हैं
(घ) दोनों के अतिरिक्त कोई अन्य पद प्रधान है

110. 'रुपया-पैसा' द्वन्द्व समास है, क्योंकि इसमें :
(क) पूर्व पद प्रधान है

(ख) उत्तर पद प्रधान है
(ग) दोनों पद प्रधान है
(घ) दोनों के अतिरिक्त कोई अन्य पद प्रधान है

111. तत्पुरुष समास में कौन-सा पद प्रधान होता है?
(क) पूर्व पद
(ख) उत्तर पद
(ग) दोनों पद
(घ) दोनों के अतिरिक्त कोई अन्य पद

112. 'भरपेट' कौन-सा समास है?
(क) अव्ययीभाव (ख) कर्मधारय
(ग) द्विगु (घ) द्वन्द्व

113. 'हस्तलिखित' कौन-सा समास है?
(क) बहुब्रीहि (ख) तत्पुरुष
(ग) अव्ययीभाव (घ) द्विगु

114. 'गजानन' कौन-सा समास है?
(क) बहुब्रीहि (ख) अव्ययीभाव
(ग) द्विगु (घ) द्वन्द्व

115. जिस समास का पहला पद संख्यावचक विशेषण हो, उसे क्या कहते हैं?
(क) अव्ययीभाव (ख) द्वन्द्व
(ग) द्विगु (घ) बहुब्रीहि

116. 'त्रिलोकी' कौन-सा समास है?
(क) द्विगु (ख) बहुब्रीहि
(ग) अव्ययीभाव (घ) तत्पुरुष

117. 'सेनानायक' कौन-सा समास है?
(क) तत्पुरुष (ख) अव्ययीभाव
(ग) बहुब्रीहि (घ) कर्मधारय

118. 'ऋणमुक्त' कौन-सा समास है?
(क) अव्ययीभाव (ख) तत्पुरुष
(ग) बहुब्रीहि (घ) कर्मधारय

119. 'चन्द्रमुख' कौन-सा समास है?
(क) तत्पुरुष (ख) कर्मधारय
(ग) बहुब्रीहि (घ) अव्ययीभाव

120. 'ग्रंथकर्ता' कौन-सा समास है?
(क) बहुब्रीहि (ख) द्वन्द्व
(ग) द्विगु (घ) तत्पुरुष

121. 'काम-काज' कौन-सा समास है?
(क) द्वन्द्व (ख) द्विगु
(ग) कर्मधारय (घ) अव्ययीभाव

122. 'जन्मांध' कौन-सा समास है?
(क) बहुब्रीहि (ख) द्वन्द्व
(ग) कर्मधारय (घ) तत्पुरुष

123. 'चरणकमल' कौन-सा समास है?
(क) कर्मधारय (ख) द्विगु
(ग) बहुब्रीहि (घ) अव्ययीभाव

124. 'जानकीनाथ' कौन-सा समास है?
(क) अव्ययीभाव (ख) तत्पुरुष
(ग) बहुब्रीहि (घ) द्वन्द्व

125. निम्नलिखित में से किस समास में अन्य पद प्रधान नहीं है?
(क) सप्तऋषि (ख) दशानन
(ग) गजानन (घ) चतुर्भुज

अलंकार

1. अलंकार के कितने मुख्य भेद होते हैं?
(क) दो (ख) तीन
(ग) चार (घ) पाँच

2. काव्य का अस्थिर धर्म क्या है?
(क) रस (ख) शब्द शक्ति
(ग) अलंकार (घ) छंद

3. जहाँ एक साथ शब्द और अर्थ दोनों में विशेषता हो, वहाँ–
(क) शब्दालंकार होता है
(ख) अर्थालंकार होता है
(ग) अनुप्रास अलंकार होता है
(घ) उभयालंकार होता है

4. जब किसी कविता में एक शब्द का

एक ही प्रयोग हो, परन्तु उसके दो या अधिक अर्थ हों, तब कौन-सा अलंकार होता है?
(क) रूपक (ख) उपमा
(ग) प्रतीप (घ) श्लेष

5. निम्न में कौन-सा शब्दालंकार नहीं है?
(क) उपमा, रूपक
(ख) व्यतिरेक, दृष्टांत
(ग) अनुप्रास, यमक
(घ) श्लेष, वक्रोक्ति

6. 'कुन्द इन्दु सम देह, उमा रमन करुण अयन'
उक्त पद में कौन-सा अलंकार है?
(क) श्लेष (ख) उपमा
(ग) अनुप्रास (घ) रूपक

7. 'कनक कनक ते सौ गुनी मादकता अधिकाय। वा खाये बौराय जग या पाये बौराय।'
उक्त पद में कौन-सा अलंकार है?
(क) यमक (ख) अनुप्रास
(ग) रूपक (घ) प्रतीप

8. 'स्वर्ग की तुलना उचित ही है यहाँ किन्तु सुरसरिता कहाँ सरयू कहाँ? वह मरों को मात्र पार उतारती, यह यहाँ से जीवितों को तारती।'
उक्त प्रद में कौन-सा अलंकार है?
(क) श्लेष (ख) व्यतिरेक
(ग) रूपक (घ) भ्रान्तिमान

9. 'हनुमान की पूँछ में लगन न पाई आग। लंका सिगरी जल गई, गए निसाचर भाग।'
उक्त पद में कौन-सा अलंकार है?
(क) उत्प्रेक्षा
(ख) भ्रान्तिमान
(ग) दृष्टान्त
(घ) अतिशयोक्ति

10. 'एक राज्य न हो तो बहुत से हों जहाँ, राष्ट्र का बल बिखर जाता है वहाँ, बहुत तारे थे अँधेरा कब मिटा, सूर्य का आना सुना जब तब मिटा।'
उक्त पद में कौन-सा अलंकार है?
(क) दृष्टांत (ख) व्यतिरेक
(ग) भ्रान्तिमान (घ) उपमा

11. 'मेरी भव बाधा हरौ, राधा नागरि सोई। जो तन की झाईं परत, स्यामु हरित दुति होई।'
उक्त पद में कौन-सा अलंकार है?
(क) व्यतिरेक (ख) श्लेष
(ग) उपमा (घ) अनुप्रास

12. जब शब्द (पद) में एक या कई व्यंजन एक से अधिक बार एक ही क्रम में आएँ, वह कौन-सा अलंकार होता है?
(क) यमक (ख) दृष्टान्त
(ग) भ्रांतिमान (घ) अनुप्रास

13. काव्य में शब्दगत और अर्थगत सौंदर्य की वृद्धि उत्पन्न वाले साधन को क्या कहते हैं?
(क) अलंकार (ख) रस
(ग) छन्द (घ) शब्द-शक्ति

14. निम्न पंक्तियों में कौन-सा अलंकार है? "बहुरि अंजली बांधि ध्यान विधि को विधिवत गहि। माँगी गंग उमंग सहित पूरब प्रसंग कहि।।"
(क) अनुप्रास (ख) उत्प्रेक्षा
(ग) मालोपमा (घ) भ्रान्तिमान

15. अनुप्रास के कितने भेद होते हैं?
(क) दो (ख) तीन
(ग) चार (घ) पाँच

16. जब कविता में एक ही शब्द दो या अधिक बार आये और हर बार उसका अर्थ भिन्न हो, तो कौन-सा अलंकार होता है?

(क) यमक
(ख) अतिशयोक्ति
(ग) अनुप्रास
(घ) प्रतीप

17. किस अलंकार में लक्षण से चमत्कार घटित होता है?
(क) प्रतीप
(ख) रूपक
(ग) अतिशयोक्ति
(घ) अनन्वय

18. किस अलंकार में प्रसिद्ध उपमानों को उपमेय के रूप में कर लिया जाता है?
(क) रूपक (ख) अनुप्रास
(ग) प्रतीप (घ) उपमा

19. प्रस्तुत वर्ण्य-विषय को बढ़ा-चढ़ाकर अतिरंजित रूप में अभिव्यक्त करने से कौन-सा अलंकार होता है?
(क) अतिशयोक्ति
(ख) दृष्टान्त
(ग) विभावना
(घ) विशेषोक्ति

20. किस अलंकार में कविता में उपमेय और उपमान बिंब-प्रतिबिंब भाव से होते हैं?
(क) अतिशयोक्ति
(ख) प्रतीप
(ग) विशेषोक्ति
(घ) दृष्टान्त

21. जब भ्रमवश किसी एक चीज को देखकर उसके समान की किसी अन्य वस्तु का भ्रम हो तो कौन-सा अलंकार होता है?
(क) विभावना (ख) उत्प्रेक्षा
(ग) भ्रान्तिमान (घ) विशेषोक्ति

22. उपमान की अपेक्षा उपमेय के वर्णन में जब उत्कृष्टता दिखाइ जाती है, तो कौन-सा अलंकार होता है?
(क) प्रतीप (ख) विभावना
(ग) उत्प्रेक्षा (घ) व्यतिरेक

23. किस अलंकार में उपमेय में उपमान की सम्भावना की जाती है?
(क) उत्प्रेक्षा (ख) विभावना
(ग) प्रतीप (घ) अनुप्रास

24. कविता में जब बिना पर्याप्त कारण के कार्य सम्पन्न होने का चमत्कार घटित होता है, तो कौन-सा अलंकार होता है?
(क) प्रतीप
(ख) उत्प्रेक्षा
(ग) अतिशयोक्ति
(घ) विभावना

25. प्रबल कारणों के उपस्थित होते हुए भी जब कार्य सिद्ध न होने का वर्णन किया जाए तो कौन-सा अलंकार होता है?
(क) विशेषोक्ति (ख) विभावना
(ग) व्यतिरेक (घ) प्रतीप

26. जहाँ किसी उक्ति में वक्ता के अभिप्रेत आशय से भिन्न अर्थ की कल्पना की जाये, वहाँ कौन-सा अलंकार होता है?
(क) प्रतीप (ख) अनुप्रास
(ग) वक्रोक्ति (घ) विभावना

27. जहाँ सादृश्य के कारण किसी वस्तु को देखकर यह निश्चय न हो सके कि यह वही वस्तु है या अन्य; अर्थात् दोनों में दुविधा बनी रहे, वहाँ कौन-सा अलंकार होता है?
(क) भ्रान्तिमान (ख) विभावना
(ग) सन्देह (घ) प्रतीप

28. जहाँ सामान्य कथन का विशेष कथन द्वारा और विशेष कथन का सामान्य कथन द्वारा समर्थन किया जाता है,

वहाँ कौन-सा अलंकार होता है?

(क) विशेषोक्ति (ख) विभावना

(ग) अर्थान्तरन्यास (घ) वक्रोक्ति

29. जहाँ कविता में एक ही चीज उपमान और उपमेय भाव से कही जाती है, वहाँ कौन-सा अलंकार होता है?

(क) प्रतीप (ख) अनन्वय

(ग) अनुप्रास (घ) रूपक

30. वर्णन में जो प्रस्तुत विषय के रूप में होता है (जैसे सीता का मुख) उसे क्या कहते हैं?

(क) उपमेय (ख) उपमान

(ग) धर्म (घ) वाचक

31. वर्ण्य वस्तु की शोभा बढ़ाने के लिए जिस अप्रस्तुत (जैसे चन्द्रमा) की कल्पना की जाती है, उसे क्या कहते हैं?

(क) धर्म (ख) वाचक

(ग) उपमान (घ) उपमेय

32. जिस गुण के कारण उपमेय और उपमान में समानता स्थापित की जाती है (जैसे सुन्दर), उसे क्या कहते हैं?

(क) उपमेय (ख) उपमान

(ग) वाचक (घ) धर्म

विपरीतार्थक शब्द

विपरीतार्थक शब्द वे शब्द होते हैं जो किसी शब्द के ठीक विपरीत अथवा उल्टा अर्थ प्रकट करते हैं। इन्हें विलोम और विपर्याय भी कहा जाता है। अंग्रेजी में ऐसे, शब्द 'एण्टानिम्स' कहे जाते हैं।

निर्देश : *चार विकल्पों में से सही विपरीतार्थक शब्द छांट कर उस पर निशान लगाइये।*

1. अकथ

(क) कथनीय (ख) मान्य

(ग) कथ्य (घ) चिन्तनीय

2. अचल

(क) अस्थिर (ख) चल

(ग) जंगम (घ) कंपायमान

3. अटल

(क) अस्थिर (ख) चल

(ग) टलना (घ) अदृढ़

4. अति

(क) न्यून (ख) कम

(ग) अल्प (घ) नगण्य

5. अथ

(क) अन्त (ख) समाप्ति

(ग) इति (घ) विश्राम

6. अन्त

(क) आरम्भ (ख) आदि

(ग) अथ (घ) शुरुआत

7. अदूरदर्शी

(क) गीध दृष्टि (ख) दूर दृष्टि

(ग) दूरदर्शी (घ) भविष्य दृष्ट

8. अदूषित

(क) कलुषित (ख) पंकिल

(ग) रुग्ण (घ) दूषित

9. अलभ्य

(क) मिलना (ख) लभ्य

(ग) आशा (घ) प्राप्त

10. अधर्म

(क) धर्मयुत (ख) सुधर्म

(ग) धर्म (घ) आपद्धर्म

11. अमावस्या

(क) प्रतिपदा (ख) प्रदोष

(ग) चतुर्दशी (घ) पूर्णिमा

12. अमृत

(क) काटकूट (ख) विष

(ग) गरल (घ) हलाहल

13. **अशक्य**
(क) शक्य (ख) साध्य
(ग) सुगम (घ) संभव

14. **आकर्षण**
(क) घृणा (ख) जुगुप्सा
(ग) पलायन (घ) विकर्षण

15. **आकांक्षा**
(क) अनिच्छा (ख) अनाकांक्षा
(ग) विमुखता (घ) घृणा

16. **आकाश**
(क) गगन (ख) पाताल
(ग) धरा (घ) रसातल

17. **आग**
(क) शीत
(ख) पानी
(ग) बर्फ
(घ) उपल (ओला)

18. **आमिष**
(क) शाक (ख) अन्न
(ग) निरामिष (घ) भोज्य

19. **आमोद**
(क) अप्रसन्नता (ख) विषाद
(ग) क्रोध (घ) निर्गंध

20. **आय**
(क) व्यय (ख) खर्च
(ग) मितव्यय (घ) बचत

21. **आरोहण**
(क) अपरोहण (ख) अवरोहण
(ग) पतन (घ) विनाशन

22. **आर्य**
(क) असभ्य (ख) अजान
(ग) अनार्य (घ) दस्यु

23. **आश्रय**
(क) आलंबहीन (ख) निरालंब
(ग) निराश्रय (घ) बेसहारा

24. **इष्ट**
(क) अप्रिय (ख) अवांछित
(ग) अनिष्ट (घ) शुभ

25. **ईर्ष्या**
(क) स्नेह (ख) प्रसन्नता
(ग) उत्फुल्लता (घ) शीतलता

26. **उगलना**
(क) लील जाना (ख) निगलना
(ग) खाना (घ) चबाना

27. **उग्र**
(क) विनम्र (ख) शान्त
(ग) भीरु (घ) विनयी

28. **उत्कर्ष**
(क) पराभव (ख) अनुत्कर्ष
(ग) अवनति (घ) पतन

29. **उत्कृष्ट**
(क) निम्न (ख) असुन्दर
(ग) क्षुद्र (घ) निकृष्ट

30. **उत्साह**
(क) अनुत्साह (ख) उत्साहहीन
(ग) आलसी (घ) भीरु

31. **उदय**
(क) पराभव (ख) अस्त
(ग) अवसान (घ) ग्रस्त

32. **उल्लास**
(क) ह्रास (ख) म्लानता
(ग) कष्ट (घ) अप्रसन्नता

33. **ऊर्ध्व**
(क) निम्न (ख) लघु
(ग) अधो (घ) अल्प

34. **एकता**
(क) अनेकता (ख) विभिन्नता
(ग) असहयोग (घ) अलग-अलग

35. **एकांत**
(क) भीड़-भाड़ (ख) जन संकुल
(ग) मेला (घ) बाजार

36. **एकीकरण**
(क) अलगाव
(ख) विभाजन

(ग) विलगीकरण
(घ) फैलाना

37. **ओजस्वी**
(क) कान्तिहीन (ख) म्लान
(ग) रोगी (घ) कामुक

38. **औचित्य**
(क) अनुचित (ख) बुरा
(ग) अनौचित्य (घ) अनुपयुक्त

39. **कंजूस**
(क) उदार
(ख) फिजूलखर्ची
(ग) बहुव्ययी
(घ) व्यर्थव्ययी

40. **कटु**
(क) कषाय (ख) मधु
(ग) नमकीन (घ) मधुर

41. **कदाचित्**
(क) निश्चित (ख) प्रायः
(ग) अवश्यमेव (घ) नित्य

42. **कन्या**
(क) औरत (ख) महिला
(ग) पुरुष (घ) वर

43. **कनिष्ठ**
(क) ज्येष्ठ (ख) समवयस्क
(ग) मध्यम (घ) वृद्ध

44. **कायर**
(क) शायर (ख) शूर/वीर
(ग) बहादुर (घ) उत्साही

45. **किशोर**
(क) बाल (ख) प्रौढ़
(ग) वृद्ध (घ) रुग्ण

46. **कुटिल**
(क) दुष्ट (ख) सरल
(ग) मृदुल (घ) चंचल

47. **कुकृत्य**
(क) सुकर्म (ख) भलाई
(ग) शुभकर्म (घ) सुकृत्य

48. **कुमति**
(क) मन्दमति (ख) सन्मति
(ग) मतिवान (घ) सुमति

49. **कुशाग्र**
(क) मन्द (ख) नीच
(ग) मूढ़ (घ) अल्प

50. **कुसंग**
(क) सुसंग/सत्संग
(ख) भक्ति
(ग) शुभ संग
(घ) साधु संग

51. **खाद्य**
(क) अखाद्य (ख) नीरस
(ग) अभक्ष्य (घ) अग्राह्य

52. **खोटा**
(क) अच्छाई (ख) अदूषण
(ग) खरा (घ) निर्दोष

53. **गद्य**
(क) पद्य (ख) काव्य
(ग) तुकबन्दी (घ) कवित्त

54. **गप**
(क) सही (ख) ठीक
(ग) सच (घ) उचित

55. **गायन**
(क) वादन (ख) रुदन
(ग) नर्त्तन (घ) हास्य

56. **घरेलू**
(क) बाहरी (ख) शहरी
(ग) बाजारू (घ) आपसी

57. **चंचल**
(क) अचंचल (ख) स्थिर
(ग) शान्त (घ) गंभीर

58. **चन्द्रमा**
(क) प्रकाश (ख) धूप
(ग) ऊषा (घ) सूर्य

59. **चिढ़ना**
(क) प्रसन्न होना (ख) हँसना

(ग) मुस्कराना (घ) रोना

60. छली
(क) साधु (ख) सज्जन
(ग) भला (घ) निश्छली

61. जंगम
(क) स्थिर (ख) स्थावर
(ग) ठहराव (घ) पंगु

62. ज्ञान
(क) विज्ञान (ख) अज्ञान
(ग) मूर्खता (घ) सीमित ज्ञान

63. ज्ञेय
(क) अनबूझ (ख) अज्ञेय
(ग) नासमझ (घ) विज्ञेय

64. ज्येष्ठ
(क) कनिष्ठ (ख) लघु
(ग) अल्प (घ) छोटा

65. ज्योतिर्मय
(क) श्याममय
(ख) कालिमायुक्त
(ग) अंधकारमय
(घ) धुंधयुक्त

66. झूठ
(क) सत्य (ख) अर्द्धसत्य
(ग) यथार्थ (घ) नग्नसत्य

67. टाट
(क) मखमल
(ख) कपड़ा (सूती)
(ग) रेशम
(घ) कीनखाब

68. टोटा
(क) लाभ (ख) फायदा
(ग) मुनाफा (घ) बचत

69. ठण्डा
(क) गर्म
(ख) शीतोष्ण
(ग) समशीतोषण
(घ) तापित

70. ढीठ
(क) सज्जन (ख) शरीफ
(ग) भला (घ) विनयी

71. तनय
(क) भगिनी (ख) अनुजा
(ग) तनया (घ) भतीजी

72. तप्त
(क) शीतल (ख) अतप्त
(ग) अदग्ध (घ) ठंडा

73. तमोगुण
(क) रजोगुण (ख) शतोगुण
(ग) अवगुण (घ) गुणाक गुण

74. तिक्त
(क) कषाय (ख) मधुर
(ग) अम्ल (घ) लावण्य

75. तिरस्कार
(क) स्वागत (ख) सम्मान
(ग) आदर (घ) प्रशंसा

76. त्यागना
(क) मिला लेना
(ख) लेना
(ग) अपनाना
(घ) ग्रहण करना

77. थकान
(क) स्वस्थ
(ख) प्रसन्न
(ग) थकान रहित
(घ) स्फूर्ति

78. दक्षिण
(क) पूर्व (ख) पश्चिम
(ग) उत्तर (घ) सर्वत्र

79. दानव
(क) मानव (ख) देव
(ग) यक्ष (घ) किन्नर

80. दरिद्र
(क) सम्पन्न
(ख) समृद्धिशाली

(ग) भूपति
(घ) श्रीपति

81. दुर्बल
(क) तपोबले (ख) आत्मबल
(ग) धनबल (घ) सबल

82. दुर्भाग्य
(क) निर्भाग (ख) सौभाग्य
(ग) भाग्यवान (घ) भाग्यशाली

83. दुश्चरित्र
(क) सच्चरित्र (ख) सदाचारी
(ग) भद्र (घ) सुशील

84. दृश्य काव्य
(क) श्रव्यकाव्य (ख) खण्डकाव्य
(ग) महाकाव्य (घ) गीतिकाव्य

85. देशी
(क) प्रान्तीय
(ख) ग्रामीण
(ग) शहरी/नगरीय
(घ) विदेशी

86. धनवान
(क) गरीब (ख) निर्धन
(ग) फकीर (घ) भिखारी

87. धर्म
(क) अधर्म (ख) पाप
(ग) पातक (घ) अघ

88. धूप
(क) छाँव (ख) बरसात
(ग) रात (घ) चाँदनी

89. स्वर्ग
(क) कान
(ख) मृत्युलोक
(ग) पाताललोक
(घ) नरक

90. नायक
(क) नायिका (ख) युवती
(ग) प्रेमिका (घ) सुन्दरी

91. नास्तिक
(क) व्यावहारिक (ख) आस्तिक
(ग) बौद्धिक (घ) भौतिक

92. निराश
(क) आशा (ख) आशान्वित
(ग) आशामय (घ) आशावन

93. निःश्वास
(क) श्वासहीन (ख) मृतक
(ग) उच्छवास (घ) ऊर्ध्वश्वास

94. निशाचर
(क) देव (ख) मनुष्य
(ग) दिवाचर (घ) खेचर

95. निशि
(क) दिवा (ख) दिन
(ग) दिवस (घ) सवेरा

96. निश्चय
(क) अनिश्चय (ख) विनिश्चय
(ग) सुनिश्चय (घ) कुनिश्चय

97. निस्संकोच
(क) संकोच (ख) संतोषी
(ग) सलज्ज (घ) संकोचवान

98. निष्पाप
(क) अपवित्र (ख) पापात्मा
(ग) पापी (घ) अघी

99. नूतन
(क) पुराना (ख) जीर्ण
(ग) वृद्ध (घ) पुरातन

100. नृशंस
(क) दयावान (ख) करुणापूर्ण
(ग) मेहरबान (घ) कृपालु

101. नेक
(क) बुरा (ख) निर्दय
(ग) पापी (घ) हीन

102. नेत्रवान
(क) नेत्ररहित (ख) अज्ञानी
(ग) नेत्रहीन (घ) अंधा

103. नैसर्गिक
(क) कृत्रिम (ख) ब[illegible]

(ग) रचित (घ) विरचित

104. न्याय
(क) अन्याय (ख) अनर्थ
(ग) बेइंसाफी (घ) बुरा बर्ताव

105. न्यून
(क) अत्यधिक (ख) पर्याप्त
(ग) बहुत (घ) अधिक

106. पत्थर
(क) कुसुम (ख) पादप
(ग) फूल (घ) काष्ठ

107. परमात्मा
(क) धर्मात्मा (ख) पापात्मा
(ग) आत्मा (घ) महात्मा

108. परिचित
(क) अपरिचित (ख) अनजान
(ग) अभिज्ञ (घ) अज्ञात

109. परिपक्व
(क) अधपका (ख) सुपक्व
(ग) कच्चा (घ) पक्व

110. परिहार्य
(क) अपरिहार्य (ख) अनिवार्य
(ग) आवश्यक (घ) अटल

111. पर्दा
(क) खुला
(ख) अबाध
(ग) आवरण विहीन
(घ) बेपर्दा

112. पवित्र
(क) चरित्र (ख) अपवित्र
(ग) अपावन (घ) अशौच

113. पारदर्शी
(क) अल्पदर्शी (ख) अपारदर्शी
(ग) दूरदर्शी (घ) स्वप्नदर्शी

114. पार्थिव
(क) स्वप्निल (ख) अलौकिक
(ग) असंसारी (घ) अपार्थिव

115. पैर
(क) मस्तक (ख) सिर
(ग) हाथ (घ) ललाट

116. प्रचंड
(क) शान्त (ख) विनम्र
(ग) निर्बल (घ) सह्य

117. प्रिय
(क) द्वेषी (ख) अप्रिय
(ग) बैरी (घ) दुश्मन

118. प्रीति
(क) वैर (ख) दुश्मनी
(ग) शत्रुता (घ) द्वेष

119. प्रेम
(क) विराग (ख) स्नेहहीन
(ग) घृणा (घ) कलह

120. प्रत्याशा
(क) अप्रत्याशा (ख) निराशा
(ग) आशारहित (घ) हताशा

121. प्रत्यय
(क) अज्ञान (ख) मूर्खता
(ग) उपसर्ग (घ) असम्मति

122. प्राप्य
(क) अनुपलब्ध (ख) अप्राप्य
(ग) दुर्गम (घ) अनुपस्थित

123. फायदेमन्द
(क) हानिप्रद (ख) नुकसान
(ग) बुरी (घ) अलाभकर

124. फूल
(क) कली (ख) बौर
(ग) पल्लव (घ) काँटा

125. बावला
(क) सज्ञान (ख) बुद्धिमान
(ग) संयमित (घ) चतुर

126. ब्रह्म
(क) जीव (ख) माया
(ग) जगत (घ) अज्ञान

127. भद्र
(क) असज्जन (ख) अभद्र

(ग) अवांछित (घ) धूर्त

128. भयंकर
(क) सौम्य (ख) कान्त
(ग) आकर्षक (घ) मनोहर

129. भिक्षु
(क) राजा (ख) नृप
(ग) भूप (घ) भूपाल

130. मंद
(क) तेज (ख) तीव्र
(ग) गतिमान (घ) गतिशील

131. मान
(क) अपमान (ख) अनादर
(ग) असम्मान (घ) बेइज्जती

132. मिट्टी
(क) राख (ख) सोना
(ग) चाँदी (घ) हीरामोती

133. मूक
(क) वाचाल (ख) बातून
(ग) बकवादी (घ) वक्ता

134. मूढ़
(क) बुद्धिमान (ख) योग्य
(ग) चतुर (घ) अक्लमन्द

135. मूर्त
(क) निराकार (ख) पिंडहीन
(ग) अमूर्त्त (घ) अशरीरी

136. मृत्यु
(क) जन्म (ख) पैदायश
(ग) आगमन (घ) उत्पत्ति

137. मृदु
(क) रूखा (ख) कठोर
(ग) पाषाणी (घ) काष्ठवत

138. योग
(क) विषयभोग (ख) आनन्द
(ग) सुख (घ) भोग

139. रंक
(क) नृप (ख) भूपति
(ग) नृपाल (घ) राजा

140. रवि
(क) चन्द्र (ख) सुधाकर
(ग) राकेश (घ) शशि

141. रीझना
(क) नाराज़ होना
(ख) दुखी होना
(ग) बुरा मानना
(घ) परेशान होना

142. रुदन
(क) हास्य (ख) प्रसन्नता
(ग) मुस्कान (घ) अट्टहास

143. रूपवान
(क) कुरूप (ख) असुन्दर
(ग) अंगहीन (घ) निर्लज्ज

144. लघु
(क) लम्बा (ख) दीघ
(ग) बृहद् (घ) गुरु

145. लज्जावान
(क) लज्जारहित
(ख) लज्जाहीन
(ग) निर्लज्ज
(घ) बेशर्म

146. लाचार
(क) समर्थ
(ख) सशक्त
(ग) सबल
(घ) सामर्थ्यशाली

147. लौकिक
(क) असंसारी
(ख) अस्वाभाविक
(ग) अलौकिक
(घ) दैवी

148. वर्तमान
(क) भविष्य
(ख) भूत
(ग) अनद्यतनभूत
(घ) कालहीन

149. बहिरंग
(क) अन्तरंग (ख) रंगारंग
(ग) जलतरंग (घ) रामरंग

150. हँसना
(क) रोना (ख) चिल्लाना
(ग) मौन रहना (घ) मुस्कराना

151. हट्टा-कट्टा
(क) कमजोर (ख) दुर्बल
(ग) निस्तेज (घ) असमर्थ

152. हर्ष
(क) क्रोध (ख) चिन्ता
(ग) शोक (घ) परेशान

153. हित
(क) अनहित (ख) अनुपकार
(ग) नुकसान करना
(घ) सताना

154. हिंसा
(क) अहिंसा (ख) निर्वैर
(ग) दयावान (घ) करुणा

155. हृदयहीन
(क) सहृदय (ख) दया
(ग) कठोर (घ) साधु

पर्यायवाची शब्द

समानार्थी शब्दों को पर्यायवाची शब्द भी कहा जाता है। प्रत्येक शब्द की अपनी अलग पहचान, गरिमा तथा विशिष्टता होती है। कमल के कई पर्यायवाची हैं, किन्तु उन सब की अपनी विशिष्टताएँ हैं, यथा—पुण्डरीक श्वेत कमल के लिए, इन्दीवर नील कमल के लिए, अरविन्द और सरसी रुह लाल कमल के लिए प्रयुक्त होते हैं। सभी प्रकार के कमलों के लिए प्रायः वारिज, पंकज, सरसिज आदि शब्दों का प्रयोग किया जाता है। यही बात दया, करुणा, कृपा आदि शब्दों के लिए भी कही जा सकती है। आम बोलचाल में इनका प्रयोग बोध होने पर इनका उपयुक्त प्रयोग करना सुलभ होता है।

निर्देश : *नीचे कुछ शब्द दिए गए हैं। प्रत्येक के पर्यायवाची के चार विकल्प दिए गए हैं। इनमें से एक विकल्प सही पर्यायवाची है, उसका चयन कीजिए :*

1. अग्नि
(क) अनिल
(ख) अनल
(ग) गर्म
(घ) ताप

2. अमृत
(क) पीयूष
(ख) गरल
(ग) सरस
(घ) जीवनदायनी

3. आँख
(क) लोचन
(ख) आस्थि
(ग) वदन
(घ) जलज

4. आकाश
(क) अनन्त
(ख) पाताल
(ग) वितल
(घ) तल

5. कपड़ा
(क) परिधान
(ख) पटिका
(ग) पीताम्बर
(घ) लहँगा

6. कमल
(क) सरोज
(ख) सरोवर
(ग) पंक
(घ) पुष्प

7. गंगा
(क) पाताल नदी
(ख) हिमनदी
(ग) भागीरथ
(घ) त्रिपथगा

8. चाँद
(क) मयंक
(ख) भानु
(ग) दिनकर
(घ) रवि

9. नदी
(क) सरिता
(ख) प्रवाह
(ग) धारा
(घ) जलधर

10. पर्वत
(क) पत्थर
(ख) चट्टान
(ग) शिखर
(घ) मेरू

11. पवन
(क) अनिल
(ख) अनल
(ग) अग
(घ) विहग

12. पति
(क) साजन
(ख) प्रिया
(ग) भार्या
(घ) दारा

13. पानी
(क) मही
(ख) मेदिनी
(ग) अम्बु
(घ) तरणी

14. पुत्र
(क) आत्मज
(ख) तनया
(ग) सुता
(घ) आत्मजा

15. पुत्री
(क) सुता
(ख) सुत
(ग) आत्मज
(घ) नन्दन

16. फूल
(क) बहार
(ख) मधु
(ग) माधव
(घ) सुमन

17. वृक्ष
(क) विटप
(ख) अभ्र
(ग) प्रसून
(घ) रसा

18. बादल
(क) अज
(ख) व्यामोह
(ग) नीरद
(घ) मधुप

19. बिजली
(क) चंचला
(ख) खटका
(ग) त्रास
(घ) संत्रास

20. माता
(क) धात्री
(ख) धरणी
(ग) धरित्री
(घ) श्यामा

21. घोषणा
(क) आवाज
(ख) पुकारना
(ग) ऐलान
(घ) ललकारना

22. उत्कर्ष
(क) आकर्षण
(ख) विकर्षण
(ग) उन्नति
(घ) निष्कर्ष

23. उदय
(क) अन्त
(ख) विकास
(ग) प्रगट
(घ) व्यस्त

24. दक्ष
(क) निपुण
(ख) समर्थ
(ग) कर्मठ
(घ) मेहनती

25. संवाद
(क) विवाद
(ख) झगड़ा
(ग) सम्बोधन
(घ) वार्तालाप

26. इन्द्र
(क) सुरेन्द्र
(ख) जगदीश
(ग) महीप
(घ) हरि

27. ईश्वर
(क) लम्बोदर
(ख) प्रभु
(ग) रवि
(घ) पन्नग

28. पक्षी
(क) खग
(ख) जलधर
(ग) सोम
(घ) कानन

29. पृथ्वी
(क) भू
(ख) अम्बा
(ग) गात
(घ) दारा

30. घर
(क) निलय
(ख) विपिन
(ग) अहि
(घ) भाग

31. जंगल
(क) अरण्य
(ख) नग
(ग) मारुत
(घ) रूख

32. दिन
(क) गूधर
(ख) हिय
(ग) वासर
(घ) गात

33. मनुष्य
(क) सुधाकर
(ख) भानु
(ग) करि
(घ) मनुज

34. हाथी
(क) वामा
(ख) हस्ती
(ग) हिया
(घ) भारती

35. मित्र
(क) तनय
(ख) सहचर
(ग) मयंक
(घ) पन्नग

36. राजा
(क) नृप
(ख) विनायक
(ग) देव
(घ) अमर

37. आनन्द
(क) लालसा
(ख) विधु
(ग) हर्ष
(घ) वृषा

38. आम
(क) रसाल
(ख) उत्पल
(ग) अंशु
(घ) सोम

39. आश्रम
(क) गृह
(ख) विहार
(ग) सदन
(घ) अचल

40. इच्छा
(क) मयूख
(ख) रासभ
(ग) स्पृहा
(घ) कुंमिल

41. इन्द्राणी
(क) शची
(ख) रश्मि
(ग) धनद
(घ) विधु

42. कामदेव
(क) सुरपग
(ख) कन्दर्प
(ग) यक्षराज
(घ) विनायक

43. क्रोध
(क) पटु
(ख) इषु
(ग) रोष
(घ) त्रिदश

44. गणेश
(क) भानु
(ख) मधवा
(ग) आदित्य
(घ) लम्बोदर

45. **गधा**
(क) वैशाखनन्दन
(ख) डागर
(ग) मार
(घ) आपगा

46. **चोर**
(क) रजनीचर
(ख) सारंग
(ग) अमर्ष
(घ) वृषा

47. **यमुना**
(क) तरिणी
(ख) तिया
(ग) अजा
(घ) कालिन्दी

48. **दास**
(क) गीर्वाण
(ख) निशाकर
(ग) नाराच
(घ) चाकर

49. **द्रव्य**
(क) धन
(ख) प्रसून
(ग) पाथ
(घ) सर

50. **नर्क**
(क) यमलोक
(ख) कटक
(ग) विहायस
(घ) मनुजाद

51. **नौका**
(क) अर्णव
(ख) दन्ती
(ग) जलधर
(घ) नाव

52. **विष्णु**
(क) जनार्दन
(ख) छायानाथ
(ग) चन्द्रशेखर
(घ) कणधर

53. **समुद्र**
(क) धराधर
(ख) द्विरेक
(ग) अण्डज
(घ) जलधि

54. **सर्प**
(क) भुजंग
(ख) हाटक
(ग) तपन
(घ) भूतेश

55. **सोना**
(क) सारंग
(ख) मनोहर
(ग) कंचन
(घ) दिनेश

56. **सिंह**
(क) केशरी
(ख) व्याल
(ग) बलाहक
(घ) अज

57. **सुन्दर**
(क) वारण
(ख) सुरम्य
(ग) समग्र
(घ) मुंचन

58. **स्त्री**
(क) करी
(ख) भारती
(ग) त्रियामा
(घ) वनिता

59. पत्नी
(क) भार्या
(ख) आपगा
(ग) अर्कजा
(घ) कौमुदी

60. बाण
(क) तुंग
(ख) विशिख
(ग) भृत्य
(घ) अनंग

61. पार्वती
(क) उमा
(ख) मेदिनी
(ग) तरिणजा
(घ) देवापगा

62. सब
(क) समग्र
(ख) हेम
(ग) भर्ता
(घ) वसु

63. घमण्ड
(क) वक्र
(ख) द्वेष
(ग) तन्तु
(घ) गर्व

64. लता
(क) बेलि
(ख) कैथ
(ग) भयद
(घ) लाख

65. बटोही
(क) पथिक
(ख) नृपाल
(ग) तात
(घ) सारंग

निर्देश : *नीचे चार-चार शब्दों के समूह दिए गए हैं। प्रत्येक समूह में एक शब्द बेमेल है तथा शेष तीन शब्द पर्यायवाची हैं, आपको उस शब्द का चयन करना है, जो बेमेल है :*

66. (क) तम
(ख) अंधकार
(ग) तिमिर
(घ) अंश

67. (क) अनल
(ख) आग
(ग) दहन
(घ) तमिस्त्रा

68. (क) अतुल
(ख) अद्वितीय
(ग) अनुपम
(घ) शुष्मा

69. (क) अहं
(ख) अहंकार
(ग) दर्प
(घ) निराला

70. (क) पता
(ख) खोज
(ग) जाँच
(घ) शोध

71. (क) गरल
(ख) पीयूष
(ग) सुधा
(घ) सोम

72. (क) कानन
(ख) जंगल
(ग) पादप
(घ) वन

73. (क) अश्व
(ख) गज

(ग) घोड़ा
(घ) तुरंग

74. (क) दानव
(ख) मानव
(ग) दैत्य
(घ) राक्षस

75. (क) आँख
(ख) चक्षु
(ग) नयन
(घ) मुख

76. (क) अन्तरिक्ष
(ख) वसुन्धरा
(ग) आसमान
(घ) गगन

77. (क) इच्छा
(ख) अभिलाषा
(ग) कामना
(घ) प्रयोजन

78. (क) कपड़ा
(ख) चीर
(ग) वसन
(घ) पोशाक

79. (क) अब्ज
(ख) कमल
(ग) राजीव
(घ) आम्र

80. (क) कोयल
(ख) पिक
(ग) वनचर
(घ) वनप्रिय

81. (क) गंगा
(ख) देवनदी
(ग) गोदावरी
(घ) भागीरथी

82. (क) गणेश
(ख) एकदन्त
(ग) देवराज
(घ) गणपति

83. (क) घर
(ख) निलय
(ग) निकेतन
(घ) झोपड़ी

84. (क) चाँद
(ख) हिमांशु
(ग) विनायक
(घ) सुधांशु

85. (क) नदी
(ख) तरणी
(ग) तटिनी
(घ) सरिता

86. (क) पक्षी
(ख) चिड़िया
(ग) सुमन
(घ) विहग

87. (क) पवन
(ख) अचला
(ग) वात
(घ) वायु

88. (क) समीर
(ख) पृथ्वी
(ग) भू
(घ) भूमि

89. (क) पानी
(ख) समीर
(ग) अम्बु
(घ) जल

90. (क) पुत्र
(ख) तनया

(ग) तनय
(घ) सुत

91. (क) पुत्र
(ख) तनया
(ग) सुता
(घ) कन्या

92. (क) गृहिणी
(ख) आदमी
(ग) पुरुष
(घ) नर

93. (क) मधु
(ख) फूल
(ग) पुष्प
(घ) सुमन

94. (क) माधव
(ख) तरु
(ग) पेड़
(घ) वृक्ष

95. (क) माता
(ख) अम्बु
(ग) अम्मा
(घ) जननी

96. (क) क्रोध
(ख) अमर्ष
(ग) स्वत्व
(घ) कोप

97. (क) मोर
(ख) केकी
(ग) शिखी
(घ) शिखण्डी

98. (क) अश्म
(ख) बृषभ
(ग) बलीवर्द
(घ) बैल

99. (क) सुषमा
(ख) शोभा
(ग) सुन्दरता
(घ) रमणी

100. (क) तरंगिणी
(ख) तटिनी
(ग) तरिणी
(घ) सरिता

101. (क) भवन
(ख) भुवन
(ग) निकेतन
(घ) सदन

102. (क) खगेश
(ख) शृंगाल
(ग) सियार
(घ) जम्बुक

103. (क) शशि
(ख) हिमकर
(ग) शशांक
(घ) रूपक

104. (क) हेरम्ब
(ख) गाय
(ग) भद्रा
(घ) धेनु

105. (क) द्रौपदी
(ख) द्रुपदसुता
(ग) पांचाली
(घ) रमणी

106. (क) द्रव्य
(ख) द्रव
(ग) सम्पदा
(घ) दौलत

107. (क) तनय
(ख) सुता
(ग) आत्मजा
(घ) दुहिता

108. (क) सरोज
(ख) अरविन्द
(ग) सलिल
(घ) पंकज

109. (क) जंगल
(ख) कान्ता
(ग) कान्तार
(घ) कानन

110. (क) तलवार
(ख) असि
(ग) कृपण
(घ) खड्ग

111. (क) पत्ता
(ख) पर्ण
(ग) पल्लव
(घ) प्रसून

112. (क) युद्ध
(ख) संग्राम
(ग) समर
(घ) सार

113. (क) सरस्वती
(ख) वीणापाणि
(ग) शारदा
(घ) धनद

114. (क) तुरंग
(ख) शेर
(ग) मृगराज
(घ) व्याघ्र

115. (क) झण्डा
(ख) पताका
(ग) प्रस्तर
(घ) ध्वज

116. (क) पत्नी
(ख) कलत्र
(ग) दौहित्र
(घ) भार्या

117. (क) जानकी
(ख) वैदेही
(ग) जनकसुता
(घ) वामा

118. (क) कुबेर
(ख) श्वान
(ग) कोषपाल
(घ) धनपति

119. (क) पुष्प
(ख) सुमन
(ग) प्रसून
(घ) निलय

120. (क) अग्र
(ख) अगला
(ग) ज्येष्ठ
(घ) दावा

121. (क) हनुमान
(ख) पवनपुत्र
(ग) बजरंगबली
(घ) यक्षपति

122. (क) रात
(ख) रैन
(ग) रजनी
(घ) कामिनी

123. (क) अरुण
(ख) आदित्य
(ग) दिनकर
(घ) महीप

124. (क) मोक्ष
(ख) मुक्ति
(ग) कैवल्य
(घ) कृतान्त

125. (क) संन्यासी
(ख) माधव
(ग) तापस
(घ) संत

शब्दार्थ

निर्देशः *चार विकल्पों में से सही अर्थ छाँटकर उस पर निशान लगाइये।*

1. अंग सौष्ठव
(क) शक्ति
(ख) सुकुमारता
(ग) कमनीयता
(घ) शारीरिक सौन्दर्य

2. अन्तर्घट
(क) घड़े का भीतरी-भाग
(ख) मन/हृदय
(ग) चित्त
(घ) अन्त:करण

3. अंतःशुद्धि
(क) घर के भीतरी-भाग की स्वच्छता
(ख) मन की शुद्धि
(ग) समाज के विभिन्न अंगों में शुद्धता
(घ) शरीर के भीतरी भागों की सफाई

4. अपकीर्त्ति
(क) अप्रसिद्धि (ख) निन्दा
(ग) अनिष्ट (घ) नीचता

5. अर्चना
(क) आराधना
(ख) खींचना
(ग) याचना करना
(घ) उपार्जन करना

6. अकूत
(क) अछूत
(ख) तंबा-चौड़ा
(ग) बलशाली
(घ) जिसकी गिनती न की जा सके

7. अनिच्छु
(क) असहमत
(ख) जिसे चाह न हो
(ग) उदास
(घ) वैरागी

8. अतिरेक
(क) साहस
(ख) व्याकुलता
(ग) बहुत अधिकता
(घ) प्रचंडता

9. अनित्य
(क) अचूक
(ख) सदा न रहने वाला
(ग) आकस्मिक
(घ) जो डाँवाडोल न हो

10. अनुपमेय
(क) विचित्र
(ख) अपूर्व
(ग) विस्तीर्ण
(घ) जिसकी तुलना किसी से न की जा सके

11. अनुर्वर
(क) कमजोर (ख) अनुपजाऊ
(ग) कल्पित (घ) व्यर्थ

12. अपंग
(क) निर्जीव
(ख) सुन्न
(ग) बेहोश
(घ) जिसके किसी अंग में कमी हो

13. आँकना
(क) तोलना
(ख) परखना
(ग) मोलभाव करना
(घ) अनुमान लगाना

14. आदृत
(क) गुणी (ख) श्रद्धावान
(ग) सम्मानित (घ) समृद्ध

15. इतस्ततः
(क) इत्यादि (ख) सब जगह

(ग) इधर-उधर (घ) फैला हुआ

16. **उपदेष्टा**
(क) शिक्षक
(ख) उपदेश देने वाला
(ग) विद्वान
(घ) अधिकारी

17. **उजागर**
(क) निर्मल (ख) उजला
(ग) निष्पक्ष (घ) प्रकाशमान

18. **उच्छिन्न**
(क) पूरी तरह से नष्ट
(ख) निराश
(ग) नकली
(घ) जूठा

19. **उपादान**
(क) अल्प दान (ख) सामग्री
(ग) सूत्र (घ) कल-पुरजे

20. **एकात्म**
(क) संचित
(ख) जिसकी आत्मा एक हो
(ग) अकेला
(घ) निश्चित

21. **ऋचा**
(क) अध्याय (ख) पूजा
(ग) वेद-मंत्र (घ) कर्मकांड

22. **कंठाग्र**
(क) गरदन का ऊपरी भाग
(ख) चोंच
(ग) मुँहबोला
(घ) जबानी याद

23. **कंटक**
(क) हैरानी (ख) काँटा
(ग) बुरी दशा (घ) आपत्ति

24. **कटाक्ष**
(क) गुस्सा (ख) टेढ़ी नजर
(ग) हमला (घ) आक्षेप

25. **कुयोग**
(क) मुसीबत (ख) बुरा नतीजा
(ग) षड्यंत्र (घ) बुरी घड़ी

26. **कतिपय**
(क) शायद (ख) कुछ
(ग) अनेक (घ) न्यून

27. **खगेश**
(क) गिद्ध (ख) सिंह
(ग) गरुड़ (घ) इन्द्र

28. **खचित**
(क) खिंचा हुआ
(ख) जड़ा हुआ
(ग) छकड़ा
(घ) पुराना

29. **गरिष्ठ**
(क) अहंकारपूर्ण
(ख) क्रुद्ध
(ग) शान्त
(घ) भारी

30. **गुरुतर**
(क) विशाल
(ख) भीषण
(ग) श्रेष्ठ
(घ) जो अपेक्षाकृत अधिक भारी या महत्त्वपूर्ण हो

31 **गतप्राण**
(क) मरणासन्न
(ख) मृत
(ग) कम आयु वाला
(घ) शिथिल

32. **गरिमा**
(क) गौरव (ख) परिणाम
(ग) अनुकूलता (घ) लाभ

33. **गूढ़ार्थ**
(क) रहस्य
(ख) जटिल अभिप्राय
(ग) अंतर
(घ) मूर्खता

34. गौरवान्वित
(क) सुशोभित (ख) उन्नत
(ग) गर्वयुक्त (घ) सम्मानित

35. गुम्फित
(क) हर्षित
(ख) गुंथी हुई/गुंथा हुआ
(ग) बचा हुआ
(घ) छिपा हुआ

36. ग्लानि
(क) अरुचि
(ख) अवसन्न
(ग) क्रोध
(घ) मानसिक व्यथा

37. गृहीत
(क) अधिकृत
(ख) स्वीकृत/प्राप्त किया हुआ
(ग) सम्मानित
(घ) विदीत

38. घृणित
(क) घृणा से परे
(ख) घृणा करने वाला
(ग) घृणा के योग्य
(घ) घृणा का पात्र

39. घ्राणेन्द्रिय
(क) इन्द्रियों से अंगोचर
(ख) रसबोध कराने वाली इन्द्रिय
(ग) स्पर्श कराने वाली इन्द्रिय
(घ) गन्ध बोध कराने वाली इन्द्रिय

40. चरितावली
(क) बहुत चरित्रों या जीवनियों का संकलन
(ख) आत्म-कथा
(ग) लोगों का गुणगान
(घ) किसी के चरित्र स्वभाव आदि का वर्णन

41. चित्तवृत्ति
(क) स्वभाव
(ख) मन की अवस्था
(ग) चंचलता
(घ) स्थिर मन

42. चमत्कार
(क) उत्सव
(ख) अनहोनी बात
(ग) अद्भुत बात
(घ) नाटक

43. छलावा
(क) दिखावट
(ख) धोखा
(ग) भूल
(घ) विश्वासघात

44. छरहरा
(क) अकेला
(ख) प्रसन्न
(ग) सुन्दर
(घ) इकहरे बदन का

45. छद्मवेश
(क) अभिनय
(ख) तड़क-भड़क
(ग) नकली-वेश
(घ) धोखाधड़ी

46. जीवट
(क) उत्साह (ख) साहस
(ग) श्रम (घ) कर्तव्य

47. जलतरंग
(क) लहर
(ख) बाजा
(ग) बड़वानल
(घ) उमंगों का अंत

48. झकोरा
(क) मंद हवा
(ख) पंखा
(ग) तूफानें
(घ) तेज हवा का झोंका

49. **ठनठन गोपाल**
(क) सुखी
(ख) चिंताहीन
(ग) मूर्ख
(घ) निर्धन व्यक्ति

50. **तत्त्वावधान**
(क) देखरेख (ख) संगठन
(ग) अनुपालन (घ) अनुग्रह

51. **दत्तक**
(क) रक्षित
(ख) गोद लिया हुआ
(ग) त्याज्य
(घ) दानी

52. **द्वंद्वातीत**
(क) लड़ाई से विमुख
(ख) चिन्तारहित
(ग) सुख दुःख से परे
(घ) विरक्त

53. **दावानल**
(क) मुठभेड़
(ख) जंगल की आग
(ग) मुकदमेंबाजी
(घ) विस्फोट

54. **धनैषणा**
(क) लालच
(ख) धन की लालसा
(ग) सम्पत्ति की चाह
(घ) मितव्यय

55. **धाराबद्ध**
(क) अधिक समय तक प्रवाही
(ख) निरंतर/सतत
(ग) धीरे-धीरे
(घ) बँधा हुआ

56. **धीरोदात्त**
(क) सदाचारी
(ख) धैर्यवान एवं उदार
(ग) पराक्रमी
(घ) विजयी

57. **धृष्ट**
(क) धीर (ख) स्थिरचित्त
(ग) निर्लज्ज (घ) उत्साही

58. **नकारना**
(क) रोकना
(ख) अस्वीकृत
(ग) इनकार करना
(घ) उलटना

59. **नमित**
(क) झुका हुआ
(ख) विनीत
(ग) जो कठोर न हो
(घ) जिसका दमन किया गया हो

60. **नैसर्गिक**
(क) स्वर्गिक (ख) सरल
(ग) सुन्दर (घ) प्राकृतिक

61. **निष्ठा**
(क) निष्ठुर (ख) वचनबद्ध
(ग) दृढ़
(घ) किसी में श्रद्धा रखने वाला

62. **निःस्व**
(क) धनहीन
(ख) दुर्बल
(ग) जिसे अभिमान न हो
(घ) स्वार्थरहित

63. **निठल्ला**
(क) बेकार
(ख) आलसी
(ग) बेईमान
(घ) बेकार/खाली

64. **पदरज**
(क) पाँव की धूल
(ख) पाँव तले की धूल
(ग) रास्ते की गर्द
(घ) पैरों से रौंदी गई कोई चीज़

65. **प्रतियोगी**
(क) साथ देने वाला

(ख) किसी मुकाबले में भाग लेने वाला
(ग) शत्रु
(घ) परिश्रमी

66. पुजापा
(क) पूजन की सामग्री
(ख) पूज्यभाव
(ग) भोग सामग्री
(घ) पूजा करना

67. बल
(क) शक्ति (ख) स्फूर्ति
(ग) चेतनता (घ) पौरुष

68. बतियाना
(क) बातून
(ख) बातचीत करना
(ग) समझाना-बुझाना
(घ) वाद-विवाद करना

भंगिमा
क) अभिव्यक्ति (ख) चेष्टा
(ग) एक जाति (घ) संकेत

70. भंग
(क) टूटना (ख) परेशान
(ग) बांकपन (घ) विच्छेदन

71. भावबोध
(क) विचारधारा
(ख) कल्पना
(ग) किसी विचार का ज्ञान
(घ) भावना

72. भाराक्रान्त
(क) बोझ से दुखी
(ख) पीड़ित
(ग) परेशान
(घ) डरा हुआ

73. मनोरथ
(क) मनरूपी रथ
(ख) इच्छा/मनोकामना
(ग) मनोज्ञ
(घ) अभीष्ट

74. मीमांसा
(क) प्रतिपादन
(ख) प्रशंसा
(ग) मीन-मांस
(घ) गंभीर चिन्तन के बाद लिया गया निर्णय

75. यथेष्ट
(क) काफी मात्रा में
(ख) पर्याप्त
(ग) मनोनुकूल
(घ) प्रभूत

76. यातना
(क) कष्ट
(ख) बहुत अधिक वेदना
(ग) वह पीड़ा तथा कष्ट जो यमलोक में भोगनी पड़ती है
(घ) यात्रा

77. युवराज
(क) राजकुमार
(ख) राजकुमार जो भविष्य में राजा बनेगा
(ग) दो राजा
(घ) नया राज्य

78. रंक
(क) निर्धन (ख) रंग
(ग) कौड़ी (घ) उद्विग्न

79. रागारुण
(क) क्रोध से लाल हुआ
(ख) प्रेम से रक्तिम हुआ
(ग) रक्तवर्णी
(घ) परेशान

80. राजीव
(क) पद्म
(ख) नीलकमल
(ग) एक व्यक्ति विशेष

(घ) राजा का

81. **राज्याभिषेक**
(क) राजतिलक
(ख) राजा का स्नान
(ग) राजा का आक्रमण करने जाना
(घ) राजनिवास

82. **लंपट**
(क) लम्बा वस्त्र
(ख) एक प्रकार का जेवर
(ग) व्यभिचारी/धूर्त्त
(घ) भुक्खड़

83. **ललाम**
(क) मस्तक (ख) सुन्दर
(ग) वल्गा (घ) अद्भुत

84. **लोहित**
(क) कुंकुम (ख) रक्त
(ग) चितकबरा (घ) एक घास

85. **वंचक**
(क) कथा बाँचने वाला
(ख) धूर्त्त/ठग
(ग) तनिक/किंचित
(घ) एक नीव

86. **वहिर्गमन**
(क) विरोध स्वरूप बाहर चले जाना
(ख) देशाटन करने जाना
(ग) शौच जाना
(घ) बाहर चले जाना

87. **विश्लेषण**
(क) किसी पदार्थ के तत्त्वों को पृथक करना
(ख) संयोजन करना
(ग) अनुसंधान करना
(घ) समीक्षा करना

88. **संरचना**
(क) बनावट या गठन
(ख) सुघर
(ग) उपाचार
(घ) रचित

89. **हस्तगत**
(क) प्राप्त (ख) लिखावट
(ग) सहज (घ) हस्ताक्षर

90. **होतव्यता**
(क) प्रारब्ध (ख) सामर्थ्य
(ग) दाँव (घ) अभिप्राय

वाक्य/वाक्यांश के लिए एक शब्द

नीचे कुछ वाक्य या वाक्यांश दिये गये हैं। उनके नीचे चार अलग-अलग शब्द दिये गये हैं, जिनमें से एक का अर्थ वही है जो वाक्या या वाक्यांश का है। उस शब्द को छांटकर उस पर निशान लगाइये।

1 जो आयु में बड़ा हो–
(क) गुरु (ख) अग्रज
(ग) वरिष्ठ (घ) सहोदर

जो बिना समझे-बूझे किसी बात को सत्य मान कर उस पर विश्वास कर लेते हैं–
(क) विवेकहीन
(ख) मूर्ख
(ग) अज्ञानी
(घ) अन्धविश्वासी

जिस तर्क का कोई जवाब न हो–
(क) अकाट्य (ख) जोरदार
(ग) तीखा (घ) सटीक

4. जिसे आँखों से देखा न जा सके–
(क) सूक्ष्म
(ख) अगोचर
(ग) मायावी
(घ) अस्तित्वहीन

5. ऐसा मार्ग जिस पर जा सकना कठिन हो–
(क) ऊबड़-खाबड़
(ख) दुर्गम
(ग) असम
(घ) सँकरा

6. जिसका कोई शत्रु पैदा न हुआ हो–
(क) शत्रुहीन (ख) सर्वप्रिय
(ग) अजातशत्रु (घ) सर्वमित्र

7. जिसे जीता न जा सके–
(क) परमवीर (ख) अज्ञेय
(ग) अजेय (घ) अगम

8. जो ईश्वर में विश्वास न करता हो–
(क) अनीश्वर (ख) नास्तिक
(ग) राक्षस (घ) विधर्मी

9. जिस बालक के माँ-बाप न हों (मर चुके हों)–
(क) असहाय (ख) अनाथ
(ग) अबोध (घ) निरीह

10. छोटे भाई के लिए शब्द है–
(क) भैया (ख) अनुज
(ग) अग्रज (घ) भ्राता

11. किसी की लम्बी दुखपूर्ण कथा–
(क) राम कहानी (ख) विपदा
(ग) दुखड़ा (घ) विलाप

12. तीन वेदों को जानने वाला–
(क) द्विवेदी (ख) त्रिवेदी
(ग) विद्वान (घ) चतुर्वेदी

13. जिसकी उपमा न दी जा सके–
(क) अद्वितीय (ख) अनुपमेय
(ग) आदर्श (घ) अकथ्य

14. दूसरों पर अकारण अत्याचार करने वाला–
(क) पानी (ख) आततायी
(ग) हिंसक (घ) दुष्ट

15. जो सब कुछ जानने वाला है–
(क) धुरन्धर (ख) सर्वव्यापी
(ग) निष्णात (घ) सर्वज्ञ

16. जो रोग सम्पर्क से फैलता है–
(क) घातक (ख) सम्पर्क
(ग) असाध्य (घ) संचारी

17. पुराने जमाने में राजा-बादशाह जिस स्थान से अपनी प्रजा को दर्शन देते थे–
(क) वातायन (ख) कबन्ध
(ग) दरबार (घ) झरोखा

18. आकाश में उड़ने वाले जीव-जन्तु–
(क) पक्षी (ख) खगोल
(ग) नभचर (घ) गगनचुम्बी

19. जो एहसान न माने–
(क) कृतज्ञ (ख) कृतकार्य
(ग) कृतघ्न (घ) एहसानमंद

20. जो दूसरों की सहायता की अपेक्षा न करे–
(क) आत्मनिर्भर
(ख) पुरुषार्थी
(ग) आत्मविश्वासी
(घ) स्वाभिमानी

21. जो अपने ढंग का अनोखा हो–
(क) चमत्कारी (ख) विरला
(ग) असमान (घ) अद्वितीय

22. जो किसी का पक्ष न ले–
(क) न्यायी (ख) निस्वार्थी
(ग) निर्भर (घ) निष्पक्ष

23. जिसका अन्त न हो–
(क) अन्तस (ख) अनन्त
(ग) अनअन्त (घ) निअंत

24. उच्च कुल में जन्म लेने वाला–
(क) कुली (ख) कुलीन
(ग) कुलिश (घ) कुलिज

25. किसी वस्तु को प्राप्त करने की प्रबल इच्छा–
(क) लालच (ख) ललक
(ग) लोभ (घ) लाव

26. जो सेवा बिना वेतन, पारिश्रमिक या पारितोष के की जाये–
(क) अर्थहीन (ख) अनार्थिक
(ग) अवैतनिक (घ) निरर्थक

27. जिसका बध निषिद्ध हो–
(क) निर्बध
(ख) अबध्य
(ग) अनबध
(घ) बधहीन

28. जिसने गृहस्थ जीवन का त्याग कर दिया हो–
(क) साधु (ख) संन्यासी
(ग) योगी (घ) तपस्वी

29. जो या जिसे पहले न सुना गया हो–
(क) अश्रुत (ख) अश्रव्य
(ग) अश्राव्य (घ) अनश्रव्य

30. वह डण्डा या छड़ जिस पर पहिया घूमता है–
(क) धनुष (ख) धुर्र
(ग) धुरी (घ) धृति

शुद्ध वाक्य ढूँढना

निर्देशः *नीचे चार-चार वाक्यों के समूह दिये गये हैं। प्रत्येक समूह में एक वाक्य शुद्ध है। शुद्ध वाक्य छाँटकर उस पर निशान लगाइये।*

1. (क) निर्धनों के लिए दान दी जानी चाहिए
(ख) छमाही परीक्षा आरंभ होने वाला है
(ग) आजकल छतरी का फैशन नहीं है
(घ) खोदाई में अनेक वस्तुएँ निकाले गए

2. (क) शीला गाना गाती है
(ख) शीला को बाजा बजाया
(ग) शीला और मोहन आ रहा है
(घ) अध्यापक ने विद्यार्थी को कहानी सुनाया

3. (क) माँ ने नौकर को रुपये दिया
(ख) रमेश अभी आ गया
(ग) हम ऊँचे पर्वत पर जायेंगे
(घ) सूर्य उदय हो गया है

4. (क) हवा तेजी से चलती है
(ख) वर्षा होने लग गई
(ग) अनर्थ हो गया
(घ) तुमको यह बात किसने कहा?

5. (क) अनेकों लोग उनके साथ थे
(ख) लड़कियाँ खेल रही हैं
(ग) आपके एक-एक वाक्य प्रभावी होते हैं
(घ) हमारे घर पर बहुत आटा रखा है

6. (क) काम पर लगन रखो
(ख) राम, श्याम, मोहन ने आम खाया
(ग) आपकी वाणी के भीतर मिठास है
(घ) उसकी गाय बहुत दूध देती है

7. (क) आप उनको बोल दो
(ख) आज बादल घिर आई
(ग) बार-बार चालबाजी मत करो
(घ) श्याम ने वंशी बजाया

8. (क) जो सोते हैं, सो खायेंगे
(ख) अपने उनको क्या कह दिया?
(ग) यह उसके इज्जत का प्रश्न है
(घ) राधा ने नौकर को पीटा

9. (क) माली फूल को तोड़ते हैं
(ख) राम और श्याम कविता करते हैं
(ग) उन्हें कल स्कूल नही आना है
(घ) इस लिस्ट में 10 पुस्तकों के नाम हैं

10. (क) जी लगाकर काम को करो
(ख) गुरु में श्रद्धा रखो

(ग) मनुष्य एक सामाजिक प्राणी है
(घ) धर्म प्रेम का जड़ है

11. (क) मैं आपकी श्रृद्धा करता हूँ
(ख) शोभा काम से दौड़ती है
(ग) आपकी बहनजी आये हैं
(घ) इतने नम्बर बहुत हैं

12. (क) दीवार पर नहीं लिखो
(ख) आम के आम गुठलियों का दाम
(ग) मेरा वश न चला और मैंने रो दिया
(घ) यह काम आप ही कर सकते हैं

13. (क) बड़ों से आदर करना चाहिए
(ख) पढ़ने पर मन लगाओ
(ग) उसने बड़ी मेहनत से हिन्दी को सीखा
(घ) उसने अपना नाम बताया

14. (क) इस पर माता ने हँस दिया
(ख) स्वयं को खतरे में डालकर उसने बच्चे को बचाया
(ग) यह काम तुम्हारे लाभ की प्राप्ति का होगा
(घ) पुस्तक दे दो आप हमें

15. (क) हमारा काम तुमको करना पड़ा
(ख) धर्म जीवन की सार है
(ग) उसने स्कूल नहीं जाना है
(घ) तुम किसके साथ बात कर रहे हो

16. (क) वह पानी नहीं खाते हैं
(ख) उनके मन के भीतर बड़ा दुख है
(ग) संतों के उपदेश ध्यान देकर सुनो
(घ) उन्होंने हिन्दी सीखी

17. (क) गरीब से गरीब भी रोटी खा लेता है
(ख) तुम उधर को क्यों गए थे?
(ग) मेरे को उनसे कुछ लेना-देना नहीं है
(घ) इतने रुपयों में घर का खच कैसे चलेगा?

18. (क) वह स्वभाव का मितव्ययी है
(ख) उसने अपनी पुस्तक खो दिया
(ग) उसे बन्दीगृह में बन्दी बनाया गया
(घ) अपने कर्त्तव्य का पालन करो

19. (क) यह सब आप की कृपायें हैं
(ख) उनके नाम सूची में नहीं हैं
(ग) उसने गन्ने खरीदे
(घ) अहंकार विनाश का जड़ है

20. (क) मुझे हिन्दी सीखना है
(ख) क्या तुमने हिन्दी सीखा?
(ग) तुम्हारे को हिन्दी कौन पढ़ाता है?
(घ) तुम्हें हिन्दी आती है

21. (क) कृपया शीघ्र से पत्र का उत्तर दें
(ख) पढ़ने में आलस्य न करें
(ग) उनको मनीआर्डर आया है
(घ) अभी वह घर तक नहीं आया है

22. (क) यह सुनकर रानी ने हँस दिया
(ख) अब तुम जा सकते हो
(ग) कल इतवार है
(घ) उसने मुझको चोरी लगाई

23. (क) वह धर्म का विश्वास नहीं करता
(ख) उसकी पत्नी ने हँस कर बोला
(ग) उसके फल हाथों-हाथ बिक गए
(घ) खीझ कर उसने रो दिया

24. (क) जल को गंदा मत करो
(ख) लगन से काम करने पर सफलता मिलेगी
(ग) दया धर्म की मूल है
(घ) इस पुस्तक की मूल्य बहुत है

25. (क) समय को व्यर्थ न गँवाओ
(ख) पुस्तक को जल्दी-जल्दी पढ़ो

(ग) दवात मत छुओ
(घ) धन का सदुपयोग करो

26. (क) कृष्ण वहाँ शाम जायेगा
(ख) इतना कहकर वह खिसक गया
(ग) उसके नाम पर तूती बोलती है
(घ) उसे अपने धन को लेकर बड़ा घमंड है

27. (क) गांधी जी ने अनेक उपदेश दिये
(ख) उनकी सारी करतूतों के पर्दे फाश हो गए
(ग) दिन-रात की मेहनत से सेहत खराब होने का अंदेशा होगा
(घ) क्या तुमने परीक्षा दिया है?

28. (क) उसको बुलावा आया है
(ख) आपने जो देखा, वह सत्य नहीं थी
(ग) मैं हँस कर चल पड़ा
(घ) सभा में उनको बहुत अपमान हुआ

29. (क) सबने अपनी-अपनी राम कहानी सुनाया
(ख) इस मौसम में आम बहुत महंगे हैं
(ग) टेलीफोन पर व्यर्थ की बात नहीं करना चाहिए
(घ) आपने उनको सम्पर्क किया या नहीं?

30. (क) आपने अपना नाम नहीं बताया
(ख) कृपया ध्यान दें, किसी ने इस नल का पानी नहीं पीना है
(ग) पुस्तकों के लिए एक अलमारी खरीदा है
(घ) आपको सुपुत्र कौन-सी कक्षा में पढ़ते हैं

मुहावरे और लोकोक्तियाँ

निर्देशः *सही विकल्प पर निशान लगायें।*

1. अंग-अंग ढीला होना
(क) शिथिल कर देना
(ख) बहुत मारना
(ग) मालिश करना
(घ) सताना

2. अंग-अंग मुस्काना
(क) अत्यन्त प्रसन्न होना
(ख) भाव-विभोर होना
(ग) हाव भाव प्रकट करना
(घ) व्यायाम करना

3. अंगारे उगलना
(क) क्रोध में आकर कठोर शब्द कहना
(ख) आग फेंकना
(ग) लाल पीला होना
(घ) उतावली करना

4. अंगारों पर लेटना
(क) बहुत परेशान होना
(ख) दुःखी होना
(ग) चिन्ता करना
(घ) उतावली करना

5. अँगुली उठाना
(क) निन्दित होना
(ख) हानि पहुँचाना
(ग) बुराई करना
(घ) संकेत करना

6. अँगुली पर नचाना
(क) वश में रखना
(ख) इशारा करना
(ग) बहुत काम करना
(घ) संत्रास देना

7. अंगूठा दिखाना
(क) मौके पर काम न करना
(ख) चिढ़ाना

(ग) बेबस करना
(घ) परेशान करना

8. आँचल पसारना
(क) भीख माँगना
(ख) रक्षा की याचना करना
(ग) बहुत रोना
(घ) विनत हो जाना

9. अँतड़ियों में बल पड़ना
(क) बहुत रोना
(ख) बहुत हँसना
(ग) बीमार होना
(घ) दौड़ धूप करना

10. अंधा क्या चाहे दो आँखें
(क) आवश्यक वस्तु की प्राप्ति
(ख) आगे आना
(ग) मुराद पूरी होना
(घ) पशेमान होना

11. अंध बन जाना
(क) टाल देना
(ख) अनजान बन जाना
(ग) धोखे में आ जाना
(घ) लालायित होना

12. अंधेर नगरी चौपट राजा
(क) अव्यवस्था होना
(ख) किसी की बात न सुनना
(ग) किसी राजा की कहानी
(घ) बेपरवाह होना

13. अक्ल का दुश्मन
(क) बेवकूफ (ख) महा मूर्ख
(ग) पागल (घ) बुद्धिहीन

14. अक्ल चरने जाना
(क) बुद्धि से काम न करना
(ख) बाहर घूमने जाना
(ग) हाजिर जवाब होना
(घ) आमोद-प्रमोद करना

15. अक्ल बड़ी की भैंस
(क) सशक्त शरीर में ही बुद्धि का निवास नहीं होता
(ख) शक्ति-सम्पन्न ही मात्र बुद्धिमान होते हैं
(ग) भैंस और अक्ल का क्या मुकाबला
(घ) अक्लमन्द ही बड़े होते हैं भैस नहीं

16. अखाड़ा मारना
(क) हरा देना
(ख) विजय प्राप्त करना
(ग) कुश्ती लड़ना
(घ) परेशान करना

17. आग में घी डालना
(क) क्रोध बढ़ाना
(ख) हवन करना
(ग) उद्विग्न करना
(घ) प्रज्ज्वलित करना

18. अच्छे दिन देखना
(क) सुखपूर्वक यात्रा करना
(ख) तीर्थ दर्शन करना
(ग) सुख-सुविधा से जीवन यापन करना
(घ) शुभ मुहूर्त में उठना

19. अठखेलियाँ करना
(क) दिल्लगी करना
(ख) मजे में रहना
(ग) खेल खेलना
(घ) हँसना

20. अपने पाँव में कुल्हाड़ी मारना
(क) कष्ट सहना
(ख) अपना नुकसान खुद करना
(ग) बीमारी बुलाना
(घ) काम करते नुकसान होना

21. आँख उठाकर भी न देखना
(क) चुप रहना
(ख) जी चुराना
(ग) ध्यान तक न देना
(घ) अनसुनी करना

22. आँखें नीची होना
(क) आँखों की बीमारी होना
(ख) धूप सहन न करना
(ग) सोच समझकर चलना
(घ) शर्मिन्दा होना/लजा जाना

23. आँखें चुराना
(क) शर्म के कारण सामने न आना
(ख) जान बचाना
(ग) मारे-मारे फिरना
(घ) चुप बैठना

24. आँखें मिलाना
(क) प्यार करना
(ख) साहस करना
(ग) बदहवास होना
(घ) चिन्ता करना

25. आँखें बिछाना
(क) श्रद्धा करना
(ख) सम्मानपूर्वक प्रेम करना
(ग) प्रतीक्षा करना
(घ) स्वागत करना

26. आग लगने पर कुआँ खोदना
(क) मुसीबत बुलाना
(ख) पानी का प्रबंध करना
(ग) कठिनाइयों से निपटने के लिए तत्काल उपाय करना
(घ) आपत्ति आने पर उसका उपाय ढूँढना

27. आपे में न होना
(क) होश में न रहना
(ख) मिथ्या बकवाद करना
(ग) क्रोध में भड़क उठना
(घ) अपनी सुध खो देना

28. आस्तीन का साँप होना
(क) साँप पास रखना
(ख) छुपा दुश्मन होना
(ग) संकट सामने होना
(घ) दुश्मनी रखना

29. आसमान से बातें करना
(क) ऊपर उड़ान भरना
(ख) तेज गाड़ी चलाना
(ग) तेज दौड़ना/दौड़ाना
(घ) डींग हाँकना

30. इति श्री करना
(क) समाप्त करना
(ख) पूजा करना
(ग) पारायण करना
(घ) किसी चीज़ की माँग करना

31. इधर-उधर की लगाना
(क) निन्दा करना
(ख) चुगली करना
(ग) भेद खोलना
(घ) झगड़ा कराना

32. ईंट से ईंट बजाना
(क) तकरार करना
(ख) इमारत बनवाना
(ग) ध्वंस कर देना
(घ) बहादुरी दिखाना

33. उड़ती चिड़िया पहचानना
(क) पक्षियों की विशेषज्ञ होना
(ख) चालाकी भाँप जाना
(ग) सावधान रहना
(घ) अटकलें लगाना

34. उल्लू बनाना
(क) बेवकूफ बनाना
(ख) लुकाछिपी खेलना
(ग) परेशान करना
(घ) बे-सिर-पैर की बात सिखाना

35. उँची दुकान, फीका पकवान
(क) नाम अधिक वास्तविकता कम
(ख) नाम बड़े दर्शन थोड़े
(ग) वस्तु का बेजायका होना
(घ) कोरी विज्ञापन बाज़ी

36. ऊसर में बीज होना
(क) बेमतलब का काम करना

(ख) नुकसान उठाना
(ग) गलत जमीन में खेती करना
(घ) निरर्थक परिश्रम करना

37. एक पंथ दो काज
(क) एक रास्ते में दो काम करना
(ख) एक ढेले से दो पक्षी मारना
(ग) उठाई गिरी करना
(घ) एक उद्योग से दोहरा फायदा उठाना/कमाना

38. ओखली में सिर देना
(क) धान कूटते चोट लगना
(ख) आपत्तियाँ मोल लेना
(ग) जान बूझकर स्वयं को विपत्ति में फँसाना
(घ) परेशान होना

39. औंधी खोपड़ी
(क) निपट मूर्ख
(ख) बेवकूफ आदमी
(ग) खोपड़ी उल्टी होना
(घ) गाते रहना

40. कंघी चोटी से फुरसत न मिलना
(क) बनिज व्यापार करना
(ख) वेश बनाना
(ग) सदा सिंगार करते रहना
(घ) बेकार के काम करना

41. कंगाली में आटा गीला
(क) विपत्ति पर विपत्ति आना
(ख) कष्ट भोगना
(ग) गरीबी में गुजारा करना
(घ) बेबसी में सत्तू खाना

42. कंचन बरसना
(क) अच्छी बरसात होना
(ख) समय पर पानी बरसना
(ग) सुखपूर्वक जीवन यापन करना
(घ) अधिक धन की प्राप्ति होना

43. कपाल क्रिया करना
(क) अंतिम क्रिया करना
(ख) सिर फोड़ देना
(ग) सताना
(घ) मार-पीट करना

44. कच्चा चिट्ठा खोलना
(क) पूरी कथा कहना
(ख) हिसाब बताना
(ग) पोल खोलना
(घ) सही स्थिति बताना

45. कलेजा पसीजना
(क) दिल बैठ जाना
(ख) हाल खराब होना
(ग) गर्मी लगना
(घ) दया उत्पन्न होना

46. कलेजे से लगाकर रखना
(क) संभाल कर रखना
(ख) प्यार से रखना
(ग) बहुत प्रेम करना
(घ) छिपाए रखना

47. कागज़ी घोड़े दौड़ाना
(क) केवल लिखा-पढ़ी करते रहना
(ख) बेकार का काम करना
(ग) खिलौने बनाना
(घ) खबर फैलाना

48. काटो तो खून नहीं
(क) बहुत कमजोर होने की दशा
(ख) बहुत भयभीत होने की दशा
(ग) बेहोश हो जाने की दशा
(घ) मृतवत हो जाना

49. कानों में तेल डाकर बैठना
(क) किसी की बात न सुनना
(ख) खुदगर्ज़ होना
(ग) बेकार बैठना
(घ) कहीं न जाना

50. काम का न काज का दुश्मन अनाज का
(क) बेकार के काम करना
(ख) स्वार्थी होना

(ग) बकार का आदमी
(घ) किसी उपयोग लायक न होना

51. ख्याली घोड़े दौड़ाना
(क) सोचते रहना
(ख) विचार अधिक काम कम करना
(ग) कल्पनाएँ करते रहना
(घ) काम बताना

52. खिसियानी बिल्ली खंभा नोचे
(क) लज्जित होकर किसी दूसरे पर क्रोध करना
(ख) दूसरों से लड़ पड़ना
(ग) लज्जित होना
(घ) परेशान होना

53. खुशामदी टट्टू
(क) भार ढोना
(ख) बिना लाभ के काम करना
(ग) अमीरों की चापलूसी करना
(घ) खुशामद करना

54. खून उबलना
(क) भागकर जाना
(ख) बहुत क्रोध करना
(ग) उत्साह में भर जाना
(घ) साहसी होना

55. खून सूखना
(क) बहुत डर जाना
(ख) हार मानना
(ग) बेबस होना
(घ) गुमसुम हो जाना

56. खून से हाथ रँगना
(क) किसी को परेशान करना
(ख) किसी की हत्या करना
(ग) प्रताड़ित करना
(घ) हत्या में शामिल होना

57. खेल बिगाड़ना
(क) बना बनाया काम बिगाड़ना
(ख) खेल ठीक से न खेलना
(ग) हार जाना
(घ) ज़िद करना

58. गधों को हलवा खिलाना
(क) अनाज बरबाद करना
(ख) गलत भोजन देना
(ग) ऊट-पटाँग काम करना
(घ) नीचों का सत्कार करना

59. गरदन झुकाना
(क) रोगी होना
(ख) वृद्ध होना
(ग) गला टूट जाना
(घ) शर्मिन्दा होना

60. गला फँसना
(क) मौत सामने आना
(ख) लाचार होना
(ग) फेर में पड़ जाना
(घ) मुसीबत में पड़ना

61. घर आया कुत्ता भी नहीं निकाला जाता
(क) किसी का अपमान नहीं करना चाहिए
(ख) अतिथि का अपमान नहीं करना चाहिए
(ग) कितना भी हीन व्यक्ति क्यों न हो उसका निरादर नहीं करना चाहिए
(घ) घर में सबको स्थान देना चाहिए

62. घर का भेदी लंका ढावे
(क) घर का निकम्मा आदमी बोझ होता है
(ख) घर की फूट से घर का नाश होता है
(ग) जान-बूझकर घर बरबाद करना
(घ) बाहर का आदमी घर को बरबाद कर देता है

63. घर में नहीं दाने, बुढ़िया चली भुनाने
(क) झूठा आडम्बर करना
(ख) अधिक दिखावा करना

(ग) डींग हाँकना
(घ) मुश्किल से गुज़ारा करना

64. चंगुल में फँसना
(क) परवश होना
(ख) बेबस होना
(ग) मुसीबत मोल लेना
(घ) चपेट में आना

65. चिकना घड़ा
(क) जिस पर पानी का असर न हो
(ख) परिस्थितियों में सुरक्षित
(ग) निर्लज्ज
(घ) लापरवाह

66. चुल्लू भर पानी में डूब मरना
(क) लज्जावश मुँह न दिखाना
(ख) थोड़े पानी से काम चलाना
(ग) आत्महत्या करना
(घ) छोटे तालाब में डूब जाना

67. चोर चोर मौसेरे भाई
(क) एक ही पेशे तथा स्वभाव के व्यक्तियों का मेल
(ख) चोर आपस में रिश्तेदार होते हैं
(ग) बेईमान की मदद बेईमान करते हैं
(घ) नाता-रिश्ता जोड़ना

68. जंगल में मंगल
(क) वन में पूजा-पाठ
(ख) जंगल में मांगलिक कार्य
(ग) वन में महोत्सव
(घ) निर्जन स्थान में चहल-पहल

69. जिस डाल पर बैठना उसी को काटना
(क) आश्रयदाता का अनिष्ट करना
(ख) पेड़ की छाया खत्म करना
(ग) पेड़ की काट-छाँट करना
(घ) पेड़ों का विनाश करना

70. जी चुराना
(क) मोहित करना
(ख) डोरे डालना
(ग) सुस्ती करना
(घ) बचना

71. जीवन की घड़ियाँ गिनना
(क) वर्षगाँठ मनाना
(ख) मृत्यु का समीप आना
(ग) जीवन का हिसाब रखना
(घ) जीवन में खरीदी गई घड़ियों का हिसाब रखना

72. ज्यों-ज्यों भीजे कामरी, त्यों-त्यों भारी होय
(क) कमली भीगने पर भारी हो जाती है
(ख) जैसे जैसे कमली भीगती जाती है वह और भी भारी होती जाती है
(ग) कर्ज को चुकाते रहना चाहिए नहीं तो वह बढ़ता जाता है
(घ) कमली को भीगने से बचाना चाहिए

73. झंडा गाड़ना
(क) अधिकार स्थापित करना
(ख) निशान बनाना
(ग) संकेत देना
(घ) मर्यादाएँ सुनिश्चित करना

74. झटक जाना
(क) दुखी होना
(ख) उतावली करना
(ग) दुर्बल होना
(घ) फटकारा जाना

75. टपक पड़ना
(क) पानी का रिसना
(ख) अकस्मात् आ जाना
(ग) गुस्सा होना
(घ) गुस्से में बोल पड़ना

76. टीका-टिप्पणी करना
(क) समालोचना करना

(ख) बात-बढ़ाना
(ग) अर्थ करना
(घ) टीका लगाकर पाठ करना

77. **ठंडा पड़ जाना**
(क) शीतांग होना
(ख) बुखार उतरना
(ग) क्रोध का शान्त होना
(घ) उत्साहहीन होना

78. **ठोकर खाते फिरना**
(क) बेकार भटकते फिरना
(ख) जगह-जगह ठोकरें लगना
(ग) लड़खड़ाना
(घ) परेशान होना

79. **डंका बजना**
(क) शोहरत/प्रसिद्ध होना
(ख) शादी होना
(ग) बुलाना
(घ) आतंक फैलना

80. **डूबते को तिनके का सहारा**
(क) डूबते हुए बच जाना
(ख) मामूली सहायता पहुँचना
(ग) निराशा में किंचित आशा का होना
(घ) व्यर्थ की आशा करना

81. **डपोर शंख**
(क) बड़ा शंख
(ख) झूठा, बे-सिर-पैर की कहने वाला
(ग) एक विशेष प्रकार का शंख
(घ) जल्दबाज

82. **तकदीर चमकना**
(क) मस्तक ऊँचा उठना
(ख) भाग्योदय होना
(ग) लाभ होना
(घ) खजाना मिलना

83. **तीर की तरह जाना**
(क) दौड़कर भाग जाना
(ख) तेजी करना
(ग) जल्दबाजी करना
(घ) दुबला होना

84. **त्यौरी चढ़ाना**
(क) डोरी चढ़ाना
(ख) लताएँ ऊपर करना
(ग) क्रुद्ध होना
(घ) कष्ट देना

85. **थू-थू होना**
(क) बदनामी फैलना
(ख) थूकना
(ग) चर्चा होना
(घ) व्यर्थ की बातें फैलना

86. **दंग रह जाना**
(क) घबरा जाना
(ख) भयभीत होना
(ग) आश्चर्य में पड़ जाना
(घ) चिन्ता करना

87. **दिल पसीजना**
(क) दिल का बैठ जाना
(ख) दया आना
(ग) डर जाना
(घ) विनती मानना

88. **धमा चौकड़ी करना**
(क) खेलना-कूदना
(ख) कबड्डी खेलना
(ग) बेकार घूमना
(घ) इकट्ठा होकर शोरगुल मचाना

89. **नंग बड़े परमेश्वर से**
(क) दुष्ट खतरनाक होते हैं
(ख) दुष्ट लोगों से सभी डरते हैं
(ग) बदमाशों को भगवान से भी बड़ा कहना चाहिए
(घ) दुष्टों की वंदना पहले करनी चाहिए

90. **नाक रगड़ना**
(क) विनती करना
(ख) खुशामद करना

(ग) अधीन होना
(घ) बीमार पड़ना

91. नीद हराम होना
(क) अत्यधिक चिन्ता
(ख) फिक्र के कारण नींद न आना
(ग) विपत्ति में पड़ना
(घ) बहुत दुःखी होना

92. नौ दिन चलै अढ़ाई कोस
(क) बहुत सुस्ती से काम करना
(ख) ऊँची चढ़ाई चढ़ना
(ग) चक्करदार रास्ते से जाना
(घ) गड़बड़ी के काम करना

93. पगड़ी उतारना
(क) विश्राम करना
(ख) सेवा करना
(ग) बेइज्जती करना
(घ) आवभगत करना

94. पट्टी पढ़ाना
(क) शिक्षा आरंभ करना
(ख) बहकाना
(ग) तख्ती में लिखनो सिखाना
(घ) शुरुआत करना

95. पर्वत पर कुवाँ खोदना
(क) असंभव को संभव करना
(ख) पानी की व्यवस्था करना
(ग) वृथा परिश्रम करना
(घ) बेसहारा को सहारा देना

96. पाप का घड़ा भर जाना
(क) कुकर्मों का फल मिलना
(ख) दिन पूरे हो जाना
(ग) पापों का फल पाना
(घ) भेद खुल जाना

97. फन्दे में पड़ जाना
(क) विपत्ति में पड़ना
(ख) छला जाना/धोखे से फँसना
(ग) बंध जाना
(घ) बेबस होना

98. फूला न समाना
(क) अधिक खा जाना
(ख) सन्तुष्ट होना
(ग) शेखी बघारना
(घ) बहुत प्रसन्न होना

99. फूल सूँघकर रहना
(क) बहुत अल्प आहार करना
(ख) फूलों से प्रेम करना
(ग) अनशन करना
(घ) कुछ न खाना

100. बंटाधार करना
(क) काम बिगाड़ना
(ख) विनाश करना
(ग) काम चौपट कर डालना
(घ) काम में देर करना

101. बाप-दादों का नाम डुबाना
(क) बाप-दादों की कमाई खाना
(ख) बाप-दादों की सम्पत्ति मिट्टी में मिलाना
(ग) बाप-दादों की बदनामी करना
(घ) बाप-दादों के यश को मटिया-मेट करना

102. बिजली गिरना
(क) वज्रपात होना
(ख) झटका लगना
(ग) बड़ी विपत्ति का आना
(घ) बरसात में बिजली का चमकना

103. भंग खाना
(क) भाँग खाने की लत होना
(ख) बुद्धि से काम न लेना
(ग) सोते रहना
(घ) ऊँघना

104. भंडा फोड़ना
(क) भेद खोलना
(ख) भंडार खोलना
(ग) बर्तन तोड़ना
(घ) मार-पीट करना

105. भभूत रमाना
(क) संन्यासी बन जाना
(ख) फकीरी में गुजारा करना
(ग) शंकर की भक्ति करना
(घ) अनासक्त होना

106. भरी थाली में लात मारना
(क) अन्न का अपमान करना
(ख) मिली वस्तु का त्याग करन.
(ग) बेवकूफी करना
(घ) अन्न बिखेरना

107. भीगी बिल्ली बनना
(क) डर जाना (ख) भाग जाना
(ग) छिप जाना (घ) घात लगाना

108. मक्खी मारना
(क) जीव-हत्या करना
(ख) कीड़े-मकोड़े मारना
(ग) घिनौने काम करना
(घ) खाली बैठना

109. मिरचें लगाना
(क) मिरचों की खेती करना
(ख) तीखी बात कहना
(ग) नाराज करना
(घ) लड़वा देना

110. मुँह में पानी भर आना
(क) लालच आ जाना
(ख) लार टपकाना
(ग) इन्तजार करना
(घ) भूख लगना

111. मुट्ठी गरम करना
(क) हाथ सेंकना
(ख) रिश्वत देना
(ग) मदद करना
(घ) मारना

112. यथा नाम तथा गुण
(क) जैसा नाम वैसे ही गुण
(ख) नाममात्र की उपयोगिता
(ग) उपयोगिता विहीन
(घ) गुणवान

113. यमपुर भेजना
(क) दूर की यात्रा कराना
(ख) मार डालना
(ग) मजा चखाना
(घ) दंडित करना

114. यज्ञ में आहुति देना
(क) पुण्य कार्य करना
(ख) आग भड़काना
(ग) क्रोध बढ़ाना
(घ) यज्ञ में समिधा डालना

115. रंग फीका पड़ना
(क) मुख की कान्ति बिगड़ जाना
(ख) रंग-रूप बिगड़ जाना
(ग) घबड़ा जाना
(घ) उदास होना

116. रंग में भंग होना
(क) मनमुटाव होना
(ख) उत्सव में उदासी छा जाना
(ग) गड़बड़ करना
(घ) मारपीट हो जाना

117. राई का पर्वत बनाना
(क) धीरे धीरे संचय करना
(ख) छोटे से बड़ा होना
(ग) उद्यमी होना
(घ) छोटी बात को बढ़ा-चढ़ा कर कहना

118. लंगोटिया यार
(क) बचपन का साथी
(ख) फकीर मित्र
(ग) बेकाम साथी
(घ) फक्कड़ दोस्त

119. लीपा-पोती करना
(क) सफाई करना
(ख) ऐब छिपाना
(ग) लीपना-पोतना
(घ) घर साफ करना

120. लोट-पोट होना
(क) क्रुद्ध होना
(ख) लेटने लगना
(ग) बहुत प्रसन्न होना
(घ) गिर पड़ना

121. वेद वाक्य मानना
(क) प्रामाणिक मानना
(ख) श्रद्धेय मानना
(ग) आदरणीय कथन समझना
(घ) पुराना समझना

122. शरीर में आग लगना
(क) क्रोधित होना
(ख) जलन मालूम होना
(ग) खुजली होना
(घ) जल जाना

123. शेर के मुँह में हाथ डालना
(क) ताकत दिखाना
(ख) ताकतवार से लड़ने का जोखिम उठाना
(ग) शेर का शिकार करना
(घ) मरने की तैयारी करना

124. सठिया जाना
(क) बुद्धि भ्रष्ट होना
(ख) बुढ़ापा आ जाना
(ग) साठ की उम्र में पहुँचना
(घ) कमज़ोर होना

125. सब्ज बाग़ दिखाना
(क) घुमाने ले जाना
(ख) बाग की हरियाली दिखाना
(ग) प्रकृति का निरीक्षण करना
(घ) झूठा आश्वासन देना

126. सितम ढ़ाना
(क) अत्याचार करना
(ख) अन्याय करना
(ग) दीवाल गिराना
(घ) मुसीबत में डालना

127. सिंहासन हिलाना
(क) भयभीत करना
(ख) सत्तारहित करने का उपक्रम करना
(ग) सिंहासन तोड़ने का प्रयास करना
(घ) सिंहासन को क्षति पहुँचाना

128. हक्का-बक्का होना
(क) अचरज में पड़ना
(ख) भयभीत होना
(ग) भाग जाना
(घ) छुप जाना

129. हजम करना
(क) पचा जाना
(ख) हाज़मा ठीक करना
(ग) किसी की वस्तु हड़प लेना
(घ) पाचक चूर्ण खाना

130. हज़ामत बनाना
(क) दाढ़ी के बाल बनाना
(ख) मुख शोभा बढ़ाना
(ग) मज़ाक बनाना
(घ) ठगना या धोखा देना

उत्तरमाला

भाषा और व्याकरण

1	2	3	4	5	6	7	8	9	10
(ग)	(ग)	(ग)	(ग)	(ग)	(क)	(ग)	(क)	(क)	(घ)
11	**12**	**13**	**14**	**15**	**16**	**17**	**18**	**19**	**20**
(ग)	(घ)	(ग)	(ख)	(घ)	(ग)	(ग)	(घ)	(क)	(ग)

21	22	23	24	25	26	27	28	29	30
(ख)	(ख)	(ख)	(ग)	(घ)	(क)	(क)	(ग)	(क)	(क)
31	32	33	34	35	36	37	38	39	40
(ग)	(ख)	(घ)	(ग)	(क)	(घ)	(ख)	(क)	(घ)	(घ)
41	42	43	44	45	46	47	48	49	50
(क)	(क)	(ग)	(घ)	(क)	(ख)	(ग)	(घ)	(ख)	(क)
51	52	53	54	55	56	57	58	59	60
(ख)	(ख)	(क)	(ख)	(क)	(क)	(ख)	(ग)	(ख)	(घ)
61	62	63	64	65	66	67	68	69	70
(ग)	(ग)	(ख)	(ख)	(ग)	(क)	(क)	(ख)	(क)	(ख)
71	72	73	74	75	76	77	78	79	80
(ग)	(ग)	(क)	(ख)	(ख)	(ख)	(ग)	(क)	(क)	(क)
81	82	83	84	85	86	87	88	89	90
(ग)	(क)	(घ)	(घ)	(ख)	(ख)	(क)	(ग)	(ख)	(क)
91	92	93	94	95	96	97	98	99	100
(घ)	(क)	(क)	(क)	(ग)	(ख)	(क)	(ग)	(ग)	(ख)
101	102	103	104	105	106	107	108	109	110
(ख)	(ख)	(क)	(ग)	(क)	(ख)	(ग)	(ख)	(घ)	(ख)
111	112	113	114	115	116	117	118	119	120
(क)	(ग)	(घ)	(ख)	(क)	(ग)	(घ)	(ग)	(ग)	(क)
121	122	123	124	125	126	127	128	129	130
(ख)	(क)	(क)	(ग)	(क)	(घ)	(क)	(क)	(क)	(ख)
131	132	133	134	135	136	137	138	139	140
(क)	(ग)	(घ)	(ग)	(ग)	(ख)	(ख)	(घ)	(क)	(ख)
141	142	143	144	145	146	147	148	149	150
(क)	(क)	(घ)	(ग)	(ग)	(ग)	(क)	(ग)	(ग)	(घ)
151	152	153	154	155					
(ग)	(ख)	(ग)	(ख)	(ख)					

वर्तनी

1	2	3	4	5	6	7	8	9	10
(ग)	(क)	(ख)	(ख)	(ग)	(क)	(घ)	(घ)	(ख)	(घ)
11	12	13	14	15	16	17	18	19	20
(ख)	(ख)	(ख)	(ग)	(घ)	(ग)	(क)	(ग)	(क)	(घ)
21	22	23	24	25	26	27	28	29	30
(ग)	(घ)	(ख)	(ग)	(क)	(ग)	(ग)	(घ)	(ग)	(ग)
31	32	33	34	35	36	37	38	39	40

(क)	(घ)	(ग)	(क)	(घ)	(ख)	(क)	(ग)	(घ)	(ग)
41	**42**	**43**	**44**	**45**	**46**	**47**	**48**	**49**	**50**
(ग)	(ख)	(ख)	(क)	(घ)	(ग)	(ख)	(ख)	(ख)	(ख)
51	**52**	**53**	**54**	**55**	**56**	**57**	**58**	**59**	**60**
(क)	(ग)	(क)	(क)	(घ)	(ख)	(ख)	(ग)	(ख)	(ग)
61	**62**	**63**	**64**	**65**	**66**	**67**	**68**	**69**	**70**
(क)	(ग)	(ख)	(घ)	(ख)	(क)	(ख)	(घ)	(क)	(ग)
71	**72**	**73**	**74**	**75**	**76**	**77**	**78**	**79**	**80**
(ख)	(ग)	(ख)	(घ)	(ख)	(क)	(घ)	(ख)	(ख)	(क)
81	**82**	**83**	**84**	**85**	**86**	**87**	**88**	**89**	**90**
(ख)	(ग)	(ग)	(क)	(ग)	(घ)	(क)	(घ)	(ग)	(क)
91	**92**	**93**	**94**	**95**	**96**	**97**	**98**	**99**	**100**
(ख)	(ख)	(ख)	(ग)	(घ)	(ग)	(ख)	(घ)	(ख)	(ख)
101	**102**	**103**	**104**	**105**	**106**	**107**	**108**	**109**	**110**
(ख)	(घ)	(ग)	(घ)	(ख)	(ग)	(ख)	(ग)	(घ)	(ग)
111	**112**	**113**	**114**	**115**	**116**	**117**	**118**	**119**	**120**
(क)	(ग)	(ख)	(ख)	(ग)	(घ)	(क)	(घ)	(ख)	(क)
121	**122**	**123**	**124**	**125**	**126**	**127**	**128**	**129**	**130**
(ग)	(ख)	(ख)	(ग)	(घ)	(ग)	(ग)	(ग)	(घ)	(घ)
131	**132**	**133**	**134**	**135**	**136**	**137**	**138**	**139**	**140**
(ग)	(घ)	(घ)	(ग)	(ख)	(घ)	(घ)	(ग)	(घ)	(ग)

प्रत्यय और उपसर्ग

1	**2**	**3**	**4**	**5**	**6**	**7**	**8**	**9**	**10**
(ख)	(क)	(ग)	(घ)	(ख)	(क)	(क)	(ख)	(ग)	(ग)
11	**12**	**13**	**14**	**15**	**16**	**17**	**18**	**19**	**20**
(क)	(ख)	(ग)	(क)	(ग)	(ग)	(ख)	(ग)	(क)	(ख)
21	**22**	**23**	**24**	**25**	**26**	**27**	**28**	**29**	**30**
(ख)	(ग)	(क)	(ग)	(ग)	(क)	(ख)	(ख)	(ग)	(ख)
31	**32**	**33**	**34**	**35**	**36**	**37**	**38**	**39**	**40**
(घ)	(ग)	(ख)	(ग)	(क)	(ख)	(ग)	(ग)	(ग)	(क)
41	**42**	**43**	**44**	**45**	**46**	**47**	**48**	**49**	**50**
(ग)	(ख)	(ख)	(ख)	(क)	(क)	(ख)	(घ)	(ख)	(ख)
51	**52**	**53**	**54**	**55**	**56**	**57**	**58**	**59**	**60**
(घ)	(ख)	(घ)	(ख)	(क)	(ग)	(ग)	(ग)	(क)	(क)
61	**62**	**63**	**64**	**65**	**66**	**67**	**68**	**69**	**70**
(ग)	(घ)	(ख)	(ख)	(ग)	(क)	(ग)	(ख)	[illegible]	(घ)

71	72	73	74	75	76	77	78	79	80
(ग)	(ग)	(ख)	(ग)	(घ)	(ख)	(ख)	(ग)	(ग)	(ग)
81	**82**	**83**	**84**	**85**	**86**	**87**	**88**	**89**	**90**
(ख)	(ख)	(क)	(घ)	(ग)	(घ)	(क)	(क)	(क)	(ग)
91	**92**	**93**	**94**	**95**	**96**	**97**	**98**	**99**	**100**
(ख)	(ग)	(ख)	(ग)	(क)	(ग)	(ख)	(ग)	(घ)	(ग)

संधि विचार

1	2	3	4	5	6	7	8	9	10
(क)	(ग)	(क)	(ग)	(ख)	(क)	(ग)	(क)	(घ)	(ख)
11	**12**	**13**	**14**	**15**	**16**	**17**	**18**	**19**	**20**
(ख)	(ग)	(क)	(घ)	(ख)	(ख)	(ख)	(ग)	(घ)	(क)
21	**22**	**23**	**24**	**25**	**26**	**27**	**28**	**29**	**30**
(ग)	(ग)	(क)	(क)	(ख)	(ख)	(ग)	(ग)	(ख)	(ग)
31	**32**	**33**	**34**	**35**	**36**	**37**	**38**	**39**	**40**
(घ)	(क)	(क)	(ख)	(ग)	(ग)	(घ)	(ग)	(ख)	(ख)
41	**42**	**43**	**44**	**45**	**46**	**47**	**48**	**49**	**50**
(घ)	(ख)	(ग)	(ख)	(ग)	(ग)	(ग)	(ग)	(ख)	(ख)
51	**52**	**53**	**54**	**55**	**56**	**57**	**58**	**59**	**60**
(क)	(ख)	(क)	(क)	(ग)	(ख)	(ग)	(ख)	(ग)	(ग)
61	**62**	**63**	**64**	**65**	**66**	**67**	**68**	**69**	**70**
(ख)	(क)	(ग)	(ग)	(ख)	(ग)	(ग)	(क)	(ख)	(क)

समास विचार

71	72	73	74	75	76	77	78	79	80
(ग)	(ग)	(ख)	(ग)	(घ)	(क)	(ग)	(क)	(क)	(क)
81	**82**	**83**	**84**	**85**	**86**	**87**	**88**	**89**	**90**
(ग)	(ख)	(ग)	(ख)	(ख)	(क)	(ख)	(क)	(क)	(घ)
91	**92**	**93**	**94**	**95**	**96**	**97**	**98**	**99**	**100**
(घ)	(ग)	(क)	(घ)	(ख)	(क)	(ख)	(घ)	(ग)	(घ)
101	**102**	**103**	**104**	**105**	**106**	**107**	**108**	**109**	**110**
(ग)	(क)	(ख)	(ग)	(घ)	(घ)	(क)	(ख)	(घ)	(ग)
111	**112**	**113**	**114**	**115**	**116**	**117**	**118**	**119**	**120**
(ख)	(क)	(ख)	(क)	(ग)	(क)	(क)	(ख)	(ख)	(घ)
121	**122**	**123**	**124**	**125**					
(क)	(घ)	(क)	(ग)	(—)					

अलंकार

1	2	3	4	5	6	7	8	9	10
(क)	(ग)	(घ)	(घ)	(ख)	(ग)	(क)	(ख)	(घ)	(क)
11	**12**	**13**	**14**	**15**	**16**	**17**	**18**	**19**	**20**
(ख)	(घ)	(क)	(क)	(घ)	(क)	(ख)	(ग)	(क)	(घ)
21	**22**	**23**	**24**	**25**	**26**	**27**	**28**	**29**	**30**
(ग)	(घ)	(क)	(घ)	(क)	(ग)	(ग)	(ग)	(ख)	(क)
31	**32**								
(ग)	(घ)								

विपरीतार्थक शब्द

1	2	3	4	5	6	7	8	9	10
(ग)	(ख)	(ग)	(क)	(ग)	(ख)	(ग)	(घ)	(ख)	(ग)
11	**12**	**13**	**14**	**15**	**16**	**17**	**18**	**19**	**20**
(घ)	(ख)	(क)	(घ)	(ख)	(ख)	(ख)	(ग)	(ख)	(क)
21	**22**	**23**	**24**	**25**	**26**	**27**	**28**	**29**	**30**
(ख)	(ग)	(ग)	(ग)	(क)	(ख)	(ख)	(ख)	(घ)	(क)
31	**32**	**33**	**34**	**35**	**36**	**37**	**38**	**39**	**40**
(ख)	(ख)	(ग)	(क)	(ख)	(ग)	(क)	(ग)	(क)	(घ)
41	**42**	**43**	**44**	**45**	**46**	**47**	**48**	**49**	**50**
(ख)	(घ)	(क)	(ख)	(ख)	(ख)	(घ)	(घ)	(क)	(क)
51	**52**	**53**	**54**	**55**	**56**	**57**	**58**	**59**	**60**
(क)	(ग)	(क)	(ग)	(ख)	(ग)	(क)	(घ)	(क)	(घ)
61	**62**	**63**	**64**	**65**	**66**	**67**	**68**	**69**	**70**
(ख)	(ख)	(ख)	(क)	(ग)	(क)	(क)	(ग)	(क)	(घ)
71	**72**	**73**	**74**	**75**	**76**	**77**	**78**	**79**	**80**
(ग)	(ख)	(ख)	(ख)	(ख)	(घ)	(घ)	(ग)	(ख)	(क)
81	**82**	**83**	**84**	**85**	**86**	**87**	**88**	**89**	**90**
(घ)	(ख)	(क)	(क)	(घ)	(ख)	(क)	(क)	(घ)	(क)
91	**92**	**93**	**94**	**95**	**96**	**97**	**98**	**99**	**100**
(ख)	(घ)	(ग)	(ग)	(क)	(क)	(क)	(ग)	(घ)	(क)
101	**102**	**103**	**104**	**105**	**106**	**107**	**108**	**109**	**110**
(क)	(ग)	(क)	(क)	(घ)	(ग)	(ख)	(क)	(ग)	(क)
111	**112**	**113**	**114**	**115**	**116**	**117**	**118**	**119**	**120**
(घ)	(ख)	(ख)	(घ)	(ग)	(क)	(ख)	(क)	(ग)	(क)
121	**122**	**123**	**124**	**125**	**126**	**127**	**128**	**129**	**130**
(ग)	(ख)	(ख)	(घ)	(घ)	(क)	(ख)	(घ)	(ग)	(ख)

131	132	133	134	135	136	137	138	139	140
(क)	(ख)	(क)	(ग)	(ग)	(क)	(ख)	(घ)	(घ)	(घ)
141	**142**	**143**	**144**	**145**	**146**	**147**	**148**	**149**	**150**
(क)	(क)	(क)	(घ)	(ग)	(क)	(ग)	(ख)	(क)	(क)
151	**152**	**153**	**154**	**155**					
(ख)	(ग)	(क)	(क)	(क)					

पर्यायवाची शब्द

1	2	3	4	5	6	7	8	9	10
(ख)	(क)	(क)	(क)	(क)	(क)	(घ)	(क)	(क)	(घ)
11	**12**	**13**	**14**	**15**	**16**	**17**	**18**	**19**	**20**
(क)	(क)	(ग)	(क)	(क)	(घ)	(क)	(ग)	(क)	(क)
21	**22**	**23**	**24**	**25**	**26**	**27**	**28**	**29**	**30**
(ग)	(ग)	(ग)	(क)	(घ)	(क)	(ख)	(क)	(क)	(क)
31	**32**	**33**	**34**	**35**	**36**	**37**	**38**	**39**	**40**
(क)	(ग)	(घ)	(ख)	(ख)	(क)	(ग)	(क)	(ख)	(ग)
41	**42**	**43**	**44**	**45**	**46**	**47**	**48**	**49**	**50**
(क)	(ख)	(ग)	(घ)	(क)	(क)	(घ)	(घ)	(क)	(क)
51	**52**	**53**	**54**	**55**	**56**	**57**	**58**	**59**	**60**
(घ)	(क)	(घ)	(क)	(ग)	(क)	(ख)	(घ)	(क)	(ख)
61	**62**	**63**	**64**	**65**	**66**	**67**	**68**	**69**	**70**
(क)	(क)	(घ)	(क)	(क)	(घ)	(घ)	(घ)	(घ)	(क)
71	**72**	**73**	**74**	**75**	**76**	**77**	**78**	**79**	**80**
(क)	(ग)	(ख)	(ख)	(घ)	(ख)	(घ)	(घ)	(घ)	(ग)
81	**82**	**83**	**84**	**85**	**86**	**87**	**88**	**89**	**90**
(ग)	(ग)	(घ)	(ग)	(ख)	(ग)	(ख)	(क)	(ख)	(ख)
91	**92**	**93**	**94**	**95**	**96**	**97**	**98**	**99**	**100**
(क)	(क)	(क)	(क)	(ख)	(ग)	(घ)	(क)	(घ)	(ग)
101	**102**	**103**	**104**	**105**	**106**	**107**	**108**	**109**	**110**
(ख)	(क)	(घ)	(क)	(घ)	(ख)	(क)	(ग)	(ख)	(ग)
111	**112**	**113**	**114**	**115**	**116**	**117**	**118**	**119**	**120**
(घ)	(घ)	(घ)	(क)	(ग)	(ग)	(घ)	(ख)	(घ)	(घ)
121	**122**	**123**	**124**	**125**					
(घ)	(घ)	(घ)	(घ)	(ख)					

शब्दार्थ

1. (घ) : तनुजा के अंग-सौष्ठव की सभी प्रशंसा करते हैं।

2. (ख) : अन्तर्घट को निर्मल रखना चाहिए क्योंकि उसमें हरि का निवास होता है।

3. (ख) : अन्तःशुद्धि, काया शुद्धि से श्रेष्ठ होती है।
4. (ख) : अपकीर्तिमय जीवन से मृत्यु श्रेष्ठ होती है।
5. (क) : नित्य कर्म से निवृत्त होकर आश्रमवासी आराधना में लग गये।
6. (घ) : निज़ाम के पास अकूत सम्पत्ति थी।
7. (ख) : कुछ व्यक्ति नौकरी के प्रति अनिच्छु होते हैं।
8. (ग) : अतिरेक हानिकर होता है।
9. (ख) : आत्मा नित्य है किन्तु शरीर अनित्य है।
10. (घ) : राधा का सौन्दर्य अनुपमेय था।
11. (ख) : बजर भूमि अनुर्वर होती है।
12. (घ) : सरकारी उपक्रमों में अपंगों के लिए भी रोज़गार के द्वार खुल गए हैं।
13. (घ) : सर्वव्यापी भ्रष्टाचार का ठीक-ठीक आंकना कठिन है।
14. (ग) : पं॰ मदनमोहन मालवीय राजनीतिज्ञों में नहीं वरन् साहित्यकारों में भी समादृत थे।
15. (ग) : उसके कमरे में पुस्तकें इतस्ततः पड़ी हुई थीं।
16. (ख) : आजकल आचरणकर्ताओं की नहीं अपितु उपदेष्टाओं की बहुलता है।
17. (घ) : जय कपीश तिहुं लोक उजागर।
18. (क) : चाणक्य आश्रम के समीप उगे सभी कुशों को उच्छिन्न करना चाहता था।
19. (ख) : भवन निर्माण के सभी उपादान एकत्र हो गए थे।
20. (ख) : दोनों में एकात्म प्रेम है।
21. (ग) : वेदों की ऋचाएँ सस्वर गाई जाती हैं।
22. (घ) : उसको पाठ्यक्रम की सभी कविताएँ कंठाग्र हैं।
23. (ख) : अकबर महाराणा प्रताप को अपने मार्ग का कंटक मानता था।
24. (ख) : सींक लै काजर दे री गवांरन आंगुरी तेरी कटेगी कटाक्षन।
25. (घ) : कुयोग में कोई साथ नहीं देता।
26. (ख) : वह कतिपय प्रश्नों के ही उत्तर देने में समर्थ रहा।
27. (ग) : गरुड़ पक्षियों का स्वामी माना जाता है।
28. (ख) : राज मन्दिर में मूल्यवान मणियाँ खचित थीं।
29. (घ) : गरिष्ठ भोजन विलम्ब से पचता है।
30. (घ) : वह मंत्रिपद का गुरुतर भार वहन करने में सक्षम है।
31. (ख) : चिकित्सकीय सहायता पहुँचने से पूर्व ही वह गतप्राण हो चुका था।
32. (क) : प्रधानमंत्री का पद बड़ा गरिमापूर्ण होता है।
33. (ख) : सूर के पदों का गूढ़ार्थ समझना सबके बूते की बात नहीं।
34. (घ) : आपने मेरे घर पधार कर मुझे गौरवान्वित किया है।
35. (ख) : इस हार में गुम्फित एक-एक मणि बहुमूल्य है।
36. (घ) : अपने अशिष्ट व्यवहार पर उसे बड़ी ग्लानि हुई।
37. (ख) : ग्रह गृहीत व्यक्ति का उत्थान संभव नहीं होता।
38. (घ) : अपने कुकर्मों से वह समाज में घृणित हो गया है।

39. (घ) : वृद्धावस्था में अन्य इन्द्रियों की भाँति घ्राणेन्द्रिय भी शिथिल हो जाती हैं।
40. (क) : चैतन्य चरितावली एक अनूठी पुस्तक है।
41. (ख) : आजकल सुधा की चितवृत्ति अच्छी नहीं है।
42. (ग) : कुछ लोग साधना के चमत्कार दिखाकर दूसरों को प्रभावित कर लेते हैं।
43. (ख) : छलावा करके प्रेम का नाटक नहीं करना चाहिए।
44. (घ) : छरहरे बदन का जवान बड़ा फुर्तीला है।
45. (ग) : छद्मवेश में घूम कर राजा अपने राज्य की सही स्थिति देखते थे।
46. (ख) : कभी सूरमा हैं न जीवन गंवाते
बलाएं उड़ाते हैं, चुटकी बजाते।
47. (ख) : जलतरंग एक अच्छा बाजा है।
48. (घ) : हवा का झकोरा आने से वृक्ष गिर गया।
49. (घ) : बेचारा ठनठनगोपाल है; मकान खरीदने के लिए पैसा कहाँ से लाता।
50. (क) : यह गोष्ठी किसके तत्वाधान में हो रही है।
51. (ख) : रानी झांसी के एक दत्तक पुत्र था।
52. (ग) : सच्चे संत-महात्मा द्वंद्वातीत होते हैं।
53. (ख) : दावानल ने पूरा वन जला डाला।
54. (ख) : धनैषणा मनुष्य के पतन का कारण बनती है।
55. (ख) : जल प्रपात का धाराबद्ध जल दर्शनीय होता है।
56. (ख) : मानस में राम का धीरोदात्त चरित्र तुलसी की काव्य कला का ज्वलन्त प्रतीक है।
57. (ग) : करै दौष निरसंक जो, डरे न तिय के मान;
लाज धरै मन में नहीं, नायक धृष्ठ निदान।
58. (ग) : उसने भाई को आर्थिक सहायता देने से नकार दिया।
59. (क) : नमित राष्ट्रध्वज देखकर शंका हो जाती है।
60. (घ) : हिमालय का नैसर्गिक सौन्दर्य दर्शनीय है।
61. (घ) : श्याम अपने आराध्य देव शिव पर पूरी निष्ठा रखता है।
62. (क) : निःस्व व्यक्ति आज के युग में बहुत कम आदर के पात्र होते हैं।
63. (क) : निठल्ले घूमने से क्या लाभ, थोड़ा-बहुत काम करना ही चाहिए।
64. (क) : श्रीराम की पद रज पाकर ही भक्त कृतार्थ हो गए।
65. (ख) : प्रतियोगिता परीक्षा में उत्तीर्ण होने पर ही सरकारी नौकरी के द्वार खुलते हैं।
66. (क) : श्री सत्यनारायण की कथा से पूर्व पुजापा एकत्र करना आवश्यक होता है।
67. (क) : बलहीन (शक्तिहीन) की कोई परवाह नहीं करता।
68. (ख) : मोहन की आदत बतियाने की अधिक, काम करने की कम है।
69. (ख) : अपनी भंगिमा से ही उसने अपनी कला का परिचय दे डाला।
70. (क) : भंग का अर्थ टूटना होता है जैसे धनुषभंग, अंगभंग आदि। स्कूटर से गिरने

से उसका अंगभंग हो गया है।

71. (ग) : अद्वैत दर्शन का भाव बोध आसान नहीं है।

72. (क) : भाराक्रान्त अश्व लड़खड़ा कर गिर पड़ा।

73. (ख) : सुफल मनोरथ होहिं तुम्हारे,
राम लखन सुनि भये सुखारे।

74. (घ) : पूर्व मीमांसा और उत्तर सीमांसा भारतीय गंभीर चिन्तन के अन्यतम उदाहरण हैं।

75. (ख) : रसोईघर में एक मास के लिए यथेष्ठ सामग्री रख दी गई है।

76. (ग) : आजकल के भ्रष्टाचारी कानून तथा यम-यातना की भी परवाह नहीं करते।

77. (ख) : राजा दशरथ ने **राम** को युवराज बनाने की इच्छा व्यक्त की थी।

78. (क) : एक दिन सब ही जायेगा, राजा, रंक, फकीर।

79. (क) : रागारुण राजकन्या यवन सरदार की धमकी से तनिक भी भयभीत नहीं हुई।

80. (ख) : नव राजीव नयन अति सुन्दर,
अधराधर मुस्कान मनोहर।

81. (क) : राज्याभिषेक की तैयारी पूरी हो जाने के बावजूद राम को वन जाना पड़ा।

82. (ग) : लंपट व्यक्ति को कोई अपने पास नहीं बैठने देता।

83. (ख) : सीता की मुख छवि ललित ललाम थी।

84. (ख) : शरीर में अनेक लोहित वाहिनी नाड़ियाँ होती हैं।

85. (ख) : वंचक व्यक्ति मित्र को भी अपनी दुष्टता का शिकार बनाने में नहीं हिचकते।

86. (घ) : कुछ संसद-सदस्यों ने विरोध स्वरूप संसद भवन से वहिर्गमन किया।

87. (क) : वैज्ञानिक मिट्टी तथा जल तक का विश्लेषण करके वास्तविकता का पता लगाते हैं।

88. (क) : ताजमहल की संरचना देखकर लोग आश्चर्यचकित रह जाते हैं।

89. (क) : हस्तगत राशि का सदुपयोग करना बुद्धिमानी है।

90. (क) : जैसी ही होतव्यता, तैसी मिले सहाय,
आपु न आवै ताहि पै, ताहि वहाँ लै जाये।

वाक्य/वाक्याश के लिए एक शब्द

1	**2**	**3**	**4**	**5**	**6**	**7**	**8**	**9**	**10**
(ग)	(घ)	(क)	(ख)	(ख)	(ग)	(ग)	(ख)	(ख)	(ख)
11	**12**	**13**	**14**	**15**	**16**	**17**	**18**	**19**	**20**
(क)	(ख)	(ख)	(ख)	(घ)	(घ)	(घ)	(ग)	(ग)	(क)

21	22	23	24	25	26	27	28	29	30
(घ)	(घ)	(ख)	(ख)	(ख)	(ग)	(ख)	(ख)	(क)	(ग)

शुद्ध वाक्य ढूँढना

1	2	3	4	5	6	7	8	9	10
(ग)	(क)	(ग)	(ग)	(ख)	(घ)	(ग)	(घ)	(घ)	(ग)
11	**12**	**13**	**14**	**15**	**16**	**17**	**18**	**19**	**20**
(घ)	(घ)	(घ)	(ख)	(क)	(घ)	(घ)	(घ)	(ग)	(घ)
21	**22**	**23**	**24**	**25**	**26**	**27**	**28**	**29**	**30**
(ख)	(ख)	(ग)	(ख)	(ग)	(ख़)	(क)	(ग)	(ख)	(क)

मुहावरे और लोकोक्तियाँ

1. (ख) : अध्यापक ने ऐसी मार लगाई कि शरारती छात्र का अंग-अंग ढीला हो गया।

2. (क) : परीक्षा में प्रथम आने पर मोहन का अंग-अंग मुस्करा उठा।

3. (क) : व्यर्थ की बातों में आकर वह अंगारे उगलने लगा।

4. (क) : परीक्षाफल अनुकुल न आने के कारण सोहन को सारी रात ऐसा लग रहा हो मानों अंगारों पर लेट रहा हो।

5. (क) : संदेहास्पद चरित्र के कारण मोहिनी को ओर उसके पड़ोसी भी अँगुली उठाते हैं।

6. (क) : नई-नई बहू अभी से अपने पति को अँगुली पर नचाने लगी है।

7. (क) : पहले तो दिलासा देता रहा किन्तु कन्या की शादी पर साहूकार ने रमेश को अँगूठा दिखा दिया।

8. (ख) : माँ ने आँचल पसार कर जज से निवेदन किया कि मेरे निर्दोष पुत्र को छोड़ दिया जाये।

9. (ख) : चुटकुला सुनते ही हँसते-हँसते उसकी अंतड़ियों में बल पड़ गए।

10. (क) : दीनू की मकान की लालसा पूरी हो गई, अन्धा क्या चाहे दो आँखें।

11. (ग) : समझदार व्यक्ति भी कभी-कभी मीठी बातों में आकर अन्धे बन जाते हैं।

12. (क) : मूल्य नियंत्रण मजाक बन गया है जिसके कारण लोग कहते हैं कि अंधेर नगरी चौपट राजा, कोई सुनने वाला ही नहीं रहा। गरीब अपना दुखड़ा किससे कहे।

13. (घ) : चारुदत्त अक्ल का दुश्मन है, उसको समझाने से क्या लाभ।

14. (क) : बातें तो केशव समझदारी की करता है किन्तु काम करते समय उसकी अक्ल चरने चली जाती है।

15. (क) : ज्ञान ने सरोज को ऐसा चकमा दिया कि दिन भर वह खाक ही छानता रहा। तन्दुरुस्त होने पर भी सरोज उसकी चालाकी न समझ सका। ठीक ही है अक्ल बड़ी की भैंस।

16. (ख) : मोहन ने जयसिंह को कुश्ती में पछाड़ कर अखाड़ा मार लिया।

17. (क) : लक्ष्मण के मर्मान्तक शब्द परशुराम के लिए अग्नि में घी डालने के समान हुए।

18. (ग) : कठोर परिश्रम के बाद ही कालू को अच्छे दिन देखने का अवसर मिला।

19. (क) : मेरा पांच सौ रुपये का नुकसान हो गया और तुम्हें अठखेलियाँ सूझ रही हैं।

20. (ख) : व्यापार में ज्यादा धन न लगाने की सीख न मान कर राजन ने अपने पैरों पर आप ही कुल्हाड़ी मार ली।

21. (ग) : मंत्री के आने पर जनता ने उन्हें आँख उठाकर भी नहीं देखा।

22. (घ) : सच्चाई प्रकट हो जाने पर व्यापारी की आँखे नीची हो गईं।

23. (क) : कर्ज लेने के बाद से अब सोम आँखें चुराए फिर रहा है, कि कहीं महाजन कड़ा तकाज़ा न कर बैठे।

24. (क) : अपने से बड़ों के सामने वह अपनी प्रेयसी से आँख मिलाने का साहस कैसे करे।

25. (ख) : अपने गुरुदेव के आने पर उसने आँखें बिछा दीं।

26. (घ) : पहले तो दीपा ने कुछ सोचा नहीं। अब कन्या का विवाह सिर पर आ जाने पर वह प्रबन्ध करता फिरता है, जो आग लगने पर कुआँ खोदने के समान है।

27. (ग) : किसी अजनबी को देखकर कुत्ते आपे में नहीं रहते, भों-भों करने लग जाते हैं।

28. (ख) : जिसे प्यार से पाला था, वह आस्तीन का सांप हो गया। बचपन का साथी था वह अब मेरे लिए अभिशाप बन गया।

29. (ग) : देखते ही देखते दौड़ में कृष्णावल का घोड़ा आसमान से बातें करने लगा।

30. (क) : भारतेन्दुजी ने पूर्वजों की सम्पत्ति की इतिश्री कर डाली।

31. (घ) : संतोष को इधर-उधर की लगाने में न जाने क्या मज़ा आता है, दो भाइयों में अकारण मन-मुटाव करा दिया।

32. (ग) : अकबर ने अपने छल-बल से अनेक राजपूतों के किलों की ईंट से ईंट बजा दी थी।

33. (ख) : राधे लाल ने विनय को राजी करने की बड़ी कोशिश की किन्तु विनय तो उड़ती चिड़िया पहचानता था, वह उसकी मीठी बातों में नहीं आया।

34. (क) : शेर-गीदड़ वाली कहानी में गीदड़ ने अपनी चतुराई से शेर को उल्लू बना दिया।

35. (ख) : घण्टे वाले हलवाई की दुकान का सोहन हलवा खाकर जब सुमति को आनन्द न आया, तो स्वभावतः उसके मुँह से निकल पड़ा 'ऊँची दुकान फीके पकवान'।

36. (घ) : मोहन ने एल-एल॰बी॰ करके वकालत तो की नहीं, उसका यह श्रम ऊसर

में बीज बोने के समान है।

37. (घ) : सफेदा बोना एक पंथ दो काज जैसा है; जलाने के लिए लकड़ी तथा खर्च के लिए पैसा दोनों ही इससे प्राप्त होते हैं

38. (ग) : किरायेदार से लड़ाई करके उसने ओखली में सिर दे दिया है।

39. (क) : कन्हाई को समझाना बेकार है, वह तो औंधी खोपड़ी है।

40. (ग) : नई बहू को तो कंघी चोटी से ही फुरसत नहीं मिलती, वह फिर घर का काम-काज कैसे करेगी।

41. (क) : बरसात में मकान का गिरना तथा बाढ़ से खेतों का चौपट हो जाना दीनू के लिए कंगाली में आटा गीला होने के समान है।

42. (घ) : कपड़े की दुकान चल जाने से लाला छिद्दूमल के घर कंचन बरस रहा है।

43. (ख) : उसने चोर को मार-मार कर उसकी कपाल क्रिया कर दी।

44. (ग) : सीमा रक्षा पुलिस की पूछताछ से तंग होकर जासूस ने सारा कच्चा चिट्ठा खोल दिया।

45. (घ) : दुर्घटना का दृश्य देखकर माया का कलेजा पसीज गया।

46. (ग) : माँ अपने बच्चे को कलेजे से लगाकर रखती है।

47. (क) : कागजी घोड़े दौड़ाने से तब तक कोई फायदा नहीं होता जब तक मुलाकात करके सही बात न बता दी जाए।

48. (ख) : पुलिस के आ जाने पर चोर की हालत ऐसी थी कि काटो तो खून भी नहीं।

49. (क) : 'राशनिंग दफ्तर के बाबू कानों मे तेल डाल कर बैठे हैं, राशन कार्ड बनाकर ही नहीं देते।

50. (घ) : चाहे कितना समझाओ मोहन कोई उद्यम करने के लिए तैयार ही नहीं होता, घर में बेकार पड़ा रहता है। ऐसी दशा में चिढ़कर उसकी मां कहती है 'काम का न काज का दुश्मन अनाज का'।

51. (ग) : आज तक तो उसने कुछ भी नहीं किया, घर में बैठे-बैठे ख्याली घोड़े दौड़ाया करता है।

52. (क) : स्कूल में सोहन को डाँटा अध्यापक ने, पर बाद में वह चमन से लड़ पड़ा कि तू मेरी किताब क्यों ले गया था। ऐसे में कहते हैं, खिसियानी बिल्ली खम्बा नोचे।

53. (ग) : बिस्सो तो पूरा खुशामदी टट्टू है; दिन भर बैठा सेठ लक्ष्मी दास की चापलूसी करता है।

54. (ख) : चोर को रंगे हाथों पकड़ने के बाद दरोगा ने उससे कहा कि सारी बात सच-सच बता दो। लेकिन चोर यही कहता रहा कि उसने चोरी की ही नहीं। चोर की ढिठाई पर दरोगा का खून उबलने लगा।

55. (क) : क्रूर मालिक को देखकर नौकर का खून सूख जाता है।

56. (ख) : निरपराध परिन्दों के खून से हाथ रंगने में कोई लाभ नहीं है। आखिर परिन्दे भी भगवान ने ही बनाए हैं।

57. (क) : लाइसेंस तो बन ही जाता, किन्तु इन्सपेक्टर से टक्कर लेकर राधे ने अपना बना बनाया खेल बिगाड़ लिया है।

58. (घ) : इस गाँव की रीति निराली है; यहाँ गायों का तो तिरस्कार होता है तथा गधों को हलवा खिलाया जाता है।

59. (घ) : पिता द्वारा फटकारे जाने पर सीमान्त की गरदन झुक गई।

60. (ख) : श्याम व राम ने बराबर पूंजी लगाकर व्यापार शुरू किया। व्यापार चल जाने पर राम हिसाब-किताब में बेईमानी करने लगा। श्याम व्यापार से अलग होना चाहता था किन्तु बदनामी का भय था, अतः वह यही सोचता था कि अब तो गला फँसा बैठा।

61. (ग) : बेचारे भिखारी को क्यों दुत्कारते हो, घर आया कुत्ता भी नहीं निकाला जाता, फिर वह तो इन्सान है।

62. (ख) : रावण का भाई विभीषण राम से मिल गया और लंका का विनाश हो गया। ऐसी स्थिति में कहा जाता है, घर का भेदी लंका ढावे।

63. (क) : किसी अमीर को फँसाने के लिए तेजराम के आडम्बरों को देखकर यही कहना पड़ता है घर में नहीं दाने, बुढ़िया चली भुनाने।

64. (क) : राजन बहुत बनते फिरते थे, अब पुलिस के चंगुल में फँस गए हैं, जमानती भी ढूंढे नहीं मिलते।

65. (ग) : कितना भी समझाओ किन्तु नशेड़ी सम्पत राम तो चिकना घड़ा है; उस पर किसी बात का असर ही नहीं होता।

66. (क) : अरे! तुम्हें तो चुल्लू भर पानी में डूब मरना चाहिए, अपने कुकृत्य से परिवार की थरन धूल में मिला दी।

67. (क) : चाहे ऋतुराज हो अथवा हेमन्त दोनों ही एक जैसे हैं– चोर-चोर मौसेरे भाई।

68. (घ) : प्रधान मंत्री के अभयारण्य देखने जाने पर जंगल में भी मंगल होने लगेगा।

69. (क) : बेचारे मोहन ने अपने साथी नीहार को बैठने को ठौर दिया किन्तु उसने तो जिस डाल पर बैठा, उसी को काटना शुरू कर दिया।

70. (घ) : "बेकार बैठने से काम नहीं चलेगा बेटा! काम से जी न चुराया कर" माँ ने यशोधन को समझाते हुए कहा।

71. (ख) : श्यामू तो अब जीवन की घड़ियाँ गिन रहा है, कैंसर के भयानक रोग ने उसे बुरी तरह जकड़ रखा है।

72. (ग) : कर्ज़ लेकर दादू ने उसे ब्याज सहित चुकाने में देर कर दी। फलतः वह बढ़कर इतना अधिक हो गया है कि उसके बूते में चुकाना नहीं रहा। किसी ने ठीक ही कहा है ज्यों-ज्यों भीगै कामरी त्यों-त्यों भारी होय।

73. (क) : अंग्रेजी हुकूमत के खिलाफ बगावत करने वालों में श्री सुभाष चन्द्र बोस ने अपने कृत्यों से अपनी देशभक्ति का झण्डा गाड़ दिया।

74. (ग) : आजकल पर्याप्त देखभाल के अभाव में मनोहर का घोड़ा झटक गया है।

75. (ख) : खाना खाने के समय न जाने कहाँ से नीरज टपक पड़ा।
76. (क) : प्रोफेसर का भाषण इतना जोरदार था कि किसी को टीका-टिप्पणी करने की हिम्मत ही नहीं पड़ी।
77. (घ) : बार-बार घाटा उठाने के कारण प्रेम कुमार व्यापार के मामले में ठण्डा पड़ गया है।
78. (क) : मिली नौकरी को छोड़कर दयाराम अब ठोकरें खाता फिर रहा है।
79. (क) : स्पष्ट रूप से स्वतंत्रता की माँग करने के कारण श्री गंगाधर तिलक के नाम के डंके बजने लगे।
80. (ग) : रघुनाथ की वचनावली प्रिय मातु श्री को भा गई।
दुःख-सिंधु में लघुतोष तिनके का सहारा पा गई।।
81. (ख) : निरे डपोरशंख राम कुमार की बातों में आकर आपने भी पैसा और समय बर्बाद किया।
82. (ख) : तिहनों का व्यापार करने से नागेश की तकदीर चमक उठी है।
83. (क) : प्याज का भाव दो रुपए किलो सुनकर सन्तोष तीर की तरह दुकान पर पहुँचा।
84. (ग) : परशुराम की त्योरी चढ़ी देख कर जनकपुर में सारी सभा आतंकित हो उठी।
85. (क) : काला बाजारी करते पकड़े जाने के कारण गोपीराम की र्स्वत्र थू-थू हो गई।
86. (ग) : परीक्षा में रामनरेश की प्रथम श्रेणी आई देखकर उसके साथी दंग रह गए।
87. (ख) : भिखारी की दीन दशा देखकर रघुपति का दिल पसीज गया।
88. (घ) : बच्चे छत पर धमा चौकड़ी मचा रहे थे तभी घर वालों ने उन्हें मना किया।
89. (ख) : गोस्वामी तुलसीदास ने भी पहले दुष्टों की वन्दना की है, क्योंकि 'नंग बड़े परमेश्वर से'।
90. (ख) : बार-बार नाक रगड़ने पर भी पुलिस ने नन्हूक को नहीं छोड़ा।
91. (क) : फूलनदेवी ने उत्तर प्रदेश तथा मध्य प्रदेश में लोगों की नींद हराम कर रखी थी।
92. (क) : केदारनाथ की चढ़ाई के बारे में मशहूर है कि 'नौ दिन चलै अढ़ाई कोस'।
93. (ग) : क्षणभर में दरोगा ने मोहन की पगड़ी उतार कर रख दी क्योंकि वह बहुत दिन बाद उनके हाथ आया था।
94. (ख) : मुझे पट्टी मत पढ़ाइए मैं आपकी बातों में आने वाली नहीं – शीला ने मोहन से कहा।
95. (ग) : प्रतियोगिता परीक्षा में पास होने के लिए किया गया उसका प्रयास पर्वत पर कुआँ खोदने के समान है।
96. (क) : पाप का घड़ा भर जाने पर कंस का निधन श्री कृष्ण के हाथों हुआ था।

97. (ख) : ठगों के फन्दे में फँस कर मन्नू ने अपनी गाँठ की पूँजी भी गवाँ दी।
98. (घ) : लाटरी खुल जाने के कारण जगदीश फूला नहीं समा रहा था।
99. (क) : रानी-महारानियाँ फूल सूँघकर गुजारा करती हैं।
100. (ग) : दिन भर खेलते रहने के कारण सुधा ने अपनी पढ़ाई का बंटाधार कर डाला।
101. (घ) : अपने कुलक्षणों के कारण रमेश ने अपने बाप-दादों का नाम डुबा दिया है।
102. (ग) : बीमारी तथा व्यापार में घाटा होने के कारण बेचारे रामदेव पर बिजली ही गिर पड़ी है।
103. (ख) : लगता है आप भंग खाकर बैठे हैं तभी बार-बार सवाल गलत कर रहे हैं।
104. (क) : विभीषण ने राम की सेना में जाकर रावण का भंडा फोड़ कर दिया।
105. (क) : उद्धव ने गोपिकाओं के पास जाकर उन्हें भभूत रमाने को कहा।
106. (ख) : भरी थाली में लात मार कर उसने अपना ही नुकसान किया है।
107. (क) : पिताजी के आगे रामू भीगी बिल्ली बन जाता है किन्तु साथियों से झगड़ा करता है।
108. (घ) : कोई काम न करके श्रीमती रेखा दिन भर मक्खी मारा करती है।
109. (ग) : साफ बात कह कर तुमने रवीन्द्र को मिरचें लगा दीं।
110. (क) : गरम-गरम गुलाब जामुन देखकर आनन्द के मुँह में पानी भर आया।
111. (ख) : आजकल भ्रष्टाचार इतना बढ़ गया है कि लोगों की मुट्ठी गर्म किये बिना कोई काम होता ही नहीं।
112. (क) : महाराजा दशरथ यथा नाम तथा गुण थे।
113. (ख) : हिंसक शेर को शिकारी ने बंदूक की एक गोली से ही यमपुरी भेज दिया।
114. (ग) : परशुराम के प्रति कहे गए लक्ष्मण के शब्दों ने यज्ञ में आहुति का काम किया।
115. (ग) : शेर को देखकर अन्य जानवरों के रंग फीके पड़ जाते हैं।
116. (ख) : विवाहोत्सव के समय संयुक्ता के हरण से रंग में भंग हो गया।
117. (घ) : मानसिंह के प्रति कही गई मामूली सी बात ने राई का पहाड़ बना दिया।
118. (क) : भगवान श्री कृष्ण के मित्र सुदामा उनके लंगोटिया यार थे।
119. (ख) : अच्छे लोग बुराइयों पर लीपा-पोती करना पसन्द नहीं करते।
120. (ग) : अकबर-बीरबल विनोद नामक पुस्तक पढ़कर आदमी लोट-पोट हो जाता है।
121. (क) : शिष्य गण अपने गुरु के वाक्यों को वेद वाक्य मानते थे।
122. (क) : अपशब्द सुनकर भले आदमियों के शरीर में भी आग लग जाती है।
123. (ख) : गांव के जमींदार का अपमान करके सरजू ने शेर के मुँह में हाथ डालने का दुस्साहस किया।
124. (क) : बच्चों से दिल्लगी करते करते शर्म नहीं आती, लगता है आप सठिया गए हैं। मोहन ने खीझकर कहा।

125. (घ) : सब्ज बाग दिखाकर रहीम ने मोहन से एक हजार रुपए ठग लिए।

126. (क) : नादिरशाह ने दिल्ली पर जो सितम ढाया उसे आज भी नादिरशाही के नाम से घृणा से याद किया जाता है।

127. (ख) : विपक्षी पार्टियाँ सत्ताधारी पार्टी का सिंहासन हिलाने की चेष्टाएँ करती रहती हैं।

128. (क) : एकाएक प्रधानाचार्य को आया देखकर आपस में लड़ रहे विद्यार्थी हक्का बक्का हो गए।

129. (ग) : किसी का माल हजम कर जाना आसान नहीं। पाप की कमाई फूट-फूट कर निकलती है।

130. (घ) : साड़ी खरीदने में ऐसी हजामत बनी कि जीवन भर याद रहेगी। बेईमान दुकानदार ने रेशमी साड़ी की जगह बनावटी सिल्क की घटिया साड़ी मत्थे मढ़ दी।

Physics

1. The resistance between point A and D in the figure given below (neglecting the resistance of connecting wires AOC and BQD) is

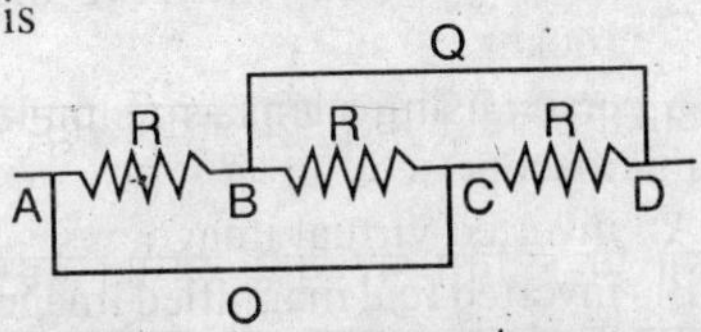

A. 3R B. R/3

C. 2/3R D. 3R/2

2. A fuse is fixed in a circuit in order to
   A. decrease the amount of current flowing.
   B. increase the amount of current flowing.
   C. increase the power consumed in the circuit.
   D. safeguard circuit against excessive currents.
3. Waves that can be transmitted through empty space are
   A. sound waves
   B. earth-quake waves
   C. electro-magnetic waves
   D. ultrasonic waves
4. In mechanical wave notion
   A. no medium is required.
   B. particles of the medium travel along the wave.
   C. particles of the medium remain at rest throughout.
   D. particles of the medium vibrate about their mean position.
5. The temperature of the boiling water in a steam engine boiler may be as high as 350°C because
   A. the boiler is well insulated.
   B. there are impurities dissolved in the water.
   C. there is a high pressure inside the boiler.
   D. the find under the boiler is at a high temperature.
6. A convex lens makes a real image of 4 cm length on a screen. When the lens is shifted to a new position without disturbing the object or the screen, we again get a real image on the screen which is 16 cm long. The length of the object must be
   A. 12 cm B. 20 cm
   C. 8 cm D. 1/4 cm
7. Three bulbs with power ratings of 40W, 60W and 100W at 220 V are connected in series to a 220V mains. Energy consumption will be
   A. the highest for 100W bulb
   B. the highest for 60 W bulb
   C. the highest for 40 W bulb
   D. the same for all the three bulbs
8. The variation of force applied to a particle and the distance moved along a straight line is shown in the graph below :

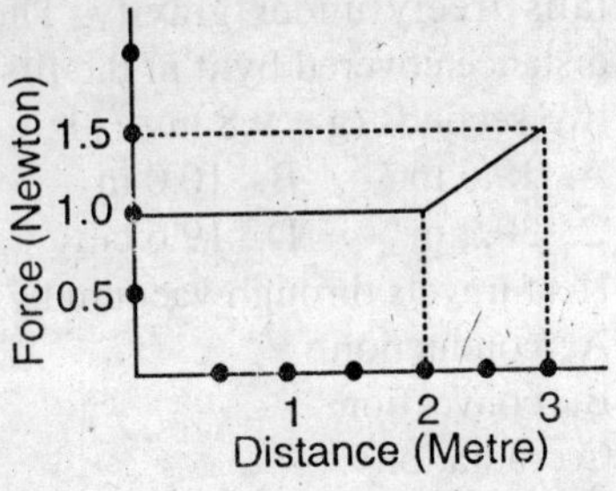

The kinetic energy of the particle at distance 3 metre is

A. 3.0 joule B. 4.5 joule

C. 3.25 joule D. 3.50 joule

9. Hard water does not lather with soap owing to the formation of

A. acetates of calcium and magnesium

B. stearates of calcium and magnesium

C. carbonates of calcium and magnesium

D. sulphates of calcium and magnesium

10. If the kinetic energy is increased by 300%, then the momentum is increased by

A. 300% B. 200%

C. 100% D. 150%

11. A body weighs 121 gm and 125.44 gm on two different pans of a faulty balance. Its true weight will be

A. 4.44 gm B. 120.00 gm

C. 123.22 gm D. 130.00 gm

12. The temperature, of which the same value on both the Centigrade and the Fahrenheit scales exists, is

A. 40° B. – 40°

C. 32° D. – 32°

13. A stone is dropped from rest and falls freely under gravity. The distance covered by it in the first two seconds ($g = 9.8\ ms^{-2}$) is

A. 19.6 m B. 10.0 m

C. 39.2 m D. 19.6 cm

14. Heat travels through vacuum by

A. conduction

B. convection

C. radiation

D. both A and B

15. Rocket engines lift a rocket from the earth surface, because hot gases with high velocity

A. Push against the earth

B. Push against the air

C. React against the rocket and push it up

D. Heat up the air which lifts the rocket

16. A person using a lens as a simple microscope sees an

A. inverted virtual image

B. inverted real magnified image

C. upright real magnified image

D. upright virtual image

17. Mirage is a phenomenon that results from

A. total internal reflection of light

B. reflection of light

C. refraction of light

D. diffraction of light

18. When the speed of a body is doubled, its kinetic energy becomes

A. double B. half

C. quadruple D. one-fourth

19. A person climbing to hill bends forward in order to

A. avoid slipping

B. increase speed

C. reduce fatique

D. increase stability

20. An iron ball and a wooden ball of the same mass arc released from a height h in air. Neglecting the viscous drag of air

A. the iron ball will hit the ground earlier.

B. the wooden ball will hit the ground earlier.

C. both will reach the ground at the same time.

D. there is equal probability for the wooden and iron ball to hit the ground earlier.

21. Two masses of 10 kg and 20 kg respectively are connected by a massless spring as shown below :

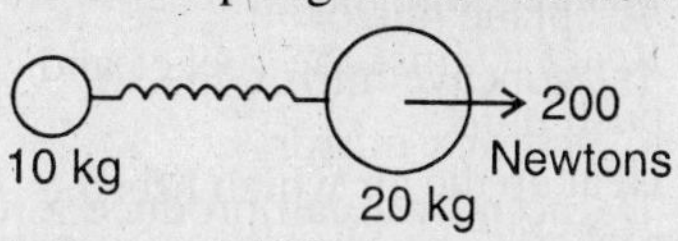

A force of 200 Newtons acts on the 20 kg mass. At the instant shown the 10 kg mass has acceleration of 12 m/sec^2. What is the acceleration of 20 kg mass?

A. 12 m/sec^2 B. 4 m/sec^2
C. 10 m/sec^2 D. Zero

22. Which of the following properties a fuse wire for normal electrical appliances should have?

1. Thick wire
2. Thin wire
3. Lower melting point alloy
4. High melting point alloy

A. 1 and 3 B. 1 and 4
C. 2 and 3 D. 2 and 4

23. In a lamp, oil rises up the wick because,

A. oil is very light
B. of the capillary action phenomenon
C. oil is highly volatile
D. of surface tension

24. Which of the following techniques is used to transmit audio signals in television broadcasts?

A. Time division multiplexing
B. Pulse code modulation
C. Amplitude modulation
D. Frequency modulation

25. An irregular shaped body has a weight of 12 kg in air and 8 kg in water. What is the density in kg/m^3?

A. $\frac{3}{2}$ B. 3
C. 3000 D. $\frac{2}{3}$
E. None of these

26. An elastic spring has a force constant K. It is cut into three equal parts. The force constant of each part is

A. K B. $\frac{K}{3}$
C. 3K D. $K\sqrt{3}$
E. None of these

27. All objects experience the same acceleration due to the gravity of the earth. This is because the gravitational force is proportional to

A. density B. mass
C. force D. weight
E. None of these

28. The apparent depth of a quantity of a liquid in a vessel is 15 cm. If its real depth is 20 cm, then the refractive index of the liquid is

A. 0.75 B. 21.33
C. 300 D. 1.33

29. Which type of mirror is used by dentists to concentrate light on the tooth to be examined?

A. Concave
B. Convex
C. Plane
D. Planeoconvex

30. The Sun and Moon appear elliptical near the horizon due to

A. optical illusion
B. interference
C. refraction
D. actual change in shapes

31. A wooden block is floating in water. If $\frac{4}{5}$ of its volume is immersed in water and volume of the water displaced in 800 ml, the volume of the block is

A. 1000 ml B. 800 ml

C. 640 ml D. 200 ml

32. The minimum possible temperature beyond which matter cannot be cooled is

A. – 98.10°C B. – 100.00°C

C. – 273.15°C D. – 459.40°C

33. Which one of the following will take place when a watch based on oscillating spring is taken to the moon?

A. It will become slow

B. It will become fast

C. It will indicate the same time as on earth

D. It will stop working

34. The type of mirror used in the handlamps of cars is the

A. plane mirror

B. spherical convex mirror

C. spherical concave mirror

D. parabolic concave mirror

35. The process of fission occurs mainly in

A. nuclear reactors

B. chemical reactions

C. the hydrogen bomb

D. the Sun

36. Air is completely removed from an electric bulb to prevent

A. oxidation of tungsten filament

B. busting of the bulb

C. loss of light due to absorption

D. None of these

37. The function of fuse in an electrical circuit is

A. to avoid electric shocks

B. to regulate the flow of current

C. to break the circuit in case of over-loading

D. None of these

38. What type of mirror can be used to obtain the real image of an object?

A. plane mirror

B. concave mirror

C. convex mirror

D. no mirror can produce a real image

39. A physical balance works on the principle of

A. gravitation

B. gravity

C. law of falling bodies

D. law of moments

40. Sound waves cannot travel through

A. solids B. liquids

C. gases D. vacuum

41. Which type of water is used in atomic reactors?

A. Hard water

B. Soft water

C. Heavy water

D. Mineral water

42. An electric motor rated at one horsepower of mechanical power will consume how much of electrical power?

A. 1 kilogram B. 2000 watts

C. 745 watts D. 500 watts

43. Which type of mirror with always form virtual image?

A. Concave

B. Convex

C. Plane

D. Plane as well as convex

44. A washing machine works on the principle of

A. angular momentum

B. law of conservation

C. gravitational force

D. centrifugal force

45. As a gas-filled balloon ascends in

atmosphere, its weight

A. increases

B. decreases

C. remains the same

D. nothing can be said

46. A concave mirror of focal length 'f' is immersed in water of refractive index 1.3. Its focal length in water will be

A. equal to f B. $f \times 1.3$

C. $\frac{f}{1.3}$ D. zero

47. A stone is thrown in the vertically upward direction. It comes the thrower after sometime. Which one of the given graphs represents the graph of upward velocity vs time?

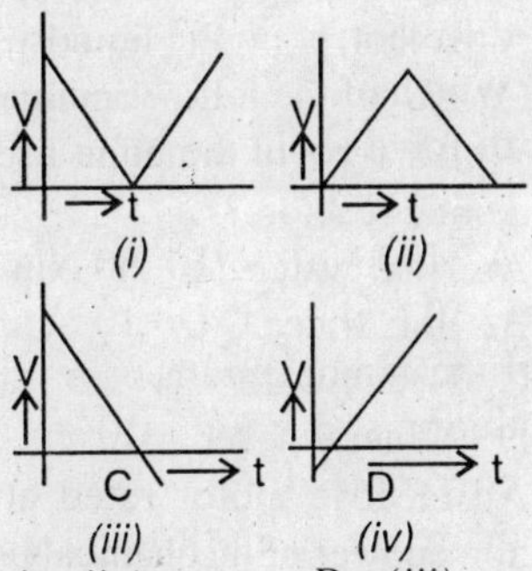

A. (iv) B. (iii)

C. (ii) D. (i)

48. Which of the following is not a part of an external combustion engine?

A. Cylinder B. Spark plug

C. Boiler D. Piston

49. A racing automobile has a uniform acceleration of 4 m/s^2. The distance covered in 10 seconds after the start from rest is

A. 100 m B. 200 m

C. 300 m D. 400 m

50. A body is placed on a table. The earth acts a gravitational force on it. The reaction of this force acts

A. on the table

B. on the earth

C. on the body

D. partly on the body and on the table

51. A ball of mass 1 kg, moving with velocity 10 m/s hits a free stationary target of mass 9 kg and stuck to it. The kinetic energy lost in the process in the form of heart is

A. zero B. 25 J

C. 45 J D. 50 J

52. A solid body of density 0.5 g/cc floats on a liquid of density 0.9 g/cc. The fraction of solid volume above the liquid surface is

A. $\frac{4}{9}$ B. $\frac{5}{9}$

C. $\frac{2}{3}$ D. Zero

53. A body is in equilibrium under three forces $\vec{A}, \vec{B}, \vec{C}$. If $\vec{A}$ equals 40 N along horizontal (x = axis) and $\vec{B}$ equals – 30 N along vertical (y-axis), then the magnitude of $\vec{C}$ is

A. 70 N B. 10 N

C. 50 N D. 35 N

54. An acceleration time curve is plotted for a motion. What relates to the area between the curve and the time axis between l_1 and l_2

A. the displacement between l_1 and l_2

B. the change in velocity between l_1 and l_2

C. the average velocity between l_1 and l_2

D. the average acceleration between l_1 and l_2

55. The graph shows the variations in a physical quantity p due to change in another quantity q.

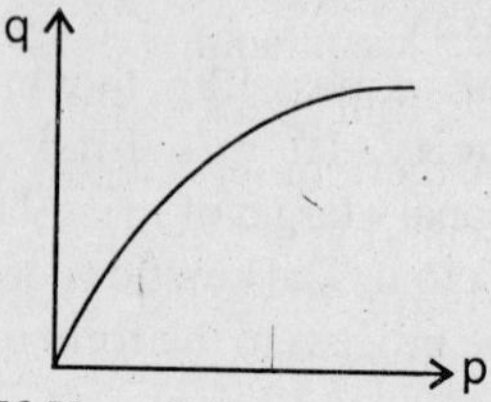

If K and C are constants, which of the following equation most appropriately expresses the relation between p and q?

A. $p = q + c$ B. $pq = K$
C. $p = Kq$ D. $p = Kq^2$

56. In which of the following pairs the two units can be used for the measurement of the same quantity?

A. kg m^2/s^2, J/s
B. kg m^2/s^2, Ws
C. kg m/s^2, Nm
D. kg m/s^2, Ws

57. In a hydroelectric power project water falls freely from a height of 30 m at the rate 10^5 kg per second. If we could convert 30% of this energy into electricity and assume acceleration due to gravity g = 10 m/s^2, the electrical power produced would be

A. 9 MW B. 27 MW
C. 90 MW D. 100 MW

58. Which part of solar spectrum is primarily absorbed by the ozone layer?

A. Infrared B. Visible
C. Ultraviolet D. Far Infrared

59. Two bulbs A and B when connected in parallel across a battery (with no internal resistance) consume 100 W and 300 W power. If they are connected in series across the same battery the total power consumption would be

A. 400 W B. 200 W
C. 100 W D. 75 W

60. The acceleration due to gravity g at the surface of the earth in 9.8 m/s^2. At a height of one earth radius above the earth's surface the value of g is

A. 9.80 m/s^2 B. 4.90 m/s^2
C. 2.45 m/s^2 D. 19.60 m/s^2

61. A metre-scale of uniform section is balanced at its mid point, M, on a pivot. A small weight of mass 10 g is hung from the scale at different points (g = 10 ms^{-2}). Which of the following moments of force about the point M is not possible

A. 100 Nm B. 50 Nm
C. 0 Nm D. 10 Nm

62. Linear momentum of a body is decreased by 20%. The corresponding percentage decrease in its kinetic energy would be

A. 36% B. 40%
C. 44% D. 48%

63. Half-life of a radioactive substance is 28 years. The time required by a sample of this substance to get reduced to 3.125% of its original mass will be

A. 84 years B. 112 years
C. 140 years D. 168 years

64. The weight of an object in air, in a liquid of density ρ and in another liquid of density ρ′ is 750 N, 500 N and 400 N, respectively.

The ratio $\rho : \rho'$ will be

A. 4 : 5 B. 5 : 4

C. 7 : 5 D. 5 : 7

65. Two metal balls A and B have their radii in the ratio 3 : 1 and densities in the ratio 1 : 3, respectively. The ratio of mass of A to that of mass B is

A. 3 : 1 B. 1 : 3

C. 1 : 1 D. 9 : 1

66. What value must the resistor R_1 have in order that the total resistance between the terminals A and B shall be R?

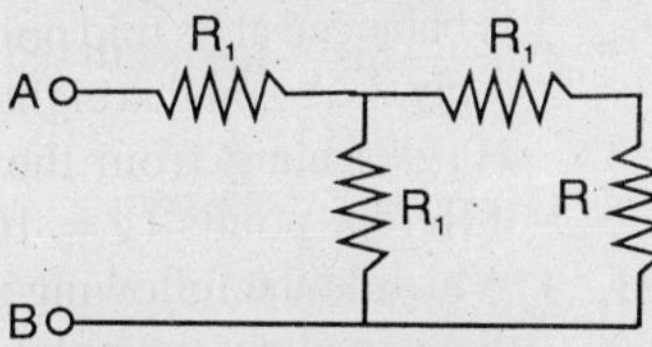

A. 2R B. $\sqrt{3}$ R

C. $\frac{R}{\sqrt{3}}$ D. $\frac{R}{2}$

67. Colour of a Star is guide to its temperature. Which of the following Stars would you expect to be hottest?

A. Yellow-white Canopus

B. Red Betelgeuse

C. Blue-white Sirius

D. Yellowish Alpha Centauri

68. In the propagation of sound waves in air, the angle between the direction of vibration of air molecules and the direction of wave propagation

A. is 0°

B. varies between – 90° to 90°

C. varies between 0 to 90°

D. is 90°

69. Mass of an object A is four times that of the mass of object B. If the kinetic energies of A and B be equal, then the momentum of A will be

A. more than that of B

B. equal to that of B

C. less than that of B

D. four times of B

70. A thermometer with an arbitrary scale has ice point at – 10° and steam point at 140°. If the temperature measured by this thermometer is 20°, the corresponding reading on the Celcius scale will be

A. 13.3°C B. 20°C

C. 30°C D. 45°C

71. The speed of sound will be highest in

A. dry air at 0°C

B. dry air at 30°C

C. humid air at 0°C

D. humid air at 30°C

72. The figure shows the arrangement in which three identical bulbs X, Y and Z connected to a battery with a switch S.

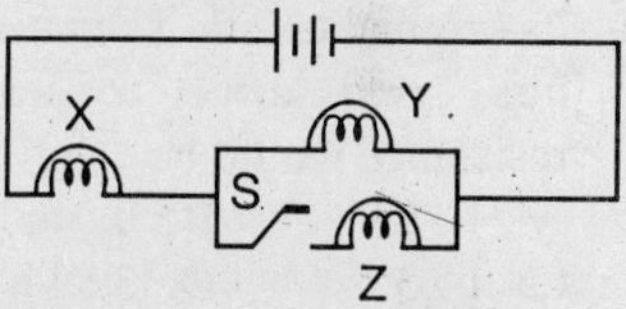

Which of the following changes to the brightness of the bulbs will occur when the switch S is closed?

A. X stays the same, Y decreases

B. X decreases, Y decreases

C. X increases, Y remains the same

D. X increases, Y decreases

73. A ball rolling along the ground with an initial speed v comes to a stop after a time t. Which of the following pictures shows the correct distance-time graph of the motion? (In the graph the distance is shown by s)

A. 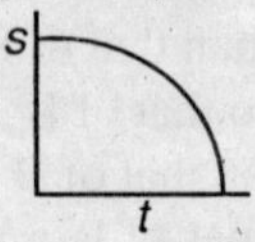

B. 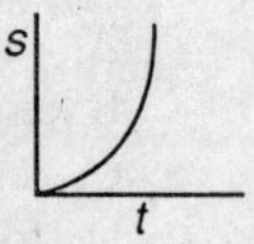

C. 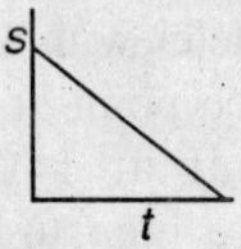

D. 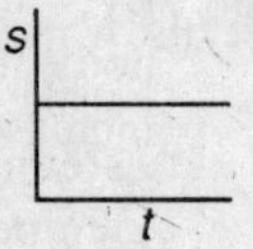

74. Television and Computers display picture on

A. Fluorescent tubes
B. Discharge tubes
C. G.M. tubes
D. Cathode ray tubes

75. Which of the following statements best explains the fact that a pinhole camera forms a real image?

A. Light travels in a straight line
B. Light can be refracted
C. Light can be displaced
D. Light is a form of energy

76. A wire stretched to three times of its original length. The ratio of its ness resistance to original resistance would be

A. 1 : 9 B. 9 : 1
C. 1 : 3 D. 3 : 1

77. If 300 crests of a wave on a water surface pass through a point is one minute, then the frequence of the wave is

A. 0.2 Hz B. 5.0 Hz
C. 7.5 Hz D. 0.3 kHz

78. The average distance between the earth and INSAT satellite about 5 times the radius of the earth. If aceleration due to gravity at earths' surface be 10 m/s^2, its value on the sattelite will be

A. 4 m/s^2 B. 2 m/s^2
C. 0.4 m/s^2 D. zero

79. A body spends 20 joules of energy in 5 seconds. What is its power?

A. 100 W B. 20 W
C. 5 W D. 4 W

80. A particle is moving eastwards, with a velocity of 5 ms^{-1}. In 10 s, the velocity changes to 5 ms^{-1} northwards. The average acceleration is

A. $\frac{1}{2}$ms^{-1} due north
B. zero
C. $\frac{1}{\sqrt{2}}$ms^{-1} due north-east
D. $\frac{1}{2}$ms^{-2} due west

81. The position-time graph for two objects A and B is shown in figure below. If V_A and V_B are the velocities of the objects A and B, respectively, then the correct option is

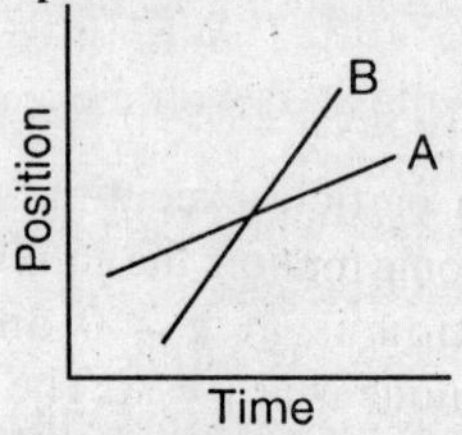

A. $V_A = V_B$
B. $V_A < V_B$
C. $V_A > V_B$
D. $V_A > V_B$ upto certain time and after that $V_A < V_B$

82. A ball is dropped from a height of 90 m. Its velocity just at the time of touching the floor is (g = 10 ms^{-1})

A. 900 ms^{-1} B. $30\sqrt{2}$ ms^{-1}
C. $\frac{30}{\sqrt{2}}$ ms^{-1} D. 1800 ms^{-1}

83. **Consider :** A second pendulum will not lose time if ;

I. its length is increased

II. it is taken to a high altitude

III. it is taken deep under the earth's surface

Which one of the above are correct? Choose the answer from one of the choices mentioned below.

A. I only
B. II only
C. III only
D. None of these

84. A given object has mass m and weight w on the surface of the earth. The same object has a mass m' and weight w' on the moon. Which one is the correct statement?

A. $m = m', w = w'$

B. $m = m', \frac{w}{6} = w'$

C. $\frac{m}{6} = m', w = w'$

D. $m \neq m', w \neq w'$

85. For a particle executing simple harmonic motion, the equilibrium position is at $x = 0$ and the amplitude is at $x = A$. The KE of the particle will be equal to the potential energy at

A. $x = 0$

B. $x = A$

C. $x = \frac{A}{2}$

D. a point where $x > \frac{A}{2}$ but $x < A$

86. A ball is thrown up with a velocity of 19.6 ms^{-1}. How high did the ball go, if ($g = 9.8\ ms^{-2}$)?

A. 18.6 m B. – 19.6 m
C. 19.4 m D. 19.9 m

87. What would be the weight of 100 kg of steel at the centre of the earth?

A. 1000 kg B. 980 kg
C. 0 D. 1200 kg

88. By what factor, will the KE of a body increase if its velocity is increased three times?

A. 8 B. 4
C. 9 D. 27

89. Area of acceleration time graph indicates

A. velocity
B. velocity and speed
C. speed
D. distance travelled

90. Refer to the velocity time graph given below :

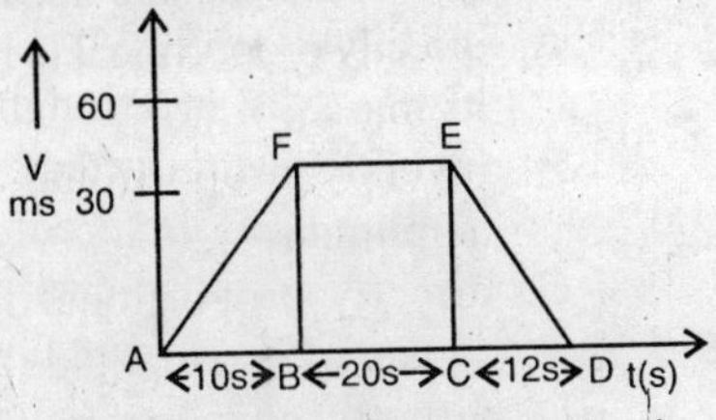

What is the average velocity between points A and F?

A. 40 ms^{-1} B. 30 ms^{-1}
C. 18 ms^{-1} D. 20 ms^{-1}

91. Refer to figure of Q.No. 90, what is the distance travelled during the interval BC?

A. 1800 m B. 1600 m
C. 1000 m D. 1200 m

92. Refer to figure of Q.No. 90, what is the total distance travelled by the body during its entire journey?

A. 1200 m B. 1600 m
C. 1860 m D. 1960 m

93. Refer to figure Q.No. 90, what is the uniform acceleration while the body travels from A to B?

A. 10 ms^{-2} B. 6 ms^{-2}

C. 12 ms^{-2} D. 60 ms^{-2}

94. A body has a linear momentum of p and a mass of m. What is its kinetic energy?

A. p^2m B. $2p^2m$

C. $\frac{p^2}{m}$ D. pm

95. A particle of mass 6 kg is rotating in a circle of radius 3 m, at a velocity of 10 ms^{-1}. What is the magnitude of force that must be made to act on it in order to maintain its motion?

A. 400 N B. 300 N

C. 100 N D. 200 N

96. In a simple harmonic motion, the energy of the particle in SHM is

A. directly proportional to half of its mass

B. inversly proportional to its amplitude

C. directly proportional to the square of its amplitude

D. directly proportional to its angular velocity

97. A body of mass 1 kg was moving with a velocity of 5 ms^{-1} when it was suddenly stopped stopped by a force. The body came to a halt. What was the magnitude of the force?

A. 2.5 N B. 3.2 N

C. 1.0 N D. 1.9 N

98. An aircraft takes off a the speed of 100 km/hr^{-1} at an angle of 30° with the runway. What is the velocity of the aircraft along the runway?

A. 100 km/hr^{-1}

B. 80 km/hr^{-1}

C. 86.6 km/hr^{-}

D. 76.6 km/hr^{-1}

99. If a vector $\vec{v} = 4\vec{i} + 3\vec{j}$ is multiplied by 3, resultant vector would be

A. $9\vec{i} + 12\vec{j}$ B. $12\vec{i} + 9\vec{j}$

C. $\vec{i} + \vec{j}$ D. $16\vec{i} + 12\vec{j}$

100. A vector $\vec{V}$ can be defined as follows :

$\vec{v} = 6\vec{i} + 8\vec{j}$

What is the angle made by $\vec{V}$ with x-axis?

A. $\theta = \tan^{-1}\frac{8}{6}$

B. $\theta = \tan^{-1}\frac{12}{13}$

C. $\theta = \tan^{-1}\frac{4}{3}$

D. $\theta = \tan^{-1}\frac{3}{4}$

101. A car has a mass m at rest. In time t, its velocity becomes v under the influence of force F. What does the expression $\frac{mv}{t}$ represent?

A. Acceleration (a)

B. Momentum (p)

C. Force (F)

D. All of the above

102. What is the energy present in 40 MT of water at a height of 200 m, the water still not being released?

A. 7,84,000 J

B. 7,84,00,000 J

C. 78,40,000 J

D. 78,40,00,000 J

103. A water fall is 84 m. If half of the KE gets converted into heat, what is the rise in the temperature of water?

A. 9.8 °C B. 0.98°C

C. 98°C D. 0.098°C

104. Two identical bodies move on two concentric circular paths. The speed and radius of the path of the outer body is double than that of the inner body. The force experienced by them will be

A. more for outer body
B. more for inner body
C. same for both the bodies
D. insufficient information to predict

105. When a body of mass m revolves with a uniform speed of v on a circular track of radius r. The work done by the body in one revolution will be

A. $3\pi mv^2$

B. $\left(2\pi - \frac{1}{2}\right) mv^2$

C. $2\pi mv^2$

D. 0

106. A bob of mass 150 gms is replaced by a mass of 200 gms in a simple pandulum. The time period of the simple pandulum will

A. decrease
B. increase
C. not be affected
D. depend upon the material at the new bob

107. What would happen if friction were missing?

A. Cars would stop with the help of hydraulic brakes
B. Machines with V belts would not work
C. Walking would be easier
D. Writing on the paper would be smoother

108. What are the dimensions of force?

A. ML^2T^{-1} B. MLT^{-2}
C. $M^0L^1T^{-3}$ D. LT^{-2}

109. Two circular discs have masses in the ratio of 1 : 2 and diameters in the ratio of 2 : 1. The ratio of their moments of inertia is

A. 1 : 1 B. 2 : 1
C. 4 : 3 D. 3 : 4

110. The time period of a simple pendulum is 2s. If its length be increased from times, the new time period would become

A. 6 seconds B. 8 seconds
C. 4 seconds D. 4π seconds

111. The momentum of body of mass 5 kg is 15 kg-m-s^{-1}. What is its kinetic energy?

A. 20.5 J B. 22.5 J
C. 29.3 J D. 26.5 J

112. The formula F = ma is a deduction of

A. Newton's First Law of Motion
B. Newton's Second Law of Motion
C. Newton's Third Law of Motion
D. None of the above

113. A ball P is dropped vertically from a point. Another ball Q is thrown horizontally from the same point. When would they reach the ground?

A. At the same time
B. Ball A would reach first
C. Ball B would reach first
D. Cannot be predicted

114. The velocity of a body is given by the equation

$$v = a + \frac{b}{t} + ct^2$$

What would be the unit of b?

A. ms^{-2} B. ms^{-1}

C. m D. s^{-1}

115. A particle covers one-half of a circle of radius r. The distance travelled by the particle and displacement covered by it are

A. $2\pi rt, r$ B. $\pi r, 2r$

C. $\pi r, \frac{r}{2}$ D. $\pi r^2, \frac{r^2}{2}$

116. A copper disc has a circular hole at its centre. When the copper disc is heated to raise its temperature, the diameter of the hole will

A. increase

B. decrease

C. first increase, then decrease

D. first decrease, then increase

117. Why does a table tennis ball keep on dancing on a water jet with pressure?

A. The ball has the tendency to do so

B. The ball remains at the top of the jet due to the thrust of water and is not able to change its state

C. The ball falls down occasionally

D. None of the above

118. The centripetal force

A. always works in the direction of motion

B. always acts at right angle to the direction of motion

C. always acts parallel to the path of motion

D. None of the above

119. Two weights have been connected to a pulley through a weightless string, as shown below :

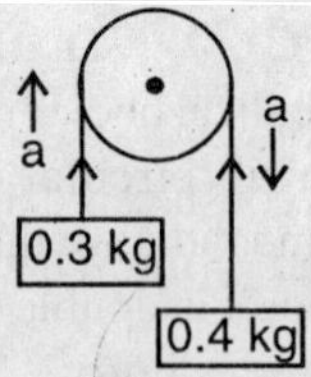

The weights are 0.3 kg and 0.4 kg. The pulley is smooth. The tension in the stiring is

A. 3.00 N B. 3.4 N

C. 3.35 N D. 12.35 N

120. The graph between the force on and position of a particle has been shown below. The work donw by the force for displacing the particle from $x = 1$ cm to $x = 5$ cm is

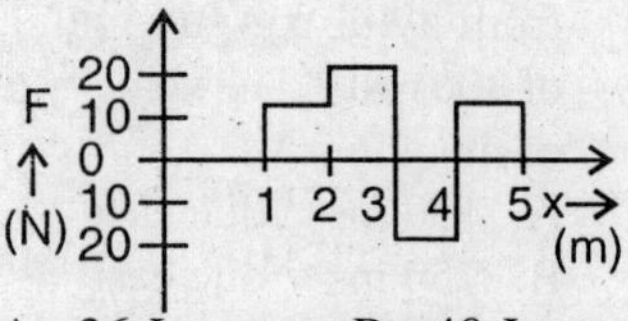

A. 36 J B. 40 J

C. 23 J D. 20 J

121. Two bodies of 5 kg and 4 kg are tied to a string as shown in figure below. If the table and the pulley are smooth, the acceleration of the body with mass 5 kg is

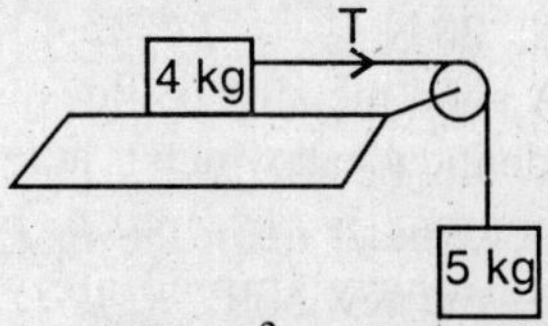

A. $6.4\ ms^{-2}$ B. $5.45\ ms^{-2}$

C. $9.75\ ms^{-2}$ D. $5.9\ ms^{-2}$

122. The stretched membranes of areas $2m^2$ and $3m^2$ are placed in a liquid at the same depth. The ratio of pressure on them is

A. $\sqrt{2}:\sqrt{3}$ B. $2^2 : 3^2$

C. $\frac{1}{2}:\frac{1}{3}$ D. $1^2 : 1^2$

123. Planck's constant is defined by the equation E = hv. What is the unit of h?

A. Js^{-1} B. Js

C. Ws^{-2} D. Js^{-2}

124. An iceberg floats in the sea and is partly immersed in it. The density of water is 1.03 g cm^{-3} and that of ice is 0.92 g cm^{-3}. The fraction of the total volume of the iceberg above the sea level is

A. 18% B. 14%

C. 22% D. 11%

125. A 10 kg shot is fired eastwards from a 400 kg gun with a speed of 300 ms^{-1}. The velocity of recoil of the gun is

A. 130 ms^{-1} due east

B. 750 ms^{-1} due east

C. 130 ms^{-1} due west

D. 75 ms^{-1} due west

126. A small rocket is ejecting 0.05 kg of gases per second at a velocity of 400 ms^{-1}. The accelerating force on the rocket is

A. 41.4 N B. 200 N

C. 20 N D. 45.4 N

127. A solid metallic collides with an identical ball which is at rest. The first one is observed to become stationary immediately upon collision. The second ball

A. will remain at rest

B. will go forward with one-third of the velocity of the first hall (in motion)

C. will go forward with the same velocity as that of the first ball (in motion)

D. None of the above

128. A block of steel of size 5 cm × 5 cm × 5 cm is weighed in water. If the relative density of steel is 7, its apparent weight is

A. 6 × 5 × 5 × 5 g

B. 7 × 5 × 5 × 5 g

C. 9 × 5 × 5 × 5 g

D. 125 g

129. Under isothermal conditions, the elasticity of a gas is equal to its

A. pressure

B. volume

C. molar volume

D. None of the above

130. When a piece of metal weighing 48.3 g at 10°C was immersed in a current of steam at 100°C. What is the specific heat of the metal?

A. 0.058 B. 0.069

C. 0.085 D. 0.095

131. Two spheres of the same size are made of the same metal. But one is hollow and the other one is solid. They are heated to the same temperature,

A. the hollow sphere will expand more

B. the solid sphere will expand more

C. both spheres with expand almost equall

D. None of the above

132. A piece of Al of 20 g mass, gives out 560 J of heat on cooling from 50°C. What is the specific heat of Al?

A. 600 J kg^{-1} k^{-1}

B. 800 J kg^{-1} k^{-1}

C. 550 J kg^{-1} k^{-1}

D. 850 J kg^{-1} k^{-1}

133. Which one of the following changes in the parameters of an ideal gas will change its volume four times?

A. Both temperature and

pressure are doubled

B. Temperature is reduced to one half and pressure is doubled

C. Temperature is reduced to one-fourthand there is no change in pressure

D. Pressure is reduced to one-fourth and there is no change in temperature

134. The value of absolute zero on the Fahrenheit scale is

A. + 450.4°C B. – 459.4°C

C. + 459.4°C D. – 550.3°C

135. Equal volumes of copper and mercury have the same thermal capacity. Mercury has a specific heat of 0.046 gm per cc and density of 13.6 gm per cc. Find the density of copper if its specific heat is 0.092.

A. 2.9 gm per cc

B. 6.9 gm per cc

C. 6.8 gm per cc

D. 2.8 gm per cc

136. Choose the correct statement.

A. $\alpha:\beta:\gamma = 1:3:2$

B. $\alpha:\beta:\gamma = 3:2:1$

C. $\alpha:\beta:\gamma = 2:3:1$

D. $\alpha:\beta:\gamma = 1:2:3$

137. The pressure of a gas in a metal cylinder is 4 atmospheres at 27°C. The pressure at 54°C is (in atmosphere)

A. 3.36 atm B. 4.36 atm

C. 6.23 atm D. 5.36 atm

138. The pressure of a given mass of an ideal gas is changed isothermally and a graph is plotted between pressure and the reciprocal of the volume. What would be the resultant graph?

A. 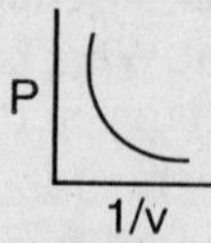

B. 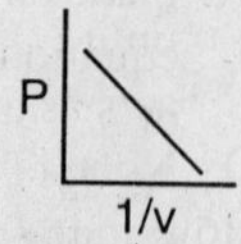

C. 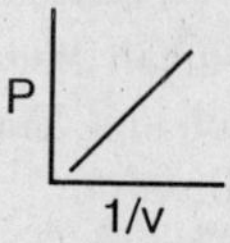

D. 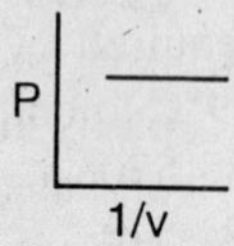

139. A bar, 50 cm long, is heated from 14°C to 98°C. If the increase in length is 0.7 mm, what is the coefficient of linear expanse?

A. 0.00017 B. 0.000017

C. 0.000023 D. 0.00023

140. The coefficient of linear expansion for a solid is 0.000231°C. The coefficient of volume expansion of the same solid will be

A. double the coefficient of linear expansion

B. thrice the coefficient of linear expansion

C. one-half of the coefficient of linear expansion

D. equal to the coefficient of linear expansion

141. Specific heat of a gas at constant pressure is greater than specific heat of that gas at constant volume. It is so because

A. at constant volume, work is done against external pressure

B. at constant pressure, work is done while expanding the gas

C. at constant pressure, force of attraction of molecules of the gas is greater

D. none of the above

142. A perfect white body is a body, which

A. reflects all the energy falling

on it

B. absorbs all the energy falling on it

C. acts as a black body at times

D. None of the above

143. How many calories of heat are required by 1 gram of water at 99°C to boil off?

A. 530 B. 640

C. 540 D. 500

144. What is the relative humidity of a place when it is raining?

A. 50% B. 80%

C. 0% D. 100%

145. If 60 g of ice at 0°C is mixed with 40 g of water at 60°C, then the resultant mixture will consist of

A. 70 g of water and 30 g of ice at 0°C

B. 40 g of water and 60 g of ice at 0°C

C. 120 g of water at 0°C

D. 60 g of water at 0°C

146. The mean kinetic energy of gas molecule is proportional to

A. $\sqrt{T}$

B. T^2

C. T

D. None of the above

147. Which one of the following is not an internal combustion engine?

A. Steam engine

B. Truck engine

C. Motorcycle engine

D. Diesel engine set's engine

148. The temperature, to which a gas must be cooled before it can be liquefied by pressure alone, is known as its

A. saturation point

B. freezing point

C. liquification temperature

D. critical temperature

149. A pressure cooker works on the basis of the following principle

A. boiling point is lowered by increasing the pressure on the surface of the liquid

B. boiling point is raised by increasing the pressure on the surface of the liquid

C. more heat energy is consumed when the pressure is lowered

D. more heat energy is consumed when the quantity of liquid is increased

150. Find the amount of heat required to boil off 10 gm of ice at – 8°C. Given latent heat of ice = 80 cals per gm. Latent Heat of Steam = 540 cals per gm. Specific Heat of Ice = 0.5.

A. 7,000 cals B. 7,240 cals

C. 8,240 cals D. 6,240 cals

151. Latent heat of ether at 0°C is 90 cal per g. How much ether should be evaporated to freeze 60 g of water at 60°C?

A. 60 g B. 35 g

C. 33 g D. 30 g

152. The water equivalent of a body is 10 gm. Its thermal capacity is

A. 10 J per°K

B. 10 cal per°K

C. 10 kcal per°K

D. 10 g per°K

153. 6 gm of steam at 100°C are mixed with 250 gm of water at 0°C. The temperature of the mixture is

A. 20°C B. 28°C

C. 15°C D. 10°C

154. The surface water of a lake is about to freeze. What is the temperature of water at the bottom of the lake?

A. 4°C B. – 4°C
C. 3°C D. – 3°C

155. The rate at which, a hot body loses heat, is proportional to the

A. temperature of the body
B. square of temperature of the body
C. difference between the temperature of the body and the temperature of the surroundings
D. square root of the temperature of the body

156. What is the speed of heat radiations in vacuum?

A. 3,000 ms^{-1}
B. 3×10^8 ms^{-1}
C. 6×10^4 ms^{-1}
D. 8×10^4 ms^{-1}

157. A sample of gas 0°C. To what temperature, must the temperature be raised in order to double the speed of molecules of the gas?

A. – 273°C B. 273°K
C. 273°C D. – 273°K

158. At what rate will the ice melt in a wooden box. 2 cm thick and of inside measurement of 100 × 60 × 60 cms, if external temperature is 20°C and the conductivity of the wood is 0.0004.

A. 2.92 gs^{-1} B. 3.94 gs^{-1}
C. 1.96 gs^{-1} D. 1.56 gs^{-1}

159. If the scale of temperature is in degrees F instead of in degrees C, the value of specific heat will be

A. greater
B. same in both the cases
C. lesser
D. cannot predict

160. The most important principle of kinetic theory of gases is that

A. lighter gas molecules have higher average energies than heavier gas molecules
B. lighter gas molecules have lower average energies than heavier gas molecules
C. all the molecules in a gas have the same average energy value
D. All of the above are true

161. In isothermal expansion of in ideal gas

A. heat content remains constant
B. temperature remains constant
C. both heat and temperature remain constant
D. pressure and temperature of the gas remain constant

162. Which one of the following statements is true?

A. Ventilation of rooms is essential for good health because fresh air can enter into the room
B. The direct formation of a vapour from a solid is known as vaporisation
C. Ice is a good refrigeration because it has a high specific heat
D. The temperature of boiling water in steam engine boiler may be as high as 300°C as there is high pressure inside the boiler

163. The boiling point of water

I. can be increased by adding salt to it
II. can be increased by increasing nor be decreased
III. is 100°C and can neither be increased nor be decreased

Which one these statements (I, II

and III) is correct?

A. I is correct

B. II and III are correct

C. II is correct

D. I, II and III are correct

164. Mercury is used as a thermometric substance because

A. it is a metal available in liquid state

B. it has high density and so, the length of the mercury column will be small

C. its vapour pressure will be the same

D. it has a uniform coefficient of volume expansion

165. When a liquid boils, the vapour pressure of the vapour is

A. equal to the atomspheric pressure

B. less than the atmospheric pressure

C. more than the atmospheric pressure

D. None of the above

166. It is easy to fuse platinum into glass because

A. A coefficient of expansion of platinum is greater than that of glass

B. coefficient of expansion of platinum is less than that of glass

C. coefficient of expansion of platinum is equal to that of glass

D. None of the above

167. The rate of cooling of the body depends upon

A. surface area of the body

B. the temperature difference between the body and its surroundings

C. the material of the body

D. Both (A) and (B)

168. The door of a refrigerator, which is working, is left open

A. the temperature of the room will fall

B. the temeprature of the room will rise

C. the room will have the same temperature as has been maintained within the refrigerator

D. None of the above

169. What is Latent Heat?

A. It is the heat given to a body and simultaneously the body releases it to the atmosphere

B. It is the heat given to a body to heat it by 1°C

C. It is the heat given to body to change its state at constant temperature

D. None of the above

170. If a substance is dissolved in water, at agiven temperature, then

A. the saturated vapour pressure of water will be lowered

B. the saturated vapour pressure of water will be raised

C. there will be no effect on the saturated vapour

D. None of the above

171. What will be the state of gas below to critical temperature?

A. Vapour

B. Solid

C. Liquid

D. Solid and vapours

172. Hot water in a beaker takes 10 minutes to cool from 90°C to 80°C. The time taken by it to cool from 80°C to 70°C is

A. more than 10 minutes

B. 10 minutes
C. less than 10 minutes
D. None of the above

173. Which one of the following does not have a melting point?
A. Glass B. Oxygen
C. Mercury D. Aluminium

174. Why cotton cloth (double layer) acts as a warm cloth in winter?
A. Cotton has insulating property
B. The layer of air trapped between the two layers acts as a bad conductor of heat
C. The human body adjusts its temperature
D. All of the above

175. A gas molecule has mass in and it strikes the wall of its container with a velocity *v*. The momentum after the collision is
A. *mv* B. – *mv*
C. 2*mv* D. $\frac{mv}{2}$

176. Which formula is correct for representing Graham's Law of Diffusion (terms used are standard)?
A. $r_1 r_2 = \sqrt{\rho_2 \rho_1}$ B. $\frac{r_1}{r_2} = \frac{\sqrt{\rho_2}}{\sqrt{\rho_1}}$
C. $\frac{r_1}{r_2} = \frac{\sqrt{\rho_1}}{\sqrt{\rho_2}}$ D. $\frac{r_1}{r_2} = \rho_1 \rho_1$

177. How do the molecules of a gas behave?
A. Flexible, inelastic spheres
B. Flexible, elastic spheres
C. Rigid, perfectly elastic spheres
D. Depends upon the type of the gas

178. $\frac{P}{T}$ is constant provided *n* and *v* are constants. What is the law governing this statement?
A. Charle's Law
B. Boyle's Law
C. Regnault's Law
D. Avogadro's Law

179. Two sound waves, passing through air, have their wavelength in the ratio of 4 : 5. Their frequencies are the ratio of
A. 4 : 5 B. 3 : 4
C. 5 : 4 D. 1 : 1

180. The ratio of frequency of a fundamental note in an open pipe to that in a closed pipe of the same length is
A. 2 : 1 B. 2 : 3
C. 3 : 2 D. 1 : 2

181. Two coupled vibrating systems are said to be in resonance if their
A. amplitudes are equal
B. frequencies are equal
C. damping factors are equal
D. temperature are equal

182. In which medium, would you be able to hear the sound of a train (the train is at a great distance from you)?
A. From the air
B. From the steel rails
C. From the wooden planks under the rails
D. It is not possible to hear the sound

183. The distance between two successive crests or troughs is 1 m and the velocity of the waves is 320 ms^{-1}. What is the frequency?
A. 340 Hz B. 400 Hz
C. 320 Hz D. 420 Hz

184. Why the auditoria walls are provided with carboard panels and porons wall furnishings?

A. So that the sound from the stage may be heard properly
B. So that the echo effect may be minimised
C. So that the sound may appear to be pleasing on the ears of the listeners
D. All of the above

185. A musical sound is one that is produced

A. at regular intervals
B. in quick succession
C. Both (A) and (B)
D. None of (A) and (B)

186. Which relationship, out of those given below, represents the velocity of sound wave?

A. $v=\frac{\lambda}{n}$ B. $v=n\lambda$
C. $v=\frac{n}{\lambda}$ D. $v=n\lambda+1$

187. The loudness of sound depends upon

A. its velocity
B. its pitch
C. its amplitude
D. its frequency

188. The audible range of a person is 20 to 18,000 Hz. If speed of sound in air is 330 ms^{-1}, calculate the longest wavelength of sound, which he can detect?

A. $\frac{18000}{330}$ m B. $\frac{330}{18000}$ m
C. $\frac{20}{330}$ m D. $\frac{330}{20}$ m

189. A thunder is heard 4 seconds after the lighting. At what distance, the lightning occured?

A. 1,480 m B. 1,380 m
C. 2,380 m D. 1,000 m

190. What is the frequency of a fundamental note of 0.2 m long pipe. Given, the velocity of sound in air = 332 ms^{-1}.

A. 430 B. 730
C. 840 D. 830

191. Transverse waves cannot travel through

A. lubricating oil
B. a stretched nylon string
C. hydrogen gas
D. an iron rod

192. The ratio of velocity of sound in air at 4 atmospheric pressure and that at 1 atmospheric pressure would be

A. 2 : 1 B. 1 : 2
C. 1 : 1 D. 1 : 4

193. For an organ pipe, the wavelength of the fundamental note is

A. equal to the length of the pipe
B. half the length of the pipe
C. one-fourth the length of the pipe
D. twice the length of the pipe

194. The frequency of sound can remain unchanged even if we double the length of the wire, provided

A. tension of the wire is doubled
B. tension of the wire is decreased four-fold
C. tension of the wire is halved
D. tension of the wire is increased four-fold

195. A closed pipe has a fundamental frequency of 312 Hz. Its first overtone is

A. 336 Hz B. 936 Hz
C. 836 Hz D. 736 Hz

196. The velocity of sound at 15°C and 380 mm pressure is 340 ms^{-1}. If the temperature remains constant and pressure is doubled, the velocity of sound will be

A. 680 ms^{-1} B. 170 ms^{-1}

C. 340 ms^{-1} D. 1360 ms^{-1}

197. Which characteristics of sound enables us to distinguish two musical notes coming from different sources but having the same frequency and loudness?

A. Timber

B. Pitch

C. Loudness

D. None of the above

198. As the length of a vibrating column increases, its frequency

A. decreases

B. increases

C. remains the same

D. increases if the vibrating column is in not air

199. The sound of frequency 512 Hz is higher than the sound of frequency 256 Hz by

A. one octave

B. two cotaves

C. half on octave

D. three octaves

200. You have two identical organ pipes with same length and diameter. One is closed at one end while the other one is open at both the ends. The quality of sound is superior in the open-ended pipe because

A. presence of two harmonics—one odd and one even

B. presence of two odd harmonics

C. presence of two even harmonics

D. harmonic

201. In gases, the sound waves can at any two temperature can be represented by the following expression.

A. $\frac{v_1}{v_2} = \sqrt{\frac{T_2}{T_1}}$ B. $\frac{v_1}{v_2} = T_2T_1$

C. $\frac{v_1}{v_2} = \frac{T_2}{T_1}$ D. $\frac{v_1}{v_2} = \sqrt{\frac{T_1}{T_2}}$

202. Which one of the following rays has the greatest value of wavelength?

A. Red B. Yellow green

C. Ultraviolet D. Infrared

203. The velocity of sound in a gas in 4 times that in air at the same temperature. When a tuning fork is sounded in air, a wave of frequency 480 cs^{-1} and wavelength λ, is generated. The same fork is sounded in a gas and the wavelength of the wave produced in the gas is λ_2. Then $\frac{\lambda_2}{\lambda_1}$ is

A. $\frac{1}{4}$ B. 4

C. $\frac{1}{2}$ D. 2

204. When a train arriving at a railway platform approaches a person standing on the platform, the noise produced by the engine increases. This phenomenon is governed by

A. Kundt's Rule

B. Law of Tension

C. Law of Mass

D. Doppler's Effect

205. What is the fundamental frequency of a sonometer wire 20 cm long?

$T = 20$, $m = 5.2 \times 10^{-3}$ kg m^{-1}

A. 160 Hz B. 155 Hz

C. 225 Hz D. 250 Hz

206. Plane waves are incident on a concave reflector. The reflected waves will be
A. plane
B. circular
C. parabolic
D. None of the above

207. Antinodes are the points of
A. minimum displacement
B. maximum displacement
C. nil displacement
D. None of the above

208. For a sound wave in air, the vibrations of the particles of a medium
A. are parallel to the direction of propagation
B. are perpendicular to the direction of propagation
C. may either be parallel or perpendicular to the direction of propagation
D. None of the above

209. For sound waves in air, the vibration are
A. electromagnetic
B. longitudinal
C. transverse
D. None of the above

210. If two vibrating systems are in rasonance, then
A. their amplitudes are equal
B. their frequencies are equal
C. their temperature are equal
D. their intensities are equal

211. If the temperature of a room is 30°C, what will be the velocity of sound?
A. 350 ms^{-1} B. 333 ms^{-1}
C. 380 ms^{-1} D. 300 ms^{-1}

212. How many nodes and antinodes are there in a tuning fork?
A. 6 B. 5
C. 3 D. 4

213. Two waves of amplitudes a_1 and a_2 interface. The maximum amplitude will be
A. $a_1 a_2$ B. $a_1 + a_2$
C. $\frac{a_1}{a_2}$ D. $\frac{a_2}{a_1}$

214. When a wave of sound enters our ears and produces the sensation of sound, then this sensation persists for
A. 0.3 second B. 0.1 second
C. 0.42 second D. 0.52 second

215. In which type of waves, there is no flow of energy?
A. Longitudinal
B. Transverse
C. Progressive
D. Stationary

216. The distance between two consecutive compressions is
A. 2λ B. 3λ
C. 4λ D. λ

217. The longer the length of the prong iof a tuning fork is the frequency of vibration produced.
A. lower
B. higher
C. same
D. cannot be predicted

218. What is interference?
A. Two waves of different amplitudes travel in the same direction
B. Two waves of same amplitude travel in opposite directions
C. Two waves of different amplitudes travel in opposite directions
D. None of the above

219. The distance between two nearest troughs of a wave is called
A. time period B. trough bar

C. wavelength D. trough tide

220. The phenomenon of echo of sound waves is due to
A. reflection
B. interference
C. diffraction
D. all of the above

221. The musical interval between two tone is determined by
A. the actual difference of their frequencies
B. the difference of square roots of their frequencies
C. the ratio of their frequencies
D. the ratio of square of their frequencies

222. Velocity of sound in a medium is
A. independent of its density
B. inversely proportional to its density
C. directly proportional to its density
D. inversely proportional to the square root of its density

223. Can two persons hear each other's voice on the moon?
A. Yes! Easily
B. No! There is no conducting medium for sound waves
C. May be! Depends upon the pitch of the sound waves
D. Insufficient information to predict

224. What is the audible range of sound?
A. 0-200 Hz
B. 0-20,000 Hz
C. 0-2000 Hz
D. 300 to 2000 Hz

225. Which one of the following has the longest wavelength?
A. Radio waves
B. Sound waves
C. X-rays
D. Infrared ray

226. The sum of potential energy and kinetic energy of a string is
A. directly proportional to the square of the amplitude
B. directly proportional to the square of the frequency
C. inversely proportional to the square of the frequency
D. None of the above

227. In order to hear an echo of a sound wave, the minimum distance between the sound producing body and the reflecting surface should be
A. 20 m B. 17.5 m
C. 21.6 m D. 24.0 m

228. A broadcasting station is sending wavesof frequency 71×10^4 Hz. What is the wavelength? (Given, velocity of waves = $8 \times 10^8\ ms^{-1}$.)
A. 423.5 m B. 425 m
C. 425 m D. 430 m

229. Which one of the following mirrors can form a virtual image?
A. Concave Mirror
B. Convex mirror
C. Both (A) and (B)
D. None of (A) and (B)

230. A person is suffering from myopia. What type of lens should be used by him to rectify his vision?
A. A cylindrical lens
B. A convex lens
C. A concave lens
D. None of the above

231. When a ray of light goes from a denser medium to a rarer medium, then the angle of refraction goes on
A. increasing

B. decreasing
C. no change takes place
D. insufficient information to predict

232. Which one of the following waves has the lowest wavelength?
A. Heat radiations
B. X-rays
C. Light radiations
D. Sound waves

233. The critical angle for glass is 45°. What is the refractive index of glass?
A. 1.32 B. 1.41
C. 1.2 D. 1.25

234. Why does a diamond shine so brightly?
A. Due to refraction
B. Due to total internal reflection
C. Due to reflection
D. None of the above

235. Which one of the following colours suffers maximum deviation after dispersion through a prism?
A. Green B. Red
C. Yellow D. Violet

236. Two plane mirrors are inclined at angles of 30°, 40°, 50° and 60°, turn by turn. At which angle of the mirrors, there would be the maximum number of images?
A. At 30° B. At 40°
C. At 50° D. At 60°

237. If in the case of a convex lens, the objective is at infinity, then the nature of the image is
A. real, diminished and inverted
B. real and highly diminished
C. vertical and dminished
D. None of the above

238. The power of a telescope to see the two objects distinctly is called its
A. dispersive power
B. magnifying power
C. resolving power
D. None of the above

239. What is the unit of power of a lens?
A. Candela B. Dioptre
C. Metre D. Lux

240. A ray of light is incident on a plane mirror at an angle of 60°. If the mirror is rotated by an angle of 10°, what is the new angle of reflection?
A. 60° B. 80°
C. 40° D. 100°

241. Which one of the following mirrors is free from spherical abberration?
A. Convex
B. Concave
C. Parabolic
D. None of the above

242. If $f = \frac{R}{2}$, then this relationship indicates that the mirror is
A. convex B. parabolic
C. plane D. convex

243. A concave mirror is a part of a sphere of radius 36 cm. At what distance should an object be placed so that we get a real image magnified three times that of the size of the object?
A. 0.4 m B. 0.44 m
C. 0.43 m D. 0.49 m

244. A person can see clearly up to 3 metres. What shoud be the power of the lens in his spectacles so that he could see clearly up to 12 metres.
A. 0.25 D B. – 0.25 D
C. 0.5 D D. – 0.75 D

245. Which one of the following represents Lambert's cosine law?

A. $I = \frac{L\cos\theta}{r}$

B. $I = \frac{L\cos^2\theta}{r^2}$

C. $I = \frac{L\cos\theta}{r^2}$

D. None of the above

246. The critical angle of a liquid in 30°. Find its refractive index.

A. 3.1 B. 2.3

C. 2.5 D. 2.0

247. Why the rainbow is formed after rains?

A. The tiny water molecules act as slabs

B. The tiny water molecules act as prisms

C. The tiny water molecules act as convex lenses

D. None of the above

248. Which type of mirror (reflector) is used in headlights of cars?

A. Convex

B. Concave

C. Either (A) or (B)

D. None (A) or (B)

249. When reflection takes place from a spherical mirror, positions of the object and its image are known as

A. poles

B. conjugate foci

C. focal lengths

D. None of the above

250. The focal lengths of the objective and the eye-piece of an astronomical telescope are 60 cm an 10 cm, respectively. Its magnifying power is

A. 6 B. $\frac{1}{6}$

C. 60 D. $\frac{1}{60}$

251. Cylindrical lenses are used to cure the following optic disease.

A. Myopia

B. Hypermetropia

C. Astigmatism

D. Presbyopia

252. Presbyopia is an eye defect in which, a person can see

A. nearer objects clearly

B. distant objects clearly

C. both distant and nearer objects clearly

D. None of the above

253. Why does the illusion of mirage occur?

A. Light gets reflected from the sandy surface

B. Refractive index of air continuously drecreases with height

C. Refractive index of air continuously increases with height

D. None of the above

254. Light waves are similar in nature to

A. Gamma Rays

B. X-Rays

C. Cathode Rays

D. None of the above

255. Which one of the following is more monochromatic ?

A. Laser beam

B. White light

C. Sodium light

D. Mercury light

256. The velocity of light in diamond, glass and water decreases in the following order.

A. Diamond > Water > Glass

B. Water > Glass > Diamond

C. Diamond = Glass = Diamond
D. None of the above

257. Critical angle for the passage of light from glass to air is minimum in value for
A. green rays B. yellow rays
C. violet rays D. red rays

258. If there were no atmosphere on the earth, duration of daylight on the earrth would
A. increase
B. decrease
C. remain the same
D. depends upon the weather

259. The dispersive power of a prism depends upon
A. the material of the prism
B. the angle of the prism
C. the size of the prism
D. None of the above

260. A beam of monochromatic light is passing from one medium to another. Which one of the following quantities does not change?
A. Amplitude B. Velocity
C. Frequency D. Wavelength

261. Monochromatic light of wavelength 600 mm is incident from air on a glass surface whose refractive index is 1.5. The wavelength of the refracted light is
A. 200 mm B. 400 mm
C. 600 mm D. 900 mm

262. The refractive index of glass is 1.5. What is the speed of light in glass, if speed of light in vacuum $= 3 \times 10^8$ ms^{-1}?
A. 2×10^8 ms^{-1}
B. 2.8×10^8 ms^{-1}
C. 3.2×10^8 ms^{-1}
D. None of the above

263. A convex lens of focal length 1 metre is placed in contact with another concave lens of equal focal length. What is the focal length of the new lens so formed?
A. + 1 m
B. + 2 m
C. Infinity
D. None of the above

264. A coin is dropped in water of refractive index $\frac{4}{3}$. The real depth of the coin in 28 cm. The coin would be apparently appear to be at a depth of
A. 14 cm B. 21 cm
C. 24 cm D. 20 cm

265. The totally dark part of the shadow is known as
A. umbra
B. penumbra
C. eclipse
D. None of the above

266. A parallel beam of light having intensity I_0 passes through two thin parallel ordinary glass sheets normally. The intensity of light after the transmission will be nearly
A. I_0 B. $0.96\ I_0$
C. $0.92\ I_0$ D. $0.81\ I_0$

267. The human eye can see both nearly and distant objects clearly. The reason is that
A. the muscles connected to the eye lens can adjust their focus
B. the retina can change position
C. the least distance of distinct human vision is 25 cm
D. the iris and the eyelids are responsible for regulation of light

268. A piece of cloth is red in colour.

It is viewed in yellow light. What would be the colour of the cloth before our eyes?

A. Red B. Orange
C. Yellow D. Black

269. If a glass rod is put in a beaker containing colourless liquid, the glass rod seems to disappear. It is so because

A. the liquid and the glass have the some colour
B. the liquid and the glass have the same density
C. the liquid and the glass have the same refractive index
D. None of the above

270. Light travels through a glass plate of thickness *t* and refractive index *n*. If *c* is the velocity of light in vacuum, the time taken to travel through this thickness is

A. $\frac{t}{nc}$ B. *mc*
C. $\frac{nt}{c}$ D. $\frac{tc}{n}$

271. When a glass slab of RI = 1.7 is placed on a cross marked on a sheet of paper, it appears to be raised by 1.2 cm. The thickness of the glass slab is

A. 2.90 cm B. 2.914 cm
C. 2.814 cm D. 2.8 cm

272. A man is standing between two plane mirrors inclined at an angle to 60°. The number of images that he will be able to see is

A. 4 B. 5
C. 6 D. 3

273. A drive is inside the pond while the Sun is setting. The angle to the horizon at which he sees the Sun setting is

A. 0°C B. Nearly 31°
C. 49° D. 90°

274. Total internal reflection cannot take place when a ray passes from

A. glass to air
B. air to glass
C. glass to water
D. water to air

275. When a plane mirror is rotated through a certain angle, the reflected ray turns through double the angle. The size of the image

A. is doubled
B. becomes infinite
C. ishalved
D. remains the same

276. In a compound microscope, the nature of final image is

A. virtual, inverted, magnified
B. real, inverted, diminished
C. virtual, inverted, diminished
D. real, inverted, magnified

277. If the angle of incidence is equal to the critical angle, the angle of refraction will be

A. 0° B. 45°
C. 90° D. 180°

278. If refractive index of glass is 1.5 and the velocity of light in a vacuum is 3×10^8 ms^{-1}, the time taken by light for travelling a distance of 300 m in glass will be

A. 1.5×10^{-5} s
B. 1.6×10^{-5} s
C. 1.5×10^{-7} s
D. 1.5×10^{-6} s

279. The magnetic field due to a magnetic dipole of magnetic moment M at a point on the axis of the dipole and at a distance *d* from it is given by

A. $\frac{2M}{d^2}$ B. $\frac{M}{d^2}$

C. Md^3 D. $2Md^2$

280. A steel wire of length L has a magnetic moment M. It is then bent into a semicircular arc. The new magnetic moment is

A. $M\pi$ B. $\frac{M}{\pi}$

C. ML D. $\frac{M}{L}$

281. The angle of dip is the angle

A. between the magnetic meridian and the geographical meridian

B. between the direction of earth's magnetic field and the horizontal direction

C. between the vertical component of earth's magnetic field and magnetic meridian

D. None of the above

282. If the pole strength as well as the distance between the two magnetic poles is doubled, the force between them

A. reduces by one-half

B. remains unchanged

C. increases two times

D. increases four times

283. What is the value of 1 wbm^{-2}?

A. 10^4 gauss B. 10^{-4} gauss

C. 10^{-3} gauss D. 100 gauss

284. The magnetic field produced by electrons in atoms and molecules is

A. due to their spin motions

B. due to their orbital motions

C. due to both of their spin and orbital motions

D. neither due to their spin motions nor due to their orbital motions

285. What is angle between geographical and magnetic meridian known as?

A. Angle of magnetic dip

B. Angle of declination

C. Angle of deflection

D. None of the above

286. At the centre of a magnetic bar, the magnetism is

A. maximum

B. minimum

C. zero

D. cannot be predicted

287. If a metal is weakely repelled by a magnet, then the metal is expected to be

A. non-magnetic

B. paramagnetic

C. diamagnetic

D. ferromagnetic

288. The vertical plane, which passes through the magnetic axis of a freely suspended magnet, is known as

A. magnetic moment

B. magnetic length

C. magnetic axis

D. magnetic meridian

289. For protecting a sensitive equipment from external magnetic field, it should be

A. placed inside an iron box

B. wrapped with insulated material around it and current passed through it

C. surrounded with fine copper gauge

D. None of the above

290. If a bar magnet gets broken up into two parts as shown in figure below, the polarity of end A, B, C

and D will be

A. A, C-North Poles; B, D-South Poles
B. A, B-North Poles; C, D-South Poles
C. A, B, C-North Poles; D-South Pole
D. A-North Pole; D-South Pole. Polarity of B and C cannot be determined

291. The magnet attracts both ends of a rod of magnetic substance (but not magnetised) due to the phenomenon of
A. electric field
B. magnetic induction
C. polarisation
D. None of the above

292. The conductivity of a magnetic substance for the lines of force with respect to air is called
A. magnetic permeability
B. magnetic induction
C. magnetic flux density
D. None of the above

293. A magnet can be demagnetised by
A. hammering a magnet
B. putting it in water
C. cooling it
D. putting it in contact with iron

294. The magnetic flux is expressed in
A. Oersted B. Gauss
C. Weber D. Lux

295. Magnetic storms are due to
A. the rotation of the earth around its axis
B. the revolution of the earth around the sun
C. the sun sports
D. None of the above

296. The force acting on a current carrying conductor placed in a magnetic field depends upon
A. the strength of the current
B. the strength of the magnetic field
C. the length of the conductor
D. All of the above

297. If a charged particle moves in a magnetic field, the direction of the force on the charge is given by
A. Fleming's Left Hand Rule
B. Maxwell's Rule
C. Fleming's Right Hand Rule
D. None of the above

298. The line, which joins the North Pole and the South Pole of a magnet, is called its
A. Magnetic Meridian
B. Magnetic Axis
C. Magnetic Flux
D. None of the above

299. The effective length of a bar magnet is ....its geometrical length
A. one-sixth B. five-fourth
C. two-third D. three-fourth

300. What is the approximate magnetic field at the centre of a circular coil of radius 4 cm when a current of 0.5 A is flowing through it?
A. 7.85×10^{-7} tesla per A-m
B. 7.84×10^{-6} tesla per A-m
C. 7.8×10^{-5} tesla per A-m
D. 7.85×10^{-4} tesla per A-m

301. In the relationship $B = \frac{2\mu_0 r}{\pi I}$, what is μ_0?
A. Permeability
B. magnetic intensity
C. Susceptibility
D. Magnetic moment

302. At the magnetic poles, the angle of dip is equal to

A. 180° B. 90°
C. 120° D. 0°

303. What is Curic point?

A. A point on the equator where there is no magnetic moment
B. A temperature above which, all ferromagnetic substances lose their magnetism
C. A temperature at which all the ferromagnetic substances become diamagnetic
D. None of the above

304. In the phenomenon of magnetic hysterisis

A. the magnetic flux density lags behind the external field strength
B. the magnetic flux density is ahead of the external field strength
C. the magnetic flux density does not vary
D. All of the above

305. What are basic ingredients of ALNICO?

A. Aluminium, Copper, Tin
B. Copper, Tin, Cobalt
C. Aluminium, Nickel, Copper
D. The composition can vary

306. Which one of the following is a diamagnetic substance?

A. Platinum B. Aluminium
C. Copper D. Nickel

307. "The susceptibility of some paramagnetic substances is inversely proportional to the thermodynamic temperature." This statement is also known as

A. Curie's Law
B. Kundt's Rule
C. Faraday's Law
D. Lenze's Law

308. In which product, would you find the application of magnets?

A. AC Motor
B. Dynamo
C. Steam locomotive
D. Loudspeaker

309. This permeability of a diamagnetic material is

A. less than one
B. greater than one
C. equal to one
D. difficult to determine

310. Which one of the following cannot be magnetised?

A. Iron B. Cobalt
C. Nickel D. Mica

311. Which one of the following does not show the property of hysterisis?

A. AC Transformer
B. AC Current
C. AC Motor
D. AC Fan

312. In the formula $F = \frac{1}{\mu} \frac{m_1 \times m_2}{d^2}$, what is the value of μ for air?

A. 2 B. 1
C. $\frac{1}{2}$ D. 2.3

313. The vertical commponent of the total intensity of earth's magnetic field is equal to

A. $H \cos\theta$ B. $H \cot\theta$
C. $H \tan\theta$ D. $(H \tan\theta)^2$

314. If a bar magnet is suspended in the air, what would be the angle made by its axis with the axis of rotation of the earth?

A. 87° B. 17°
C. 73° D. 60°

315. What is the amount of force on a moving charge in a magnetic field?

A. $B = Fqv\sin\theta$

B. $B = Fqv\sin^2\theta$

C. $F = Bqv\sin\theta$

D. $F = \dfrac{Bqv}{\sin\theta}$

316. The magnetic lines of force inside a bar magnet flow

A. from North Pole to South Pole

B. from South Pole to North Pole

C. sometimes from North Pole and at other time from South Pole

D. Cannot be predicted

317. What is the permeability of vacuum?

A. $4\pi\times10^{-7}$ TmA^{-1}

B. $4\pi\times10^{7}$ TmA

C. $2\pi\times10^{-7}$ TmA

D. $2\pi\times10^{-7}$ TmA

318. Two parallel currents, flowing in the same direction

A. repel one another

B. attract one another

C. do not exert any force on one another

D. None of the above

319. A geyser of 2.5 kW is connected to a battery of 220 V. An iron of 1.5 kW is also connected to the battery. To prevent any failure of the equipment the fuse wire must have a current rating of

A. $\dfrac{400}{22}$ A B. $\dfrac{4000}{22}$ A

C. 400 A D. 22 A

320. In the process of electroplating, the object to be coated is used as

A. cathode

B. anode

C. cathode or anode, which depends upon the material to be electroplated

D. None of the above

321. Two parallel wires carry currents in opposite directions. They will

A. attract each other

B. repel each other

C. neither attract nor repel

D. Cannot be predicted

322. Five identical resistance coils are connected in a circuit, as shown in the figure below. The resistance measured between A and B is found to be 1Ω. The individual coils must have a resistance of

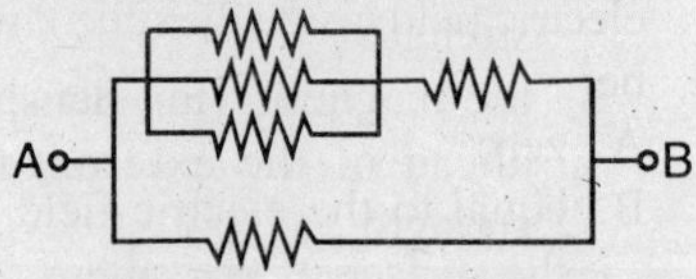

A. $\dfrac{7}{3}\Omega$ B. $\dfrac{4}{7}\Omega$

C. $\dfrac{7}{4}\Omega$ D. 7Ω

323. When the temperature of a metal is raised, its conductance

A. increases

B. decreases

C. reamains the same

D. None of the above

324. What value must be resistance R_1 have in order that the resistance between terminal A and B shall be R?

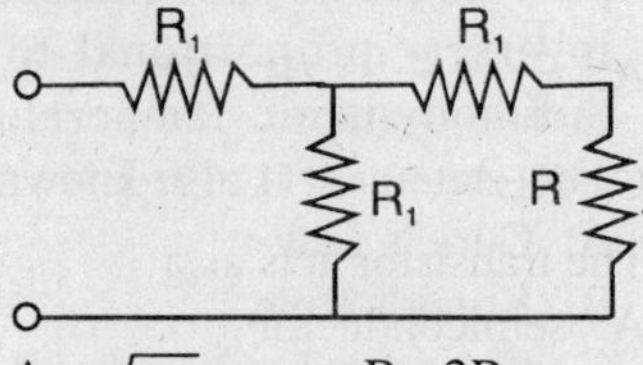

A. $\sqrt{3}R$ B. 2R

C. $\frac{R}{\sqrt{3}}$ D. $\frac{R}{2}$

325. Which device is used to step up or step down AC power?

A. Resistivity
B. Melting point
C. Transformer
D. DC generator

326. The safety fuse is able to protect the electrical devices because it has a low

A. resistivity
B. melting point
C. conductivity
D. None of the above

327. A hollow sphere of copper has been given positive charge. The electric field inside the sphere will be

A. zero
B. equal to the electric field on the surface of the sphere
C. less than the electric field on the surface of the sphere
D. greater than the electric field on the surface of the sphere

328. A battery is used for charging on air-filled capacitor and is removed when the capacitor is fully charged. Some mica sheets are now inserted between the two plates of the capacitor. If E is the energy of the capacitor and the dielectric constant of mica sheets is K, then energy stored in mica capacitor would be

A. $\frac{E}{K}$ B. KE

C. KE^2 D. $\sqrt{KE}$

329. The transistor acts as a

A. semiconductor
B. rectifier
C. thermionic value
D. insulator

330. Two lamps, one of 100 W and other of 50 W rating, are connected in series with a 220 V AC supply. What is the power consumed by the circuit?

A. 100 W B. 180 W
C. 150 W D. 200 W

331. The force acting on a charge is given by

A. $\vec{F} = \vec{E}q$

B. $\vec{F} = \frac{\vec{E}}{q}$

C. $\vec{F}q = \frac{1}{\vec{E}}$

D. None of the above

332. When the capacitors C_1 and C_2 are in parallel, their joint capacitance is equal to

A. $\frac{1}{C_1} + \frac{1}{C_2}$ B. C_1C_2

C. $C_1 + C_2$ D. $\sqrt{C_1 + C_2}$

333. Power in single phase circuit is equal to

A. $P = \sqrt{3}\ VI \cos\theta$

B. $P = \sqrt{3}\ VI$

C. $P = VI \cos\theta$

D. $P = VI$

334. What is the electrolyte is used in a voltaic cell?

A. Dilute HCl
B. Dilute H_2SO_4
C. DIlute HNO_3
D. Concentrated H_2SO_4

335. What is one watt equal to?

A. $1\ Js^{-1}$ B. $1\ ergs^{-1}$
C. $100\ Js^{-1}$ D. 746 HP

336. A body has a negative charge of 1

coulomb. That means it has

A. lost one electron

B. gained one electron

C. lost 6.25×10^8 electrons

D. gained 6.25×10^8 electrons

337. According to Coulombs's law, what are the units of the constant of proportionality (K_0)?

A. N - m C^{-2} B. N - m^2 C^{-2}

C. N - m C D. N - m^2

338. Two 30 μF capacitors are joined in parallel. Then this combination is joined with the 30 μF capacitors in series. The effective capacitance will be

A. 30 μF B. 12 μF

C. 32 μF D. 10 μF

339. The commonly used material used in heating appliances is Nichrome, which is an alloy of

A. Nickel and Lead

B. Nickel and Chromium

C. Lead and Chromium

D. Nickel, Lead and Chromium

340. A current of 4 A, from 250 V source, flows through an electric iron for one hour. The energy consumed is

A. 2 kWh B. 4 kWh

C. 1 Wh D. 1 kWh

341. If the length and cross-section of a wire are doubled, then

A. its resistance will increase four times

B. its resistance will decrease four times

C. its resistance will increase two times

D. its resistance will remain unchanged

342. The potential at a point due to an electric charge varies

A. directly as distance from the charge

B. inversely as the distance from the charge

C. inversely as the square of the distance from the charge

D. directly as the square of the distance from the charge

343. The charge of a hollow sphere would reside on its

A. inner surface

B. outer surface

C. partly on its inner surface and partly on its outer surface

D. None of the above

344. What is the unit of conductance?

A. Ohm B. Henry

C. Mho D. Oersted

345. What type of material is used for making the cores of transfoermers?

A. CRGO B. Steel

C. Chromium D. Copper

346. If silver is the best conductor of electricity, then why is it not used in transformers and motor?

A. Difficult of obtain

B. Difficult to draw in wires

C. Costly

D. All of the above

347. In which of the following materials, will there be a reduction in electrical resistance with the rise of its temeprature?

A. Nichrome B. Platinum

C. Selenium D. Gold

348. Flux is changed from 20 T to 10 T in 1 second. Then, the magnitude of induced emf is

A. 20 V B. 40 V

C. 30 V D. 10 V

349. An electric appliance operates on 120 V. Then, the best produced by each electron that passes through it is

A. 1.9×10^{-10} J

B. 1.92×10^{-17} J

C. 1.2×10^{-12} J

D. None of the above

350. The amount of copper deposited when a current of 1 A is passed for one second is

A. 3.29×10^{-8} kg

B. 3.3×10^{-2} kg

C. 3.29×10^{-4} kg

D. 3.3×10^{-6} kg

351. Which one of the following graphs has been drawn according to Ohm's Law?

A. 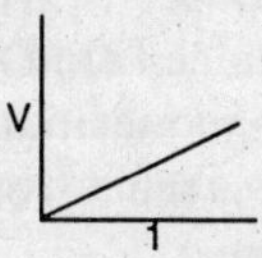

B. 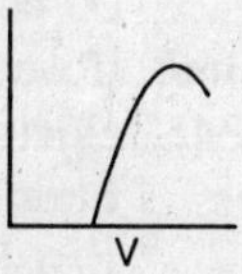

C. 

D. 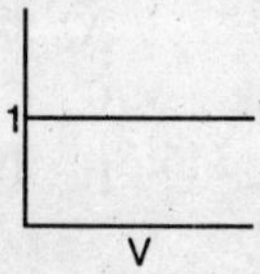

352. When the cells are connected in parallel, the total emf will be equal to

A. sum of emf values of all the cells

B. the emf of a single cell

C. half the sum of emf values of all the cells

D. None of the above

353. An electric line of force is

A. a curve, the tangent to which at any point gives the direction of electric field at the point

B. the path along which a unit positive charge would move, if free to do so, when place in the electric field

C. Both of the above

D. None of the above

354. Twenty-four cells of internal resistance 1Ω each and emf of 1.5 V each are used to send a maximum current through an external resistance of 3Ω. How should the cells be connected?

A. In parallel

B. In series

C. Six in series and rest in parallel

D. None of the above

355. The electron in a hydrogen atom revolves around the proton at the speed of 1.18×10^6 ms^{-1} in an orbit of radius 0.53 Å. What is the equivalent current?

A. Nearly 10^{-2} A

B. Nearly 10^{-4} A

C. Nearly 10^{-6} A

D. Nearly 10^{-3} A

356. Find the equvalent resistant between A and B

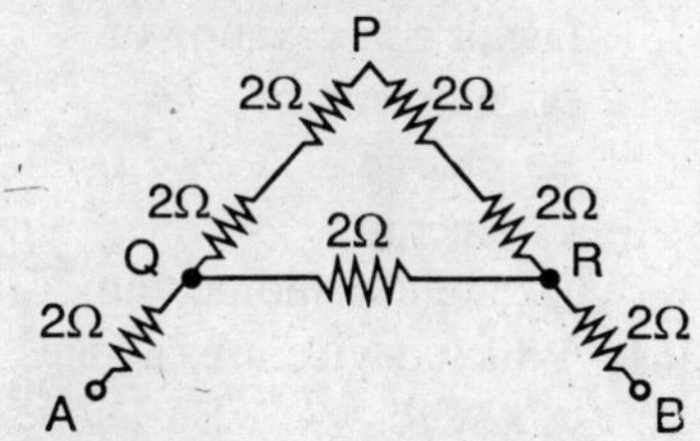

A. $\frac{1}{2}\Omega$ B. $\frac{3}{2}\Omega$

C. $\frac{4}{3}\Omega$ D. $\frac{3}{4}\Omega$

357. Two bulbs (of 100 W and 200 W) have been connected in parallel and 220 V AC fed to them from common point. Which bulb will have more current flowing through it?

A. Bulb of 100 W

B. Bulb of 200 W

D. Cannot be predicted

358. The capacitance of a parallel plate condenser

A. varies linearly with the common area of the plates
B. varies directly with the separation of the plates
C. depends upon the metal used to make the plates
D. varies inversely with the dielectric constant of the material between the plates

359. Two point charges of $+4\,\mu C$ and $+8\,\mu C$, respectively repel each other with a force of 10 N. If a charge of $-4\,\mu C$, is given to each one of these charges, the new forces of attraction is

A. 10 N   B. 20 N
C. zero   D. 4 N

360. Lenz's law is a consequence of the law of conservation of

A. momentum
B. charge
C. energy
D. angular momentum

361. Which device uses a gate?

A. SCR   B. Diode
C. Rectifier   D. Convertor

362. An elector with a charge *e* moves with a constant velocity v parallel to the lines of force of a uniform magnetic field B. The force experienced by the electron is

A. Bev   B. Be/v
C. zero   D. Bev^2

363. The magnetic field due to a current is given by

A. $\Delta B = k\dfrac{I\Delta/\sin\theta}{r^2}$

B. $\Delta B = k\dfrac{I\sin\theta}{r^2}$

C. $\Delta B = \dfrac{k.A/I\cos\theta}{r}$

D. None of the above

364. Heat generated by electrical current in a resistance circuit is expressed in

A. IR   B. IR^2
C. I^{2}R   D. $\sqrt{IR}$

365. The magnetic field produced in a solenoid coil and depend inversely upon

A. current
B. length
C. number of turns
D. constant K

366. If we combine Faraday's Law of electromagnetic induction and Lenz's law, then arrive at

A. $E = n\dfrac{d\phi}{dt}$

B. $E = -n\dfrac{d\phi}{dt}$

C. $nE = \dfrac{d^2\phi}{dt^2}$

D. None of the above

367. The potential difference between any two phases of a three phase-phase line of 440 V AC is

A. 410 V AC
B. 230 V AC
C. 440 V AC
D. Cannot be determined

368. In which device would you find the commutator?

A. AC generator
B. DC generator
C. AC motor
D. All of the above

369. The main source of energy of the sun is

A. fusion of heavy nuclei
B. fusion of light nuclei

C. fission of light nuclei

D. fission of heavy nuclei

370. A nuclear reactor is a device, which produces energy with the help of

A. nuclear fusion

B. nuclear fission

C. thermonuclear reaction

D. simple chemical reactions

371. If the chain reaction of the nuclear power plant were not controlled, the power plant would

A. become defunct

B. explode like a nuclear bomb

C. generate pollution due to leakage of chemicals

D. continue to work

372. Which material is used to produce nuclear power?

A. Platinum

B. Radium

C. Uranium

D. All of the above

373. The uranium series starts from ^{235}U and ends at

A. ^{207}Sn B. ^{207}Pb

C. ^{207}Pt D. ^{207}PO

374. The best method to find the life of an old wooden log is to

A. use carbon dating technique

B. count the number of rings in its stem

C. burn the piece of wood and find the amount of carbon in it

D. use either of the aforesaid methods

375. N_0 is the original number of nucleii of a radioactive metal. At the end of half-life, the number nucleii would remain equal to

A. N_0 B. $2N_0$

C. $\frac{N_0}{2}$ D. N_0^2

376. For which atomic number onwards, the radioactivity of elements is inherent?

A. $Z > 80$ B. $Z > 82$

C. $Z > 114$ D. $Z > 90$

377. Which was the first nuclear research reactor of India?

A. Apsara B. Zerlina

C. Purnima D. Kaiga

378. What is the approximate energy level of thermal neutrons?

A. 10 eV B. 1 eV

C. 0.1 eV D. 100 eV

379. What is the mass of an electron?

A. 9.1×10^{-22} g

B. 9.1×10^{-28} g

C. 9.1×10^{-26} g

D. 9.1×10^{-24} g

380. What is the charge on a proton?

A. 1.5×10^{-22} coulomb

B. 1.6×10^{-24} coulomb

C. 1.6×10^{-22} coulomb

D. 1.6×10^{-20} coulomb

381. Nucleii with the same atomic number are called

A. isomers B. isotopes

C. isotones D. isobars

382. If the atom is to be electrically neutral, then

A. protons = neutrons

B. neutrons = electrons

C. protons = electrons

D. protons + electrons = neutrons

383. In the nuclear reaction $^{10}_{52}Te + ^{1}_{2}H \rightarrow ^{131}_{53}I + X$ the particle X is

A. beta particle

B. neutron

C. alpha particle

D deutron

384. When an electron and a positron combine, a new particle emerges.

It is a/an

A. alpha particle

B. positron

C. neutron

D. None of the above

385. What is molecular weight of heavy water?

A. 20 B. 22

C. 18 D. 16

386. $^{9}_{4}Be$ is bombarded by an α particle. One of the byproducts is $^{12}_{6}C$. Which one is the other byproduct?

A. neutron

B. positron

C. a proton

D. None of the above

387. Which one of the following isotopes is used to detect brain tumours?

A. ^{12}C B. ^{24}Na

C. ^{10}Te D. ^{14}C

388. Why is heavy water used in nuclear power reactors?

A. To stop the flow of electrons

B. To regulate the speed of fast neutrons

C. To absorb the harmful radiations of the nuclear chain reaction

D. None of the above

389. What is the value of 1 eV?

A. 1.602×10^{-17} J

B. 1.602×10^{-20} J

C. 1.602×10^{-12} J

D. 1.602×10^{-10} J

390. What is the difference between the parts of a diode and those of a triode?

A. The anode missing in diode

B. The cathode missing in triode

C. The grid missing in triode

D. None of the above

391. The amu is equal to

A. one-twelth of the mass of an atom of ^{12}C

B. 1.66×10^{-14} kg

C. mass of an atom of ^{14}C

D. None of the above

392. Which one of the following represents 1 Curie (Ci)?

A. 3.7×10^{8} dis per second

B. 3.7×10^{10} dis per second

C. 3.8×10^{8} dis per second

D. 3.8×10^{10} dis per second

393. Which one of the following has the maximum value of penetration?

A. α - rays

B. β - rays

C. γ - rays

D. All have equal penetration

394. Which one of the following has the maximum speed?

A. α - rays

B. β - rays

C. γ - rays

D. All have equal speed

395. What is the half-life of U^{235}_{92}?

A. 4.5×10^{9} years

B. 4.2×10^{3} years

C. 4.5×10^{11} years

D. 4.2×10^{9} years

396. Which particle initiates a chain reaction in uranium?

A. Newton

B. α - particle

C. Electron

D. Any one of the above

397. Why fusion reaction is difficult to achieve?

A. Light nucleii are not available

B. High values of temperature and pressure required to

initiate the reaction

C. Heavy nucleii are not available

D. None of the above

398. What is the number of protons in an atom of U_{92}^{235}?

A. 239 B. 142

C. 92 D. 98

399. The diameter of a nucleus is of the order of

A. 10^{-15} m B. 10^{-2} m

C. 10^{-21} m D. 10^{-19} m

400. What is the full from of LASER?

A. Light Amplified by Strict Emission Radio

B. Light Amplification by Stimulated Emission of Radiation

C. Lighter Amplitude due to Struck Emission of Radio-isotopes

D. None of the above

401. What is the number of electrons in 1 cubic cm of copper?

A. 8.4×10^{22} B. 2.4×10^{12}

C. 4.2×10^{11} D. 8.4×10^{9}

402. The penetrating power of X-rays increases with

A. increase in frequency

B. increase in intensity

C. increase in voltage

D. increase in pressure inside the X-ray tube

403. If an electron in an atom jumps from a higher orbit to a lower orbit, it

A. gains energy

B. loses energy

C. neither gains nor loses energy

D. depends upon the chemical reaction

404. In which place out of the following, heavy water is not being manufactured?

A. Nangal B. Tuticorin

C. Managuru D. Vizag

405. Berilium rods are used in nuclear power plan to

A. generate neutrons

B. absorb extra neutrons

C. initiate the chain reaction

D. generate particles

406. Which element can be enriched to produce nuclear fission material?

A. Thorium B. Iridium

C. Silicon D. Lead

407. The energy required to ionise an atom of Hydrogen is equal to

A. 13.6 eV B. 18.2 eV

C. 12.4 eV D. 12.6 eV

408. The threshold wavelength of sodium metal is 6800Å. The work function of the metal is

A. 1.29 eV B. 1.82 eV

C. 12.4 eV D. 1.72 eV

409. The junction of a NPN transistor is rich in

A. electrons

B. holes

C. neutrons

D. None of the above

410. What is *n*-type doping?

A. Mixing impurities in a semiconductor to generate free electrons

B. Mixing impurities in a semiconductor to generate free holes

C. Changing the composition of a semiconductor by adding metal to it

D. Changing the thermal properties of a semiconductor

411. A transistor can be used effectively as a/an

A. diode

B. amplifier
C. rectifier
D. All of the above

412. Balmer series, in the emission spectrum of a hydrogen atom, lie in the
A. ultra-violet region
B. violet region
C. infrared region
D. visible region

413. The first spectral line of sodium atom is 5890 Å. The first excitation potential of sodium is
A. 2.1 V B. 4.2 V
C. 2.9 V D. 3.4 V

414. According to Bohr's model of hydrogen atom
A. the angular velocity of the electron is quantised
B. the linear velocity of the electron is quantised
C. the angular momentum of the electron is quantised
D. the linear momentum of the electron is quantised

415. The work function of a metallic surface is 4 eV. The threshold wavelength is
A. 2956 Å B. 3056 Å
C. 3112 Å D. 3012 Å

416. Which one of the following cannot be released naturally by a radioactive element?
A. α-rays B. β-rays
C. X-rays D. γ-rays

417. After the completion of four half-lives, the percentage of original radioactive substance left is
A. 6.0% B. 6.25%
C. 7.25% D. 8.25%

418. Plutonium for the atom bomb is produced from
A. U^{239}
B. U^{235}
C. U^{238}
D. None of the above

419. An astronaut orbiting the earth in a circular orbit 120 kms above the surface of the earth, gently drops a spoon out of the spaceship. The spoon will
A. leave the spaceship and head towards the space
B. move along with the spaceship
C. fall back on the earth
D. head towards the moon and start revolving around it

420. The planet which has no satellite is
A. Neptune B. Mercury
C. Jupiter D. Mars

421. The red shift suggest that the universe is
A. revolving B. oscillating
C. contracting D. expanding

422. The planet closest to sun is
A. Earth B. Jupiter
C. Mercury D. Pluto

423. Why a rocket is made to lose its fuel cylinders while it moves up in space?
A. It must lose weight
B. It must remove fuel cylinders elese it could catch fire
C. It must become streamlined
D. All of the above

424. Atmosphere is present on earth due to
A. gravitational attraction
B. air
C. cloud
D. surface tension

425. The cause of weightlessness in spaceships revolving round the

earth is
A. zero gravity
B. acceleration
C. inertia
D. surface tension

426. The escape velocity of a body projected from the surface of a planet does not depend upon
A. the mass of the earth
B. the direction of projection of the body
C. the mass of the planet
D. radius of the planet

427. The weight of a body of mass *m* when taken to the bottom of deep mine
A. decrease
B. increase
C. its mass increases
D. its mass decreases

428. Newton's law of gravitation is valid for
A. all bodies
B. only heavenly bodies
C. only for small bodies
D. only for charged bodies

429. The intensity of gravitation field inside a hollow sphere is
A. maximum B. minimum
C. zero D. constant

430. The escape velocity from moon is
A. 11.2 km/s B. 42 km/s
C. 2.41 km/s D. 7.2 km/s

ANSWERS

1	**2**	**3**	**4**	**5**	**6**	**7**	**8**	**9**	**10**
B	D	C	D	C	C	A	C	B	C
11	**12**	**13**	**14**	**15**	**16**	**17**	**18**	**19**	**20**
C	B	A	C	C	D	A	C	D	A
21	**22**	**23**	**24**	**25**	**26**	**27**	**28**	**29**	**30**
B	C	B	B	B	B	B	D	B	C
31	**32**	**33**	**34**	**35**	**36**	**37**	**38**	**39**	**40**
A	C	C	D	D	A	C	B	D	D
41	**42**	**43**	**44**	**45**	**46**	**47**	**48**	**49**	**50**
C	C	D	D	B	A	C	B	B	A
51	**52**	**53**	**54**	**55**	**56**	**57**	**58**	**59**	**60**
C	B	C	C	B	B	A	C	A	A
61	**62**	**63**	**64**	**65**	**66**	**67**	**68**	**69**	**70**
C	A	D	B	D	C	B	D	C	C
71	**72**	**73**	**74**	**75**	**76**	**77**	**78**	**79**	**80**
D	A	A	D	A	B	A	D	D	B
81	**82**	**83**	**84**	**85**	**86**	**87**	**88**	**89**	**90**
B	B	D	B	B	B	C	D	A	B
91	**92**	**93**	**94**	**95**	**96**	**97**	**98**	**99**	**100**
D	C	B	C	D	A	C	A	A	A
101	**102**	**103**	**104**	**105**	**106**	**107**	**108**	**109**	**110**
C	B	D	A	D	C	B	B	B	C

111	112	113	114	115	116	117	118	119	120
B	B	A	C	B	A	B	B	C	B
121	**122**	**123**	**124**	**125**	**126**	**127**	**128**	**129**	**130**
B	D	B	D	D	C	C	A	A	D
131	**132**	**133**	**134**	**135**	**136**	**137**	**138**	**139**	**140**
C	B	D	B	C	A	B	C	B	B
141	**142**	**143**	**144**	**145**	**146**	**147**	**148**	**149**	**150**
C	A	C	D	A	C	A	D	B	B
151	**152**	**153**	**154**	**155**	**156**	**157**	**158**	**159**	**160**
D	B	C	C	D	B	C	D	C	C
161	**162**	**163**	**164**	**165**	**166**	**167**	**168**	**169**	**170**
B	D	C	D	A	B	D	C	A	A
171	**172**	**173**	**174**	**175**	**176**	**177**	**178**	**179**	**180**
A	A	A	B	B	B	C	C	C	A
181	**182**	**183**	**184**	**185**	**186**	**187**	**188**	**189**	**190**
B	B	C	B	D	A	C	A	B	D
191	**192**	**193**	**194**	**195**	**196**	**197**	**198**	**199**	**200**
C	C	D	C	B	C	A	A	A	C
201	**202**	**203**	**204**	**205**	**206**	**207**	**208**	**209**	**210**
C	D	B	D	C	B	B	A	B	B
211	**212**	**213**	**214**	**215**	**216**	**217**	**218**	**219**	**220**
A	D	D	B	A	D	D	C	C	A
221	**222**	**223**	**224**	**225**	**226**	**227**	**228**	**229**	**230**
C	D	B	C	B	A	B	B	A	D
231	**232**	**233**	**234**	**235**	**236**	**237**	**238**	**239**	**240**
A	B	B	B	C	B	B	B	B	B
241	**242**	**243**	**244**	**245**	**246**	**247**	**248**	**249**	**250**
B	A	A	B	C	D	B	B	B	A
251	**252**	**253**	**254**	**255**	**256**	**257**	**258**	**259**	**260**
C	A	C	A	B	B	C	B	A	C
261	**262**	**263**	**264**	**265**	**266**	**267**	**268**	**269**	**270**
B	A	C	B	A	A	A	B	C	C
271	**272**	**273**	**274**	**275**	**276**	**277**	**278**	**279**	**280**
B	B	C	B	D	A	D	D	A	B
281	**282**	**283**	**284**	**285**	**286**	**287**	**288**	**289**	**290**
B	B	B	C	B	C	C	D	A	A
291	**292**	**293**	**294**	**295**	**296**	**297**	**298**	**299**	**300**
B	A	A	C	C	D	A	B	B	A
301	**302**	**303**	**304**	**305**	**306**	**307**	**308**	**309**	**310**
A	B	B	A	C	C	A	C	A	D
311	**312**	**313**	**314**	**315**	**316**	**317**	**318**	**319**	**320**
B	B	C	B	C	B	A	C	A	A
321	**322**	**323**	**324**	**325**	**326**	**327**	**328**	**329**	**330**
B	C	B	C	C	B	A	B	B	C

331	332	333	334	335	336	337	338	339	340
A	C	C	B	A	D	B	B	B	D
341	342	343	344	345	346	347	348	349	350
D	B	B	C	A	C	C	D	B	A
351	352	353	354	355	356	357	358	359	360
B	B	D	B	B	B	B	A	C	C
361	362	363	364	365	366	367	368	369	370
A	C	A	C	A	B	C	B	B	B
371	372	373	374	375	376	377	378	379	380
B	C	B	A	C	B	A	C	B	C
381	382	383	384	385	386	387	388	389	390
B	C	B	A	A	B	B	B	A	C
391	392	393	394	395	396	397	398	399	400
A	B	C	C	A	A	B	C	A	B
401	402	403	404	405	406	407	408	409	410
A	A	B	D	B	A	A	B	B	A
411	412	413	414	415	416	417	418	419	420
B	D	A	C	A	C	B	C	B	B
421	422	423	424	425	426	427	428	429	430
D	C	A	A	B	B	A	A	C	C

EXPLANATORY ANSWERS

80. $\vec{v}_1 = 5,\ \vec{v}_2 = 5,\ t = 10\text{ s}$

$$\therefore\ \vec{a} = \frac{\vec{v}_2 - \vec{v}_1}{t}$$

In magnitude, $|a| = \dfrac{|\vec{v}_2| - |\vec{v}_1|}{t}$

$$= \frac{5-5}{10} = \frac{0}{10} = 0$$

82. $v = ?$ $\quad u = 0$

$g = 10$ $\quad x = 90\text{ m}$

$v^2 - u^2 = 2gs$

$v^2 - 0 = 2 \times 10 \times 90$

$v^2 = 1800$

$v = 30\sqrt{2}\text{ m}$

83. $T = 2\pi\sqrt{\dfrac{l}{g}}$

If length is increased, T will increase. If g is decreased, T will increase. At high altitude or in the earth, the value of g would vary and so T would also vary.

Hence, correct choice is (D).

86. $u = 19.6\text{ ms}^{-1}$

$v = 0$

$v^2 - u^2 = 2gs$

$0 - (19.6)^2 = 2 \times 9.8 \times s$

$$s = \frac{-19.6 \times 19.6}{2 \times 9.8}$$

$= -19.6\text{ m}$

Negative sign indicates movement of the ball against gravity

$\Rightarrow s = 19.6\text{ m}$

88. $KE_1 = \dfrac{1}{2}mv^2$

Now, $v = 3v$

$KE_2 = \dfrac{1}{2}m(3v)^2 = 27\dfrac{1}{2}m(v)^2$

$$\Rightarrow \frac{KE_2}{KE_1} = \frac{(27)\frac{1}{2}m(v)^2}{\frac{1}{2}mv^2} = 27$$

90.

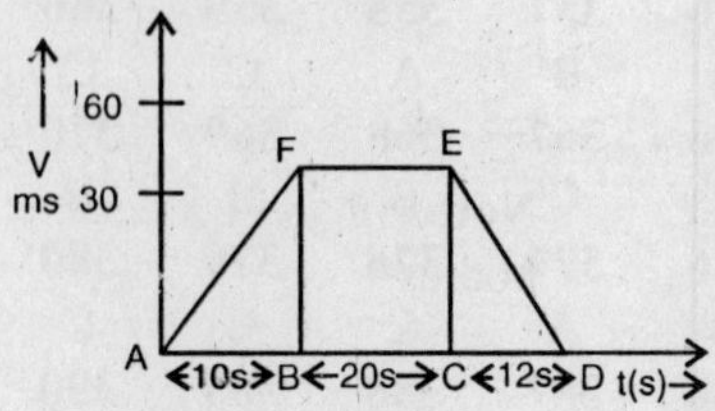

Average velocity

$$= \frac{\text{Distance travelled}}{\text{Time taken}}$$

$$= \frac{\text{Area of } \Delta\text{ABF}}{\text{Time taken}} = \frac{\frac{1}{2}\text{AB} \times \text{BF}}{\text{AB}}$$

$$= \frac{\frac{1}{2} \times 10 \times 60}{10} = \frac{300}{10} = 30 \text{ ms}^{-1}$$

91. Distance travelled during time interval BC
= Area of rectangle of BCEF
= BC × CF
= 20 × 60 = 1200 m

922. Total distance travelled
= Area of ΔABF + Area of rectangle BCEF + Area of ΔDCE

$$= \frac{1}{2}\text{AB} \times \text{BF} + \text{BC} \times \text{CE} + \frac{1}{2} \times \text{DC} \times \text{CE}$$

$$= \frac{1}{2}10 \times 60 + 20 \times 60 + \frac{1}{2} \times 12 \times 60$$

= 300 + 1200 + 360 = 1860 m

93. Uniform acceleration during

$$\text{AB} = \frac{v_2 - v_1}{t_2 - t_1}$$

$v_2 = 60$
$v_1 = 0$
$t_2 = 10$
$t_1 = 0$

⇒ Uniform acceleration

$$= \frac{60 - 0}{10 - 0} = 6 \text{ ms}^{-2}$$

94. Linear momentu = p

$$p = \text{mv} \Rightarrow v = \frac{p}{m}$$

$$\text{KE} = \frac{1}{2}mv^2$$

$$= \frac{1}{2}m \times \left(\frac{p}{m}\right)^2$$

$$= \frac{1}{2}m \times \frac{p^2}{m^2} = \frac{1}{2}\frac{p^2}{m}$$

95. $m = 6$ kg
$v = 10 \text{ ms}^{-1}$
$r = 3$

The force that must act to maintain the motion

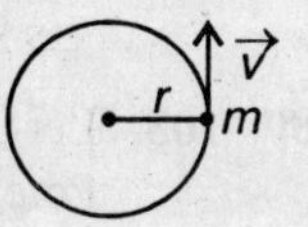

$$= \frac{mv^2}{r} = \frac{6 \times (10)^2}{3}$$

$$= \frac{6 \times 100}{3} = 200 \text{ N}$$

96. In SHM, Total Energy $= \frac{1}{2}ma^2w^2$

97. $m = 1$ kg, $u = 5 \text{ ms}^{-1}$
$v = 0, t = 5$ s

$v = u + at$
$0 = 5 + a \times 5$
$-5 = 5a$
$a = -1 \text{ ms}^{-2}$

Negative sign of a shows retardation.

Now F = ma
$= 1 \times 1 = 1$ N

98. $\vec{OP} = 100 \text{ km hr}^{-1}$

$\angle$MOP = 30°

$$\frac{\overrightarrow{OM}}{\overrightarrow{OP}} = \cos 30°$$

$$\overrightarrow{OM} = \overrightarrow{OP} \cos 30°$$

$$(OM) = |OP| \cos 30°$$

$$= 100 \times \frac{\sqrt{3}}{2} = 50 \times 1.732$$

$$= 86.600 = 86.6 \text{ km hr}^{-1}$$

99. $\vec{V} = 4\vec{i} + 3\vec{j}$

$$\Rightarrow 3\vec{V} = 3(4\vec{i} + 3\vec{j})$$

$$= 3.4\vec{i} + 3.3\vec{j} = 12\vec{i} + 9\vec{j}$$

100. $\vec{V} = 6\vec{i} + 8\vec{j} \Rightarrow x = 6, y = 8$

$$\tan\theta = \frac{y}{x} = \frac{8}{6} = \frac{4}{3}$$

$$\Rightarrow \theta = \tan^{-1}\frac{4}{3}$$

103. Let mass of water = m gms

Potential Energy of water

$= mgh = m \times 980 \times 8400$

The potential energy of water at the top would be converted into kinetic energy as the water comes down.

$\Rightarrow$ KE of water $= m \times 980 \times 8400$

Half of the KE is converted into heat.

$$\Rightarrow \text{Heat} = \frac{1}{2} m \times 980 \times 84006$$

$$= m \times 0.098$$

Now Heat $= ms\theta$

where s = specific heat, θ = temp. rise

$$\Rightarrow ms\theta = m \times 0.098$$

$$s\theta = 0.098$$

$s = 1$ for water

$$\Rightarrow \theta = 0.098°C$$

104. Force $= \frac{mv^2}{r}$

$$\Rightarrow F_1 = \frac{mv^2}{r_1}; \; F_2 = \frac{mv^2}{r_2}$$

Note : m and v are same for both bodies.

$$\frac{F_1}{F_2} = \frac{\frac{mv^2}{r_1}}{\frac{mv^2}{r_2}} = \frac{r_1}{r_2}$$

But $r_2 = 2r_1$

$$\Rightarrow \frac{F_1}{F_2} = \frac{r_1}{2r_2} = \frac{1}{2} \Rightarrow 2F_1 = F_2$$

Hence the outer body would experience greater force.

108. $F = ma = MLT^{-2}$

109. Moment of inertia of a circular disc is given by $= \frac{1}{2}MR^2$

Let, mass of first disc = m

So, mass of second disc = $2m$

Let, diameter of first disc = 2D

So, diameter of second disc = D

But $D = \frac{R}{2}$

Radius of first disc = 2D

$$= \frac{2R}{2} = R$$

Radius of second disc = 2D

$$= \frac{R}{2}$$

where R = radius

$$\Rightarrow \frac{MI_1}{MI_2} = \frac{\frac{1}{2}MR^2}{\frac{1}{2}MR^2}$$

$$= \frac{\frac{1}{2}m \times R^2}{\frac{1}{2}2m \times \left(\frac{R}{2}\right)^2}$$

$$= \frac{R^2}{2\frac{R^2}{4}} = \frac{1}{\frac{1}{2}} = \frac{2}{1}$$

$\Rightarrow MI_1 : MI_2 = 2 : 1$

110. $T = 2\pi\sqrt{\frac{l}{g}}$

Case I: $T_1 = 2 = 2\pi\sqrt{\frac{l}{g}}$ $T_1 = 2s$

$\Rightarrow \sqrt{\frac{l}{g}} = \frac{1}{\pi}$

Case II:

New Length = $4l$

$\Rightarrow T_2 = 2\pi\sqrt{\frac{4l}{g}} = 2\pi\, 2\sqrt{\frac{l}{g}}$

Put $\sqrt{\frac{l}{g}} = \frac{1}{\pi}$ in this eqn.

$T_2 = 2\pi \times 2 \times \frac{1}{\pi} = 4$ seconds

114. $v = a + \frac{b}{t} + ct^2$

v is the velocity of the body. So all the elements of the RHS would also have the units of velocity, i.e. ms^{-1}. The term $\frac{b}{t}$ has time as in its denominator.

$$LT^{-1} = \frac{b}{t}$$

$$LT^{-1} = b \times T^{-1}$$

$\Rightarrow \quad b = L$

$\Rightarrow b$ would have units of length. In the answer set, the units are in metres.

$\Rightarrow b$ would be in metres.

132. $Q = ms\theta$

$$560 = \frac{20}{1000} \times s \times (50 - 15)$$

$$= \frac{1}{50} \times s \times 35$$

$$s = \frac{560 \times 50}{35} = 800 \text{ J kg}^{-1} \text{ K}^{-1}$$

143. $\frac{F - 32}{180} = \frac{273}{100}$

$$F = \frac{180 \times 273}{100} + 32 = -459.4 \text{ °C}$$

135. Thermal capacity = $m \times s$

Let v be the volume of mercury.

$\Rightarrow$ Volume of copper = v

Thermal capacity of mercury $= v \times 13.6 \times 0.046$ calories

Thermal capacity of copper $= v \times d \times 0.092$

$\Rightarrow v \times d \times 0.092 = v \times 13.6 \times 0.046$

d = Density of copper

$$= \frac{13.6 \times 0.046}{0.092} = 6.8 \text{ gm per cc}$$

137. The gas equation is

$$\frac{P_1V_1}{T_1} = \frac{P_2V_2}{T_2}$$

$P_1 = 4$ atm.

$V_1 = V_1 = V$

$T_1 = 27 + 273 = 300°K$

$T_2 = 54 + 273 = 327°K$

$$\frac{4 \times V}{300} = \frac{P_2 \times V}{327}$$

$$P_2 = \frac{4 \times 327}{300} = 4.36 \text{ atm.}$$

150. There are four stages in the process.

(*a*) Heat needed to bring 10 gm of ice at – 8°C to 0°C = 10 × 0.5 × 8 = 40 cals

(*b*) Heat required to meet 10 gm

of ice at 0°C into water at 0°C
= 10 × 80 = 800 cals

(*c*) Heat required to convert 10 gm of water at 0°C into 10 gm of water at 100°C
= 10 × 100 = 1000 cals

(*d*) Heat required to convert 10 gm of water at 100°C to 10 gm of steam at 100°C
= 10 × 540 = 5400 cals

Total heat required
= 40 + 800 + 1000 + 5400 = 7240 cals

158. Thickness= d = 2 gm
High Temp.= T_1 = 20°C
Low Temp. = T_2 = 0°C
k= 0.0004 and t = 1 sec
Total area of six sides
= 2 [100 × 60 + 100 × 60 + 100 × 60] = 31,200 m²

$$Q = \frac{kAt(T_1 - T_2)}{d}$$

Here, Q is the rate of melting of ice.

$$Q = \frac{0.0004 \times 31200 \times 20}{2}$$

= 124.8 cals

So, amount of ice melting per second

$$= \frac{1248}{80} = 1.56 \text{ g}$$

179. $v = n\lambda$

where v = velocity of wave
n = frequency of wave
λ = wavelength of wave

$n_1 : n_2 : : 4 : 5$

$v = n_1\lambda_1 = 4\lambda_1$

$v = n_2\lambda_2 = 5\lambda_2$

As the velocity of the wave remains the same

$\Rightarrow \quad 4\lambda_1 = 5\lambda_2$

$$\frac{\lambda_1}{\lambda_2} = \frac{5}{4}$$

$\lambda_1 : \lambda_2 :: 5 : 4$

183. λ = 1 m
v = 320 ms^{-1}

$$n = \frac{v}{\lambda} = \frac{320}{1} = 320 \text{ Hz}$$

190. v = 332 ms^{-1}
l = 0.2 m

$$n = \frac{v}{2l} = \frac{332}{2 \times 0.2} = 830$$

196. The velocity of sound does not vary with variation in pressure.

244.

$$\frac{1}{u} + \frac{1}{v} = \frac{1}{f}$$

$$\frac{1}{1200} + \frac{1}{-300} = \frac{1}{f}$$ (u and v are in cms)

f = – 400 cm

$$\text{Power} = \frac{100}{f} \text{ in cm}$$

$$= \frac{100}{-400} = -0.25 \text{ Dioptre}$$

246. $$u = \frac{1}{\sin C} = \frac{1}{\sin 30°} = \frac{1}{1/2} = 2.00$$

261. RI of medium

$$= \frac{\text{Wavelength in vacuum/air}}{\text{Wavelength in medium}}$$

$$\lambda_{medium} = \frac{\lambda_{air}}{\mu} = \frac{600}{1.5} = 400 \text{ mm}$$

262. $$l_{\mu_g} = \frac{\text{Velocity of light in vacuum}}{\text{Velocity of light in glass}}$$

Now l_{μ_g} = 1.5

Velocity of light in vacuum
$= 3 \times 10^8$ ms^{-1}

$$\Rightarrow 1.5 = \frac{3 \times 10^5}{\text{Velocity of light in glass}}$$

$\Rightarrow$ Velocity of light in glass

$$= \frac{3 \times 10^8}{1.5} = 2 \times 10^8 \text{ ms}^{-1}$$

263. $\frac{1}{F} = \frac{1}{f_1} + \frac{1}{f_2}$

Here $f_1 = -f_2$

$$\Rightarrow \frac{1}{F} = \frac{1}{f_1} - \frac{1}{f_2} = 0$$

$$\Rightarrow F = \frac{1}{0} = \infty$$

264. Refractive Index

$$= \frac{\text{Real Depth}}{\text{Apparent Depth}}$$

Apparent Depth

$$= \frac{\text{Real Depth}}{\text{Refractive Index}}$$

$$= \frac{28}{4/3} = \frac{28 \times 3}{4} = 21 \text{ cm}$$

271.

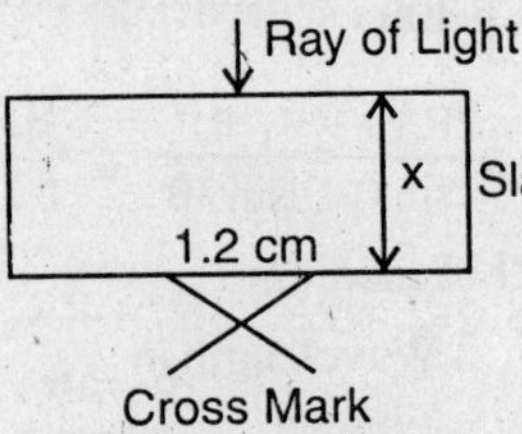

Let thickness of slab = x cm
The cross mark seems to be raised by = 1.2 cm
Real Depth = x
Apparent Depth = $x - 12$
Refractive Index = 1.7

$$\text{RI} = \frac{\text{Real Depth}}{\text{Apparent Depth}}$$

$$1.7 = \frac{x}{(x-12)}$$

$(1.7)(x - 12) = x$
$1.7x - 2.04 = x$
$1.7x - x = 2.04$
$0.7x = 2.04$

$$x = \frac{204}{70}$$

$= 2.914$ cm

319. Rating of geyser = 2.5 kW
Rating of iron= 1.5 kW
Total load= 4.0 kW
So, Total load = 4000 W
The battery must develop this power to run two applicances
$\Rightarrow$ Battery power required = 4000 W

$P = VI$
$4000 = 220 \times I$

$$I = \frac{4000}{200} = \frac{400}{22} \text{ A}$$

Hence, the rating of the fuse will be $\frac{400}{22}$ A

322.

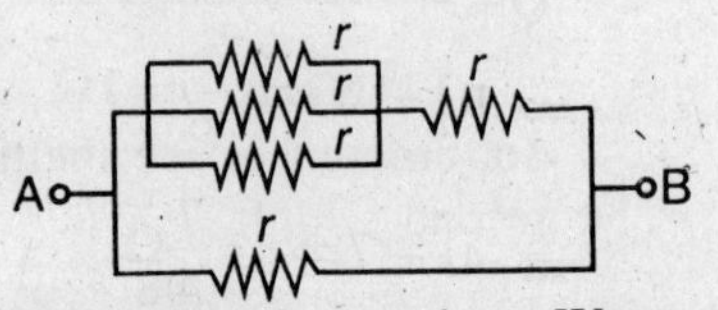

Let each resistance be r. We can add resistance in parallel branch as follows :

$$\frac{1}{R} = \frac{1}{r} + \frac{1}{r} + \frac{1}{r} = \frac{3}{r} \Rightarrow R = \frac{r}{3}$$

This resistance can be added in series with the resistance r.

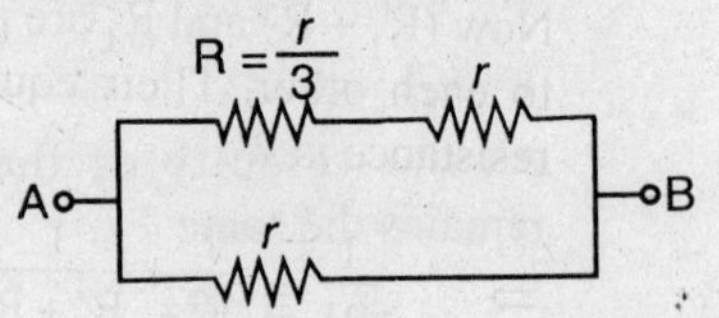

Resistance of upper branch

$= R_1 = R + r = \frac{r}{3} + r = \frac{4r}{3}$

$\Rightarrow R_1 = \frac{4r}{3}$

This resistance (R_1) is in parallel with resistance r. The equivalent resistance of these two is the total resistance across A and B.

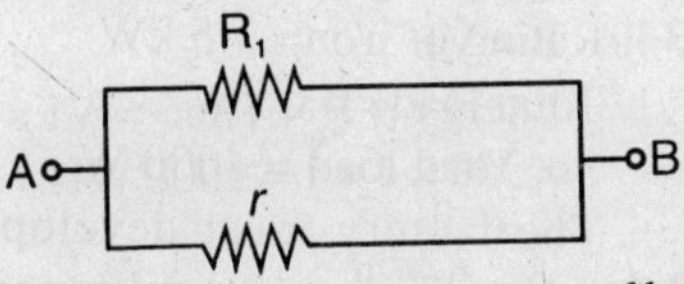

Resistance of two parallel resistors

$= \frac{1}{R_2} = \frac{1}{R_1} + \frac{1}{r} = \frac{1}{4r/3} + \frac{1}{r}$

$= \frac{3}{4r} + \frac{1}{r} = \frac{3+4}{4r} = \frac{7}{4}r$

$\Rightarrow R_2 = \frac{4}{7}r$

But R_2 is given as 1Ω.

$\Rightarrow R_2 = 1\Omega \Rightarrow \frac{4}{7}r = 1\Omega$

$\Rightarrow 4r = 7 \Rightarrow r = \frac{7}{4}\Omega$

324. The equivalent grant is

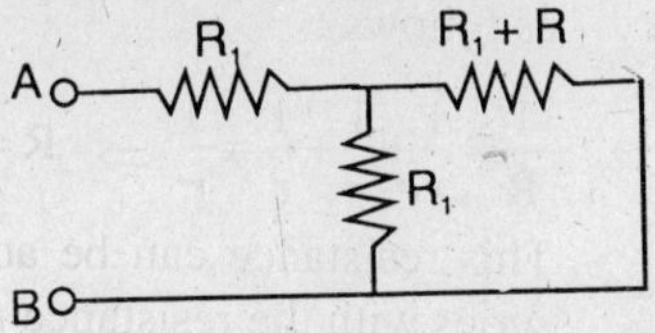

Now ($R_1 + R$) and R_1 are parallel to each other. Their equivalent resistance is R'.

$\Rightarrow \quad \frac{1}{R'} = \frac{1}{R'} + \frac{1}{R' + R}$

$= \frac{R_1 + R_1 + R}{(R_1 + R) R_1}$

$= \frac{2R_1 + R}{(R_1 + R) R_1}$

$\Rightarrow R' = \frac{(R_1 + R) R_1}{2R_1 + R}$

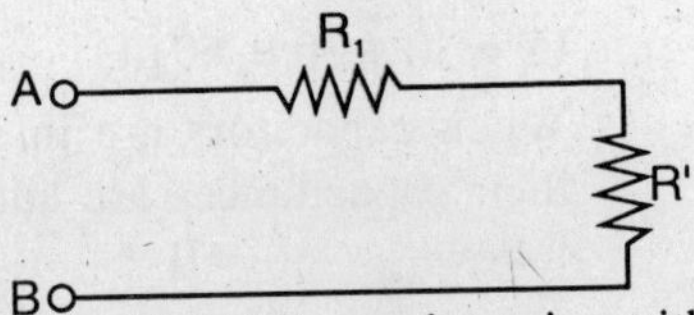

Now R' and R_1 are in series with each other. Their resistance (total) is R'' say.

$R'' = R_1 + R'$

$= R_1 + \frac{(R_1 + R) R_1}{2R_1 + R}$

$= \frac{2R_1^2 + RR_1 + (R_1 + R) R_1}{2R_1 + R}$

$= \frac{2R_1^2 + RR_1 + R_1^2 + RR_1}{2R_1 + R}$

But R'' = R
(as per the statement)

$\Rightarrow \frac{2R_1^2 + RR_1 + R_1^2 + RR_1}{2R_1 + R} = R$

$\Rightarrow 2R_1^2 + RR_1 + R_1^2 + RR_1 = R(2R_1 + R)$

$\Rightarrow 2R_1^2 + RR_1 + R_1^2 + RR_1 = 2RR_1 + R^2$

$\Rightarrow 2RR_1 + 3R_1^2 = 2RR_1 + R^2$

$\Rightarrow 3R_1^2 = R^2$

$\Rightarrow 2R_1^2 = \frac{R^2}{3}$

$$\Rightarrow R_1 = \sqrt{\frac{R^2}{3}} = \frac{R}{\sqrt{3}}$$

338. 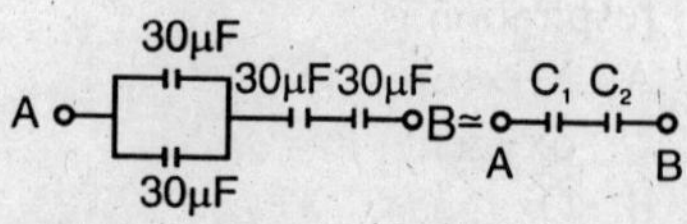

When capacitors are in parallel, their capacitances are added

$C_1 = 30 + 30 = 60\ \mu F$

When capacitors are in series, their capacitances are added as follows :

$$\frac{1}{C_2} = \frac{1}{30} + \frac{1}{30}$$

$$= \frac{1+1}{30} = \frac{2}{30} = \frac{1}{15}$$

$$\Rightarrow C_2 = 15\ \mu F$$

C_1 and C_2 have to added as follows to get the effective capacitance

$$\frac{1}{C} = \frac{1}{C_1} + \frac{1}{C_2} = \frac{1}{60} + \frac{1}{15}$$

$$= \frac{1+4}{60} = \frac{5}{60} \Rightarrow C = \frac{60}{5}$$

$$= 12\ \mu F$$

340. $P = VI$

Energy $= P \times \text{Time} = VI \times \text{Time}$
$= 250 \times 4 \times 1 = 1000\ \text{WH} = 1\ \text{kWh}$

365. $B = \frac{k2\pi nl}{I} \Rightarrow B = \frac{1}{I}$

367. The p.d. between phase would also remain 440 V.

368. The commutator is used to produce unidirectional DC current in a DC generator.

Chemistry

1. Which of the following is a synthetic polymer?
A. Neoprene B. Cellulose
C. Latex D. All of these

2. Which of the following is a form of natural calcium carbonate?
A. Malachite B. Marble
C. Magnox D. Oleum

3. Which of the following is not required for combustion of coal?
A. Oxygen
B. Fuel
C. Flame
D. All of the above

4. Which of the following elements has the greatest number of compounds?
A. Hydrogen B. Carbon
C. Oxygen D. Silicon

5. 'Dry ice' is the name given to
A. supercooled ice
B. solid carbon dioxide
C. solid ammonia
D. All of the above

6. Most favourable conditions for storing foodgrains are
A. low temperature and high humidity
B. high temperature and low humidity
C. high temperature and high humidity
D. low temperature and low humidity

7. Litmus paper is used for checking
A. purification of water
B. acidity/alkalinity of water
C. hardness of water
D. chlorine-content of water

8. The gas supplied to sea-divers for respiration is
A. Mixture of helium with oxygen
B. Oxygen
C. Helium
D. None of these

9. The rate of dillusion, is
A. faster in solids than in liquids and gases.
B. faster in gases than in liquids and solids.
C. faster in liquids than in solids and gases.
D. eqiual to solids, liquids and gases.

10. Which of the following substances is used, in the laboratory, for fast drying of netural gases?
A. Sodium phosphate
B. Phosphorous pentoxide
C. Sodium sulphate
D. Anhydrous calcium chloride

11. The equivalent weight of an acid is equal to
A. molecular weight *x* acidity
B. molecular weight *x* basicity
C. molecular weight/basicity
D. molecular weight/acidity

12. The pH of aquesous solution of sodium hydroxide is
A. 10 B. 12
C. 20 D. 24
E. 32

13. Wood charcoal is commonly prepared by the process of burning wood
A. in contact with air
B. in contact with pure pure

oxygen

C. out of contact with air

D. in contact with nitrogen and inert gas

14. An example of a compound containing both ionic and covalent bonds is

A. sodium oxide

B. sodium hydroxide

C. sodium chloride

D. carbon tetrachloride

15. The most reactive compound, for the electrophilic nitration, is

A. benzene

B. nitrobenzene

C. benzoic acid

D. toulene

16. Chemically, dry ice is

A. Ice formed from pure distilled water

B. Solid Carbon dioxide

C. Solid Sulphur dioxide

D. A mixture of ice and common salt

17. The position of an element in the Periodic Table is Class V and Period III. It atomic number is

A. 7 B. 13

C. 15 D. 25

18. The specific heat of a metal is 0.16 and its weight is 12. What is its atomic weight?

A. 40 B. 36

C. 3.3 D. 60

19. A conductor having the positive charge of 8.0×10^{-19} coulomb, will have

A. 5 electrons more

B. 5 electrons less

C. 8 electrons more

D. 8 electrons less

20. Two electric bulbs are connected with a source of constant voltage is parallel having the resistances in the ration 1 : 2. What will be the ratio of consumption of electric energy between the two bulbs?

A. 4 : 1 B. 2 : 1

C. 1 : 2 D. 1 : 4

21. The use of gypsum is recommended mainly in soils which are

A. alkaline

B. saline

C. water logged

D. acidic

22. A liquid of α coefficient of volume expansion is heated in a vessel of metal with $\frac{\alpha}{3}$ coefficient of linear expansion. The level of liquid in the vessel will

A. rise

B. fall

C. remain unchanged

D. Cannot be said

23. $BaCl_2 + H_2SO_4 \rightarrow BaSO_4 + 2HCl$ is a

A. Displacement reaction

B. Oxidation-Reduction reaction

C. combination reaction

D. Double Decomposition reaction

24. Which of the following ores is related with the extraction of aluminium?

A. Azurite B. Bauxite

C. Limonite D. Siderite

25. The nature of aqua solution of ammonium chloride is

A. Coloured B. Neutral

C. Acidic D. Alkaline

26. What is the chemical formula of water gas?

A. $C + H_2O$ B. $CO + H_2$

C. $CO_2 + H_2$ D. $N_2 + H_2$

27. The difference between isotopes of an element is due to the presence of a difference number of

A. protons B. neutrons
C. electrons D. photons

28. Which of the following will result in the oxidation of the halide ions?

A. Chlorine is added to hydrogen iodide.
B. Iodine is added to hydrochloride acid
C. Bromide is added to aquous sodium floride
D. Sodium chloride is added to aquous hydrochloric acid

29. While water (H_2O) is a liquid under ordinary conditions, hydrogen sulphide (H_2S) is gas despite higher molecular weight. This anomaly results from the fact that

A. sulphur atom is larger than oxygen atom.
B. sulphur is more electro negative than oxygen.
C. O—H bond is more polar than S—H bond
D. water is a neutral substance while hydrogen sulphide is weakly acidic.

30. The main difference between the procaryotic cell and eucaryotic cell is that in the procaryotic cell, there is no

A. cell wall.
B. internal membrane system
C. genetic system
D. nucleus with a nuclear membrane

31. The nitrogenous fertilizers with the highest percentage of nitrogen is

A. ammonium nitrate
B. urea
C. calcium nitrate
D. ammonium sulphate

32. Synthetic detergents have an advantage over soaps in this that

A. they do not form micelles when dissolved in water.
B. they are easily broken down by micro organisms present in water bodies.
C. they can be produced on a large scale.
D. they lather well even in hard waters.

33. Of the following, the metal described as a "strategic metal" is

A. Silicon B. Titanium
C. Uranium D. Germanium

34. In which of the following industries is mica used as a raw material?

A. electrical
B. iron and steel
C. toys
D. glass and pottery

35. Which one of the following forms is the basis of modern periodic table?

A. Atomic volume
B. Atomic number
C. Atomic mass
D. Atomic size
E. None of these

36. The substance widely employed as an inhalation anaesthetic is

A. Nitrous oxide
B. Nitrogen peroxide
C. Ammonia
D. Nitrogen

37. There are four gas jars containing O_2, CO_2, H_2 and N_2 respectively.

Which of the following tests would identify the four gases?

A. Inserting burning splinters into the jars
B. Inserting a piece of burning magnesium
C. Passing the glass through lime water
D. Dissolving the gas in water.

38. Natural rubber in made strong and bouncy by adding to it

A. sponge
B. sulphur
C. chlorine
D. sulphuric acid

39. Which of the following is employed as a lubricant?

A. Silica B. Diamond
C. Graphite D. Iron Oxide

40. Amalgams are alloys

A. that are highly coloured
B. that contain mercury as one of the constituents
C. that have great resitance to abrasion
D. that contain carbon

41. Which of the following types of glass is used in making lenses and prisms?

A. jena glass B. flint glass
C. soft glass D. pyrex glass

42. Of the following, the best way to put out a petrol fire is to use

A. water
B. soda-water fire exitinguisher
C. rags
D. carbon tetrachloride extinguisher

43. Of the following, the item with the greatest susceptibility to spontaneous heating is

A. kerosene B. candles
C. turpentine D. alcohol

44. Which of the following are fossil fuels?

A. Coal and petroleum
B. Petroleum and natural gas
C. Coal and natural gas
D. Coal, petroleum and natural gas

45. A common fluorescent tube contains

A. sodium vapour
B. argon at less pressure
C. mercury vapour at low pressure
D. mercuric oxide and neon

46. Of the following items, the one for which the most care should be taken to prevent moth damage is

A. woolen blankets
B. cotton clothes
C. synthetic textiles
D. canvas bags

47. Carbon tetrachloric can be used as

A. industrial solvent for fats and resins
B. fire extinguisher
C. dry cleaning agent
D. All the above purposes

48. Which of the following is not a natural fibre?

A. Flax B. Cotton
C. Rayon D. Silk

49. At what temperature will the hydrogen molecules escape from earth surface?

A. 10^4K B. 10^3K
C. 10^2K D. 10 K

50. Milk is an example of

A. Gel B. Suspension
C. Emulsion D. Foam

51. The substance most commonly used as a food preservative is

A. Sodium bicarbonate
B. Tartaric acid

C. Acetic acid
D. Benzoic acid

52. Gun powder consists of a mixture of
A. TNT and sand
B. Sulphur, sand and charcoal
C. Sulphur, nitre and charcoal
D. TNT and charcoal

53. Radio carbon dating is used to estimate the ages of
A. babies
B. fossils
C. rocks
D. ancient buldings

54. For the production of iron the raw material used is
A. limestone B. coke
C. petrol D. rubber

55. One gram of a gas occupies 0.16 litres at STP. The molecular weight of the gas is
A. 64 B. 140
C. 160 D. 224

56. The pH value value of an acidic buffer solution is 4.6. When the concentration of weak acid present in it is increased ten times, the p^{OH} of the solution will be
A. 4.6 B. 9.2
C. 10.4 D. 10.0

57. Which of the following compounds are responsible for acid rain
A. NO_2 B. SiO_2
C. SO_2 D. CO

58. Potassium nitrate is used in
A. Salt B. Fertiliser
C. Medicine D. Glass

59. Which among the following compounds possess molecules having both covalent and ionic bonds?
A. Sodium hydroxide
B. Sodium chloride
C. Carbon dioxide
D. Water (H_2O)

60. Cooking gas contains more than 90 per cent of
A. Helium
B. Sulphur dioxide
C. Hydrogen
D. Butane

61. In the preparation of Soap, the vegetable oil is subjected to
A. Catalytic hydrogenation
B. Alkaline hydrolysis
C. Aerial oxidation
D. Thermal decomposition

62. The nitrogen content of fertiliser urea is approximately
A. 19.5 per cent
B. 17 per cent
C. 20 per cent
D. 46 per cent

63. Soda water is saturated with which of the following gases?
A. Carbon-dioxide
B. Carbon monoxide
C. Ammonia
D. Sulphur

64. Which of the following minerals can be considered a type of coal?
A. Bauxite B. Chromite
C. Anthracite D. Haematite

65. Natural rubber is a polymer of
A. ethylene B. acetylene
C. isoprene D. acetylene

66. The acid present in lemons and organes is
A. acetic acid
B. hydrochloric acid
C. critic acid
D. oxalic acid

67. Which of the following is not a natural fibre?
A. Nylon B. Cellulose

C. Cotton D. Starch
E. None of these

68. Which of the following is a poisonous gas?
A. Carbon dioxide
B. Carbon monoxide
C. Nitrogen
D. All of these

69. Which of the following elements is essentially present in human blood?
A. Silicon B. Radon
C. Nickel D. Iron

70. Which of the element common to brass and bronze?
A. Copper B. Iron
C. Zinc D. Aluminium

71. Which of the following is used as an anti-rusting agent?
A. Lead oxide
B. Zinc oxide
C. Iron oxide
D. Copper oxide

72. Which of the following substances is used as invisible ink?
A. Ferrous sulphate
B. Nickel chloride
C. Cobalt chloride
D. All of the above

73. The pairs of colours which, when combined (mixed), give the effect of 'white', are called
A. complementary colours
B. secondary colours
C. primary colours
D. surface colours

74. During galvanization, the substance which is coated on the surface of iron to protect it from rusting is
A. galium B. aluminium
C. tin D. zinc

75. Diamond finds many industrial uses because of its hardness. The substance that is alterantively used in place of diamond is
A. quartz
B. silicon carbide
C. bauxite
D. graphite

76. The element common to bone and cement is
A. silicon
B. calcium
C. nitrogen
D. phosphorous

77. The raw material common to cement and glass is
A. soda B. rock
C. gypsum D. sand

78. Which of the following is themost abundant element in the universe?
A. Calcium B. Silicon
C. Hydrogen D. Helium

79. Which of the following elements is synthetic?
A. Argon B. Lauthanum
C. Californium D. Thalium

80. Water for drinking purpose can be purified by
A. chloronation
B. aeration
C. ultra-violet radiation
D. All of the above techniques

81. Which of the following allotropes of carbon is conductor of hbeat and electricity?
A. Wood Charcoal
B. Fuel Charcoal
C. Graphite
D. Diamond

82. Which of the following metals reacts with cold water?
A. Sodium B. Aluminium
C. Iron D. Copper

83. Which of the following metals is most tensile?

A. Copper B. Silver
C. Aluminium D. Gold

84. Gases are conductors of electricity at

A. high pressure
B. low pressure
C. low temperature
D. high temperature

85. The oxygen is accumulated on which of the following during electrolysis of water?

A. Anode
B. Cathode
C. Both electrodes
D. None of these

86. In the ordinary fire extinguisher, carbon dioxide is generated by the reaction of

A. Magnesite and dilute HCl
B. Sodium bicarbonate and dilute
C. Marble powder and dilute HCl
D. Limestone and dilute H_2SO_4

87. Which one of the following electronic configurations is NOT possible?

A. $1s^2$
B. $1s^2, 2s^2, 2p^6, 2d^{10}, 3s^2$
C. $1s^2, 2s^2, 2p^5$
D. $1s^2, 2s^2, 2p^6, 3s^1$

88. Which one of the following is a bio-fertiliser?

A. Spirogyra B. Agaricus
C. Fern D. Nostoc

89. The coded information for synthesizing a protein is carried from the nucleus to the ribosome in the form of

A. DNA B. *m*RNA
C. *r*RNA D. *t*RNA

90. Which one of the following is an example of redox reaction?

A. $CuSO_4 + Fe \rightarrow FeSO_4 + Cu$
B. $Ca(OH)_2 + 2HCl \rightarrow CaCl_2 + 2H_2O$
C. $CaO + 2HCl \rightarrow CaCl_2 + H_2O$
D. $CaCO \rightarrow CaO + CO_2$

91. The mixture of cement, sand and water is called

A. Canker B. Concrete
C. Mortar D. RCC

92. Which of the following chemicals is being investigated as an fueld alternative to gasoline?

A. Hydrochloric acid
B. Alcohols
C. Esters
D. Hydrocarbon

93. Which of the following statements is not correct about ionic compounds?

A. They are solids under ordinary conditions.
B. They conduct electricity in molten state.
C. They are insoluble in polar solvents.
D. They have high melting and boiling points.

94. The group number of an element (from groups 1 to 8) in the periodic table indicates

A. the valency with respect to hydrogen.
B. the number of electrons in the outermost orbit of the atom.
C. the chemical reactivity
D. the atomicity

95. When nitrogen and phosphorus combine with hydrogen

A. there occurs sharing of their electrons with hydrogen.

B. there occurs transference of electrons

C. there is sharing of electrons in the case of nitrogen but transference of electrons in the case of phosphorus.

D. There is transference of electrons in the case of phosphorus.

96. A charged polythene rod is held near a thin stream of water running from a tap. The water bends towards the rod. The best explanation for this observation is

A. water contains H^+ and OH^- ions

B. water molecules are held together by a weak electrical force

C. water molecules have more of one kind of charge than the other

D. a water molecule has an uneven distribution of change

97. Which one of the following substances burns to form an oxide which is gaseous at room temperature?

A. Hydrogen B. Magnesium
C. Sodium D. Sulphur

98. Which one of the following should be present for the bleaching action of chlorine?

A. Dry air B. Moisture
C. Sunlight D. Pure oxygen

99. The presence of a gas is increased by 50% at constant temperature. The fractional decrease in volume will approximately be

A. 66% B. 33%
C. 17% D. 8%

100. An electron and a proton are projected with same kinetic energy at right angles to a uniform magnetic field. The radius of trajectories in the magnetic field will be

A. greater in case of electron

B. greater in case of proton

C. same for both electrons and proton

D. zero for electron and infinite for proton

101. Nitrogen, phosphorous and potassium are essential for plant growth. They are known as

A. Micronutrients

B. Macronutrients

C. Trace Elements

D. None of these

102. When one gram ethane burns it produces x gram of CO_2 where x is

A. 0.293 B. 2.93
C. 3.66 D. 2.52

103. The compound used as refrigerant is

A. CF_2Cl_2 B. CCl_4
C. CF_4 D. CH_2F_2

104. Fat molecules are composed of

A. one molecule of glycerol and two molecules of fatty acids

B. two molecules of glycerol and one molecule of fatty acids

C. one molecule of glycerol and three molecules of fatty acids

D. one molecule of glycerol and one molecule of fatty acids

105. The total number of electrons in molecule of ethyne is

A. 8 B. 10
C. 12 D. 14

106. Which one of the following represents the electronic configuration of Al^{3+} ions?

A. $1s^2\ 2s^2\ 2p^6\ 3s^2\ 3p^5$

B. $1s^2\ 2s^2\ 2p^6\ 3s^2\ 3p^4$
C. $1s^2\ 2s^2\ 2p^6$
D. $1s^2\ s^2\ 2p^6\ 3s^1$

107. The atomic mass of gold is 197. The mass of 1.2×10^{23} atoms of gold would be
A. 1.2 g B. 16.4 g
C. 39.4 g D. 236.4 g

108. The elements W, X, Y and Z have atomic numbers 8, 9, 11 and 17 respectively. Which one of the following is not likely to exist?
A. Y_2W B. WX
C. YZ D. XZ

109. Aparent nucleus emits a β-particle to produce a daughter nucleus. The place of the daughter element with respect to parent element in periodic table will be
A. one place to the right
B. one place to the left
C. one place below in the same group
D. one place above in the same group

110. Which one of the following contains the same number of the atoms as is contained in 12 g of magnesium? (**Given :** Atomic Masses C = 12, Mg = 24, Ca = 40)
A. 12 g of Carbon
B. 20 g of Calcium
C. 24 g of Carbon
D. 40 g of Calcium

111. The atomic numbers of elements A, B, C and D are 7, 9, 10 and 11, respectively. Which one of the following pairs of elements will form ionic compounds?
A. A and B B. B and C
C. C and D D. B and D

112. Which one of the following fuels has the highest calorific value?
A. Natural Gas B. Coke
C. Coal D. Wood

113. A white solid has the following characteristics
melting point 450°C
boiling point 1390°C
does not conduct electricity when solid conducts electricity in a molten state.
The solid is probably a
A. metal element
B. non-metal element
C. compound of metal and non-metal
D. compound of two non-metals

114. The number of electrons, protons and neutrons in X^{3+}, obtained from the element X (atomic mass 27 and atomic number 13) will be respectively
A. 10, 13 and 14
B. 13, 13 and 17
C. 13, 16 and 14
D. 16, 13 and 14

115. Which one of the following extraction presses is used for obtaining zinc metal?
A. Electrolysis of its fused salt
B. Reduction with carbon monoxide
C. Reduction with carbon
D. Amalgamation

116. Which one of the following represents the use of Ca(OCl)Cl?
A. Bleaching agent
B. Dehydrating agent
C. Hardening agent for making
D. Reducing agent

117. Which one of the following substances is not used as a fertilizer?
A. Ammonium Sulphate

B. Potassium Nitrate
C. Calcium Superphosphate
D. Calcium Carbonate

118. Magnalium is an alloy containing
A. Magnesium, Iron
B. Aluminium, Lead
C. Magnesium, Aluminium
D. Magnesium, Zinc

119. When natural gas burns, heat is produced due to the formation of
A. C=O bonds only
B. O—H bonds only
C. C=O and O—H bonds both
D. C—H bonds only

120. Which one of the following is a synthetic rubber?
A. Neoprene
B. Ethylene
C. Chlorobutadiene
D. Isoprene

121. Azurite is the name for
A. $Cu(OH)_2, 2CuCO_3$
B. Cu_2O
C. $CuFeS_2$
D. $Cu(OH)_2, CuCO_3$

122. 'Calcium is more metallic than Bismuth'. The best experimental evidence to support this statement is
A. Calcium is harder and more rigid than Bismuth.
B. Calcium is farther to the left in the periodic table than Bismuth.
C. Calcium hydroxide is a stronger base than Bismuth hydroxide
D. Bismuth has more valence electrons than Calcium

123. The following tests were made to identify a gas
Lighted match stick : match stick went out and gas did not burn
Lime water : no change
Which one of the following gases could it be
A. Nitrogen
B. Oxygen
C. Carbon dioxide
D. Hydrogen

124. Which one of the following is the correct formula of the compound which is formed by the combination of the elements A and B whose atomic number are 9 and 12 respectively?
A. A_2B_7 B. A_2B
C. BA_2 D. B_7A_2

125. A pure substance melts at 113°C and does not conduct electricity in either the solid or the liquid state. The bonding in this substance is primarily
A. molecular B. covalent
C. metallic D. ionic

126. Which one of the following contain the same number of atoms?
A. 2 g of H_2 and 16 g of O_2
B. 2 g of H_2 and 8 g of O_2
C. 1 g of H_2 and 32 g of C_2
D. 2 g of H_2 and 32 g of C_2

127. The atomic weights of hydrogen oxygen and sulphur are 1, 16 and 32 respectively. The equivalent weight of sulphuric acid would be
A. 98 B. 96
C. 64 D. 49

128. Everyone in a group of students individually heated some potassium permanganate in a test tube. Each one of them measured the volume of the gas evolved and the change in mass. A graph plotted from their results is shown here

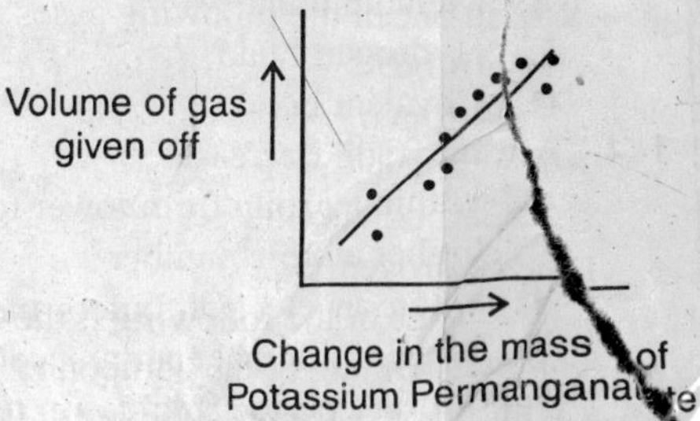

From these results we can infer that

A. the student did not work as carefully as they should
B. the sample of potassium permangnate was not pure
C. a hotter gas flame gives more gas
D. a greater change in mass gives more gas

129. Which one of the following substances consists of a long hydrocarbon chain with a sodium or potassium atom at one end?

A. Soap
B. Vitamins
C. Proteins
D. Hydrogenated fatty acids

130. A crucible containing a few pieces of Magnesium was weighed in a balance and then heated strongly. The crucible was weighed again after heating and found to have gained in total weight. There is a gain in total weight because

A. mangesium is replaced by another element
B. another element has been added
C. the heat caused greater movement of the molecules
D. the magnesiumin the crucible expanded due to heat

131. Which ones of the folowing species are isoelectronic?

A. Cl^- and Br^-
B. Na^+ and Mg^{++}
C. Ar and Ne
D. Mg^{++} and Ca^{++}

132. The *e/m* ratio for an electron is constant at

A. very high speeds of electrons
B. very slow speeds of electrons
C. moderate speeds on electrons
D. None of the above

133. An element has atomic mass 19 and atomic number 2, 8, 19. Which one of the following ions will be formed by it after losing one electon?

A. A^+ ion
B. A^{--} ion
C. A^{++} ion
D. None of these

134. If a neutron is added to the nucleus of an atom, then

A. its atomic meas will increase
B. its nuclear charge will decrease
C. its atomic mass will remain the same
D. it will become negative in polarity

135. Which one of the following was studied by Bohr while he propounded his atomic model?

A. The Stark effect
B. The spectra hydrogen atom
C. The Zeeman effect
D. None of the above

136. Mg has three natural isotopes with isotopic masses and relative abundance of 23.98 (78.60%), 24.98 (10.11%) and 25.98 (11.29%) respectively. The atomic mass of Mg is

A. 23.42 B. 23.95
C. 24.00 D. 24.95

137. The maximum number of electrons that can be occupied by a sub-level of a *p*-orbital of atomic structure is

A. 8 B. 6
C. 4 D. 2

138. The maximum number of electrons that can be accommodated in the *n*th energy levels is equal to

A. $4n^2$ B. $2n^2$
C. $\frac{n^2}{4}$ D. $\frac{n^2}{2}$

139. The bond angle H—C—H in a molecule of methane is

A. 100° B. 109°
C. 103° D. 102°

140. The electronic configuraiton of an ion of Mg^{++} is

A. 2, 8, 1 B. 2, 8
C. 2, 8, 2 D. 2, 8, 3

141. In a covalent bond the electrons are .... between the two participating atoms

A. transferred completely
B. shared
C. neither transferred nor shared
D. insufficient information to predict

142. Why the H—Cl bond is polar ionic?

A. The nucleus of hydrogen is stronger
B. The nucleus of chlorine is stronger
C. Both the nucleii are equally stronger
D. None of the above

143. Which bond is the weakest among the following?

A. Ionic bond
B. Metallic bond
C. Hydrogen bond
D. Covalent bond

144. Atomic radii decrease

A. within a group from lower to higher atomic number
B. when an electron enters the higher principal energy level
C. within a period from lower to higher atomic number
D. None of the above

145. In a metal chloride, the weights of the metal and chlorine are in the ratio of 2 : 1. What is the equivalent weight of the metal?

A. 71 B. 77.4
C. 67.8 D. 79.2

146. Which one of the following is not an electrovalent compound?

A. Common salt
B. Sylvine
C. Aluminium chloride
D. Carbon tetrachloride

147. The vapour density of compound having molecular formula $(CO)_x$ is 70. The value of *x* is

A. 6 B. 5
C. 9 D. 7

148. Which one of the following groups has the strongest tendency to lose an electron?

A. F, Cl, Br B. Li, Na, K
C. C, Si, Pb D. Cu, Ag, Au

149. Electrovalent linkage is formed by

A. transfer of electrons
B. mutual sharing of electrons
C. transfer as well as mutual sharing of electrons
D. None of the above

150. How many atoms of sulphur form

one molecule of sulphuric acid?

A. One B. Two

C. Three D. Eight

151. Why is carbon the hardest substance in the world when it is found as a diamond?

A. The C—C bonds are strongest due to heat and pressure during the formation

B. The C—H bonds are strongest in diamond

C. The structure is a tetrahderon which has a stable configuration

D. Carbon is pure and hence, the hardest

152. What is the state of sodium chloride under ordinary conditions?

A. Acqueous solid

B. Alkaloid

C. Crystalline structure

D. None of the above

153. The *e/m* ratio in anode rays

A. is constant

B. depends upon the nature of the gas

C. depends upon the temperature of the gas

D. depends upon the potential difference across the gas

154. The maxmium number of electrons that can be accomodated in K, L, M, N, ..., etc., level in an atom is given by

A. Bohr Bury scheme

B. Pauli's exclusion principle

C. Rutherford's atomic model

D. Bohr's atomic model

155. The oxidation number of sulphur in H_2SO_4 is

A. 6 B. 8

C. 10 D. 2

156. Which one of the following is an alkyne?

A. 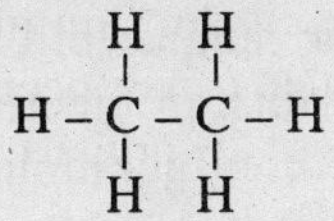

B. 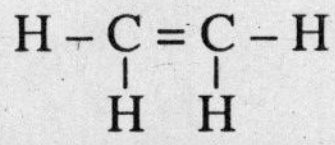

C. H – C ≡ C – H

D. 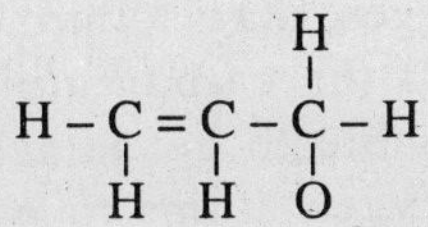

157. What is the valency of alkali metals?

A. + 1 B. – 2

C. – 1 D. + 2

158. The atomic number of an elemen is 11. What is the number of electrons in the M shell of the atom?

A. 2 B. 1

C. 0 D. 3

159. The valency of elements in the perodic table towards hydrogen

A. decreases regularly from 1 to 8

B. first increases from Group 1 to Group IV and then, decreases

C. first decreases from Group I to Group IV and then, increases

D. None of the above

160. The bond formed between the atoms of the same element is a/an.

A. covalent bond

B. ionic bond

C. metallic bond

D. depends upon the condition of temperature and pressure

161. Which one has more ability to

gain an electron?

A. F B. Na

C. C D. Mg

162. The atomic number of Cl is 17. After it gains an electron, the electronic configuration of Cl^- becomes

A. 2, 8, 7 B. 2, 8, 9

C. 2, 8, 8 D. 2, 8, 7, 1

163. If coal is burned in limited supply of oxygen, CO is formed. Why?

A. All the carbon atoms are unable to get attached to oxygen atoms to produce molecules of CO_2

B. O is less electrovalent that C

C. Oxygen is sufficient to produce bonds with C such that CO_2 may be formed

D. C and O do never produce CO_2

164. Which one of the following gave the long form of the periodic table?

A. Mendeelev

B. Dalton

C. Lother Mayer

D. Mosley

165. NaOH is an alkali becuase it releases

A. hydrogen ion - -H^+

B. sodium ion —Na^+

C. hydroxal ion —OH^+

D. None of the above

166. The existence of a number of free and mobile electrons in some elements make them good

A. conductors

B. insulators

C. partial conductors

D. All of the above

167. Among the following, which one has 11 neutrons, 10 electrons and 9 protons?

A. Isotopes

B. Neutral atoms

C. Cations

D. Anions

168. The correct order of electro-negativity is

A. F > O > N > C

B. F < O < N < C

C. F < N > O < C

D. None of the above

169. What is the formula for phosgene?

A. $CaClO_3$

B. $COCl_2$

C. $CO(OH)_2$

D. CH_3COOCO

170. In a redox reaction, MnO_4^{--} has been converted to MnO_2. The number of electrons involved in the conversion is

A. 2 B. 4

C. 3 D. 1

171. The electronic configuration of chromium (Z = 24) is

A. $1s_2 2s_2 2p_6 3s_2 3p_6 3d_4 4s_2$

B. $1s_2 2s_2 2p_6 3s_2 3p_6 3d_4$

C. $1s_2 2s_2 2p_6 3s_2 3p_6 3d_5 4s_1$

D. None of the above

172. The relative atomic masses of the elements are usually not whole numbers because

A. it is often impossible to obtain a pure sample of an element

B. methods for determining relative atoms masses are not very accurate

C. most elements occur naturally as a mixture of isotopes

D. the number of neutrons present in the nucleus of an atom differs from the number of proton present in it

173. A compound is made up of

elements X and Y. The equivalent weight of X is one-fourth its atomic weight and the equivalent weight of Y is half its atomic weight. The formula of the compound is

A. XY B. XY_2
C. X_2Y D. X_4Y_2

174. Which one of the following is true with respect to atomic size?

A. H > F > Cl > Br > l
B. H < F < Cl < Br < l
C. H < Br < H < Cl < l
D. Br < Cl < H < F < l

175. Nitrogen combines with oxygen to form several gaseous oxides, like N_2O_5, N_2O, NO, N_2O_3 and NO_2. This proves

A. Law of Constant Proportions
B. Law of Multiple Proportions
C. Gay Lussac's Law
D. None of the above

176. Which one of the following groups of elements forms a coloured ion?

A. *s*-block
B. *p*-block
C. *d*-block
D. *d*-block as wells as *f*-block

177. In Lother Meyer's curve, the peaks are occupied by

A. alkali metals
B. halogens
C. alkaline earth metals
D. inert gases

178. Variable valency is exhibited by

A. elements with vacant orbitals
B. elements with completely filled orbitals
C. transition elements only
D. None of the above

179. An element A is a member of Group V of the periodic table and an element B is a member of Group I of the periodic table. When A and B combine, the compound so formed will have the following formula.

A. BA B. B_2A
C. A_2B D. AB_3

180. The elements from I B to VII B, VIII are known as

A. noble gases
B. transition elements
C. lanthbanides
D. actinides

181. The seventh period is a/an

A. short period
B. long period
C. incomplete period
D. complete period

182. Who enunciated the Law of Triad in order to arrange elements in the periodic table?

A. John Dalton
B. John A Newland
C. Doberenier
D. Mendeleev

183. The number of groups present in the long form of the periodic table is

A. 16 B. 18
C. 8 D. 6

184. Elements of Group VII A most readily combine with the elements of the following group

A. VII A B. I A
C. IV A D. VIII A

185. How many elements are present in the sixth period of the periodic table?

A. 32 B. 28
C. 18 D. 8

186. According to Mendeleev's periodic law, the physical and chemical properties of elements are the periodic functions of their

A. atomic weights

B. atomic numbers

C. valencies

D. number of neutrons

187. The elements of Group I A are called

A. alkaline earth metals

B. noble gases

C. transition elements

D. alkali metals

188. As we move from left to right within a period, the metallic character

A. increases

B. decreases

C. remains the same

D. cannot be predicted

189. Arrange the following atoms in the increasing order of ionisation energies : O, S, Se, Te, Po

A. Se, Te, S, Po, O

B. Po, Te, Se, S, O

C. O, S, Se, Te, Po

D. Te, O, S, Po, Se

190. With respect to chlorine, hydrogen will be

A. electronegative

B. neutral

C. electropositive

D. None of these

191. In which part of the periodic groups, noble gases are present?

A. Group VI

B. Period V and VI

C. Group V

D. Group O or VIII

192. In which block, does the element with following electrons arrangement exist?

$1s_2 2s_2 2p_6 3s_2 3p_6 3d_{10} 4s_2 4p_2$

A. *s*-block B. *p*-block

C. *d*-block D. *f*-block

193. Halogens have been put in the periodic table in

A. Group O B. Group VII

C. Group VI D. Group III

194. "When elements are arranged in increasing order of their weights, the eighth element resembles the first one." Who propounded this law?

A. Moseley B. Mendeleev

C. Graham D. Newland

195. Elements in the same vertical group of the periodic table have generally

A. the same atomic size

B. the same electronic configuration

C. the same number of electrons in the outermost shell of their atoms

D. None of the above

196. Aluminium is the third group of the periodic table. Hence, the formula for its oxide is

A. AlO_3 B. Al_2O_3

C. AlO D. A_3O_3

197. In the periodic table, each horizontal row is called a

A. group B. period

C. subgroup D. subperiod

198. The molecular mass of water is

A. 20 B. 30

C. 18 D. 16

199. Solid carbondioxide is also known as

A. dry ice B. carbon ice

C. wet ice D. slaked ice

200. Non-reacting gases have a tendency to mix with each other. This phenomenon is known as

A. chemical reaction

B. diffusion

C. effusion

D. explosion

201. Nitrolum is a mixture of
A. calcium and nitrogen
B. nitrogen and aluminium
C. calcium cynamide and coke
D. calcium carbide and nitrogen

202. Aqua regia is a mixture of
A. HNO_3 and HCl (1 : 3)
B. HCl and H_2SO_4 (1 : 1)
C. H_2SO_4 and HNO_3 (2 : 3)
D. HCl, HNO_3 and H_2SO_4 (1 : 3 : 2)

203. How do CO_2 and SO_2 differ from one another?
A. Reaction with litmus solution
B. Reaction with basic oxides
C. Action on acidified $K_2Cr_2O_7$ solution
D. Action on a strip of blue litmus paper

204. Which one of the following is a mono-basic salt?
A. HNO_3 B. H_3PO_3
C. H_2SO_4 D. H_2CO_3

205. The basicity of an acid is defined as
A. the number of replaceable OH^- ions
B. the number of OH^+ ions that can be formed from one mole of the acid
C. the power of the acid to form salts
D. None of the above

206. The most stable hydride is
A. NH_3 B. PH_3
C. AsH_3 D. SbH_3

207. CO_2 would turn lime water
A. white B. blue
C. milky D. brown

208. The percentage of oxygen in pure water is
A. 19% B. 81%
C. 89% D. 52%

209. The mass of one mole of atoms of an element (is grams) is equal to
A. the gram molecular mass
B. the gram atomi mass
C. the gram ionic mass
D. None of the above

210. The solute particle in a colloidal solution will
A. not settle down
B. settle down
C. behave according to temperature
D. None of the above

211. The purity of a solid is determined by measuring its
A. melting point
B. boiling point
C. freezing point
D. None of the above

212. A mixture of sodium chioride and ammonium chloride can be most easily separated by
A. sedimentation
B. steam distillation
C. fractional crystallisation
D. sublimation

213. The numerical value of the standard temperature of a gas is
A. 0°C B. 40°C
C. 150°C D. 0°C

214. The ratio of weights by which, carbon and oxygen combine in a molecule of carbon monoxide is equal to
A. 3 : 2 B. 3 : 4
C. 4 : 3 D. 3 : 1

215. The element with maximum electron affinity is
A. N B. H
C. He D. F

216. Which one of the following

behaves sometimes as a metal and sometimes as a non-metal?

A. Cu B. Ag
C. Sb D. Zn

217. Water is a

A. homogeneous mixture
B. heterogeneous mixture
C. colloid
D. compound

218. An atom that can neither gain nor lose electron, is known as

A. metallic B. non-metallic
C. inert D. reactive

219. The allotropic form of oxygen is

A. ozone B. CO_2
C. O_4 D. SO_2

220. What is the basic nature of NH_2?

A. Acidic
B. Basic
C. Neutral
D. Depends upon the solvent

221. What is nitrochalk?

A. Nitrogen plus chalk
B. NH_4NO_3 plus chalk
C. NH_4 plus NH_3 plus chalk
D. None of the above

222. Which one of the following is not a thermoplastic?

A. Teflon B. Orlon
C. Bakelite D. Flint Glass

223. In which case, the coavlent bonds all likely to break earlier and with ease?

A. Alkanes
B. Alkenes
C. Alkynes
D. All of the above

24. Which one of the following is a purely covalent compound?

A. HCl B. $CHCl_3$
C. CCl_4 D. $AlCl_3$

225. Which one of the following has highest oxidation potential?

A. Na B. Ag
C. Al D. Zn

226. Which one of the given statements is/are true of the reaction given below?

$C(s) + O(g) \rightarrow CO_2(g) + 94.3\,k\,cal$

I. One mole of CO_2 is prroduced for every two moles of oxygen consumed
II. The reaction is endothermic
III. The reaction is exothermic

A. I and II B. II alone
C. III alone D. I and III

227. Which one of the following chemical equations represents a decomposition reaction?

A. $Ca(OH)_2 + CO_2 \rightarrow CaCO_2 + H_2O$
B. $CaO + H_2O \rightarrow Ca(OH)_2 + \text{Heat}$
C. $CaCO_2 \xrightarrow{\text{Heat}} CaO + CO_2$
D. $Zn + CuSO_4 \rightarrow ZnSO_4 + Cu$

228. In the Ostwaed process of the manufacture of HNO_3, the main reaction is

$4HN_3 + 5O_2 \rightarrow 4NO + 6H_2O$

This reaction is catalysed by

A. Fe B. Ni
C. Mn D. V_2O_5

229. During the hydrogenation of unsaturated fats, the catalyst used is

A. Fe B. Ni
C. Mn D. V

230. Consider the following reaction

$Zn + CuSO_4 \rightarrow ZnSO_4 + Cu$

A. Zn is oxidised
B. Zn is reduced
C. Cu is oxidised
D. None of the above

231. The process of oxidation involves
A. gain of electrons
B. gain of protons
C. loss of electrons
D. loss of protons

232. In the process of electrorefining of metals, pure metals is made the
A. cathode
B. anode
C. electrolyte stolution
D. both electrode and anode

233. A dibasic acid will produce
A. an acidic salt and a normal salt
B. a normal salt
C. a double salt
D. a complex salt

234. Which one of the following gets hydrolysed in an acqueous solution?
A. salt of weak acid and strong base
B. salt of weak acid and weak base
C. salt of strong acid and weak base
D. All of the above

235. When NH_4Cl is added to a solution of NH_4OH, the
A. dissociation of NH_4OH increases
B. dissociation of NH_4OH decreases
C. concentration of OH^- increases
D. concentration of OH^- as well as NH_4^+ increases

236. During electrolysis, reduction takes place at
A. anode
B. cathode
C. both anode and cathode
D. None of the above

237. Consider the following reaction

$Na^-(l) + e^- \not\rightarrow Na(s)$

$Cl(l) \rightarrow Cl + e^-$

Which one has been reduced?
A. Cl^- ion
B. Na^+ ion
C. Both Na^+ and Cl^- ions
D. Neither has been reduced

238. Which one of the following reactions is the fastest?
A. Rusting of iron in moist air
B. Electrolysis of fused calcium chloride
C. Precipitation of silver chloride when solutions of silvernitrate and sodium chloride are mixed
D. Burning of wood

239. The rate of reaction is
A. directly proprotional to the concentration of each of its reactions
B. inversely proportional to concentration of each of its reactions
C. inversely proportional to the concentration of each of its reactants and products
D. All of the above

240. Active nitrogen is obtained by
A. passing electric discharge through nitrogen gas at low pressure
B. thermal decomposition of nitrogen
C. action of acids on nitrogen
D. heating of nitrides of active metals

241. When two colourless gases are mixed, dense white fumes are obtained. The gases are
A. $NH_3 + SO_2$
B. $NH_3 + HCl$
C. $NH_3 + NO_2$

D. None of the above

242. The following reaction is in equilibrium

$2SO_2(g) + O_2(g) \rightleftharpoons 2SO_3(g) +$ Heat

Which one of the altered conditions would increase the concentration of SO_2?

A. Decreased temperature and increased pressure

B. Decreased pressure and increased temperature

C. Both temperature and pressure decreased

D. Non alteration required

243. A system is represented by 3A + 2B = C

If k is the equilibrium constant, then

A. $k = [3A] \times [2B]/[C]$

B. $k = [C]/[3A] \times [2B]$

C. $k = [C]/[A]^2 \times [B]^2$

D. None of the above

244. Which one of the following chemical reactions is correct?

A. ${}^{14}_{7}N + {}^{0}n_1 \rightarrow {}^{14}_{6}C + {}^{4}_{2}He$

B. ${}^{238}_{92}U \rightarrow {}^{231}_{39}Th + {}^{4}_{2}He$

C. ${}^{90}_{38}Sr \rightarrow {}^{90}_{39}Y + {}^{4}_{2}He$

D. None of the above

245. A balloon (filled with ethylene, i.e., C_2H_4) is pricked with a sharp-pointed needle and quickly plunged into a tank of hydrogen at the same pressure. After sometime, the balloon will

A. get enlarged

B. collapse completely

C. shrink in size

D. remain unchanged in size

246. In which of the following chemical reactions, does sulphuric acid function as an oxidising agent?

A. $H_2SO_3 + Br_2 + H_2O \rightarrow H_2SO_4 + 2HBr$

B. $H_2SO_3 + 2H_2O \rightarrow 3H_2O + S$

C. $H_2SO_3 + 2FeCl_3 + H_2O \rightarrow H_2SO_4 2FeCl_3 + 2HCl$

D. None of the above

247. In the reaction

$H_3PO_4 + Ca(OH)_2 = CaHPO_4 + 2H_2O$

The equivalent of phosphoric acid is

A. 49.0 B. 98.0

C. 147.0 D. 24.5

248. Yellow ammonium sulphide can separate

A. CdS and As_2S_3

B. Bi_2S_3 and CuS

C. PbS and Bi_2S_3

D. HgS and PbS

249. When $k_2Cr_2O_7$ is converted into k_2CrO_4, then the change in the oxidation number of chromium is

A. 3 B. 4

C. 5 D. 0

250. When 28 g of N_2 gas, having volume 22.4 litres at 0°C and at a pressure of 1 atmosphere were heated to 273°C, the pressure of the gas became 2 atmospheres. The new volume of the gas in litres is

A. 26.2 B. 22.8

C. 22.4 D. 25.4

251. The amount of Al deposited, when a current of 49 A is passed through its electrolyte for 30 minutes (equivalent weight of Al = 8.99) is

A. 6.71 g B. 5.71 g

C. 22.4 g D. 6.28 g

252. The reaction

$2H_2S + SO_2 \rightarrow 2H_2O + S$

is an example of

A. an exothermic reaction

B. an oxidation reduction reaction

C. a complex formation reaction

D. a displacement reaction

253. Conversion of $KMnO_4$ to $MnSO_4$ is a process of

A. reduction

B. oxidation

C. dehydrogenation

D. dehydration

254. If 100 ml of $\frac{N}{10}$ H_2SO_4 are mixed with 200 ml of $\frac{N}{5}$ H_2SO_4, then the normality of the acid in the mixture is

A. $\frac{N}{5}$ B. $\frac{N}{6}$

C. $\frac{N}{3}$ D. $\frac{N}{10}$

255. In a displacement reaction

A. the ion of a compound replaces the ion of another compound

B. the ion of an element replaces the ion another element in a compound

C. there is no replacement of ions

D. All of the above are true

256. Which one of the following is a redox reaction?

A. $Na \rightarrow Na^+ + e^-$

B. $Cl + e^- \rightarrow Cl$

C. $CuO + H_2 \rightarrow Cu + H_2O$

D. None of the above

257. Complete the following reaction

$2Al_2O_3 \xrightarrow{\text{Electricity}} 4Al + ...?$

A. ? = O B. ? = O_2

C. ? = $3O_2$ D. ? = $3H_2O$

258. Which one of the following is more reactive metal than hydrogen?

A. Silver B. Platinum

C. Mercury D. Tin

259. In the process of isomerism

A. the molecular formula of the compound changes

B. the rearrangement of the atoms of a compound within a molecule takes place

C. molecular formula change and atoms are also rearranged

D. None of the above

260. When one mole of $^{238}_{92}U$ emits alpha particles, 1×10^{15} ergs of energy are released. How much energy is lost when 0.5 mole of $^{238}_{92}U$ emits alpha particles?

A. 5.0×10^{14} erg

B. 6.2×10^{10} erg

C. 9.2×10^{14} erg

D. 5.9×10^{12} erg

261. A solution always has

A. a lower boiling point than that boiling point of pure solvent

B. a boiling point equal to the boiling point of the pure solvent

C. a higher boilint point than the boiling point of the pure solvent

D. None of the above

262. In the preparation of sulphur trioxide by the reaction

$2SO_2(g) + O_2(g) \rightleftharpoons 2SO_3 + \Delta$

the most favourable conditions for

the maximum generation of SO_3 are

A. low temperature and low pressure

B. high temperature and high pressure

C. medium temperature and medium pressure

D. medium temperature and high pressure

263. According to Le Chatlier's principle, when a system in equilibrium is subjected to a change in concentration, temperature or pressure, the equilibrium shifts in a direction that tends to

A. support the change

B. oppose the change

C. neither support nor oppose the change

D. Cannot be predicted

264. As a general rule, the rise in temperature will favour

A. an exothermic reaction

B. an exothermic and an endothermic reaction

C. an endothermic reaction

D. None of the above

265. Dissolution of $CaCl_2$ in water is accompanied by

A. absorption of heat

B. evolution of heat

C. absorption and evolution of heat

D. None of the above

266. Which one of the following best explains the action of a catalyst in enhancing the rate of a chemical reaction?

A. It decreases the energy of activation of the reaction

B. It prevents the reverse reation from occurring

C. It increases the value of equilibrium constant of the reaction

D. It increases the kinetic energy of the molecules

267. At the equilibrium state in a reaction

A. the amount of product formed is equal to the amount of unreacted reaction

B. the rate of forward reaction is equal to the rate of backward reaction

C. R_1 (velocity constant for forward reaction) and R_2 (velocity constant for reverse reactions) are equal

D. the reaction comes to an end completely

268. Which one of the following could be used as a reducing agent (beside carbon) to reduce M_2O_3 to the metal M?

A. Iron B. Aluminium

C. Zinc D. Copper

269. Which one of the following metals has the least reactivity towards water?

A. Iron B. Zinc

C. Magnesium D. Sodium

270. Which one of the following is an important zinc are?

A. Calamine B. Crystalite

C. Malachite D. Gibbsite

271. Which one of the following elements is extracted commercially by the electrolysis of an acqueous solution of one of its compounds?

A. Na B. Al

C. Br D. Cl

272. Heating of zinc oxide with carbon

yields zinc along with
A. carbon monoxide
B. carbon dioxide
C. zinc oxide
D. No other by product

273. Which types of ores are concentrated by the froth floatation process?
A. Bromide ore B. Chloride ore
C. Sulphate ore D. Sulphide ore

274. If we roast copper pyrites, we would obtain $Cu_2O.SO_2$ and
A. Fe_2O_2
B. FeO
C. FeS
D. None of the above

275. A burning piece of magnesium continues to burn in oxygen until all the oxygen in the gas jar is consumed. The colour of the powder formed inside the jar is
A. red B. black
C. white D. brown

276. What is the essential element of an amalgam?
A. Alkali B. Alkali Metal
C. Mercury D. Silver

277. Which one of the following is a metalloid?
A. Arsenic B. Tellurium
C. Bolonium D. Selenium

278. Bauxite is an oxide mineral of
A. Aluminium B. Zinc
C. Copper D. Lead

279. Which one of the following is not a conductor of electric current?
A. Indium B. Gallium
C. Thallium D. Boron

280. Which one of the following elements has the strongest tendency to form covalent bonds?
A. Ca B. Be
C. Mg D. Ba

281. Which one of the following is least ionic in nature?
A. NaCl
B. $BeCl_2$
C. $CaCl_2$
D. All are equally ionic

282. What we obtain from a blast-furnace is
A. pig iron B. wrought iron
C. mild steel D. cast iron

283. Which metal is normally used for converting cooking oil into vegetable ghee through the process of hydrogenation?
A. Zinc B. Lithium
C. Nickel D. Silver

284. The most malleable metal is
A. sodium B. gold
C. potassium D. platinum

285. Which one of the following is used for electrical purification of Al?
A. Hoop's process
B. Bayer's process
C. Serpeck's process
D. None of these

286. Which one of the following is pearl ash?
A. $MgCO_3$ B. $CaCO_3$
C. K_2CO_3 D. Na_2CO_3

287. Which category of metals generally exists as halide ores?
A. Alkali metals
B. Alkaline earth metals
C. Methalloids
D. None of the above

288. An alloy is a homogeneous mixture of
A. two or more metals
B. a metal and non-metal
C. metals as well as non-metals
D. None of the above

289. Sodium Nitrate is not used in the

preparation of gun powder because
A. it is deliquescent
B. it is an explosive
C. it does not decompose easily
D. None of the above

290. Solvay's process is used for preparing washing soda. It cannot be used for the preparation of K_2CO_3 because
A. K_2CO_3 is not stable under ordinary conditions
B. K_2CO_3 is highly soluble in water and hence, it cannot be filtered out
C. potassium is the most reactive metal
D. None of the above

291. Which one of the following pairs shows diagonal relationship?
A. Na and Mg B. Li and Mg
C. Li and Na D. Al and C

292. Froth floatation, ore concentration and ore roasting are the process related to
A. organic chemistry
B. stoichiometry
C. metallurgy
D. chemical kinetics

293. Which one of the following will not form oxygen on heating?
A. Potassium chloride
B. Red lead
C. Potassium permanganate
D. Ammonium nitrate

294. An explosive compound containing nitrogen is
A. Ammonium chloride
B. Nitrogen tri-chloride
C. Ammonium nitrate
D. Ammonium phosphate

295. The halogen, which can exist as a liquid under normal atmospheric conditions, is
A. iodine B. bromine
C. chlorine D. fluorine

296. Antichlor is a compound which
A. liberates chlorine easily from the bleaching powder
B. converts chlorine to hydrogen chloride
C. acts as a catalyst in the manufacture of dyes and paints
D. absorbs other halogen easily

297. Deacon's process is used for the manufacture of
A. bleaching powder
B. sulphuric acid
C. chlorine
D. nitric acid

298. CO_2 is used in fire extinguishers because
A. it has relatively low critical temperature
B. it behaves as dry ice in the solid state
C. it is heavier than air and is colourless
D. it is neither combustible nor a supporter of combustion

299. The amount of N_2 in air by volume is (nearly)
A. 92% B. 78.1%
C. 62% D. 38%

300. Calgon is the name given to
A. sodium zeolite
B. sodium hexameta phosphate
C. disodiumhydrogen phosphate
D. trisodium phosphate

301. The most abundant element in the universe is
A. hydrogen B. oxygen
C. helium D. silicon

302. Which phosphorus combines in the atmosphere of chlorine to

form

A. PCl_5 B. PCl_3

C. PCl_6 D. PCl_4

303. NH_3 and HCl combine to form

A. ammonium hydroxide

B. dense white fumes

C. white precipitates

D. black precipitates

304. When $CuSO_4.5H_2O$ is treated in concentrated H_2SO_4, it turns

A. dirty yellow B. brown

C. white D. crimson

305. The reactivity of halogens has the following order

A. Cl > I > Br

B. Br > I > Cl

C. Cl > Br > I

D. All the three have same reavtivity

306. Red phosphorus is a

A. hard crystalline solid without any smell

B. soft crystalline solid without any smell

C. soft waxy solid with a particular smell

D. hard solid with a peculiar smell

307. The super-phosphate of lime is used as

A. an oxidising agent

B. a reducing agent

C. a fertiliser

D. None of these

308. Absorption of H_2 by Pd is known as

A. oxidation

B. reduction

C. hydrogenation

D. occlusion

309. Water gas is a mixture of

A. $CO + N_2$ B. $CO_2 + H_2$

C. $CO + H_2$ D. $CO_2 + N_2$

310. Metal oxides are

A. covalent in nature

B. ionic in nature

C. coordinate in nature

D. All of the above.

311. The boiling point of liquid H_2 is

A. – 253°C B. – 272°C

C. – 203°C D. – 200°C

312. Hydrogen sulphide turns a filter paper soaked in the solution of lead acetate, to

A. red B. black

C. blue D. white

313. Which one of the following alloys does not contain zinc?

A. German silver

B. Bronze

C. Brass

D. Gun metal

314. A sample of water, is drawn from a well, became milky after boiling. It most probably contains

A. dissolved magnesium carbonate

B. dissolved calcium hydrogen carbonate

C. dissolved sodium chloride

D. dissolved calcium carbonate

315. Which one of the following is not correct for yellow (white) phosphorus?

A. It is transparent and waxy

B. It has a low kindling temperature

C. Its molecular mass corresponds to P_4

D. It is kept in CS_2

316. $KMnO_4$ is not decolorised by ordinary hydrogen but when put in a mixture of zinc and H_2SO_4, it is decolorised. This is because hydrogen obtained is

A. Nascent hydrogen

B. Molecular hydrogen
C. Atomic hydrogen
D. None of the above

317. Dry powder fire extinguisher has the following ingredients?
A. Sand and backing soda
B. Sand and aluminium sulphate
C. Sand and H_2SO_4
D. Sand and calcium carbonate

318. The purest form of H_2S gas is prepared through the reaction of
A. antimony trisulphide with concentrated hydrochloric acid
B. iron sulphide with diluted H_2SO_4
C. heating of magnesium hydrogen sulphide
D. None of the above

319. Skin, silver and leather become yellow on contact with NHO_3 because of the formation of
A. NO_2
B. Nitrates
C. Xantho proteins
D. NO

320. Plants absorb nitrates nitrites of the soil and convert them into
A. urea
B. ammonia
C. ammonium hydrogen
D. oxides of nitrogen

321. Fuels in automobiles are mixtures of
A. saturated hydrocarbons
B. unsaturated hydrocarbons
C. saturated and unsaturated hydrocarbons
D. None of the above

322. What is the IUPAC name of $CH_2CH_2CH(CH_2)$?
A. Butane
B. 2-methyl butane
C. π-butane
D. None of these

323. Which one of the following forms of carbon absorbs colours?
A. Wood
B. Charcoal
C. Bone charcoal
D. Coke

324. $CH_2{=}C{=}CH_2$ contains
A. π-bonds in conjugation
B. π-bonds perpendicular to one another
C. a combination of π-bonds in conjugation and at right angles
D. None of the above

325. What is the name of the compound whose structure has been shown below?

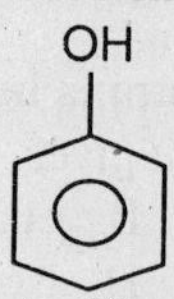

A. Phenol
B. Benzoic acid
C. Benzyl alcohol
D. Benzaldehyde

326. Which one of the following statements is correct?
A. Carbon reduces hot and concentrated H_2SO_4
B. Carbon reduces hot and concentrated HNO_3
C. Carbon forms binary compounds with metals and non-metals
D. All of the above are correct

327. The atomic weights of elements are measured by taking the weight of atom (as standard) of
A. O – 16 B. C – 12
C. N – 14 D. H – 1

328. Octance number is a scale for counting
A. the quality of petrol
B. the percentage of LPG in a given sample of petrol
C. the count of knocking of a fuel
D. None of the above

329. Which compound would have a ring structure?
A. Pentane
B. Ethylene
C. Benzoic acid
D. Propane

330. Which one of the following is a functional group of organic acids?
A. $>C=O$ B. 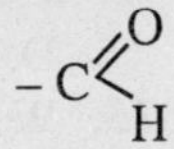
C. – OH D. 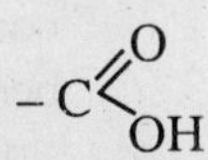

331. When chloroform is heated with silver powder, it gives
A. ethylene B. ethane
C. ethyne D. iso-propane

332. When ethyl chloride reacts with alcoholic KOH, it gives
A. ethyl alchohol
B. ethane
C. ethylene
D. diethyl ether

333. The general formula for alkanes is
A. C_nH_{2n+1} B. C_nH_{2n-1}
C. C_nH_{2n-2} D. C_nH_{2n+2}

334. Formaldehyde is used in the preparation of
A. ethyl alcohol
B. aniline
C. utropine
D. None of these

335. The atoms of carbon in diamond are connected to one another through
A. ionic bonds
B. coordinate bonds
C. hydrogen bonds
D. None of these

336. The members of a homologous series have
A. same melting point
B. different boiling points
C. same boiling point
D. None of the above

337. The IUPAC name of CH_3CHO is
A. acetaldehyde
B. formaldehyde
C. ethanol
D. ethane

338. Acetylene decolorises the purple colour of alkaline potassium permanganate due to the formation of
A. oxalic acid
B. acetaldehyde
C. formaldehyde
D. acetic acid

339. Which one of the following is used as a fuel?
A. CO_2 B. CH_3COOH
C. CH_4 D. CH_3CHO

340. The total number of sigma bonds in C_2H_6 is
A. four B. five
C. six D. seven

341. Chlorination of methane in the presence of diffused sunlight and halogen carrier will form, beside CCl_4,
A. Mono-chloro methane
B. di-chloro methane
C. tri-chloro methane
D. All of these

342. Which one of the following is not a petroleum products?
A. Kerosene oil
B. Petrol
C. Paraffin wax

D. Phenol

343. In which one of the following hydrocarbons, the four valencies of carbon are fuly saturated?

A. Alkenes
B. Alkynes
C. Alkanes
D. None of these

344. The shape of molecule of methane is

A. tetrahedral B. octahaderal
C. circular D. pentahedral

345. Graphite is used as a lubricant in heavy machinery because

A. it has layers, which readily slip over one another
B. it has lubricating property because it contains carbon only
C. its atoms are loosely connected
D. None of the above

346. The type of coal having the highest content of carbon is

A. lignite
B. bituminous coal
C. peat
D. anthracite

347. What is ethylene oxide used as?

A. As a fumigant
B. As a solvent
C. As an anti-freeze
D. None of the above

348. The number of isotopes of carbon is

A. two B. three
C. four D. one

349. When methane is heated in the absence of air or O_2, it breaks up to give carbon and hydrogen. The process is called

A. pyrolysis
B. cracking
C. polymerisation
D. None of these

350. When hydrocarbons burn in air, they yield

A. CO_2, heat and water
B. CO_2 and water
C. heat and water
D. heat and other bi-products, which depend upon temperature

351. The Iodoform test is used to identify

A. alcohols
B. carboxylic acids
C. armines
D. None of these

352. Crystalline allotropic forms of carbon are

A. graphite and coke
B. graphite and diamond
C. diamond and coke
D. diamond and lamp black

353. When a few drops of bromine water are added to acetylene, its brown colour is decolorised due to formation of

A. ethyl chloride
B. propyl bromide
C. acetylene dibromide
D. ethyl bromide

354. Aldehyde reacts with Tollen's reagent to form

A. formaldehyde
B. silver mirror
C. ethane
D. acetylene

355. Saturated hydrocarbons undergo

A. substitution reaction
B. polymerisation
C. addtion reaction
D. All of the above

356. If sodium bicarbonate is added to a solution of carboxylic acid, the gas so produced will be

A. H_2 B. CH_4

C. O_2 D. CO_2

357. Methane is also known as

A. water gas

B. producer gas

C. marsh gas

D. methane producer

358. Aromatic hydrocarbons give all the following reactions except

A. burning with a non-smoky flame

B. burning with a smoky flame

C. substitution reactions

D. giving CO_2 and water on drastic oxidation

359. Regenerated fibre is

A. cotton B. rayon

C. nylon D. decron

360. Which one of the following fibres contains protein units in its molecule?

A. Nylon B. Wool

C. Cotton D. Rayon

361. CO reacts with haemoglobin to form a compound which stops blood from absorbing oxygen. The compound formed is

A. oxyhaemoglobin

B. carboxy haemoglobin

C. nitro haemoglobin

D. phosgene

362. What is writing paper?

A. Cellulose

B. Starch

C. Protein

D. Carbohydrate

363. Power alcohol (gasohol) can be derived from

A. sugar cane juice

B. molasses

C. methyl alcohol

D. fruit juice

364. When acetic acid combines with ethyl alcohol in the presence of concentrated H_2SO_4, it will give

A. an ester

B. an aldehyde

C. an alcohol

D. a carboxylic acid

365. The high polymer of ethylene is known as

A. polystyrene B. polythene

C. tyrene D. tetralene

366. Ethylene, on ozonolysis, give ozonide, which, on hydrolysis, gives

A. acetaldehyde

B. glycol

C. formaldehyde

D. glyoxal

367. Breakage or higher hydrocarbon into lower ones through heat is known as

A. neutralisation

B. polymerisation

C. cracking

D. acetylation

368. Ethylene is prepared in the laboratory by heating a mixture of sulphuric acid (concentrated) and

A. butyl alcohol

B. ethyl alcohol

C. proply alcohol

D. None of these

369. What is the valency of carbon in ethylene?

A. four B. three

C. two D. one

370. The bond angles in the molecule of methane (CH_4) is

A. 108°, 28' B. 109°, 28'

C. 110° D. 118°, 28'

371. Acetylene reacts with ammoniacal cuprous chloride to form a

reddish brown precipitate of
A. copper acetylide
B. ethyl chloride
C. methyl chloride
D. None of these

372. In combined state, carbon occurs in nature as
A. carbon dioxide only
B. carbon monoxide and carbonates
C. carbon dioxide and carbonates
D. carbonates only

373. In *Gobar* Gas Plants of Indian villages, the normally produced gas is
A. acetylene
B. propylene
C. methane
D. None of the above

374. An atom or a group of atoms present in an organic compound that shows nearly the same behaviour in chemical reactions, is known as
A. a functional group
B. a free radical
C. a reactive radical
D. None of these

375. Which one of the following groups is present in CH_3COOCH_3?
A. Alcohol B. Acid
C. Ester D. Aldehyde

376. Which one of the following tests is used to check the unsaturation of hydrocarbons?
A. Chromyl chloride test
B. Beyer's reagent test
C. Lake test
D. Ring test

377. Greases would be obtained after the fractional distallation of
A. crude kerosene
B. crude diesel
C. crude petroleum
D. None of these

378. What is the content of acetic acid in household vinegar?
A. 2% B. 3%
C. 4% D. 5%

379. Dehydration of ethanol gives
A. CH_2OH B. $CH_2{=}CH_2$
C. CH_2CHO D. $CH{=}CH$

380. Wood charcol is used in gas masks because it
A. has a good smell
B. dissolves poisonous gases
C. absorbs poisonous gases
D. None of the above

381. Saturated and unsaturated hydrocarbons that contain ring of carbon atoms are called
A. alkenes
B. cyclic compounds
C. alkanes
D. aromatic compounds

382. Which one of the following compounds is an aromatic hydrocaron?
A. Chloroform B. Urea
C. Glycerol D. Phenol

383. When calcium carbide reacts with water, it gives
A. ethane
B. propane
C. acetylene
D. None of these

384. Acetylene polymerises to give
A. octane
B. benzene
C. hexane
D. None of the above

385. The allotrope of carbon, which is

a good conductor of heat and electricity, is

A. diamond
B. sugar charcoal
C. graphite
D. wood charcoal

386. When a mixture of nitrogen and acetylene is subjected to spark, the product so formed is

A. hydrocyanic acid
B. acetylene nitride
C. nitroacetylene
D. acetylene nitric acid

387. What is the disadvantage of using coal as a fuel?

A. Cheap
B. Transportation is difficult
C. Gives ash and polluting gases upon cambustion
D. All of the above

388. Acetylene is a

A. colourless gas
B. blue coloured gas
C. yellow coloured gas
D. brown coloured gas

389. C_4H_{10} has two isomers. One of them is *n*-butane. The other one is

A. *n*-propane
B. iso-butane
C. *n*-pentane
D. None of these

390. Which one is not the amorphous form of carbon?

A. Sugar B. Coke
C. Lamp black D. Graphite

391. More the number of bonds between two carbon atoms

A. lesser will be its bond length
B. more will be its bond length
C. no effect would be observed on the bond length
D. lesser would be the reactivity of that molecule

392. What is the calorific value of biogas?

A. 13 kJ-kg^{-1}
B. 35-40 kJ-kg^{-1}
C. 80 kJ-kg^{-1}
D. 140 kJ-kg^{-1}

393. Kindling temperature is the lowest temperature at which

A. the substance can be melted
B. the substance can catch fire
C. the substance can produce flames with bluish tinge
D. All of the above

394. Which one of the following is not a solid fuel?

A. Dung Cake B. Ethanol
C. Wood D. Charcoal

395. We can use the following to extinguish fires (depending upon the nature of burning material), except one, which should never be used?

A. Soda acid B. Water
C. Acetylene D. CCl_4

396. Charcoal is a better fuel than wood because

A. it produces more heat per kg than wood
B. it produces more smoke per kg than wood
C. it produces less heat per kg than wood
D. None of the above

397. Why is LPG mixed with a gas having smell?

A. So that it could be smelled
B. So that its pressure could be measured
C. So that it could be confumed with doubt that there is a leakage of LPG
D. All of the above

398. What is LPG?
A. *n*-propane B. Iso-propane
C. Ethylene D. Butane

399. Which are of the India is not rich in crude oil reserves?
A. Gujarat
B. Assam
C. Bombay High
D. Andhra Pradesh

400. Look at the following reaction. If we want to produce methane from coal, what is the missing item in this reaction?

$$\text{Coal} + 2H_2 \xrightarrow{\text{catalyst}} CH_4 + \text{residues}$$

A. C_2H_6 would be liberated
B. Pressure has to be applied
C. Catalyst is not needed
D. No change needed as the reaction is correct

401. In which one of the following processes, energy is absorbed?
A. Burning of methane in oxygen
B. Respiration by man
C. Photosynthesis by green plants
D. Burning of coal

402. Which energy source would to produce any pollution?
A. Coal B. Kerosene
C. Solar rays D. Petroleum

403. Producer gas is a mixture of
A. gaseous hydrocarbons
B. nitrogen and CO
C. CH_4 and H_2
D. None of the above

404. When fuel burns in oxygen, the reaction is known as
A. an endothermic reaction
B. an exothermic reaction
C. an intrinsic reaction
D. an extrinsic reaction

405. Which one would be obtained after the fraction distillation of crude oil?
A. Fuel oil
B. Kerosene
C. Greases and oils
D. All of the above

406. The fuel in Appollo rocket was a mixture of
A. butane + acetylene
B. methyl hydrazine and dinitrogen tetraoxide
C. pentane + octane-87
D. None of the above

407. Which one of the following is not a fuel?
A. Paraffin wax
B. Petroleum gas
C. Marsh gas
D. High speed diesel

408. Which one of the following is not a secondary fuel?
A. Coal gas B. Water gas
C. Petroleum D. Producer gas

409. Which of the following would have more calorific value?
A. Methane B. Ethane
C. Propane D. Butane

410. Which would be an ideal fuel for the rural househols of India?
A. LPG B. *Gobar* gas
C. Water gas D. CNG

411. Which one of the following is not a nuclear fuel?
A. Plutonium
B. Radium
C. Uranium
D. All of the above

412. Synthesic fuel oil is obtained after processing
A. marsh gas B. coal
C. producer D. iso-propane

413. In order to sustain the human and biological lives on the planet, we

should
A. conserve fossil fuels
B. use non-conventional fuels
C. reduce the number of vehicles that pollute the air
D. only (A) and (B)

414. Which one of the following would extinguish a fire?
A. CO B. CO_2
C. CH_4 D. C_2H_4

415. Which fuel would be ideal for the engine of a bus as it is heavy?
A. Petrol
B. Diesel
C. Alcohol
D. All of the above

416. Coal gas is a mixture of
A. H_2, CH_4 and CO
B. H_2, CH_4 and CO
C. H_2 and CH_4
D. CH_4 and CO

417. What is the application of flint glass?
A. Manufacture of mirrors
B. Manufacture of optical instruments
C. Manufacture of glass crockery
D. All of the above

418. Hydraulic cement is made by burning of a mixture of
A. limestone and sodium carbonate
B. limestone and nickel carbonate
C. limestone and ammonium caronate
D. limestone and clay

419. Which one of the following is not used in the households on a daily basis?
A. Phosphorus B. Fluorine
C. Arsenic D. Calcium

420. Which one of the following is a detergent?
A. Sodium sulphate
B. Sodium hydroxide
C. Sodium lauryl sulphate
D. Sodium thiosulphate

421. Which one of the following is *kissan khad*?
A. $Ca(NO_3)NH_4NO_3$
B. $Ca(NO_3)NH_4NO_36H_2O$
C. $Ca(NO_3)NH_3NO_2$
D. None of the above

422. Which one of the following is not a raw material for the manufacture of glass?
A. Soda ash B. Sand
C. Limestone D. Chalk

423. The gloves used in surgery and medical examinations are made up of
A. PVC
B. natural latex
C. synthetic rubber
D. All of the above

424. If selenium is added to the basic raw materials for manufacture of glass, the resultant colour of the glass sheet would be
A. green B. blue
C. orange red D. yellow

425. Which one of the following cannot be moulded again as desired?
A. Nylon B. Polythene
C. Bakelite D. Teflon

426. Rayon is made from
A. nylon B. cellulose
C. wood pulp D. polyster

427. Natural rubber can be hardened by adding the following material during its vulcanisation
A. ferric oxide
B. clay
C. carbon black

D. coal dust

428. How does a detergent remove dirt?

A. It forms weak hydrogen bonds with washing clothes dirt during the process of washing clothes

B. It detaches dirt molecules through a peaceful action of the washing machine

C. It softens dirt so that it can be carried away by water

D. None of the above

429. Natural rubber is a linear polymer of

A. 2-methyl butane

B. 2-methyl propane

C. *n*-hexane

D. 2-methyl butadiene

430. Which one would generate maximum lather when used with soap?

A. Distilled water

B. Soft water from underground

C. Hard water from underground

D. All the three would produce the same amount of lather

431. Which one of the following is man-made material?

A. Latex

B. PVC

C. Natural rubber

D. Coal

432. In soda-acid fire extinguisher, the fire is extinguished mainly due to

A. dilute H_2SO_4

B. formation of CO_2

C. presence of sodium bicarbonate

D. formation of water as a product

433. Why is gelatin used in the manufacture of ice cream?

A. It helps the mixture to solidfy

B. It improves the flavour of ice-cream

C. It prevents the formation of colloids

D. It stablises the colloids and prevents the crystal formation

434. The glass obtained after reaction involving potash and lead is known as

A. flint glass

B. safety glass

C. crom glass

D. None of these

435. The process of making a soap by hydrolysis of a fat with a strong alkali is called

A. aponification

B. esterification

C. emulsification

D. None of these

436. Which chemical is frequently used by doctors for oral treatments and ear treatments?

A. Sodium hydroxide

B. Hydrogen paroxide

C. Hydrochloric acid

D. Aqua Regia

437. Which one of the following is not a source of chemical or items of everyday usage?

A. Petroleum B. Coal

C. Sea water D. Dacron

438. Which alcohol is used to make wines, liquours and liquers?

A. Methyl alcohol

B. Ethyl alcohol

C. Iso-propyl alcohol

D. Butanol

439. Which one of the following is commoly used in household kitchens?

A. Oil of vitriol B. Blue vitriol

C. Cinnabar D. Baking soda

440. Which one of the following is used by doctors to fix and heal broken legs?

A. $CaSO_4 \frac{1}{2} H_2O$

B. MnO_2

C. $NaNO_3$

D. $Na_2CO_3 10H_2O$

441. The difference between baking powder and baking soda is that

A. baking powder has tartaric acid in addition to baking soda

B. baking soda is absent in baking powder

C. baking powder is a liquid but baking soda is not

D. there is not difference

442. What are the basic constituents of German silver?

A. Cu and Ni

B. Ni, Zn and Sn

C. Zn, Ni and Cu

D. Ni and Sn

443. What is slaked lime?

A. $Ca(OH)_2$

B. CaO

C. $Ca_3(POH)_2$

D. $CaSO_4 \frac{1}{2} H_2O$

444. Glass is soluble in

A. H_2SO_4 B. HCl

C. HF D. HNO_3

445. PVC is used in

A. manufacture of bags

B. manufacture of cables

C. manufacture of bed linen

D. None of the above

446. When hard water is treated with zeolite, the ions exchanged would include

A. Na^+ and H^+

B. Na^+ and Mg^+

C. Na^+ and OH^-

D. Na^+ and SO_4^{--}

447. Which one of the following nitrogeneous fertilisers is not very effective in acidic soils?

A. Ammonium sulphate

B. Urea

C. Nitrolin

D. Calcium nitrate

448. High-alumina cement can be prepared by heating a mixture of bauxite and

A. tri-calcium aluminate

B. dicalcium silicate

C. limestone

D. gypsum

449. A compound has three elements X (with oxidation number of + 2), Y (with oxidation number of + 5) and Z (with oxidation number of – 2). The molecular formula of the compound is

A. $X_2(YZ_3)_6$

B. $X_3(YZ_4)_2$

C. $X_5(Y_2Z_2)_2$

D. None of the above

450. The mole of a compound is composed of 6.02×10^{23} atoms of hydrogen, 35.5 g of chlorine and 48 g of oxygen. The compound is

A. HCIO B. $HCIO_2$

C. $HCIO_3$ D. $HCIO_4$

ANSWERS

1	2	3	4	5	6	7	8	9	10
A	B	B	B	B	D	B	A	B	D
11	12	13	14	15	16	17	18	19	20
C	B	C	B	D	B	C	A	B	B
21	22	23	24	25	26	27	28	29	30
A	C	D	B	C	B	B	A	C	B
31	32	33	34	35	36	37	38	39	40
B	D	B	A	B	A	B	B	C	C
41	42	43	44	45	46	47	48	49	50
B	B	C	D	C	A	D	C	A	C
51	52	53	54	55	56	57	58	59	60
D	C	B	B	B	C	B	C	A	D
61	62	63	64	65	66	67	68	69	70
B	D	A	C	C	C	A	B	D	A
71	72	73	74	75	76	77	78	79	80
A	C	A	D	B	B	D	C	C	D
81	82	83	84	85	86	87	88	89	90
C	A	D	D	A	B	B	D	B	A
91	92	93	94	95	96	97	98	99	100
C	B	C	B	A	A	D	C	B	A
101	102	103	104	105	106	107	108	109	110
B	B	A	C	D	C	C	B	A	B
111	112	113	114	115	116	117	118	119	120
D	A	B	A	B	A	D	C	C	A
121	122	123	124	125	126	127	128	129	130
A	B	A	A	B	A	D	D	A	C
131	132	133	134	135	136	137	138	139	140
B	C	A	A	B	B	B	B	B	B
141	142	143	144	145	146	147	148	149	150
B	B	D	C	A	D	B	B	A	A
151	152	153	154	155	156	157	158	159	160
A	C	B	A	A	C	A	B	B	A
161	162	163	164	165	166	167	168	169	170
A	C	A	A	C	A	D	A	B	A
171	172	173	174	175	176	177	178	179	180
C	C	B	B	B	D	A	A	D	B
181	182	183	184	185	186	187	188	189	190
C	C	A	B	A	A	D	B	B	C
191	192	193	194	195	196	197	198	199	200
D	B	B	D	[illegible]	B	B	C	A	C

201	202	203	204	205	206	207	208	209	210
C	A	C	A	B	A	C	C	B	A
211	212	213	214	215	216	217	218	219	220
A	D	A	B	D	C	D	C	A	B
221	222	223	224	225	226	227	228	229	230
B	C	C	C	A	C	C	C	B	A
231	232	233	234	235	236	237	238	239	240
C	A	A	D	B	B	B	C	A	A
241	242	243	244	245	246	247	248	249	250
B	A	C	B	D	B	A	A	D	C
251	252	253	254	255	256	257	258	259	260
A	B	A	A	B	C	C	D	B	A
261	262	263	264	265	266	267	268	269	270
C	D	B	C	A	A	B	B	A	A
271	272	273	274	275	276	277	278	279	280
A	A	D	B	C	C	A	A	D	B
281	282	283	284	285	286	287	288	289	290
B	A	C	D	A	C	A	C	A	B
291	292	293	294	295	296	297	298	299	300
A	C	D	B	B	B	C	D	B	B
301	302	303	304	305	306	307	308	309	310
A	B	B	A	C	A	C	D	C	B
311	312	313	314	315	316	317	318	319	320
A	B	B	B	D	A	A	A	C	C
321	322	323	324	325	326	327	328	329	330
C	B	C	A	A	D	B	A	C	D
331	332	333	334	335	336	337	338	339	340
C	C	C	C	B	B	B	A	C	D
341	342	343	344	345	346	347	348	349	350
C	D	C	A	A	D	A	B	A	A
351	352	353	354	355	356	357	358	359	360
A	B	C	B	C	D	C	A	B	C
361	362	363	364	365	366	367	368	369	370
B	A	B	A	B	C	C	B	A	B
371	372	373	374	375	376	377	378	379	380
A	C	C	A	D	B	C	D	B	C
381	382	383	384	385	386	387	388	389	390
B	D	C	B	C	A	C	A	B	D
391	392	393	394	395	396	397	398	399	400
A	B	B	B	C	A	C	D	D	B
401	402	403	404	405	406	407	408	409	410
C	C	B	B	D	B	A	C	A	B
411	412	413	414	415	416	417	418	419	420
B	B	D	B	B	B	B	D	C	C

421	422	423	424	425	426	427	428	429	430
B	D	B	C	C	B	C	A	D	A
431	**432**	**433**	**434**	**435**	**436**	**437**	**438**	**439**	**440**
B	B	A	A	A	B	D	B	D	A
441	**442**	**443**	**444**	**445**	**446**	**447**	**448**	**449**	**450**
A	C	A	C	B	B	D	A	B	C

Biology

1. Which of the following tissues can be used to demonstrate?
   A. Root top B. Shoot apex
   C. Antherlobes D. Stem
2. The main controlling centre of the cell is the
   A. nucleus
   B. mitochondria
   C. ribosome
   D. endoplastic reticulam
3. The gland that contains the body's thermostat is
   A. Pineal
   B. Pituitary
   C. Thyroid
   D. Hypothalamus
4. 'Myopia' is
   A. Colour blindness
   B. Night blindness
   C. Short Sightedness
   D. Long Sightedness
5. Syphilis is caused by
   A. spirochaete B. vibrio
   C. gonococcus D. bacillus
6. $KMNO_4$ can be used is
   A. Pesticide B. Insecticide
   C. Disinfectant D. Fertilizer
   E. None of these
7. Which of the following contains cobalt?
   A. Chlorophyll
   B. Haemoglobin
   C. Vitamin B_{12}
   D. Vitamin K
   E. None of these
8. Which of the following diseases is caused by bacteria?
   A. Small pox B. Dysentry
   C. Influenza D. Cholera
9. The life span of human red corpuscles is
   A. uncertain
   B. 120 days
   C. 180 days
   D. as long as the individual survives
10. The bacteria responsible for 'nitrogen fixation' is found in the roots of
    A. grass
    B. citrus plants
    C. leguminous plants
    D. neem trees
11. The phenomenon involved in the process of dialysis, used on patients with affected kidney, is
    A. diffusion
    B. osmosis
    C. absorption
    D. electrophoresis
12. Which of the following contains the largest quantity of poly-unsaturated fatty acids [PUFA]?
    A. Cottonseed oil
    B. Soyabeen oil
    C. Sunflower oil
    D. Coconut oil
    E. None of these
13. Any enzyme that works in an acidic medium is
    A. Maltose B. Trypsin
    C. Pepsin D. Ptyalin
14. Which of the following is most important for the growth of children up to the age of 14?
    A. Protein B. Vitamins
    C. Fat D. Milk
15. In termites, the cellulose wood is digested by
    A. protozoans

B. bacteria
C. protozoans bacteria
D. cellulose breaking enzyme— β amalyse

16. Which one of the following is a product of the dark reactions of photosynthesis?
A. ATP B. NADH 2
C. NaDPH 2 D. Sugar

17. The rate of which the heart beats per minute in an adult averages
A. 60 B. 72
C. 84 D. 92

18. The least toxic nitrogenous wastes is
A. urea B. creatinine
C. uric acid D. creatine

19. The transport of organic substances in plants is through
A. fibres B. phloem
C. xylem D. wood

20. Which of the following living things is useful to mankind?
A. Earthworm B. Tapeworm
C. Sandworm D. Paramecium

21. Which of the following is not required by the plants to grow?
A. Nitrogen
B. Carbon dioxide
C. Sunlight
D. Sand

22. A valuable drug obtained from a plant is
A. aspirin
B. morphine
C. cimetadine
D. streptomycin

23. Which of the following diseases is caused by virus?
A. Small pox
B. Tuberculosis
C. Tetanus
D. Cholera

24. The main use of "magnesia" is as a/an
A. Mild Laxatire
B. Antiseptic
C. Antibiotic
D. Pain-killer

25. Gene is a segment of
A. Chromosome
B. DNA
C. RNA
D. Both DNA and RNA

26. In higher plant, usually the haploid (half) set of chromosomes are present in
A. Shoot apex B. Endosperm
C. Pollen D. Embryo

27. Which one of the following is the best method for temporarily preventing pregnancy in a woman?
A. IUD B. Tubectomy
C. Vasectomy D. Lapertomy

28. There are four groups of human blood, A, B, AB and O. Which of the following is called universal blood group?
A. O B. A
C. B D. AB

29. Which of the following is not a contagious disease?
A. Measles
B. Tuberculosis
C. Cancer
D. Syphilis

30. During food making process in plants, the gas removed from air is
A. carbon dioxide
B. oxygen
C. nitrogen
D. rare gases

31. Alcohol and Carbon dioxide are formed from carbohydrates by the action of

A. viruses B. bacteria

C. yeasts D. fungus

32. Which of the following is not directly involved with excretory system of our body?

A. Skin

B. Large intestine

C. Lungs

D. Kidneys

33. Haemoglobin contained in the blood is present in

A. plasma

B. white corpuscles

C. red corpuscles

D. All of the above

34. Which of the following elements is not present in human body?

A. Sodium B. Phosphorus

C. Potassium D. Thorium

35. Excess of amino acids are broken down to form urea in

A. Kidney B. Liver

C. Spleen D. Rectum

36. The fertility of the soil can be in created by growing

A. Cereals B. Fibre Crops

C. Legumes D. Root Crops

37. Small pox is caused by

A. bacteria B. germs

C. virus D. worms

38. A person is said to be anaemic if his body has deficiency of

A. calcium and phosphorus

B. vitamins

C. red blood corpuscles

D. white blood corpuscles

39. Virus may be classified as

A. a plant

B. an animal

C. plant as well as animal

D. none of these

40. Which of the following organisms is the smallest?

A. Bacteria B. Virus

C. Protozoa D. Germ

41. Polio is a disease caused due to

A. bacterial infection

B. virus infection

C. protozoal infection

D. food poisoning

42. Which of the following does not contain carbohydrates?

A. Honey B. Potato

C. Saccharine D. Rice

43. The main function of the haemoglobin present in the bloods is to act as

A. oxygen carrier to the cells

B. blood purifier

C. iron store in the body

D. All the above

44. In human body, Vitamin A is stored in

A. skin B. liver

C. spleen D. pancreas

45. Jaundice is caused due to which of the following reasons?

A. Bacterial infection

B. Virus infection

C. Nematodes

D. Sand-fly bite

46. Which of the following vitamins are not 'fat soluble'?

A. Vitamin A, B, O

B. Vitamin A, D, E

C. Vitamin B, C

D. Vitamin A, K

47. Which type of nerve carry impulses from sense organs in response to stimuli; pain, light, heat, sound?

A. Motor nerves

B. Sensory nerves

C. Secretory nerves

D. All the above

48. Which of the following is called "Sunshine Vitamin"?
A. Vitamin A B. Vitamin D
C. Vitamin E D. Vitamin K

49. Deficiency of Vitamin A can cause
A. abnormal clotting of blood
B. night-blindness
C. rickets
D. abnormal functioning of nerves

50. Scurvy is caused by the deficiency of
A. Vitamin C B. Vitamin B
C. RBCs D. WBCs

51. Which of the following acts as the building blocks of proteins?
A. Carbohydrates
B. Amino acids
C. DNA
D. Liquids

52. While cooking food, the compounds lost to the maximum extent are
A. fats
B. carbohydrates
C. proteins
D. vitamins

53. What is essentially required to digest the food in stomach?
A. Air B. Water
C. Enzymes D. Minerals

54. Which of the following is not present is the human body?
A. Lactic acid
B. Hydrochloric acid
C. Nitric acid
D. Amino acid

55. Cynocobalamine is the chemical name of
A. Vitamin A B. Vitamin B_2
C. Vitamin B_6 D. Vitamin B_{12}

56. An enzyme that converts starch into maltose during brewing is known as
A. maltase B. diastase
C. estrase D. anatase

57. In human beings, the two lungs are separated from each other by
A. heart
B. liver
C. pituitary gland
D. kidney

58. The chemical name of vitamin B_1 is
A. niainamide B. pyridoxine
C. thiamine D. riboflavine

59. Iron supplied to the human body in the form of food or medicine, is usually present in
A. ferrous state
B. ferric state
C. elemental state
D. None of the above

60. Power of regeneration is lowest in
A. brain cell B. liver cell
C. bone cell D. muscle cell

61. Crop rotation is used by farmers to increase
A. Soil fertility
B. nitrogenous content of soil
C. organic content of soil
D. All of these

62. Mitochondrial DNA in an individual is derived from
A. father
B. mother
C. both the parents
D. neither of parents

63. In human beings, sex is determined in the sex chromosomes X and Y. What would then, be the genetic constitution of a normal woman?
A. XO B. XX
C. XY D. YY

64. Which of the following is least

infectious?
A. Leprosy
B. Tuberculosis
C. Conjuctivites
D. Hepatitis

65. Which one of the following animals is called a living fossil?
A. Sea cucumber
B. Polystomelia
C. Peripatus
D. Sacculina

66. The normal blood pressure of human beings is the range of
A. 120/80 mm B. 110/70 mm
C. 110/75 mm D. 140/80 mm

67. Most food nutrients are absorbed into the blood from the
A. stomach
B. mouth
C. small intestine
D. large intestine

68. Which one of the following secretions does not contain enzymes?
A. Saliva
B. Pancreatic juice
C. Bile
D. Gastric juice

69. Sex chromosomes may be defined as
A. X-chromosome
B. Y-chromosome
C. Chromosome concerned with sex determination
D. SAT chromosome

70. A pungent odour or the smell of a fine perfume is interpreted in the brain in the
A. Cerebrum
B. Cerbral Hemlspheres
C. Temporal Cortex
D. Cerebellum

71. Transfer of generatic information from one generation to the other is accomplished by
A. DNA
B. Transfer RNA
C. Messenger RNA
D. Messenger and transfer RNA

72. The enzyme found in saliva which converts starch into glucose is
A. phieleam B. zymes
C. lypes D. erepsin

73. Where would you look for active cell division in plants?
A. In cortical cells
B. In pith cells
C. At intermodes of stem
D. At the tip of stem and root

74. Obligate parasites are those organisms which
A. live only on living host
B. live only on dead and decaying organic matter
C. are essentially parasites but can also become saprophytes
D. are essentially saprophytes but can also become parasites

75. A class of hormones which regulate the menstrual cycle and support gamete formation is
A. Progesterone
B. Estrogen
C. Testosterone
D. All the above

76. The most abundant source of iron is
A. milk
B. green vegetables
C. eggs
D. beens

77. Which one of the following is performed by phloem in plants?
A. Photosynthesis
B. Conduction of food
C. Absorption of minerals and

water

D. None of these

78. During blood clotting, platelets release

A. Thrombin

B. Prothrembin

C. Thromobinase

D. Fibrinogen

79. Which one of the following organs is responsible for the water balance of the human body?

A. Lungs B. Kidney

C. Liver D. Heart

E. None of these

80. A sexual reproduction in protozoa is by

A. binary fission

B. fertilisation

C. conjugation

D. None of the above

81. Oxygen balance in the atmosphere is maintained through the process of

A. photosynthesis

B. fat synthesis

C. protein synthesis

D. amino synthesis

82. Non-vascular plants do not contain:

A. parenchyma cells

B. xylem vessel

C. meristematic cells

D. epidermis

83. A tissue is a group of cells having similar

A. origin and function

B. origin, structure and function

C. origin and structure

D. structure and function

84. A link between the living and non-living is provided by

A. bacteria B. viruses

C. plankton D. vibries

85. Agar-commonly used as a synthetic growth medium and in bakery, is obtained from

A. algae B. mosses

C. cycas D. pine

86. Blood is formed in the human adult by the

A. heart

B. spleen

C. red bone marrow

D. yellow bone marrow

87. The largest part of most diets is made up of

A. nucleic acid

B. proteins

C. carbon hydrates

D. vitamin

88. A person with blood group AB is sometimes called a universal recipient because of

A. lack of antigens

B. lack of antibodies

C. lack of both antigens and antibodies

D. the presence of antibodies

89. Haemophilia, a human disease, is caused by

A. bacterial infection

B. fungal infection

C. mutant gene

D. viral infection

90. Chromosomes not related to sex-inheritance are called

A. allosomes B. autosomes

C. centrosomes D. mesosomes

91. The bacteria responsible for 'nitrogen fixation' is found in the roots of

A. grass

B. citrus plants

C. leguminous plants

D. neem trees

92. In hospitals, the oxygen tubes for

respiration contain oxygen and
A. nitrogen
B. helium
C. argon
D. carbon dioxide

93. For a given liquid, the rate of evaporation depends on
A. the temperature of the liquid
B. the temperature of air
C. the surface area of the liquid
D. All these factors

94. Chlorophyll enables the plants to
A. absorb oxygen from the atmosphere
B. absorb carbon dioxide from the atmosphere
C. absorb a little of Sun's energy for food manufacture
D. store starch in the cells of the leaf

95. A typical plant has red flowers if it grown in a slightly acidic soil but has blud flowers if the soil is neutral. Which of the following substances could be added to the soil to change the colour of the flowers of this plant from blue to red?
A. sodium bicarbonate
B. table salt
C. lime
D. vinegar

96. Secondary growth in plants refers to the
A. development of secondary organs after the plant attains maturity
B. development of flowers and fruits
C. growth in length and development of new branches after the plant starts flowering
D. formation of secondary tissues by the activity or lateral meristems

97. Gene control heredity in man and other organism, this gene is
A. A bead-like structure on the chromosomes
B. A protein molecule
C. A segment of RNA
D. A segment of RNA of DNA

98. A balanced fertiliser for plants is
A. compost
B. ammonium sulphate
C. super phosphate of lime
D. urea

99. "Pectin", used in the preparation of certain food belongs to the class of compound called
A. proteins
B. vitamins
C. carbohydrates
D. harmones
E. None of these

100. Which one of the following is non-biodegradable?
A. Glucose
B. A sheet of cellophene
C. Cellulose
D. Latex of a rubber plant

101. A patient was not able to digest the fats. It could be because he was not producing
A. bile juice B. ptyalin
C. amylase D. gastic juice

102. Which one of the following could be preserved only as a mold fossil in sedimentary rock?
A. The foot prints of a dinosaur
B. The body of the insect
C. The skeleton of a fish
D. The tissues of a mammal

103. Which one of the following helped the scientists to develop the cell theory?

A. Discovery of ribosomes
B. Explanation of DNA structure
C. Identification of vacuole
D. Invention of the microscope

104. One difference between sexual reproduction and asexual reproduction is that asexual reproduction produces more

A. differences among individuals in a species
B. similarity between parent and off spring
C. variety among off spring of a single parent
D. similarity among off spring of two parents

105. Which one of the following substances is likely to be present in the urine of a person suffering from the disease diabetes mellitus?

A. Insuline B. Lactose
C. Maltose D. Glucose

106. Which one of the following components does not circulate in a cyclic manner in an ecosystem?

A. Minerals
B. Water
C. Energy
D. Atmospheric gas

107. Which one of the following elements is present in Chlorophyll?

A. Iodine B. Calcium
C. Iron D. Magnesium

108. Which one of the following is known as Tissue?

A. Group of organs
B. Group of system
C. Group of cells
D. Group of vessels

109. Transpiration in green plants is higher in the presence of

A. dry air and high temperature
B. moist air and high temperature
C. moist air and low temperature
D. dry air and low temperature

110. Which one of the following food chains will be more advantageous in terms of energy?

A. 2 trophic levels
B. 3 trophic levels
C. 4 trophic levels
D. 5 trophic levels

111. The element which is good for teeth in small amounts but discolours the teeth and leads to calcification of bones on prolonged use is

A. Phosphorus B. Fluorine
C. Magnesium D. Calcium

112. Which part of brain controls the heart beat in voluntary action?

A. Crebellum
B. Cerebrum
C. Hypothalmus
D. Medulla Oblongata

113. The class of compounds of which the cell wall of plants is made of, is

A. Amino Acid
B. Polysaccharide
C. Protein
D. Lipid

114. The body of reptiles is covered with scales whereas that of birds is covered with feathers, but scales are found in the legs of both of them. It can be inferred from the information that

A. birds and reptiles have common ancestors
B. birds have evolved from reptiles
C. reptiles have evolved from

birds

D. there is no relation between birds and reptiles

115. Which one of the following is not found in birds?

A. Urinary Bladder

B. Intestine

C. Liver

D. Kidneys

116. Which one of the following diseases is not caused by a bacteria?

A. Cholera

B. Dermatitis

C. Rinderpest

D. Tuberculosis

117. Which one of the following deficiency diseases is called an endemic disease?

A. Beri-beri B. Goitre

C. Rickets D. Scurvy

118. You are most likely to find dividing cells in

A. a mature leaf

B. xylem tissue

C. petals of a flower

D. a root tip

119. Digestion of food is aided by the action of

A. antibiotics B. enzymes

C. hormones D. vitamins

120. An animal with a hard, saw-toothed mouth parts is likely to be a

A. blood sucking insect

B. leaf chewing herbivore

C. sap sucking herbivore

D. nector sucking insect

121. Sexual reproduction always involves

A. pollination

B. internal fertilisation

C. the production of sex cells

D. forming of new individuals identical to the parents

122. Tetanus is a disease caused by

A. Fungi B. Bacteria

C. Virus D. Protozoa

123. Molecular weight of glucose is

A. 78 B. 180

C. 110 D. 120

124. A number of organisms are involved in different activities of nitrogen cycle. *Nitrosomonas* and *Nitrobacter* take part in

A. Nitrogen fixation

B. Ammonification and Nitrification

C. Denitrification

D. Immobilization

125. A number of glands are present in human body. Which of the following glands controls the growth of human body?

A. Thyroid B. Adrenal

C. Pituitary D. Pancreas

126. Different parts of a seed are : embryo, cotyledons, endosperm and seed coat. Plumule is a part of

A. Embryo B. Endosperm

C. Cotyledons D. Seed Coat

127. Micro-organisms and enzymes are most active in the temperature range

A. 10°C-20°C B. 20°C-30°C

C. 30°C-40°C D. 40°C-50°C

128. Catract, a disease of the eye is due to

A. eye lens turning opaque

B. damage to cornea

C. tearing of retina

D. dislodgement of retina

129. Which one of the following tissues are not found in animals?

A. Connective tissue

B. Meristematic tissue
C. Epithelial tissue
D. Muscle tissue

130. Which of the following is not a single celled organism?
A. Euglena
B. Hydra
C. Paramoecium
D. Amoeba

131. Ammonia is converted into urea in
A. pancreas B. liver
C. kidney D. stomach

132. Microvilli are found in the
A. oesophagus
B. stomach
C. small intestine
D. large intestine

133. Photosynthesis takes place
A. during a sunny day only
B. during a cloudy day only
C. during the night only
D. Both during day and night

134. Which one of the following is a hermaphrodite?
A. Frog B. Man
C. Hydra D. Donkey

135. The site of energy production in the cell is
A. ribosomes
B. golgi bodies
C. mitochondria
D. chloroplast

136. The pyramids in human kidney are found in
A. cortex B. medulla
C. ureter D. pelvis

137. Organs having same origin and structure but perform different functions are
A. homologous organs
B. analogous organs
C. vestigeal organs
D. None of the above

138. Vestigeal organ is
A. fully developed and non-functional
B. rudimentary with special function
C. vermiform appendix only
D. rudimentary and non-functional

139. Which of the following includes the remaining three?
A. Biome B. Ecosystem
C. Biosphere D. Community

140. The percentage of nitrogen in the atmosphere is about
A. 21 per cent B. 78 per cent
C. 52 per cent D. 82 per cent

141. One of the following is not able to fix free atmospheric nitrogen
A. blue green algae
B. non-leguminous plants like *Gingko*
C. non-leguminous plants like wheat and maize
D. All leguminous plants

142. Which of the following Indian animal is a protected species?
A. Horse B. Rhinoceros
C. Cow D. Snake

143. Biennial plants are those which
A. produce flowers twice in their life-cycle
B. produce flowers many times in their life-cycle
C. remains vegetative in one growing season
D. complete their life-cycle in one season only

144. A pollen grain of angiosperm may be best defined as
A. a male sperm cell
B. a spore mother cell
C. a partially developed embryo

D. a partially developed male. gametophyte

145. How many miotic cell divisions will be required to get 16 cells?
A. 2 B. 4
C. 8 D. 15

146. Leaves are modified into spines in cactus because
A. they protect the plant
B. they prevent loss of water (transpiration)
C. the plant does not need leaves
D. None of the above

147. A camel does not perspire in summer because
A. it reduces the body temperature by 7°C from the surrounding environment
B. it increases the body temperature upto 42°C
C. it has no sweat glands
D. the pores through which sweat comes out get choked with sand

148. From the list given find out the main characteristics of a fish
A. carnivorous
B. swimming
C. gill breathing
D. egg and egg laying

149. Plant cells differ from animal cells as
A. plant cells have cellulose walls
B. plant cells are larger
C. plant cells have vacuoles
D. plant cells are smaller

150. Iodine is required for the activity of
A. adrenal gland
B. liver
C. spleen
D. thyroid

151. Iron is necessary for the formation of
A. nerve cells
B. parietal cells
C. red blood cells
D. white blood cells

152. The cerebrum which is the largest part of human brain is responsible for
A. the reflex action
B. coordinating the movements of body
C. memory and learing
D. controlling the heart and breathing

153. Pepsin is secreted by
A. liver B. pancreas
C. stomach D. intestine

154. Which of the following salivary glands are largest in size?
A. Parotid glands
B. Submandibular
C. Sublingual
D. All of the same size

155. Which of the following type of food will provide more energy?
A. Carbohydrate
B. Proteins
C. Fats
D. Vitamins

156. Hydrochloric acid producing cells of stomach are
A. pareital cells
B. chief cells
C. mucous cells
D. goblet cells

157. Enzymes producing cells of stomach are
A. parietal cells
B. chief cells
C. mucous cells
D. goblet cells

158. Muscularis mucosae is well

developed in

A. duodenum B. jejunum
C. stomach D. rectum

159. The enzyme pepsin is

A. secreted in the vertebrate stomach that acts in an acidic medium
B. secreted in the vertebrate stomach that acts in an acidic mdeium
C. secreted in vertebrate small intestine that acts in an acidic medium
D. secreted in the vertebrate small intestine that acts in an acidic medium

160. Which of the following gland is known as 'graveyard' of red blood cells?

A. Pancreas B. LIver
C. Kidney D. Spleen

161. Teeth are derived from

A. epidermic of skin
B. both epidermis and dermis of skin
C. dermis of skin
D. bone of the jaw skeleton

162. Liver can synthesise

A. vitamin A B. vitamin B
C. vitamin D D. vitamin K

163. Respiration in all animals is similar in that it involves

A. intake of oxygen to the blood
B. expulsion of carbon dioxide from the blood
C. production of energy
D. All of the above

164. The centre for the regulation of respiration is present in the

A. cerebrum
B. medulla oblongata
C. olfactory lobes
D. optic lobes

165. The capacity of tissues to use oxygen is lost in

A. asphyxia
B. anemic hypoxia
C. histotoxic hypoxia
D. All of the above

166. The common passage for food and air in mammals is the

A. oesophagus B. nasal cavity
C. larynx D. pharynx

167. Maximum carbon dioxide from the tissues is collected in the form of

A. carbonic acid
B. sodium and potassium bicarbonates
C. in the gaseous state
D. dissolved with haemoglobin

168. The nervous control of the respiratory system is done by

A. central nervous system
B. atomic nervous system
C. central and peripheral systems
D. parasympathetic nervous system

169. Glottis of frog leads to

A. tracheal chamber
B. pharyngo-tracheal chamber
C. laryngo-tracheal chamber
D. bucco-pharyngeal chamber

170. With the increase of carbon dioxide concentration in the blood, breathing becomes

A. slow and deep
B. faster and deeper
C. slow and superificial
D. there is no effect on breathing

171. Arteries supplying blood to the heart are

A. hepatic arteris
B. pulmonary arteries
C. cardiac arteries
D. coronary arteries

172. Haemoglobin in the blood is present to
A. impart red colour to the blood
B. transport oxygen from lungs to tissues
C. transport carbondioxide from tissues to lungs
D. make the blood concentrated in proteins

173. The artery carrying deoxygenated blood is
A. pulmonary B. gastric
C. renal D. coronary

174. The heart of a fish is
A. one-chambered
B. two-chambered
C. three-chambered
D. four-chambered

175. Veins can best be defined as
A. blood vessels carrying oxygenated blood
B. blood vessels carrying deoxygenated blood
C. blood vessels that bring blood from body organs to the heart
D. blood vessels that carry blood from heart to body organs

176. The number of pulmonary veins present in mammals are
A. one B. two
C. three D. four

177. The largest artery in the body is
A. pulmonary artery
B. gastric artery
C. aorta
D. renal artery

178. Adult human heart weighs about
A. 180 grams B. 300 grams
C. 500 grams D. 750 grams

179. At the time of birth
A. there are more WBC than RBC
B. there are less WBC than RBC
C. WBC and RBC and equal in number
D. None of the above

180. Presence of urea in the blood is called as
A. uremia
B. diurea
C. haematuria
D. None of the above

181. Yellow colour of the urine is due to the presence of
A. uric acid B. cholestrol
C. urochrome D. bile salts

182. The loop of Henle in the nephron is absent from
A. frog B. man
C. rabbit D. dog

183. The normal blood flow through arteries in human is about
A. 25 litres/hour
B. 50 litres/hour
C. 100 litres/hour
D. 200 litres/hour

184. Which of the following is not an excretory activity?
A. Removal of carbon dioxide
B. Removal of faecal matter
C. Removal of sweat due to perspiration
D. Removal of urine

185. Kidney stones are mainly made of
A. uric acid and calcium carbonate
B. uric acid and calcium oxalate
C. uric acid and phosphates of calcium and magnesium
D. uric acid and calcium metabi-sulphite

186. Urine is
A. acidic in nature
B. alkaline in nature
C. neutral in nature
D. None of the above

187. The number of nephrons in a kidney of human beings is about
A. 2×10^6 B. 2×10^9
C. 2×10^{12} D. 2×10^{15}

188. The region of the brain that coordinates various involuntary actions of the body are
A. cerebrum
B. medulla oblongata
C. cerebellum
D. optic lobes

189. Which of the following nerve is purely sensory?
A. Olfactory B. Hypoglossal
C. Vagus D. Trochlear

190. A spinal nerve divides into
A. ramus dorsalis and ramsu ventralis
B. ramus dorsalis, ramus ventralis, and communicans
C. ramus communicans only
D. ramus dorsalis only

191. Autonomic nervous system consist of
A. two longitudinal sympathetic chains of ganglia
B. one longitudinal sympathetic chain of ganglia
C. two longitudinal sympathetic chains of ganglia
D. one longitudinal parasympathetic chain of ganglia

192. Which of the following layer is present only in mammals
A. Duramater
B. Pia mater
C. Archnoid
D. None of these

193. Which of the following portion of brains should be destroyed for the loss of intelligence?
A. Cerebellum
B. Cerebral hemispheres
C. Olfactory lobes
D. Optic lobes

194. In man, total number of muscles present is
A. 639 B. 650
C. 550 D. 450

195. The total number of vertebrae in an adult human being is
A. 33 B. 26
C. 36 D. 56

196. The longest bone of the body
A. humerus B. femur
C. tibia D. radius

197. The activity of the anterior pituitary gland is regulated by
A. posterior pituitary
B. somatogenic hormone in the blood
C. hypothalamus
D. All of the above

198. The disease 'acromegaly' is caused due to the hyper activity of
A. pituitary B. thyroid
C. parathroid D. pineal

199. If a person of 40 years of age is given the extracts of pituitary gland, he will suffer from
A. gigantism
B. acromegaly
C. his life span will increase
D. his reproductive abilities will increase

200. The egg of human being is
A. alecithal and mesolectithal
B. microlecithal and telolecithal
C. alecithal and isolecithal
D. alecithal and centrolecithal

201. The term 'puberty' refers to the stage when
A. the animal becomes fully mature
B. the secondary sexual

characters start appearing
C. the ovum is released from the ovary or the first discharge from penis occur
D. the male and female reproduce

202. What will happen, if a fresh water *Amoeba* is put in a sea water?
A. The number of food vacuoles will increase
B. The amount of plasmasol will decrease and the amount of plasmagel increase
C. The animal will die
D. The animal will lose water and contractile vacuole

203. Time required for binary fission in *Amoeba* is
A. 15 minutes B. 30 minutes
C. 60 minutes D. 120 minutes

204. Asexual reproduction in a sponge *Leucosolenia* occurs by
A. binary fission
B. sporulation
C. gemmule formation
D. budding

205. *Hydra* is usable to digest
A. carbohydrates
B. proteins
C. fats
D. starch

206. The male mosquitoes are unable to suck the blood because
A. they have reduced mandibles
B. mandibles are absent
C. they have reduced antennae
D. they have reduced eyes

207. The prawns are
A. herbivorous
B. carnivorous
C. omnivorous
D. insectivorous

208. The largest living bird is
A. kiwi B. ostrich
C. emu D. crane

209. The smallest mammal is the
A. screw B. mouse
C. platypus D. mole

210. The largest living mammal is
A. elephant
B. tiger
C. whale
D. hippopotamus

211. Life first originated in the
A. sea water B. fresh water
C. air D. land

212. The process of organic evolution is
A. slow and discontinuous
B. slow and continuous
C. rapid and discontinuous
D. rapid and continuous

213. Sense organs get degenerated in
A. aquatic animals
B. terrestrial animals
C. cave-dwellers
D. desert animals

214. Modern man *Homo sapiens* originated from
A. monkey B. gorilla
C. chimpanze D. proconsul

215. Protoplasm is a
A. heterogenous fluid
B. homogenous fluid
C. gel-like fluid
D. sol-like fluid

216. A microscope used to study the three diamensional image of an object is
A. phase contrast microscope
B. scanning electron microscope
C. *uv*-microscope
D. electron microscope

217. A dead cell differs from a living

cell in that

A. it has separated from other cells

B. its vital process are destroyed

C. a change in its specific organisation has occured

D. a change in its surrounding atmosphere has occured

218. The chief component of protoplasm is

A. glucose B. fat

C. water D. alcohol

219. Plasm membrane is a

A. fully permeable structure

B. non-permeable structure

C. semi-permeable structure

D. selectively permeable structure

220. The most important function of lysosomes is in

A. bone formation

B. intercellular digestion

C. interacellular digestion

D. autolysis

221. The nucleus of a cell helps in

A. cell maintenance

B. cell replication

C. control of cell activities

D. All of the above

222. An organised nucleus is absent from

A. green algae

B. parasitic angiosperms

C. bacteria

D. fungi

223. Chemically nucleus consists of

A. DNA and proteins

B. RNA and proteins

C. RNA and DNA

D. RNA, DNA and proteins

224. Mendel was successful over his predecessors because

A. he established relationships between the individuals and their parents by keeping the pedigree records of several generations

B. he made quantitative studies to establish certain mathematical hypothesis

C. he used pea as the plant material

D. All of the above

225. DNA replication is done by the activity of the enzyme

A. DNA synthatase

B. DNA polymerase

C. RNA polymerase

D. deoxyribonuclease

226. The DNA contents in a cell

A. is same throughout the cell cycle

B. increases sharply during the period just before chromosome duplication

C. decreases during the process of cell division

D. increases after the mitosis is completed

227. Length of a plant is increased by the tissues of

A. lateral meristems

B. apical meristems

C. intercalary meristems

D. All of the above

228. In the process of osmosis

A. both cell wall and protoplasm act as a membrane

B. the whole prtoplasms act as a membrane

C. only the outer layer of protoplasm acts as a membrane

D. cell wall only acts as a membrane

229. The process of transpiration takes

place through the
A. stomata
B. cuticle
C. lenticels
D. All of the above

230. Grafting in monocot stems is not possible because they
A. do not have acambium
B. have scattered vascular bundles
C. have no collenchymatous hypodermis
D. All of the above

231. Most of the plants obtain nitrogen from the soil in the form of
A. free nitrogen
B. nitric acid
C. nitrites
D. nitrates

232. Which of the following is a micronutrient?
A. Nitrogen
B. Magnesium
C. Potassium
D. Molybdenum

233. Potassium is required by the plant body in the process of
A. photosynthesis
B. synthesis of chromophyll
C. opening and closing of stomata
D. All of the above

234. Magnesium and iron are needed by plants in the
A. energy transfer mechanisms
B. synthesis of chlorophyll
C. stomatal opening and closing
D. translocation of carbohydrates

235. In plants, a common symptom caused by the deficiencies P, K, Ca and Mg is
A. curling of leaf tip
B. formation of anthocyanin pigments
C. poor development of venation
D. appearance of dead necrotic tissues

236. Leaves appear green because they
A. absorb green light
B. reflect green light
C. both absorb and reflect green light
D. None of the above

237. The first step in photosynthesis is the
A. joining of 3-carbon atoms to form glucose
B. photophosphorylation
C. excitement of chlorophyll molecule by light
D. photolysis of water

238. The process of taking in CO_2 and release of O_2 by plants occurs in
A. transpiration
B. respiration
C. photosynthesis
D. osmosis

239. The role of light in photosynthesis is to
A. activate chloroplast
B. split water
C. reduce carbon dioxide
D. synthesize glucose

240. Dark reaction of photosynthesis is so called because
A. it can also occur in dark
B. it does not require light energy
C. both the above
D. none of the above

241. Which of the following equation is most correct for photosynthesis?
A. $CO_2 + H_2O \rightarrow CH_2O + O_2$
B. $6CO_2 + 6H_2O \rightarrow C_6H_{12}O_6 + 6O_2$

C. $6CO_2 + 12H_2O \rightarrow C_6H_{12}O_6 + 6H_2O + 6O_2\uparrow$

D. $C_6H_{12}O_6 + O_2 \rightarrow CO_2 + H_2O$

242. One of the following is not a limiting factor in the process of photosynthesis

A. oxygen

B. carbondioxide

C. chlorophyll

D. availability of sunlight

243. The percentage of light energy utilised for photosynthesis by higher plant is

A. 99% B. 50%

C. 10% D. 1-9%

244. The rate of photosynthesis is independent of

A. quality of light

B. quantity of light

C. duration of light

D. temperature

245. The photosynthesis pigments present in the green plants are

A. chlorophyll a

B. chlorophyll b

C. carotene and xanthophyll

D. All of the above

246. In the dark reaction, CO_2 is (in C_4 plants)

A. PGA B. PEP

C. RuDP D. glucose

247. In C_4 plants, carbon dioxide fixation occurs in the chloroplasts of

A. palisade parenchyma

B. spongy parenchyma

C. bundle sheath

D. guard cells

248. The end product of respiration in plants are

A. carbon dioxide and water

B. carbon dioxide, water and energy

C. water and energy

D. sugar and energy

249. The immediate source of energy in cellular activity is

A. DNA B. RNA

C. NAD D. ATP

250. The movement of plant hormones is in

A. longitudinal direction

B. horizontal direction

C. any direction

D. hormones do not move

251. Sugar cane is an example of

A. Long Day Plant (LDP)

B. Short Day Plant (SDP)

C. Day Neutral Plant (DNP)

D. None of the above

252. The primary function of the stem is

A. to bear the leaves

B. to absorb water and mineral salts

C. to fix the plant to the soil

D. to help in vegetative propagation

253. 'Eyes' are present in

A. rhizome B. bulb

C. tuber D. corm

254. Bipinnate compound leaf is present in

A. rose B. peepal

C. gold mohar D. china rose

255. Branching in a tree provides

A. large amount of timber

B. large number of leaves

C. sufficient light for photosynthesis

D. provides mechanical supoort

256. The edible part of apple is

A. epicarp

B. mesocarp

C. endocarp

D. fleshy thalamus

257. The plant which buries its fruits in the soil is
A. potato B. radish
C. groundnut D. sweet potato

258. The type of fruit of water melon is
A. drupe B. peop
C. pome D. berry

259. Double fertilisation means
A. one male gamete fuses with two female gametes
B. two male gamates fuse with one female gamete
C. one male gamete fuses with one female gamete twice
D. two male gametes fuse with two female gametes separately

260. Seeds are sensitive to light because of the presence of
A. chlorophyll
B. embryonal axis
C. phytochromes
D. endosperms

261. Yeast is abundantly found in
A. moist bread
B. organic matter rich in carbohydrates
C. organic matter rich in proteins
D. organic matter rich in fats

262. The main cause that has led to increase in population all over the world is
A. decrease in death rate
B. increase in birth rate
C. decrease in birth rate
D. increase in death rate

263. Leaching of soil generally occurs in
A. dry regions
B. arctic regions
C. humid regions
D. can be any region

264. The soil nutrients are mainly lost due to
A. soil erosion
B. over cropping
C. leaching
D. All of these

265. The antibiotic chlorellin is obtained from
A. an alga B. a fungus
C. a virus D. a bacterium

266. Most of the pulses we eat belong to the family
A. Cuccurbotaceae
B. Umbelliferal
C. Pepilionaceal
D. Cruciferal

267. Genes are made of
A. Histones
B. Polynucleotides
C. Hydrocarbons
D. Lipoproteins

268. Which of the following diseases are sex-linked?
A. Colour blindness
B. Malignancy
C. Hepatitis
D. Leukemia

269. The mechanical tissue consisting of living cells is
A. collenchyma
B. selerenchyma
C. parenchyma
D. chlorenchyma

270. Which of the following is micronutrient?
A. Mg B. K
C. Ca D. Zn

271. The protein part of an enzyme is termed
A. apoenzyme
B. holoenzyme
C. coenzyme

D. prostheic group

272. Chlorosis in leaves is due to
A. lack of water
B. pathogenic disease
C. lack of certain minerals
D. None of these

273. Sexual reproduction is absent in
A. blue-green algae
B. green algae
C. brown algae
D. red algae

274. DNA is
A. single stranded
B. double stranded
C. single or double stranded
D. None of these

275. RNA is
A. single stranded
B. double stranded
C. single or double stranded
D. None of these

276. The first event in photosynthesis is
A. photolysis of water
B. release of oxygen
C. formation of ATP and $NADPH_2$
D. photroexitation of chlorophyll and ejection of an electron

277. Many of the biological proteins are determined largely by the
A. kinds of amino acids present
B. order in which amino acids are linked together in the polypeptide chain
C. spatial relationship of one amino acid to another
D. All of the above

278. Total number of amino acids in nature
A. 20
B. 22
C. 23
D. 200 approximately

279. Enzyme contained in the tears, nasal mucous and sputum is
A. lysozyme
B. isozyme
C. ribonuclease
D. None of these

280. Malaria is transmitted by
A. female *Anopheles*
B. feamle *Culex*
C. male *Anopheles*
D. both male and female *Anophles*

281. Shivering characteristic of malaria occurs when
A. merozoitses are liberated from RBCs with toxic substance haemozoin
B. schizonts enter the RBCs
C. signet ring stage
D. trophozoite stage

282. Canal system in sponges serves for
A. nutrition
B. nutrition and respiration
C. nutrition, respiration and excretion
D. nutrition, respiration, excretion and gamete transportation

283. In the kidney, glucose is mainly absorbed in the
A. loop of Henle
B. proximal convoluted tubule
C. distal convoluted tubule
D. Bowman's capsule

284. After fertilisation the zygote will develop into a male organism in the
A. egg possesses a y-chromosome
B. sperm possesses a y-chromosome

C. sperm posses an X-chromosome

D. egg posees an Y-chromosome

285. Spinal cleavage is found in

A. annelids B. flat worm

C. molluses D. All of these

286. When DDT was applied in an orchard as a pesticide the fruit production decreased. This happened because

A. DDT is a growth retardant

B. DDT disturbed hormonoa balance essential for fruit setting

C. DDT killed the pollinating insects along with the pests

D. DDT inhibited flowering

287. A chemical that prevents blood clotting is most useful in the treatment of

A. leukaemia

B. anaemia

C. coronary thrombosis

D. haemophilia

288. Red blood corpuscles are manufactured in

A. bone marrow

B. liver only

C. spleen only

D. All the above three

289. The beating of heart is referred to

A. expansion of auricle

B. expansion of ventricle

C. expansion of contraction of both auricle

D. contraction of auricle and ventricle

290. The middle ear is made up of

A. bone

B. cartilage

C. muscles

D. bone and muscles

291. Which of the following function is not done by kidney?

A. Respiration

B. Ultrafilteration

C. Reabsorption

D. Recreation

292. Plants give out during day and take in during night

A. oxygen and nitrogen

B. oxygen

C. carbon dioxide and oxygen

D. carbon dioxide and nitrogen

293. The head region of virus contains

A. ammonia

B. nucleic acid

C. amino acids

D. deoxy ribo nucleic acid

294. Thorns grow in place of leaves in

A. mesophyte B. halophyte

C. tropophytes D. xerophytes

295. The principal cereal crop in India is

A. wheat B. rice

C. maize D. sorghum

296. Insulin is

A. an enzyme which digests sugar

B. an enzyme which converts invertage into glucose

C. a hormone which helps metabolism of sugar

D. a hormone which promotes growth

297. A clone is produced

A. sexually from a single sexually produced ancestor

B. sexually from single asexually produced ancestor

C. by artificial insemination from a single sexually produced ancestor

D. *in vitro* from a single sexually produced ancestor

298. Life of a RBC in human blood

is of

A. 30 days

B. 120 days

C. 15 hours

D. None of these

299. Pasteurisation is a heat treatment that destroys

A. all the micro-organisms

B. enzymes

C. part but not all the micro-organisms

D. catalysts

300. Ranikhet disease is a disease affecting

A. pigs B. poultry

C. cattle D. horse

ANSWERS

1	**2**	**3**	**4**	**5**	**6**	**7**	**8**	**9**	**10**
A	A	D	C	D	C	C	D	B	C
11	**12**	**13**	**14**	**15**	**16**	**17**	**18**	**19**	**20**
B	C	C	A	B	D	B	A	B	A
21	**22**	**23**	**24**	**25**	**26**	**27**	**28**	**29**	**30**
D	B	A	A	A	C	A	A	C	A
31	**32**	**33**	**34**	**35**	**36**	**37**	**38**	**39**	**40**
C	B	C	D	B	C	C	C	D	B
41	**42**	**43**	**44**	**45**	**46**	**47**	**48**	**49**	**50**
B	C	A	B	B	C	B	B	B	A
51	**52**	**53**	**54**	**55**	**56**	**57**	**58**	**59**	**60**
B	D	C	C	D	B	A	C	A	A
61	**62**	**63**	**64**	**65**	**66**	**67**	**68**	**69**	**70**
A	B	B	A	C	A	C	C	C	B
71	**72**	**73**	**74**	**75**	**76**	**77**	**78**	**79**	**80**
A	A	D	A	B	B	B	C	B	A
81	**82**	**83**	**84**	**85**	**86**	**87**	**88**	**89**	**90**
A	B	D	B	A	C	C	B	C	B
91	**92**	**93**	**94**	**95**	**96**	**97**	**98**	**99**	**100**
C	B	D	B	A	D	D	A	C	D
101	**102**	**103**	**104**	**105**	**106**	**107**	**108**	**109**	**110**
A	A	D	B	D	A	D	C	A	A
111	**112**	**113**	**114**	**115**	**116**	**117**	**118**	**119**	**120**
B	D	D	C	A	B	B	B	B	B
121	**122**	**123**	**124**	**125**	**126**	**127**	**128**	**129**	**130**
D	B	B	B	C	D	D	A	B	B
131	**132**	**133**	**134**	**135**	**136**	**137**	**138**	**139**	**140**
B	C	A	C	C	B	A	D	C	B
141	**142**	**143**	**144**	**145**	**146**	**147**	**148**	**149**	**150**
C	B	B	D	D	B	B	C	A	D
151	**152**	**153**	**154**	**155**	**156**	**157**	**158**	**159**	**160**
C	C	C	A	C	A	B	C	A	D

161	**162**	**163**	**164**	**165**	**166**	**167**	**168**	**169**	**170**
B	D	C	B	C	D	B	C	C	B
171	**172**	**173**	**174**	**175**	**176**	**177**	**178**	**179**	**180**
D	B	A	B	C	D	C	B	A	A
181	**182**	**183**	**184**	**185**	**186**	**187**	**188**	**189**	**190**
C	A	A	B	C	A	A	C	A	B
191	**192**	**193**	**194**	**195**	**196**	**197**	**198**	**199**	**200**
A	C	B	A	B	B	C	A	B	C
201	**202**	**203**	**204**	**205**	**206**	**207**	**208**	**209**	**210**
B	D	B	D	D	B	C	B	A	C
211	**212**	**213**	**214**	**215**	**216**	**217**	**218**	**219**	**220**
A	B	C	D	A	A	B	C	D	C
221	**222**	**223**	**224**	**225**	**226**	**227**	**228**	**229**	**230**
D	C	D	D	B	B	B	C	D	B
231	**232**	**233**	**234**	**235**	**236**	**237**	**238**	**239**	**240**
D	D	D	B	D	B	C	C	A	B
241	**242**	**243**	**244**	**245**	**246**	**247**	**248**	**249**	**250**
B	A	D	C	D	B	C	B	D	A
251	**252**	**253**	**254**	**255**	**256**	**257**	**258**	**259**	**260**
C	A	C	C	B	D	C	B	D	C
261	**262**	**263**	**264**	**265**	**266**	**267**	**268**	**269**	**270**
B	A	C	D	A	C	B	A	B	D
271	**272**	**273**	**274**	**275**	**276**	**277**	**278**	**279**	**280**
A	C	A	A	A	D	D	D	A	A
281	**282**	**283**	**284**	**2285**	**286**	**287**	**288**	**289**	**290**
A	D	B	B	D	C	C	A	C	A
291	**292**	**293**	**294**	**295**	**296**	**297**	**298**	**299**	**300**
A	B	D	D	B	C	A	B	D	B

QUANTITATIVE APTITUDE

1

NUMBERS

A number tells us how many times a unit is contained in a given quantity. It therefore signifies one or more units, or denotes one or more distinct objects of the same kind. For example, *one* rupee, *six* pencils, *nine* cats, *thirty* paise, etc. The words in italics denote numbers.

Whole Numbers: The numbers 0, 1, 2, 3, 4, 5, 6, 7, 8, 9, 10, 11, ... are called whole numbers or integers. So 84 is an integer while 6¼ is not an integer.

Even Numbers: The numbers, which are divisible by two are called even numbers. *For example,* 2, 4, 6, 8, 10, 12, 28, 36, etc.

Odd Numbers: The numbers, which cannot be divided by two are called odd numbers. *For example,* 1, 3, 5, 7, 9, 11, 13, 15, 17, 19, etc.

Prime Numbers: The numbers, which are divisible only by themselves and one are called prime numbers. *For example,* 2, 3, 5, 7, 11, 13, etc.

Composite Numbers: The numbers, which are not prime called composite numbers. Thus, the prime numbers and composite numbers make up the set of natural numbers.

Consecutive Numbers: A collection of numbers is consecutive if each number is the successor of the number which precedes it. *For example,* 4, 5, 6, 7, 8 and 9 are consecutive, but 4, 5, 6, 8, 10 are not. 6, 8, 10, 12 are consecutive even numbers. 11, 13, 17, 19 are consecutive prime numbers.

Any whole number can be written as a product of factors which are prime numbers.

How to write a number as a product of prime factors?

(*i*) Divide the number by 2 if possible; continue to divide by 2 until the factor you get, is not divisible by 2.

(*ii*) Divide the result from (i) by 3 if possible; continue to divide by 3 until the factor you get, is not divisible by 3.

(*iii*) Divide the result from (ii) by 5 if possible; continue to divide by 5 until the factor you get, is not divisible by 5.

(*iv*) Continue this procedure by dividing by 7, 11, 13, and so on; until all the factors are prime.

EXAMPLES :

Example 1. *Express 2310 as a product of prime factors.*

Solution.

2	2310
2	1155
5	385
7	77
	11

$\therefore$ 2310 = 2 × 3 × 5 × 7 × 11.

Example 2. *Resolve 1026 into prime factors.*

Solution.

2	1026
3	513
3	171
3	57
	19

$\therefore$ 1026 = 2 × 3 × 3 × 3 × 19

A number n is a common multiple of two other numbers a and b if it is a multiple of each of them. For example, 24 is a common multiple of 2 and 3, since 2 × 12 = 24 and 3 × 8 = 24. But 21 is not a common multiple of 3 and 6, because 21 is not a multiple of 6.

A number *x* is a common factor of two other numbers *a* and *b* if *x* is a factor of *a* and *x* is a factor of *b*.

L.C.M.: The least common multiple of two numbers is the smallest number which is a common multiple of both numbers.

How to find the least common multiple of two numbers *a* and *b*?

(i) Write *a* and *b* as products of *primes* separately.

(ii) If there are any common factors delete them in one of the products.

(iii) Multiply the remaining factors to get L.C.M.

PROPERTIES OF NUMBERS

1. The product of any two consecutive numbers is divisible by 2

For example,

2 × 3 = 6 is divisible by 2

3 × 4 = 12 is divisible by 2

4 × 5 = 20 is divisible by 2

15 × 16 = 240 is divisible by 2

2. The product of any three consecutive numbers is divisible by 6.
For example,

$2 \times 3 \times 4 = 24$ is divisible by 6
$3 \times 4 \times 5 = 60$ is divisible by 6
$4 \times 5 \times 6 = 120$ is divisible by 6
$10 \times 11 \times 12 = 1320$ is divisible by 6
$40 \times 41 \times 42 = 68880$ is divisible by 6

3. The product of any four consecutive numbers is divisible by 24.
For example,

$2 \times 3 \times 4 \times 5 = 120$ is divisible by 24.

$$4 \times 5 \times 6 \times 7 = 24 \times 5 \times 7$$
$$6 \times 7 \times 8 \times 9 = 3 \times 2 \times 7 \times 8 \times 9 = 24 \times 2 \times 7 \times 9$$
$$10 \times 11 \times 12 \times 13 = 2 \times 5 \times 11 \times 12 \times 13 = 24 \times 5 \times 11 \times 13$$

4. The product of any five consecutive numbers is divisible by 120.
For example,

$$2 \times 3 \times 4 \times 5 \times 6 = 120 \times 6$$
$$3 \times 4 \times 5 \times 6 \times 7 = 120 \times 21$$
$$4 \times 5 \times 6 \times 7 \times 8 = 120 \times 56$$

5. Every square number is a multiple of 3 or exceeds of multiple of 3 by unity.
For example,

$$3^2 = 9 = 3 \times 3$$
$$4^2 = 16 = 3 \times 5 + 1$$
$$5^2 = 25 = 3 \times 8 + 1$$
$$6^2 = 36 = 3 \times 12$$
$$7^2 = 49 = 3 \times 16 + 1$$

6. Difference of the squares of any two odd numbers is always divisible by 8.
For example,

$$5^2 - 3^2 = 25 - 9 = 16 = 8 \times 2$$
$$7^2 - 5^2 = 49 - 25 = 24 = 8 \times 3$$
$$9^2 - 5^2 = 81 - 25 = 56 = 8 \times 7$$
$$11^2 - 3^2 = 121 - 9 = 112 = 8 \times 14$$

7. A number is exactly divisible by 11 when the difference between the sums of the digits in the odd and even places respectively is zero or a multiple of 11.
For example, Consider the number 1569942

Sum of the odd digits = $1 + 6 + 9 + 2 = 18$
Sum of the even digits = $5 + 9 + 4 = 18$

Difference between the sums of the odd and even digits

$$= 18 - 18 = 0$$

Hence, 1569942 is divisible by 11.

8. The product of two consecutive odd or even numbers increased by unity is a perfect square.

For example,

$$3 \times 5 + 1 = 16 = 4^2$$
$$4 \times 6 + 1 = 25 = 5^2$$
$$5 \times 7 + 1 = 36 = 6^2$$
$$6 \times 8 + 1 = 49 = 7^2$$

9. The sum of any two consecutive numbers is equal to the difference of their squares.

For example,

$$3 + 4 = 7 = 4^2 - 3^2 = 7$$
$$5 + 4 = 9 = 5^2 - 4^2 = 9$$
$$7 + 6 = 13 = 7^2 - 6^2 = 13$$

10. The sum of the cubes of any three consecutive numbers is divisible by the sum of the numbers themselves.

For example, $2^3 + 3^3 + 4^3 = 8 + 27 + 64 = 99 = (2 + 3 + 4)\ 11$

$4^3 + 5^3 + 6^3 = 64 + 125 + 216 = 405$

$= (4 + 5 + 6)\ 27$

EXERCISE

1. 2, 4, 6, 8, 10, ... are:

A. prime numbers
B. odd numbers
C. even numbers
D. natural numbers

2. 1, 2, 3, 4, ... are :

A. Natural numbers
B. Odd numbers
C. Prime numbers
D. Composite numbers

3. 1, 2, 3, 4, 5, 7, 11 and 13 are:

A. even numbers
B. odd numbers
C. prime numbers
D. natural numbers

4. The prime numbers between 1 to 100 are:

A. 20 B. 22
C. 25 D. 30

5. The only even prime number is:

A. 2 B. 67
C. 79 D. 98

6. Which of the following is not a prime number?

79, 83, 87, 97

A. 79 B. 83
C. 87 D. 97

7. Which of the following is a prime number?

117, 147, 149, 159

A. 117 B. 147
C. 149 D. 159

8. The next number in the sequence 1, 7, 3, 9, 5, 11, ... is :
A. 7 B. 13
C. 15 D. 17

9. In the sequence 4, 9, ...25, 36, the missing number is :
A. 14 B. 16
C. 20 D. 21

10. In the sequence 17, ..., 18, 15, 19, 14, 20, 13, the missing number is:
A. 5 B. 10
C. 12 D. 16

Directions. *For questions 11 to 14, let * means add the first number to twice the second number.*

11. The value of 5*4 is:
A. 20 B. 9
C. 11 D. 13

12. The value of 7*0 is:
A. 7 B. 9
C. 14 D. 0

13. The value of [1*2] * 3 is:
A. 5 B. 7
C. 9 D. 11

14. The value of 3* [0*6] is:
A. 18 B. 23
C. 27 D. 29

Directions. *For questions 15 to 17, let Δ means square the first number and add the second.*

15. The value of 2 Δ 10 is:
A. 12 B. 14
C. 27 D. 102

16. The value of 6 Δ 7 is:
A. 42 B. 43
C. 54 D. 59

17. The value of [3 × 2] Δ 9 is :
A. 42 B. 45
C. 87 D. 91

Directions. *For questions 18 to 20, let ** means increase the first number by 2 and then multiply by the second number.*

18. The value of 5** 3 is :
A. 15 B. 25
C. 21 D. 17

19. The value of [3**3]**4 is:
A. 68 B. 60
C. 54 D. 36

20. The value of [5**0]**3 is :
A. 0 B. 6
C. 15 D. 21

21. The smallest whole number which is divisible by 3 and also by the next two greater prime number is:
A. 15 B. 21
C. 60 D. 105

22. A number is called perfect, when it is equal to the sum of all its divisions excluding the number itself, e.g., 6 = 1 + 2 + 3. The other perfect number less than 32 is:
A. 8 B. 12
C. 16 D. 28

23. The smallest number of four digits is:
A. 1001 B. 0001
C. 0010 D. 1000

24. The largest number of four digits is:

A. 1000 B. 9000

C. 9009 D. 9999

25. If 'a' is an odd number, 'b' is an even number and 'c' is odd then, $a + b + c$ is:

A. odd number

B. even number

C. prime number

D. any number

26. The product of two prime numbers is a :

A. prime number

B. even number

C. odd number

D. composite number

27. Prime factors of a number are 2, 2, 3, 7. The number is :

A. 14 B. 41

C 48 D. 84

28. The largest number which is a factor of 56 as well as 84 is :

A. 2 B. 7

C. 14 D. 28

29. H.C.F. of 72, 108, 56 is :

A. 3 B. 4

C. 6 D. 8

30. L.C.M. of 6, 9, 12, 18 is :

A. 28 B. 36

C. 38 D. 42

31. If 'x' and 'y' are both odd numbers, which of the following numbers must be an even number?

A. $x + y$

B. $x \times y$

C. $xy + 2$

D. $2x + y$

32. 'a' is less than 'b', which of the following numbers is greater than 'a' and less than 'b' :

A. $\frac{a+b}{2}$ B. $\frac{ab}{2}$

C. $b^2 - a^7$ D. ab

33. $a + b + c + d$ is a positive number, a minimum of 'x' of the numbers a, b, c and d must be positive, where 'x' is equal to :

A. 1 B. 2

C. 3 D. 4

34. Which of the following is largest? $[2 + 2 + 2]^2$, $[(2 + 2)^2]^2$, $[2 \times 2 \times 2]^2$, $[4]^2$

A. $[2 + 2 + 2]^2$

B. $[(2 + 2)^2]^2$

C. $[2 \times 2 \times 2]^2$

D. $[4]^2$

35. The sum of two numbers is 84. If one of them exceeds the other by 12, the numbers are :

A. 62, 22 B. 36, 24

C. 48, 36 D. 35, 47

36. Take a number. Double it and add 15 to it. If the result is 81, the number is :

A. 30 B. 32

C. 33 D. 66

37. Take a number, find its square root and add 20 to it. If the result is 30, the number is :

A. 5 B. 1

C. 20 D. 100

38. There are four numbrs A, B, C and D. Average of the first three, i.e., A, B and C is 15 and that of

B, C and D is 16. If the last number, i.e. D is 19, then the first number is:

A. 15 B. 16
C. 17 D. 18

39. Think of a number, divide it by 9 and add 9 to it, if the result is 27, the number is :

A. 18 B. 21
C. 100 D. 162

40. Of the three numbers, the first is twice the second and thrice the third. If the average of three is 22, the three numbers are:

A. 12, 18, 36 B. 18, 12, 36
C. 36, 12, 18 D. 36, 18, 12

41. The number which when added to itself 10 times gives 264. The number is:

A. 20 B. 22
C. 24 D. 26

42. If a person is standing on the sixth number in the queue from both the ends, the total persons in the queue are:

A. 9 B. 11
C. 12 D. 13

43. A number increased by itself and 5 gives 17. The number is :

A. 2 B. 3
C. 5 D. 6

44. Consider a number 'x'. Divide it by 4 and add 9. If the result is 15, the value of 'x' is :

A. 20 B. 24
C. 23 D. 28

45. A number 'x' when multiplied by 5 and added to three times its own gives 64, the number is:

A. 8 B. 12
C. 14 D. 18

46. If the sum of two numbers 'x' and 'y' is equal to twice the first number, the second number 'y' is:

A. $> x$
B. $< x$
C. $= x$
D. negative number

47. The excess of thrice a certain number over 11 is 19. The number is:

A. 8 B. 9
C. 10 D. 11

48. The difference between the squares of two consecutive numbers is 25. The numbers are:

A. 13, 12 B. 12, 13
C. 15, 14 D. 14, 13

49. The sum of two digits of a number is 15. If 9 is added to the number, the digits are reversed. The number is :

A. 78 B. 87
C. 69 D. 96

50. A number which when multiplied by 11 is as much above 180 as it was originally below it. The number is:

A. 25 B. 30
C. 40 D. 45

51. Divide ₹ 53 among X, Y, Z so that X may receive ₹ 7 more than Y, and Y may receive ₹ 8 more than Z.

A. 10, 15, 18 B. 18, 10, 25
C. 20, 12, 27 D. 25, 18, 10

EXPLANATORY ANSWERS

1. C : The numbers divisible by 2 are called even numbers since, 4, 6, 8, 10, are divisible by 2, hence these are even numbers.

2. A : The numbers written in natural sequence are natural numbers.

3. C : The numbers which are not divisible by 2, 3, 5, 7, 11 and 13 (*i.e.*, by any numbers except themselves and one) are called prime numbers.

4. C : To find out prime numbers between 1 and 100, write all numbers between 1 to 100.

✱	(2)	(3)	4	(5)	6	(7)	8	9	10
(11)	12	(13)	14	15	16	(17)	18	(19)	20
21	22	(23)	24	25	26	27	28	(29)	30
(31)	32	33	34	35	36	(37)	38	39	40
(41)	42	(43)	44	45	46	(47)	48	49	50
51	52	(53)	54	55	56	57	58	(59)	60
(61)	62	63	64	65	66	(67)	68	69	70
(71)	72	(73)	74	75	76	77	78	(79)	80
81	82	(83)	84	85	86	87	88	(89)	90
91	92	93	94	95	96	(97)	98	99	100

(*i*) Cross out 1 which is not a prime number.

(ii) Cross out all numbers divisible by 2, except 2 which is a prime number.

(*iii*) Cross out all numbers divisible by 3, except 3 itself.

(*iv*) Cross out all numbers divisible by 5, except 5 itself.

(*v*) Cross out all numbers divisible by 7, except 7 itself.

The numbers remaining are the prime numbers between 1 and 100 which are circled and are 25 in all.

5. A : 2 is the only even prime number.

6. C : 87 is divisilble by 3, therefore it is not a prime number.

7. C : 149 is not divisible by any number, therefore it is a prime number.

8. A : In the sequence 1, 7, 3, 9, 5, 11..... the alternate numbers differ by 2, i.e., first and third number differ by 2, similarly the difference of second and fourth number is 2. Thus, next number in the series should be 5 + 2 = 7.

9. B : The sequence 4, 9, ..., 25, 36 contains the square of natural numbers, *i.e.*, 2^2, 3^2, 4^2, 5^2, 6^2. Thus the missing number is 4^2, *i.e.*, 16.

10. D : In the sequence 17, ..., 18, 15, 19, 14, 20, 13, the next alternate number is one more than the previous alternate number, i.e., 17 + 1 = 18, 18 + 1 = 19, 19 + 1 = 20. Also the second number and fourth number differ by 1, i.e.. 13 + 1 = 14, 14 + 1 = 15, 15 + 1 = 16 is the required missing number).

[**means add the first number to the twice of the second number*].

11. D : 5 + [2 × 4] = 5 + 8 = 13

12. A : 7 + [2 × 0] = 7 + 0 = 7.

13. D : [1 * 2]* 3 = [1 + 2 × 2]* 3 = 5* 3 = 5 + 3 × 2 = 11.

14. C : 3 * [0 * 6] = 3 *[0 + 2 × 6] = 3* 12 = 3 + 2 × 12 = 27

[Δ *means square the first number and add the second number.*]

15. B : 2 Δ 10 = 2 × 2 + 10 = 14

16. B : 6 Δ 7 = 6 × 6 + 7 = 43

17. B : [3 × 2] Δ 9 = 6 Δ 9 = 6 × 6 + 9 = 45

[** *means increase the first number by 2 and then multiply by the second number*].

18. C : 5**3 = [5 + 2] × 3 = 21

19. A : [3**3]**4 = [(3 + 2) × 3]**4 = 15**4 = [15 + 2] × 4 = 68

20. B : [5**0]**3 = [(5 + 2) × 0] = **3 = 0**3 = [0 + 2] × 3 = 6

21. D : The number should be divisible by 3, 5, and 7. Thus L.C.M. of 3, 5, 7 is equal to 105 which is the required number.

22. D : 28 is multiple of 1, 2, 4, 7, 14.
Also 1 + 2 + 4 + 7 + 14 = 28

23. D. 24. D.

25. A : Out of *a, b, c* ; a is odd and *c* is odd while b is even. The sum of two odd numbers is even, *i.e.*, $a + c$ = even = d. Also the sum of two even numbers is even, i.e., d + b = even.
$\therefore\ a + b + c$ = Even number.

26. D : Product of two prime numbers is not a prime number but it is always composite number.

27. D : The number is equal to the product or prime factors.
$\therefore$ 2 × 2 × 3 × 7 = 84 is the required number.

28. D : Find H.C.F. of 56, 84 which is equal to 28.

29. B.

30. B.

31. A : Since the sum of two odd numbers is always even number, therefore, $x + y$ is even number.

32. A : Average of two different numbers is always between the two numbers.

33. A : If all the numbers were not positive, then the sum could not be positive. If a, b, c were all –1 and d were 5, then $a + b + c + d$ would be positive, so B, C, D are incorrect.

34. B :

$$(2 + 2 + 2)^2 = 6^2 = 36$$

$$[(2 + 2)^2]^2 = [4^2]^2 = [4 \times 4]^2 = 16 \times 16 = 256$$

$$[2 \times 2 \times 2]^2 = (8)^2 = 64$$

$$(4)^2 = 4 \times 4 = 16.$$

35. C : Let the numbers be x and y

$$x + y = 84$$

$$x + (x + 12) = 84, \text{ or } 2x = 84 - 12 = 72,$$

or $$x = \frac{72}{2} = 36$$

$$y = x + 12 = 36 + 12 = 48.$$

36. C : Let the number be x

$\therefore$ $$2x + 15 = 81, \text{ or } 2x = 81 - 15 = 66$$

$\therefore$ $$x = \frac{66}{2} = 33.$$

37. D : Let the number be x

$\therefore$ $$\sqrt{x} + 20 = 30, \text{ or } \sqrt{x} = 30 - 20 = 10$$

$\therefore$ $$\left(\sqrt{x}\right)^2 = (10)^2, \text{ or } x = 100.$$

38. B : $$\frac{A+B+C}{3} = 15, \text{ or, } A + B + C = 15 \times 3 = 45 \quad \text{...}(i)$$

$$\frac{B+C+D}{3} = 16, \text{ or } B + C + D = 48 \quad \text{...}(ii)$$

$$D = 19$$

$\therefore$ $B + C + 19 = 48$ or, $B + C = 48 - 19 = 29$

But, $A + B + C = 45$

Putting the value of $B + C = 29$ in the above equationi (i), we get

$$A + 29 = 45$$

$\therefore$ $$A = 45 - 29 = 16$$

39. D : Let the number be x.

$\therefore \quad \frac{x}{9}+9 = 27$ or, $\frac{x}{9} = 27 - 9 = 18$

$\therefore \quad x = 18 \times 9 = 162$

40. D : Let the third number $= x$

$\therefore$ First number $= 3x$, Second number $= \frac{3x}{2}$

$\therefore \quad \frac{1}{3}\left[x+3x+\frac{3x}{2}\right] = 22$ or, $\frac{11}{2}\ x = 66$

or, $x = \frac{66\times 2}{11} = 12 =$ Third number,

$12 \times 3 = 36 =$ First number,

$\frac{12\times 3}{2} = 18 =$ Second number.

41. C : Let the number be x.

Then, $x + 10x = 264$

or, $11x = 264, \ \therefore \ x = \frac{264}{11} = 24$

42. B : If the person is standing at sixth number in the queue from both sides, that means there are five persons ahead and five persons behind him. Hence, total number of person in the queue is $5 + 1 + 5 = 11$.

43. D : Let the number is x.

$\therefore \quad x + x + 5 = 17$, or $2x = 17 - 5 = 12$

$\therefore \quad x = \frac{12}{2} = 6$

44. B : $\frac{x}{4}+9 = 15$

$\frac{x}{4} = 15 - 9 = 6$

$\therefore \quad x = 6 \times 4 = 24.$

45. A : $5 \times x + 3x = 64$ or, $8x = 64$, $\quad \therefore x = \frac{64}{8} = 8$

46. C : $x + y = 2x$

$\therefore \quad y = 2x - x = x$

47. C : Let the number be x.

$\therefore \quad 3x - 11 = 19, \quad$ or $3x = 19 + 11 = 30$

$\therefore \quad x = \frac{30}{3} = 10.$

48. A : Let the numbers are x and $(x + 1)$

$\therefore \quad (x + 1)^2 - x^2 = 25$

or, $\quad x^2 + 1 + 2x - x^2 = 25$

or, $\quad 2x + 1 = 25$

or, $\quad 2x = 25 - 1 = 24, \quad \therefore x = \frac{24}{2} = 12$

$\therefore \quad x + 1 = 12 + 1 = 13$

Hence, the numbers are 12, 13.

49. A : Let x be the digit in units place. Digit in ten's place is then $15 - x$.

$\therefore$ The number $= 10(15 - x) + x$

The new number with reserve digits $= 10 \times x + (15 - x)$

$\therefore \quad 10(15 - x) + x + 9 = 10x + 15 - x$

$150 - 10x + x + 9 = 9x + 15$

or, $\quad 18x = 144, \quad \therefore x = \frac{144}{18} = 8$

The digit of ten's place $= 15 - 8 = 7$

$\therefore$ The required number $= 78$

50. B : Let the number is x

$\therefore \quad 180 - x = 11x - 180$

or, $\quad 180 + 180 = 11x + x, 360 = 12x,$

or, $\quad x = \frac{360}{12} = 30$

51. D : Let Y receives ₹ a.

Then X receives ₹ $a + 7$ and Z receives ₹ $a - 8$.

But, $a + 7 + a + a - 8 =$ ₹ 53

or, $\quad 3a - 1 = 53, 3a = 53 + 1$

$\therefore \quad 3a = 54$, or, $a = \frac{54}{3}$

= ₹ 18. = Y's share

X's share= $a + 7 = 18 + 7 =$ ₹ 25,

Z's share= $a - 8 = 18 - 8 =$ ₹ 10.

2

FRACTIONS AND DECIMALS

A fraction is a number that represents a ratio or division of two whole numbers. A fraction is written in the form x/y, the number on the top, 'x' is called numerator; the number on the bottom, 'y' is called denominator. The denominator tells how many equal parts there are; and the numerator tells how many of these equal parts are taken.

> **Sets of equal fractions can be obtained by multiplying, or dividing, the numerator and denominator by the same number.**

For example,

$$\frac{3}{4}=\frac{3\times 2}{4\times 2}=\frac{3\times 2\times 2}{4\times 2\times 2}=\frac{3\times 3}{4\times 3}=\frac{3\times 4}{4\times 4}$$

Mixed Numbers: A mixed number consists of a whole number and a fraction.$3\frac{1}{4}$ is a mixed number, it means $3 + \frac{1}{4}$.

How to change mixed number into fraction?

(*i*) Multiply the whole number by the denominator of the fraction.

(*ii*) Add the numerator of the fraction to the result of step (*i*)

(*iii*) Use the result of step (*ii*) as the numerator and use the denominator of the fractional part of the mixed number as the denominator. This fraction is equal to the mixed number.

> **In calculations involving mixed numbers, always change the mixed numbers into fractions.**

Multiplication of Fractions: While multiplying, two fractions multiply their numerators and divide this by the product of their denominators.

Note: *In word problems,* **of** *always indicates multiplication.*

Division of Fractions: This can be done either by multiplying by the L.C.M. of the denominators of the fractions, or by multiplying by such a number which can make the denominator 1.

It may be noted that one fraction is a reciprocal of another if their product is 1. So $\frac{1}{3}$ and 3 are reciprocals. To find the reciprocal of a fraction, simply interchange the numerator and deno-minator. This is known as inverting fractions. To divide one fraction by another fraction, invert the divisor and multiply. *For example :*

$$\frac{3}{8} \div \frac{1}{2} = \frac{3}{8} \times 2 = \frac{6}{8} = \frac{3}{4}$$

Addition of Fractions: If the fractions have same denominator, then the denominator is called a common denominator. In such cases, add the numerators and use this sum as the new numerator with the common denominator as the denominator of the sum. *For example,*

$$\frac{3}{15} + \frac{7}{15} = \frac{3+7}{15} = \frac{10}{15} = \frac{2}{3}$$

If the fractions have different denominators, then L.C.M. is called the least common denominator and as has been said for the case when the fractions had the same denominator, *For example,*

$$\frac{1}{3} + \frac{9}{4} + \frac{3}{5} = ?$$

In this case, common denominator is L.C.M. of 3, 4, 5, which is equal to 60,

$$\frac{1}{3} = \frac{20}{60}, \frac{9}{4} = \frac{135}{60}, \frac{3}{5} = \frac{36}{60}$$

$$= \frac{20}{60} + \frac{135}{60} + \frac{36}{60} = \frac{191}{60}$$

Subtracting Fractions: When the fractions have the same denominator, subtract the numerators and place the result over the denominator.
For example,

$$\frac{5}{8} - \frac{3}{8} = \frac{5-3}{8} = \frac{2}{8}$$

When the fractions have different denominators,

(*i*) First of all, find the common denominator:

(*ii*) Express the fractions as equivalent fractions with the same denominator.

(*iii*) Subtract as has been said above, *for example,*

$$\frac{5}{8} - \frac{1}{5} = ?$$

Common denominator in this case is 40,

$$\frac{5}{8} = \frac{25}{40}, \frac{1}{5} = \frac{8}{40}$$

$$\frac{25}{40} - \frac{8}{40} = \frac{25-8}{40} = \frac{17}{40}$$

Equivalent Fractions: Two fractions may be equivalent or equal if they represent the same ratio of number. *For example,*

$$\frac{2}{5}=\frac{4}{10}=\frac{6}{15}=\frac{20}{50}$$

Combined Operations: Sometimes in simplifying fractions, we may come across the following signs :

(*i*) Brackets – ( ), { }, [ ]

(*ii*) Of – means multiplication

while dealing with such problems,

(*i*) first of all brackets should be removed,

(*ii*) then *of* followed by,

(*iii*) division and multiplicaiton, then

(*iv*) addition and subtraction.

Note: *Terms enclosed within brackets are to be treated as one quantity.*

When an expression within a bracket is preceded by the sign (+), the bracket may be removed without making any change in the sign of the quantities or terms within the bracket.

When an expression within a bracket is preceded by the sign (–), the bracket may be removed only after changing the sign of every term within it.

Complex Fractions: A fraction whose numerator and denominator are themselves fractions is called a complex fraction.

For example, $\frac{3/8}{4/5}$

It can be simplified by dividing the fractions. Thus,

$$\frac{3/8}{4/5}=\frac{3}{8}\div\frac{4}{5}=\frac{3}{8}\times\frac{5}{4}=\frac{15}{32}$$

DECIMALS

A collection of digits after a period (decimal point) is called decimal fraction. *For example,* .513, .317, .219, .6, etc. Every decimal represents a fraction.

How to find a fraction represented by decimal?

(*i*) Take a fraction whose denominator is 10, and whose numerator is the first digit to the right of decimal point.

(*ii*) Take the fraction whose denominator is 100, and whose numerator is the second digit to the right of decimal point.

(*iii*) Continue the procedure untill all the digits to the right of the decimal point have been used up. The denominator in each case is 10 times the denominator in the previous step.

(*iv*) The sum of the fractions obtained in (i), (ii) and (iii) is the fraction represented by the decimal point. For example, the fraction represened by 0.317 may be found out as follows:

$$\frac{3}{10}+\frac{1}{100}+\frac{7}{1000}=\frac{300}{1000}+\frac{10}{1000}+\frac{7}{1000}=\frac{317}{1000}$$

Any number of zeros may be added to the right of a decimal fraction without changing its value.

Addition and Subtraction of Decimals: While adding decimals we put decimal under decimal, units under units, tens under tens and hundreds under hundreds.

For example, 23.4621 + 102.019 + 0.961 =?

$$\begin{array}{r} 23.4621 \\ 102.0190 \\ 0.9610 \\ \hline 126.4421 \\ \hline \end{array}$$

Multiplicaiton of Decimals: When we multiply the decimal fractions by 10, the hundredths become tenths (10 × 1/100 = 1/10), the tenths become units (10 × 1/10 = 1) and the units become tens (1 × 10 = 10) and so on.

For example, 2.45 × 10 = 24.5.

Decimals are multiplied like whole numbers. The decimal point of the product is placed in such a way that the number of decimal places in the product is equal to the total of the number of decimal places in all the numbers multiplied.

Division of Decimals: While dividing one decimal by another decimal :

(*i*) Move the decimal point in the divisor to the right until there is no decimal fraction in the divisor.

(*ii*) Move the decimal point in the dividend the sâme number of places to the right as you moved the decimal point in step *(i)*.

(*iii*) Divide the result of *(ii)* by the result of *(i)*.

(*iv*) The number of decimal places in the result should be equal to the number of decimal places in the result of step *(ii)*.

For example, 66.957 ÷ 0.11

$$=\frac{66.957}{0.11}=\frac{66.957\times 100}{0.11\times 100}=\frac{6695.7}{11}=608.7$$

Relation between Decimal Fraction and Normal Fraction: A fraction can be converted into a decimal fraction by dividing the numerator by denominator. *For example*, 1/2 = 1.0/2 = 0.5.

$$\frac{1}{5}=\frac{1.0}{5}=0.2, \qquad \frac{1}{10}=\frac{1\cdot 0}{10}=0\cdot 1$$

$\frac{1}{4}=\frac{1\cdot00}{4}=0\cdot25,$ $\frac{1}{100}=\frac{1\cdot00}{100}=0\cdot01$

$\frac{3}{4}=\frac{3\cdot00}{4}=0\cdot75,$ $\frac{1}{1000}=\frac{1\cdot000}{1000}=0.001$

$\frac{1}{20}=\frac{1\cdot00}{20}=0.05,$ $\frac{3}{8}=\frac{3.000}{8}=0\cdot375$

$\frac{1}{16}=\frac{1\cdot0000}{16}=0\cdot0625,$ $\frac{7}{8}=\frac{7\cdot000}{8}=0\cdot875$

EXERCISE

1. Which of the following is equivalent to $\frac{15}{25}$?

A. $\frac{150}{25}$ B. $\frac{15}{250}$

C. $\frac{3}{5}$ D. $\frac{60}{75}$

2. Which of the following is not equivalent to $\frac{13}{20}$?

A. $\frac{26}{40}$ B. $\frac{130}{200}$

C. $\frac{39}{60}$ D. $\frac{52}{60}$

3. If $\frac{9*3}{3*7}$ is equivalent to $\frac{9}{7}$, the sign * is replaced by :

A. ÷ B. ×

C. + D. –

4. $\frac{5}{6}$ of an hour is equal to :

A. half an hour B. 40 minutes

C. 50 minutes D. 55 minutes

5. An aircraft uses 2/5 of its fuel in flying 1,250 kilometres. The distance travelled on remaining fuel is :

A. 1875 km B. 2125 km

C. 250 km D. 475 km

6. If $\frac{4}{3}*\frac{3}{4}=\frac{16}{9}$, then * means :

A. + B. –

C. × D. ÷

7. If $\frac{3}{15}*\frac{17}{5}=\frac{51}{75}$, then * means :

A. + B. –

C. × D. ÷

8. If $5x = 1$, then x is equal to :

A. .20 B. .02

C. $\frac{1}{2}$ D. 5

9. Which of the following is the largest fraction?

A. $\frac{3}{15}$ B. $\frac{5}{20}$

C. $\frac{8}{64}$ D. $\frac{25}{1000}$

10. Which of the following is the smallest fraction?

A. $\frac{1}{10}$ B. $\frac{1}{100}$

C. $\frac{9}{1000}$ D. $\frac{500}{10000}$

11. Six times x increased by 12 is equal to :

A. $\frac{x}{2}$ B. $2x$

C. $6x + 12$ D. $12x + 6$

12. Five times y diminished by 20 is equal to :

A. $5y - 20$ B. $5y + 20$

C. $y/4$ D. $4y$

13. The number less than 15 by 7 is:

A. $15x - 7$ B. 15/7

C. 15 D. 8

14. The excess of thrice a certain number over 16 is 32. The number is :

A. 17 B. 16

C. 12 D. 10

15. If 21 is added to four times a number, the result is 57. The number is :

A. 7 B. 8

C. 9 D. 10

16. A number, the sum of whose fourth and fifth parts exceeds their third part by 28, is :

A. 120 B. 240

C. 220 D. 160

17. Which fraction should be added to the sum of $5\frac{3}{4}$, $4\frac{4}{5}$ and $7\frac{3}{8}$ to make the result a whole number?

A. $\frac{1}{40}$ B. $\frac{2}{40}$

C. $\frac{3}{40}$ D. $\frac{4}{40}$

18. $\frac{1}{15}+\frac{3}{15}+\frac{5}{15}+\frac{6}{15}=?$

A. $\frac{10}{15}$ B. $\frac{3}{5}$

C. $\frac{4}{5}$ D. 1

19. A number one-sixth of which exceeds its one-ninth by 100 is :

A. 600 B. 900

C. 1500 D. 1800

20. The sum of $\frac{1}{2}, \frac{1}{4}$ and $\frac{1}{8}$ of a number is 28. The number is :

A. 28 B. 32

C. 36 D. 42

21. The sum of $\frac{1}{9}, \frac{1}{3}, \frac{1}{6}$ and $\frac{7}{18}$ of a number is 150. The number is :

A. 120 B. 130

C. 140 D. 150

22. Which is the greatest? .999, .1011, .1995, .9985

A. .999 B. .1011

C. .1995 D. .9985

23. In decimal system, $9\frac{1}{8}$ may be represented as:

A. 9.18 B. 9.125

C. 9.025 D. 9.225

24. $2.205 \div 0.15 = ?$

A. 1.47 B. 14.7

C. 147 D. 0.147

25. G.C.M. of .24, 3.2 and 16.0 is :
A. 80 B. 8
C. .8 D. .08

26. L.C.M. of .24, 3.2 and 16.0 is :
A. .48 B. 4.8
C. 48 D. 480

27. A pole has 0.5 of its length in mud, 0.25 of its length in water and 2 metres above water. The total length of the pole is :
A. 8 metres B. 5 metres
C. 4 metres D. 2 metres

28. $\sqrt{1/3}$ is equal to :
A. 0.57 B. 0.35
C. 0.30 D. 3.00

29. How many times does 2/3 of 1/2 go into half of one third?
A. 2 B. 1/2
C. 1/3 D. 2/3

30. The eleventh part of $990\frac{990}{990}$ is:
A. 99.0 B. 99.99
C. 90 D. 90.9

31. A train started from Delhi at 6.00 A.M. On the next (second) station 1/3 passengers got down and 96 got in. On the next (third) station, 1/2 of the total passengers present in the train got down and 12 came in. Now there were 248 passengers in the train. When the tain started from Delhi, total number of passengers were :
A. 435 B. 564
C. 654 D. 736

32. 1 ÷ [1 + 1 ÷ {1 + 1 ÷ 1(1 + 1 ÷ 2)}] is equal to:
A. 1 B. 2
C. $\frac{5}{8}$ D. zero

33. L.C.M. of 6, 7, 8 and 10 is equal to :
A. 840 B. 830
C. 820 D. 800

34. By how much does $\frac{6}{7/8}$ exceed $\frac{6/7}{8}$:
A. $6\frac{2}{3}$ B. $6\frac{3}{4}$
C. $7\frac{1}{2}$ D. $8\frac{3}{4}$

35. $\frac{.03}{1000}$ is equal to :
A. 3×10^5 B. 3×10^{-3}
C. 3×10^{-6} D. 3×10^{-5}

36. $10\frac{1}{25}$ is equal to :
A. 10.25 B. 10.125
C. 10.04 D. 10.025

37. 1.25 × 1.25 + 2.75 × 2.75 + 2 × 1.25 × 2.75 is equal to :
A. 4.000 B. 16.000
C. 26.1250 D. 28.3250

38. What fraction of an hour is a second ?
A. $\frac{1}{24}$ B. $\frac{1}{60}$
C. $\frac{1}{120}$ D. $\frac{1}{3600}$

39. G.C.M. of 1.6 and 0.72 is equal to :
A. 8 B. .8
C. .08 D. .008

40. $\frac{4}{5}$ of 0.025 is equal to :
A. 0.0002 B. 0.002
C. 0.02 D. 0.2

EXPLANATORY ANSWERS

1. C : $\frac{15}{25}=\frac{3\times5}{5\times5}=\frac{3}{5}$.

2. D : $\frac{26}{40} = \frac{2\times13}{2\times20} = \frac{13}{20}, \frac{39}{60} = \frac{13\times3}{20\times3} = \frac{13}{20}$

$\frac{130}{200} = \frac{13\times10}{20\times10} = \frac{13}{20}, \frac{52}{60} = \frac{13\times4}{20\times3} = \frac{13}{20}\cdot\times\frac{4}{3}$

Hence, $\frac{52}{60}$ is not equal to $\frac{13}{20}$.

3. B : $\frac{9*3}{3*7}=\frac{9}{7}$, or, $\frac{9\times3}{7\times3}=\frac{9}{7}$, $\therefore$ The sign * is $\times$.

4. C : $\frac{5}{6}$ of 1 hr = $\frac{5}{6}\times 60$ minutes = 50 minutes.

5. A : Remaining fuel = $1-\frac{2}{5}=\frac{5-2}{5}=\frac{3}{5}$

Distance flown by $\frac{2}{5}$ of fuel = 1250 km.

Distance flown by full fuel = $\frac{1250}{2/5} = \frac{1250\times5}{2}$ km.

Distance flown by $\frac{3}{5}$ of fuel = $\frac{1250\times5\times3}{2\times5}=1875$ km.

6. D. **7. C.**

8. A : $5x = 1$, $\therefore x = \frac{1}{5} = .20$.

9. B : $\frac{3}{15}=\frac{1}{5}, \frac{8}{64}=\frac{1}{8}, \frac{5}{20}=\frac{1}{4}, \frac{25}{1000}=\frac{1}{40}$,

$\frac{1}{5},\frac{1}{4},\frac{1}{8},\frac{1}{40}$, $\frac{16,\ 20,\ 10,\ 2}{80}$

$\therefore$ The largest fractin is $\frac{1}{4}=\frac{5}{20}$.

10. C : $\frac{1}{10} = .1,\ \frac{9}{1000} = .009$

$\frac{1}{100} = .01.\ \frac{500}{10000} = \frac{5}{100} = .05$

The smallest of these quantities is $.009 = \frac{9}{1000}$.

11. C : $x \times 6 + 12 = 6x + 12$.

12. A : $5 \times y - 20 = 5y - 20$.

13. D : $15 - 7 = 8$.

14. B : Let the number be x

$$3x - 16 = 32$$

$$\therefore \quad 3x = 32 + 16 = 48, \text{ or } x = \frac{48}{3} = 16.$$

15. C : Let the number is x

$\therefore\ 4x + 21 = 57$ or, $4x = 57 - 21 = 36$, or, $x = \frac{36}{4} = 9$.

16. B : Let the number is x.

$\therefore \frac{x}{4} + \frac{x}{5} = \frac{x}{3} + 28,\ \frac{9x}{20} = \frac{x}{3} + 28$, or, $\frac{9x}{20} - \frac{x}{3} = 28$

or, $\frac{27x - 20x}{60} = 28$ or, $7x = 28 \times 60 \therefore\ x = \frac{28 \times 60}{7} = 240$.

17. C : $5\frac{3}{4} + 4\frac{4}{5} + 7\frac{3}{8} = \frac{23}{4} + \frac{24}{5} + \frac{59}{8} = \frac{717}{40}$

717/40 becomes whole number when 3/40 is added to it, i.e.,

$\frac{717}{40} + \frac{3}{40} = \frac{720}{40} = 18$ which is a whole number.

18. D : $\frac{1}{15} + \frac{3}{15} + \frac{5}{15} + \frac{6}{15} = \frac{1+3+5+6}{15} = \frac{15}{15} = 1$.

19. D : Let the number is x.

$\frac{x}{6} = \frac{x}{9} + 100$ or, $\frac{x}{6} - \frac{x}{9} = 100$, or, $\frac{x}{18} = 100$

or, $x = 100 \times 18 = 1800$.

20. B : Let the number is x.

$\therefore \quad \frac{x}{2}+\frac{x}{4}+\frac{x}{8}=28$, or, $\frac{7x}{8}=28 \;\therefore\; 7x = 28 \times 8$ or, $x=\frac{28\times 8}{7}=32$.

21. D : Let the number is x.

$\therefore \frac{x}{9}+\frac{x}{3}+\frac{x}{6}+\frac{7x}{18}=150$ or, $\frac{2x+6x+3x+7x}{18}=150 \Rightarrow \frac{18x}{18}=150$

or, $x=\frac{150\times 18}{18}=150$.

22. A : .999 is the greatest.

23. B : $9\frac{1}{8}=9+\frac{1}{8}=9+.125=9.125$.

24. B : $2.205 \div 0.15=\frac{2.205}{0.15}=\frac{2205}{1000}\times\frac{100}{15}=\frac{2205}{150}=14.7$.

25. D : G.C.M. of .24, 3.2 and 16.0

$=$ G.C.M. of $\frac{24,\ 320 \text{ and } 1600}{100}=\frac{8}{100}=0.08$.

26. C : L.C.M. of .24, 3.2 and 16.0 = L.C.M. of

$\frac{24,\ 320 \text{ and } 1600}{100}=\frac{4800}{100}=48$.

27. A : Let total length of the pole $= x$
Pole above water $= x - [0.5x + 0.25x] = 0.25x$;
$0.25x = 2$ metres

$\therefore\ x=\frac{2\times 100}{25}=8$ metres.

28. A : $\sqrt{\frac{1}{3}}=\frac{\sqrt{1}}{\sqrt{3}}=\frac{1}{\sqrt{3}}=\frac{1}{1.732}=\frac{1000}{1732}=0.57$.

29. B : $\frac{2}{3}$ of $\frac{1}{2}=\frac{2}{3}\times\frac{1}{2}=\frac{1}{3}$, $\frac{1}{2}$ of $\frac{1}{3}=\frac{1}{6}$ $\therefore\ \frac{1}{6}\div\frac{1}{3}=\frac{1}{6}\times\frac{3}{1}=\frac{1}{2}$.

30. C : Eleventh part of $990\frac{990}{990}=990\frac{990}{990}\div 11=\frac{991}{11}=90.09$.

31. B : When train started from Delhi let number of passengers was x. On next station, 1/3 got down and 96 got in.

Now passengers in train $= x - \frac{x}{3} + 96 = \frac{2x}{3} + 96$

On next station 1/2 of it got down and 12 got in, i.e.,

$\frac{1}{2}\left[\frac{2x}{3} + 96\right]$ got down and 12 got in

Now passengers in train $= \frac{2x}{3} + 96 - \left[\frac{x}{3} + 48\right] + 12$

$= \frac{2x}{3} - \frac{x}{3} + 96 - 48 + 12 = 248 \quad \therefore x = [248 - 60] \times 3 = 188 \times 3 = 564.$

32. C.

33. A : The L.C.M. of 6, 7, 8 and 10 is calculated as follows :

2	6, 7, 8, 10
3	3, 7, 4, 5
4	1, 7, 4, 5
5	1, 7 1, 5
7	1, 7, 1, 1
	1, 1, 1, 1

L.C.M. = 2 × 3 × 4 × 5 × 7 = 840.

34. B : $6 \div \frac{7}{8} = \frac{6}{1} \times \frac{8}{7} = \frac{48}{7}$ or $\frac{6}{7} \div 8 = \frac{6}{7} \times \frac{1}{8} = \frac{3}{28}$

$\frac{48}{7} - \frac{3}{28} = \frac{192 - 3}{28} = \frac{189}{28} = 6\frac{21}{28} = 6\frac{3}{4}.$

35. D. **36. C.**

37. B : Put 1.25 = a and 2.75 = b, then,

1.25 × 1.25 + 2.75 × 2.75 + 2 × 1.25 × 2.75

$= a^2 + b^2 + 2ab = (a + b)^2 = (1.25 + 2.75)^2 = (4)^2 = 16.000.$

38. D. **39. C.**

40. C : $\frac{4}{5} \times 0.025 = \frac{4}{5} \times \frac{25}{1000} = \frac{1}{50} = 0.02.$

3

POWERS, EXPONENTS AND ROOTS

If 'x' is any number and 'n' is a whole numbr greater than 0, x^n means that the product of n factors each of which is equal to x. Thus,

$$x^n = x \,.\, x \,.\, x \,.\, x \,\ldots\ldots\ldots\ldots x \; n \text{ times}$$

$$2^4 = 2 \times 2 \times 2 \times 2 = 16$$

$$3^5 = 3 \times 3 \times 3 \times 3 \times 3 = 243$$

$$\left(\frac{x}{y}\right)^n = \frac{x^n}{x^n}$$

$$\left(\frac{3}{7}\right)^2 = \frac{3\times3}{7\times7} = \frac{9}{49}.$$

In the expression x^n, x is called the base and n is called the exponent. The laws of exponents are :

$$x^n \times x^m = x^{n+m}$$

$$\frac{x^n}{x^m} = x^{n-m}$$

$$(x^m)^n = x^{mn}$$

$$(xy)^m = x^m y^m$$

Negative Exponents: $x^0 = 1$, for any non-zero number x. By one of the law of exponents,

$$x^n \times x^0 = x^{n+0} = x^n$$

i.e., $x^0 = 1$

Also, $x^{-n} = \dfrac{1}{x^n}$

Roots : If a number 'x' is raised to nth power and the result is 'a', then 'x' is called the *nth* root of 'a', which is usually written as $\sqrt[n]{a} = x$, *For example,*

$$2^4 = 16, \text{ or } \sqrt[4]{16} = 2$$

The second root is called the square root, the third root is called the cube root.

$$x^{1/n} \times y^{1/n} = (x.y)^{1/n}$$

or,

$$\sqrt[n]{x \times y} = \sqrt[n]{x} \times \sqrt[n]{y}$$

A number which is a prfect square must end in one or another of the digits 0, 1, 4, 5, 6, 9.

It may be noted that the square of,

1 & 9 both end in 1.
2 & 8 both end in 4.
3 & 7 both end in 9.
4 & 6 both end in 6.
5 end in 5.

(1, 9); (2, 8); (3, 7); (4, 6); (5, 5) are pairs of complementary digits, i.e., the sum of the digits in each pair is 10.

If two numbers end in complementary digits, their squares will have the same final digit.

If a number end in zero, its square should contain 2 zero and if a number ends in 2 zeros, its square should end in 4 zeros, and so on.

A number ending in an odd number of zeros cannot be a perfect square.

EXERCISE

1. $\sqrt{\frac{1}{3}} = ?$

A. 0.30
B. 0.57
C 0.89
D. 3.00

2. $\frac{6^4}{3^3} = ?$

A. 24
B. 42
C 48
D. 2

3. $\left(\frac{1}{2}\right)^{-1} = ?$

A. $-\frac{1}{2}$

B. $+\frac{1}{2}$

C. -2

D. $+ 2$

4. $125° = ?$

A. 125 B. 1
C. 1250 D. 12.5

5. $8^{1/3} = ?$

A. $\frac{8}{3}$ B. $\frac{3}{8}$

C. 4 D. 2

6. $4^4 \times 4^{17} = ?$

A. 8^{17} B. 4^{21}

C. 8^{21} D. 4^{13}

7. $\frac{10x^8}{5x^4} = ?$

A. $2x^4$ B. $2x^2$

C. $2x^8$ D. $2x^{12}$

8. $2^{3^2} = ?$

A. 2^6 B. 2^9

C. 2^5 D. 8^4

9. $(2^3)^2 = ?$

A. 8 B. 64

C. 312 D. 512

10. $(36)^{1/2} = ?$

A. 18 B. 9

C. 6 D. 3

11. $x^{3/4} . x^{3/4} = ?$

A. $2x^{3/1}$ B. $x^{9/16}$

C. $x^{6/8}$ D. $x^{3/2}$

12. $(x^{3/4})^{1/2} = ?$

A. $x^{3/8}$ B. $x^{4/6}$

C. $x^{2/5}$ D. $x^{3/2}$

13. $\sqrt{32} = ?$

A. 4 B. $2\sqrt{4}$

C. $4\sqrt{2}$ D. $2^3\sqrt{2}$

14. $5\sqrt{3} = ?$

A. $\sqrt{75}$ B. $\sqrt{50}$

C. $\sqrt{25}$ D. $\sqrt[3]{5}$

15. $x^{b-c} \times X^{c-a} \times X^{a-b} = ?$

A. x^{a+b+c} B. x^{a-b-c}

C. $x^{2a-2b-2c}$ D. 1

16. When 16000 is expressed as a product of powers of 4 and 10, then it equals :

A. $4^2 \times 10^2$ B. $4^2 \times 10^3$

C. $4^3 \times 10^3$ D. $4^2 \times 10^4$

17. When 1800 is expressed as a product of powers of prime numbers, then it equals :

A. $2 \times 9 \times 10^2$ B. $2 \times 3^2 \times 10^2$

C. $2 \times 3^2 \times 5^2$ D. $2^3 \times 3^2 \times 5^2$

18. 27×243 is equal to :

A. 3^8 B. 3^9

C. 3^{10} D. 3^{11}

19. The sum of the squares of two numbers is 26 and difference is 8. The numbers are :

A. 9, 17 B. 3, 17

C. $9, \sqrt{17}$ D. $3, \sqrt{17}$

20. $\left[\left(\frac{x}{y}\right)^3\right]^{-2} = ?$

A. $\left(\frac{x}{y}\right)^{-6}$ B. $\left(\frac{x}{y}\right)^{1}$

C. $\left(\frac{x}{y}\right)^{6}$ D. $\left(\frac{x}{y}\right)^{5}$

21. $(x^4)^3$ is equal to :

A. x^{6+2} B. x^{12}

C. $x^{4/13}$ D. x^{4-3}

22. $(27)^{-4/3}$ is equal to :

A. 81 B. 54

C. $\frac{1}{21}$ D. $\frac{1}{81}$

23. $x^{1/8} \div x^{3/4}$ is equal to :

A. $x^{5/8}$ B. $x^{2/4}$

C. $x^{2/3}$ D. $\frac{1}{x^{5/8}}$

24. $\left[27^{-2/3}\right]^{1/2}$ is equal to :

A. $\frac{27}{54}$ B. $\frac{2}{3}$

C. $\frac{1}{3}$ D. $\frac{1}{9}$

25. $\sqrt{72}$ is equal to :

A. $6\sqrt{2}$

B. $4\sqrt{6}$

C. $9\sqrt{6}$

D. $2\sqrt{6}$

EXPLANATORY ANSWERS

1. B : $\sqrt{\frac{1}{3}} = \sqrt{0.3333} = 0.57$.

2. C : $\frac{6^4}{3^3} = \frac{6\times6\times6\times6}{3\times3\times5} = 2\times2\times2\times6 = 48$.

3. D : $\left(\frac{1}{2}\right)^{-1} = (2)^{+1} = 2$.

4. B : Any number raise to power zero = 1.

5. D : (8)1/3 = $(\sqrt[3]{8})^1 = \sqrt[3]{8} = 2$.

6. B : Since, $a^x \times a^x = a^{x+y}$

$\therefore$ $4^4 \times 4^{17} = 4^{4+17} = 4^{21}$.

7. A : $\frac{10x^8}{5x^4} = \frac{2x^8}{x^4} = 2x^8 \times x^{-4} = 2x^{8-4} = 2x^4$.

8. B : $2^{3^2} = 2^{3\times3} = 2^9$.

9. B : $(2^3)^2 = (2\times2\times2)^2 = 2\times2\times2\times2\times2\times2 = 64$.

10. C : $(36)^{1/2} = \sqrt{36} = 6$.

11. D : $x^{3/4}.x^{3/4} = x^{3/4+3/4} = x^{6/4} = x^{3/2}$.

12. A : $(x^{3/4})^{1/2} = x^{3/4.1/2} = x^{3/8}$.

13. C : $\sqrt{32} = \sqrt{4\times4\times2} = \sqrt{(4)^2.2} = 4\sqrt{2}$.

14. A : $5\sqrt{3} = \left(\sqrt{5}\right)^2.\sqrt{3} = \sqrt{5}.\sqrt{5}.\sqrt{3} = \sqrt{5.5.3} = \sqrt{75}$.

15. D : $x^{b-c} \cdot x^{c-a} \cdot x^{a-b} = x[b - c + c - a + a - b] = x^0 = 1.$

16. B : $16000 = 16 \times 1000 = (4)^2 \times (10)^3 = 4^2 \times 10^3.$

17. D : The prime factors of 1800 are, $2 \times 2 \times 2 \times 3 \times 3 \times 5 \times 5$

$= 2^3 \times 3^2 \times 5^2.$

18. A : $27 \times 243 = [3 \times 3 \times 3] \times [3 \times 3 \times 3 \times 3 \times 3] = 3^3 \cdot 3^5 = 3^8.$

19. D : Let the numbers are x and y

$\therefore$ $$x^2 + y^2 = 26 \quad ...(i)$$
$$x^2 - y^2 = 8 \quad ...(ii)$$

Adding (i) and (ii), we get

$$2x^2 + y^2 - y^2 = 26 + 8 = 34$$

or, $2x^2 = 34,$ or $x^2 = \frac{34}{2} = 17$

$\therefore$ $x = \sqrt{17}$

Since, $x^2 + y^2 = 26$

or, $17 + y^2 = 26$

$\therefore$ $y^2 = 26 - 17 = 9$

$\therefore$ $y = \sqrt{9} = 3$

Hence, the numbers are 3 and $\sqrt{17}$.

20. A : $\left[\left(\frac{x}{y}\right)^3\right]^{-2} = \left(\frac{x}{y}\right)^{3\times-2} = \left(\frac{x}{y}\right)^{-6}$

21. B : $(x^4)^3 = x^4 \cdot x^4 \cdot x^4 = x^{4+4+4} = x^{12}.$

22. D : $(27)^{-4/3} = \frac{1}{(27)^{4/3}} = \frac{1}{\sqrt[3]{(27)^4}} = \frac{1}{3^4} = \frac{1}{3\times3\times3\times3} = \frac{1}{81}.$

23. D : $x^{1/8} \div x^{3/4}$

or $x^{1/8 - 3/4}$

or $x^{-5/8} = \frac{1}{x^{5/8}}.$

24. C : $[27^{-2/3}]^{1/2} = 27^{-2/3\times1/2} = 27^{-1/3} = \frac{1}{27^{1/3}} = \frac{1}{3}.$

25. A : $\sqrt{72} = \sqrt{36\times2} = \sqrt{6\times6\times2} = 6\sqrt{2}.$

4

PERCENTAGE

Percent, or per centum means 'for every hundred'. A percentage is a fraction expressed with 100 as its denominator and the rate per cent as its numerator. Thus, 5 per cent means 5 out of 100, or it can be expressed as 5/100 = 1/20. The symbol % is used to denote the term 'per cent'.

A decimal is converted to percentage by multiplying the decimal by 100, or by moving the decimal point two places to the right.

A percentage can be converted into decimal by dividing it by 100, or by moving the decimal point two places to the left.

For example, 12.5% = 0.125

and, 25% = .25

A fraction can be converted into a percentage by changing the fraction to a decimal and then changing the decimal to a percentage. A percentage can be changed into a fraction by first converting the percentage into a decimal and then changing the decimal to a fraction. *For example,*

1% = .01 = 1/100, 100% = 1.0 = 1

2% = .02 = 2/100, 120% = 1.2 = 12/10

5% = .05 = 1/20, 12.5% = 0.125 = 1/8

Remember :

1. To change a fraction or mixed number to a per cent; multiply the fraction or mixed number by 100. Reduce, if possible and add % sign.
2. To remove a % sign attached to a decimal and to keep it as decimal, divide the decimal by 100.
3. To remove a % sign attached to a decimal and to change the number to a fraction; divide the decimal by 100, change the result to a fraction, and reduce if necessary.
4. To remove a % sign attached to a fraction or mixed number and to keep it as fraction, divide the fraction or mixed number by 100.
5. To remove a % sign attached to a fraction or mixed number and to change the number to a decimal; divide the fraction by 100 and change the result to decimal.
6. In percentage problems, the whole is 100%. *For example,* if a problem involves 20% of a quantity, the rest of the quantity is 100 – 20 = 80%.

EXERCISE

1. 20% is equal to :

A. $\frac{1}{3}$ B. $\frac{1}{4}$

C. $\frac{1}{5}$ D. $\frac{2}{5}$

2. 5/8 may be expressed as:

A. 50/80%

B. 62.5%

C. 55.5%

D. 70.5%

3. 15% of ₹ 50 is equal to:

A. ₹ 25 B. 12.50

C. ₹ 9.50 D. 7.50

4. What rate per cent is one minute 12 seconds to an hour?

A. 2% B. 3%

C. 4% D. 5%

5. A student has to secure 40 per cent marks to pass. If he gets 20 marks and fails by 20 marks, the maximum marks are:

A. 20 B. 40

C. 80 D. 100

6. A person spends 75% of his salary and saves ₹ 150 per month. His monthly salary is:

A. ₹ 750 B. ₹ 600

C. ₹ 400 D. ₹ 300

7. Standard gold contains 22 parts of pure gold to 2 parts of alloy. The percentage of alloy in a sovereign which is made of standard gold is:

A. 11% B. 12%

C. $8\frac{1}{3}\%$ D. $11\frac{1}{3}\%$

8. The catalogue price of an article is ₹ 250. A reduction of 12% is made for cash purchase. The case price is:

A. ₹ 250

B. ₹ 220

C. ₹ 200

D. ₹ 180

9. 20% of ₹ 5 is :

A. Re. 1 B. ₹ 2

C. ₹ 3 D. ₹ 4

10. 15% of 3 metres is :

A. 30 cm

B. 45 cm

C. 60 cm

D. 25 cm

11. 5% of a number is 15. The number is :

A. 150 B. 200

C. 250 D. 300

12. 75% of what area is 15 square metres?

A. 10 square metres

B. 15 square metres

C. 20 square metres

D. 25 square metres

13. What per cent of ₹ 30 is ₹ 10?

A. 30% B. 33.3%

C. 35% D. 40%

14. What per cent of 6.25 is 1.25?

A. 10% B. 15%

C. 20% D. 25%

15. What per cent of 3 metres is 75 cm?

A. 10% B. 15%

C. 20% D. 25%

16. 62.5% may be written as :

A. $\frac{3}{8}$ B. $\frac{4}{8}$

C. $\frac{5}{8}$ D. $\frac{6}{8}$.

17. 125% may be expressed in fractions as :

A. $\frac{4}{5}$ B. $\frac{5}{4}$

C. $\frac{3}{5}$ D. $\frac{6}{5}$

18. 97% of students were present in a school and 18 students were absent. The total number of students in the school is:

A. 400 B. 450

C. 500 D. 600

19. The population of a town increased from 50,000 to 52,000. The increase per cent is:

A. 4%

B. 3%

C. 2%

D. 1%

20. At a clearance sale, goods were sold at a reduction of 20 per cent. A student purchased a pen for ₹ 12 at the clearance sale. The usual price of the pen was:

A. ₹ 12

B. ₹ 13

C. Rs 14

D. ₹ 15

21. In a college election, a candidate who got 40% of total votes was defeated by his rival by 160 votes. the total number of votes polled was:

A. 900 B. 800

C. 700 D. 600

22. In an election, 4000 votes were polled. One of the candidates got 40% votes. He was defeated by:

A. 2400 votes

B. 1600 votes

C. 800 votes

D. 600 votes

23. The selling price of a certain commodity was reduced by 25%. As a result of it, the sales increased by 30%. What was the effect of it on cash collected by daily sales?

A. 5% increase

B. 5% decrease

C. 2.5% increase

D. 2.5 decrease

24. If the price of kerosine be raised by 10%, find by how much per cent a house holder must reduce his consumption of kerosine so that not to increase his expenditure?

A. 10%

B. 9.09%

C. 9.0%

D. 8.25%

25. A towel was 50 cm broad and 100 cm long. When bleached, it was found to have lost 20% of its length and 10% of breadth. The percentage of decrease in area is:

A. 28%

B. 20%

C. 10.08%

D. 10%

EXPLANATORY ANSWERS

1. C : $20\% = \frac{20}{100} = \frac{1}{5}$.

2. B : $\frac{5}{8} \Rightarrow \frac{5}{8} \times 100 = \frac{500}{8} = 62.5\%$.

3. D : 15% of ₹ 50 = $\frac{15}{100}$ × ₹ 50 = ₹ 7.50.

4. A : 1 minute 12 seconds = 60 + 12 = 72 second

1 hour = 60 × 60 = 3600 seconds

$\therefore \quad \frac{72 \times 100}{3600} = 2\%$.

5. D : Marks required to pass = 40% = 20 + 20

$\therefore \quad \text{Maximum marks} = \frac{100 \times 40}{40} = 100$.

6. B : Saving = 100% – 75% = 25% = ₹ 150

$\therefore$ Total salary = $\frac{100}{25}$ × 150 = ₹ 600.

7. C : Total parts = 22 parts + 2 parts = 24 parts; 24 parts contain 2 parts alloy

$\therefore$ 100 parts contain $\frac{2}{24} \times 100 = \frac{25}{3} = 8\frac{1}{3}\%$.

8. B : Reduction at 12% on ₹ 250 = $\frac{12}{100}$ × 250 = ₹ 30

$\therefore$ Cash price = Catalogue price – Reduction

= ₹ 250 – ₹ 30 = Rs. 220.

9. A : 20% of ₹ 5 = $\frac{20}{100} \times 5$ = Re. 1.

10. B : 15% of 3 metres = 15% of 300 cm = $\frac{15}{100} \times 300$ = 45 cm.

11. D : Let the number = x

$\therefore$ $$5\% \text{ of } x = 15$$

or, $$\frac{5}{100} \times x = 15$$

$\therefore$ $$x = \frac{15 \times 100}{5} = 300.$$

12. C : Let the area = x m^2

$\therefore$ $$75\% \text{ of } x = 15 \text{ sq. m}$$

or $$\frac{75}{100} \times x = 15$$

$\therefore$ $$x = \frac{15 \times 100}{75} = 20 \text{ sq. m.}$$

13. B : $\frac{10}{30} \times 100 = 33.3\%.$

14. C : $\frac{1.25}{6.25} \times 100 = 20\%.$

15. D : $\frac{75}{300} \times 100 = 25\%.$

16. C : $62.5\% = \frac{62.5}{100} = \frac{625}{1000} = \frac{5}{8}.$

17. C : $125\% = \frac{125}{100} = \frac{5}{4}.$

18. D : Number of students absent = 100% – 97% = 3% = 18

$\therefore$ $$100\% = \frac{18 \times 100}{3} = 600.$$

19. A : Increase in population = 52,000 – 50,000 = 2000

$\therefore$ $$\% \text{ increase} = \frac{2000}{50,000} \times 100 = 4\%.$$

20. D : S.P. = ₹ 12 = 80% of usual price

$\therefore$ $$\text{Usual price} = \frac{100}{80} \times 12 = ₹\ 15.$$

21. B : Candidate who won the election got 100 – 40 = 60% votes;

Difference of votes = 60% – 40% = 20% = 160

$$\therefore \quad \text{Total votes polled} = \frac{160}{20} \times 100 = 800.$$

22. C : Candidates who lost election got 40% of 4000

$$= \frac{40}{100} \times 4000 = 1600 \text{ votes}$$

Candidates who won the election got 60% of 4000

$$= \frac{60}{100} \times 4000 = 2400 \text{ votes}$$

Difference of votes = 2400 – 1600 = 800 votes.

23. D : Selling price = 100 – 25 = 75%, Daily sales = 100 + 30 = 130%;

0.75 × 1.30 = 0.975 = Cash collected = 97.5%;

100% – 97.5% = 2.5% decrease.

24. B : Raised price of kerosine is 110/100 of the original price. Hence, the consumption should become 100/110 of the original consumption so as to keep the expenditure same.

$$\therefore \quad \text{Reduction} = \left(1 - \frac{100}{110}\right) \text{ of original consumtion}$$

$$= \frac{10}{110} \text{ of original consumption}$$

$$\text{Reduction } \% = \frac{10}{110} \times 100 = 9.09\%.$$

25. A :

Original area = 100 × 50 = 5000 sq. cm.

Reduced length = 80% of 100 cm = 80 cm.

Reduced breadth = 90% of 50 cm. = 45 cm.

Reduced area = 80 × 45 = 3600 sq. cm.

Reduction in area = 5000 – 3600 = 1400 sq. cm.

$$\therefore \quad \% \text{ Reduction} = \frac{1400}{5000} \times 100 = 28\%.$$

5

RATIO AND PROPORTION

Ratio: The relation which one quantity bears to another quantity of the same kind, showing the number of times one quantity is contained in another, is called ratio between the two quantities. Thus, the relation between ₹ 48 and ₹ 6 is the same as the relation between ₹ 8 and Re. 1. This relation or the ratio is written as 8 : 1.

Since, a ratio is a fraction, it is not altered if both of its terms are divided or multiplied by the same number.

For example,

$$\frac{2}{3}=\frac{4}{6}=\frac{8}{12}=\frac{20}{30}$$

Both the quantities are called the terms of the ratio. The quantity in the numerator is called *antecedent* and the quantity in the denominator is called *consequent.*

Inverse Ratio: When antecedent and consequent of one ratio become respectively the consequent and antecedent of the other, the second ratio is called the inverse or reciprocal ratio of the first.

For example, 3/5 or 3 : 5 is the inverse ratio of 5/3 or 5 : 3.

Compound Ratio: When the antecedents and consequents of two or more ratios are multiplied to get a new antecedent and a new consequent, the new ratio formed is called their compound ratio.

For example,

the compound ratio of 2 : 3, 3 : 4, 5 : 6 is

$$\frac{2}{3}\times\frac{3}{4}\times\frac{5}{6}=\frac{5}{12} \text{ or } 5 : 12$$

Proportion: Four quantities may be in proportion when the ratio of first to the second is the same as the ratio of third to the fourth. Thus the ratio 2 : 5 and 12 : 30 are equal and the four numbers 2, 5, 12 and 30 are in proportion and are writen as 2 : 5 : :12 : 30

If four quantities are in proportion, the product of the extremes is equal to the product of the means.

EXERCISE

1. The ratio between two numbers is 3 : 4 and their sum is 490. The numbers are:
A. 200 and 290
B. 210 and 280
C. 220 and 270
D. 230 and 260

2. The ratio between two numbers is 3 : 4 and the sum of their squares is 625. The numbers are:
A. 6 and 8 B. 15 and 20
C. 18 and 24 D. 20 and 25

3. Which of the following is greatest?
3 : 4, 4 : 5, 5 : 6, 6 : 7
A. 3 : 4 B. 4 : 5
C. 5 : 6 D. 6 : 7

4. In an examination, 25 students out of 70 scored less than 50% marks. The ratio of number of students who scored 50% marks or more to the number of students who scored less than 50% marks is:
A. 1 : 2 B. 3 : 5
C. 9 : 5 D. 5 : 7

5. The fraction that bears the same ratio to 4/9 that 3/11 does to 5/33 is:
A. 4 : 5 B. 5 : 6
C. 6 : 5 D. 7 : 5

6. If the consequent be 15 and the value of the ratio 3/5, then the value of antecedent is:
A. 7 B. 8
C 9 D. 10

7. If A : B = 5 : 7 and B : C = 9 : 11, then A : C = ?
A. 9 : 11 B. 45 : 77
C. 45 : 66 D. 39 : 77

8. Three numbers are in the ratio of 2 : 3 : 4 and the sum of the squares of the numbers is 116. The numbers are:
A. 4 : 6 : 8
B. 5 : 6 : 7
C. 6 : 9 : 12
D. 8 : 12 : 16

9. Sides of two squares are in the ratio of 3 : 4. Their perimeters are in the ratio of:
A. 3 : 4 B. 7 : 8
C. 5 : 6 D. 6 : 7

10. Two cubical boxes made of card-board have their edges in the ratio of 3 : 4. The ratio of the amounts of card-board in each of them is:
A. 3 : 4 B. 5 : 6
C. 6 : 7 D. 9 : 16

11. The angles of a triangle are in the ratio of 1 : 2 : 3. The largest angle is of:
A. 30° B. 60°
C. 90° D. 120°

12. The salaries of two persons are in the ratio of 4 : 7. Both of them spend 80 per cent of salaries and save rest of the money. The ratio of their savings is:
A. 8 : 2
B. 4 : 7
C. 7 : 5
D. 5 : 3

13. The mean proportion between 9 and 25 is:

A. 10 B. 12
C. 15 D. 17

14. The third proportional to 12 and 30 is:

A. 40 B. 45
C. 50 D. 75

15. The fourth proportional to 3, 4 and 15 is:

A. 20 B. 18
C. 17 D. 15

16. 75 : 15 = x : 7, the value of x is:

A. 25 B. 35
C. 40 D. 45

17. x : 7.5 = 7 : 17.5, the value of x is:

A. 1.0 B. 2.5
C. 3.0 D. 3.5

18. The mean proportional to 5 and 125 is:

A. 10 B. 15
C. 20 D. 25

19. The inverse ratio of 12 to 18 is:

A. $\frac{3}{2}$ B. $\frac{2}{3}$
C. $\frac{1}{3}$ D. $\frac{3}{1}$

20. Two numbers are in the ratio of 2: 3 and if 8 is added to each of them, they become in the ratio of 3 : 4. The number are:

A. 2 and 3
B. 4 and 6
C. 8 and 12
D. 16 and 24

21. If $x : y = 3 : 2$, then $(x + y) : (x - y) = ?$

A. 1 : 5 B. 5 : 1
C. 3 : 5 D. 5 : 2

22. If $x : y = y : z$, then $x = ?$

A. z B. $\frac{z}{y^2}$
C. $\frac{y^2}{z}$ D. $\frac{y}{z}$

EXPLANATORY ANSWERS

1. B : Ratio is 3 : 4, sum = 490

If sum is 7, the numbers are 3 and 4.

If sum is 490, the numbers are $\frac{3}{7} \times 490$ and $\frac{4}{7} \times 490$ *i.e.*, 210 and 280.

2. B : Ratio is 3 : 4. Sum of the squares of 3 and 4 is 9 + 16 = 25. If sum of the squares is 25, the squares of numbers are 9 and 16.

If sum of the squares is 625, the squares of numbers are $\frac{9}{25} \times 625$ and $\frac{16}{25} \times 625$ *i.e.*, 225 and 400.

Hence, the numbers are $\sqrt{225}$ and $\sqrt{400}$, *i.e.*, 15 and 20.

3. D : $\frac{3}{4}, \frac{4}{5}, \frac{5}{6}, \frac{6}{7}$

$\frac{315,\ 336,\ 350,\ 360}{420}$. Hence, the ratio 6 : 7 is the greatest.

4. C : Total students = 70.

Number of students scoring less than 50% marks = 25; Number of students scoring 50% or more than 50% marks = 70 – 25 = 45.

∴ The ratio of number of students who scored 50% marks or more to the number of students who scored less than 50% marks

$$= 45 : 25 = 9 : 5.$$

5. A : Let the required fraction is x. Then

$$\frac{x}{4/9} = \frac{3/11}{5/33} = \frac{3}{11} \times \frac{33}{5} = \frac{9}{5}$$

$$\therefore \quad x = \frac{9}{5} \times \frac{4}{9} = \frac{4}{5}, \text{ or }, 4 : 5.$$

6. C :

$$\text{Ratio} = \frac{3}{5} = \frac{\text{Antecedent}}{\text{Consequent}} = \frac{x}{15}$$

$$\therefore \quad x = 9, \text{ only then } \frac{9}{15} = \frac{3}{5}$$

7. B : $A : B = 5 : 7$; $B : C = 9 : 11$; $A : C = ?$

$$\frac{A}{B} = \frac{5}{7}, \quad \frac{B}{C} = \frac{9}{11}, \quad \frac{A}{C} = x$$

$$\frac{A}{B} \times \frac{B}{C} = \frac{5}{7} \times \frac{9}{11}, \text{ or, } \frac{A}{C} = \frac{45}{77}$$

$$\therefore \quad A : C = 45 : 77$$

8. A : Ratio of numbers = 2 : 3 : 4.

Ratio of squares of numbers = 4 : 9 : 16

If sum of the squares is 29, the squares of the numbers are 4, 9, 16.

If sum of the squares is 116, the squares of the numbers are

$$\frac{4}{29} \times 116, \frac{9}{29} \times 116, \frac{16}{29} \times 116 = 16, 36, 64$$

∴ The numbers are $\sqrt{16}$, $\sqrt{36}$, $\sqrt{64}$ = 4, 6, 8.

9. A : Let the sides of two squares are $3x$ and $4x$.
Their perimeters are $4(3x)$ and $4(4x) = 12x$ and $16x$.
Ratio of permieters = $12x : 16x = 3 : 4$.

10. D : Let the sides of two cubes are $3x$ and $4x$. Surface areas of two cubes are $6(3x)^2$ and $6(4x)^2$.
Ratio of surface areas = $6(3x)^2 : 6(4x)^2 = 54x^2 : 96x^2 = 9 : 16$.

11. C : Ratio of the angles of triangle = $1 : 2 : 3$
Sum of the angles of triangle = 180°

$$\text{Largest angle} = \frac{3}{6} \times 180 = 90^\circ$$

12. B : Let the salaries be $4x$ and $7x$.
Savings are $100 - 80 = 20\%$

$$\text{Ratio of savings} = 20\% \text{ of } 4x : 20\% \text{ of } 7x$$

$$= \frac{20}{100} \times 4x : \frac{20}{100} \times 7x = 4 : 7$$

13. C : The mean proportion between any two numbers is equal to the square root of their product.
Let x be the mean proportion between 9 and 25.

$\therefore$ $$9 : x = x : 25$$

or, $$x^2 = 25 \times 9, \text{ or, } x = \sqrt{25 \times 9} = \sqrt{225} = 15.$$

14. D : Let x be the third proportional to 12 and 30.

Then, $$12 : 30 = 30 : x$$

or, $$12x = 30 \times 30$$

$\therefore$ $$x = \frac{30 \times 30}{12} = 75.$$

15. A : Let x be the fourth proportional to 3, 4, 15.

Then, $3 : 4 = 15 : x$

Since, product of the extremes = Product of the means

$\therefore$ $$3x = 15 \times 4, \text{ or, } x = \frac{15 \times 4}{3} = 20.$$

16. B : $$75 : 15 = x : 7$$

$$75 \times 7 = 15 \times x \text{ or, } x = \frac{75 \times 7}{15} = 35.$$

17. C : $x : 7.5 = 7 : 17.5$

$$x \times 17.5 = 7.5 \times 7.0$$

$$\therefore \quad x = \frac{7.5 \times 7.0}{17.5} = 3.0.$$

18. D : Let x be the mean proportional to 5 and 125.

Then, $5 : x = x : 125$ or, $x^2 = 125 \times 5$

$$\therefore \quad x = \sqrt{125 \times 5} = \sqrt{625} = 25.$$

19. A : The inverse ratio of 12 : 18 *i.e.,*

$\frac{12}{18}$ is $\frac{18}{12} = \frac{3}{2}$.

20. D : Let the numbers be $2x$ and $3x$.

Then we have, $\frac{2x+8}{3x+8} = \frac{3}{4}$, or, $8x + 32 = 9x + 24$

or, $9x - 8x = 32 - 24$, or, $x = 8$

$\therefore$ The numbers are 2×8 and 3×8 *i.e.,* 16 and 24

21. B : $x : y = 3 : 2$, $x + y = 3 + 2$

and $x - y = 3 - 2$

$\therefore$ $(x + y) : (x - y) = 5 : 1$

22. C : $x : y = y : z$, or, $\frac{x}{y} = \frac{y}{z}$

$$\therefore \quad x = \frac{y}{z} . y = \frac{y^2}{z}$$

6

PROFIT AND LOSS

Profit and Loss: The terms profit and loss are largely used in business. When the selling price (S.P.) is greater than cost price (C.P.) there is always some profit. When the selling price is less than the cost price, there is always loss.

> **It should be noted that profit or loss is calculated on the cost price, generally in the form of per cent.**

For example, a man buys an article for ₹ 50 and sells it for ₹ 65. The gain per cent is calculated as follows:

$$\text{Profit} = \text{Selling Price} - \text{Cost Price}$$
$$= ₹\ 65 - ₹\ 50 = ₹\ 15$$

$$\%\ \text{Profit} = \frac{15}{50} \times 100 = 30\%$$

When cost price and profit or loss % are given, then

$$\text{S.P.} = \frac{[100 + \text{gain}\%]}{100} \times \text{C.P.}$$

or

$$\text{S.P.} = \frac{[100 - \text{Loss}\%]}{100} \times \text{C.P.}$$

When selling price and profit or loss % are given,

$$\text{C.P.} = \frac{\text{S.P.} \times 100}{100 + \text{Gain}\ \%} \quad \text{or} \quad \text{C.P.} = \frac{\text{S.P.} \times 100}{100 - \text{Loss}\ \%}$$

(i) To find the cost price when the selling price and the % profit based on cost price is given:

Establish a relation between S.P. and C.P. and solve it to find C.P.

For example, an article is sold for Rs.10 which is a 10% profit of C.P.

In this case, S.P. = ₹ 10 = C.P. + 10% of C.P. (Profit)

∴ S.P. = 100% of C.P.

or, $$\text{C.P.} = ₹\ \frac{10 \times 100}{110} = ₹\ 9.09.$$

(ii) To find the S.P. when the profit based on S.P. is given:

Establish a relation between the S.P. and C.P. and solve it to find the S.P.

For example, a person buys a book for ₹ 27 and sells it at a profit of 10% of S.P. Find the S.P.

₹ 27 + Profit = S.P.

Since, profit is 10% of S.P., the C.P. must be 90% of S.P.

∴ ₹ 27 = 90% of S.P.

$$\therefore \quad \text{S.P.} = \frac{27 \times 100}{90} = ₹\ 30.$$

(iii) To find S.P. when the % loss on the S.P. is given:

Establish a relation between C.P. and S.P. and solve it to find S.P.

For example, an article was bought for ₹ 10. Due to some breakage, it was sold for 25% loss on the S.P. Find the S.P. of the article.

₹ 10 – Loss = S.P.

Since, the loss is 25% of the S.P., the C.P. must be 125% of S.P.

∴ ₹ 10 = 125% of S.P.

$$\therefore \quad \text{S.P.} = \frac{\text{Rs. } 10 \times 100}{125} = ₹\ 8.$$

(iv) To find S.P. when the list price and % discount are given:

Multiply the list price by % discount to find the discount in terms of money and subtract it from the list price.

For example, the list price of an article is ₹ 90. Find its selling price if it is sold at 10% discount.

List price = ₹ 90.00, Discount = 10% of ₹ 90.00

$$= \frac{10 \times 90}{100} = ₹\ 9.00$$

∴ Selling price = ₹ 90.00 – ₹ 9.00 = ₹ 81.00

(v) To find S.P. when list price and a series of discounts are given:

(*a*) Multiply the list price by first % discount.

(*b*) Subtract it from the list price.

(*c*) Multiply the remainder by second discount.

(*d*) Subtract the product from the remainder.

(*e*) Continue the same procedure if more discounts are given.

For example, find the selling price of an article listed at ₹ 200 on which there are discounts of 10% and 20%.

First discount = 10% of ₹ 200

$$= \frac{10 \times 200}{100} = ₹\ 20$$

First selling price = ₹ 200 – ₹ 20 = ₹ 180.

Second discount = 20% of ₹ 180

$$= \frac{20 \times 180}{100} = ₹\ 36$$

Second selling price = ₹ 180 – ₹ 36 = ₹ 144

(vi) To find the single equivalent discount of a series of discounts :

(a) Add first two discounts.

(b) Multiply first two discounts.

(c) Subtract this product from the sum to find the equivalent discount of the first two discounts.

(d) If there is third discount, add the equivalent of first two discounts to the third.

(e) Multiply the equivalent of first two discounts by third.

(f) Subtract this product from the sum to find the equivalent of the three discounts.

(g) Continue the same procedure, if there are more discounts.

For example, what is the single discount equivalent to discount series 10%, 20%, 30%.

10% + 20% = 0.1 + 0.2 = 0.3

10% × 20% = 0.1 × 0.2 = 0.02

0.30 – 0.02 = 0.28

0.28 + 30% = 0.28 + 0.3 = 0.580

0.28 × 30% = 0.28 × 0.3 = 0.084

0.580 – 0.084 = 0.496 = 49.6%

Hence, the single equivalent discount of 10%, 20% and 30%, is 49.6%.

EXERCISE

1. A man buys an article for ₹ 25 and sells it for ₹ 30. His profit is:

A. 16.67% B. 20%

C. 25.5% D. 25.67%

2. If an article is sold at 10% profit, then the selling price in terms of cost price is:

A. 10/11 B. 11/10

C. ₹ 110 D. ₹ 90

3. If an article is sold at gain of x%, the cost price in terms of selling price is:

A. $\frac{100}{100+x}$ B. $\frac{100+x}{100}$

C. $\frac{100}{100-x}$ D. $\frac{100-x}{100}$

4. If an article is sold at gain of y%, the selling price in terms of cost price is:

A. $\frac{100}{100-y}$ B. $\frac{100-y}{100}$

C. $\frac{100}{100+y}$ D. $\frac{100+y}{100}$

5. If an article is sold at a loss of 25%, the selling price in terms of cost price is:

A. $\frac{1}{2}$ B. $\frac{2}{3}$

C. $\frac{3}{4}$ D. $\frac{4}{5}$

6. If an article is sold at a loss of 50%, the cost price in terms of selling price is:

A. $\frac{1}{2}$

B. 2

C. 2.5

D. None of the above

7. If S.P. of an article is 4/3 of C.P., the profit is:

A. $\frac{1}{3}\%$ B. $33\frac{1}{3}\%$

C. $25\frac{1}{5}\%$ D. $20\frac{1}{2}\%$

8. If C.P. of an article is 3/2 of S.P., the profit or loss percentage is:

A. $33\frac{1}{3}\%$ loss B. $33\frac{1}{3}\%$ profit

C. $33\frac{1}{8}\%$ loss D. $33\frac{1}{8}\%$ profit

9. If S.P. of an article is 6 times the loss, the loss percentage is:

A. $14\frac{5}{9}\%$ B. $15\frac{2}{8}\%$

C. $16\frac{3}{5}\%$ D. $14\frac{2}{7}\%$

10. If gain is 1/4 of C.P., the profit percentage is:

A. 4% B. 25%

C. 50% D. 75%

11. If loss is 1/3 of S.P., the loss percentage is:

A. 33% B. 25%

C. 20% D. 17%

12. A man bought certain articles at 8 for ₹ 7 and sold them at 6 for ₹ 5. The gain or loss percentage is:

A. $4\frac{16}{21}\%$ gain

B. $4\frac{16}{21}\%$ loss

C. No profit no loss

D. None of the above

13. A man bought a number of oranges at 3 for a rupee and an equal number at 2 for a rupee. At what price per dozen should be sell them to make a profit of 20%?

A. ₹ 4 B. ₹ 5

C. ₹ 6 D. ₹ 7

14. A machine was bought for ₹ 9000. For how much should it be sold to gain 15%?

A. ₹ 10,150 B. ₹ 10,250

C. ₹ 10,300 D. ₹ 10,350

15. Find the selling price if a fountain pen costing ₹ 6.20 is sold at a loss of 10%?

A. ₹ 6.92 B. ₹ 5.58

C. ₹ 6.00 D. ₹ 5.92

16. A carpet is sold for ₹ 585 at a loss of 10%. The cost price is:

A. ₹ 650 B. ₹ 640

C. ₹ 630 D. ₹ 620

17. A machine is sold at a profit of 20%. If it had been sold at a profit of 25%, it would have fetched ₹ 35 more. The cost price of the machine is:

A. ₹ 650 B. ₹ 700
C. ₹ 750 D. ₹ 800

18. By selling a book for ₹ 31 a person loses 7% of his outlay. If he sells the same book for ₹ 35, the bargain is:

A. 4% loss B. 4% profit
C. 5% loss D. 5% profit

19. The cost price of 12 articles is equal to the selling price of 9 articles. The gain per cent is:

A. 25.0% B. 33.3%
C. 30.0% D. 67.7%

20. At a clearance sale, the prices had been reduced by 20%. If a transistor was being sold at ₹ 150 before reduction, the price at clearance sale was:

A. ₹ 130
B. ₹ 125
C. ₹ 120
D. ₹ 115

EXPLANATORY ANSWERS

1. B : Profit = ₹ 30 – ₹ 25 = ₹ 5, % Profit = $\frac{5}{25} \times 100 = 20\%$.

2. B : If the profit is 10%, then S.P. = 110% of C.P. = $\frac{110}{100}$ of C.P. = $\frac{11}{10}$ of C.P.

3. A : Gain = x%, S.P. = $[100 + x]$ % of C.P. $\therefore$ C.P. $= \frac{100}{100+x}$ S.P.

4. D : Gain = y%, S.P. = $[100 + y]$ % of C.P.

$$\text{S.P.} = \frac{100+y}{100} \times \text{C.P.}$$

5. C : Loss = 25%, C.P. = 100, S.P. = 100 – 25 = 75

or, S.P. = 75% of C.P. = $\frac{3}{4}$ of C.P.

6. B : Let C.P. = 100, Loss = 50%, S.P. = 100 – 50 = 50%;
or, S.P. = 50% of C.P. or, C.P. = 200% of S.P. or, C.P. = 2 × S.P.

7. B : C.P. = 1, S.P. = $\frac{4}{3}$, Profit = $\frac{4}{3} - 1 = \frac{1}{3}$

% Profit = $100 \times \frac{1}{3} = 33\frac{1}{3}\%$.

8. A : C.P. = 1, S.P. = $\frac{2}{3}$ of C.P., Loss = $1 - \frac{2}{3} = \frac{1}{3}$.

% Loss = $\frac{1}{3} \times 100 = 33\frac{1}{3}\%$.

9. D : S.P. = 6 times the Loss or, Loss = $\frac{1}{6}$ of S.P.

C.P. = S.P. + Loss = S.P. + $\frac{1}{6}$ of S.P. = $\frac{7}{6}$ of S.P.

or, S.P. = $\frac{6}{7}$ of C.P. ∴ Loss = 1 – $\frac{6}{7}$ of C.P. = $\frac{1}{7}$ of C.P.

% Loss = 100 × $\frac{1}{7}$ = $14\frac{2}{7}\%$

10. B : C.P. = 1, Gain = $\frac{1}{4}$ of C.P. = $\frac{1}{4}\times 1 = \frac{1}{4}$

% Gain = $\frac{1}{4}\times 100 = 25\%$.

11. B : Loss = $\frac{1}{3}$ of S.P.

C.P. = S.P. + Loss = S.P. + $\frac{1}{3}$ of S.P. = $\frac{4}{3}$ of S.P.

or, S.P. = $\frac{3}{4}$ of C.P. ∴ Loss = $\frac{1}{4}$ of C.P.

% Loss = $\frac{1}{4}$ × 100 of C.P. = 25% of C.P.

12. B : C.P. of one article = ₹ $\frac{7}{8}$, S.P. of one article = ₹ $\frac{5}{6}$

Loss = C.P. – S.P. = $\frac{7}{8}-\frac{5}{6}=\frac{1}{24}$

% Loss = $\frac{1}{24}\times\frac{8}{7}\times 100 = \frac{100}{21} = 4\frac{16}{21}\%$

13. C : Let 1 dozen oranges were bought at 3 for a rupee and one dozen oranges were bought at 2 for a rupee.

∴ C.P. of 1 dozen = ₹ 4

C.P. of 1 dozen = ₹ 6

C.P. of 2 dozens = ₹ 6 + ₹ 4 = ₹ 10

% Profit 20% = 20% of ₹ 10 = ₹ 2

∴ S.P. = C.P. + Profit = ₹ 10 + ₹ 2

= ₹ 12

S.P. of 2 dozen oranges = ₹ 12

∴ S.P. of 1 dozen oranges = ₹ $\frac{12}{2}$ = ₹ 6

14. D : C.P. = ₹ 9000, Gain = 15% of ₹ 9000 = $\frac{15}{100} \times 9000$ = ₹ 1350.

∴ S.P. = ₹ 9000 + ₹ 1350 = ₹ 10,350.

15. B : C.P. = ₹ 6.20, Loss = 10% of C.P. = 10% of ₹ 6.20

$= \frac{10}{100} \times 6.20$ = 62 paise

S.P. = C.P. – Loss = ₹ 6.20 – 62 paise

= ₹ 5.58

16. A : S.P. = ₹ 585, Loss = 10% of C.P.

$$\text{C.P.} = \frac{\text{S.P.} \times 100}{[100 - \text{Loss\%}]} = \frac{585 \times 100}{100 - 10} = \frac{585 \times 100}{90} = ₹\ 650.$$

17. B : Let, C.P. = ₹ 100

Ist S.P. = ₹ 120, IInd S.P. = ₹ 125

Difference = ₹ 125 – ₹ 120 = ₹ 5

If difference is ₹ 5, C.P. = ₹ 100

If difference is ₹ 35, C.P. = $\frac{100}{5} \times 35$ = ₹ 700

18. D : S.P. = ₹ 31, Loss = 7%

∴ C.P. = $\frac{31 \times 100}{93}$ = ₹ $\frac{100}{3}$

IInd S.P. = ₹ 35, Profit = ₹ 35 – ₹ $\frac{100}{3}$ = ₹ $\frac{5}{3}$

∴ % Profit = $\frac{5}{3} \times \frac{3}{100} \times 100 = 5\%$.

19. B : Let C.P. of one article = ₹ 1

∴ C.P. of 12 articles = ₹ 12

C.P. of 12 articles = S.P. of 9 articles = ₹ 12

∴ S.P. of 12 articles = $\frac{12}{9} \times 12$ = ₹ 16

Profit = ₹ 16 – ₹ 12 = ₹ 4

% Profit = $\frac{4}{12} \times 100 = 33.3\%$

20. C : S.P. before reduction = ₹ 150

S.P. after reduction = 100 – 20 = 80% of ₹ 150

$= \frac{80}{100} \times 150$ = ₹ 120.

7

INTEREST

Interest is the sum which is paid for the use of other's money. If it is payable yearly, it is called rate per cent per annum. Thus, 6% per annum means ₹ 6 paid as interest on each ₹ 100 for one year. The money borrowed is called *Principal.* The sum of the principal and interest is called *Amount.*

In the Case of Simple Interest:

$$\text{Simple Interest} = \frac{\text{Principal} \times \text{Rate\%} \times \text{Time (in years)}}{100}$$

$$\text{Amount} = \text{Principal} + \text{Interest}$$

When time, rate% and interest are given,

$$\text{Principal} = \frac{\text{Interest} \times 100}{\text{Rate} \times \text{Time (in years)}}$$

When principal, interest and time are given,

$$\text{Rate} = \frac{\text{Interest} \times 100}{\text{Principal} \times \text{Time}}$$

When principal, interest and rate are given,

$$\text{Time} = \frac{\text{Interest} \times 100}{\text{Principal} \times \text{Rate}}$$

Example 1. A sum of money amounts to ₹ 6000 in 2 years. If the interest on the sum for that time is ₹ 1000. Find the rate of simple interest.

Solution. Amount = ₹ 6000, Interest = ₹ 1000

Principal = ₹ 6000 – ₹ 1000 = ₹ 5000

Time = 2 years

$$\text{Rate} = \frac{\text{Interest} \times 100}{\text{Principal} \times \text{Time}} = \frac{1000 \times 100}{5000 \times 2} = 10\%$$

Example 2. What principal with yield ₹ 600 as simple interest at 12% per annum in 1 year?

Solution. Interest = ₹ 600, Rate = 12%, Time = 1 year

$$\text{Principal} = \frac{\text{Interest} \times 100}{\text{Rate} \times \text{Time}} = \frac{\text{Rs. } 600 \times 100}{12 \times 1} = ₹\ 5000.$$

Example 3. At what time will the interest on a sum of money will equal to the principal at 10% per annum?

Solution. Let, Principal = x, ∴ Interest = x, Rate = 10%

$$\text{Time} = \frac{\text{Interest} \times 100}{\text{Principal} \times \text{Rate}} = \frac{x \times 100}{x \times 10} = 10 \text{ years.}$$

Example 4. Three years back, a sum of money was remitted in a bank at 12% per annum S.I. The accounts are now cleared, the bank paying a sum of ₹ 6,800. What was the sum originally invested?

Solution. Interest for 3 years = 3 × 12 = 36% of the principal. The amount in 3 years = 100 + 36 = 136% of the principal = ₹ 6800.

$$\therefore \quad \text{Original sum invested} = \frac{6800 \times 100}{136} = ₹\ 5000.$$

In the Case of Compound Interest:

$$\text{Amount} = \text{Principal}\left[1+\frac{\text{Rate}}{100}\right]^{\text{Time(in year)}}$$

If rate of compound interest differs from year to year, then

$$\text{Amount} = \text{Principal}\left[1+\frac{\text{Rate}_1}{100}\right]\left[1+\frac{\text{Rate}_2}{100}\right]\left[1+\frac{\text{Rate}_3}{100}\right]\text{..........}$$

Example 5. Find the compound interest on ₹ 2000 for 2 years at 10%.

Solution. $$\text{Amount} = \text{Principal}\left[1+\frac{\text{Rate}}{100}\right]^2$$

$$= ₹\ 2000\left[1+\frac{10}{100}\right]^2 = ₹\ 2000 \times \frac{11}{10} \times \frac{11}{10}$$

$$= ₹\ 2420$$

$$\text{Compound Interest} = ₹\ 2420 - ₹\ 2000 = ₹\ 420$$

Example 6. Find the compound interest on ₹ 4000 for 1.5 years at 10% interest payable half- yearly.

Solution. (In such cases, double the time and half the rate)

$$\text{Amount} = 4000\left(1+\frac{5}{100}\right)^3$$

$$= ₹\ 4000 \times \frac{21}{20} \times \frac{21}{20} \times \frac{21}{20} = ₹\ 4630.50$$

$$\text{Compound Interest} = ₹\ 4630.50 - ₹\ 4000 = ₹\ 630.50$$

Example 7. In what time ₹ 12000 will amount to ₹ 13230 at 5% C.I.?

Solution. Principal $\left[1+\frac{\text{Rate}}{100}\right]^n$ = Amount

$$\therefore \quad ₹\ 13230 = ₹\ 12000\left[1+\frac{5}{100}\right]^n$$

$$\therefore \quad \left[1+\frac{5}{100}\right]^n = \frac{\text{Rs. } 13230}{\text{Rs. } 12000}$$

or,
$$\left[\frac{21}{20}\right]^n = \frac{441}{400} = \frac{21}{20}\times\frac{21}{20} = \left[\frac{21}{20}\right]^2$$

$$\therefore \quad n = 2 \text{ years}$$

When interest is calculated half-yearly, halve the rate and double the time. When interest is calculated quarterly, divide the rate by 4 and multiply the time by 4.

EXERCISE

1. S.I. on ₹ 5000 for 5 years at 10% p.a. is equal to:
A. ₹ 250 B. ₹ 2000
C. ₹ 2500 D. ₹ 2800

2. What principal will yield ₹ 120 as S.I. at 6% p.a. in 10 years?
A. ₹ 100 B. ₹ 125
C. ₹ 150 D. ₹ 200

3. In how many years will the sum of money double itself at 10% per annum S.I.?
A. 4 years B. 5 years
C. 8 years D. 10 years

4. What sum of money will produce an interest of ₹ 80 in 5 years at the rate of 5% per annum?
A. ₹ 320 B. ₹ 380
C. ₹ 420 D. ₹ 500

5. If S.I. on ₹ 5000 in 2 years is ₹ 500, the amount is:
A. ₹ 4500 B. ₹ 5500
C. ₹ 5575 D. ₹ 6000

6. The simple interest on a certain sum of money is ₹ 49 and the rate per cent is equal to the number of years. The rate per cent is:
A. 10% B. 9%
C. 7% D. 6%

7. If the rate of interest is 2 paise per rupee per month, then the interest on ₹ 200 in one year will be:
A. ₹ 4 B. ₹ 24
C. ₹ 48 D. ₹ 50

8. What annual payment will discharge a debt of ₹ 440 due in 5 years? Simple interest reckoned at 5%.
A. ₹ 80 B. ₹ 90
C. ₹ 100 D. ₹ 105

9. Compound interest on ₹ 2000 for 3 years at 5% p.a. is:
A. ₹ 300 B. ₹ 315.25
C. ₹ 325.50 D. ₹ 333.75

10. Find the compound interest on ₹ 1000 is one year at 5% per annum when the interest is calculated half-yearly?

A. ₹ 50.20 B. ₹ 50.62
C. ₹ 50.82 D. ₹ 55.62

11. The difference between C.I. and S.I. on ₹ 2500 for 2 years at 4% p.a. is:

A. ₹ 2 B. ₹ 3
C. ₹ 4 D. ₹ 5

12. What sum lent at C.I. at 5% p.a. will amount to ₹ 441 in 2 years?

A. ₹ 200 B. ₹ 250
C. ₹ 450 D. ₹ 400

13. For a sum of ₹ 1000, during same time at the same rate, highest quantity will be:

A. S.I. B. C.I.
C T.D. D. B.G.

14. S.I. is equal to C.I. for a certain sum when:

A. rate is same
B. time is same
C. interest is computed annually and time is one year
D. None of the above

15. Simple interest on the sum due of a bill for the time from when the bill is discounted to the due date of bill is called:

A. Simple Interest
B. Compound Interest
C. True Discount
D. Banker's Discount

16. A sum becomes double in 15 years at simple interest. It will become triple in:

A. 20 years B. 30 years
C. 35 years D. 40 years

17. In 5 years the interest on certain sum amounts to one-fourth of the sum. The rate of interest per annum is:

A. 4% B. 5%
C. 6% D. 10%

EXPLANATORY ANSWERS

1. C : $\text{S.I.} = \dfrac{\text{Principal} \times \text{Time} \times \text{Rate}}{100} = \dfrac{5000 \times 5 \times 100}{100} = ₹\ 2500.$

2. D : $\text{Principal} = \dfrac{\text{S.I.} \times 100}{\text{Time} \times \text{Rate}} = \dfrac{120 \times 100}{6 \times 10} = ₹\ 200$

3. D : Let Principal = x

$\therefore$ Amount = $2x$, Hence, Interest = $2x - x = x$

$$\text{Rate} = 10\%, \text{ Time} = \frac{\text{Interest} \times 100}{\text{Principal} \times \text{Rate}} = \frac{x \times 100}{x \times 10} = 10 \text{ years.}$$

4. **A** : Principal $= \dfrac{\text{Interest} \times 100}{\text{Rate} \times \text{Time}} = \dfrac{80 \times 100}{5 \times 5} = ₹\ 320.$

5. **B** : Amount = ₹ 5000 + ₹ 500 = ₹ 5500.

6. **C** : Let the Principal = ₹ 100, Time = x years, Rate = $x\%$

$$\text{S.I.} = \frac{100 \times x \times x}{100} = x^2 = ₹\ 49$$

$$\therefore \quad x = \sqrt{49} = 7 = 7\%$$

7. **C** : Rate of interest = 2% per month
= 24% per year

$$\therefore \quad \text{Interest} = \frac{200 \times 24 \times 1}{100} = ₹\ 48$$

8. **A.**

9. **B** :

$$\text{Amount} = ₹\ 2000 \left(1 + \frac{5}{100}\right)^3$$

$$= ₹\ 2315.25$$

$$\text{C.I.} = \text{Amount} - \text{Principal} = 2315.25 - 2000$$

$$= ₹\ 315.25.$$

10. **B** : When interest is calculated half-yearly, convert 1 year into 2 half years and take half of the rate.

Thus, rate = 2.5%, $n = 2$

$$\text{Amount} = ₹\ 1000 \left(1 + \frac{2.5}{100}\right)^2$$

$$= ₹\ 1050.62$$

$$\text{Interest} = 1050.62 - 1000 = ₹\ 50.62.$$

11. C. 12. D. 13. B. 14. C. 15. D. 16. B.

17. **B** : Let sum = x, ∴ Interest = $x/4$,
Time = 5 years,

$$\text{Rate} = \frac{\text{Interest} \times 100}{\text{Sum} \times \text{Time}} = \frac{x/4 \times 100}{x \times 5} = 5\%.$$

8

DISCOUNT

Discount in the general term is the reduction or an allowance made from the amount of a bill in lieu of its immediate cash payment. The reduction made in consideration of making immediate payment is called discount or true discount. The immediate cash payment or cash equivalent is called present worth or present value.

$$\text{Sum Due} = \text{Present Worth} + \text{True Discount}$$

$$\text{True Discount} = \text{Sum Due} - \text{Present Worth}$$

$$\text{True Discount on Sum Due} = \text{Interest on Present Worth}$$

$$\text{Present Worth} = \frac{100 \times \text{Sum Due}}{100 + [\text{Rate} \times \text{Time}]}$$

$$\text{True Discount} = \frac{\text{Sum Due} \times \text{Rate} \times \text{Time}}{100 + [\text{Rate} \times \text{Time}]}$$

Example. *Find the present worth and true discount on ₹6000 due 2 years at 10% per annum S.I.*

Solution.

$$\text{P.W.} = \frac{100 \times \text{Sum Due}}{100 + [\text{Rate} \times \text{Time}]}$$

$$= \frac{100 \times 6000}{100 + [10 \times 2]} = \frac{100 \times 6000}{120} = ₹\ 5000$$

$$\text{T.D.} = \frac{\text{Sum Due} \times \text{Rate} \times \text{Time}}{100 + [\text{Rate} \times \text{Time}]}$$

$$= \frac{6000 \times 10 \times 2}{100 + [10 \times 2]} = \frac{6000 \times 10 \times 2}{120} = ₹\ 1000.$$

Banker's Discount: In business when a trader buys goods from a wholesaler, the payment is generally made by a bill of exchange which is a kind of undertaking in writing to pay for the goods after a certain time. When the wholesaler wants money at earlier date, in such case, the bill is sold to the banker for ready money and it is said to be discounted and the amount which the banker deducts is called Banker's discount.

Banker's Discount (B.D.) is the same as the simple interest on the amount of bill for the number of days the bill has yet to run.

Banker's Gain (B.G.) = Banker's Discount – True Discount

Banker's Discount = True Discount + Interest on True Discount

$$\text{Sum Due} = \frac{\text{B.D.} \times \text{T.D.}}{\text{B.D.} - \text{T.D.}}$$

$$\text{T.D.} = \sqrt{\text{P.W.} \times \text{B.G.}}$$

Example 1. *True discount on a certain sum of money due 1 year hence is ₹ 48 and interest on the same sum for the same time is ₹ 50. Find the sum and the rate per cent.*

Solution.

$$\text{Sum} = \frac{\text{Interest} \times \text{Discount}}{\text{Interest} - \text{Discount}}$$

$$= \frac{\text{Rs. } 50 \times \text{Rs. } 48}{\text{Rs. } 50 - \text{Rs. } 48} = ₹\ \frac{50 \times 48}{2} = ₹\ 1200$$

Now, ₹ 50 is the interest on ₹ 1200 in one year,

$$\therefore \quad \text{Rate} = \frac{50 \times 100}{1200 \times 1} = 4\frac{1}{6}\%$$

Example 2. The banker's discount and true discount on a certain sum of money at 5% S.I. are ₹ 30 and ₹ 25 respectively. Find the sum.

Solution.

$$\text{Sum} = \frac{\text{B.D.} \times \text{T.D.}}{\text{B.D.} - \text{T.D.}} = \frac{30 \times 25}{30 - 25} = ₹\ 150$$

Example 3. *Find the banker's discount and banker's gain on a bill of ₹ 4000 at 10% if it is cashed 3 months in advance.*

Solution.

$$\text{Banker's discount} = \frac{\text{Rs. } 4000 \times 10 \times 3}{12 \times 100} = ₹\ 100$$

Cash received by the bill holder = ₹ 4000 – ₹ 100 = ₹ 3900

Interest on ₹ 100 = ₹ 2.50

Amount = ₹ 100 + ₹ 2.50 = ₹ 102.50

If amount is ₹ 102.50, T.D. = ₹ 2.50

If amount is ₹ 4000,

$$\text{T.D.} = \frac{2.50}{102.50} \times 4000 = ₹\ 97.56$$

B.G. = B.D. – T.D. = ₹ 100 – ₹ 97.56 = ₹ 2.44.

Example 4. *Banker's gain on a bill is ₹ 18 whose present worth is ₹ 450. Find true discount.*

Solution.

$$\text{T.D.} = \sqrt{\text{P.W.} \times \text{B.G.}}$$

$$= \sqrt{450 \times 18} = \sqrt{8100} = ₹\ 90.$$

Example 5. *True discount on a bill of ₹ 5400 is ₹ 900. Find the banker's discount and also banker's gain.*

Solution. Amount = ₹ 5400, T.D. = ₹ 900,

P.W. = Amount − T.D. = ₹ 5400 − ₹ 900

= ₹ 4500

S.I. on ₹ 4500 = ₹ 900

$\therefore$ S.I. on ₹ 5400 = ₹ $\frac{900 \times 5400}{4500}$ = ₹ 1080

$\therefore$ B.D. = ₹ 1080

$\therefore$ B.G. = B.D. − T.D. = ₹ 1080 − ₹ 900 = ₹ 180.

EXERCISE

1. Present worth of a money is equal to:

A. $\frac{100 \times \text{Sum Due}}{100 + \text{Rate} + \text{Time}}$

B. $\frac{100 \times \text{Sum Due}}{(100 + \text{Rate})\ \text{Time}}$

C. $\frac{100 + (\text{Rate} \times \text{Time})}{100 \times \text{Sum Due}}$

D. $\frac{100 \times \text{Sum Due}}{100 + (\text{Rate} \times \text{Time})}$

2. Find the present worth of ₹ 1248 due 2 years hence at 2% per annum simple interest

A. ₹ 1200 B. ₹ 1210
C. ₹ 1220 D. ₹ 1242

3. Find the present worth of ₹ 460 due 3 years hence at 5% per annum S.I.

A. ₹ 450 B. ₹ 420
C. ₹ 410 D. ₹ 400

4. Find the discount on ₹ 1010 due 3 months hence at 4% p.a. S.I.

A. ₹ 8 B. ₹ 9
C. ₹ 10 D. ₹ 12

5. Find the reduction made on a bill of ₹ 1150 paid 1.25 years before it is due when the rate of interest is 12%

A. ₹ 100 B. ₹ 150
C. ₹ 200 D. ₹ 225

6. Find the difference between S.I. and T.D. on ₹ 5100 for half-year at 4% p.a.

A. Re. 0.50 B. Re. 1.00
C. ₹ 1.50 D. ₹ 2.00

7. If the true discount on a bill due 2 years hence at 5% p.a. is ₹ 25, the amount of the bill is:

A. ₹ 125 B. ₹ 220
C. ₹ 250 D. ₹ 275

8. If the present worth of a bill of ₹ 660 due 2 years hence is ₹ 600, the rate per cent per annum is:

A. 4% B. 5%
C. 6% D. 10%

9. The true discount on a sum of money due 1 year is ₹ 100 and banker's discount on the same sum and for the same time is ₹ 104. The sum is:

A. ₹ 2500 B. ₹ 2550
C. ₹ 2600 D. ₹ 2700

10. The true discount on a sum of money due 12 months is ₹ 200 and banker's discount on the same sum and for the same time is ₹ 208. The rate of interest is:

A. 4% B. 5%
C. 6% D. 7%

11. The true discount on a certain sum of money for 2 years is 3/4 the banker's discount. The rate of interest is:

A. 15% B. 16.67%
C. 20% D. 20.33%

12. The T.D. on a bill is 5/6 of B.D. and the rate is 4%. The time is:

A. 5 years B. 4 years
C. 3 years D. 2 years

13. A trader's terms are 20% discount for cash payment and interest is charged after one year. What rate of interest per annum does the customer get on his money for cash payment?

A. 15% B. 20%
C. 25% D. 30%

14. The T.D. on a bill due 1 year hence at 5% p.a. is ₹ 40. The amount is:

A. ₹ 840 B. ₹ 900
C. ₹ 950 D. ₹ 1000

15. The interest on ₹ 5000 is equal to the true discount on ₹ 5050 at 4% p.a. The latter is due after:

A. 3 months B. 4 months
C. 5 months D. 6 months

EXPLANATORY ANSWERS

1. D : $\text{P.W.} = \dfrac{100 \times \text{S.D.}}{100 + (\text{Rate} \times \text{Time})}$.

2. A : $\text{P.W.} = \dfrac{100 \times \text{S.D.}}{100 + (\text{Rate} \times \text{Time})} = \dfrac{100 \times 1248}{100 + (2 \times 2)} = \dfrac{100 \times 1248}{104} = ₹\ 1200.$

3. D : $\text{P.W.} = \dfrac{100 \times \text{S.D.}}{100 + (\text{Rate} \times \text{Time})} = \dfrac{100 \times 460}{100 + (3 \times 5)} = \dfrac{100 \times 460}{115} = ₹\ 400.$

4. C : $\text{T.D.} = \dfrac{\text{Sum} \times \text{Rate} \times \text{Time}}{100 + (\text{Rate} \times \text{Time})} = \dfrac{1010 \times 1/4 \times 4}{100 + (1/4 \times 4)} = \dfrac{1010}{101} = ₹\ 10$

5. B : $\text{Reduction} = \text{T.D.} = \dfrac{1150 \times 12 \times 5/4}{100 + (12 \times 5/4)} = \dfrac{1150 \times 15}{115} = ₹\ 150.$

6. D :

$\text{S.I.} = \dfrac{5100 \times 4 \times 1/2}{100} = ₹\ 102$

$\text{T.D.} = \dfrac{5100 \times 4 \times 1/2}{100 + (4 \times 1/2)} = \dfrac{5100 \times 2}{102} = ₹\ 100$

$\text{S.I.} - \text{T.D.} = ₹\ 102 - ₹\ 100 = ₹\ 2.$

7. D : Let P.W. = ₹ 100

S.I. on ₹ 100 at 5% for 2 years $= \dfrac{100 \times 5 \times 2}{100} = ₹\ 10$

Amount = 100 + 10 = ₹ 110,
₹ 10 is the T.D. on ₹ 110
If T.D. is ₹ 10, amount = ₹ 110

If T.D. is ₹ 25, amount = $\frac{110}{10} \times 25$ = ₹ 275.

8. B : P.W. = ₹ 600, Interest = ₹ 660 – ₹ 600 = ₹ 60,

Time = 2 years, Rate = $\frac{60 \times 100}{600 \times 2} = 5\%$.

9. C : Sum = $\frac{\text{B.D.} \times \text{T.D.}}{\text{B.D.} - \text{T.D.}} = \frac{104 \times 100}{104 - 100} = \frac{104 \times 100}{4}$ = ₹ 2600.

10. A : Sum = $\frac{\text{B.D.} \times \text{T.D.}}{\text{B.D.} - \text{T.D.}} = \frac{208 \times 200}{208 - 200} = \frac{208 \times 200}{8}$ = ₹ 5200.

Now, ₹ 208 is the interest on ₹ 5200 for 1 year.

∴ Rate = $\frac{208 \times 100}{5200 \times 1} = 4\%$.

11. B : If B.D. = x, T.D. = $3/4x$, Sum = $\frac{x \times 3/4x}{x - 3/4x} = 3x$,

Since, B.D. is the interest on sum due, ∴ Rate = $\frac{x \times 100}{3x \times 2} = \frac{100}{6} = 16.67\%$.

12. A : If, B.D. = x, T.D. = $6/5x$, Sum = $\frac{x \times 5/6x}{x - 5/6x} = 5x$

Since, B.D. is the interest on sum due, ∴ Time = $\frac{x \times 100}{5x \times 4}$ = 5 years.

13. C : Let amount of Bill = ₹ 100, Discount for cash payment = 20% = ₹ 20

∴ Cash price = ₹ 100 – ₹ 20 = ₹ 80

i.e., ₹ 20 is interest earned on ₹ 80 for one year.

∴ Rate = $\frac{20 \times 100}{80 \times 1}$ = ₹ 25%.

14. A : T.D. = Interest on P.W. = ₹ 40

Time = 1 year, Rate = 5% P.W. = $\frac{40 \times 100}{5 \times 1}$ = ₹ 800.

∴ Amount = 800 + 40 = ₹ 840

15. A : Interest on P.W. = T.D. on amount

Now, Interest on ₹ 5000 = T.D. on ₹ 5050

∴ ₹ 5000 is the P.W. of ₹ 5050 due at 4%

∴ Interest on ₹ 5000 = Sum due – P.W. = ₹ 5050 – ₹ 5000 = ₹ 50

∴ Time = $\frac{50 \times 100}{5000 \times 4} = \frac{1}{4}$ year = 3 months

9

TIME, WORK AND WAGES

While dealing with problems of time and work, it should be kept in mind that,

(*i*) If a man can do a piece of work in 5 days, It is evident that in one day he will finish 1/5 of his whole work; and vice versa.

(*ii*) If the number of persons engaged to do a certain job be increased in a certain ratio, the time required to do the same job will be decreased in the same ratio, and vice-versa. Thus, if the number of persons be changed in the ratio of 3 : 5, the time required to finish the job will be changed in the ratio of 5 : 3.

(*iii*) If A is twice as good workman as B, then A will take one-half of the time taken by B to do the same job.

(*iv*) While dealing with problems on wages, it may be kept in mind that the money obtained is always divided in the ratio of the work done by each person.

In the problems based on time and work, it is always assumed that a person works at uniform rate, unless and until specified in the problem.

Example. *A can do a piece of work in 4 days and B can do the same work in 6 days. How long will A and B take to do the work together?*

Solution. A's work in one day = $\frac{1}{4}$ of the total work

B's Work in one day = $\frac{1}{6}$ of the total work

$(A + B)$'s work in one day = $\frac{1}{4}+\frac{1}{6} = \frac{5}{12}$ of the total work

$\therefore$ Number of days taken by A + B to finish the work = $\frac{12}{5}$ = 2.4 days.

EXERCISE

1. A can do a certain job in 6 days and B can finish the same job in 10 days. A and B together will finish the same job in:

A. less than 10 days but more then 6 days

B. more than 10 days

C. less than 6 days

D. 2 days

2. A can make a table in 3 days while his friend can make it in 6 days. A and his friend together will make the table in:

A. 3 days B. 2 days
C. 1 day D. 1/2 days

3. X and Y together can do a certain job in 10 days while X alone can do the same job in 15 days. Y alone will do the same job in:

A. 15 days B. 20 days
C. 25 days D. 30 days

4. Amit can do 1/2 of a piece of work in 8 days, while Aslam can do 1/3 of the same work in 8 days. In how many days can both do it together?

A. 9.6 days B. 10.5 days
C. 11.2 days D. 16.0 days

5. X, Y and Z together can do a piece of work in 8 days while X and Z together can do it in 12 days. Y alone will do the same work in:

A. 16 days B. 20 days
C. 24 days D. 28 days

6. 24 persons can assemble a machine in 12 days. In how many days 36 persons will assemble the same machine?

A. 8 days B. 12 days
C. 16 days D. 20 days

7. X, Y and Z can do a certain job in 8, 10 and 8 days respectively. How long would they take to complete the same job when all work together?

A. $2\frac{1}{7}$ days B. $2\frac{3}{7}$ days

C. $2\frac{5}{7}$ days D. $2\frac{6}{7}$ days

8. If m men can do $1/n$ of a piece of work in P days, find the expression for the number of persons required to do the whole work in q days?

A. mn/pq B. mnq/p
C. mnp/q D. mp/nq

9. In the above Q. No. 8 if $m = 15$, $n = 4$, $p = 12.5$ and $q = 20$, then the number of persons required to do the same work is:

A. 38 B. 34
C. 30 D. 26

10. A piece of work can be done by 6 men and 5 women in 6 days or 3 men and 4 women in 10 days. In how many days can it be done by 9 men and 15 women?

A. 1 day B. 2 days
C. 3 days D. 4 days

11. X and Y undertook a contract to do a certain job for ₹ 4200. X alone could do the job in 3 weeks and Y alone in 4 weeks. If both of them finished the job working together, in what ratio should money be divided (X : Y)?

A. 3 : 4 B. 4 : 3
C. 1 : 1 D. 2 : 3

12. X and Y did a piece of work together and received ₹ 300. If X alone can do that piece of work in 2 weeks and Y alone in 3 weeks, how should the money be divided between them?

A. X = ₹ 180, Y = ₹ 120
B. X = ₹ 120, Y = ₹ 180
C. X = ₹ 150, Y = ₹ 150
D. X = ₹ 200, Y = ₹ 100

13. A, B and C did a work together and earned ₹ 195. If the ratio of work of A : B : C be as 4 : 6 : 3, the money obtained by C is:

A. ₹ 90 B. ₹ 60

C. ₹ 45 D. ₹ 30

14. To finish a certain job X takes twice as long as Y and Z together and Z three times as long as X and Y together. If X, Y and Z working together complete the job in 6 days, how long would X take to complete the work alone?

A. 16 days B. 18 days

C. 24 days D. 28 days

15. In the above question, how long would Z take to complete the work alone?

A. 16 days B. 18 days

C. 20 days D. 24 days

SOME SELECTED EXPLANATORY ANSWERS

1. C : Work done by A in one day = $\frac{1}{6}$

Work done by B in one day = $\frac{1}{10}$

Work done by (A + B) in one day = $\frac{1}{6}+\frac{1}{10} = \frac{8}{30}$

$\therefore$ A + B together will finish the work in $\frac{30}{8}$ days = $3\frac{6}{8}$ days which is less than 6 days.

2. B : Work done by A and his friend in one day = $\frac{1}{3}+\frac{1}{6}=\frac{3}{6}$

$\therefore$ Both will finish the work in $\frac{6}{3}$ = 2 days

3. D : Work done by X + Y in one day = $\frac{1}{10}$

Work done by X alone in one day = $\frac{1}{15}$

Work done by Y alone in one day = $\frac{1}{10}-\frac{1}{15}=\frac{1}{30}$

$\therefore$ Y alone will finish the work in 30 days.

4. A : Amit alone can do the whole work in 8 × 2 = 16 days

$\therefore$ Work done by Amit in one day = $\frac{1}{16}$

Aslam alone can do the whole work in 8 × 3 = 24 days

$\therefore$ Work done by Aslam in one day = $\frac{1}{24}$

Work done by Amit and Aslam in one day = $\frac{1}{16}+\frac{1}{24}=\frac{5}{48}$

$\therefore$ Amit and Aslam will finish the work in $\frac{48}{5}$ = 9.6 days.

5. C : Work done by X + Y + Z in one day = $\frac{1}{8}$

Work done by X + Z in one day = $\frac{1}{12}$

Work done by Y in one day = $\frac{1}{8}-\frac{1}{12}=\frac{1}{24}$

$\therefore$ Y alone will finish the work in 24 days.

6. A : $\because$ 24 persons can assemble in 12 days.
$\therefore$ 1 person can assemble in 12 × 24 days

$\therefore$ 36 persons can assemble in $\frac{12 \times 24}{36}$ = 8 days

7. D : Work done by X + Y + Z in one day = $\frac{1}{8}+\frac{1}{10}+\frac{1}{8}=\frac{7}{20}$

$\therefore$ X + Y + Z will complete the work in $\frac{20}{7} = 2\frac{6}{7}$ days.

8. C : *m* men can do 1/*n* of work in *p* days
$\therefore$ Number of men required to do the work in one day = *mnp*
Hence, number of men required to do the whole work in *q* days = *mnp*/*q*.

9. A : *mnp*/*q* = $\frac{15 \times 4 \times 12.5}{20}$ = 38.

10. C :

$$6 \text{ days} \rightarrow 6\,m + 5\,w$$
$$1 \text{ day} \rightarrow 36\,m + 30\,w$$

Similarly,

$$10 \text{ days} \rightarrow 3\,m + 4\,w$$
$$1 \text{ day} \rightarrow 30\,m + 40\,w$$
$$36\,m + 30\,w = 30\,m + 40\,w$$

or, $$6\,m = 10\,w$$

or, $$1\,m = \frac{5}{3}\,w$$

Therefore, $$6\,m + 5\,w = 15\,w$$

and $$9\,m + 15\,w = 30\,w$$

The problem now reduce to

$$15\,w \rightarrow 6 \text{ days}$$

$$\therefore \quad 30\,w \rightarrow 6 \times \frac{15}{30} = 3 \text{ days}$$

11. B : Ratio of working capacity of X and Y is 4 : 3

$\therefore$ Ratio of money to be divided = 4 : 3

12. A : Ratio of working capacity of X and Y is 3 : 2

$$\therefore \quad \text{X's share} = \frac{3}{5} \times 300 = ₹\ 180,$$

$$\text{Y's share} = \frac{2}{5} \times 300 = ₹\ 120.$$

13. C : Money obtained byC $= \frac{3}{13} \times 195 = ₹\ 45.$

14. B : 2 times X's daily work = (Y + Z)'s daily work

Adding X's daily work to both sides we get

3 times X's daily work = (X + Y + Z)'s daily work = 1/6

$\therefore$ X's daily work $= \frac{1}{6} \times \frac{1}{3} = \frac{1}{18}$

$\therefore$ X alone can finish the work in 18 days.

15. D : 3 times Z's daily work = (X + Y)'s daily work

Adding Z's daily work to both sides, we get

4 times Z's daily work = (X + Y + Z)'s daily work = 1/6

$\therefore$ Z's daily work $= \frac{1}{6} \times \frac{1}{4} = \frac{1}{24}$

$\therefore$ Z alone can finish the work in 24 days.

10

SPEED, TIME AND DISTANCE

Important Formulae :

$$\text{Distance} = \text{Speed} \times \text{Time}$$

$$\text{Speed} = \frac{\text{Distance}}{\text{Time}}$$

$$\text{Time} = \frac{\text{Distance}}{\text{Speed}}$$

EXERCISE

1. Speed of a moving car is 36 km/hr. Its speed in metres per second is:

A. 10 m/s B. 15 m/s
C. 20 m/s D. 25 m/s

2. Two trains start at the same time from two stations X and Y, 900 km apart; and proceed towards each other at an average speed of 38 and 22 km per hour respectively. They will meet after

A. 12 hours B. 13 hours
C. 14 hours D. 15 hours

3. A scooterist completes a journey in 10 hours, the first half at the rate of 21 km/hr and the second half at the rate of 24 km/hr. The total distance travelled is :

A. 256 km B. 224 km
C. 204 km D. 192 km

4. A train 100 m long is running at the speed of 60 km per hour. Time taken by the train to pass a telegraph post is:

A. 4 sec B. 5 sec
C. 6 sec D. 3 sec

5. A train 150 m long is running at the speed of 90 km/hr. Time taken by the train to pass through a tree is :

A. 3 sec B. 4 sec
C. 6 sec D. 8 sec

6. A train 100 m long is running at the speed of 65 km/hr. Time taken by the train to pass through a man walking at the rate of 5 km/hr in the direction of the train is :

A. 8 sec B. 6 sec
C. 4 sec D. 2 sec

7. A train 100 m long is running at the rate of 55 km/hr. Time taken by the train to pass through a man walking at the rate of 5 km/hr moving in opposite direction is :

A. 10 sec B. 8 sec
C. 6 sec D. 4 sec

8. Two persons start from the same place and walk in the opposite directions at 5 km and 4 km per hour respectively. At the end of 3 hours, distance between them is

A. 12 km B. 15 km
C. 27 km D. 30 km

9. A person starts from a place *P* at 6 A.M. and walks to *Q* at 3 km per hour. Another person starts from *P* at 8 A.M. and follows the first on bicycle at 6 km per hour. Both of them reach *Q* at the same time. The distance from *P* to *Q* is:

A. 12 km B. 10 km
C. 8 km D. 6 km

10. A person can row at the rates of *x* km/hr up a stream and at the rate of *y* km/hr down the stream. The rate in still water is:

A. $x+y$ B. $x-y$
C. $\frac{x-y}{2}$ D. $\frac{x+y}{2}$

11. In Q. 10, the rate of flow of stream is :

A. $x+y$ B. $x-y$
C. $y-x$ D. $\frac{y-x}{2}$

12. A person can row down a stream at 6 km/hr and up the same stream at 3 km/hr. His rate in still water is :

A. 9 km/hr B. 4.5 km/hr
C. 1.5 km/hr D. 1.0 km/hr

13. In Q. 12, the rate of flow of the stream is :

A. 1.5 km/hr B. 2.5 km/hr
C. 4.5 km/hr D. 18.0 km/hr

14. A man can row at the rate of 9 km per hr in still water. At what rate can he row against a stream flowing 7 km per hour?

A. 8 km/hr B. 7 km/hr
C. 2 km/hr D. –2 km/hr

15. To walk one kilometre *A* takes m minutes and *B*, n minutes. In one hour, the difference of distance travelled by *A* and *B* is:

A. $m-n$ B. $60m-60n$
C. $\frac{60}{m}-\frac{60}{n}$ D. $\frac{60}{mn}$

EXPLANATORY ANSWERS

1. A : Speed $= \frac{36\text{ km}}{1\text{ hr}} = \frac{36000\text{ m}}{3600\text{ sec}} = 10$ m/s.

2. D : Distance covered by two trains in 1 hour = 38 + 22 = 60 km.

Distance = 900 km

Time taken $= \frac{900}{60} = 15$ hours.

3. B : Let distance = x km.

Time taken in travelling $\frac{x}{2}$ km at the rate of 21 km/hr

$$= \frac{1}{21} \times \frac{x}{2} = \frac{x}{42} \text{ hr.}$$

Time taken in travelling $\frac{x}{2}$ km at the rate of 24 km/hr

$$= \frac{1}{24} \times \frac{x}{2} = \frac{x}{48} \text{ hr.}$$

But $\frac{x}{42} + \frac{x}{48} = 10$

$$\frac{8x + 7x}{336} = 10$$

$$15x = 3360$$

$\Rightarrow$ $x = 224$ km.

4. C : Distance = 100 m

$$\text{Speed} = \frac{60 \text{ km}}{1 \text{ hr}} = \frac{60000 \text{ m}}{3600 \text{ sec}} = \frac{50}{3} \text{ m/sec}$$

$$\text{Time} = \frac{\text{Distance}}{\text{Speed}} = \frac{100}{50/3} = \frac{100 \times 3}{50} = 6 \text{ sec.}$$

5. C : $\text{Speed} = \frac{90 \text{ km}}{1 \text{ hr}} = \frac{90000 \text{ m}}{3600 \text{ sec}} = 25 \text{ m/sec.}$

Distance = 150 m.

$$\text{Time} = \frac{\text{Distance}}{\text{Speed}} = \frac{150}{25} = 6 \text{ sec.}$$

6. B : Net speed = Speed of train – speed of man = 65 – 5 = 60 km/hr

$$\text{Speed} = \frac{60 \text{ km}}{1 \text{ hr}} = \frac{60000 \text{ m}}{3600 \text{ sec}} = \frac{50}{3} \text{ m/s}$$

$$\text{Time} = \frac{\text{Distance}}{\text{Speed}} = \frac{100}{50/3} = \frac{100 \times 3}{50} = 6 \text{ sec.}$$

7. C : Net speed = speed of train + speed of man = 55 + 5 = 60 km/hr

For rest of the answer see Q. 6.

8. C : Since, both the persons are moving in opposite direction and start from the same place, distance them after one hour = 5 + 4 = 9 km.

$\therefore$ Distance after 3 hours = 9 × 3 = 27 km.

9. A : Let distance from P to $Q = x$ km

Speed of first person = 3 km/hr

$$\text{Time taken} = \frac{x}{3} \text{ hr}$$

Speed of second person = 6 km/hr

$$\text{Time taken} = \frac{x}{6} \text{ hr}$$

According to problem, $\frac{x}{3} - \frac{x}{6} = 2$

$$\frac{2x - x}{6} = 2$$

$$x = 12$$

$\therefore$ Distance from P to Q = 12 km.

10. D : Rate in still water = $\frac{x + y}{2}$.

11. D : Rate of flow of stream = $\frac{y - x}{2}$.

12. B : Rate of still water = $\frac{6+3}{2}$ = 4.5 km/hr.

13. A : Rate of flow of stream = $\frac{6-3}{2}$ = 1.5 km/hr.

14. C : Rate of rowing against flowing water

= Rate of rowing of man – Rate of flow of the stream

= 9 – 7 = 2 km/hr.

15. C : Distance travelled by A in 1 hour = $\frac{60}{m}$ km

Distance travelled by B in 1 hour = $\frac{60}{n}$ km

$\therefore$ Difference of distance travelled by A and B in 1 hour = $\frac{60}{m} - \frac{60}{n}$.

11

AVERAGE

EXERCISE

1. The heights of 5 students (in cm) are 140, 135, 142, 138, 140. Their average height is :
   A. 136
   B. 138
   C. 139
   D. 140
2. Marks obtained by 10 students are 22, 35, 37, 38, 29, 27, 34, 36, 28, 34. The average marks are :
   A. 30 B. 31
   C. 32 D. 34
3. Average of class I to class V is 29. Average of class I to class III is 31. Average of class IV to class V is:
   A. 25 B. 26
   C. 27 D. 28
4. The average age of a group of 13 boys is 13 years. When two more boys joined the group, the average rose by 2 years. The sum of the ages of the two new boys is :
   A. 50 years
   B. 30 years
   C. 56 years
   D. 26 years
5. A boy of height 165 cm is replaced by another, which decreases the average height of the group of 34 boys by 1 cm. The height of the new boy is :
   A. 132 cm B. 129 cm
   C. 130 cm D. 131 cm
6. The average of five consecutive even numbers, starting with 2, is:
   A. 4 B. 6
   C. 7 D. 5
7. The average of 4, 5, 3.5, 7.5, 9.5 and 6.5 is :
   A. 6.0 B. 5.2
   C. 5.5 D. 5.0
8. The average of 8 numbers is 12. If each number is increased by 2, the average of the new set of numbers is:
   A. 14 B. 12
   C. 15 D. 13
9. The weights of 5 balls in gms are as under 50, 54, 53, 56, 52. The average weight is :
   A. 53 B. 54
   C. 52 D. 51
10. The lengths of 5 pieces of a string in cms are : 5, 5.2, 6.3, 7.2, 6.3. The average length of a piece is:
    A. 5.8 B. 6.0
    C. 6.1 D. 6.2

EXPLANATORY ANSWERS

1. C : Average height $= \frac{140+135+142+138+140}{5} = \frac{695}{5} = 139.$

2. C : Average marks $= \frac{22+35+37+38+29+27+34+36+28+34}{10}$

$= \frac{320}{10} = 32.$

3. B : Total students in class I to V = 29 × 5 = 145

Total students in class I to III = 31 × 3 = 93

Total students in class IV and V = 145 – 93 = 52

Average of class IV and V $= \frac{52}{2} = 26.$

4. C : Total age of 13 boys = 13 × 13 = 169 years

Total age of 15 boys = 15(13 + 2) = 15 × 15 = 225 years

Total age of two new boys = 225 – 169 = 56 years.

5. D : Average decrease in height of 34 boys = 1 cm

Total decrease in height of 34 boys = 34 × 1 = 34 cm

∴ Height of the new boy = 165 – 34 = 131 cm.

6. B : Sum of five consecutive even numbers starting with 2

= 2 + 4 + 6 + 8 + 10 = 30

Average = 30 ÷ 5 = 6.

7. A.

8. A : New average = 12 + 2 = 14.

9. A : Average weight $= \frac{50+54+53+56+52}{5} = \frac{265}{5} = 53.$

10. B : Average length $= \frac{5+5.2+6.3+7.2+6.3}{5} = \frac{30.0}{5} = 6.0.$

12

PARTNERSHIP

EXERCISE

1. X, Y and Z invested in a common business. X invested ₹ 6000 for 2 months, Y invested ₹ 7000 for 4 months and Z invested ₹ 6400 for 5 months. Out of a profit of ₹ 900, X's share is:
   A. ₹ 400 B. ₹ 350
   C. ₹ 150 D. ₹ 110
2. X, Y and Z invested ₹ 2400, ₹ 3600 and ₹ 4800 in a business. Out of a profit of ₹ 1260, X's share is :
   A. ₹ 280 B. ₹ 420
   C. ₹ 560 D. ₹ 140
3. A, B and C invested in a common business. A invested ₹ 5000 for 2 months, B invested ₹ 6000 for 3 months and C invested ₹ 4000 for 5 months. Out of a profit of ₹ 960, A's share is:
   A. ₹ 360 B. ₹ 200
   C. ₹ 400 D. ₹ 300
4. A, B and C invested in a common business. A invested ₹ 10000 for 3 months, B invested ₹ 15000 for 4 months and C invested ₹ 12000 for 5 months. Out of a profit of ₹ 1020, A's share is :
   A. ₹ 204 B. ₹ 408
   C. ₹ 612 D. ₹ 816
5. X, Y and Z invested in a common business. X invested ₹ 4000 for 2 months, Y invested ₹ 2500 for 4 months and Z invested ₹ 3000 for 6 months. Out of a profit of ₹ 1800, X's share is :
   A. ₹ 400 B. ₹ 500
   C. ₹ 800 D. ₹ 900
6. X, Y and Z invested ₹ 4800, ₹ 7200 and ₹ 9600 in a business. Out of a profit of ₹ 2520, Z's share is:
   A. ₹ 280 B. ₹ 560
   C. ₹ 840 D. ₹ 1120
7. A, B and C invested ₹ 600, ₹ 900 and ₹ 1200 in a business. Out of a profit of ₹ 549, A's share is:
   A. ₹ 61 B. ₹ 122
   C. ₹ 183 D. ₹ 244
8. A, B and C invested in a common business. A invested ₹ 2000 for 5 months, B invested ₹ 1200 for 6 months and C invested ₹ 2500 for 3 months. Out of a profit of ₹ 494, A's share is :
   A. ₹ 144 B. ₹ 200
   C. ₹ 150 D. ₹ 300
9. X, Y and Z invested ₹ 10000, ₹ 7200 and ₹ 7500 in a common business. Out of a profit of ₹ 988, X's share is :
   A. ₹ 400 B. ₹ 288
   C. ₹ 300 D. ₹ 247

10. *A*, *B* and *C* invested ₹ 1200, ₹ 1800 and ₹ 2400 in a common business. Out of a profit of ₹ 1098, *A*'s share is :

A. ₹ 244 B. ₹ 586

C. ₹ 488 D. ₹ 366

11. *A* and *B* invested ₹ 30000 and ₹ 34000 in a common business. Out of a profit of ₹ 1600, *A*'s share is :

A. ₹ 800 B. ₹ 750

C. ₹ 850 D. ₹ 900

12. Mohan and Ramesh invested ₹ 8000 and ₹ 10,000 respectively in a common business. Out of a profit of ₹ 9630, Mohan's share is:

A. ₹ 3210 B. ₹ 4280

C. ₹ 5350 D. ₹ 6420

13. *X*, *Y* and *Z* invested ₹ 2800, ₹ 3600 and ₹ 1600 in a common business. Out of a profit of ₹ 9600, *X*'s share is :

A. ₹ 3360 B. ₹ 4200

C. ₹ 2100 D. ₹ 6300

14. *A*, *B* and *C* invested ₹ 2400, ₹ 3600 and ₹ 4800 in a common business. Out of a profit of ₹ 981, *A*'s share is :

A. ₹ 109 B. ₹ 218

C. ₹ 327 D. ₹ 436

EXPLANATORY ANSWERS

1. C : *X*'s investment for 1 month = ₹ 6000 × 2 = ₹ 12000

Y's investment for 1 month = ₹ 7000 × 4 = ₹ 28000

Z's investment for 1 month = ₹ 6400 × 5 = ₹ 32000

12000 : 28000 : 32000

3 : 7 : 8

Sum of ratio = 3 + 7 + 8 = 18

$$X\text{'s share in the profit} = \frac{3}{18}\times 900 = ₹\ 150.$$

2. A :

X		*Y*		*Z*
₹ 2400	:	₹ 3600	:	₹ 4800
2	:	3	:	4

Sum of ratio = 2 + 3 + 4 = 9

$$X\text{'s share in the profit} = \frac{2}{9}\times 1260 = ₹\ 280.$$

3. B : *A*'s investment for 1 month = ₹ 5000 × 2 = ₹ 10000

B's investment for 1 month = ₹ 6000 × 3 = ₹ 18000

C's investment for 1 month = ₹ 4000 × 5 = ₹ 20000

Ratio = 10000 : 18000 : 20000

5 : 9 : 10

Sum of ratio = 5 + 9 + 10 = 24

$$A\text{'s share in the profit} = 960\times\frac{5}{24} = ₹\ 200.$$

4. A : A's investment = ₹ 10000 × 3 = ₹ 30000

B's investment = ₹ 15000 × 4 = ₹ 60000

C's investment = ₹ 12000 × 5 = ₹ 60000

Ratio = 30000 : 60000 : 60000

1 : 2 : 2

Sum of ratio = 1 + 2 + 2 = 5

A's share in the profit = ₹ $1020 \times \frac{1}{5}$ = ₹ 204.

5. A : X's investment = ₹ 4000 × 2 = ₹ 8000

Y's investment = ₹ 2500 × 4 = ₹ 10000

Z's investment = ₹ 3000 × 6 = ₹ 18000

X : Y : Z = 8000 : 10000 : 18000

4 : 5 : 9

Sum of ratio = 4 + 5 + 9 = 18.

X's share in the profit = $\frac{4}{18} \times 1800$ = ₹ 400.

6. D :

X		Y		Z
4800	:	7200	:	9600
2	:	3	:	4

Sum of ratio = 2 + 3 + 4 = 9

Z's share in the profit = $\frac{4}{9} \times 2520$ = ₹ 1120.

7. B :

A		B		C
600	:	900	:	1200
2	:	3	:	4

Sum of ratio = 2 + 3 + 4 = 9

A's share in the profit = $\frac{2}{9} \times 549$ = ₹ 122.

8. b : A's investment = ₹ 2000 × 5 = ₹ 10000

B's investment = ₹ 1200 × 6 = ₹ 7200

C's investment = ₹ 2500 × 3 = ₹ 7500

Ratio = 10000 : 7200 : 7500

100 : 72 : 75

Sum of ratio = 100 + 72 + 75 = 247

A's share in the profit = $\frac{100}{247} \times 494$ = ₹ 200.

9. A :

X		Y		Z
10000	:	7200	:	7500
100	:	72	:	75

Sum of ratio = 100 + 72 + 75 = 247

X's share in the profit = $\frac{100}{247} \times 988$ = ₹ 400.

10. A :

A		B		C
1200	:	1800	:	2400
2	:	3	:	4

Sum of ratio = 2 + 3 + 4 = 9

A's share in the profit = $\frac{2}{9} \times 1098$ = ₹ 244.

11. B :

A		B
30000	:	34000
15	:	17

Sum of ratio = 15 + 17 = 32

A's share in the profit = $\frac{15}{32} \times 1600$ = ₹ 750.

12. B : Mohan's investment = ₹ 8000

Ramesh's investment = ₹ 10000

Ratio = 8000 : 10000 = 4 : 5

Sum of ratio = 4 + 5 = 9

Mohan's share in the profit = $\frac{4}{9} \times \text{Rs.}9630$ = ₹ 4280.

13. A :

X		Y		Z
2800	:	3600	:	1600
7	:	9	:	4

Sum of ratio = 7 + 9 + 4 = 20

X's share in the profit = $\frac{7}{20} \times 9600$ = ₹ 3360.

14. B :

A		B		C
2400	:	3600	:	4800
2	:	3	:	4

Sum of ratio = 2 + 3 + 4 = 9

A's share in the profit = $\frac{2}{9} \times 981$ = ₹ 218.

13

MIXTURE AND ALLIGATION

1. Rule of Alligation:

$$\frac{\text{Amount of Cheaper ingredient}}{\text{Amount of Dearer ingredient}} = \frac{\text{Cost price of Dearer} - \text{Mean Price}}{\text{Mean Price} - \text{Cost Price of Cheaper}}$$

Here cost price of unit quantity of the mixture is called the *Mean Price*. The above rule may be represented schematically as under:

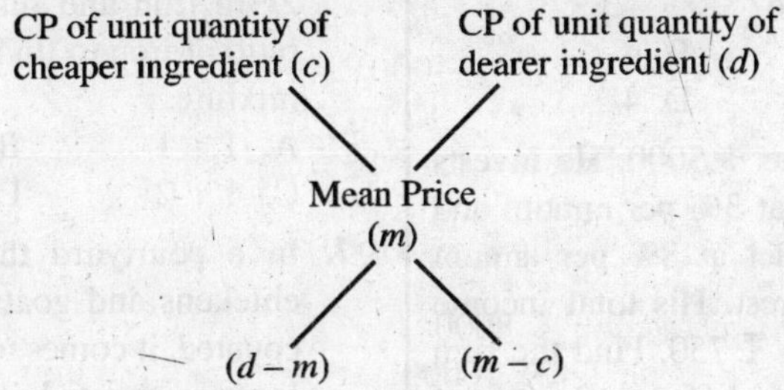

(Cheaper quantity) : (Dearer quantity) = $(d - m) : (m - c)$

This relationship is very helpful in solving problems on mixture involving percentage values, rates, prices, speeds etc.

2. m gm of sugar solution has x % sugar in it. To increase the sugar content in the solution to y %,

quantity of sugar need to be added $= \dfrac{m(y-x)}{100-y}$

3. A vessel contains x litres of liquid A. y litres are withdrawn and replaced by liquid B. Next y litres of the mixture is withdrawn and again replaced by liquid B.
This operation is repeated n times.

$$\frac{\text{Quantity of liquid A left after } n\text{th operation}}{\text{Whole quantity of liquid A initially present}} = \left(\frac{x-y}{x}\right)^n \text{ or } \left(1-\frac{y}{x}\right)^n$$

EXERCISE

1. Two vessels A and B contain mixture of milk and water in the ratio 4 : 1 and 9 : 11 respectively. They are mixed in the ratio of 3 : 2. Find the ratio of milk : water in the resulting mixture.

A. 34 : 16 B. 33 : 17
C. 16 : 34 D. 17 : 33

2. In what ratio must water be added to spirit to gain 25% by selling it at cost price?

A. 1 : 4 B. 4 : 1
C. 3 : 4 D. 4 : 3

3. A person has ₹ 5000. He invests a part of it at 3% per annum and the remainder at 8% per annum simple interest. His total income in 3 years is ₹ 750. Find the sum invested at different rates of interest.

A. ₹ 2000 and ₹ 3000
B. ₹ 2500 and ₹ 2500
C. ₹ 3000 and ₹ 2000
D. ₹ 2750 and ₹ 2250

4. A person covers a distance of 100 kms in 10 hours, partly by walking at 7 km/hr and rest by running at 12 km/hr. Find the distance covered in each part.

A. 48 kms B. 72 kms
C. 108 kms D. 124 kms

5. A vessel contains 80 litres of milk. 16 litres of milk was taken out of the vessel and replaced by water. Then 16 litres of mixture was withdrawn and again replaced by water. The operation was repeated for third time. How much milk is now left in the vessel?

A. 96.40 litres
B. 50.36 litres
C. 40.96 litres
D. 32.76 litres

6. If 4 kg of an alloy made of 1/4th iron and rest is mixed with 6 kg of another alloy made of 2/3rd iron and rest tin, find the ratio of iron to tin in the resultant mixture.

A. 1 : 1 B. 2 : 1
C. 1 : 2 D. 3 : 2

7. In a courtyard there are many chickens and goats. If heads are counted, it comes to 100 but when legs are counted, it comes to 320. Find the number of chickens and goats in the courtyard.

A. 20, 50 B. 30, 70
C. 40, 60 D. 50, 50

8. A container is full of milk. One-third of milk is taken out of it and replaced by same quantity of water. Then again one-third of the mixture is taken out of it and replaced by the same quantity of water. The process is repeated 4 times. If 16 litres of milk is left in the container at the end of 4th operation, find the capacity of the container.

A. 76 litres B. 81 litres
C. 82 litres D. 85 litres

9. The cost of type-I rice is ₹ 15 per kg and type-II is ₹ 20 per kg. If both type I and type II are mixed in the ratio of 2 : 3, then find the price per kg of the mixed variety.

A. ₹ 19.50
B. ₹ 19
C. ₹ 18.50
D. ₹ 18

10. A cask full of wine from which 8 litres are drawn and is then filled with water. This operation is performed three more times. The ratio of quantity of wine left in the cask to that of the water is 16 : 81. How much wine did the cask hold originally?

A. 42 litres B. 32 litres
C. 24 litres D. 18 litres

EXPLANATORY ANSWERS

1. B:

Fraction is	*Milk*	*Water*
A :	$\frac{4}{5}$	$\frac{1}{5}$
B :	$\frac{9}{20}$	$\frac{11}{20}$
(3A + 2B) = A and B :	$\left(\frac{12}{5}+\frac{9}{10}\right)$	$\left(\frac{3}{5}+\frac{11}{10}\right)$
	$\frac{33}{10}$	$\frac{17}{10}$

So, Ratio of milk : water in the resulting mixture = 33 : 17.

2. A: Let cost price of spirit be Re. 1 per litre.

Then SP of mixture = Re. 1 per litre

Gain = 25%

So, CP of mixture $= 1 \times \frac{100}{125} = \text{Re. } \frac{4}{5}$

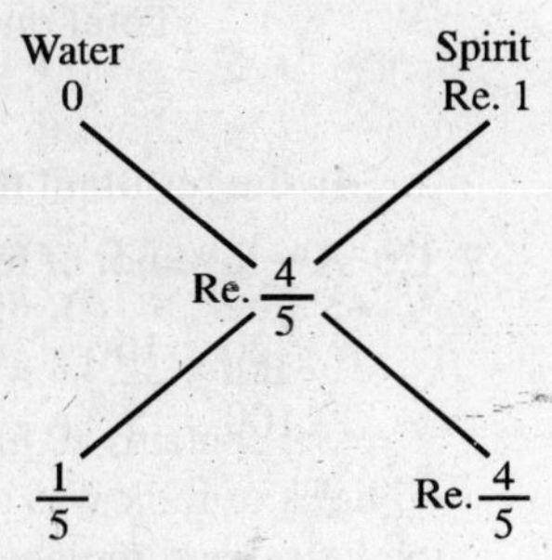

We assume that CP of water is zero.

Using alligation rule on cost price,

Water should be mixed to spirit in the ratio $\frac{1}{5} : \frac{4}{5}$ or 1 : 4.

3. C: Average rate of interest $= \dfrac{100 \times 750}{5000 \times 3} = 5\%$ per annum

Investment at 3% per annum

$= \dfrac{3}{3+2} \times 5000 = ₹\ 3000$

Investment at 8% per annum

$= \dfrac{2}{3+2} \times 5000 = ₹\ 2000.$

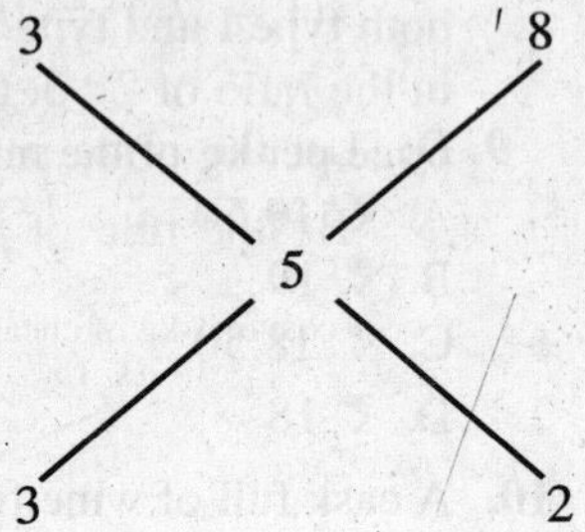

4. B: Average speed $= \dfrac{100}{10} = 10$ km/hr.

Ratio of time taken at 7 km/hr to 12 km/hr = 2 : 3

Time taken at 7 km/hr $= \dfrac{2}{2+3} \times 10 = 4$ hrs.

Distance covered at 7 km/hr = 7 × 4 = 28 km.

Distance covered at 12 km/hr = 100 – 28 = 72 km.

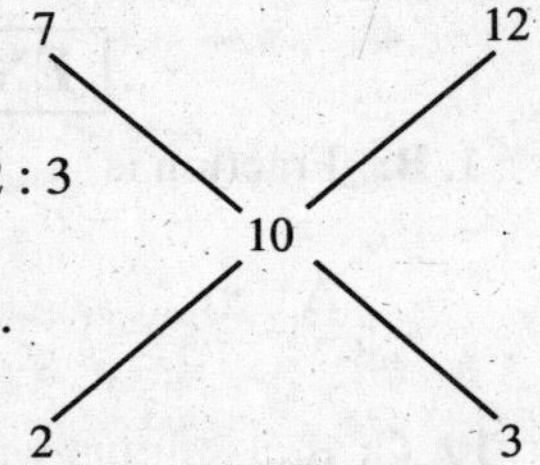

5. C: Amount of milk left $= 80\left(1-\dfrac{16}{80}\right)^3 = 80\left(\dfrac{4}{5}\right)^3$

$80 \times \dfrac{64}{125} = 40.96$ litres.

6. A: Total quantity of iron $= 4\left(\dfrac{1}{4}\right)+6\left(\dfrac{2}{3}\right) = 1+4 = 5$ kg.

Total quantity of tin $= (4+6)-5$

$= 5$ kg.

In the resultant mixture, iron : tin = 5 : 5 or 1 : 1.

7. C: Average no. of legs per head

$= \dfrac{320}{100} = \dfrac{16}{5}$

or, 3 : 2

No. of goats $= \dfrac{3}{3+2} \times 100 = 60$

No. of chickens $= 100 - 60 = 40.$

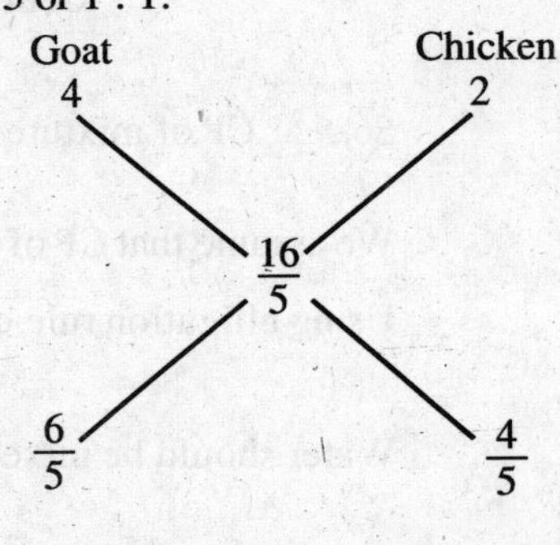

8. B: Let capacity of the container be x litre; then

$$x(1-1/3)^4 = 16 \Rightarrow x\left(\frac{2}{3}\right)^4 = 16 \quad \Rightarrow x \times \frac{16}{81} = 16 \quad \therefore x = 81 \text{ litres}$$

9. D: Let the price per kg of mixed variety be ₹ x; then

By the rule of alligation,

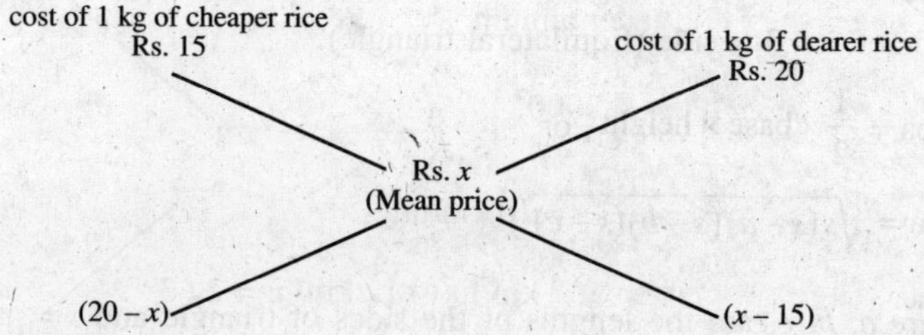

Now, $\frac{20-x}{x-15} = \frac{2}{3} \quad \Rightarrow 60 - 3x = 2x - 30 \quad \Leftrightarrow 5x = 90 \therefore x = ₹\ 18$

10. C: Let x litres wine cask hold originally, then

$$\frac{x\left(1-\frac{8}{x}\right)^4}{x} = \frac{16}{81} \Rightarrow \left(1-\frac{8}{x}\right)^4 = \left(\frac{2}{3}\right)^4 \Rightarrow \left(1-\frac{8}{x}\right) = \frac{2}{3}$$

$$\Rightarrow \frac{8}{x} = 1 - \frac{2}{3} \quad \Rightarrow \frac{8}{x} = \frac{1}{3} \quad \therefore x = 24 \text{ litres}$$

14

MENSURATION

Triangle

1. Perimeter = 3 × side (Equilateral triangle)

2. Area = $\frac{1}{2} \times \text{base} \times \text{height}$, or

Area = $\sqrt{s(s-a)(s-b)(s-c)}$

where *a, b, c,* are the lengths of the sides of triangle and $s = \frac{a+b+c}{2}$

Equilateral Triangle : All three sides are equal in length and all three angles are equal to 60°.

$$\text{Area} = \frac{\sqrt{3}}{4} \times (\text{Side})^2$$

Isosceles Triangle : Two sides are equal in lengths.

1. Area = $\frac{b}{4}\sqrt{4a^2 - b^2}$

where a = lengths of equal sides b = length of unequal side

2. In an isosceles right triangle,

(a) Hypotenuse = $\sqrt{2} \times \text{congruent side (a)}$

(b) Area = $\frac{1}{2} \times a^2$

(c) Perimeter = $\sqrt{2} \times a\left(\sqrt{2}+1\right)$

Rectangle :

1. Area = length(l) × breadth(b)

2. Perimeter = $2(l + b)$

3. Diagonal = $\sqrt{l^2 + b^2}$

Square :

1. Area = $(\text{Side})^2$
2. Perimeter = 4 × side
3. Diagonal = $\text{side} \times \sqrt{2}$

Parallelogram: Area = Base × Height.

Trapezium : Area = $\frac{1}{2} \times$ Height × (Sum of parallel sides). Here, height is the distance between the two parallel sides.

Rhombus :

1. Area = $\frac{1}{2} \times$ Product of diagonals
2. Side = $\sqrt{\left(\frac{d_1}{2}\right)^2 + \left(\frac{d_2}{2}\right)^2}$, where d_1 and d_2 are diagonals
3. Perimeter = 4 × side

Quadrilateral : Area = $\frac{1}{2} \times$ One diagonal × (Sum of perpendicular to it from the opposite vertices) = $\frac{1}{2} \times d \times (a+b)$

Circle :

1. Diameter = 2 × Radius
2. Area = $\pi r^2 = \frac{\pi}{4} d^2$; where d = diameter = $\sqrt{\frac{4A}{\pi}}$
3. Circumference = $2\pi r = \pi d$
4. Radius = $\frac{\text{Circumference}}{2\pi} = \frac{\sqrt{\text{Area}}}{\pi}$
5. Length of an Arc = $\frac{\theta}{360°} \times 2\pi r$
6. Area of sector = $\frac{\theta}{360°} \times \pi r^2 = \frac{1}{2} \times \text{Arc} \times r$

Polygon :

1. Interior angle + Exterior angle = 180°
2. Each interior angle = $\left(\frac{2n-4}{n}\right) \times 90°$

where n = number of sides

3. Sum of Exterior angles = 360°
4. Perimeter = Number of sides × Length of side.
5. For an equilateral triangle of side 'a'

(*a*) radius of inscribed circle $=\frac{a}{2\sqrt{3}}$

and side of the triangle $= 2\sqrt{3}r$,

(*b*) radius of circumcircle $= \frac{a}{\sqrt{3}}$

6. Area of regular polygon $=\frac{1}{2}$(No. of sides) (Radius of the inscribed circle)
7. Area of regular hexagon $= \frac{3\sqrt{3}}{2}(\text{side})^2 = 2.598\ (\text{side})^2$
8. Area of a regular octagon $= 2\left(\sqrt{2}+1\right)(\text{side})^2 = 4.828\ (\text{side})^2$
9. Area of quadrilateral, A $= \sqrt{s(s-a)(s-b)(s-c)(s-d)}$

where, $s = \frac{a+b+c+d}{2}$

VOLUME AND SURFACE AREA OF SOLIDS

Cuboid : A cuboid has six faces, each one a ractangle. It has 12 edges. For example, a rectangular brick.

Let Length = l, Breadth = b and Height = h, then,

1. Volume = (Length × Breadth × Height)
2. Whole Surface Area = $2(lb + bh + lh)$
3. Diagonal $= \sqrt{l^2 + b^2 + h^2}$
4. Area of 4 walls of a room $= 2 \times h\ (l + b)$

Cube : In a cube, Length = Breadth = Height

1. Volume = $(l)^3$
2. Length $= \sqrt[3]{\text{Volume}}$
3. Whole Surface Area = $6\ l^2$
4. Diagonal $= l \times \sqrt{3}$
5. Lateral Surface Area = $4\ l^2$

Cylinder :

1. Volume = $\pi r^2 h$
2. Curved Surface Area = $2\pi rh$
3. Total Surface Area = $2\pi r(r + h)$

where r = radius, h = height

Spherical Cell :

1. Volume = $\frac{4}{3}\pi\left(R^3 - r^3\right)$
2. Total Surface Area= $4\pi(R^2 - r^2)$

where R = Outer radius

r = Inner radius

Sphere :

1. Volume = $\frac{4}{3}\pi r^3$
2. Surface Area = $4\pi r^2$

Semi-sphere :

1. Volume = $\frac{2}{3}\pi r^3$
2. Curved surface area = $2\pi r^2$
3. Total surface area = $3\pi r^2$

Cone :

1. Slant height (l) = $\sqrt{r^2 + h^2}$
2. Volume = $\frac{1}{3}\pi r^2 h$
3. Curved surface area = πrl
4. Total surface area = $\pi r(l + r)$
5. If the depth of the frustum of a cone be k and the radii of its ends are r_1 and r_2, then

(i) Slant height of the frustum of a cone

$$= \sqrt{k^2 + (r_1 - r_2)^2}$$

(ii) Curved surface of the frustum = $\pi(r_1 + r_2)\, l$.

(iii) Volume = $\frac{\pi k}{3}\left(r_1^2 + r_1 r_2 + r_2^2\right)$

EXERCISE

1. What is the area of a circle whose radius is equal to the side of a square whose perimeter is 112 metres?

A. 176 sq m
B. 2504 sq m
C. 284 sq m
D. None of these

2. The sum of the circumference of a circle and the perimeter of a rectangle is 132 cm. The area of the rectangle is 112 sq cm and breadth of the rectangle is 8 cms. What is the area of the circle?

A. 616 sq cm
B. 540 sq cm
C. 396 sq cm
D. Cannot be determined

3. The total area of a circle and a rectangle is equal to 1166 sq cm. The diameter of the circle is 28 cm. What is the sum of the circumference of the circle and the perimeter of the rectangle if the length of the rectangle is 25 cm?

A. 186 cm
B. 182 cm
C. 184 cm
D. Cannot be determined

4. What would be the cost of laying a carpet on a floor which has its length and breadth in the respective ratio of 32 : 21 and where its perimeter is 212 feet, if the cost per square foot of laying the carpet is ₹ 2.5?

A. ₹ 6,720
B. ₹ 5,420
C. ₹ 7,390
D. None of these

5. A triangle's perimeter is 25 cms Which of the following may be true or is a possibility?

(*a*) The sides are 7 cms., 7 cms and 11 cms.
(*b*) It is an equilateral triangle.
(*c*) The value of sides can be in integer only.

A. Only (*a*)
B. Only (*a*) and (*b*)
C. Only (*c*)
D. Only (*b*) and (*c*)

6. What will be the cost of building a fence around a circular field with area equal to 18,634 sq. metres; if the cost of building the fence per metre is ₹ 365?

A. ₹ 1,76,660 B. ₹ 68,01,410
C. ₹ 2,43,250 D. ₹ 56,60,220

7. The area of a square is 196 sq cms whose side is half the radius of a circle. The circumference of the circle is equal to breadth of a rectangle. If perimeter of the rectangle is 712 cm. What is the length of the rectangle?

A. 196 cm B. 186 cm
C. 180 cm D. 190 cm

8. The circumference of a circular plot is 484 metres Find out the area of that circular plot—

A. 15246 metre^2
B. 18634 metre^2
C. 20328 metre^2
D. 13552 metre^2

9. A room measures 22 dm by 16 dm. I wish to buy a carpet for the floor leaving an uncarpeted margin 2 dm wide along each of the shorter sides of the room and a margin 0.5 dm wide along each of the longer sides of the room. If the price of the carpet is ₹ 500 per sq. metre, what is the cost of the whole carpet required?

A. ₹ 500 B. ₹ 2700
C. ₹ 2000 D. ₹ 1350

10. A paper is in the form of a rectangle ABCD where AB = 22 cm and BC = 14 cm. A semi-circular portion with segment BC as a diameter is cut off. Find the area of remaining paper.

A. 231 cm^2 B. 213 cm^2
C. 321 cm^2 D. 200 cm^2

11. How many plants can be put in a circular flower bed whose circumference is 880 dm allowing 35 dm^2 for each plant?

A. 880 B. 1760
C. 1000 D. 1500

12. An athletic track 14 m wide consists of two straight sections 120 m long joining semi-circular ends whose inner radius is 35 m. Calculate the area of the track :

A. 5670 m^2 B. 7065 m^2
C. 5670 m^2 D. 7056 m^2

13. A square park has each side of 100 m. At each corner of the park, there is a flower bed in the form of a quadrant of radius 14 m. Then the area of the remaining part of the park is :

A. 9384 m^2 B. 9834 m^2
C. 9000 m^2 D. 8900 m^2

14. The length of minute hand of a clock is 14 cm. Then the area swept by the minute hand in one minute.

A. 10 m^2 B. 12.26 m^2
C. 20.26 m^2 D. 10.26 m^2

15. Find the area of ring between two concentric circles whose circumference are 77 cm and 55 cm.

A. 770 cm^2 B. 321 cm^2
C. 231 cm^2 D. 230 cm^2

16. A rectangle water reservoir is 10.8 metres long and 3.75 metres wide at base. Water flows into it at the rate of 18 m per sec. through the pipe having the cross section 7.5 cm × 4.5 cm. Then the height to which the water will rise in the reservoir in 30 minutes is :

A. 7.2 m B. 2.7 m
C. 3.7 m D. 7.3 m

17. A rectangular sheet of 44 cm × 18 cm is rolled along its length and a cylinder is formed. Then the volume of cylinder is :

A. 7227 cm^2 B. 7272 cm^2
C. 2727 cm^2 D. 2772 cm^2

18. How many metres of cloth 5 metre wide will be required to make a conical tent, the radius of whose base is 7 metre and height is 24 metre?

A. 100 m B. 110 m
C. 550 m D. 55 m

19. The surface area of a sphere whose volume is 4851 cubic metres is :

A. 1386 m^2 B. 1380 m^2
C. 1286 m^2 D. 3186 m^2

20. A hollow sphere of external and internal diameter 4 cm and 2 cm respectively, is melted into a cone of base diameter 8 cm. Then the height of the cone is :

A. 12 cm B. 14 cm
C. 20 cm D. 24 cm

21. The diamensions of a metallic rod are 19 cm × 4 cm × 2 cm and each side of a metallic cube is 4 cm. Both are melted and recast into a new cube. Find the length of edge of cube so formed.

A. 4 cm B. 5 cm
C. 6 cm D. 7 cm

22. An agricultural field is in the form of a rectangle of length 35 metres and width 15.4 metres. A pit 5.5 metres long, 4 metres wide and 2.5 metres deep is dug in the corner of the field and the earth taken out of the pit is spread uniformly over the remaining area of the field. The extent to which the level of the field has been raised is :

A. 16.6 cm B. 10.6 cm
C. 16.1 cm D. 6.10 cm

23. The side of a square exceeds the side of the another square by 4 cm and the sum of areas of two squares is 400 sq. cm. Find the dimensions of the square.

A. 8 cm, 12 cm
B. 10 cm, 14 cm
C. 12 cm, 16 cm
D. 14 cm, 18 cm

24. The cost of levelling a rectangular field at the rate of 85 paise per square metre is ₹ 624.75. Then the perimeter of the field if its sides are in the ratio of 5 : 3 is :

A. 35 m B. 21 m
C. 112 m D. 49 m

25. The diagonal of a rectangular field is 15 m and its area is 108 sq. m. What will be the total expenditure in fencing the field at the rate of ₹ 5 per metre?

A. ₹ 441 B. ₹ 420
C. ₹ 210 D. ₹ 120

26. The minute hand of a clock is 10 cm long. The area of the face of the clock described by the minute hand between 9 AM and 9.35 AM is :

A. 140 cm^2 B. 183.3 cm^2
C. 180 cm^2 D. 175.3 cm^2

27. The length of a rectangular plot is 60% more than its breadth. If the difference between the length and the breadth of that rectangle is 24 cm, what is the area of that rectangle?

A. 2400 sq. cm
B. 2480 sq. cm
C. 2560 sq. cm
D. Data inadequate

28. The area of a rectangle is 460 square metres. If the length is 15% more than the breadth, what is the breadth of the rectangular field?

A. 15 metres
B. 26 metres
C. 34.5 metres
D. None of these

29. The ratio between the length and the breadth of a rectangular field is 3 : 2. If only the length is increased by 5 metres, the new area of the field will be 2600 sq. metres. What is the breadth of the rectangular field?

A. 40 metres
B. 60 metres
C. 65 metres
D. Cannot be determined

30. If the length and breadth of a rectangular plot be increased by 50% and 20% respectively, then how many times will its area be increased?

A. $1\frac{1}{3}$ B. 2
C. $3\frac{2}{5}$ D. None of these

31. The length of a rectangle is decreased by *r*%, and the breadth is increased by $(r + 5)$%. Find *r*, if the area of the rectangle is unaltered.

A. 5 B. 8
C. 10 D. 20

32. The length and breadth of the floor of the room are 20 feet and 10 feet respectively. Square tiles of 2 feet length of different colours are to be laid on the floor. Black tiles are laid in the first row on all sides. If white tiles are laid in the one-third of the remaining and blue tiles in the rest, how many blue tiles will be there?

A. 16 B. 24
C. 32 D. 48

33. A park square in shape has a 3 metre wide road inside it running along its sides. The area occupied by the road is 1764 square metres. What is the perimeter along the outer edge of the road?

A. 576 metres
B. 600 metres
C. 640 metres
D. Data inadequate

34. What will be the length of the diagonal of that square plot whose area is equal to the area of a rectangular plot of length 45 metres and breadth 40 metres?

A. 42.5 metres
B. 60 metres
C. 75 metres
D. Data inadequate

35. The length of one pair of opposite sides of a square is increased by 5 cm on each side; the ratio of the length and the breadth of the newly formed rectangle becomes 3 : 2. What is the area of the original square?

A. 25 sq. cm B. 81 sq. cm
C. 100 sq. cm D. 225 sq. cm

36. What will be the ratio between the area of a rectangle and the area of a triangle with one of the sides of the rectangle as base and a vertex on the opposite side of the rectangle?

A. 1 : 2
B. 2 : 1
C. 3 : 1
D. None of these

37. A cow is tethered in the middle of a field with a 14 feet long rope. If the cow grazes 100 sq. ft. per day, then approximately what time will be taken by the cow to graze the whole field?

A. 2 days B. 6 days
C. 18 days D. 24 days

38. A circular ground whose diameter is 35 metres, has a 1.4 m broad garden around it. What is the area of the garden in square metres?

A. 160.16
B. 176.16
C. 196.16
D. None of these

39. The cost of the paint is ₹ 36.50 per kg. If 1 kg of paint covers 16 square feet, how much will it cost to paint outside of a cube having 8 feet each side?

A. ₹ 692 B. ₹ 768
C. ₹ 876 D. ₹ 972

40. The capacity of a cylindrical tank is 246.4 litres. If the height is 4 metres, what is the diameter of the base?

A. 1.4 m B. 2.8 m
C. 14 m D. 28 m

EXPLANATORY ANSWERS

1. D: $\because$ Radius of the circle $= \dfrac{112}{4} = 28$ m

$\therefore$ Area of the circle $= \dfrac{22}{7} \times 28 \times 28 = 2464 \text{ m}^2$.

2. A: Length of the rectangle $= \dfrac{112}{8} = 14$ cm.

$\therefore$ Perimeter of the rectangle $= 2(14 + 8) = 44$ cm.

$\therefore$ Circumference of the circle $= 132 - 44 = 88$ cm.

$\therefore \quad r = \dfrac{88 \times 7}{2 \times 22} = 14$ cm

$\therefore$ Area of the circle $= \dfrac{22}{7} \times 14 \times 14 = 616$ sq cm.

3. B: From question—

$\because$ Diameter of the circle = 28 cm.

$\Rightarrow$ Area of the circle = $\frac{22}{7}\times(14)^2$ = 616 cm^2

$\therefore$ Area of the rectangle = 1166 – 616 = 550 cm^2

$\Rightarrow$ Breadth of the rectangle = $\frac{550}{25}$ = 22 cm.

$\therefore$ Required sum = $2\times\frac{22}{7}\times(14)+2(25+22)$

= 88 + 94 = 182 cm.

4. A: Length of the floor = $\frac{212\times32}{2\times(32+21)}$ = 64 ft.

and breadth the floor = $\frac{64\times21}{32}$ = 42 ft.

$\therefore$ Area of the floor = 64 × 42 = 2688 sq. ft.

$\therefore$ Reqd. cost = ₹ 2688 × 2.5 = ₹ 6720.

5. A: Only statement A may be true or possibility.

6. A: Area of the circular field = 18634 m^2

$\therefore$ πr^2 = 18634

$\therefore$ $r^2 = 18634\times\frac{7}{22}$ = 5929

$\therefore$ r = 77 m

$\therefore$ Length of the fence = $2\times\frac{22}{7}\times77$ = 484 m

$\therefore$ Total cost = 484 × 365 = ₹ 176660.

7. C: One side of the square = $\sqrt{196}$ = 14 cm

$\therefore$ Radius of the circle = 28 cm

$\therefore$ Circumference of the circle = $2\times\frac{22}{7}\times28$ = 176 cm

$\therefore$ Breadth of the rectangle = 176 cm

$\therefore$ Length of the rectangle = $\frac{712}{2}-176$ = 356 – 176 = 180 cm.

8. B: Let r be the radius of the circular plot then from problem,

$\because$ The circumference of the circular plot = 484 m

$$\Rightarrow \qquad 2\pi r = 484$$

$$r = 484 \times \frac{7}{22} \times \frac{1}{2} = 77 \text{ metres}$$

$\therefore$ Area of the circular plot = $\pi r^2 = \frac{22}{7} \times (77)^2 = 18634 \text{ m}^2$.

9. D.

10. A: Area of the whole paper ABCD = $22 \times 14 = 308 \text{ cm}^2$

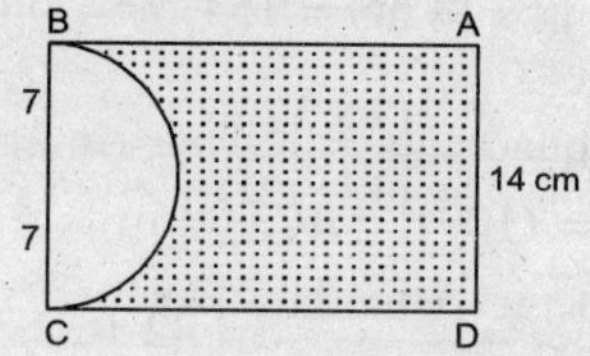

Radius of the semi-circle = $\frac{1}{2} \times 14 \text{ cm} = 7 \text{ cm}$

$\therefore$Area of the semi-circle = $\frac{1}{2}\pi r^2 = \frac{1}{2} \times \frac{22}{7} \times 7 \times 7 = 77 \text{ cm}^2$

$\therefore$ Area of the remaining part of the paper

$$= 308 \text{ cm}^2 - 77 \text{ cm}^2 = 231 \text{ cm}^2.$$

11. B: Circumference of flower bed = 880 dm

$$\Rightarrow \qquad 2\pi r = 880 \text{ dm}$$

$$\Rightarrow \qquad r = \frac{880}{2\pi} \text{ dm} = \frac{880 \times 7}{2 \times 22} = 140 \text{ dm}$$

Area of flower bed = $\pi r^2 = \frac{22}{7} \times (140)^2 \text{ dm}^2$

$\therefore$ Required number of plants

$$= \frac{\frac{22}{7} \times 140 \times 140}{35} \text{ dm}^2$$

$$= \frac{22}{7} \times \frac{140 \times 140}{35} = 1760.$$

12. D.

13. A: Area of each quadrant = $\frac{\theta}{360} \times \pi r^2$

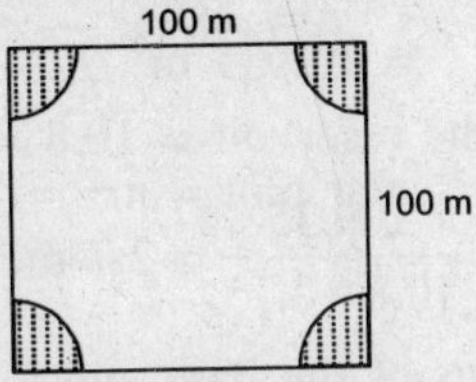

$$= \frac{90}{360} \times \frac{22}{7} \times 14 \times 14 \text{ m}^2 = 154 \text{ m}^2$$

$\therefore$ Area of 4 quadrants = 154 × 4 m² = 616 m²

Area of park = $(100)^2$ = 10,000 m²

Hence area of the remaining part of the park

$$= 10{,}000 - 616 = 9{,}384 \text{ m}^2.$$

14. D: Length of minute hand of clock = r = 14 cm

Central angle covered in 1 minute = $\frac{360}{60} = 6°$

$\therefore$ Area swept in one minute = Area of sector with central angle 6°

$$= \frac{\theta}{360} \times \pi r^2 = \frac{6}{360} \times \frac{22}{7} \times 14 \times 14$$

$$= \frac{154}{15} = 10.26 \text{ cm}^2.$$

15. C: Let R be the radius of outer circle and r the radius of inner circle.
Circumference of outer circle = 77 cm

$$\therefore\ 2\pi R = 77 \Rightarrow R = \frac{77}{2\pi} = \frac{77 \times 7}{2 \times 22} = \frac{49}{4} \text{ cm}$$

Circumference of inner circle = 55 cm

$$\therefore\quad 2\pi r = 55 \quad \Rightarrow r = \frac{55}{2\pi} = \frac{55 \times 7}{2 \times 22} = \frac{35}{4} \text{ cm}$$

$$\therefore\quad \text{Area of ring} = \pi(R^2 - r^2)$$

$$= \frac{22}{7} \times \left(\frac{49}{4} + \frac{35}{4}\right)\left(\frac{49}{4} - \frac{35}{4}\right) = 231 \text{ cm}^2$$

16. B: Volume of water that flows in one second

$= (18 \times 0.075 \times 0.045)\ m^3$

Volume of water that flows in 30 minutes

$= 18 \times 0.075 \times 0.045 \times 30 \times 60$

$= 109.35\ m^3.$

Area of the base of the reservoir $= 10.8 \times 3.75\ m^2$

$\therefore$ Height of water $= \dfrac{109.35}{10.8 \times 3.75} = 2.7$ metres.

17. D: Let r cm be the radius of the base and h cm be the height.

Then, $h = 18$ cm.

Now, circumference of the base = Length of the sheed

$\Rightarrow$ Circumference = 44 cm

$\Rightarrow$ $2\pi r = 44$

$\Rightarrow$ $2 \times \dfrac{22}{7} \times r = 44$

$\Rightarrow$ $r = 7$ cm

Volume of the cylinder= $\pi r^2 h\ cm^3$

$= \dfrac{22}{7} \times (7)^2 \times 18\ cm^3$

$= 2772\ cm^3$

18. B: Slant height, $l = \sqrt{r^2 + h^2}$

$= \sqrt{7^2 + 24^2} = 25$ metres

Area of curved surface of cone $= \pi rl$

$= \dfrac{22}{7} \times 7 \times 25 = 550\ m^2$

$\therefore$ Area of the cloth required $= 550\ m^2$

$\therefore$ Length of the cloth $= \dfrac{550}{5} = 110$ metres.

19. A.

20. B.

21. C: Volume of the metallic rod $= 19 \times 4 \times 2 = 152$ cu.cm.

Volume of the cube $= 4^3 = 64$ cu. cm.

Total volume of both after melting them

$$= 152 + 64 = 216 \text{ cu.cm.}$$

$\therefore$ Volume of new cube = 216 cu. cm.

$\Rightarrow$ Side = 6 cm.

22. B.

23. C: Let S_1 and S_2 be the two squares. Let the side of the square S_1 be x cm. Then the side of the square $S_2 = (x + 4)$ cm.

$\therefore$ Area of square $S_1 = x^2$

and, Area of square $S_2 = (x + 4)^2$

$\therefore$ From question,

$\Rightarrow$ $x^2 + (x + 4)^2 = 400$

Solving the equation,

$\Rightarrow$ $x = -16$ and 12

But x cannot be negative

$\therefore$ Side of the square $S_1 = 12$ cm

$\therefore$ that of square $S_2 = x + 4 = 12 + 4 = 16$ cm.

24. C: Area of the field $= \left(\dfrac{\text{Total cost}}{\text{Rate/metre}^2}\right)$

$$= \frac{624.75}{0.85} = 735 \text{ sq. metres}$$

Let the length and breadth of the field be $5x$ and $3x$ metres respectively.

Then, its area $= 5x \times 3x = 15x^2$ sq. metres

$\therefore$ $15x^2 = 735$

$\Rightarrow$ $x^2 = \dfrac{735}{15} = 49$

$\Rightarrow$ $x = 7$

$\therefore$ Length $= 5x = 5 \times 7 = 35$ metres

and breadth $= 3x = 3 \times 7 = 21$ metres

$\therefore$ Perimeter $= 2\,(35 + 21) = 112$ metres.

25. C.

26. B: Angle described by minute hand in 60 minutes = 360°

Angle described by minute hand in 35 minutes $= \dfrac{360}{60} \times 35 = 210°$

$\therefore$ The required area swept by the minute hand = Area of sector $r = 10$ cm

and, $\theta = 210°$

$$= \frac{22}{7} \times 10 \times 10 \times \frac{210}{360}$$

$$= 183.3 \text{ cm}^2.$$

27. C: Let breadth = x cm. Then, length = $\left(\frac{160}{100}x\right)$ cm = $\frac{8}{5}x$ cm.

So, $\frac{8}{5}x - x = 24 \Rightarrow \frac{3}{5}x = 24$

$$\Rightarrow x = \left(\frac{24 \times 5}{3}\right) = 40.$$

$\therefore$ Length = 64 cm, Breadth = 40 cm.

Area = (64×40) cm^2 = 2560 cm^2.

28. D: Let breadth = x metres. Then, length = $\left(\frac{115x}{100}\right)$ metres.

$$\therefore x \times \frac{115x}{100} = 460 \Rightarrow x^2 = \left(\frac{460 \times 100}{115}\right) = 400$$

$$\Rightarrow x = 20.$$

29. A: Let length = $(3x)$ metres and breadth = $(2x)$ metres.

Then, $(3x + 5) \times 2x = 2600$

$\Rightarrow 6x^2 + 10x - 2600 = 0$

$\Rightarrow 3x^2 + 5x - 1300 = 0$

$\Rightarrow (3x + 65)(x - 20) = 0$

$\Rightarrow x = 20.$

$\therefore$ Breadth = $2x$ = 40 m.

30. D:

31. D: Let original length = x and original breadth = y.

Then, original area = xy.

$$\text{New area} = \left[\frac{(100 - r)}{100} \times x\right]\left[\frac{(105 + r)}{100} \times y\right]$$

$$= \left[\left(\frac{10500 - 5r - r^2}{10000}\right) xy\right]$$

$\therefore \left(\frac{10500 - 5r - r^2}{10000}\right)xy = xy \quad \Rightarrow \quad r^2 + 5r - 500 = 0$

$\Rightarrow \quad (r + 25)(r - 20) = 0 \quad \Rightarrow \quad r = 20.$

32. A: Area left after laying black tiles = [(20 – 4) × (10 – 4) sq. ft = 96 sq. ft.

Area under white tiles = $\left(\frac{1}{3} \times 96\right)$ sq. ft = 32 sq. ft

Area under blue tiles = (96 – 32) sq. ft = 64 sq. ft

Number of blue tiles = $\frac{64}{(2 \times 2)} = 16.$

33. B: Let the length of the outer edge be x metres. Then, length of the inner edge = $(x - 6)$ m.

$\therefore \quad x^2 - (x - 6)^2 = 1764$

$\Rightarrow \quad x^2 - (x^2 - 12x + 36) = 1764$

$\Rightarrow \quad 12x = 1800$

$\therefore \quad x = 150.$

$\therefore$ Required perimeter = $(4x)$ m = (4×150) m = 600 m.

34. B: Area = $(45 \times 40)\ m^2 \quad \Rightarrow \quad \frac{1}{2} \times (\text{diagonal})^2 = 1800$

$\Rightarrow$ diagonal = 60 m.

35. C: Let original length of each side = x cm.

Then, its area = $(x^2)\ cm^2$.

Length of rectangle formed = $(x + 5)$ cm and its breadth = x cm.

$\therefore \quad \frac{x+5}{x} = \frac{3}{2} \quad \Rightarrow \quad 2x + 10 = 3x \quad \Rightarrow \quad x = 10.$

$\therefore$ Original length of each side = 10 cm and its area = $100\ cm^2$.

36. B: Area of rectangle = lb sq. units.

Area of the triangle = $\frac{1}{2} lb$ sq. units.

$\therefore$ Required ratio = $lb : \frac{1}{2} lb = 2 : 1.$

37. B: Area of the field grazed = $\left(\frac{22}{7}\times14\times14\right)$ sq. ft

$= 616$ sq. ft.

Number of days taken to graze the field = $\frac{616}{100}$ days = 6 days (approx.).

38. D: Radius of the ground = 17.5 m.

Radius of inner circle = (17.5 – 1.4) m = 16.1 m.

Area of the garden = $\pi \times [(17.5)^2 - 16.1)^2]$ m²

$= \left[\frac{22}{7}\times(17.5+16.1)(17.5-16.1)\right] m^2$

$= \left(\frac{22}{7}\times33.6\times1.4\right) m^2 = 147.84\ m^2.$

39. C: Surface area of the cube = (6×8^2) sq. ft = 384 sq. ft.

Quantity of paint required = $\left(\frac{384}{16}\right)$ kg = 24 kg.

∴ Cost of painting = ₹ (36.50 × 24) = ₹ 876.

40. D: Volume of the tank = 246.4 litres = 246400 cm³.

Let the radius of the base be *r* cm. Then,

$$\left(\frac{22}{7}\times r^2\times400\right) = 246400 \Rightarrow r^2 = \left(\frac{246400\times7}{22\times400}\right) = 196 \Rightarrow r = 14.$$

∴ Diameter of the base = $2r = 28$ cm.

15

ALGEBRAIC IDENTITIES

It is the branch of mathematics that uses letters and symbols to represent variable quantities and numbers, and to express generalizations about them.

SOME IMPORTANT FORMULAE

A. $a^2 - b^2 = (a + b)(a - b)$
B. $(a + b)^2 = a^2 + 2ab + b^2$
C. $(a - b)^2 = a^2 - 2ab + b^2$
D. $a^3 + b^3 = (a + b)(a^2 - ab + b^2)$
E. $a^3 + b^3 = (a + b)^3 - 3ab(a + b)$
F. $a^3 - b^3 = (a - b)(a^2 + ab + b^2)$
G. $a^3 - b^3 = (a - b)^3 + 3ab(a - b)$
H. $(a + b)^2 = (a - b)^2 + 4ab$
I. $(a - b)^2 = (a + b)^2 - 4ab$
J. $a^3 + b^3 + c^3 - 3abc = (a + b + c)(a^2 + b^2 + c^2 - ab - bc - ca)$
K. If $a + b + c = 0$, then $a^3 + b^3 + c^3 = 3abc$

EXERCISE

1. If $x = 12$ and $y = 4$, the value of $(x+y)^{x/y}$ will be:

A. 4096 B. 3896
C. 4196 D. 5086

2. If $x = 9$, $y = \sqrt{17}$, then the value of $\left(x^2 - y^2\right)^{-1/2}$ will be:

A. 2^{-4} B. 2^2
C. 3^{-3} D. 2^{-3}

3. If $x + y = 2z$, then the value of $\left(\frac{x}{x-z} + \frac{z}{y-z}\right)$ will be:

A. 1 B. 4
C. 3/2 D. 2

4. If $x + y + z = 0$, then the value of $\frac{(x+y)(y+z)(z+x)}{xyz}$ will be:

A. –3 B. –2
C. 0 D. –1

5. If $x + \frac{1}{x} = 3$, the value of $x^4 + \frac{1}{x^4}$ will be:

A. 49 B. 47
C. 37 D. 42

6. If $x^2 + y^2 + z^2 = 115$ and $xy + yz + zx = 27$, then the value of $x + y + z$ will be:

A. ± 15 B. ± 13
C. ± 17 D. ± 19

7. If $x = 17$, $y = 15$ and $z = 13$, then the value of $x^2 + y^2 + z^2 - 2xy - 2xz - 2yz$ will be:

A. 111 B. 109

C. 121 D. 120

8. If $x + y = 1$, then the value of $x^3 + y^3 + 3xy$ will be:

A. 1 B. 4

C. 3 D. 7

9. What will be the value of $x^3 + y^3 + z^3 - 3xyz$ if $x + y + z = 16$ and $xy + yz + zx = 78$?

A. 352 B. 452

C. 342 D. 360

10. Which of the following is equivalent to $(x^4 + y^4)(x^2 + y^2)(x + y)(x - y)$?

A. $x^8 - y^8$

B. $x^{10} - y^{10}$

C. $x^6 - y^6$

D. $x^{12} - y^{12}$

11. If $x^2 = y + z$, $y^2 = z + x$ and $z^2 = x + y$, then the value of $\left(\frac{1}{x+1} + \frac{1}{y+1} + \frac{1}{z+1}\right)$ will be?

A. 4 B. 3

C. 1 D. 2

12. If $2x = a + 3$, then what will be the value of $8x^3 - 18ax$?

A. $a^3 + 27$ B. $a^3 - 27$

C. $a^3 + 25$ D. $a^3 - 36$

13. If $x + y = 8$ and $x - y = 2$, then the value of $x^2 + y^2$ will be:

A. 38 B. 40

C. 42 D. 34

14. If $a^2 + b^2 = 30$ and $a - b = 6$, then the value of ab will be:

A. –3 B. –5

C. 2 D. –6

15. If $a + b + c = 15$ and $a^2 + b^2 + c^2 = 77$, the what will be the value of $ab + bc + ca$?

A. 22 B. 74

C. 20 D. 18

EXPLANATORY ANSWERS

1. A: $(x+y)^{x/y} = (12+4)^{12/4} = (16)^3 = 4096.$ $[\because x = 12, y = 4]$

2. D: $(x^2 - y^2)^{-1/2} = (81-17)^{-1/2}$

$$= (64)^{-1/2} = \frac{1}{\sqrt{64}} = \frac{1}{8} = 2^{-3}.$$

3. A: $\because x + y = 2z \Rightarrow x - z = z - y = -(y - z)$

$$\therefore \frac{x}{x-z} + \frac{z}{y-z} = \frac{x}{-(y-z)} + \frac{z}{y-z} = \frac{z-x}{y-z} = 1.$$ $[\because x - z = z - y]$

4. D: $\because$ $x + y + z = 0 \Rightarrow x + y = -z$

$x + y + z = 0 \Rightarrow y + z = -x$

and $x + y + z = 0 \Rightarrow z + x = -y$

$$\therefore \frac{(x+y)(y+z)(z+x)}{xyz} = \frac{-z.-x.-y}{xyz} = -1.$$

5. B:

6. B: $\because (x + y + z)^2 = x^2 + y^2 + z^2 + 2\,(xy + yz + zx)$

$\therefore (x + y + z)^2 = 115 + 2 \times 27$

$= 115 + 54 = 169$

$\therefore\ (x + y + z) = \sqrt{169} = \pm\, 13.$

7. C: The given expression is equivalent to $(x - y - z)^2$

$\therefore\ (x - y - z)^2 = (17 - 15 - 13)^2$

$= (-11)^2 = 121.$

8. A: $\because\ (x + y)^3 = x^3 + y^3 + 3xy\,(x + y)$

$\therefore\ (1)^3 = x^3 + y^3 + 3xy \times 1$

$\therefore\ 1 = x^3 + y^3 + 3xy.$

9. A: $\because\ (x + y + z) = 16 \Rightarrow (x + y + z)^2 = (16)^2$

$= x^2 + y^2 + z^2 + 2(xy + yz + zx) = 256$

$\therefore x^2 + y^2 + z^2 + 2\times 78 = 256 \Rightarrow x^2 + y^2 + z^2$

$= 256 - 156 = 100$

$\therefore\ x^3 + y^3 + z^3 - 3xyz = (x + y + z)\,[(x^2 + y^2 + z^2) - (xy + yz + zx)]$

$= 16[100 - 78]$

$= 16 \times 22 = 352.$

10. A: $\because\ (x^4 + y^4)(x^2 + y^2)(x + y)(x - y)$

$= (x^4 + y^4)(x^2 + y^2)(x^2 - y^2)$

$= (x^4 + y^4)(x^4 - y^4)$

$= x^8 - y^8.$

11. C:

12. A: $\because\ 2x = a + 3$

$\Rightarrow\ (2x)^3 = (a + 3)^3$

$\therefore\ 8x^3 = a^3 + 27 + 3 \times a \times 3(a + 3)$

$= a^3 + 9a^2 + 27a + 27$

and $18ax = 9a \times 2x$

$= 9a \times (a + 3) = 9a^2 + 27a$

$\therefore\ 8x^3 - 18ax = a^3 + 9a^2 + 27a + 27 - 9a^2 - 27a$

$= a^3 + 27.$

13. D: $\because\ x^2 + y^2 = \dfrac{(x+y)^2 + (x-y)^2}{2}$

$$= \frac{(8)^2 + (2)^2}{2} = \frac{64+4}{2} = \frac{68}{2} = 34.$$

14. A: $\because$ $$(a - b)^2 = a^2 + b^2 - 2ab$$

$\Rightarrow$ $$ab = \frac{a^2 + b^2 - (a-b)^2}{2}$$

$$= \frac{30 - (6)^2}{2}$$

$$= \frac{30 - 36}{2} = \frac{-6}{2} = -3.$$

15. B: $\because$ $(a + b + c)^2 = a^2 + b^2 + c^2 + 2(ab + bc + ca)$

$\therefore$ $$ab + bc + ca = \frac{(a+b+c)^2 - \left(a^2 + b^2 + c^2\right)}{2}$$

$$= \frac{(15)^2 - 77}{2} = \frac{225 - 77}{2}$$

$$= \frac{148}{2} = 74.$$

16

SURDS

Given a number, it is not always possible to find some whole number which when multiplied by itself will give the given number. In other words all given numbers are not perfect square numbers. For example, square root of 9, *i.e.,* $\sqrt{9}$ is 3, which is a whole number. But square root of 15, *i.e.,* $\sqrt{15}$ = 3.873, which is not a whole number.

Hence square roots of natural numbers which are not perfect squares are not rational numbers. These are irrational numbers and are called **Surds**. For example, $\sqrt{3}$, $\sqrt{7}$, $2+\sqrt{11}$, $4+\sqrt{13}$ ..... etc. are **Surds**.

Given below are a few formulas which are quite helpful in solving the problems related to surds:

1. $\sqrt{a} \times \sqrt{a} = a$

2. $\sqrt{a} \times \sqrt{b} = \sqrt{ab}$

3. $\left(\sqrt{a} + \sqrt{b}\right)^2 = a + b + \sqrt[2]{ab}$

4. $\left(\sqrt{a} - \sqrt{b}\right)^2 = a + b - \sqrt[2]{ab}$

5. $x\sqrt{a} + x\sqrt{b} = x\left(\sqrt{a} + \sqrt{b}\right)$

6. $\dfrac{1}{\sqrt{a}+\sqrt{b}} = \dfrac{1}{\sqrt{a}+\sqrt{b}} \times \dfrac{\sqrt{a}-\sqrt{b}}{\sqrt{a}-\sqrt{b}} = \dfrac{\sqrt{a}-\sqrt{b}}{a-b}$

7. $\dfrac{1}{\sqrt{a}-\sqrt{b}} = \dfrac{1}{\sqrt{a}-\sqrt{b}} \times \dfrac{\sqrt{a}+\sqrt{b}}{\sqrt{a}+\sqrt{b}} = \dfrac{\sqrt{a}+\sqrt{b}}{a-b}$

8. $a + \sqrt{b} = c + \sqrt{d} \Rightarrow a = c$ and $b = d$

9. $\sqrt{2}$ = 1.41421, $\sqrt{3}$ = 1.73205, $\sqrt{5}$ = 2.23607,

$\sqrt{6}$ = 2.4494

$\sqrt{7}$ = 2.64575, $\sqrt{8}$ = 2.82842, $\sqrt{10}$ = 3.16227,

$\sqrt{11}$ = 3.31662

EXERCISE

1. What will be the value of $\frac{1}{\sqrt{3}}$ upto 3 decimal places?
   A. 0.577 B. 0.477
   C. 0.673 D. 0.575

2. If $\sqrt{2} = 1.4122$, the value of $\frac{1}{2}\left(\frac{\sqrt{2}-1}{\sqrt{2}+1}\right)$ is:
   A. .0768 B. .0658
   C. .0858 D. .0458

3. If $\sqrt{1936} = 44$, the value of $\sqrt{19.36} + \sqrt{0.1936} + \sqrt{.001936}$ upto 3 decimal places will be:
   A. 5.679 B. 4.884
   C. 9.884 D. 6.778

4. Value of $\frac{\sqrt{2}-1}{\sqrt{2}+1}$ upto 3 decimal places will be:
   A. 0.172 B. 0.158
   C. 0.176 D. 0.188

5. $\sqrt[3]{8^4}$ is equivalent to:
   A. 15 B. 9
   C. 16 D. 25

6. If $\sqrt{6} = 2.45$, the value of $\sqrt{\frac{2}{3}} + 3\sqrt{3/2}$ will be equivalent to:
   A. 3.942 B. 4.492
   C. 4.942 D. 9.345

7. $\sqrt{72}$ is equivalent to:
   A. $3\sqrt{5}$ B. $6\sqrt{2}$
   C. $8\sqrt{2}$ D. $7\sqrt{3}$

8. What will be the value of $\left(\sqrt{80} + 3 \times \sqrt{245} - \sqrt{125}\right)$?
   A. $18\sqrt{5}$ B. $20\sqrt{5}$
   C. $22\sqrt{5}$ D. $28\sqrt{2}$

9. Value of $\left(\frac{\sqrt{5}+\sqrt{3}}{\sqrt{5}-\sqrt{3}}\right)$ will be equivalent to :
   A. $4 + \sqrt{15}$ B. $3 - \sqrt{15}$
   C. $2 + \sqrt{15}$ D. $4 - \sqrt{15}$

10. The expression $\left(\frac{\sqrt{7}+\sqrt{5}}{\sqrt{7}-\sqrt{5}}\right)$ is equivalent to:
   A. $6 - \sqrt{35}$ B. $2 + \sqrt{35}$
   C. $4 - \sqrt{35}$ D. $6 + \sqrt{35}$

EXPLANATORY ANSWERS

1. A: $\because \frac{1}{\sqrt{3}} = \frac{1}{\sqrt{3}} \times \frac{\sqrt{3}}{\sqrt{3}} = \frac{\sqrt{3}}{3} = \frac{1.732}{3} = 0.577$.

2. C: $\because \frac{1}{2}\left(\frac{\sqrt{2}-1}{\sqrt{2}+1}\right) = \frac{1}{2} \times \frac{\sqrt{2}-1}{\sqrt{2}+1} \times \frac{\sqrt{2}-1}{\sqrt{2}-1} = \frac{1}{2} \times \frac{\left(\sqrt{2}-1\right)^2}{\left(\sqrt{2}\right)^2 - 1^2}$

$$= \frac{1}{2} \times \frac{2+1-2\sqrt{2}}{2-1} = \frac{1}{2} \times \frac{3-2\sqrt{2}}{1} = \frac{1}{2} \times (3-2\times 1.4142)$$

$$= \frac{1}{2} \times 0.1716 = .0858$$

3. B: $\because \sqrt{1936} = 44 \Rightarrow \sqrt{19.36} = 4.4$

$\Rightarrow \sqrt{0.1936} = 0.44$

$\Rightarrow \sqrt{.001936} = .044$

$\therefore \sqrt{19.36} + \sqrt{0.1936} + \sqrt{.001936}$

$= 4.4 + 0.44 + .044 = 4.884.$

4. A: $\because \frac{\sqrt{2}-1}{\sqrt{2}+1} = \frac{\sqrt{2}-1}{\sqrt{2}+1} \times \frac{\sqrt{2}-1}{\sqrt{2}-1} = \frac{\left(\sqrt{2}-1\right)^2}{\left(\sqrt{2}\right)^2 - (1)^2} = \frac{2+1-2\sqrt{2}}{2-1}$

$$= \frac{3-2\sqrt{2}}{1} = 3 - 2 \times 1.414 = 0.172.$$

5. C: $\sqrt[3]{8^4} = (8)^{\frac{4}{3}} = \left(2^3\right)^{\frac{4}{3}} = 2^{3\times\frac{4}{3}} = 2^4 = 16.$

6. B: $\because \sqrt{\frac{2}{3}} + 3\sqrt{\frac{3}{2}} = \frac{\sqrt{2}}{\sqrt{3}} \times \frac{\sqrt{3}}{\sqrt{3}} + 3 \times \frac{\sqrt{3}}{\sqrt{2}} \times \frac{\sqrt{2}}{\sqrt{2}}$

$$= \frac{\sqrt{6}}{3} + \frac{3\sqrt{6}}{2} = \sqrt{6}\left[\frac{1}{3} + \frac{3}{2}\right] = \sqrt{6} \times \frac{11}{6} = \frac{11}{6} \times 2.45 = 4.492.$$

7. B: $\because \sqrt{72} = \sqrt{6 \times 6 \times 2} = \sqrt{6^2 \times 2} = 6\sqrt{2}.$

8. B: $\because \sqrt{80} + 3 \times \sqrt{245} - \sqrt{125}$

$= \sqrt{16 \times 5} + 3 \times \sqrt{49 \times 5} - \sqrt{25 \times 5}$

$= 4\sqrt{5} + 21\sqrt{5} - 5\sqrt{5} = 20\sqrt{5}.$

9. A: $\because \dfrac{\sqrt{5}+\sqrt{3}}{\sqrt{5}-\sqrt{3}} = \dfrac{\sqrt{5}+\sqrt{3}}{\sqrt{5}-\sqrt{3}} \times \dfrac{\sqrt{5}+\sqrt{3}}{\sqrt{5}+\sqrt{3}}$

$$= \frac{\left(\sqrt{5}+\sqrt{3}\right)^2}{\left(\sqrt{5}\right)^2-\left(\sqrt{3}\right)^2} = \frac{5+3+2\sqrt{15}}{5-3}$$

$$= \frac{8+2\sqrt{15}}{2} = 4+\sqrt{15}$$

10. D: $\because \dfrac{\sqrt{7}+\sqrt{5}}{\sqrt{7}-\sqrt{5}} = \dfrac{\sqrt{7}+\sqrt{5}}{\sqrt{7}-\sqrt{5}} \times \dfrac{\sqrt{7}+\sqrt{5}}{\sqrt{7}+\sqrt{5}}$

$$= \frac{\left(\sqrt{7}+\sqrt{5}\right)^2}{\left(\sqrt{7}\right)^2-\left(\sqrt{5}\right)^2}$$

$$= \frac{7+5+2\sqrt{35}}{7-5} = \frac{12+2\sqrt{35}}{2} = 6+\sqrt{35}.$$

17

TRIANGLES AND ITS VARIOUS KINDS

Properties of geometrical figures:

(*i*) **Equilateral triangle:** All sides are equal.

(*ii*) **Isosceles triangle:** Two sides are equal.

(*iii*) **Rhombus:** All sides are equal and no angle is a right angle, but diagonals are at right angles and unequal.

(*iv*) **Square:** All sides are equal and each angle is right angle. The diagonals are also equal.

(*v*) **Parallelogram:** Opposite sides are parallel and equal, diagonals bisect each other.

(*vi*) **Rectangle:** Opposite sides are equal and each angle is a right angle, diagonals are equal.

Co-ordinates of standard points:

(*i*) *Centroid of a triangle:*

The point is the intersection of the medians. This point divides each median in the ratio 2 : 1, its co-ordinates are

$$G_1\left(\frac{x_1+x_2+x_3}{3}, \frac{y_1+y_2+y_3}{3}\right)$$

(*ii*) *Incentre of a triangle:*

This is the centre of the circle which touches the sides of a given triangle, it is the point of intersection of the internal bisectors of the angles of the triangle, its co-ordinates are given by the formula

$$I=(x,y) \text{ where } x=\frac{ax_1+bx_2+cx_3}{a+b+c}$$

$$y=\frac{ay_1+by_2+cy_3}{a+b+c}$$

where (a, b, c) are the lengths of the triangle

(*iii*) *Orthocentre of a triangle:*

The point H is the intersection of the altitudes.

(*iv*) The points O, G, H are collinear and G divides OH in the ratio 1 : 2.

EXERCISE

1. The points A (12, 8), B(–2, 6) and C (6, 0) are vertices of :

A. right angled triangle

B. isosceles triangle

C. equilateral triangle

D. None of these

2. The points (1, 1) (–1, –1) and $(-\sqrt{3}, \sqrt{3})$ are the angular points of a triangle, then the triangle is:

A. right angled

B. isosceles

C. equilateral

D. None of these

3. Two vertices of a triangle are the points (1, 4) and (7, 2). Its centroid is the point (5, 3), then the third vertex is :

A. (3, 7) B. (7, 3)

C. (1, 1) D. (0, 0)

4. Let the vertices of a triangle be (0, 0), (3, 0) and (0, 4), then its orthocentre is :

A. (0, 0)

B. $\left(1, \frac{4}{3}\right)$

C. $\left(\frac{3}{2}, 2\right)$

D. None of these

5. Distance of (2, 3) from origin is:

A. 2 B. 5

C. –1 D. $\sqrt{13}$

6. Find the values of y for which the distance between the points P(2, –3) and Q(10, y) is 10 units.

A. 8, 2 B. –9, 3

C. –9, 5 D. –8, 2

7. The centroid of the triangle whose vertices are A(4, –6), B(3, –2) and C(5, 2) is :

A. 3, 2 B. 4, 1

C. 4, –2 D. 4, 3

8. If (7, 3), (6, 1), (8, 2) and (P, 4) are the vertices of a parallelogram taken in order then the value of P is :

A. 4 B. 6

C. 7 D. 9

9. If the vertices of rhombus are (3, 0), (4, 5), (–1, 4) and (–2, –1) taken in order then area of rhombus is :

A. 20 square units

B. 24 square units

C. 22 square units

D. 26 square units

10. Find the value of P for which the points A(–1, 3), B(2, P) and C(5, –1) are collinear :

A. 3 B. 1

C. 2 D. 4

EXPLANATORY ANSWERS

1. A: $BC^2 + CA^2 = AB^2$.

2. C: $BC^2 = CA^2 = AB^2$.

3. B: $5 = \frac{\Sigma x}{3},\ 3 = \frac{\Sigma y}{3}$.

4. A: The two altitudes *i.e.*, *x*-axis and *y*-axis of ΔOAB meet at origin.

5. D: A(0, 0) ———— B(2, 3)

$AB = \sqrt{(2-0)^2 + (3-0)^2} = \sqrt{4+9} = \sqrt{13}$

6. B: $\because$ PQ = 10

$\Rightarrow \sqrt{(10-2)^2 + (y+3)^2} = 10$

$\sqrt{64 + y^2 + 9 + 6y} = 10$

Squaring both sides,

$y^2 + 6y - 27 = 0$

$\Rightarrow y^2 + 9y - 3y - 27 = 0$

$\Rightarrow y(y + 9) - 3(y + 9) = 0$

$\Rightarrow (y + 9)(y - 3) = 0$

$\Rightarrow y = -9, y = 3$

$\therefore y = -9, 3$

7. C:

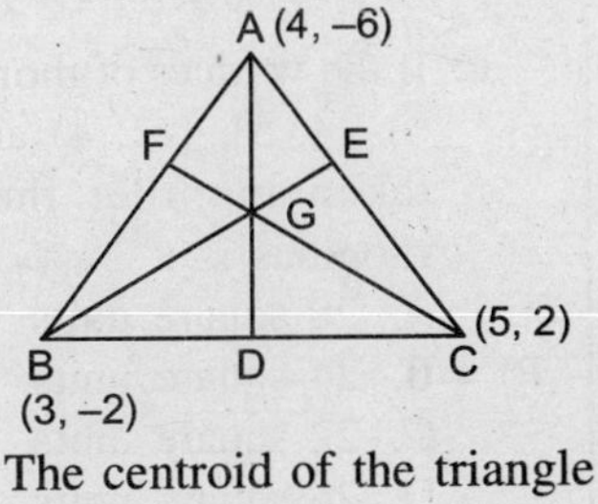

The centroid of the triangle G(*x*, *y*)

$= G\left(\frac{4+3+5}{3}, \frac{-6-2+2}{3}\right)$

= G(4, –2)

8. D:

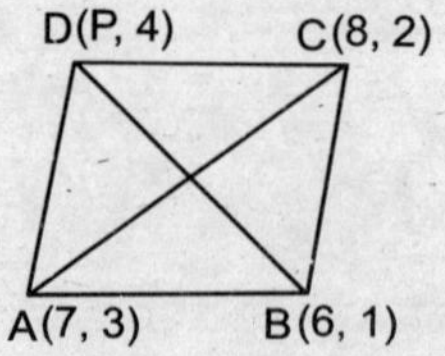

We know that the diagonals of a parallelogram bisect each other. Mid-point of AC and BD coincide.

Hence, $\left(\frac{7+8}{2}, \frac{3+2}{2}\right) = \left(\frac{6+P}{2}, \frac{1+4}{2}\right)$

$\Rightarrow \quad \left(\frac{6+P}{2}, \frac{5}{2}\right) = \left(\frac{15}{2}, \frac{5}{2}\right)$

Equating the x-co-ordinate, we get

$\frac{6+P}{2} = \frac{15}{2} \Rightarrow P = 9$

9. B: We know that area of rhombus

$= \frac{1}{2} \times AC \times BD = \frac{1}{2} \times \sqrt{(-1-3)^2 + (4-0)^2} \times \sqrt{(-2-4)^2 + (-1-5)^2}$

$= \frac{1}{2}\sqrt{32} \times \sqrt{72} = \frac{1}{2} \times 4\sqrt{2} \times 6\sqrt{2}$

$= \frac{1}{2} \times 48 = 24$ square units.

10. B: Points A, B, C are collinear

$\Rightarrow$ Area of $\Delta ABC = 0$

$\frac{1}{2}[-1\ (P + 1) + 2(-1 - 3) + 5(3 - P) = 0$

$\Rightarrow \frac{1}{2}[-6P + 6] = 0 \Rightarrow 3P = 3 \Rightarrow P = 1.$

18

SIMILARITY OF TRIANGLES

Two triangles are said to be similar, if

(*i*) their corresponding angles are equal and

(*ii*) their corresponding sides are in the same ratio (*i.e.* proportional).

Also, we know that :

(*i*) If corresponding angles of two triangles are equal, then they are known as equiangular triangles.

(*ii*) Two line segments are divided proportionally when the ratio of the lengths of the segments of one of them is equal to the ratio of the lengths of the segments of the other.

EXERCISE

1. Two similar triangles have
A. equal sides
B. equal areas
C. equal angles
D. None of these

2. Two congruent triangles have
A. proportional sides
B. equal sides
C. equal corresponding sides
D. equal corresponding angles

3. Which of the following is false for two congruent triangles
A. Corresponding angles are equal.
B. Two sides and included angles are equal.
C. Corresponding sides are equal.
D. Two angles and one side are equal.

4. If the sides of a triangle are 8 cm, 12 cm and 15 cm then the angle is
A. Right angle
B. Obtuse angle
C. Acute angle
D. None of these

5. If two triangles are on the same base and between the parallel lines then they will be
A. equilaterals
B. right angled
C. equal in area
D. congruent

6. If the three heights of a traingle are equal then it is
A. right angled triangle
B. obtuse angled triangle
C. equilateral triangle
D. None of these

7. If two corresponding sides and the angle between them of a traingle are equal to another triangle. Then the angles are :

A. congruent but not similar
B. similar but not congruent
C. neither congruent nor similar
D. congruent and similar.

8. Ratio of areas of two similar triangles is equal to :

A. ratio of squares of the corresponding altitudes
B. ratio of squares of corresponding medians.
C. Either (A) or (B)
D. (A) and (B) both

9. If the areas of two similar triangles are equal then the triangles :

A. are congruent
B. have equal length of corresponding sides
C. (A) and (B)
D. None of these

10. Two isosceles triangles have equal vertical angles and their areas are in the ratio of 9 : 25 then the ratio between their corresponding heights is :

A. 5 : 3 B. 25 : 9
C. 3 : 5 D. 16 : 9

EXPLANATORY ANSWERS

1. C: equal angles
2. C: equal corresponding sides
3. D: Two angles and one side are equal.
4. C: Acute angle
5. C: equal in area
6. C: equilateral triangle
7. C: neither congruent nor similar
8. D: (A) and (B) both
9. C. (A) and (B)
10. C: According to equestion

$$\angle A = \angle D \text{ and } \frac{ar(\Delta ABC)}{ar(\Delta DEF)} = \frac{9}{25}$$

Since, $AB = AC$ (given) ....(*i*)
$DE = DF$ (given) ....(*ii*)

Dividing (*i*) by (*ii*)

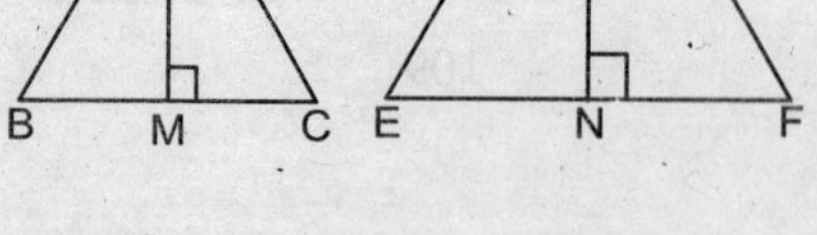

$$\frac{AB}{DE} = \frac{AC}{DF} \qquad ...(iii)$$

Hence, $\Delta ABC \sim \Delta DEF$ [By SAS criterion of similar Δs]

In ΔAMC and ΔDNF

$$\angle AMC = \angle DNF = 90°$$

$$\angle C = \angle F \qquad \text{(because } \Delta ABC \sim \Delta DEF)$$

$\therefore \angle AMC \sim DNF$ (By AA Criterion of similar Δs)

$$\therefore \quad \frac{AC}{DF} = \frac{AM}{DN}$$

and, $$\frac{ar\,(\Delta\ ABC)}{ar\,(DEF)} = \frac{AC^2}{DF^2} = \frac{AM^2}{DN^2}$$

$$\therefore \quad \frac{AM^2}{DN^2} = \frac{9}{25} \Rightarrow \frac{AM}{DN} = \frac{3}{5}$$

Hence required ratio = 3 : 5

19

CIRCLE AND TANGENTS

A circle is a set of those points in a plane that are at a given constant distance from a given fixed point in the plane. The fixed point is called the **centre of the circle** and the constant distance of every point on the circle from its centre of called the **radius of the circle**.

The fixed point O is called its centre and the constant distance r is called the radius.

Diameter is the longest chord of the circle.

Secant

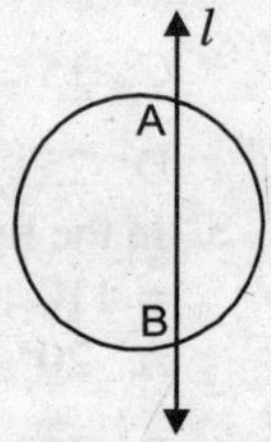

A line which interesects a circle in two distinct points is called a **secant** of the circle. In the fig. the line l intersects the circle in two distinct points A and B. The line l is a secant to the circle.

Tanget

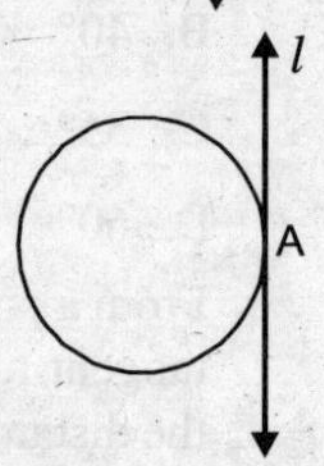

A tangent to a circle is a line that intersects the circle at exactly one point.

The point at which it meets the circle is called its point of contact and the line (tangent) is said to touch the circle at this point. In the figure, the line l meets the circle at only point A. Here A is the point of contact.

EXERCISE

1. PQ is a diameter and PQRS is a cyclic quadrilateral. If $\angle PSR$ = 150°, then measure of $\angle RPQ$ is :

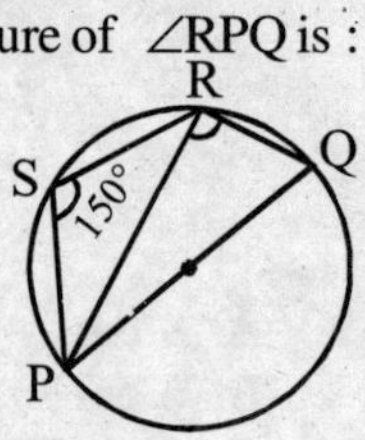

A. 90°

B. 60°

C. 30°

D. None of these

2. Determine the value of x in the figure given below.

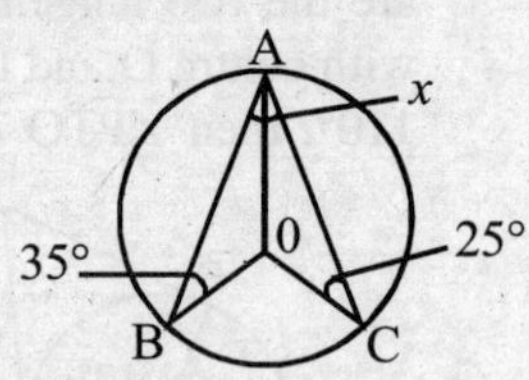

A. 35°

B. 25°

C. 30°

D. 60°

3. O is the centre of the circle. If $\angle OAB = 30°$ and $\angle OCB = 40°$, find $\angle AOC$.

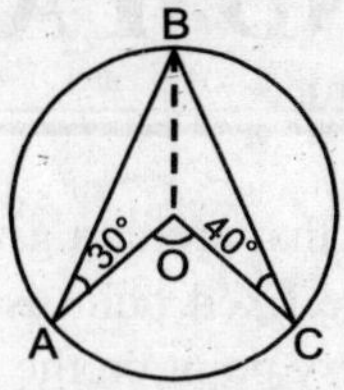

A. 120°

B. 140°

C. 110°

D. 130°

4. In fig. if $\angle ACB = 40°$, $\angle DPB = 120°$, then find *y*.

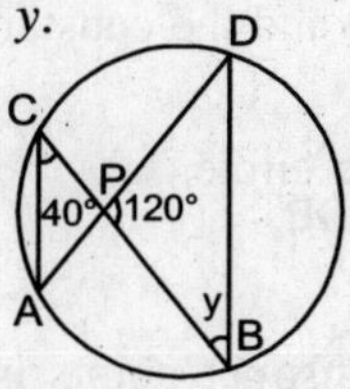

A. 10°

B. 20°

C. 15°

D. 25°

5. In the fig. if $\angle BDC = 30°$, $\angle CBA = 110°$, then find BCA.

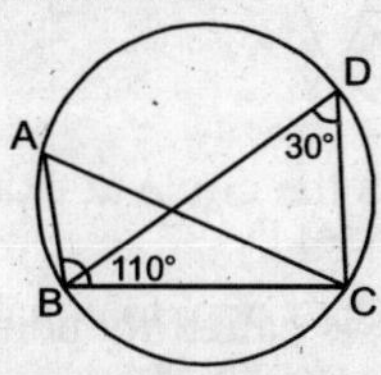

A. 20°

B. 40°

C. 35°

D. 60°

6. From a point Q, the length of the tangent to a circle is 24 cm and the distance from the centre is 25 cm. The radius of the circle is

A. 7 cm B. 12 cm

C. 15 cm D. 24.5 cm

7. In the given figure, if TP and TQ are the two tangents to a circle with centre O and that $\angle POQ = 110°$, then $\angle PTQ$ is equal to

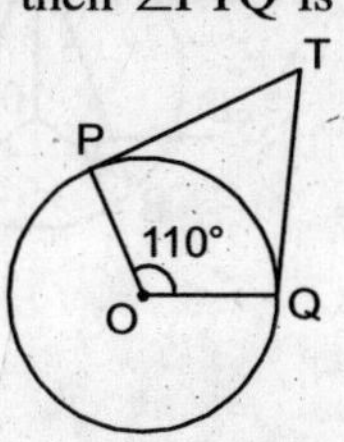

A. 60°

B. 70°

C. 80°

D. 90°

8. If tangents PA and PB from a point P to a circle with centre O are inclined to each other at angle of 80°, then $\angle POA$ is equal to

A. 50°

B. 60°

C. 70°

D. 80°

9. In Fig., a circle touches all the four sides of a quadrilateral ABCD whose sides AB = 6 cm, BC = 7 cm and CD = 4 cm. Find AD

A. 2 cm

B. 5 cm

C. 3 cm

D. 4 cm

10. If AB, AC, PQ are tangents in the figure and AB = 5 cm. The perimeter of ΔAPQ is

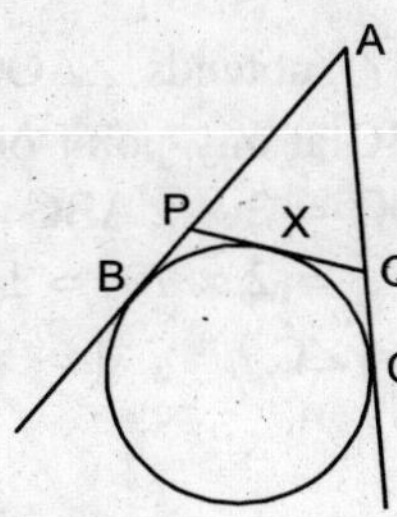

A. 8 cm

B. 6 cm

C. 10 cm

D. 5 cm

EXPLANATORY ANSWERS

1. B: $\angle PQR = 180° - 150° = 30°$

$\angle PRQ = 90°$ (Angle of a semicircle)

$\angle RPQ + 90° + 30° = 180°$

$\Rightarrow \angle RPQ = 60°$

2. D: $\angle OAB = \angle OBA \, (\because OA = OB)$

$\angle OAB = 35°$

Similarly, $\angle AOC = 25°$

$\therefore \quad \angle x = 35° + 25° = 60°$

3. B: O is the centre of the circle,

$\angle OAB = 30°$, $\angle OCB = 40°$. join OB

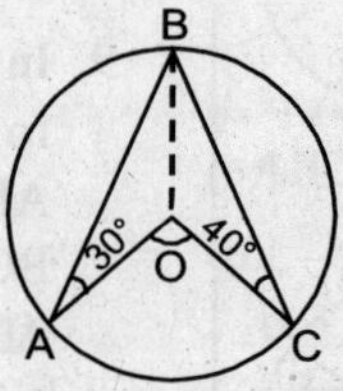

In ΔOAB,

$\therefore$ OA = OB (radii of the same circle)

$\therefore \angle OBA = \angle OAB = 30°$ ($\angle s$ opp. to equal sides of a Δ) ...(*i*)

Similarly, $\angle OBC = \angle OCB = 40°$ ...(*ii*)

Adding equations (*i*) and (*ii*), we get

$\angle OBA + \angle OBC = 30° + 40°$

$\Rightarrow \angle ABC = 70°$

$\because \widehat{AC}$ subtends $\angle AOC$ at the centre and ΔABC at any point on the circumference

$\angle AOC = 2 \times \angle ABC$

$= 2 \times 70° = 140°$

4. B: $\angle D = \angle C$ [$\because$ $\angle s$ in the same segment of a circle are equal]

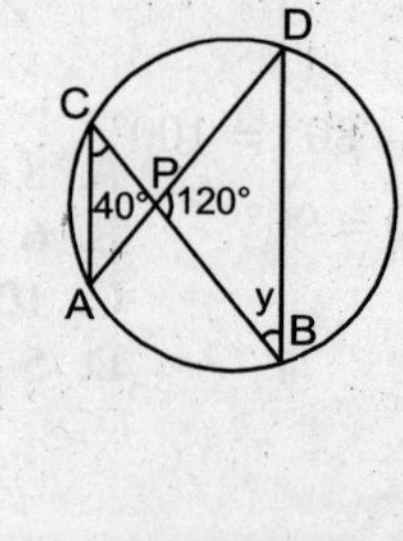

But $\angle C = 40°$ (Given)

$\therefore \angle C = 40°$

In Δ BPD, we have

$\angle BPD + \angle D + \angle B = 180°$ [$\because$ sum of three $\angle s$ of a $\Delta = 180°$]

$\Rightarrow 120° + 40° + y = 180°$

$\Rightarrow y = 180° - 160° = 20°.$

5. B: $\angle BAC = \angle BDC$ ($\angle$s in the same segment)

$= 30°$ (given)

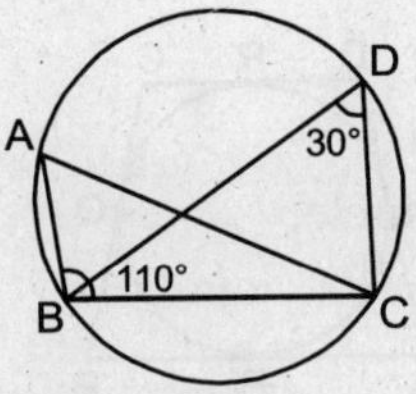

$\angle BAC + \angle CBA + \angle BCA = 180°$ ($\angle$s of ΔABC)

$\Rightarrow 30° + 110° + \angle BCA = 180°$

$\Rightarrow \angle BCA = 180° - 30° - 110° = 40°$

6. A: In rt. $\angle d$ ΔOTQ,

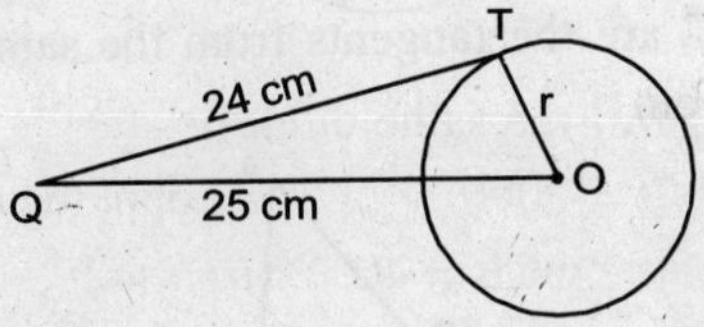

$$OT = \sqrt{OQ^2 - OT^2}$$

$$= \sqrt{25^2 - 24^2} = \sqrt{625 - 576}$$

$$= \sqrt{49} = 7 \text{ cm.}$$

7. B: Since $\angle POQ + \angle PTQ = 180°$ [$\because \angle OPT = 90°, \angle OQT = 90°$]

$\Rightarrow 110° + \angle PTQ = 180°$

$\Rightarrow \angle PTQ = 180° - 110° = 70°.$

8. A: Since $\angle APB = 80°$

$\angle AOB = 180° - 80° = 100°$

$\angle PAO = \angle PBO = 90°$

Since OP bisects $\angle AOB$

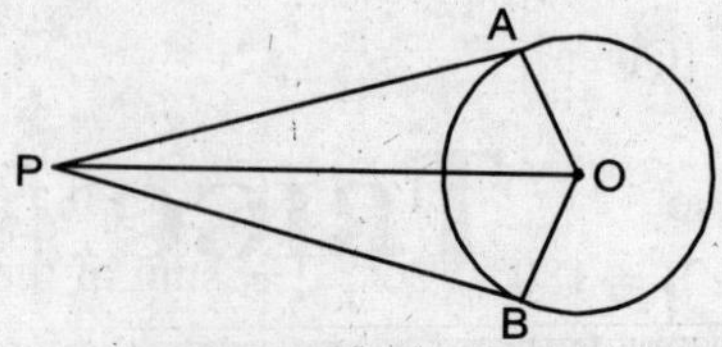

$$\angle AOP = \frac{1}{2}(100°) = 50°$$

i.e. $\angle POA = 50°$.

9. C: AD = AS + DS = AP + DR [∵ AS = AP and DS = DR]

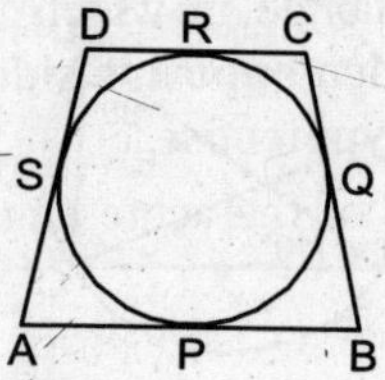

= (AB – BP) + (CD – RC)
= AB + CD – (BP + RC)
= AB + CD – (BQ + CQ) [∵ BP = BQ, RC = CQ]
= AB + CD – BC = 6 + 4 – 7 = 3 cm.

10. C: Since AB and AC are the tangents from the same point A
∴ AB = AC = 5 cm

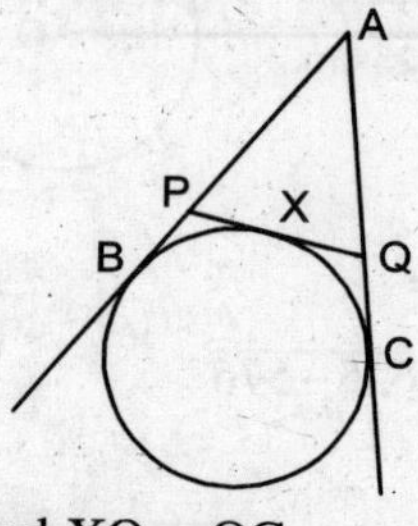

Similarly, BP = PX and XQ = QC
Perimeter of ΔAPQ = AP + AQ + PQ
= AP + AQ + (PX + XQ)
= (AP + PX) + (AQ + XQ)
= (AP + BP) + (AQ + QC)
= AB + AC = 5 + 5 = 10 cm.

20

TRIGONOMETRY

Trigonometric Ratios of Angles

There are six trigonometric ratios — sine, cosine, tangent, cotangent, secant and cosecant—upon which trigonometry is based.

ΔABC is a right- angled triangle in which $\angle ACB = \theta$. The side AB is opposite to an angle θ and is called **opposide side**. BC is the **adjacent side** in relation to angle θ; AC is the **hypotenuse**.

The six trigonometric ratios of the acute angle θ are defined as follows :

$$\sin\theta = \frac{p}{h} = \frac{AB}{AC} \qquad \cos\theta = \frac{b}{h} = \frac{BC}{AC}$$

$$\tan\theta = \frac{p}{b} = \frac{AB}{BC} \qquad \cot\theta = \frac{b}{p} = \frac{BC}{AB}$$

$$\sec\theta = \frac{h}{b} = \frac{AC}{BC} \qquad \text{cosec}\theta = \frac{h}{p} = \frac{AC}{AB}$$

IMPORTANT FORMULAE

A. (*i*) $\tan\theta = \dfrac{\sin\theta}{\cos\theta} = \dfrac{1}{\cot\theta}$ (*ii*) $\cot\theta = \dfrac{\cos\theta}{\sin\theta} = \dfrac{1}{\tan\theta}$

(*iii*) $\sec\theta = \dfrac{1}{\cos\theta}$ (*iv*) $\text{cosec}\theta = \dfrac{1}{\sin\theta}$

B. (*v*) $\sin^2\theta + \cos^2\theta = 1$

$\sin^2\theta = 1 - \cos^2\theta \Rightarrow \sin\theta = \sqrt{1-\cos^2\theta}$

$\cos^2\theta = 1 - \sin^2\theta \Rightarrow \cos\theta = \sqrt{1-\sin^2\theta}$

(*vi*) $1 + \tan^2\theta = \sec^2\theta$

$\sec^2\theta - \tan^2\theta = 1$

$\sec^2\theta - 1 = \tan^2\theta$

(*vii*) $1 + \cot^2\theta = \operatorname{cosec}^2\theta$

$\operatorname{cosec}^2\theta - \cot^2\theta = 1$

$\operatorname{cosec}^2\theta - 1 = \cot^2\theta$

C. (*viii*) $\sin(90 - \theta) = \cos\theta$

(*ix*) $\cos(90 - \theta) = \sin\theta$

(*x*) $\tan(90 - \theta) = \cot\theta$

(*xi*) $\cot(90 - \theta) = \tan\theta$

(*xii*) $\sec(90 - \theta) = \operatorname{cosec}\theta$

(*xiii*) $\operatorname{cosec}(90 - \theta) = \sec\theta$

D. (*i*) $\sin(A \pm B) = \sin A \times \cos B \pm \cos A \times \sin B$

(*ii*) $\cos(A \pm B) = \cos A \times \cos B \mp \sin A \times \sin B$

E. (*i*) $\sin 2\theta = 2\sin\theta \cdot \cos\theta$

(*ii*) $\cos 2\theta = \cos^2\theta - \sin^2\theta$

$= 1 - 2\sin^2\theta = 2\cos^2\theta - 1$

(*iii*) $\tan 2\theta = \dfrac{2\tan\theta}{1-\tan^2\theta}$

F. (*i*) $\sin 3\theta = 3\sin\theta - 4\sin^3\theta$

(*ii*) $\cos 3\theta = 4\cos^3\theta - 3\cos\theta$

T-Ratios of Standard Angles

θ	0°	30°	45°	60°	90°
$\sin\theta$	0	$\frac{1}{2}$	$\frac{1}{\sqrt{2}}$	$\frac{\sqrt{3}}{2}$	1
$\cos\theta$	1	$\frac{\sqrt{3}}{2}$	$\frac{1}{\sqrt{2}}$	$\frac{1}{2}$	0
$\tan\theta$	0	$\frac{1}{\sqrt{3}}$	1	$\sqrt{3}$	∞
$\cot\theta$	∞	$\sqrt{3}$	1	$\frac{1}{\sqrt{3}}$	0
$\sec\theta$	1	$\frac{2}{\sqrt{3}}$	$\sqrt{2}$	2	∞
$\operatorname{cosec}\theta$	∞	2	$\sqrt{2}$	$\frac{2}{\sqrt{3}}$	1

HEIGHT AND DISTANCE

Our common use for trigonometry is to measure heights and distance that are either awkward or impossible to measure by ordinary means. One of the biggest triumphs of trigonometry is being able to find the size of an object or the distance to an object (such as the moon) without going to the object. In trigonometry, we develop methods for measuring sides and angles as well as for solving related applied problems. Because of the extensive use of these concepts, trigonometry is considered one of the most practical and relevant branches of mathematics.

The Angle of Elevation

If a person is looking up at an object, the acute angle measured from the horizontal to a line of sight observation of the object is called the angle of elevation.

In the given figure, α is the angle of elevation.

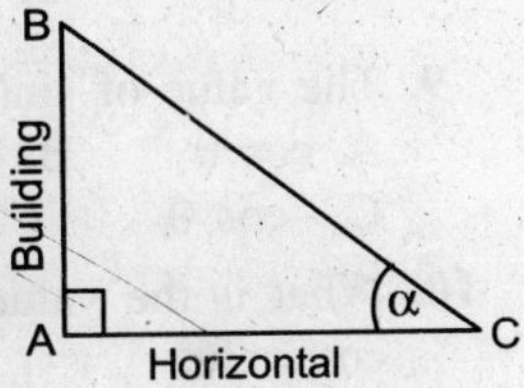

The Angle of Depression

The angle β for a point below a horizontal line is the angle formed by the horizontal line and the observer's line of sight through the point. In the following figure, β is the angle of depression.

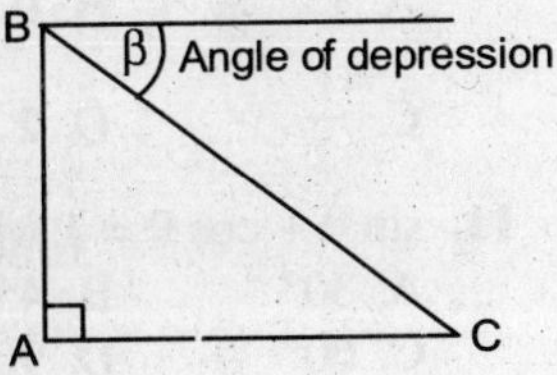

EXERCISE

1. If 2 tan θ = 1, find the value of

$$\frac{3\cos\theta + 2\sin\theta}{2\cos\theta - \sin\theta}$$

A. $\frac{8}{3}$ B. $\frac{5}{3}$

C. $\frac{2}{3}$ D. 2

2. $\cos^2 72° + \cos^2 18° = ?$

A. 0 B. 1

C. –1 D. 2

3. $3\tan^2 30° + \sec^4 45° - \tan^2 60°$ is equal to :

A. 0 B. 1

C. 2 D. 3

4. The value of $\frac{\sin 10°}{\cos 80°}$ is :

A. 0 B. 1

C. 2 D. 3

5. If θ = 45 then $\frac{2\tan\theta}{1+\tan^2\theta}$ is :

A. 1 B. 0

C. 2 D. 3

6. If θ = 30° then cos 2θ is :

A. 0 B. 1

C. $\frac{1}{2}$ D. $\frac{\sqrt{3}}{2}$

7. What is the value of $\sin^2 35° + \sin^2 55°$?

A. 0 B. 1

C. $\frac{1}{2}$ D. 2

8. The value of tan 45° × cot 45° is :

A. 0 B. 1

C. 2 D. $\frac{1}{2}$

9. The value of sin(90° – θ) is :

A. cos θ B. sin θ

C. –cos θ D. None of these

10. What is the value of sin 30° × cosec 30°

A. 1 B. 0

C. $\frac{1}{2}$ D. 2

11. sin θ + cos θ = 1 where θ = ...

A. 30° B. 45°

C. 60° D. 90°

12. tan 45° × tan 82° is

A. 1 B. 0

C. 2 D. 3

13. The angle of elevation of the top of a tower from a point on the ground, which is 30 m away from the foot of the tower is 30°. The height of the tower is :

A. $8\sqrt{3}$ m B. $9\sqrt{3}$ m

C. $10\sqrt{3}$ m D. $12\sqrt{3}$ m

14. A kite is flying at a height of 60 m above the ground. The string attached to the kite is temporarily tied to a point on the ground. The inclination of the string with the ground is 60°. Find the length of the string, assuming that there is no slack in the string.

A. $40\sqrt{3}$ m B. $30\sqrt{3}$ m

C. $20\sqrt{3}$ m D. $10\sqrt{3}$ m

15. From a point on the ground, the angles of elevation of the bottom and top of a transmission tower fixed at the top of a 20 m high building are 45° and 60° respectively. The height of the tower is :

A. $25(\sqrt{3}-1)$ m

B. $20(\sqrt{3}-1)$ m

C. 20 m

D. 10 m

16. Two poles of equal heights are standing opposite to each other on either side of a road, which is 100 metres wide. From a point between them on the road, the angles of elevation of their tops are 30° and 60°. The height of each pole is

A. 44 m B. 43.25 m

C. 50 m D. 40.5 m

17. The angle of elevation of the top of a hill at the foot of a tower is 60° and the angle of elevation of top of the tower from the foot of the hill is 30°. If the tower is 50 m high, then the height of the hill is :

A. 148 m B. 150 m

C. 152 m D. 160 m

18. The angles of elevation of the top of a tower from two points *a* and *b* from the base and in the same straight line with it are complementary. The height of the tower is :

A. ab B. $\sqrt{ab}$

C. a^2b^2 D. None of these

19. The angles of elevation of the top of a tower from two points at the distances of 4 m and 9 m from the base of the tower and in the same straight line with it are complementary. The height of the tower is :

A. 8 m B. 5 m

C. 6 m D. 4 m

20. The value of $\frac{\tan 49°}{\cot 41°}$ is :

A. 1 B. 2

C. 0 D. 3

EXPLANATORY ANSWERS

1. A: $\frac{3\cos\theta + 2\sin\theta}{2\cos\theta - \sin\theta} = \frac{3\frac{\cos\theta}{\cos\theta}+2\frac{\sin\theta}{\cos\theta}}{2\frac{\cos\theta}{\cos\theta}-\frac{\sin\theta}{\cos\theta}}$

[Dividing both the numerator and denominator by cos θ]

$= \frac{3+2\tan\theta}{2-\tan\theta} = \frac{3+2\times\frac{1}{2}}{2-\frac{1}{2}}$ [Given 2 tan θ = 1 ∴ tan θ = $\frac{1}{2}$]

$= \frac{3+1}{3/2} = 4\times\frac{2}{3} = 2\frac{2}{3}.$

2. B: $\cos^2 72° + \cos^2 18° = \cos^2 (90 - 18°) + \cos^2 18°$

$= \sin^2 18° + \cos^2 18° = 1.$

3. C: $3\left(\frac{1}{\sqrt{3}}\right)^2 + (\sqrt{2})^2 - (\sqrt{3})^2$

$= 3\times\frac{1}{3}+4-3 = 2.$

4. B: $\frac{\sin 10°}{\cos(90°-10°)} = \frac{\sin 10°}{\sin 10°} = 1.$

5. A: $\frac{2\tan 45°}{1+\tan^2 45°} = \frac{2\times 1}{1+1} = \frac{2}{2} = 1.$

6. C: $\cos 2(30°) = \cos 60° = \dfrac{1}{2}$.

7. B: $\sin^2 35° + \sin^2(90° - 35°)$

$= \sin^2 35° + \cos^2 35° = 1.$ $\quad [\because \sin^2\theta + \cos^2\theta = 1]$

8. B: $\tan 45° \times \cot 45° = 1 \times 1 = 1.$

9. A: $\sin (90° - \theta) = \cos \theta.$

10.A: $\sin 30° \times \text{cosec } 30° = \dfrac{1}{2} \times \dfrac{2}{1} = \dfrac{1}{1} = 1.$

11.D: Put $\theta = 90°$ then $\sin \theta + \cos \theta = \sin 90° + \cos 90° = 1 + 0 = 1.$

12.A: $\tan 45° \times \tan 8° \cdot \tan (90° - 8°)$

$= \tan 45° \times \tan 8° \times \cot 8° = 1 \times 1 = 1.$

13.C: Let AB be the tower. The angle of elevation of the top A of the tower from a point C on the ground which is 30 metres away from the foot of the tower is 30°.

$\therefore \quad \angle ACB = 30°$

and $\quad BC = 30$ m.

From right ΔABC, we have

$$\frac{AB}{BC} = \tan 30°$$

$$\Rightarrow \quad AB = BC \tan 30° = 30 \times \frac{1}{\sqrt{3}} = 10\sqrt{3} \text{ m.}$$

14.A: Let AB = height of kite = 60 m and the inclination of the string AC is 60°.

From right-angled ΔABC, we have

$$\frac{AC}{AB} = \text{cosec } 60°$$

$$\Rightarrow \quad \frac{AC}{60} = \frac{2}{\sqrt{3}} \Rightarrow AC = 60 \times \frac{2}{\sqrt{3}} = 40\sqrt{3} \text{ m.}$$

15.A: Let AB = 20 m be the building and AC be the transmission tower fixed at the top of building. From a point D on the ground, the angle of elevation of the bottom and top of transmission tower are 45° and 60°.

$\therefore \angle ADB = 45°$ and $\angle CDB = 60°$

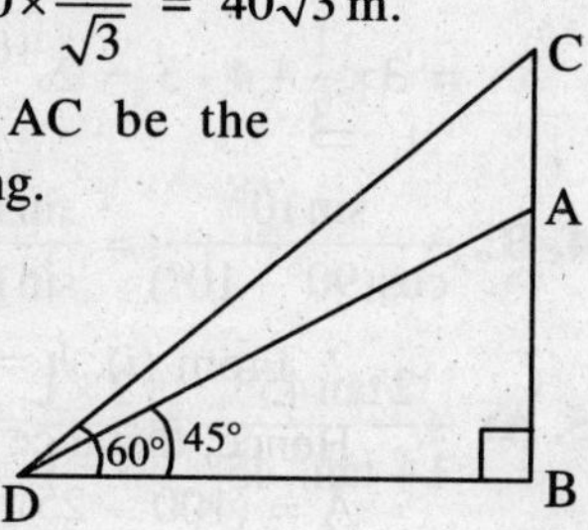

From right ΔABD, we have

$$\frac{AB}{BD} = \tan 45° = 1$$

$\therefore$ $AB = BD$

$\Rightarrow$ $BD = 20$ m $\quad [\because AB = 20 \text{ m}]$

From right-angled ΔCBD, we have

$$\frac{BC}{BD} = \tan 60°$$

$\Rightarrow$ $BC = BD \tan 60°$

$= 20 \times \sqrt{3} = 20\sqrt{3}$ m

Now $AC = BC - AB = 20\sqrt{3} - 20$

$= 20(\sqrt{3} - 1)$ m.

Hence the height of the tower $= 20(\sqrt{3} - 1)$ m.

16.B: Let AB and CD be the two poles of equal height h metres standing on either side of the road AC = 100 metres.

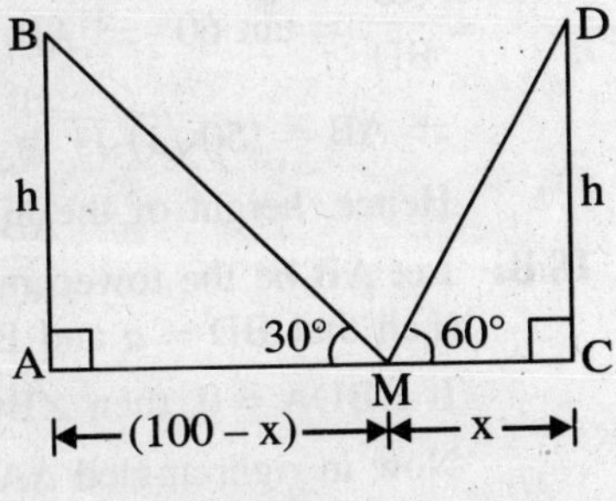

Let M be the point at which the poles AB, CD subtend angles of 30° and 60° respectively.

Let CM = x metres so that

AM = $(100 - x)$ metres

In right-angled ΔMCD, $\frac{h}{x} = \tan 60°$

$\Rightarrow$ $h = x\sqrt{3}$ ...(*i*)

In right-angled ΔMAB,

$$\frac{h}{100 - x} = \tan 30° \Rightarrow \frac{h}{100 - x} = \frac{1}{\sqrt{3}}$$

$\Rightarrow$ $h\sqrt{3} = 100 - x \Rightarrow (x\sqrt{3})\sqrt{3} = 100 - x$

$3x = 100 - x$

$4x = 100; \ x = 100 \div 4 = 25$ m

$\therefore$ From (*i*), $h = x\sqrt{3} = 25 \times 1.73 = 43.25$ m

Hence, distance of point M from C = 25 m and distance of point from A = (100 – 25)m = 75 m. Height of each pole = 43.25 m.

17.B: Let AB be the hill and CD the tower.

$$\angle BDA = 60° \text{ and } \angle DBC = 30°$$

$$CD = 50 \text{ m.}$$

Let AB = h metres

In right-angled ΔADC,

$$\frac{CD}{BD} = \tan 30°$$

$$\Rightarrow \quad BD = \frac{CD}{\tan 30°}$$

$$= CD \cot 30°$$

$$\Rightarrow \quad BD = 50\sqrt{3} \text{ metres}$$

Now in right-angled ΔABD, we have

$$\frac{AB}{BD} = \tan 60° \Rightarrow AB = BD \tan 60°$$

$$\Rightarrow AB = (50\sqrt{3})\sqrt{3} = 150 \text{ m.}$$

Hence, height of the hill is 150 m.

18.B: Let AB be the tower and C and D be the two points such that BD = a and BC = b.

If ∠BDA = θ, then ∠BCA = 90° – θ

Now in right-angled ΔABD,

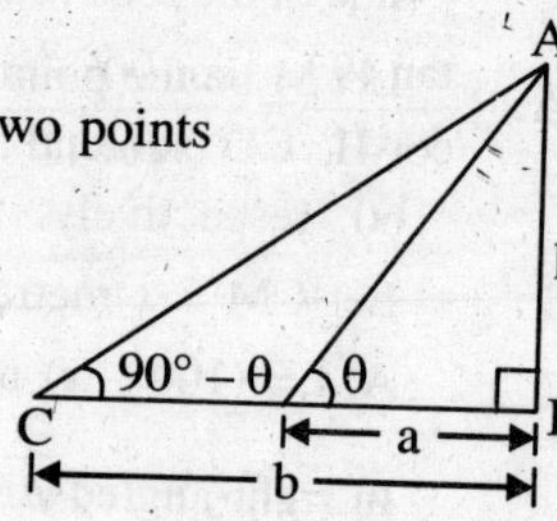

$$\frac{AB}{BD} = \tan\theta \Rightarrow \frac{h}{a} = \tan\theta$$

$$\therefore \quad h = a\tan\theta \qquad ...(i)$$

In right-angled ΔABC,

$$\frac{AB}{BC} = \tan(90° - \theta) = \cot\theta$$

$$\Rightarrow \quad \frac{h}{b} = \cot\theta \Rightarrow h = b\cot\theta \qquad ...(ii)$$

multiplying (i) and (ii), we get

$$h^2 = ab\tan\theta\cot\theta = ab\tan\theta \times \frac{1}{\tan\theta} = ab.$$

$$\therefore \quad h = \sqrt{ab}.$$

19.C: Let AB be the tower and C and D be the two points such that BD = 4 m and BC = 9 m.

If $\angle BDA = \theta$, then $\angle BCA = 90° - \theta$

Now in right-angled ΔABD,

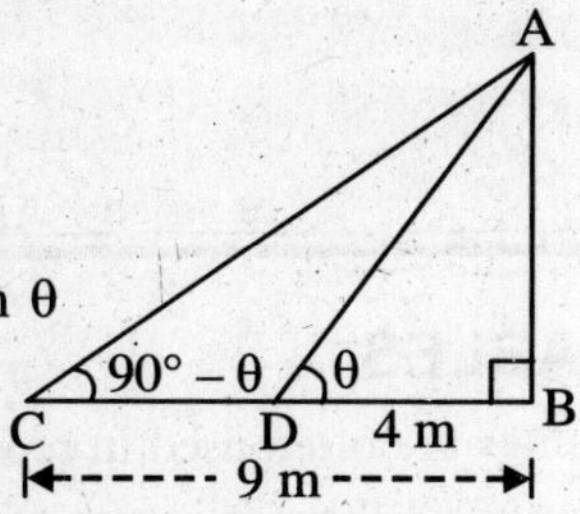

$$\frac{AB}{BD} = \tan\theta \Rightarrow \frac{h}{4} = \tan\theta$$

$$\therefore \quad h = 4\tan\theta \quad ...(i)$$

In right-angled ΔABC,

$$\frac{AB}{BC} = \tan(90° - \theta) = \cot\theta$$

$$\Rightarrow \quad \frac{h}{9} = \cot\theta \Rightarrow h = 9\cot\theta \quad ...(ii)$$

multiplying (*i*) and (*ii*), we get

$$h^2 = 36\tan\theta\cot\theta = 36\tan\theta \times \frac{1}{\tan\theta} = 36.$$

$$\therefore \quad h = \pm\sqrt{36} = 6 \text{ m}.$$

20.A: $\frac{\tan 49°}{\cot 41°} = \frac{\tan(90° - 41°)}{\cot 41°} = \frac{\cot 41°}{\cot 41°} = 1$ $\quad [\because \tan(90° - \theta) = \cot\theta]$

21

DATA TABLES

TABLES

Tables are often used in reports, magazines and newspaper to present as set of numerical data. It is one of the easiest and most accurate ways of presenting data. One of the main purposes of tables is to make complicated information easier to understand. Hence, the advantage of presenting data in a table is that one can see the information at a glance. We present below an example of tabular presentation of annual expenditure of 5 families for last 5 years.

Annual Expenditure of 5 families (in ₹ Thousands)

Years → Families ↓	**2008**	**2009**	**2010**	**2011**	**2012**
A	35	50	55	60	70
B	40	60	65	75	80
C	45	50	70	80	95
D	30	40	45	50	75
E	50	55	60	70	90

Essentials of a Tables:

(*i*) **Title:** Heading of the table

(*ii*) **Stub:** The section of the table containing row headings in called Stub.

(*iii*) **Column Captions** : The heading of each column is designated as column caption.

(*iv*) **Body**

(*v*) **Footnotes**

(*vi*) **Source**

EXERCISE

Directions (Qs. 1 to 4) : *Study the table carefully and answer the following questions.*

Division of students based on commercial streams

Stream	Department			
	Art		Science	
	Girls	Boys	Girls	Boys
1. Business management	25	45	25	65
2. Typewriting	23	186	20	32
3. Casting	25	120	12	58
4. Typewriting & casting	12	100	3	5

1. If 60% girls and 70% Boys are passed in their respective streams, then what is the total pass per cent?

A. 58 B. 66
C. 54 D. 62

2. What is the percentage difference between total number of students from Business management and casting and number of students from typewriting.

A. 44 B. 66
C. 33 D. 55

3. What is the percentage of boys in costing stream from art department?

A. 27 B. 10
C. 18 D. 15

4. What is percentage difference between total number of boys and girls?

A. 321 B. 280
C. 308 D. 250

Directions (Qs. 5 to 9) : *Study the following table to answer these questions.*

Average Hourly Wage (in ₹) by Age Group

Years	18 – 20 years		21 – 23 years	
	Male	Female	Male	Female
2007	15.1	15.1	29.7	25.1
2008	12.4	13.4	21.0	19.1
2009	10.0	13.8	14.7	16.9
2010	11.0	13.4	18.0	20.5
2011	21.2	16.3	29.1	32.7
2012	15.0	21.0	32.1	33.9

5. In 2011, for the 21-23 years age group, the wages for the females was approximately what per cent of that of the males?

A. 220 B. 30
C. 85 D. 110

6. What was the difference between the average wages of males and of females for the 21 – 23 years age group?

A. 0.80 B. 0.60
C. 0.40 D. 0.20

7. In how many years was the wage for the females higher than that of males in both the age groups?

A. Three B. Four
C. Two D. One

8. In the age group of 18–20 years, in which year was the wage-disparity maximum?

A. 2010 B. 2011
C. 2009 D. 2012

9. In the age group of 21–23 years, in which year was the wage-disparity minimum?

A. 2008 B. 2012
C. 2009 D. 2007

Directions (Qs. 10 to 15) : *Answer these questions on the basis of the data given in the following table indicating the trend in sales of four companies. The amounts given are in lakhs of rupees :*

Year	Name of the Company			
	Dowby	Alpha	Baron	Celia
2004	12.00	2.00	18.50	12.00
2005	10.00	5.00	15.00	16.00
2006	18.00	7.50	16.50	15.00
2007	20.00	11.50	14.50	36.00
2008	25.00	15.00	50.00	48.00

10. Which company has shown consistently an increasing sales average?

A. Alpha B. Baron
C. Celia D. Dowby

11. The cumulative sales of all the companies put together in 2005 was how much of the sales of 2008?

A. $\frac{3}{7}$ B. $\frac{2}{5}$

C. $\frac{1}{4}$ D. $\frac{1}{3}$

12. What was the average sales of Baron over the 5 years?

A. 22.90 B. 21.90
C. 23.90 D. 20.90

13. Which company faced a decline in sales in 2007 over its previous year?

A. Alpha B. Baron
C. Celia D. Dowby

14. The ratio of the highest turnover of any company in any year to the lowest turnover of any company in any year is

A. 25 B. 15
C. 2.5 D. 0.25

15. How many companies had the same turnover in the same year?

A. 1 B. 2
C. 3 D. 4

EXPLANATORY ANSWERS

1. D:

2. A: Number of students in Business management stream = 160 and number of students in typewriting = 261
Number of students in casting = 215

$$\text{Required percent} = \left(\frac{160+215-261}{261}\right)\times 100 = 44\% \text{ (Approx).}$$

3. A: $\text{Required percent} = \frac{(25+120)}{536}\times 100 = 27\%.$

.. A: Total number of boys = 45 + 65 + 186 + 32 + 120 + 58 + 100 + 5 = 611

Total number of girs = 25 + 23 + 25 + 12 + 25 + 20 + 12 + 13 = 145

$$\text{Required per cent} = \left(\frac{611-145}{145}\right)\times 100 = 321\%.$$

5. D: $\text{Required percentage} = \frac{32.7}{29.1} \times 100 = 112.37 \approx 110\%.$

6. B:

7. A:

Year	Wage for male 18-20 years + 21-23 years	Wage for female 18-20 years + 21 – 23 years
2007	₹ 44.8	₹ 40.2
2008	₹ 33.4	₹ 32.5
2009	₹ 24.7	₹ 30.7
2010	₹ 29.0	₹ 33.9
2011	₹ 50.3	₹ 49.0
2012	₹ 47.1	₹ 54.9

Hence, in three years the wage of females was higher than that of male.

8. D: In 2012 wage for male (18-20 years) was ₹ 15.0 white wage for female was ₹ 21.0. Obviously it is maximum wage disparity.

9. B: In 2012 wage for male (21-23 years) was ₹ 32.1 white wage for female was ₹ 33.9. Obviously it is minimum wage-disparity.

10. A: Of course, Alpha has shown consistently increasing sales average.

11. C:

Year	Total Sales of all the Companies	Cumulative Sales
2004	44.50	44.50
2005	46.00	90.50
2006	57.00	147.50
2007	82.00	229.00
2008	138.00	367.50

Let, $90.50 = K \times 367.50$

$$\Rightarrow \quad K = \frac{90.50}{367.50} = \frac{181}{735} \approx \frac{1}{4}.$$

12. A: $\frac{18.50 + 15.00 + 16.50 + 14.50 + 50.00}{5} = \frac{114.50}{5} = 22.90.$

13. B: Obviously, Baron faced a decline in sales.

14. A: $\frac{50}{2} = 25$

15. B: In 2004, Celia and Dowby.

22

BAR GRAPHS

BAR GRAPHS

Given quantity of a bar graph can be compared by the height or length. A bar graph can have either vertical or horizontal bars. You can compare different quantities or the same quantity at the different times. The bars may be placed adjacent to each other or may be separated from each other by spaces depending upon the problem.

For Illustration:

Registration of New Vehicles in Delhi (in thousands)

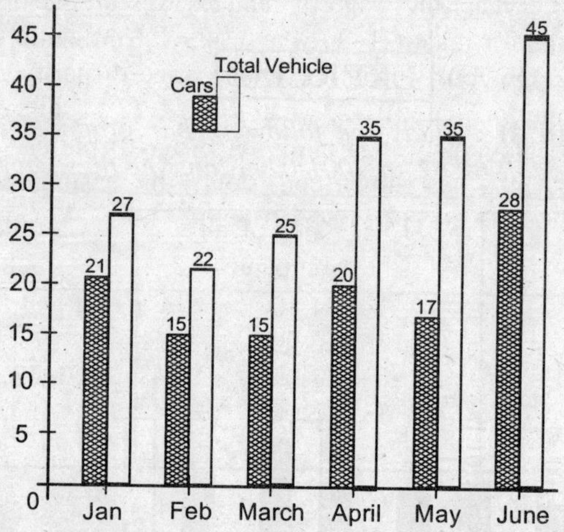

CUMULATIVE GRAPH

These are usually bar or line graphs where the height of the bar or line is divided up proportionally among various quantities presented in the graph. The representation of quantities may be done in terms of either percentage of the total or in absolute figures. These are also called sub-divided graphs. Thus, cumulative graph may be conveniently used for making comparisons.

For Illustration:

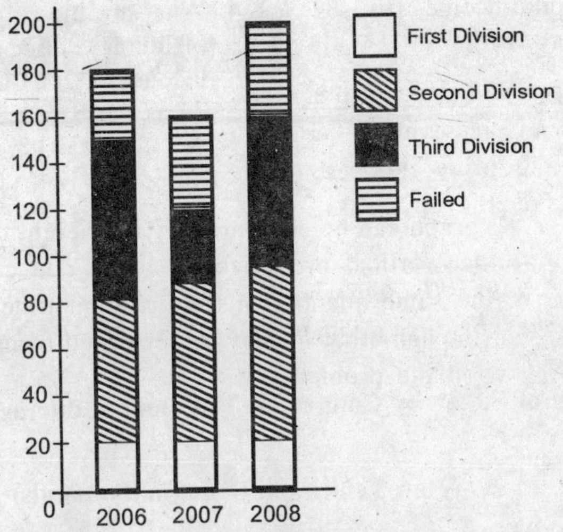

EXERCISE

Directions (Qs. 1 to 4) : *Study the following bar graph giving Economic Indices for the period 1961-62 to 2001-02 to answer these questions.*

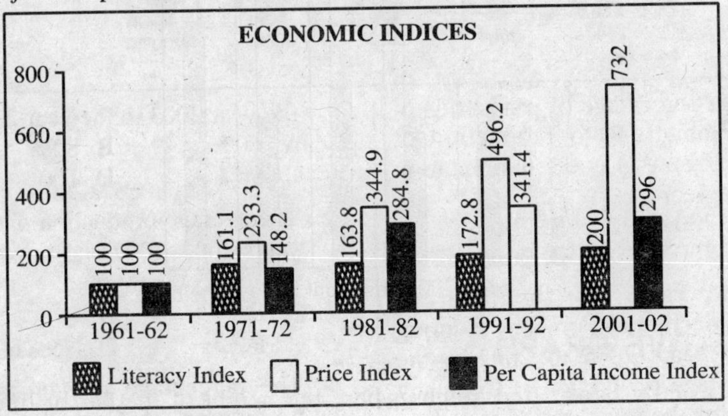

1. What is the average annual percentage increase in literacy index from 1961-62 to 2001-02?

A. 25% B. 15.8%

C. 18.3% D. 4.9%

2. Of the three economic indices which index for which period shows the maximum percentage increase as compared to the previous period?

A. Literacy, 1971-72
B. Price, 2001-02
C. Per capita income, 1981-82
D. Price, 1971-72

3. In which period the per capita income index increases at a faster rate than the price index as compared to the preceding period?

A. 1971-72 B. 2001-02
C. 1981-82 D. 1991-92

4. What are the respective indices of literacy, price and per capita income for 2001-02 taking 1971-72 as the base period?

A. 124.1, 313.8, 200
B. 313.8, 124, 201
C. 313.8, 124.1, 190
D. 124.1, 313.8, 194

Directions (Qs. 5 to 9) : *The following bar graph indicates the production of sugar (in lakh tonnes) by three different sugar companies P, Q and R over the years 2003 to 2007.*

Production of Sugar by Companies P, Q and R during 2003–2007.

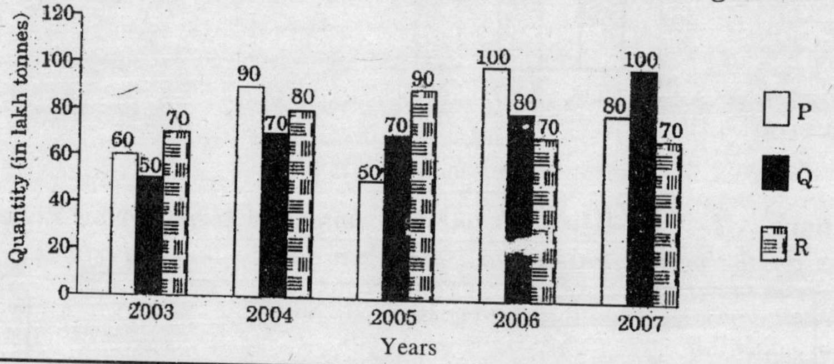

5. The percentage of production of Company R to production of Company Q is the maximum in the year

A. 2005 B. 2004
C. 2003 D. 2006

6. The ratio of the average production of Company P during the years 2005 to 2007 to the average production of Company Q for the same period is

A. 15 : 17 B. 23 : 25
C. 27 : 29 D. 9 : 11

7. The percentage increase in production of Company Q from the year 2003 to the year 2007 is

A. 60% B. 80%
C. 90% D. 100%

8. The average production over the years 2003–2007 was maximum for the Company(ies)

A. R B. Q
C. P D. None of these

9. The percentage rise or fall in production of Company Q as compared to the previous year is the maximum in the year

A. 2006 B. 2005
C. 2004 D. 2007

Directions (Qs. 10 to 13) : *Study the following graph to answer these questions.*

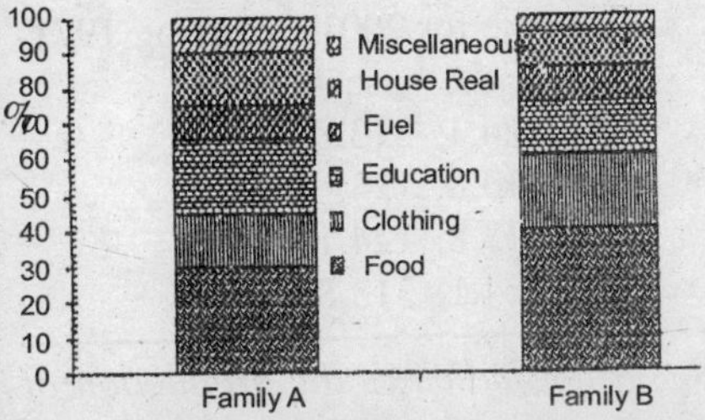

10. What fraction of the total expenditure is spent on education in family A?

A. 9/13
B. 2/3
C. 13/21
D. 1/5

11. If the total expenditure of family B is ₹ 10,000, then money spent on clothes by this family during the years is

A. ₹ 2,000 B. ₹ 600
C. ₹ 200 D. ₹ 6,000

12. If the total annual expenditure of family A is ₹ 30,000, the money spent on food, clothes and house rent is

A. ₹ 21,000 B. ₹ 18,000
C. ₹ 18,500 D. ₹ 15,000

13. What percentage is B's expenditure on food over A's expenditure on food, taking equal total expenditure?

A. 133.33% B. 70%
C. 10% D. 75%

EXPLANATORY ANSWERS

1. A: Average percentage increase = $\frac{200-100}{4}$ = 25%.

2. D: Price index of 1971-72 shows 133.3% increase which is maximum.

3. C:

Years	Per Capita Income Index	Price Index
71-72	48.20%	133.30%
81-82	67.88%	47.83%
91-92	19.87%	43.87%
01-02	Negative	47.52%

According to above table in 81-82. The Per capita income index increases at faster rate than the price index.

4. A:

5. C: In 2003, required percentage = $\frac{70}{50} \times 100 = 140\%$

In 2004, required percentage = $\frac{80}{70} \times 100 = 114.2\%$

In 2005, required percentage = $\frac{90}{70} \times 100 = 128.57\%$

Thus, in 2003 required percentage was maximum.

6. B: Required ratio = (50 + 100 + 80) : (70 + 80 + 100)
= 230 : 250 = 23 : 25

7. D: Required increase percentage

$$= \frac{100 - 50}{50} \times 100 = 100\%$$

8. A: Obviously that is R.

9. D: Obviously that year is 2007.

10. D: Required ratio = $\frac{20}{100} = \frac{1}{5}$.

11. A: Money spend on clothes by family B = $1000 \times \frac{20}{100}$ = ₹ 2000.

12. B: Required expenditure = $30000 \times \frac{(30 + 15 + 15)}{100}$ = ₹ 18000.

13. A: Required percentage = $\frac{40}{30} \times 100$ = 133.33%.

23

FREQUENCY POLYGON

FREQUENCY POLYGON

Frequency Polygon are used to show how a quantity changes continuously. If the line goes up, the quantity is increasing; if the line goes down, the quantity is decreasing; if the line is horizontal, the quantity is not changing.

For Illustration:

Demand and Production of rubber (in thousand tons) in various years

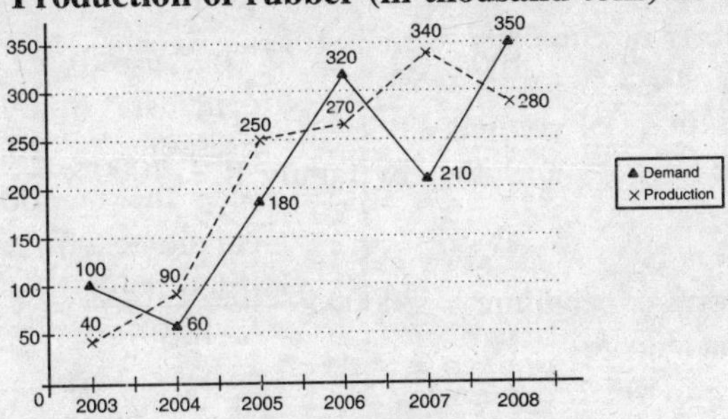

EXERCISE

Directions (Qs. 1 to 4) : *Study the given graph carefully to answer these questions.*

The following graph shows the ratio of imports to exports by two companies A and B over the years.

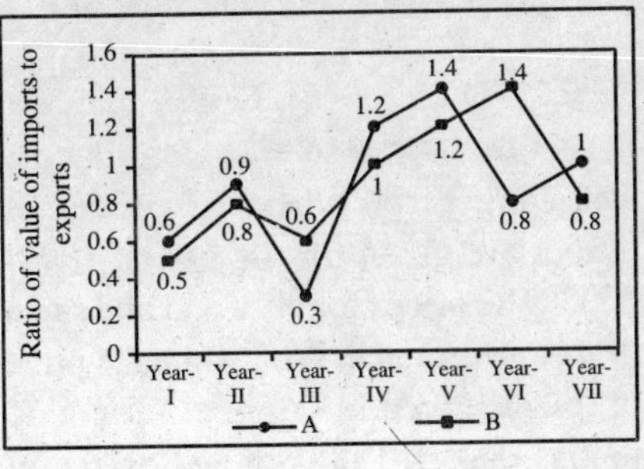

1. If the imports of company A in Year – VI were ₹ 10.40 crore, what were the exports of company A in the same year?

A. 13 crore B. 12.75 crore

C. 12.50 crore D. 13.75 crore

2. It is supposed that Imports – Exports = 'x' for company A in Year-I and the imports of company A in Year-I were ₹ 3.6 crore, and it is also supposed that Imports – Exports = 'a' for company B in Year-V and the exports of company B in Year-V were ₹ 5 crore. What is the relationship between 'a' and 'x'?

A. $x > a$ B. $x = a$
C. $a > x$ D. $x \neq a$

3. If the exports of company B in Year-III were ₹ 2.19 crore, what were the imports of company B in the same year?

A. 3.65 crore
B. 1.314 crore
C. 1.214 crore
D. 1.414 crore

4. If the imports of company A in Year-V were ₹ 8.40 crore, what were the exports of company B in Year-VII?

A. 6 crore
B. 7.40 crore
C. 7.20 crore
D. Data inadequate

Directions (Qs. 5 to 8) : *The following graph shows the number of successful candidates from different schools (A to F) in different disciplines. Study the graph carefully to answer these questions.*

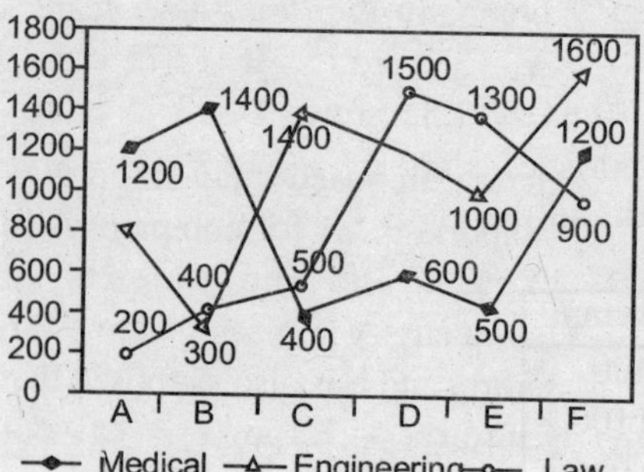

5. In which of the following institutes is the difference between the number of successful candidates in Engineering and that in Medical discipline the maximum?

A. F B. C
C. B D. D

6. The total number of successful candidates from Medical discipline is approximately what per cent more than that from Law?

A. 8% B. 15%
C. 12% D. 10%

7. The number of successful candidates from F in Engineering discipline is what per cent more than the number of successful candidates from A in Medical discipline?

A. 30% B. 25%
C. $33\frac{1}{3}\%$ D. 20%

8. In which of the following institutes is the sum of the number of successful candidates in Engineering and Law disciplines 50% of the number of Medical students of the same institute?

A. C B. E
C. D D. B

Directions (Qs. 9 to 12) : Consider the following graph where the prices of timber are given for the period 1997-2003. The prices for plywood and sawn timber are given in ₹/m^3 while the price of logs is given in ₹/tonne. Assume 1 ton is equal to 1,000 kg and one cu.m of log weigh 800 kg.

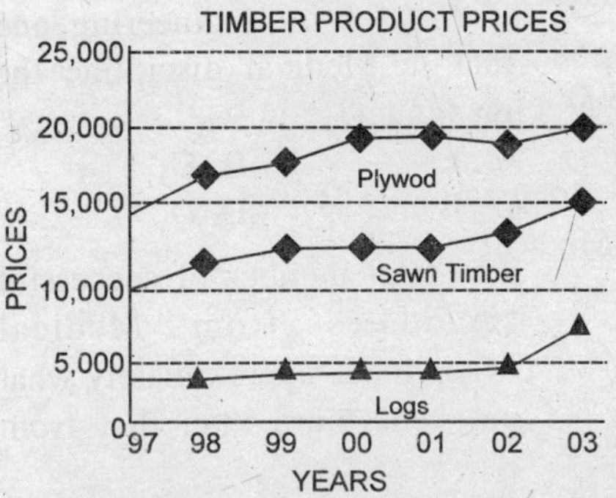

9. Which product had the largest percentage increase in price per cubic meter over the 7-year period ?

A. Sawn timber
B. Logs
C. Plywood
D. None of these

10. The maximum increase in price per cubic metre for any product over any two successive years was :

A. ₹ 2,500 B. ₹ 3,125
C. ₹ 2,000 D. ₹ 4,125

11. In 2003, the total sales of the company measured in cubic metres was made up of 40% plywood, 30% sawn timber and 30% logs. The average realisation per cubic metre in 2003 was closest to :

A. ₹ 16,500 B. ₹ 13,500
C. ₹ 15,000 D. ₹ 18,000

12. In 2004, the prices of plywood, sawn timber and logs went up by 5%, 1% and 10%, respectively, and the total sales were made up of 40% plywood, 30% sawn timber and 30% logs. The average realisation per cubic metre in 2004 was closest to :

A. ₹ 15,500 B. ₹ 16,500
C. ₹ 14,500 D. ₹ 18,500

EXPLANATORY ANSWERS

1. A:

2. C: x = ₹ 3.6 crore – ₹ $\frac{3.6}{0.6}$ crore = – ₹ 2.4 crore

a = ₹ 5 crore × 1.2 – ₹ 5 crore = ₹ 1 crore

Thus, $a > x$.

3. B: Required exports = ₹ 2.19 crore × 0.6 = ₹ 1.314 crore.

4. D: There is no relation between imports of company A in year-V and exports of company B in year-VIII and the given data is not sufficient to answer the question.

5. B:

Institute	Required difference
A	1200 – 800 = 400
B	1400 – 300 = 1100
C	1400 – 400 = 1000
D	1200 – 600 = 600
E	1000 – 500 = 500
F	1600 – 1200 = 400.

6. D: Total number of successful candidates in Medical = 5300, Law = 4800

$$\text{Required percentage} = \frac{5300 \times 4800}{4800} \times 100 = 10.4\% = 10\%.$$

7. C: Successful candidates from F in Engineering = 1600
Successful candidates from A in Medical = 1200

$$\text{Required percentage} = \frac{1600 - 1200}{1200} \times 100$$

$$= \frac{100}{3} = 33\frac{1}{3}\%.$$

8. D:

	A	B	C	D	E	F
Medical	1200	1400	400	600	500	1200
Engineering	800	300	1400	1200	1000	1600
Law	200	400	500	1500	1300	900

Hence, in B the total number of successful candidates of Engineering and Law is 50% of the number of candidates of Medical.

9. B: $$\text{Increase in plywood} = \frac{(20{,}000 - 14000)}{14000} \times 100 = 42.86\%$$

$$\text{Increase in Sawn Timber} = \frac{15000 - 10000}{10000} \times 100 = 50\%$$

$$\text{Increase in Logs} = \frac{\frac{7500}{1.25} - \frac{4000}{1.25}}{\frac{4000}{1.25}} \times 100 = 87.5\%$$

Hence, Logs had the largest increase in prices.

10. A: In plywood during 97 to 98 the price rise is about ₹ 2500 and it is maximum.

11. C: 40% of ₹ 20000 = $20000 \times \frac{40}{100}$ = ₹ 8000

30% of ₹ 15000 = $15000 \times \frac{30}{100}$ = ₹ 4500

30% of ₹ 7500 = $7500 \times \frac{30}{100}$ = ₹ 2250

Total = ₹ 8000 + ₹ 4500 + ₹ 2250 = ₹ 14750 ≈ ₹ 15000.

Hence, correct answer in C

12. A:

24

PIE CHARTS

PIE CHARTS

These are used to show the share of various sectors in the total. They usually show the percentage share of each sector in the whole (taken as 100%). In such representation the total quantity in question is distributed over a total angle of 360°. The area of each sector is proportional to the relative frequency of the class represented by the sector.

$$\text{Sector angle} = \frac{\text{Class frequency}}{\text{Total frequency}} \times 360°$$

For Illustration:

Distribution of Expenditure of a family

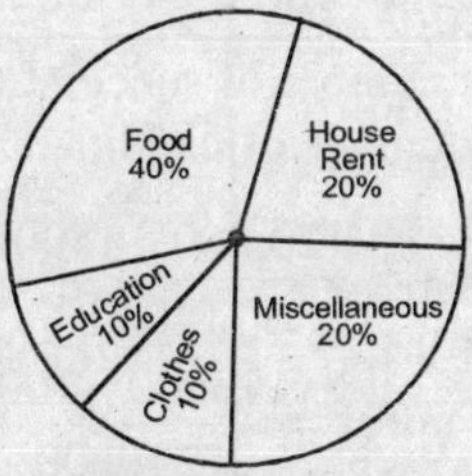

EXERCISE

Directions (Qs. 1 to 4) : *Study the pie-chart carefully to answer the questions that follow:*

Percentage-wise Break up of Students in terms of Specialization in MBA

TOTAL NUMBER OF STUDENTS = 8000

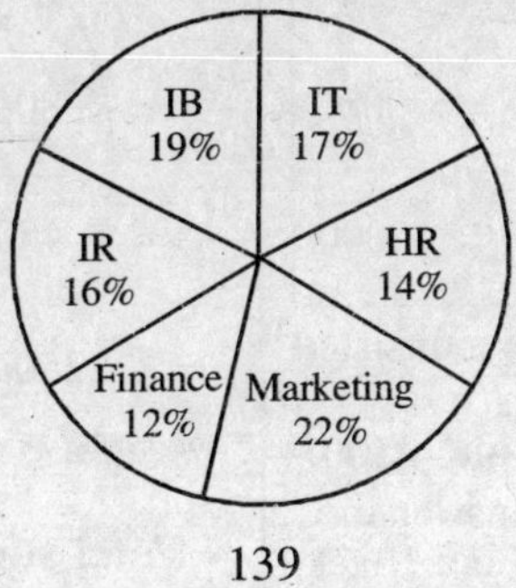

1. What is the total number of students having specialization in IR, Marketing and IT?

A. 4640 B. 4080
C. 4260 D. 4400

2. Students having IB as specialization forms **approximately** what per cent of students having Marketing as specialization?

A. 116 B. 86
C. 124 D. 74

3. What is the total number of students having IB as specilization?

A. 1520 B. 1280
C. 1360 D. 1120

4. What is the respective ratio of the students having Finance as specialization to that of students having HR as specialization?

A. 11 : 19 B. 18 : 13
C. 6 : 7 D. 12 : 21

Directions (Qs. 5 to 8) : *Study the graph below to answer these questions.*

Sale of Cycles of different colours

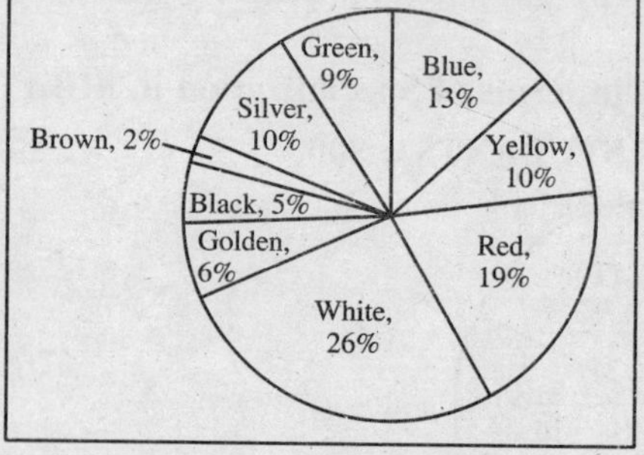

5. 50% of all the cycles consisted of which colours?

A. Black, Golden, Blue, Red
B. Blue, Black, Red, Silver
C. White, Golden, Blue, Black
D. Golden, Green, Black, White

6. Cycles of which colour when increased by two per cent and then combined with that of red cycles will make 30 per cent of the total?

A. Golden
B. Blue
C. Black
D. None of these

7. If in certain period the total production of all cycles was 95400 then how many more blue cycles were sold than green?

A. 2580 B. 3618
C. 2850 D. 3816

8. Cycles of which colour are 20% less popular than white coloured cycles?

A. Black
B. Golden
C. Blue
D. None of these

Directions (Qs. 9 to 12) : *Study the pir-chart below to answer these questions. The chart gives the composition of solar radiation.*

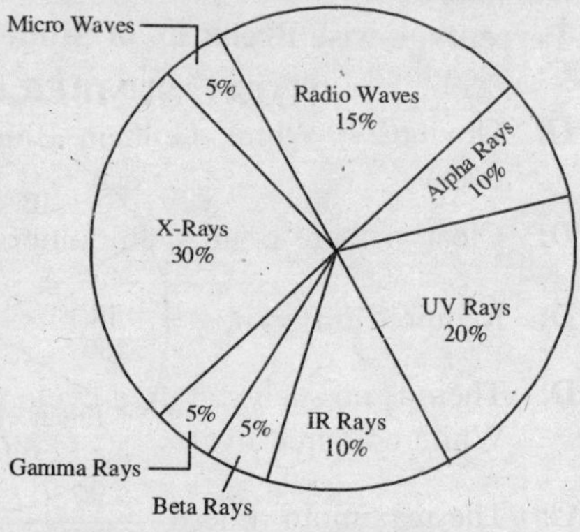

Total sun rays received in one minute = 3600 units

9. If the human body can withstand a maximum of 9720 units of IR rays when exposed to the sun continuously, then what is the maximum time in minutes that any person could stand in the sun without crossing the threshold limit of IR rays?

A. 23 B. 19

C. 27 D. 29

10. The amount of Beta rays in 10 minutes of the sun rays is how many times the amount of IR rays in 3 minutes of the sun rays?

A. 1.44 B. 1.33

C. 1.66 D. None of these

11. How many minutes of exposure to the sun in a day would be enough to ensure that the body receives enough amount of Vitamin D, given that the body requires 40 units of Vitamin D every day and that 30 units of Beta rays generate one unit of Vitamin D?

A. $5\frac{1}{3}$ B. $5\frac{2}{3}$

C. $6\frac{1}{3}$ D. $6\frac{2}{3}$

12. The amount of Alpha rays received in two minutes is how much more/ less than the amount of Radio waves received in 4 minutes?

A. 1320 units more

B. 1200 units less

C. 1440 units less

D. 1600 units more

EXPLANATORY ANSWERS

1. D:

2. B: Required percentage $= \frac{19}{22} \times 100 = 86.36\% \approx 86\%$

3. A: Required number of Students $= \frac{19}{100} \times 8000 = 1520$

4. C: Required ratio = 12 : 14 = 6 : 7

5. C: Obviously, White, Golden, Blue and Black colours consists 50% of cycles.

6. D: Clearly, there is no such colours.

7. D: Required difference $= 95400 \times \frac{(13-9)}{100} = 954 \times 4 = 3816.$

8. D: There is no such coloured cycle which is exactly 20% less popular than White coloured cycles.

9. C: The maximum time $= \frac{9720}{\frac{3600 \times 10}{100}} = 27.$

10. D:

11. D: 40 units of vitamin D generate from

$$= 40 \times 30 = 1200 \text{ units of } \beta\text{-rays}$$

The amount of β-rays received in 1 min.

$$= \frac{5}{100} \times 3600 = 180 \text{ units}$$

Hence, required time $= \frac{1200}{180} = 6\frac{2}{3}$ min.

12. C: The amount of a-rays received in 2 min.

$$= \frac{10}{100} \times 3600 \times 2 = 720 \text{ units}$$

The amount of radio waves received in 4 min.

$$= \frac{15}{100} \times 3600 \times 4 = 2160 \text{ units}$$

Required difference = 2160 − 720 = 1440 units less.

25

MISCELLANEOUS QUESTIONS

1. When three right hand side digits of a number are 1,000 the number is divisible by:

A. 4
B. 5
C. 9
D. All the above

2. When the two right hand side digits of a number are 100, the number is divisible by:

A. 2
B. 4
C. 5
D. All the above

3. When the last digit of a number is 5, the number is divisible by:

A. 3
B. 5
C. 25
D. All the above

4. The H.C.F. of the product of first six odd numbers and the product of first six even numbers is:

A. 45 B. 40
C. 34 D. 30

5. $1\frac{1}{2}+\frac{1}{7}\times 10\frac{1}{2}-2\frac{1}{3}\div 1\frac{3}{4}$ of $1\frac{1}{3}$ is equal to:

A. 1 B. 2
C. 3 D. 4

6. $6\frac{1}{2}-\left[5\frac{1}{2}-\left\{4\frac{1}{2}-\left(3\frac{1}{2}-2\frac{1}{2}-\frac{1}{2}\right)\right\}\right]$ is equal to:

A. 4 B. 3
C. 2 D. 1

7. $\frac{1}{2}+\frac{2}{3}/\frac{3}{7}-\frac{1}{6}$ is equal to:

A. $5\frac{4}{11}$ B. $3\frac{5}{11}$
C. $4\frac{5}{11}$ D. $7\frac{6}{21}$

8. The sum of $\frac{1}{2}, \frac{1}{4}, \frac{1}{8}$ of a number is 28. The number is:

A. 24 B. 28
C. 32 D. 36

9. If 20 men can finish a piece of work in 10 days, how many persons can finish the same job in 4 days?

A. 20 B. 30
C. 40 D. 50

10. If 15 men can finish a job in 20 days, 25 men will finish the same job in:

A. 8 days B. 12 days
C. 16 days D. 12 days

EXPLANATORY ANSWERS

1. D: For example, consider the number 1000. The multiples of 1000 are 125 and 8, while the multiples of 125 and 8 are 5 and 4. Hence, the number is divisible by 4, 5 as well as 8.

2. D.

3. B.

4. A: First six odd numbers are 1, 3, 5, 7, 9, 11

Product of first six odd numbers = 1 × 3 × 5 × 7 × 9 × 11

= 1 × 3 × 5 × 7 × 3 × 3 × 11

First six even numbers are 2, 4, 6, 8, 10, 12

Product of first six even numbers = 2 × 4 × 6 × 8 × 10 × 12

= 2 × 2 × 2 × 2 × 3 × 2 × 2 × 2 × 2 × 5 × 2 × 2 × 3

The common factors are 3, 3, 5.

∴ H.C.F. = 3 × 3 × 5 = 45.

5. B: $1\frac{1}{2}+\frac{1}{7}\times 10\frac{1}{2}-2\frac{1}{3}\div 1\frac{3}{4} \text{ of } 1\frac{1}{3} = \frac{3}{2}+\frac{1}{7}\times\frac{21}{2}-\frac{7}{3}\div\frac{7}{4} \text{ of } \frac{4}{3}$

$= \frac{3}{2}+\frac{3}{2}-\frac{7}{3}\div\frac{7}{3} = \frac{3}{2}+\frac{3}{2}-\frac{7}{3}\times\frac{3}{7} = \frac{3}{2}+\frac{3}{2}-1 = \frac{3}{2}+\frac{1}{2} = 2.$

6. A: $6\frac{1}{2}-\left[5\frac{1}{2}-\left\{4\frac{1}{2}-\left(3\frac{1}{2}-\overline{2\frac{1}{2}-\frac{1}{2}}\right)\right\}\right]$

$= \frac{13}{2}-\left[\frac{11}{2}-\left\{\frac{9}{2}-\left(\frac{7}{2}-2\right)\right\}\right] = \frac{13}{2}-\left[\frac{11}{2}-\left\{\frac{9}{2}-\frac{3}{2}\right\}\right]$

$= \frac{13}{2}-\left[\frac{11}{2}-3\right] = \frac{13}{2}-\frac{5}{2} = 4.$

7. C: $\frac{1}{2}+\frac{2}{3}/\frac{3}{7}-\frac{1}{6} = \frac{7}{6}/\frac{11}{42} = \frac{7}{6}\times\frac{42}{11} = \frac{49}{11} = 4\frac{5}{11}.$

8. C: Let the number be x.

$\therefore \frac{x}{2}+\frac{x}{4}+\frac{x}{8} = 28$, or $\frac{7}{x} = 28$ $\qquad \therefore x = \frac{28\times 8}{7} = 32.$

9. D: Work can be finished in 10 days by 20 men

Work can be finished in 1 day by 20 × 10 men

Work can be finished in 4 days by $\frac{20\times 10}{4}$ = 50 men.

10. B: 15 men can finish the job in 20 days

25 men can finish the job in $\frac{20\times 15}{25}$ = 12 days.

GENERAL AWARENESS

HISTORY

1. The earliest of the holy books of the Hindus is:
   A. The Gita
   B. The Ramayana
   C. The Mahabharata
   D. The Vedas
2. The relics of the pre-Aryan civilisation have been unearthed at:
   A. Taxila
   B. Rajgir
   C. Indraprastha
   D. Mohenjodaro
3. The Aryans came to India from outside and first settled in the:
   A. Samatata
   B. Pragjyotishapur
   C. Punjab
   D. Panchala
4. The poetical portion of the Vedas is known as:
   A. Brahmana
   B. Samhita
   C. Aranyaka
   D. Upanishada
5. The Vedangas were .... in number.
   A. six B. four
   C. eight D. ten
6. The earliest Hindus were divided into .... Varnas.
   A. two B. four
   C. six D. eight
7. Lord Buddha was born at:
   A. Pataliputra B. Ujjain
   C. Rajgriha D. Lumbini
8. Siddhartha attained his "enlightenment" at:
   A. Banaras B. Sarnath
   C. Kushinagar D. Gaya
9. Mahavira was born in a Kshatriya clan of the name of:
   A. Shakya B. Jnatrika
   C. Mallas D. Lichhavis
10. Lumbini the birth place of Lord Buddha is situated in:
    A. Bihar
    B. Uttar Pradesh
    C. Sikkim
    D. Nepal
11. The Indian king who opposed Alexander was:
    A. Ambhi
    B. Porus
    C. Dhanananda
    D. Chandragupta II
12. Alexander conquered the:
    A. Punjab B. Panchala
    C. Ayodhya D. Magadha
13. The French Revolution began in the year
    A. 1789 B. 1790
    C. 1796 D. 1798
14. On his way home Alexander breathed his last at:
    A. Taxila B. Babylon
    C. Persipolis D. Alexandria
15. Chandragupta was the scion of the:
    A. Nandas
    B. Magadha, the Lichhavis of Vaishali

C. Mauryas of Pippalivana
D. Sakyas of Kapilvastu

16. In the consolidation of his empire Chandragupta was greatly helped by:
A. Yaudhayana B. Upagupta
C. Chanakya D. Shudraka

17. To the court of Chandragupta Seleukos sent an ambassador of the name of:
A. Herodotus
B. Hiuen-Tsang
C. Megasthenese
D. Heleodoros

18. Chandragupta died at a place called:
A. Karnasuvarna
B. Paithan
C. Sravanvelgola
D. Nalanda

19. Megasthenese classified the Indians into .... classes.
A. five B. seven
C. nine D. eleven

20. The municipal administration of Pataliputra in the days of Chandragupta was entrusted to a Committee of .... citizens.
A. ten B. twenty
C. thirty D. forty

21. Military administration of Chandragupta was vested in ...... committees.
A. four B. six
C. eight D. ten

22. The authorship of the Artha-shastra is usually ascribed to:
A. Patanjali
B. Jaimini
C. Kautilya
D. Vatasayayan

23. The successor of Chandragupta to the throne of Magadha was:
A. Buddhagupta
B. Bimbisara
C. Bindusara
D. Udayeen

24. On the death of his father Ashoka ascended the throne of Magadha in:
A. 323 BC B. 326 BC
C. 269 BC D. 120 AD

25. Ashoka was initiated into Buddhism by:
A. Dipankara
B. Shreenjan Atisha
C. Sheelabhadra
D. Upagupta

26. For the propagation of the Buddhistic faith, Ashoka appointed new officers of the name of:
A. Rajukas
B. Yuktas
C. Amatyas
D. Dharmamahamatras

27. Ashoka sent his son and daughter for preaching of Buddhism to:
A. Sumatra B. Cambodia
C. Javadvipa D. Ceylon

28. At Pataliputra during the reign of Ashoka was held the .... Buddhistic Council or Synod.
A. first B. second
C. third D. fourth

29. The capital of Kalinga was:
A. Taxila
B. Suvarnagiri
C. Ujjain
D. Toshali

30. The administrative units except the capital of the Ashokan empire were administered by:
A. Kumaramatyas
B. Dharmamahamatras
C. Rajukas
D. Yuktas

31. The founder of the Kushana Empire in India was:
A. Menander
B. Vasudeva
C. Kujula Kadphises
D. Kanishka

32. The capital of Kanishka was:
A. Taxila
B. Multan
C. Gandhara
D. Purushapura

33. The statue of Kanishka with a broken head has been found at:
A. Mathura
B. Indraprastha
C. Brindavan
D. Hardwar

34. The fourth Buddhistic Synod was held at Purushapura, during the reign of:
A. Ashoka
B. Kanishka
C. Samudragupta
D. Harshavardhana

35. The founder of the Gupta Empire in India was:
A. Chandragupta
B. Skandagupta
C. Samudragupta
D. Budhagupta

36. The name "Napoleon of India" is usually given to:
A. Chandragupta II
B. Samudragupta
C. Kumaragupta
D. Devapala

37. Meghavarma, the King of Ceylon, was a contemporary of:
A. Ashoka
B. Kanishka
C. Samudragupta
D. Harshavardhana

38. The poet Harisena was the courtier of:
A. Samudragupta
B. Skandagupta
C. Chandragupta II
D. Lakshmana Sena

39. "Sakari" is the title usually ascribed to:
A. Kanishka
B. Gautamiputra Satakarni
C. Chandragupta Vikramaditya
D. Devapala

40. "The Council of the Nine Gems" is associated with the name of:
A. Harshavardhana
B. Devapala
C. Chandragupta II
D. Ballala Sena

41. The Chinese traveller Fa-Hien came to India during the reign of:
A. Kanishka
B. Chandragupta Maurya
C. Chandragupta Vikramaditya
D. Samudragupta

42. Tamralipti was a great seaport in:
A. Gujarat
B. Ceylon
C. Bengal
D. Andhra Pradesh

43. The author of the "Malavikagni-mitram" was:
A. Harisena B. Virasena
C. Aswaghosa D. Kalidasa

44. The "Mudrarakshasa" was composed by:
A. Shudraka
B. Vishakhadatta
C. Varahamihira
D. Aryabhatta

45. Varahamihira was a great:
A. Poet
B. Philosopher
C. Astronomer
D. Astrologer

46. The poet-philsopher Aswaghosa was a courtier of:
A. Ashoka
B. Kanishka
C. Chandragupta II
D. Harshavardhana

47. The iron-pillar of Chandraraja at Delhi is a fine-specimen of metallurgy of the:
A. Gupta Age
B. Maurya Age
C. Kushana Age
D. Pala Age

48. The Hunas attacked India during the period of the:
A. Guptas
B. Mauryas
C. Palas
D. Senas

49. The Huna leader Mihirkula was defeated by:
A. Chandragupta
B. Budhagupta
C. Yashodharman
D. Rajyavardhana

50. Pushyabhuti dynasty ruled over:
A. Thaneswar B. Ujjain
C. Sakal D. Pataliputra

51. During the Maurayan period, *Pana* was:
A. the standard coin
B. a tax
C. a common prayer hall
D. a guild of traders

52. The US Declaration of Independence was drawn up in the year
A. 1774 B. 1776
C. 1778 D. 1780

53. The place famous for its cave painting is:
A. Bagh
B. Ajanta
C. Badami
D. All the three above

54. Pulakeshin II, the King of the Chalukyas, defeated:
A. Samudragupta
B. Gautamiputra Satakarni
C. Harshavardhana
D. Govinda III

55. Yuang Chwang came to India during the reign of:
A. Dharmapala
B. Harshavardhana
C. Chandragupta II
D. Samudragupta

56. Every five years Harshavardhana held a religious fair at:
A. Thaneswar B. Kannauj
C. Prayaga D. Banaras

57. The author of the *"Kadambari"* was:
A. Harshavardhana
B. Banabhatta
C. Kalidasa
D. Charaka

58. The *"Priyadarshika"* was composed by:
A. Banabhatta
B. Bhavabhuti
C. Harshavardhana
D. Jayadeva

59. The head of the University of Nalanda was the great Bengali scholar:
A. Shreejnan Atisha
B. Nagarjuna
C. Basubandhu
D. Sheelabhadra

60. Hiuen-Tsang remained in India for ....years.
A. fourteen B. sixteen
C. eighteen D. twenty

61. The founder of the Pala dynasty in Bengal was:
A. Gopala B. Dharmapala
C. Mahipala D. Devapala

62. Dharmapala established his supremacy over the whole of northern India and placed on the throne of Kannauj:
A. Indrayudha
B. Chakrayudha
C. Amoghavarsha
D. Govinda III

63. Who among the following were the first to invade and rule the north-western India?
A. Scythians
B. Bactrian Greeks
C. Kushanas
D. Partiharas

64. Which of the following is the most popularly known name of Lord Buddha's wife?
A. Yashodhara B. Gopa
C. Bimba D. Sujata

65. After the decline of the Gupta power in the north, the Huns:
A. built a powerful empire in the South India
B. established their power in Bengal and Orissa
C. captured large tracts in the Western India
D. suffered a devastating defeat at the hands of Harsha

66. The Reign of Terror ended in France with the execution of
A. Georges Danton
B. Georges Couthon
C. Jacques Hebert
D. Maximilien Robespierre

67. Beetapala and Dhiman, the two great artists that India had ever produced belonged to the:
A. Pala Age
B. Gupta Age
C. Maurya Age
D. Pathan Age

68. He established himself as First Consul in France in the year 1799....
A. Pasquale Paoli
B. Augustin de Robespierre

C. Napoleon
D. Vicomte Paul de Barras

69. The founder of the Sena Dynasty in Bengal was:
A. Vijaya Sena
B. Samanta Sena
C. Ballala Sena
D. Lakshmana Sena

70. The first Czar of Russia was....
A. Peter I
B. Nicholas II
C. Paul I
D. Ivan the Great

71. The capital of Bengal during the days of the Senas was:
A. Karnasuvarna B. Nadia
C. Tamralipti D. Gaur

72. The *"Geetagovinda"* was composed by:
A. Dhoyee
B. Halayudha
C. Umapati Dhar
D. Jayadeva

73. The US Civil War began in the year:
A. 1855 B. 1857
C. 1859 D. 1861

74. The authorship of the *"Rajatarangini"* may be ascribed to:
A. Bakpatiraja
B. Kalhana
C. Bihlan
D. Sandhyakar Nandi

75. The *Hijira* is counted from the year:
A. 570 AD B. 622 AD
C. 632 AD D. 997 AD

76. The founder of the kingdom of Ghazni was:
A. Hijjaj
B. Sultan Mahmud
C. Alaptagin
D. Subuktagin

77. Anandapala was defeated by:
A. Subuktagin
B. Sultan Mahmud
C. Mohammad Ghori
D. Nasiruddin

78. The great scholar Alberuni was the courtier of:
A. Sultan Mahmud
B. Iltutmish
C. Subuktagin
D. Sultana Raziya

79. The great poet Firdausi adorned the court of:
A. King Solomon
B. Sultan Mahmud
C. Alauddin
D. Qutb-ud-din

80. Prithvi Raj, the Chauhan king, was finally defeated by Mohammad Ghori at the battle of:
A. Tarain B. Thaneswar
C. Chausa D. Panipat

81. The Slave dynasty in India was founded by:
A. Gyasuddin Balbal
B. Qutb-ud-din Aibak
C. Iltutmish
D. Mohammad Ghori

82. Chenghiz Khan invaded India during the reign of:
A. Alauddin Khilji
B. Mohammad-bin-Tughlak

C. Iltutmish
D. Gyasuddin Balban

83. Sultana Raziya was the .... of Iltutmish.
A. wife B. daughter
C. sister D. niece

84. Sher Shah's real name was:
A. Farid B. Bahadur
C. Faizi D. Hemu

85. The chief organiser of the campaigns of Alauddin was:
A. Ulugh Khan
B. Nasrat Khan
C. Malik Kafur
D. Khijir Khan

86. The Opium Wars of the 19th century were fought between Britain and:
A. Japan B. China
C. Indonesia D. Cambodia

87. The royal court of a Alauddin was graced by the great poet:
A. Firdausi
B. Omar Khaiyyam
C. Amir Khusrau
D. Ibn Batuta

88. The Suez canal opened in the year:
A. 1865 B. 1867
C. 1869 D. 1871

89. From Delhi Mohammad-bin-Tughlak transferred his capital to:
A. Warrangal
B. Daulatabad
C. Fatehpur Sikri
D. Ahmednagar

90. The Morroccan traveller Ibn Batuta was a contemporary of:
A. Aladuddin Khilji
B. Mohammad-bin-Tughlak
C. Sultan Mahmud
D. Gyasuddin Balban

91. Tamerlane attacked India during the reign of:
A. Firoz Tughlak
B. Mahmud Nasir-ud-din Tughlak
C. Mohammad-bin-Tughlak
D. Daulat Khan

92. The founder of Sikh religion was:
A. Kabir B. Ramanuj
C. Guru Nanak D. Ramananda

93. The first Battle of Panipat was fought in the year:
A. 1296 AD B. 1526 AD
C. 1542 AD D. 1556 AD

94. Babur defeated Sangram Singh, the Rana of Mewar, in the battle of:
A. Chausa B. Bilgram
C. Khanua D. Haldighati

95. The last battle that Humayun fought with Sher Shah was at:
A. Surajgarh
B. Bilgram (Kannauj)
C. Chausa
D. Raisin

96. Akbar was born in Sind instead of the royal palace because:
A. his mother's home was there
B. good maternity care was to be had there
C. his parents were fleeing from Sher Shah
D. his parents were on the vacation

97. Akbar permitted his regent, Bairam Khan, to go on a pilgrimage to Mecca because:
A. Akbar wanted him to go on a diplomatic mission
B. Bairam had asked to go for religious reasons
C. Bairam had been rebellious and therefore Akbar wanted him to absent himself from India for a while
D. Akbar could not go himself and therefore sent a substitute

98. Akbar tried to found a new religion because:
A. he thought the old religion was false
B. he wanted to unite the people of many religions who lived in his empire under one religion
C. he had a vision telling him to do so
D. he wanted to become famous as a religious hero

99. Akbar is famous in a way that very few kings and emperors of India are because:
A. he was a great conqueror
B. he had the most splendour at his court
C. he built the finest cities and buildings
D. he moulded the people of many religions, races and allegiances into a well-organised and contented empire

100. Akbar abolished the Hindu capitation tax (Jazia) primarily because:
A. the revenue derived from it amounted to very little
B. it made the Hindus in his reign more contented since they were not discriminated against by such a tax
C. he thought of more effective ways of raising revenue
D. he could not enforce its collection

101. The famous financial adviser to Akbar was:
A. Todar Mal
B. Abul Fazl
C. the Raja of Jodhpur
D. Bairam Khan

102. The first country in the world to grant women the right to vote was:
A. New Zealand
B. Great Britain
C. France
D. USA

103. At Akbar's death the extent of his empire was:
A. the same as Babur's
B. smaller than Babur's
C. the same as the present Indian Union
D. the same as Ashoka's

104. Abul Fazl was famous for:
A. conquering the Deccan
B. heading a rebellion
C. writing a history of Akbar's reign
D. organising land surveys

105. Akbar reigned for:
A. 25 years B. 36 years
C. 10 years D. 49 years

106. Akbar was succeeded by his son:
A. Jahangir B. Humayun
C. Shahjahan D. Aurangzeb

107. The greatest achievement of Alauddin Khilji was his:
A. invasion of South India
B. measures to improve the Standard of living
C. revenue system and control of inflation
D. contribution art

108. The Arab conquest of Sind took place in 712 A.D. under the leadership of:
A. Mohammad-bin-Qasim
B. Subuktagin
C. Mahmud Ghaznavi
D. Qutb-ud-din

109. The Vijayanagara Empire emerged during the reign of:
A. Muhammad Tughlaq
B. Alauddin Khilji
C. Humayun
D. Balban

110. In 1576 the Battle of Haldighati, was fought between Akbar and:
A. Uday Singh
B. Man Singh
C. Amar Singh
D. Rana Pratap

111. Rani Durgavati, the Queen of .... committed suicide to escape disgrace at the hands of the Mughal army.
A. Gujarat
B. Jodhpur
C. Mewar
D. Gondawana

112. Chand Sultana, the brave queen of .... was killed in an engagement with the Mughal army.
A. Golconda
B. Bijapur
C. Khandesh
D. Ahmednagar

113. The Boxer Rebellion took place in
A. South Africa B. China
C. Japan D. Burma

114. The *Akbarnama* was written by:
A. Seikh Faiji B. Abul Fazl
C. Badauni D. Kafi Khan

115. During the reign of Akbar the *Hindi Ramayana* was written by:
A. Birbal B. Surdas
C. Tulsidas D. Tansen

116. The mausoleum of Akbar at ...... is undoubtedly a fine specimen of Mughal art.
A. Secundera B. Delhi
C. Fatehpur D. Lahore

117. That Akbar was a great builder is evident from his establishment of a new town at:
A. Ahmednagar
B. Ahmedabad
C. Fatehpur Sikri
D. Jaunpur

118. The name of the wife of Salim, the eldest son of Akbar, was:
A. Hamida Banu Begum
B. Mehrunnisa (Nur Jahan)

C. Jahanara
D. Gulbadan Begum

119. Shahjahan rebelled against Jahangir because:
A. Jahangir did not like him
B. Jahangir wanted to send him away to the Deccan
C. Nurjahan wanted to place Shahryar, her own son-in-law, on the throne of Delhi
D. None of the above

120. Mahabat Khan, an Afghan Mansabdar, rose into rebellion against Jahangir and Nurjahan because:
A. the emperor wanted him to lead an expedition into Kandhar
B. Mahabat Khan failed to quell rebellious Shahjahan
C. Mahabat Khan got disgusted with the supremacy of Queen Nurjahan
D. he was called upon to lead an expedition into the Deccan

121. To the royal court of Jahangir, James I, the King of England, sent an ambassador of the name of:
A. John Hawkins
B. William Todd
C. Sir Thomas Roe
D. Sir Walter Raleigh

122. The eldest son of Jahangir was:
A. Khusro B. Khurram
C. Parvez D. Shahryar

123. *Tarabiyar Yafralaskar* is associated with:
A. Balban
B. Alauddin Khilji
C. Muhammad-bin-Tughlaq
D. Gyasuddin Tughlaq

124. World War I came to an end with the Treaty of
A. Versailles B. Riga
C. Brest-LitovskD. Bucharest

125. Suja, the second son of Shahjahan, was the governor of the:
A. Deccan
B. Kandhar
C. Bengal
D. Ahmednagar

126. Which one of the following won Sher Shah the title of the 'fore runner of Akbar'?
A. His dispensation of justice
B. His religious tolerance
C. His efficient administration
D. His military and revenue reforms

127. The eldest son of Shahjahan was:
A. Suja B. Dara
C. Murad D. Aurangzeb

128. Shahjahan had to remain in captivity for ....years.
A. eight B. fourteen
C. sixteen D. twenty

129. Which one of the following Mughal Kings had a passion for justice?
A. Akbar B. Humayun
C. Jahangir D. Shahjahan

130. The Moti Masjid was built during the reign of Shahjahan at:
A. Shahjahanabad B. Delhi
C. Agra D. Lahore

131. The *Dewan-i-Am* and the *Dewan-i-Khas* were built at:
A. Lucknow
B. Shahjahanabad
C. Jaunpur
D. Lahore

132. The Peacock Throne was caused to be built during the reign of:
A. Akbar the Great
B. Jahangir
C. Shahjahan
D. Aurangzeb

133. The fulsome development of Mughal painting was the achievement of:
A. Humayun B. Akbar
C. Babur D. Jahangir

134. Aurangzeb re-established the Jizya on the Hindus:
A. because the Mughal Exchequer was short of funds
B. because he did not like the non-conformists to his religion
C. because that was according to the tenets of the Muslim faith
D. because the Hindus were inimical to the Mughal Empire

135. Aurangzeb sentenced to death the Sikh Guru:
A. Arjun Dev
B. Hargovind Singh
C. Teg Bahadur
D. Govind Singh

136. Shivaji defeated the Moghul General:
A. Afzal Khan
B. Dilir Khan
C. Shayesta Khan
D. Murshidkuli Khan

137. Shivaji was crowned as an independent king at:
A. Surat B. Poona
C. Raigarh D. Singhagarh

138. Aurangzeb failed to defeat Shivaji because the:
A. Mughal Army grew unmanageable
B. Marathas were expert in guerrilla warfare
C. Mughals had no navy
D. Mughal generals were treacherous

139. The last of the Mughal Emperors was:
A. Jahandar Shah
B. Shah Alam II
C. Alamgir II
D. Bahadur Shah II

140. The founder of the dynasty of the Peshwas was:
A. Balaji Biswanath
B. Baji Rao
C. Balaji Baji Rao
D. Shambhaji

141. The Third Battle of Panipat was fought in the year:
A. 1526 AD B. 1556 AD
C. 1757 AD D. 1761 AD

142. Fracisco Pelasert, a Dutch trader, left an account of the reign of:
A. Akbar B. Jahangir
C. Shahjahan D. Aurangzeb

143. Manucci, an Italian adventurer, left an account of the reign of:
A. Shahjahan
B. Aurangzeb

C. Shah Alam
D. Bahadur Shah II

144. Of the modern European nations the first to come to India as traders were the:
A. English B. Portuguese
C. Dutch D. French

145. The first trading establishment of the English in India was:
A. Calcutta B. Surat
C. Bombay D. Madras

146. In 1690, the foundation of the city of Calcutta was laid by:
A. Sir Thomas Roe
B. Hawkins
C. Job Charnock
D. Clive

147. The ablest of the governors of the French settlements in India was:
A. Bussey
B. Lally
C. Dupleix
D. La Bourdonnais

148. In the Battle of Plassey in 1757 Sirajuddaula was finally defeated by the English because:
A. the English outnumbered the men of Siraj
B. the English were in a favourable position
C. Siraj was a coward and did not fight
D. some of the associates of Siraj proved treacherous

149. Sir Robert Clive committed suicide in 1775 because:
A. he failed to govern the Indian possessions properly
B. he had to disgorge the money he misappropriated
C. he was found guilty by the House of Commons
D. he wanted to escape popular ignominy

150. Sir Robert Clive first came to India as:
A. a traveller to the court of the Nawab at Murshidabad
B. a governor of the British possessions in India
C. a clerk of the East India Company
D. None of the above

151. Lord North's Regulating Act was passed during the administration of:
A. Sir Robert Clive
B. Warren Hastings
C. Lord Cornwallis
D. Sir John Shore

152. The Regulating Act was passed in the year:
A. 1784 B. 1771
C. 1776 D. 1773

153. The First Maratha War took place during the Governor-Generalship of:
A. Warren Hastings
B. Lord Cornwallis
C. Wellesley
D. Sir John Shore

154. The Treaty of Mangalore in 1784 terminated:
A. The First Maratha War
B. The Second Mysore War
C. The Second Maratha War
D. The Third Mysore War

155. The Begums of Oudh were tyrannised for extortion of money by:
A. Wellesley
B. Clive
C. Warren Hastings
D. Cornwallis

156. Warren Hastings was impeached by the House of Commons because:
A. He quarrelled with the Members of his Council
B. He did not see eye-to-eye with the British Prime Minister
C. He was accused of maladministration and oppression
D. He was not successful in the First Maratha war

157. Tipu Sultan of Mysore was killed in a bloody engagement in the:
A. First Mysore War
B. Second Mysore War
C. Third Mysore War
D. Fourth Mysore War

158. The Permanent Settlement was introduced into the British dominion in India during the administration of:
A. Sir Robert Clive
B. Warren Hastings
C. Lord Wellesley
D. Lord Cornwallis

159. The Policy of Subsidiary Alliance owed its origin to:
A. Warren Hastings
B. Lord Wellesley
C. Lord Cornwallis
D. Lord William Bentinck

160. The founder of modern Turkiye is:
A. Ismet Inonu
B. Kemal Ataturk
C. Vahideddin
D. Abdulmecid

161. The English and the Sikhs entered into friendship by:
A. The Treaty of Purandar
B. The Treaty of Wargaon
C. The Treaty of Amritsar
D. The Treaty of Lahore

162. The First Gorkha War is an important event in the administration of:
A. Lord Wellesley
B. Lord Minto
C. Lord Hastings
D. Lord Amherst

163. The Pindaris of the Western and Central India were completely subjugated by:
A. Lord William Bentinck
B. Lord Hastings
C. Lord Amherst
D. Lord Minto

164. The Third Maratha War is an important incident during the administration of:
A. Lord Hastings
B. Lord Minto
C. Lord Cornwallis
D. Lord Amherst

165. The First Burmese War occurred during the rule of:
A. Lord Amherst
B. Lord Hastings
C. Lord Minto
D. Lord Elgin

166. The system of *Sati* was abolished in India during the governor-generalship of:
A. Lord Cornwallis
B. Lord Dalhousie
C. Lord Ripon
D. Lord William Bentinck

167. The Thugs were completely quelled by:
A. Lord Hastings
B. Lord William Bentinck
C. Lord Dalhousie
D. Lord Lytton

168. The First Afghan War is an important event during the administration of:
A. Lord William Bentinck
B. Lord Auckland
C. Earl of Moira
D. Lord Amherst

169. The province of Sind was annexed to the British possessions in India during the governor-generalship of:
A. Lord Auckland
B. Lord Ellenborough
C. Lord Dalhousie
D. Lord Hastings

170. The First Sikh War was an important event in the administration of:
A. Lord Auckland
B. Lord Ellenborough
C. Lord Hardinge
D. Lord Dalhousie

171. The Doctrine of Lapse owed its origin to:
A. Lord William Bentinck
B. Lord Dalhousie
C. Lord Ripon
D. Lord Curzon

172. Telegraph and railways were first introduced into India during the governor-generalship of:
A. Lord William Bentinck
B. Lord Dalhousie
C. Lord Ripon
D. Lord Canning

173. The Sepoy Mutiny took place in the year:
A. 1757 B. 1761
C. 1836 D. 1857

174. The most important event during the administration of Lord Canning was:
A. The suppression of the Thugs
B. The abolition of the *Sati*
C. The introduction of the doctrine of Lapse
D. The Sepoy Mutiny

175. The Government of India was transferred from the hands of the East India Company to those of the British Crown during the viceroyalty of:
A. Lord Canning
B. Lord Elgin
C. Sir John Lawrence
D. Lord Mayo

176. The policy of "Masterly Inactivity" with regard to Afghanistan was adopted by:
A. Lord Auckland
B. Lord Dalhousie
C. Lord Lawrence
D. Lord Mayo

177. Entrance to the Indian Civil Service was made possible for the Indians by:
A. Lord Dalhousie
B. Lord Canning
C. Lord Lytton
D. Lord Ripon

178. The Bengal Municipal Act of 1884 was passed during the viceroyalty of:
A. Lord William Bentinck
B. Lord Dalhousie
C. Lord Canning
D. Lord Ripon

179. The Ilbert Bill was proposed to be passed during the viceroyalty of:
A. Lord Dalhousie
B. Lord William Bentinck
C. Lord Lytton
D. Lord Ripon

180. The Indian National Congress had its birth in the year:
A. 1757 B. 1775
C. 1875 D. 1885

181. The first President of the Indian National Congress was:
A. Anandamohan Basu
B. Dadabhai Naoroji
C. Raja Rammohan Roy
D. Woomesh Chandra Bannerjee

182. A Fascist government established in Italy in 1922 by
A. Ciano Galeazzo
B. Benito Mussolini
C. Emilio De Bono
D. Ivano Bonomi

183. The infamous act of the Partition of Bengal was proposed to be done during the viceroyalty of:
A. Lord Elgin
B. Lord Minto II
C. Lord Curzon
D. Lord Irwin

184. The Morley-Minto Reforms were introduced into India in the year:
A. 1904 B. 1909
C. 1919 D. 1935

185. The Simon Commission was boycotted by the Indians because:
A. No Indian was taken within it as its member
B. The Britishers wanted to perpetuate suzerainty over India
C. Gandhiji was sour about the British sense of justice
D. Nothing short of complete independence would satisfy their aspirations

186. The infamous Jallianwala Bagh Massacre, the blackest stigma in the British rule in India, was committed in the year:
A. 1919 B. 1921
C. 1926 D. 1935

187. The Non-co-operation Movement was launched by Mahatma Gandhi in:
A. 1905 B. 1920
C. 1921 D. 1926

188. The Communal Award was a creation of:
A. Lord Morley
B. Ramsay MacDonald

C. Sir Stafford Cripps
D. Sir Pethick Lawrence

189. After the failure of the Non-co-operation Movement, a new party of the Congressites, namely, "Swarjya Dal" was formed under leadership of:
A. Mahatma Gandhi
B. Vallabhbhai Patel
C. Chittaranjan Das
D. Pandit Motilal Nehru

190. The Civil Disobedience Movement was started by Mahatma Gandhi in the year:
A. 1921 B. 1930
C. 1935 D. 1942

191. The Ajad Hind Fauj was creation of:
A. Sardar Vallabhbhai Patel
B. Netaji Subhash Chandra Bose
C. Rashbehari Bose
D. Colonel Shah Nawaj

192. This Tughlaq ruler imposed the *Jaziya* tax on the Brahmins to please the *ulemas*:
A. Mohammad bin Tughlaq
B. Ghiyasuddin Tughlaq II
C. Jalaluddin Tughlaq
D. Firoz Shah Tughlaq

193. He invited Babur to invade India:
A. Sikandar Lodhi
B. Daulat Khan Lodhi
C. Ibrahim Lodhi
D. Bahlul Khan Lodhi

194. The Vijayanagar a empire was established by:
A. Devaraya and Mallikarjuna
B. Sadasiva and Tirumala
C. Harihara and Bukka
D. Saluva Narasimha and Narasa Nayaka

195. This was a revenue reform introduced during Akbar's reign:
A. *Zabti* System
B. *Mansabdari* System
C. Jagirdari system
D. Zat system

196. Akbar shifted his capital from Agra to:
A. Delhi
B. Fatehpur Sikri
C. Lahore
D. Sikandra

197. Shah Jahan defeated and expelled them from Hugli:
A. French B. Dutch
C. English D. Portuguese

198. Sher Shah constructed the Grand trunk Road to connect:
A. Agra with Sasaram
B. Agra with Assam
C. Agra with Kannauj
D. Agra with Ahmednagar

199. This Sikh guru built the Golden Temple (Harimandir):
A. Guru Angad
B. Guru Tegh Bahadur
C. Guru Arjan Dev
D. Guru Gobind Singh

200. This Mughal Emperor issued a *firman* giving the East India Company control over several villages near Calcutta and Madras:
A. Shah Alam I
B. Shah Alam II
C. Farukh Siyar
D. Muhammad Shah

ANSWERS

1	2	3	4	5	6	7	8	9	10
D	D	C	B	A	B	D	D	B	D
11	**12**	**13**	**14**	**15**	**16**	**17**	**18**	**19**	**20**
B	A	A	B	C	C	C	C	B	C
21	**22**	**23**	**24**	**25**	**26**	**27**	**28**	**29**	**30**
B	C	C	C	D	D	D	C	D	C
31	**32**	**33**	**34**	**35**	**36**	**37**	**38**	**39**	**40**
C	D	A	D	A	B	C	A	C	C
41	**42**	**43**	**44**	**45**	**46**	**47**	**48**	**49**	**50**
C	C	D	B	C	B	A	A	C	A
51	**52**	**53**	**54**	**55**	**56**	**57**	**58**	**59**	**60**
A	B	A	C	B	C	B	C	D	A
61	**62**	**63**	**64**	**65**	**66**	**67**	**68**	**69**	**70**
A	B	B	A	C	D	A	C	B	D
71	**72**	**73**	**74**	**75**	**76**	**77**	**78**	**79**	**80**
B	D	D	B	B	C	B	A	B	A
81	**82**	**83**	**84**	**85**	**86**	**87**	**88**	**89**	**90**
B	C	B	A	C	B	C	C	B	B
91	**92**	**93**	**94**	**95**	**96**	**97**	**98**	**99**	**100**
B	C	B	C	B	C	C	B	D	B
101	**102**	**103**	**104**	**105**	**106**	**107**	**108**	**109**	**110**
A	A	D	C	D	A	C	A	A	D
111	**112**	**113**	**114**	**115**	**116**	**117**	**118**	**119**	**120**
D	D	B	B	C	A	C	B	C	C
121	**122**	**123**	**124**	**125**	**126**	**127**	**128**	**129**	**130**
C	A	A	A	C	D	B	A	C	C
131	**132**	**133**	**134**	**135**	**136**	**137**	**138**	**139**	**140**
B	C	D	C	C	C	C	B	D	A
141	**142**	**143**	**144**	**145**	**146**	**147**	**148**	**149**	**150**
D	B	A	B	B	C	C	D	C	C
151	**152**	**153**	**154**	**155**	**156**	**157**	**158**	**159**	**160**
B	D	A	B	C	C	D	D	B	B
161	**162**	**163**	**164**	**165**	**166**	**167**	**168**	**169**	**170**
D	C	B	A	A	D	B	B	B	C
171	**172**	**173**	**174**	**175**	**176**	**177**	**178**	**179**	**180**
B	B	D	D	A	A	A	D	D	D
181	**182**	**183**	**184**	**185**	**186**	**187**	**188**	**189**	**190**
D	B	C	B	A	A	B	B	B	B
191	**192**	**193**	**194**	**195**	**196**	**197**	**198**	**199**	**200**
B	D	D	C	A	B	D	A	C	C

INDIAN CONSTITUTION & CIVIC LIFE

1. Administration of India was transferred to the British Crown (from the East India Company) in:
   A. 1600 B. 1857
   C. 1858 D. 1912
2. India's First War of Independence was fought in the year:
   A. 1858 B. 1857
   C. 1846 D. 1842
3. The first Governor-General and Viceroy of India was:
   A. Lord Mountbatten
   B. Lord Auckland
   C. Lord Canning
   D. Lord Irwin
4. Indian National Congress was founded by:
   A. Mahatma Gandhi in 1911
   B. A.O. Hume in 1885
   C. C.F. Andrews in 1911
   D. Lala Lajpat Rai in 1911
5. The first President of the Indian National Congress was:
   A. Jawaharlal Nehru
   B. Mahatma Gandhi
   C. W.C. Bannerjee
   D. Subhash Chandra Bose
6. The Simon Commission visited India in the year:
   A. 1922 B. 1928
   C. 1942 D. 1932
7. The first meeting of the Constituent Assembly was held in the Central Hall of Parliament on:
   A. December 6, 1946
   B. December 9, 1942
   C. January 26, 1942
   D. May 27, 1946
8. The Constitution of India was adopted and enacted, and enforced respectively on:
   A. November 26, 1949–January 26, 1950
   B. January 26, 1949–November 26, 1950
   C. August 15, 1947–November 26, 1950
   D. January 26, 1949–January 26, 1950
9. The chairman of the Drafting Committee of the Constitution was:
   A. Jawaharlal Nehru
   B. Mrs. Vijaya Laxmi Pandit
   C. Lal Bahadur Shastri
   D. Dr. Bhimrao Ambedkar
10. Preamble means:
    A. The preface of a book
    B. Preface, introduction especially that of an act of Parliament stating its aims and objectives
    C. The head of a body
    D. The top most portion of anything
11. The First Round Table Conference was held at/in:
    A. London/1930
    B. Delhi/1931
    C. London/1931
    D. Lahore/1930

12. The Congress declared its aim of attaining complete independence in the year:
A. 1929 B. 1930
C. 1942 D. 1945

13. Cripps Mission visited India in the year:
A. 1927 B. 1942
C. 1929 D. 1930

14. Mahatma Gandhi launched his 'Quit India Movement' on:
A. January 26, 1932
B. August 8, 1942
C. December 15, 1942
D. November 26, 1942

15. Indian Constitution is (perhaps) the ......in the world.
A. Lengthiest document (written)
B. Shortest document
C. Most rigid document
D. Most flexible docement

16. India is a:
A. Secular State
B. Bilingual State
C. Communist State
D. Capitalist State

17. The Indian Constitution is .... in structure.
A. federal
B. unitary
C. rigid
D. partly unitary, partly federal

18. In a federal setup of government, the powers are divided between the:
A. Centre and the units
B. Two Houses of the Legislature
C. Executive and the Legislature
D. President and the Cabinet

19. The features of the Indian Constitution (Cabinet System) have been emulated by the makers of the Constitution from the:
A. US Constitution
B. Swiss Constitution
C. British Constitution
D. Japanese Constitution

20. The Constitution of India bears the influence of the constitutions of several countries. Which country exerts the greatest influence in the framing of the 'Directive Principles of State Policy' in our Constitution?
A. Ireland B. France
C. Japan D. Russia

21. The President of India holds office for a period of:
A. 6 years B. 5 years
C. 4 years D. 7 years

22. President's Electoral College consists of:
A. Members of Parliament
B. Members of Parliament and Legislatures
C. Members of State Legislatures
D. Elected Members of Parliament and State Legislatures

23. A dispute regarding the election of the President is referred to the:
A. Election Commission
B. Parliament
C. Supreme Court
D. Vice-President

24. If the President has to resign, he sends his resignation to the:
A. Prime Minister
B. Chief Justice of India
C. Vice-President
D. Lok Sabha Speaker

25. The President should:
A. be a member of either House of Parliament
B. not be a member of either House of Parliament
C. be elected to the Parliament within six months of his election
D. the Constitution is silent on the issue of his being member of any House of the Parliament

26. Is the President of India the Supreme Commander of the three wings of the Army, the Navy and the Air Force?
A. Yes
B. No, he has nothing to do with the armed forces
C. No, it is the PM who is the Supreme Commander of the 3 wings of the armed forces
D. No, armed forces are under control of the Defence Minister

27. To contest election for the office of Vice-President of India, the candidate must have completed the age of:
A. 40 years B. 35 years
C. 30 years D 45 years

28. Which one of the following qualifications must a candidate have, to contest the election of Vice-President of India?
A. He must have served as a governor in at least one State
B. He must be eligible for contesting election to Rajya Sabha
C. He must hold an office of profit
D. He must be citizen of India and not less than 45 years of age

29. The Vice-President of India is:
A. Chairman (Ex-officio) of the Lok Sabha
B. Ex-officio Chairman of the Rajya Sabha
C. Speaker of the Lok Sabha
D. President of the Red Cross

30. The UPSC is headed by:
A. A President
B. A Chairman
C. A judge of the Supreme Court
D. A judge of the High Court

31. The President of India controls the Parliament:
A. directly
B. through the Chief Justice
C. through the Cabinet of Ministers headed by the Prime Minister
D. through the agency of the Defence Minister

32. The real powers in the Central Government are enjoyed, according to the Constitution of India, by the:
A. President of India

B. Vice-President of India
C. Prime Minister of India
D. Council of Ministers

33. The Council of Ministers is responsible to the:
A. President
B. Lok Sabha
C. Vice-President
D. Supreme Court

34. The Prime Minister is:
A. nominated by the President
B. elected by the Chief Ministers of States
C. the leader of the majority party of Lok Sabha
D. not elected; it is a hereditary post

35. The maximum number of days within which the Rajya Sabha has to return a money bill to the Lok Sabha after 'rejection' or 'acceptance' is:
A. 30 B. 14
C. 10 D. 15

36. Money bill can originate:
A. in either Houses of Parliament
B. only in the Rajya Sabha
C. only in the Lok Sabha
D. in either of the two Houses suited to the convenience of the Prime Minister

37. The ordinance promulgated by the Governor are subject to the approval by the:
A. President of India
B. State Legislature
C. Lok Sabha
D. Prime Minister

38. Which Court in India has the special responsibility of enforcing Fundamental Rights?
A. Supreme Court
B. High Court
C. District and Sessions Court
D. Any Court

39. Which one of the following is not an essential feature of the State?
A. Written Constitution
B. Territory
C. Population
D. Sovereignty

40. The Presiding Officers of the Rajya Sabha are:
A. President and Vice-President
B. The Vice-President and the Speaker
C. The Chairman and the Deputy Chairman
D. The Prime Minister and the President

41. Which of the following statements is true in respect of the Rajya Sabha?
A. One-third of its members retire every two years
B. One-third of its members retire every three years
C. Two-thirds of its members retire every two years
D. Two-thirds of its members retire every three years

42. To be eligible for the membership of the Lok Sabha a citizen of India must not be below:
A. 25 years B. 30 years
C. 35 years D. 21 years

43. The sessions judge presides over:
A. Criminal Courts
B. Civil Courts
C. Revenue Courts
D. All of the above

44. The seat of the Supreme Court is in New Delhi but it can decide to have its sitting anywhere. Who can decide?
A. The Prime Minister
B. The President
C. The Chief Justice
D. The Chief Justice with the approval of the President

45. Name the 'Law' Officers who hold office at the pleasure of the President.
A. The Chief Justice of the Supreme Court and the Attorney-General
B. The Attorney-General and the Solicitor General
C. The Law Minister and any judge of the Supreme Court or of a High Court
D. The Attorney-General and the Law Minister

46. The final power to reprieve or remit a punishment and/or to commute death sentence rests with the:
A. Chief Justice of the Supreme Court of India
B. President of India
C. Prime Minister
D. Attorney-General

47. The President's Rule is imposed in a State or in a Union Territory when the:
A. Governor of a State or the Chief Commissioner or a Lt. Governor advises the President to do so because the Government in the State/ Territory cannot be carried on in accordance with the provisions of the Constitution
B. Chief Minister of a State requests to this effect
C. Chief Justice of the State High Court recommends through the Governor
D. President knows best

48. The judges of the Supreme Court are appointed by the:
A. Prime Minister of India
B. Speaker of the Lok Sabha
C. President of India
D. Ministry of Law & Justice

49. The Rajya Sabha is:
A. dissolved once in two years
B. dissolved after every four years
C. adjourned every six months
D. not subject to dissolution

50. The President can nominate to the Rajya Sabha a maximum number of:
A. two members
B. four members
C. six members
D. twelve members

51. Normally the President can promulgate ordinances only when:
A. The Prime Minister asks him to do so
B. The Council of Ministers wants him to do so

C. The Parliament is not in session
D. The Parliament empowers him for it during a particular session

52. The ultimate authority according to the Preamble of Indian Constitution vests in:
A. the President
B. the PM
C. the Cabinet
D. the people of India

53. Money Bills in a State can be moved:
A. Only in the Legislative Council
B. Only in the Legislative Assembly
C. At the joint meeting of the LC and the LA
D. By the Chief Minister and his cabinet

54. The Legislative Council of a State is a:
A. temporary body
B. permanent body
C. semi-permanent body
D. chamber of the nominated members

55. Laws for Union Territories that don't have their own legislatures are made by the:
A. Lt Governor
B. President
C. Union Cabinet
D. Parliament

56. The Parliamentary set up of Indian nation was adopted from the constitutional set up of:
A. the UK B. the USA
C. France D. All of these

57. The Supreme Court of India has to work according to:
A. the directives of the President
B. the directives of the PM or his Cabinet
C. the directives of the Lok Sabha or the Rajya Sabha
D. the Constitution of India

58. How many members of Parliament are needed to bring a no confidence motion in the house?
A. 60 B. 50
C. 110 D. 120

59. Ministers in the Union Cabinet are appointed by the:
A. Prime Minister
B. President
C. President of India on the advice of the Prime Minister
D. Prime Minister on the advice of the Chief Justice of the Supreme Court of India

60. Who administers the Union Territories?
A. The President through the Administrators appointed by him
B. The Prime Minister of India
C. The Law Minister, Government of India
D. The Attorney-General of India

61. Which of the following states does not have a Legislative Council?
A. Bihar

B. Uttarakhand
C. Uttar Pradesh
D. Maharashtra

62. How many languages have been mentioned in the Eighth Schedule?
A. 14 B. 22
C. 13 D. 16

63. Which two of these languages are not used as State Languages in any part of India?
A. Sindhi and Sanskrit
B. Sindhi and English
C. Punjabi and Urdu
D. Tamil and Kashmiri

64. The President of India is not a member of Parliament because:
A. he has to maintain his dignity of office
B. he has to see that he remains impartial
C. he holds an office of profit under the Government
D. his position will be lowered if he becomes the member of Parliament

65. There is no law or specific provision so far to govern the President-Prime Minister relationship, yet the President acts on the advice of the Prime Minister; this is based on a convention. This convention in the Indian Constitution follows the pattern of the:
A. US Constitution
B. Russian Constitution
C. Australian Constitution
D. British Constitution

66. How long would an ordinance, issued by the President, operate after re-assembly of Parliament?
A. One fortnight
B. One month
C. Six weeks
D. Eight weeks

67. The States of India were reorganised through which Constitution Amendment Act?
A. First
B. Second
C. Seventh
D. Twenty-first

68. A list of national languages can be traced in the .... of the Indian Constitution.
A. Fifth Schedule
B. Sixth Schedule
C. Eighth Schedule
D. Seventh Schedule

69. Article 17 of the Constitution of India lays down for the:
A. abolition of untouchability
B. election of the Vice-President
C. election of the Speaker of the House of the People
D. removal of poverty

70. Indian Constitution envisages a:
A. bicameral system
B. unicameral system
C. one party government
D. Presidential government

71. The quorum of the Parliament is fixed at:
A. one-tenth of the membership of the House
B. one-third of the membership of the House

C. one-half of the membership of the House

D. four-fifths of the membership of the House

72. The members of Rajya Sabha are:

A. directly elected

B. nominated

C. indirectly elected and nominated as well

D. None of the above

73. Lok Sabha and Rajya Sabha when compared:

A. Lok Sabha is more powerful than the Rajya Sabha

B. they are equally powerful

C. Rajya Sabha is more powerful than the Lok Sabha

D. the 'intensity of Power' varies

74. The sole power to control the expenditure of the Government rests with the:

A. Parliament

B. Prime Minister

C. President of India

D. Lok Sabha

75. The right to impose reasonable restrictions on the 'Fundamental Rights of an Indian Citizen' is vested in:

A. the Supreme Court

B. the Prime Minister

C. the President

D. the Parliament

76. Supreme Court in India has to work according to the:

A. President

B. Prime Minister

C. Parliament

D. Constitution

77. Which one of the following is a regional political party?

A. Akali Dal

B. Congress

C. BJP

D. CPI

78. In the 42nd amendment to the Constitution; a new chapter has been added under which:

A. fundamental rights are modified

B. some of the fundamental rights are abolished

C. directive principles are extended

D. basic duties are added

79. Which of the following is not a fundamental right?

A. Right to speech

B. Right to vocation

C. Right to go on strike

D. Right to religion

80. Fundamental Rights of the Indian citizens are contained in .... of the 'Indian Constitution'.

A. Part I B. Part II

C. Part III D. Part IV

81. Of which fundamental right is a foreigner in India deprived of?

A. To seek justice in court

B. To seek security of life

C. To criticise policies of government

D. To vote at the time of Parliamentary election

82. Right to equality refers to:
A. Equal opportunities for education, employment or business
B. Equality before law
C. Absence of discrimination on the grounds of race, caste, religion, region etc.
D. Both B and C

83. The right to freedom refers to:
A. Right to form any lawful association
B. Right to assemble peacefully
C. Freedom of speech and expression except when it induces unlawful actions of injures the person or property of someone
D. All of these

84. The basic difference between Directive Principles and Fundamental Rights is:
A. Action can lie in the Supreme Court for violation of Fundamental Rights but no such action is possible for enforcement of Directive Principles
B. Directive Principles acquire precedence over Fundamental Rights
C. Fundamental Rights guide the Courts while Directive Principles guide the Parliament
D. There is no difference

85. President's Rule at the centre is imposed:
A. during Lok Sabha elections
B. during emergency (external or internal)
C. if the Prime Minister dies in office
D. not at all; there is no such provision in the Constitution

86. If the Parliament refers a bill to the President for his assent, then what the President can constitutionally do is to:
A. Give his assent
B. refuse his assent
C. send it for reconsideration
D. All the three above

87. Domestic and foreign policies of the Union Government are formulated constitutionally by the:
A. Council of Ministers
B. Rajya Sabha
C. Lok Sabha
D. President and the Vice-President

88. The first Chairman of the Constituent Assembly was
A. Dr. B.R. Ambedkar
B. Dr. Sachidanand
C. Dr. Abdul Ansari
D. B.N. Rao

89. The Constituent Assembly adopted the National Flag on
A. August 22, 1947
B. November 26, 1947
C. January 26, 1948
D. November 26, 1948

90. India's membership to this International Organisation was ratified in May 1949
A. United Nations

B. NAM
C. Commonwealth
D. WTO

91. The date of commencement of the Constitution is
A. January 26, 1948
B. January 26, 1949
C. January 26, 1950
D. January 26, 1951

92. The Constitution derives its authority from the
A. President
B. Citizens of India
C. Supreme Court
D. Prime Minister

93. The sole authority of interpreting the Constitution lies with the
A. Supreme Court of India
B. President
C. Lok Sabha
D. Rajya Sabha

94. Schedules can be added to the Constitution by
A. Constitutional reforms
B. Bills
C. Ordinances
D. Amendments

95. How many High Courts are presently in India?
A. 28 B. 25
C. 20 D. 18

96. The first Constitution Amendment Act was passed in the year
A. 1949 B. 1953
C. 1951 D. 1952

97. The provision for Dual Citizenship was introduced by this Act
A. Citizenship Act of 1955
B. Citizenship Act of 2003
C. Citizenship Amendment Bill of 1992
D. Dual Citizenship Act of 2005

98. This Part of the Constitution guarantees the Fundamental Rights
A. Part I B. Part II
C. Part III D. Part IV

99. Equality before law is guaranteed by
A. Article 14 B. Article 15
C. Article 16 D. Article 17

100. The Right to Information Act came into force on
A. October 12, 2003
B. October 12, 2004
C. October 12, 2005
D. October 12, 2006

101. This writ refers to an order issued by the court to prevent a person from holding office to which he is not entitled and to oust him from that office
A. Habeas Corpus
B. Mandamus
C. Certiorari
D. Quo Warrnato

102. The draft proposal for a law is called a
A. Privilege
B. Motion
C. Ordinance
D. Bill

103. The provisions for constitutional amendments are laid down in
A. Article 358 B. Article 368
C. Article 378 D. Article 388

104. The 73rd Amendment in 1993 made provisions for
A. Extending President's Rule in Punjab
B. Extending reservations for SC/STs
C. Panchayati Raj
D. Reducing the voting age from 21 to 18

105. A proposal asking for a discussion on or expressing an opinion on a matter of public importance is called a
A. Motion B. Privilege
C. Ordinance D. Resolution

106. This Article of the Constitution provides for the formation of a Finance Commission
A. Article 270
B. Article 280
C. Article 290
D. Article 300

107. This Article of the Constitution deals with the abolition of untouchability and its practice in any form
A. Article 14 B. Article 15
C. Article 16 D. Article 17

108. The Parliament reorganised the country according to ethnic and linguistic considerations under the State's Reorganisation Act of
A. 1953 B. 1956
C. 1957 D. 1959

109. Who among the following was a former Portuguese colony
A. Dadra B. Daman
C. Nagar Haveli D. Goa

110. The Capital of the Union territory of Dadra & Nagar Haveli and Daman & Diu is
A. Daman B. Dadra
C. Kavaratti D. Diu

ANSWERS

1	2	3	4	5	6	7	8	9	10
C	B	C	B	C	B	A	A	D	B
11	**12**	**13**	**14**	**15**	**16**	**17**	**18**	**19**	**20**
A	A	B	B	A	A	D	A	C	A
21	**22**	**23**	**24**	**25**	**26**	**27**	**28**	**29**	**30**
B	D	C	C	B	A	B	B	B	B
31	**32**	**33**	**34**	**35**	**36**	**37**	**38**	**39**	**40**
C	D	B	C	B	C	B	A	A	C
41	**42**	**43**	**44**	**45**	**46**	**47**	**48**	**49**	**50**
A	A	A	D	B	B	A	C	D	D

51	52	53	54	55	56	57	58	59	60
C	D	B	B	D	A	D	B	C	A
61	**62**	**63**	**64**	**65**	**66**	**67**	**68**	**69**	**70**
B	B	A	C	D	C	C	C	A	A
71	**72**	**73**	**74**	**75**	**76**	**77**	**78**	**79**	**80**
A	C	A	A	D	D	A	D	C	C
81	**82**	**83**	**84**	**85**	**86**	**87**	**88**	**89**	**90**
D	D	D	A	D	D	A	B	A	C
91	**92**	**93**	**94**	**95**	**96**	**97**	**98**	**99**	**100**
C	B	A	D	B	C	B	C	A	C
101	**102**	**103**	**104**	**105**	**106**	**107**	**108**	**109**	**110**
D	D	B	C	A	B	D	B	D	A

ECONOMY

1. A major trade partner of India in the pre-independence period was

A. USA B. UK
C. USSR D. Australia

2. Which of the following state has been announced as 'a state of total organic farming?

A. Kerala B. Karnataka
C. Sikkim D. Punjab

3. Community Development Projects were launched in

A. 1949 B. 1951
C. 1952 D. 1955

4. Currency notes in India are printed and supplied by the

A. SEBI
B. FICCI
C. IFCI
D. Reserve Bank of India

5. Deficit financing implies

A. printing new currency notes
B. replacing new currency with worn out currency
C. public expenditure in excess of public revenue
D. public revenue in excess of public expenditure

6. Depreciation means

A. closure of a plant due to lockout
B. closure of a plant due to labour trouble
C. loss of equipment over time due to wear and tear
D. destruction of a plant in a fire accident

7. Devaluation of currency leads to

A. fall in domestic prices
B. increase in domestic prices
C. no impact on domestic prices
D. erratic fluctuations in domestic prices

8. Excise duty is a tax levied on the

A. import of goods
B. export of goods
C. production of goods
D. sale of goods

9. 'UDAY Yojana' is associated with:

A. Panchayati Raj
B. Women Empowerment
C. Energy Distribution
D. Banking Sector

10. Which of the following is not a financial institution?

A. FICCI
B. IDBI
C. ICICI
D. HDFC

11. IFCI is the name of a

A. foreign bank
B. finance institution
C. fertilizer company
D. federation of industries

12. Imports into a country generate income for

A. foreign producers
B. domestic manufacturing
C. traders
D. the government

13. In the eighth plan, the emphasis has shifted from growth rate to
A. poverty eradication
B. employment generation
C. social welfare
D. None of the above

14. India Development Forum (IDF) was earlier known as the
A. Aid India Consortium
B. Aid India Bank
C. World Bank
D. None of the above

15. India's objective under the plans has been to achieve
A. growth with or without stability
B. stability, whether there is growth or not
C. growth with stability
D. None of the above

16. Jawahar Rozgar Yojana for rural employment was started in the year
A. 1959 B. 1979
C. 1969 D. 1989

17. Land is a
A. man-made resource
B. non-renewable natural resource
C. renewable natural resource
D. All of the above

18. Medium term financing is usually for a period ranging up to
A. 1 year B. 5 years
C. 3 years D. 10 years

19. MODVAT is related to
A. sales tax B. wealth tax
C. income tax D. excise duty

20. NNP is equal to
A. GNP + depreciation
B. GNP – depreciation
C. GNP + exports
D. GNP – exports

21. Paper currency first started in India in
A. 1862 B. 1542
C. 1601 D. 1680

22. Removal of poverty was the foremost objective of which of the following Five-Year Plan?
A. second B. third
C. fourth D. sixth

23. The balance of trade is also known as
A. capital transfer
B. gain from trade
C. visible balance
D. None of these

24. The basic objective of planning in India is
A. increasing employment opportunities
B. expansion of key industries
C. increase in agricultural output
D. All of the above

25. The celebrated work on Indian economic history, *The Industrial Evolution of India in Recent Times* was written by
A. R.C. Dutt
B. Dadabhai Naoroji
C. Dr. Gadgil
D. William Digby

26. The central banking functions in India are performed by the
A. UCO Bank
B. Reserve Bank of India

C. State Bank of India
D. Punjab National Bank

27. The first iron and steel unit known as the Tata Iron and Steel Company was established in the year
A. 1877 B. 1907
C. 1897 D. 1927

28. The first modern industry to develop in India was the
A. iron and steel industry
B. cottage industry
C. engineering industry
D. cement industry

29. The Food Corporation of India was established in
A. 14 January 1965
B. 1 January 1968
C. 1 June 1966
D. 1 January 1967

30. The Industrial Policy of 1956 was announced by
A. Pt. Jawaharlal Nehru
B. Sardar Patel
C. Balwant Rai Mehta
D. None of these

31. The iron and steel industry is a
A. light industry
B. basic industry
C. auxiliary industry
D. None of the above

32. The largest nationalized bank of India is the
A. State Bank of India
B. Reserve Bank of India
C. Bank of India
D. Central Bank of India

33. Who was the first Chairman of the Planning Commission?
A. Dr. S. Radhakrishnan
B. Dr. Rajendra Prasad
C. Pt. Jawaharlal Nehru
D. None of these

34. Which the following is not an international credit rating agency?
A. Standard and Poor
B. CRISIL
C. Moodys
D. Goldman Sachs

35. The Lead Bank Scheme has to formulate a plan for banking infrastructure in a
A. district B. town
C. state D. village

36. The main feature of tenancy reform may be said to be
A. reduction of rent
B. security of tenure
C. compensation for permanent improvements
D. All of the above

37. The maximum impact of direct tax is on
A. income
B. price of consumer goods
C. price of capital goods
D. price of agricultural output

38. The methods of credit control used by the RBI can be divided into
A. long-term and short-term
B. rural and urban
C. qualitative and quantitative
D. monetary and fiscal

39. The Minimum Wage Act was passed in the year
A. 1938 B. 1958
C. 1948 D. 1968

40. The National Stock Exchange of India was established in

A. 1990 B. 1991
C. 1992 D. 1993

41. The period of 'Plan Holiday' in India was

A. 1962 to 1965
B. 1966 to 1969
C. 1969 to 1972
D. 1972 to 1975

42. The NITI Aayog is a/an

A. advisory body
B. executive body
C. government body
D. autonomous body

43. The principal function of NABARD is to provide finance for the promotion of

A. agriculture
B. small scale and cottage industries
C. handicrafts and other rural craft
D. All of the above

44. The Raj Committee (1972) probed

A. direct taxes
B. indirect taxes
C. agricultural holding tax
D. no tax revenue

45. The relation of savings to the level of income is

A. positive
B. negative
C. uncertain
D. None of the above

46. The Rolling Plan concept in national planning was introduced by

A. Indira Gandhi
B. the National Front Government
C. the Janata Government
D. Rajiv Gandhi

47. The secondary sector of the Indian economy does not include

A. manufacturing
B. construction
C. mining and quarrying
D. electricity, gas and water supply

48. The Steel plant at Durgapur has been set up with assistance from

A. USA B. Russia
C. UK D. Germany

49. The tax paid by every individual is

A. an indirect tax
B. a direct tax
C. a progressive tax
D. None of these

50. Under which Five-Year Plan did agricultural register a negative growth?

A. fifth B. fourth
C. third D. second

51. What is the effect of deficit financing on the economy?

A. Inflation B. Deflation
C. Depression D. Recession

52. What percentage of the world's total area does India have?

A. 4.5 per cent B. 3.7 per cent
C. 2.4 per cent D. 2.2 per cent

53. When were the Railways nationalized?

A. 1945 B. 1946
C. 1947 D. 1951

54. Which of the following can be classified as cash crops?
A. Coffee
B. Tea
C. Rubber
D. All of the above

55. Which of the following can be used to check inflation temporarily?
A. decrease in money supply
B. increase in wages
C. decrease in taxes
D. reduction in taxes

56. 'Smart Money' is a term used for:
A. Internet Banking
B. Cash with Bank
C. Credit Card
D. Cash with Public

57. Which country is the largest Wheat producing country of the world?
A. China
B. India
C. America
D. Switzerland

58. Which of the following is considered to be a non-development expenditure?
A. Defence Services
B. Education
C. Agriculture
D. Roads and Public Works

59. Which of the following taxes has not been merged in GST?
A. Custom Duty
B. Excise Duty
C. Corporate Tax
D. Service Tax

60. SEBI was established in:
A. 1988 B. 1993
C. 1992 D. 1990

61. Which of the following years is known as the 'Year of the Great Divide'?
A. 1921 B. 1927
C. 1932 D. 1935

62. Which state has the largest drought prone area?
A. Rajasthan
B. Gujarat
C. Andhra Pradesh
D. Karnataka

63. Which state has the maximum forest area?
A. Manipur
B. Madhya Pradesh
C. Tripura
D. Nagaland

64. Who suggested the Rolling Plan for backward countries?
A. G. Myrdal
B. W.A. Lewis
C. R. Nurkse
D. A. Samuelson

65. 'World Development Report' is an annual publication of
A. United Nations Development Programme
B. International Bank of Reconstruction and Development
C. World Trade Organization
D. International Monetary Fund

66. A personal account cannot be opened in
A. a Co-operative Bank
B. a Scheduled Bank
C. Reserve Bank of India
D. None of these

67. All taxes come under
A. revenue receipts
B. capital receipts
C. public debt
D. Both A and B

68. An ad valorem duty is a tax basis of
A. the price of the commodity
B. the value added
C. the advertisement expenses
D. the unit of the commodity

69. Bank rate is the rate at which
A. a bank lends to the public
B. the Reserve Bank of India lends to the public
C. the Government of India lends to other countries
D. the Reserve Bank of India gives credit to commercial banks

70. How many banks were nationalized in 1969?
A. 16 B. 14
C. 15 D. 20

71. In which Plan was the growth rate target exceeded
A. Second B. third
C. sixth D. in none

72. Low productivity of agriculture in India is not caused by
A. inadequate availability of inputs
B. sub-division of landholdings
C. less area under cultivation
D. poor finance facilities

73. NABARD is a
A. bank B. bureau
C. board D. department

74. Reserve Bank of India was nationalized in the year
A. 1935 B. 1945
C. 1949 D. 1969

75. Small-scale industries in India are supposed to be
1. labour intensive
2. capital intensive
3. labour light
4. skill light
Choose your answer from the following codes.
A. 1 and 4 B. 2 and 3
C. 2 and 4 D. 1 and 3

76. The *Antodaya* programme was started first of all in the state of
A. Tamil Nadu
B. Odisha
C. Rajasthan
D. West Bengal

77. The budget deficit means
A. the excess of total expenditure, including loans, net of lending over revenue receipts
B. difference between revenue receipts and revenue expenditure
C. difference between all receipts and all the expenditure
D. fiscal deficit less interest payments

78. The cause of unemployment in India is not
A. population explosion
B. inadequate employment planning
C. rapid development of industry
D. Agricultural Stagnation

79. The Export Import (EXIM) Bank was set up in
A. 1980 B. 1982
C. 1981 D. 1989

80. The first Indian bank was the
A. Traders Bank
B. Imperial Bank
C. Presidency Bank, Kolkata
D. None of the above

81. The Food for Work programme has been restructured as the
A. IDLAD B. IRDP
C. MFAL D. NREP

82. The *garibi hatao* (eradicate poverty) slogan was coined during the
A. First Plan
B. Second Plan
C. Third Plan
D. Fourth Plan

83. The SEBI stands for the
A. State Earnings Board of India
B. Securities and Exchange Bank of India
C. Securities and Exchange Board of India
D. State Exchange Bank of India

84. The second nationalization of commercial banks took place in
A. 1979 B. 1980
C. 1981 D. 1982

85. The term fiscal deficit means
A. total receipts minus expeniture
B. total receipts minus interest payments on external debt
C. revenue receipts minus expenditure
D. revenue receipts minus defence expenditure

86. The Trade Unions Act was passed in
A. 1922 B. 1923
C. 1925 D. 1926

87. Which committee was set up to review the concept of the Poverty Line?
A. Chakarvarty Committee
B. Lakdawala Committee
C. Wanchooo Committee
D. Dutt Committee

88. Who was the first Indian Governor of the Reserve Bank of India?
A. C.D. Deshmukh
B. Sachindra Ray
C. S. Mukherjee
D. None of these

89. Gilt-edged market means
A. bullion market
B. market of government securities
C. market of guns
D. market of pure metals

90. In India, the public sector is the most dominant in
A. steel production
B. organized term-ending financial institution
C. transport
D. commercial banking

91. Which is the first Export Processing Zone declared as Free Trade Zone in India?
A. Santacruz B. Kandla
C. Falta D. Noida

92. 'Backwash Effect' was firstly introduced by
A. Gunnar Myrdal
B. Peter Suderland
C. Arthur Dunkel
D. Kindelberger

93. Meera Seth Committee was related to
A. Development of Handlooms
B. Sex-differentiation in employment
C. Abolition of Child Labour
D. Welfare of working women

94. 'SAPTA' is related to
A. Education
B. Trade
C. Security
D. Environment

95. National Income estimates in India is prepared by
A. NITI Aayog
B. RBI
C. Finance Ministry
D. C.S.O.

96. The definition of small scale industry in India is based on
A. Sales of a unit
B. Investment in machines and equipments
C. Market coverage
D. Export capacity

97. The book 'Politics of Charkha' is written by
A. Ashok Mehta
B. J.B. Kriplani
C. K.G. Mashruwala
D. Morarji Desai

98. Which of the following does not grant any tax rebate?
A. National Saving Certificate
B. Indira Vikas Patra
C. National Saving Scheme
D. Public Provident Fund

99. National Rural Development Institute is situated at
A. Shimla B. Hyderabad
C. Patna D. New Delhi

100. The Headquarter of World Bank is situated at
A. Manila
B. Washington D.C.
C. New York
D. Geneva

101. The main foodgrains of India is
A. Rice B. Wheat
C. Sugarcane D. Maize

102. Which sector has the maximum quantum of disguised unemployment in India?
A. Agriculture B. Industry
C. Trade D. Transport

103. The goods can be taxed heavily to earn additional revenue if they are
A. Highly elastic
B. Unit elastic
C. Perfectly elastic
D. Inelastic

104. The field given to Rangarajan Committee was
A. Modernisation of Cloth Industry
B. To probe Share scam
C. To probe Sugar scam
D. To suggest measures for controlling BOP deficit

105. Gresham's Law is related to
A. Consumption and Demand
B. Supply and Demand
C. Circulation of Money
D. Deficit Financing

106. Kelkar Committee report is related to

A. Tax Reforms
B. Financial Sector Reforms
C. Trade Reforms
D. Administrative Reforms

107. What is 'Super 301'?

A. A name of modern computer
B. A new variety of Rice
C. American trade law
D. American treatment name for Aids

108. Population Density means

A. No. of persons living per sq. km.
B. No. of persons living per kilometre
C. Ratio of population living below poverty line to total population
D. No. of persons in a village

109. Which tax is collected by Panchayat?

A. Sales Tax
B. Custom Duty
C. Land Revenue
D. Tax on local fairs

110. Centralised planning was first adopted in the economy of

A. Russia B. Poland
C. China D. India

ANSWERS

1	2	3	4	5	6	7	8	9	10
B	C	C	D	C	C	B	C	C	A
11	12	13	14	15	16	17	18	19	20
B	A	B	C	C	D	C	B	A	B
21	22	23	24	25	26	27	28	29	30
B	D	C	D	C	B	B	D	A	A
31	32	33	34	35	36	37	38	39	40
B	A	C	B	A	B	A	C	C	C
41	42	43	44	45	46	47	48	49	50
B	A	D	C	A	C	C	C	B	C
51	52	53	54	55	56	57	58	59	60
A	C	D	D	A	C	A	A	C	A
61	62	63	64	65	66	67	68	69	70
A	A	B	A	B	C	A	B	D	B
71	72	73	74	75	76	77	78	79	80
C	C	A	C	A	C	C	D	B	B
81	82	83	84	85	86	87	88	89	90
D	D	C	B	A	D	B	A	B	D
91	92	93	94	95	96	97	98	99	100
B	A	A	B.	D	B	B	B	B	B
101	102	103	104	105	106	107	108	109	110
A	A	D	D	C	A	C	A	D	A

GEOGRAPHY

1. The cause of earthquakes is mainly due to:
   A. Denudation
   B. Tectonic forces
   C. Erosion
   D. Weathering

2. The cause of soil erosion are:
   A. rocks
   B. sand
   C. wind and water
   D. none of these

3. Light takes this much time to reach the earth from the sun:
   A. 400 seconds B. 20 seconds
   C. 8 minutes D. 8 seconds

4. What is a light year?
   A. A year in which there is constant light
   B. A year in which the gravitational pull is less than normal value of 'G'
   C. The distance traversed by the light in one year
   D. A unit of time (that earth takes to go round the sun)

5. The ozone layer of the earth's atmosphere is:
   A. Stratosphere
   B. troposphere
   C. exosphere
   D. ionosphere

6. Days and nights are caused due to the earth's:
   A. rotation
   B. revolution
   C. gravitational pull
   D. nearness to the Sun

7. Change of seasons and their formation is caused by this of the earth:
   A. gravity
   B. inclination of the axis of the earth to plane of the orbit
   C. rotation
   D. revolution

8. Tides occur twice in every:
   A. 24 hours
   B. 22 hours
   C. 48 hours
   D. 24 hours and 52 seconds

9. Neap Tides occur:
   A. at half moon
   B. during the day
   C. once a month
   D. twice a week

10. Spring tides occur:
    A. during the day
    B. during the summer season
    C. during the spring season
    D. at full moon or new moon

11. Which of the following statements is true?
    A. Animals help weathering
    B. Plants help weathering
    C. Both plants and animals help weathering
    D. Both plants and animals hinder weathering

12. This water is responsible for formation of wells, springs and geysers etc:
    A. Snow water
    B. Sea water
    C. River water
    D. Underground sub-soil water

13. The sea is never full because:
A. it does not have enough water to fill the sea
B. the sea is always getting deeper and deeper
C. the earth absorbs the water therefore all the excessive rain cannot fill the sea
D. more water evaporates than rains comes down

14. Lunar Eclipse is caused when:
A. the sun, the moon and the earth are in a line
B. the earth comes between the sun and the moon
C. the sun and the earth are on either side of the moon
D. the sun comes between the earth and the moon

15. Snow line is:
A. the line above which snow never melts
B. the line below which snow never falls
C. the line above which snow is never seen
D. great mass of snow on the poles

16. Apart from the sun and the moon, the brightest object in the sky is:
A. the North Star
B. Mercury
C. Venus
D. Mars

17. Which planet is known as a blue planet?
A. Mercury B. Venus
C. Jupiter D. Earth

18. The rings of Saturn are:
A. solid sheets of rock
B. composed of billions of ice-covered rock particles
C. liquid
D. gaseous

19. Which planet is known as a Red planet?
A. Venus B. Mercury
C. Jupiter D. Mars

20. Two high tides occur after an average interval of:
A. 24 hours 2 minutes
B. 12 hours 26 minutes
C. 14 hours
D. 8 hours

21. The moon has got a diameter of about:
A. 5045 km B. 3476 km
C. 4009 km D. 2345 km

22. The smallest planets is:
A. Venus B. Mercury
C. Jupiter D. Earth

23. Pampas, the widely treeless grassy plains belongs to:
A. Africa
B. North America
C. Australia
D. South America

24. The Venus is called the:
A. Brightest planet
B. Blue planet
C. Red planet
D. None of these

25. The least important agent of erosion is:
A. streams B. glaciers
C. winds D. waves

26. The most important agent of erosion is:
A. streams B. glaciers
C. winds D. waves

27. The planets shine because:
A. they emit light
B. they are illuminated by nearby stars
C. they reflect light reaching them from the sun
D. they reflect light reaching them from the earth

28. The principal constituent of the earth's core is believed to be:
A. iron B. nickel
C. silicon D. olivine

29. The pressure of the earth's atmosphere is due to:
A. the gravitational attraction of the earth for the atmosphere
B. the heating of the atmosphere by the sun
C. the fact that most living things constantly breathe air
D. evaporation of water from the seas and oceans

30. The seasons occur because the:
A. earth's axis is tilted
B. earth's orbit is an ellipse
C. moon obstructs different amounts of sunlight at different times of year
D. sun's output of radiation varies throughout the year

31. The nearest planet to the earth is:
A. Mercury B. Saturn
C. Venus D. Jupiter

32. The mass of the moon in comparison to the earth is:
A. 1/4
B. 1/80
C. 1/200
D. none of these

33. A light-year is a unit of:
A. time B. distance
C. velocity D. energy

34. The sun obtains its energy from:
A. the nuclear fission of uranium
B. nuclear reactions in which hydrogen is converted into helium
C. nuclear reactions in which helium is converted into hydrogen
D. the burning of hydrogen and carbon

35. The outer layers of rocks around the earth are called the:
A. skin
B. rim
C. crust
D. peripheral strata

36. A fertile soil consists of:
A. sand and pebbles
B. dry dead leaves
C. sand and clay
D. loam and humus

37. The main masses of land above sea level are called:
A. continents B. islands
C. nations D. countries

38. Sedimentary rocks are easily recognized in the field because:
A. they form rounded hills
B. they are folded
C. they occur in horizontal layers
D. they occur in layers

39. Places on the same meridian experience what at the same time:

A. rain B. snow
C. midnight D. noon

40. The point of origin of an earthquake is called:

A. focus B. epicenter
C. radius D. diameter

41. When the earth is in perihelion, then it is:

A. nearest to the moon
B. nearest to sun and moon
C. farthest from sun
D. nearest to the sun

42. Of the following, which is the most direct cause of the tides on earth?

A. The tilt of the earth's poles
B. The magnetic field of the earth
C. The revolution of the earth about the sun
D. The effect of the moon's gravitational pull on earth

43. The humidity in the atmosphere is at its highest in:

A. autumn
B. monsoon
C. summer
D. winter

44. For which crop is black soil most congenial?

A. Cotton B. Gram
C. Millet D. Barley

45. Which is the crop of the longest duration?

A. Gram B. Millet
C. Barley D. Sugarcane

46. About .... of the earth's surface is covered by water.

A. 60% B. 70%
C. 79% D. 55%

47. Not all deserts are the result of changes in climate. Some are man-made. How?

A. Because of the cutting down of trees
B. Because of man's neglect of his private lawns
C. Since man started exploiting water resources for electricity generation, the land areas were adversely affected and they subsequently got converted into (man-made) deserts
D. Deserts are not man-made at all.

48. Contours are:

A. The lines drawn through places of equal heights above sea-level
B. Lines of Latitude
C. Lines of Longitude
D. Lines connecting the seaports

49. A strip of land connecting two large land masses is called the:

A. Strait B. Isthmus
C. Isotherm D. Lagoon

50. When a traveller crosses the International Date Line from west to east, he will:

A. gain one day
B. lose twelve hours
C. gain twelve hours
D. lose one day

51. What mountains traditionally serve as boundary separating Europe from Asia?
A. The Alps
B. The Himalayas
C. The Caucasus
D. The Urals

52. Durand Line is the boundary of the two countries namely:
A. India and Pakistan
B. Pakistan and Afghanistan
C. Nepal and India
D. Nepal and China

53. The length of the day at the equator is:
A. 16 h B. 14 h
C. 12 h D. 24 h

54. The greatest mass of ice on the earth's surface is found at:
A. Canada B. Greenland
C. Siberia D. Antarctica

55. The Great Barrier Reef is a:
A. plateau
B. coral formation
C. mountain
D. tidal bore

56. 49th Parallel divides:
A. India and Pakistan
B. South and North America
C. USA and Canada
D. North and South Vietnam

57. The 'Murray' river is in the country known as:
A. China B. Australia
C. Egypt D. France

58. Which country is the world's largest producer of wool?
A. New Zealand
B. Australia
C. South Africa
D. Brazil

59. Which is the largest Gulf in the world?
A. The Gulf of Mexico
B. The Gulf of Cambay
C. The Persian Gulf
D. The Gulf of China

60. The largest producer of milk in India is:
A. Uttar Pradesh
B. Rajasthan
C. Punjab
D. Gujrat

61. What is the name of the canal that joins the Pacific Ocean and the Caribbean Sea?
A. Kiel B. Panama
C. Suez D. Caledonian

62. The largest island in the world is.....
A. Tasmania B. Cyprus
C. Iceland D. Greenland

63. The Strait of Gibraltar separates Spain from:
A. Asia
B. Africa
C. North America
D. England

64. The deepest known point of the oceans is found in the:
A. Atlantic Ocean
B. Pacific Ocean
C. Indian Ocean
D. South China Sea

65. On which of the following river the Tulbul project is located?
A. Beas

B. Jhelum
C. Ravi
D. Satluj

66. The famous 'Gir' forests are located in:
A. Tamil Nadu
B. Gujrat
C. Kerala
D. Uttar Pradesh

67. Commerically speaking the world's most important canal is:
A. Panama
B. Albert
C. Suez
D. Amsterdam-Rhine

68. Which of the following is a block mountain?
A. Rocky B. Alps
C. Vosgas D. Andes

69. Which of the following is not a fertilizer mineral?
A. Nitrate B. Tungsten
C. Phosphate D. Potash

70. Suez provides a short sea-trade route between:
A. Far East, Arabian countries, and countries on Eastern Coast of Africa on one hand and Europe on the other
B. Europe and USA
C. West African countries and Europe
D. Russia and China on one hand and Europe on the other

71. The world is divided into:
A. 20 time zones
B. 12 time zones
C. 24 time zones
D. 36 time zones

72. Which of the following countries is the world's largest producer of rubber?
A. Sri Lanka
B. Nigeria
C. Zaire Republic
D. Thailand

73. The world's four largest deserts are:
A. Sahara, Gobi, Thar, Atacama
B. Sahara, Great Australian, Great Arabian, Gobi
C. Sahara, Kalahari, Takla Makan, Thar
D. Great Arabian, Sahara, Sonoran, Thar

74. Water transportation has long been important because:
A. it is the fastest means of transportation
B. it is the cheapest means of moving heavy goods
C. goods can be delivered directly to factories
D. it is the safest means of transport

75. The three longest rivers in the world are:
A. Nile, Congo, Ganges
B. Amazon, Mississipi, Amur
C. Nile, Amur, Volga
D. Nile, Amazon, Mississipi Missouri

76. Sudan and Egypt are known for:
A. Sugarcane B. Tea
C. Cotton D. Coffee

77. The northern part of Europe is called:
A. The Alpine region
B. Scandinavia
C. Benelux
D. None of the above

78. Littoral forests are rich source of:
A. bamboo
B. timber
C. firewood
D. none of these

79. ....is the capital of Morocco.
A. Muscat B. Managua
C. Rabbat D. Beijing

80. Central China, Japan, Northern New Zealand and New South Wales fall in:
A. Temperate Monsoon Region
B. Temperate Grassland
C. Mid-latitude Deserts
D. None of these

81. Cotton is grown in the Nile River Valley because:
A. The climate of Egypt is different from the rest of the Middle East
B. A warm climate and irrigated land are best for growing cotton
C. Farmers in Egypt are richer than farmers in the rest of the region
D. All the three above

82. The continent of Africa is divided into two parts by the:
A. Sahara Desert
B. Atlas Mountains
C. Congo River
D. Kalahari Desert

83. The Congo has been an important section of Africa because:
A. it lies along the trade routes from north to south
B. its mines have copper and diamonds
C. it has the only oil processing plants in Africa
D. none of the above

84. Australia may be called a 'hollow continent' because:
A. most people live along the coasts
B. it is shaped like a saucer
C. there are no rivers in the interior
D. a last part of it is a waste desert

85. Australians are able to grow large amounts of wheat because:
A. The fields are large, flat and suited to the use of machinery
B. Fields are far from the smoke-filled cities
C. They have a large labour supply and plenty of rainfall
D. All the three above

86. Australia is good for raising sheep because:
A. There is plenty of grass throughout the country
B. The warm northern lowlands are ideal for raising sheep
C. Much of the country is dry and sheep need little water
D. Both B and C

87. Which geographical region in India is the largest producer of saffron (Kesar)?

A. Konkan B. Telengana
C. Kashmir D. Coorg

88. Tropic of Cancer passes through:

A. Uttar Pradesh
B. Madhya Pradesh
C. Andhra Pradesh
D. Maharashtra

89. The right bank tributaries of the river Ganga are:

A. Gomti and Yamuna
B. Gandak and Ghaghra
C. Yamuna and Sone
D. Sone and Kosi

90. The largest of Indian peninsular rivers is:

A. Ganga B. Krishna
C. Godavari D. Narmada

91. Mention the period of blowing of South-West monsoon winds in India:

A. All the year round
B. From October to January
C. From June to September
D. From April to July

92. The Eastern and Western Ghats join at:

A. Palani Hills
B. Nilgiri Hills
C. Anamalai Hills
D. Malabar Hills

93. The 'Blue Mountains' is the epithet applicable to the:

A. Satpura mountains
B. Nilgiri mountains
C. Lushai hills
D. Aravali hills

94. The river 'Luni' is lost in:

A. Arabian Sea
B. Deltas
C. Rann of Kutch
D. Thar

95. The State in India with the largest coastline is:

A. Tamil Nadu
B. Gujarat
C. Andhra Pradesh
D. Maharashtra

96. The second largest river basin in India is:

A. Krishna basin
B. Brahmaputra basin
C. Godavari basin
D. Cauvery basin

97. 60 per cent of commercial energy in India comes from:

A. Coal
B. Wind
C. Hydel
D. Nuclear projects

98. Which one of the following rivers flows between Vindhya ranges and Satpura?

A. Mahanadi B. Narmada
C. Krishna D. Godavari

99. North India receives rain in winter because of:

A. Retreating monsoon
B. North East monsoon
C. South West monsoon
D. Western disturbances

100. River Chambal flows through:

A. Rajasthan, MP, UP
B. MP, UP, Bihar
C. MP, Rajasthan, Gujarat
D. MP, Bihar, West Bengal

101. If you go to Tuticorin, Paradip, Kandla and Mangalore, you won't have to go through:
A. Tamil Nadu B. Odisha
C. Gujarat D. Kerala

102. Which one of the following match with Khetri, Jharia, Kudremukh, Kolar respectively?
A. Coal, bauxite, iron, gold
B. Bauxite, coal, iron, gold
C. Copper, coal, iron, gold
D. Iron, copper, coal, gold

103. Bhakra, Hirakud, Nagarjuna Sagar and Ukai are situated on ....respectively.
A. Beas, Mahanadi, Godavari and Tapti
B. Beas, Mahanadi, Krishna and Narmada
C. Sutlej, Mahanadi, Krishna and Tapti
D. Ravi, Sutlej, Cauveri and Narmada

104. Irrigation is essential for India because:
A. it has variable rainfall
B. irrigated land produces higher yields
C. it is easy to dig up canals etc
D. it is cheaper and time saving

105. A place with an average rainfall of 200 cms, temperature 25°C and on sloping grounds would be suitable for the cultivation of:
A. Coffee B. Tea
C. Tobacco D. Rice

106. For seeds to remain viable, they should be stored in a:
A. cool and dry place
B. dry and warm place
C. moist and warm place
D. cool and moist place

107. Which of the following groups constitutes the basic rock forms?
A. Lignite, volcanic, sedimentary
B. Sandy, igneous, metamorphic
C. Igneous, sedimentary, metamorphic
D. Sandy, volcanic, igneous

108. The soil best suited for wheat cultivation is:
A. Red B. Laterite
C. Black D. Alluvial

109. Vijayawada city is located near the banks of this river:
A. Gomati B. Godavari
C. Krishna D. Cauvery

110. Which is the largest food crop produced in India?
A. Maize B. Rice
C. Wheat D. Jowar

111. The average annual rainfall in India is about:
A. 14 cm B. 39 cm
C. 105 cm D. 180 cm

112. The largest producer of iron ore in India is:
A. Madhya Pradesh
B. Jammu and Kashmir
C. Jharkhand
D. Odisha

113. Which is not a plant fibre crop?
A. Silk B. Cotton
C. Jute D. Flax

114. In which of the following States, mica is not found:
A. Bihar
B. Rajasthan

C. Karnataka
D. Andhara Pradesh

115. Hirakud Dam is built across the river:
A. Bargi B. Ramganga
C. Krishna D. Mahanadi

116. The Indian National Institution of Oceanography is situated in:
A. Mumbai
B. Panaji
C. Visakhapatnam
D. Port Blair

117. Surat is situated on the bank of river:
A. Tapti B. Godavari
C. Narmada D. Bhima

118. According to geological studies, the oldest mountains among the following are:
A. Nilgiris B. Himalayas
C. Aravallis D. Satpuras

119. The Satpura range runs parallel to:
A. The Ganga and the Yamuna
B. The Cauvery and the Krishna
C. The Narmada and the Godavari
D. The Narmada and the Tapti

120. Indian Institute of Petroleum is situated in which of the following cities?
A. Kandla
B. Kochin
C. Dehradun
D. Visakhapatnam

121. Tobacco in India grows in abundance in areas which are:
A. dry and sandy
B. rocky
C. hot and moist
D. cool and rocky

122. The Girnar Hills are situated in which of the following states?
A. Gujrat
B. Uttar Pradesh
C. Rajasthan
D. Madhya Pradesh

123. Tin yielding State in India is:
A. Uttar Pradesh
B. Punjab
C. Himachal Pradesh
D. Jharkhand

124. Visakhapatnam is famous for:
A. Television sets
B. Watches
C. Ship building
D. Aeroplane building

125. The important fishing harbour in India is:
A. Kolkata B. Kochin
C. Paradeep D. Mumbai

126. The river Ganga has two major sources:
A. Bhagirathi and Alaknanda
B. Bhagirathi and Yamuna
C. Bhagirathi and Saraswati
D. Alaknanda and Gandak

127. Koyana Project supplies electricity to a number of big cities which include:
A. Surat and Bharuch
B. Goa
C. Poona and Mumbai
D. Kolhapur

128. The source of the Indus river lies in the:
A. Mount Kailash region of Tibet

B. Shivalik Hills
C. Hindukush mountains
D. Chitral area

129. The Cauveri river flows into the:
A. Bay of Bengal
B. Arabian Sea
C. Palk Strait
D. Gulf of Mannar

130. One of the following rivers flow towards the north and that is:
A. Krishna B. Chambal
C. Narmada D. Tapti

131. 'Tsangpo' is the name of an Indian river which for some length flows outside India and it is:
A. Ganga B. Indus
C. Brahmaputra D. Sutlej

132. We can not find 'Laterite Soil' in an Indian state called:
A. Rajasthan B. Tamil Nadu
C. Assam D. Odisha

133. Red Soil is found in which one of the following States/UT?
A. Himachal Pradesh
B. Jammu & Kashmir
C. Karnataka
D. Assam

134. One of the following rivers flows towards the western side and that is:
A. Godavari B. Krishna
C. Mahanadi D. Periyar

135. Raniganj Coal Mine is situated in:
A. West Bengal
B. Jharkhand
C. Maharashtra
D. Andhra Pradesh

136. Chennai is hotter than Kolkata because:
A. there is no mountain nearby
B. Chennai is closer to the sea than Kolkata
C. Chennai is nearer to the Equator
D. Chennai has sandy region everywhere

137. Mumbai is colder in summer and warmer in winter because:
A. absence of any mountain range nearby
B. its nearness to the sea
C. rainfall during both the seasons
D. nearness to the Equator

138. Moscow is situated on the bank of:
A. Spree
B. Volga
C. Moskva
D. Tagus

139. The great mountain region of the Himalayas runs upto about ...... from Assam westwards.
A. 2,400 km B. 1,500 km
C. 1,000 km D. 4,324 km

140. Most of the soil of the Indo-Gangetic Plain is:
A. black soil B. rocky soil
C. alluvial soil D. sandy soil

141. 'Sabarmati' is the river that flows near a city namely:
A. Mumbai B. Ahmedabad
C. Hyderabad D. Vijayawada

142. The Indus river flows through one of the Indian States/UT also and its name is:
A. Punjab

B. Rajasthan
C. Gujarat
D. Jammu and Kashmir

143. The Mahanadi river mostly cultivates the soil of an Indian State namely:
A. Odisha
B. Madhya Pradesh
C. Maharashtra
D. Andhra Pradesh

144. The major part of ..... is cultivated by the Periyar river:
A. Tamil Nadu
B. Karnataka
C. Kerala
D. Maharashtra

145. Haldia in West Bengal is famous for its.......
A. Steel-goods
B. Radio industry
C. Oil refinery
D. Atomic power station

146. 'Lion' in India is still preserved in:
A. Gir Forests of Kathiawar
B. Kerala State
C. Rajasthan State
D. West Bengal forests

147. The Alpine races mostly live in the Indian States of:
A. Tamil Nadu and Kerala
B. Karnataka and Maharashtra
C. Gujarat and West Bengal
D. Rajasthan and Punjab

148. Cultivation by tanks is undertaken in which one of the following States of India?
A. Uttar Pradesh B. Assam
C. Rajasthan D. Karnataka

149. The Bomdila Pass is located in which state?
A. Nagaland
B. Sikkim
C. Arunachal Pradesh
D. Himachal Pradesh

150. Daman is situated at a distance of about 100 miles from Mumbai towards:
A. south B. east
C. north D. south-east

151. The first multipurpose project of independent India is:
A. Bhakra-Nangal
B. Damodar
C. Hirakud
D. Nagarjuna Sagar

152. The 'Lepchas' are mostly found in an Indian State namely:
A. Assam
B. Arunachal Pradesh
C. Sikkim
D. Jammu & Kashmir

153. The town Titagarh is associated with the industry of:
A. Cement
B. Glass
C. Coal mining
D. Paper

154. The Indian State/UT that traditionally tops in hosiery and woollen goods in India is:
A. Kerala
B. Karnataka
C. Punjab
D. Jammu and Kashmir

155. The driest part of India is:
A. Western Rajasthan
B. Jammu & Kashmir
C. Gujarat
D. Madhya Pradesh

156. Which one of the following States of India receives rainfall in winter?
A. Tamil Nadu
B. Rajasthan
C. Madhya Pradesh
D. Western Odisha

157. The landscape of Kutch is:
A. hilly
B. low-lying, flat and sandy plains
C. fertile lands having rich crops
D. only sands and nothing else

158. Which one of the following States has no coal or oil resources?
A. Gujarat B. Assam
C. Bihar D. Tamil Nadu

159. The river Damodar rises in the:
A. Rajasthan State
B. Gujarat State
C. Chhotanagpur Plateau
D. Arunachal Pradesh Hills

160. The river flowing northwards from central India in the Yamuna is:
A. Chambal B. Gandak
C. Luni D. Kosi

161. The Rihand Dam was constructed on the river:
A. Chambal B. Sone
C. Murali D. Periyar

162. Teak wood can be found in:
A. Chhattisgarh
B. Gujarat
C. Maharashtra
D. Rajasthan

163. Chilka is the name of a:
A. Lake on the east coast of India
B. Mountain in the Himalayas
C. River of Bihar
D. City in Assam

164. A monazite factory is located in one of the following places:
A. Jaipur B. Cuttack
C. Alwaye D. Kottayam

165. If we stand at one of the following stations, we can have a view of the Mount Everest and the Kanchanjungha mounts:
A. Srinagar
B. Jammu
C. Hardwar
D. Darjeeling

166. Bhubaneshwar, the capital of Odisha is also famous for:
A. its oil refinery
B. its iron and steel industry
C. its famous Lingaraja temple
D. its shipping industry

167. At which place will you find maximum sunlight in December?
A. Kanyakumari B. Pune
C. Kolkata D. Leh

168. The number of states having common boundary with the state of Madhya Pradesh:
A. 7 B. 6
C. 5 D. 8

169. "Laterite Soil" is found in India in:
A. Western Ghats
B. Eastern Ghats
C. Deccan Plateau
D. Satpura region in Madhya Pradesh

170. The winter rain in Chennai is caused by:
A. South-West Monsoons

B. North-East Monsoons
C. Intense land and sea breezes
D. Cyclonic winds in the Bay of Bengal

171. The sea territory of India extends up to:
A. 4 nautical miles
B. 12 nautical miles
C. 200 nautical miles
D. none of these

172. The crop which is sown with the commencement of Monsoon is:
A. rabi crop
B. kharif crop
C. cash crop
D. none of these

173. The chief industry located at Varanasi is:
A. Utensils
B. Carpets
C. Diesel locomotive
D. Wood work

174. Of the following, the city not situated at the bank of Ganga is:
A. Bhagalpur B. Kanpur
C. Varanasi D. Gaya

175. The cutting of forests leads to:
A. Soil erosion and incontrollable floods
B. Desilting and denaturation
C. Increase to rainfall and humidity
D. None of these

176. India provides most of the world's requirements of:
A. Jute B. Aluminium
C. Mica D. Manganese

177. In which state of India is an evergreen tropical forest to be found?
A. Arunachal Pradesh
B. Jammu & Kashmir
C. Himachal Pradesh
D. Kerala

178. The currency of Thailand is
A. Kyat B. Baht
C. Dollar D. Yen

179. Argentina is located in
A. Asia
B. Africa
C. Europe
D. South America

180. Which of the following is not an island
A. Panama B. Iceland
C. Sri Lanka D. Borneo

181. Equator, Tropic of Cancer and Tropic of Capricorn all pass through the continent of
A. Australia
B. North America
C. South America
D. Africa

182. Cabinet declared which day as 'National Space Day' in India?
A. August, 23 B. August, 20
C. August, 25 D. August, 27

183. Which of the following is a cold current
A. Kuro shio
B. Brazil
C. East Australian
D. Labrador

184. ....is an example of a seasonal wind
A. Monsoon B. Trade
C. Westerlies D. Loo

185. Which of the towns are situated on the River Nile
A. Alexandria and Bagdad
B. Alexandria and Cairo
C. Bagdad and Bangkok
D. Cairo and Bagdad

186. Mark the correct combination
A. Japan–Peso
B. Guinea–Leu
C. China–Yuan
D. Bulgaria–Kip

187. The longest day in the Northern Hemisphere is on
A. December 22nd
B. September 23rd
C. March 21st
D. June 21st

188. Qantas airlines belongs to
A. Switzerland
B. Australia
C. United Kingdom
D. Italy

189. Adam's Bridge is
A. a coral reef
B. an oasis
C. a group of islets
D. none of these

190. A mini steel plant uses this raw material in its production process
A. Scrap iron B. Iron ore
C. Steel D. Coal

191. Indian climate is an example of
A. Equatorial
B. Tropical Monsoon
C. Mediterranean
D. Sub-Tropical

192. New Moore island is located in
A. Indian Ocean
B. Arabian Sea
C. Bay of Bengal
D. Palk Strait

193. The strait located between Sri Lanka and India is
A. Cook Strait
B. Strait of Malacca
C. Palk Strait
D. Strait of Gibraltar

194. 'The Sugar Bowl' of the world is
A. Cuba B. India
C. USA D. China

195. Bauxite is an ore of
A. Iron B. Manganese
C. Mica D. Aluminium

196. Superior quality coal is
A. Anthracite B. Bituminous
C. Peat D. Lignite

197. This country lead in the production of tea
A. Sri Lanka B. Japan
C. Myanmar D. China

198. The world's longest road is
A. Grand Trunk Road
B. Monumental Axis
C. Pan Am Highway
D. Broadway Street

199. These are examples of Block Moutains in India
A. Garo and Khasi
B. Aravallis and Nilgiris
C. Vindhyas and Satpuras
D. Western and Eastern Ghats

200. The two main types of alluvial soils in India are
A. Bhangar and Terai
B. Khadar and Bhangar
C. Bhabar and Terai
D. None of these

ANSWERS

1	2	3	4	5	6	7	8	9	10
B	C	C	C	A	A	D	D	A	D
11	**12**	**13**	**14**	**15**	**16**	**17**	**18**	**19**	**20**
C	D	D	B	A	C	D	B	D	B
21	**22**	**23**	**24**	**25**	**26**	**27**	**28**	**29**	**30**
B	B	D	A	C	A	C	A	A	A
31	**32**	**33**	**34**	**35**	**36**	**37**	**38**	**39**	**40**
C	B	B	B	C	D	A	D	D	A
41	**42**	**43**	**44**	**45**	**46**	**47**	**48**	**49**	**50**
D	D	B	A	D	B	A	A	B	A
51	**52**	**53**	**54**	**55**	**56**	**57**	**58**	**59**	**60**
D	B	C	D	B	C	B	B	A	A
61	**62**	**63**	**64**	**65**	**66**	**67**	**68**	**69**	**70**
B	D	B	B	B	B	C	C	B	A
71	**72**	**73**	**74**	**75**	**76**	**77**	**78**	**79**	**80**
C	D	B	B	D	C	B	C	C	A
81	**82**	**83**	**84**	**85**	**86**	**87**	**88**	**89**	**90**
B	C	B	A	A	A	C	B	C	C
91	**92**	**93**	**94**	**95**	**96**	**97**	**98**	**99**	**100**
C	B	B	C	B	C	A	B	D	A
101	**102**	**103**	**104**	**105**	**106**	**107**	**108**	**109**	**110**
D	C	C	A	B	A	C	D	C	B
111	**112**	**113**	**114**	**115**	**116**	**117**	**118**	**119**	**120**
C	D	A	C	D	B	A	C	D	D
121	**122**	**123**	**124**	**125**	**126**	**127**	**128**	**129**	**130**
C	A	D	C	B	A	C	A	A	B
131	**132**	**133**	**134**	**135**	**136**	**137**	**138**	**139**	**140**
C	A	C	D	A	C	B	C	A	C
141	**142**	**143**	**144**	**145**	**146**	**147**	**148**	**149**	**150**
B	D	A	C	C	A	C	D	C	C
151	**152**	**153**	**154**	**155**	**156**	**157**	**158**	**159**	**160**
B	C	D	C	A	A	B	D	C	A
161	**162**	**163**	**164**	**165**	**166**	**167**	**168**	**169**	**170**
B	A	A	C	D	C	A	C	A	B
171	**172**	**173**	**174**	**175**	**176**	**177**	**178**	**179**	**180**
B	B	C	D	A	A	D	B	D	A
181	**182**	**183**	**184**	**185**	**186**	**187**	**188**	**189**	**190**
D	A	D	A	B	C	D	B	C	A
191	**192**	**193**	**194**	**195**	**196**	**197**	**198**	**199**	**200**
B	C	C	A	D	A	D	C	D	A

INDIA AT A GLANCE

1. Lambadi Embroidery belongs to which state?
A. Telangana
B. Maharashtra
C. Odisha
D. Tamil Nadu

2. The first Indian State to be ruled by the Communists is:
A. West Bengal
B. Kerala
C. Manipur
D. Andhra Pradesh

3. The largest State in area in India is:
A. UP
B. Rajasthan
C. Bihar
D. Andhra Pradesh

4. Capital of which of the following states of India is not situated on the Banks of river?
A. Bihar
B. Telangana
C. UP
D. Madhya Pradesh

5. Which of the following river does not form an estuary?
A. Yamuna
B. Narmada
C. Sharavati
D. Tapti

6. Which State in India is the highest producer of opium?
A. Madhya Pradesh
B. Uttar Pradesh
C. Gujarat
D. Bihar

7. Which Indian State is often called the heart of India?
A. UP
B. Punjab
C. Madhya Pradesh
D. West Bengal

8. Which State was formerly known as Mysore?
A. Karnataka
B. Tamil Nadu
C. Maharashtra
D. Madhya Pradesh

9. Which of the southern states of India records the maximum rainfall in a year?
A. Tamil Nadu
B. Andhra Pradesh
C. Kerala
D. Karnataka

10. The smallest State (in area) of the Indian Union is:
A. Kerala B. Tripura
C. Punjab D. Goa

11. Damodar Valley Project is a joint project of:
A. Bihar and Odisha
B. Odisha and West Bengal
C. West Bengal and Jharkhand
D. Odisha and West Bengal

12. State that has the highest urban population is:
A. Gujarat
B. Maharashtra

C. Rajasthan
D. Uttar Pradesh

13. Which State is known by the name of 'Mountain State'?
A. Arunachal Pradesh
B. Himachal Pradesh
C. Sikkim
D. Punjab

14. Which State is called the 'Cradle of Buddhism'?
A. Sikkim
B. Uttar Pradesh
C. Bihar
D. Madhya Pradesh

15. In which year Ladakh became a Union Territory?
A. 2019 B. 2020
C. 2018 D. 2017

16. In which year Jammu and Kashmir seprated into two Union Territories?
A. 2019
B. 2020
C. 2018
D. 2017

17. Which State covers about one-tenth of the entire country?
A. Bihar
B. Rajasthan
C. Madhya Pradesh
D. Odisha

18. Which one of the following lists, four states are in the descending order of the size of their total population?
A. Odisha, Rajashthan, Gujarat, Kerala
B. Kerala, Gujarat, Rajasthan, Odisha
C. Rajasthan, Gujarat, Odisha, Kerala
D. Gurajat, Kerala, Odisha, Rajasthan

19. What is meant by Bay Islands?
A. Lakshadweep Island
B. Kaccha Tivu
C. Andaman & Nicobar Islands
D. Diego Garcia

20. The foundation of New Delhi was laid on December 15, 1911. Who laid the foundation stone?
A. Lord Mountbatten
B. King George V
C. Queen Victoria
D. Lord William Bentinck

21. An industrialist wants to establish a cotton textile mill in the State of Kerala. He will face the difficulty of:
A. Electricity
B. Manpower
C. Market
D. Raw Material

22. In which Indian State has the density of population been recorded the lowest?
A. Bihar
B. Haryana
C. Rajasthan
D. Arunachal Pradesh

23. In respect of sex ratio the State which tops in respect of more females per one thousand males is:
A. Goa
B. Arunachal Pradesh

C. Kerala
D. Bihar

24. Which geographical region in India is the largest producer of *Kesar* (Saffron)?
A. Konkan B. Kashmir
C. Telengana D. Coorg

25. The shape of the Deccan Plateau is:
A. Circular
B. Rectangular
C. Triangular
D. Oblate

26. The Konark temple in Odisha is dedicated to:
A. Lord Indra
B. Lord Rama
C. The Sun God
D. None of these

27. In India, the overall percentage of literacy is (2011 census) :
A. Below 60%
B. Over 70%
C. Over 80%
D. None of these

28. The area of Lakshadweep is:
A. 199 sq km B. 56 sq km
C. 32 sq km D. 20 sq km

29. The famous Chilka Lake is situated in:
A. Rajasthan
B. Odisha
C. Karnataka
D. West Bengal

30. The Kanha National Park, tiger reserve, is located in:
A. Uttar Pradesh
B. Madhya Pradesh
C. Rajasthan
D. Punjab

31. The Panchmarhi hill station is located in which of the following States?
A. Maharashtra
B. Madhya Pradesh
C. Andhra Pradesh
D. Tamil Nadu

32. Supreme Command of all the three wings of the armed forces is vested in the:
A. Prime Minister of India
B. President of India
C. Chief of Army Staff
D. Defence Minister

33. The highest rank in the Indian Army is of:
A. General
B. Major General
C. Captain
D. Brigadier General

34. The length of Indian coastline is:
A. 5800 km
B. 5000 km
C. 7516.6 km
D. 5500 km

35. The Army Headquarters is in:
A. New Delhi B. Kolkata
C. Pune D. Patna

36. Indian Air Force was established in the year:
A. 1932 B. 1947
C. 1857 D. 1950

37. The Indian Military Academy is situated in:
A. Pune B. Dehradun
C. Patna D. Jabalpur

38. The National Defence College is situated in:
A. Mumbai B. Pune
C. New Delhi D. Ajmer

39. The slope of the Deccan Plateau is from:
A. North to South
B. East to West
C. North-West to South-East
D. North-East to South-West

40. The Territorial Army was organised in:
A. August, 1947
B. October, 1949
C. January, 1948
D. December, 1950

41. India's BSF (Border Security Force) was organised on:
A. December 1, 1965
B. August 15, 1947
C. January 30, 1948
D. April 28, 1922

42. In size, India is.....largest country in the world.
A. seventh B. second
C. third D. tenth

43. At which place do we find a natural harbour?
A. Chennai
B. Vishakhapatnam
C. Mangalore
D. Kakinada

44. The headquarter of Indian Forest College is situated at:
A. Dehradun
B. Srinagar
C. Guwahati
D. Koddaikkanal

45. Which one of the following statements is wrong?
A. India has a land frontier of about 15,200 km
B. India is well marked off from the rest of Asia by mountains and the sea
C. Tropic of Capricorn divides India in almost two equal parts
D. India is the least industrialised country in the world

46. The first Railway train 'ran' in India, from Bombay to Thana, on April 16:
A. 1805 B. 1809
C. 1853 D. 1847

47. Where is the Armed Forces Medical College located?
A. Dehradun B. Patna
C. Wellington D. Pune

48. The Reserve Bank of India performs all of the following function except:
A. To accept deposits from the people
B. Banker of Govt.
C. Banker of banks
D. Credit control

49. Leh-Manali Road connects:
A. Kullu—Shimla
B. Leh—Shimla
C. Leh—Srinagar
D. Leh—Kullu Manali

50. India's first Centre for Performing Arts is situated at:
A. Kolkata
B. Mumbai
C. New Delhi
D. Chennai

51. Which of the pairs is wrong?
A. Sarnath—Madhya Pradesh
B. Sanchi—M.P.
C. Jahaj Mahal—Mandu (M.P.)
D. Vivekanand Memorial Rocks—Kanyakumari

52. The Atomic Energy Commission was set up in:
A. August, 1948
B. October, 1947
C. January, 1949
D. May, 1950

53. Which dam provides irrigation facilities to the states of Haryana, Punjab and Rajasthan?
A. Koyna dam
B. Hirakud dam
C. Tungabhadra dam
D. Bhakra Nangal dam

54. India carried out an underground 'Peaceful Nuclear Explosion Experiment' in Rajasthan at:
A. Jaduguda
B. Bikaner
C. Sriganganagar
D. Pokhran

55. The Space Commission was set up in:
A. August, 1965
B. June, 1972
C. May, 1971
D. January, 1973

56. Where is the Vikram Sarabhai Space Centre located at?
A. Mumbai
B. Bengaluru
C. Sriharikota
D. Trivendrum

57. Bhaskara-II was launched in November, 1981 from:
A. An Aerodrome in Paris
B. A US Space Platform
C. Soviet Cosmodrome
D. Indian Launching Pad

58. Which place does India occupy among nations which have successfully launched satellites into space?
A. Seventh B. Fourth
C. Fifth D. Sixth

59. In India, marble is found in only two states. They are:
A. Madhya Pradesh—Gujarat
B. Gujarat—Rajasthan
C. Rajasthan—Madhya Pradesh
D. Madhya Pradesh—Assam

60. The first Nuclear test was undertaken in India in the year:
A. 1975 B. 1974
C. 1973 D. 1977

61. The largest concentration of diamond cutting and polishing units is located at:
A. Vadodara B. Surat
C. Panaji D. Mumbai

62. The NITI Aayog was set up in:
A. January, 2015
B. September, 2014
C. April, 2014
D. January, 2016

63. To raise the standard of consumption of the people below the poverty line, was the major specific objective of:
A. Seventh Plan
B. Fifth Plan

C. Sixth Plan
D. Eighth Plan

64. Name the ex-officio chairman of the NITI Aayog in India?
A. The President of India
B. The Union Planning Minister
C. The Union Finance Minister
D. The Prime Minister of India

65. The First Five-Year Plan accorded highest priority to:
A. Agriculture and Irrigation
B. Industry and Minerals
C. Family Planning
D. Self-reliance

66. The Second Five-Year Plan accorded highest priority to:
A. Heavy Industries
B. Poverty eradication
C. Self-reliance
D. Power

67. Which is the most irrigated state in India?
A. UP B. Punjab
C. Haryana D. Bihar

68. In India, One-rupee note is issued by:
A. Reserve Bank of India
B. Ministry of Finance, Govt. of India
C. State Bank of India
D. None of the above

69. National Flag of India was adopted on:
A. August 15, 1947
B. July 27, 1951
C. July 22, 1947
D. January 26, 1947

70. The colours of the three strips of the National Flag in order from top to bottom:
A. Blue, White, Saffron
B. White, Saffron, Green
C. Saffron, White, Green
D. Green, White, Saffron

71. The wheel on the middle strip of the National Flag has:
A. 24 spokes B. 20 spokes
C. 48 spokes D. 18 spokes

72. The words 'Satyameva Jayate' are taken from:
A. Hitopadesh
B. Mahabharata
C. Rig Veda
D. Mundaka Upanishada

73. India's National Anthem was composed by:
A. Qazi Nazrul Islam
B. Rabindra Nath Tagore
C. Bankim Chandra
D. Dr. Sir Mohd. Iqbal

74. Jana-Gana-Mana was adopted as National Anthem on:
A. January 24, 1950
B. December 27, 1957
C. September 19, 1957
D. January 30, 1948

75. National Museum is situated at:
A. New Delhi B. Kolkata
C. Mumbai D. Bengaluru

76. 14th November is celebrated in India as:
A. Health Day
B. Women's Day
C. Children's Day
D. Mrs. Indira Gandhi's Birthday

77. Kolar Gold Mines are in which state?
A. Karnataka B. Bihar
C. Odisha D. M.P.

78. The highest mountain peak in India is:
A. Kanchanjunga
B. Nanga Prabat
C. Nanda Devi
D. K-2

79. Which is the highest gateway in India?
A. Gate (main) of the Taj at Agra
B. Gateway of India, Mumbai
C. Buland Darwaza at Fatehpur Sikri
D. India Gate, New Delhi

80. The largest fresh water lake in India is:
A. Dal Lake
B. Wular Lake
C. Pushkar Lake
D. Bhatkal Lake

81. India's longest railway platform is at:
A. Varanasi
B. Hubballi (Karnataka)
C. Delhi
D. Howrah

82. India's first RV centre was set up at:
A. Bombay (Mumbai)
B. Delhi
C. Calcutta (Kolkata)
D. Lucknow

83. Famous Hindu Pilgrimage Amarnath is in:
A. Uttar Pradesh
B. Madhya Pradesh
C. Jammu and Kashmir
D. Andhra Pradesh

84. 'Seven Pagodas' is sitated at:
A. Mahabalipuram
B. Tanjore
C. Puri
D. Mumbai

85. There are five beautiful Hindu Temples built at Mount Abu in Rajasthan. These temples are known as:
A. Desert Temples
B. Mount Temples
C. Lake Temples
D. Dilwara Temples

86. The twin-city famous for Charminar, Salarjang Museum etc. is called:
A. Hubli—Dharwar
B. Mathura—Brindavan
C. Kolkata—Howrah
D. Hyderabad—Secunderabad

87. Sarnath is well-known because:
A. It has a big oil refinery
B. It is a holy place
C. It is ancient capital
D. It has a big steel plant

88. He introduced the Permanent Settlement in 1793
A. Lord Cornwallis
B. Lord Wellesley
C. William Bentinck
D. Lord Dalhousie

89. In which year was the National School of Drama set up in New Delhi?
A. 1973 B. 1970
C. 1961 D. 1959

90. What percentage of labour force in India earns its livelihood in the agriculture sector?
A. About 49% B. About 27%
C. About 80% D. About 70%

91. NABARD (The National Bank for Agriculture and Rural Development) was set up in the year:
A. 1979 B. 1982
C. 1980 D. 1981

92. World's best mulberry silk is produced in:
A. Andhra Pradesh
B. Karnataka
C. Jammu & Kashmir
D. Gujarat

93. The Sharda Sahayak Project is located in the Indian State of:
A. Uttar Pradesh B. Haryana
C. Punjab D. Bihar

94. Which Commission replaced Planning Commission?
A. Niyam Aayog
B. NAGRIC Aayog
C. NITI Aayog
D. Jan Aayog

95. The Pochampad Project irrigates the State of:
A. Tamil Nadu
B. Andhra Pradesh
C. Uttar Pradesh
D. Karnataka

96. The Tawa Project is located in the Indian State of:
A. Uttar Pradesh
B. Madhya Pradesh
C. Andhra Pradesh
D. Tamil Nadu

97. Which of the following states has the highest rate of women literacy?
A. West Bengal
B. Kerala
C. Karnataka
D. Tamil Nadu

98. India's anti-tank missible is:
A. Agni B. Prithvi
C. Nag D. Akash

99. 'Teen Beegha' is the famous name of a:
A. Missile of India
B. Film produced in Mumbai
C. Bangladesh Enclave in West Bengal
D. Forest of West Bengal

100. Krishi Vigyan Kendras (KVKs), meant to impart training to farm workers, men and women, are established by:
A. Indian Council for Agricultural Research (ICAR)
B. Afro-Asian Rural Reconstruction Organisation (AARRO)
C. Agricultural University of Rudrapur
D. National Commission on Agriculture

101. 'Electronic City' of India is:
A. Hyderabad
B. Bengaluru
C. Kolkata
D. Mumbai

102. Described as Gift of the Sea, which is the State entirely rainfed?
A. Andhra Pradesh
B. Kerala

C. Tamil Nadu
D. Tripura

103. Darjeeling is situated in which of the following states of India?
A. Himachal Pradesh
B. Sikkim
C. West Bengal
D. Assam

104. India's anti-tank missile is:
A. Agni B. Prithvi
C. Akash D. Nag

105. The State with 92 per cent hilly area is:
A. Manipur
B. Assam
C. Tripura
D. Himachal Pradesh

106. The majority of 'Khasis' people live in:
A. Meghalaya
B. Arunachal Pradesh
C. Manipur
D. Mizoram

107. The famous Khajuraho temples built in the tenth century AD were dedicated to:
A. Rama and Krishna
B. Brahma and Vishnu
C. Trimurti
D. Shiva and Parvati

108. In India agriculture contributes around:
A. One-half of the GDP
B. Three-fourths of the GDP
C. Four-fifths of the GDP
D. One-seventh of the GDP

109. The Goan Economy is based mainly upon:
A. Tourism
B. Export of Rubber
C. Agriculture
D. The earning of the Goans working in gulf countries

110. It was the Baisakhi day when the 'massacre of the Jallianwala Bagh' took place. The Jallianwala Bagh is in:
A. Lahore
B. Amritsar
C. Ahmedabad
D. Pathankot

111. The name 'Harijan' was given to the people of downtrodden classes by:
A. Swami Dayanand
B. Raja Ram Mohan Roy
C. Mahatma Gandhi
D. Acharya Vinobha Bhave

112. Which of the following is the region where Toda tribals inhabitate?
A. Ooty
B. Nilgiris
C. Garhwal
D. Darjeeling

113. According to the latest census figures, sex ratio in India is:
A. Stable B. Increasing
C. Declining D. Fluctuating

114. Which of the following international body is associated/ collaborating in the National 'Population Education Programme' in the country?
A. WHO
B. UNESCO
C. IMF
D. UNFPA

115. Lakshadweep comes under the jurisdiction of:
A. Maharashtra High Court
B. Goa High Court
C. Kerala High Court
D. Karnataka High Court

116. The most populous city in India is:
A. Kolkata B. Delhi
C. Chennai D. Mumbai

117. Raniganj is famous for its:
A. Iron ore B. Coal mines
C. Mica D. Manganese

118. The grave of Khwaja Moinuddin Chisti is situated at:
A. Jaipur B. Ajmer
C. Udaipur D. Chennai

119. Ducan passage lies between:
A. Andaman and Nicobar islands
B. South and Middle Andaman islands
C. North and Middle Andaman islands
D. North and South Andaman islands

120. In which of the following areas, pearl fishing is undertaken extensively?
A. Gulf of Mannar
B. Konkan Coast
C. Malabar Coast
D. Coromondal Coast

121. When did the regular census operations begin in India?
A. 1852
B. 1862
C. 1872
D. 1881

122. Which of the following projects supplies electricity to the Rourkela Steel Plant?
A. Damodar Valley Project
B. Tungabhadra Project
C. Hirakud Dam Project
D. Nagarjuna Project

123. The Alamatti Dam is on the river:
A. Mahanadi
B. Cauvery
C. Godavari
D. Krishna

124. The year of Saka era, except leap year, commences from:
A. April 1
B. April 15
C. March 1
D. March 22

125. The Kailash temple at Ellora is made on the:
A. Dravidian style
B. North Indian style
C. Egyptian style
D. Mexican style

126. In which State/UT is the Salal Hydroelectric Project located?
A. Jammu & Kashmir
B. Uttar Pradesh
C. Himachal Pradesh
D. Bihar

127. The depictions in Ajanta caves display the:
A. Incidents in the life of Buddha
B. Incidents pertaining to Mahavira's life
C. Legends of Vikramaditya
D. The Epic incidents

128. Who got the temples at Khajuraho built?
A. Rajputs of Chittor
B. Chaulukyas of Badami
C. Chandelas of Bundelkhand
D. Chauhans of Ajmer

129. Which city of India has the monuments of Chola period?
A. Madras (Chennai)
B. Bengaluru
C. Tanjore
D. Madurai

130. One of the following is not a rabi crop:
A. Mustard
B. Rice
C. Wheat
D. Gram

131. Jamshedpur is famous for iron and steel industry. It is located in the state of:
A. Jharkhand B. Kerala
C. Punjab D. Odisha

132. Which one of the following States in India is land locked?
A. Odisha
B. West Bengal
C. Maharashtra
D. Haryana

133. India switched over to the decimal currency system in;
A. 1955 B. 1956
C. 1957 D. 1958

134. Where is National Dairy Research Institute located?
A. Dehradun
B. Karnal
C. Chandigarh
D. Pantnagar

135. Maximum Number of daily newspapers in India are published in:
A. Bengali
B. Hindi
C. English
D. Malayalam

136. Kuchipudi dance originated from:
A. Punjab
B. Rajasthan
C. Andhra Pradesh
D. Karnataka

137. In which of the following cities is the Golden Temple located?
A. Gaya
B. Patna
C. Mathura
D. Amritsar

138. The first oil refinery in India was set up at:
A. Barauni
B. Vishakhapatnam
C. Digboi
D. Bombay (Mumbai)

139. Which one of the following is in Kerala?
A. Kovalam
B. Udupi
C. Deoghar
D. Mirik

140. What is the significance of Ajanta caves?
A. These are fine specimen of Greek architecture in India
B. These are well-known for admirable ancient rock-cut temples with fresco paintings

C. These signify the importance of secularism
D. These are well-known for the highest statue of Lord Buddha in the world

141. These princely states did not accede to the new Indian dominion after independence
A. Jodhpur, Gwalior, Hyderabad
B. Junagadh, Kashmir, Gwalior
C. Hyderabad, Mysore, Gwalior
D. Kashmir, Junagadh, Hyderabad

142. The Supreme Court of India began functioning from this year
A. 1950
B. 1951
C. 1952
D. 1953

143. During the Indo-Pak War of 1965, the Indian Prime Minister was
A. Jawaharlal Nehru
B. Indira Gandhi
C. Lal Bahadur Shastri
D. Morarji Desai

144. The Bharatiya Jan Sangh was started in 1951 by
A. Rashbehari Bose
B. Shyama Prasad Mukherjee
C. Aurobindo Ghosh
D. Ashutosh Mukherjee

145. Independent India's first general elections were held in
A. 1950
B. 1951
C. 1953
D. 1952

146. In 1954, the Panchsheel Agreement was signed between India and
A. Russia
B. Pakistan
C. China
D. Sri Lanka

147. In 1961, Operation Vijay liberated these territories from Portugal
A. Goa and Diu
B. Goa, Daman, Diu
C. Cochin, Calicut and Travancore
D. Calicut and Daman

148. Hindi was declared official language of the Union in the year
A. 1962
B. 1963
C. 1964
D. 1965

149. The Shimla Agreement is signed in 1972 between Indira Gandhi and
A. Ghulam Mohammed
B. Liaqat Khan
C. Zia-ul-Haq
D. Zulfikar Ali Bhutto

150. The Army operation to flush out Sikh terrorists from the Golden Temple was called
A. Operation Gold Star
B. Operation Kranti
C. Operation Vijay
D. Operation Blue Star

ANSWERS

1	**2**	**3**	**4**	**5**	**6**	**7**	**8**	**9**	**10**
D	B	B	D	A	A	C	A	C	D
11	**12**	**13**	**14**	**15**	**16**	**17**	**18**	**19**	**20**
C	B	C	C	A	A	B	C	C	B
21	**22**	**23**	**24**	**25**	**26**	**27**	**28**	**29**	**30**
D	D	C	B	C	C	B	C	B	B
31	**32**	**33**	**34**	**35**	**36**	**37**	**38**	**39**	**40**
B	B	A	C	A	A	B	C	C	C
41	**42**	**43**	**44**	**45**	**46**	**47**	**48**	**49**	**50**
A	A	A	A	C	C	D	A	D	D
51	**52**	**53**	**54**	**55**	**56**	**57**	**58**	**59**	**60**
A	A	D	D	B	D	C	D	C	B
61	**62**	**63**	**64**	**65**	**66**	**67**	**68**	**69**	**70**
B	A	B	D	A	A	B	B	C	C
71	**72**	**73**	**74**	**75**	**76**	**77**	**78**	**79**	**80**
A	D	B	A	A	C	A	D	C	B
81	**82**	**83**	**84**	**85**	**86**	**87**	**88**	**89**	**90**
B	B	C	A	D	D	B	A	D	A
91	**92**	**93**	**94**	**95**	**96**	**97**	**98**	**99**	**100**
B	B	A	C	B	B	B	C	C	A
101	**102**	**103**	**104**	**105**	**106**	**107**	**108**	**109**	**110**
B	B	C	D	A	A	D	D	A	B
111	**112**	**113**	**114**	**115**	**116**	**117**	**118**	**119**	**120**
C	B	B	D	C	D	B	B	A	D
121	**122**	**123**	**124**	**125**	**126**	**127**	**128**	**129**	**130**
D	C	D	D	A	A	A	C	C	B
131	**132**	**133**	**134**	**135**	**136**	**137**	**138**	**139**	**140**
A	D	C	B	B	C	D	C	A	B
141	**142**	**143**	**144**	**145**	**146**	**147**	**148**	**149**	**150**
D	A	C	B	D	C	B	D	D	D

GENERAL SCIENCE

1. When a moving train stops suddenly, a man tends to fall:
A. forward B. backward
C. upward D. All are true

2. Which of the planets does not have a moon?
A. Earth B. Venus
C. Mars D. Saturn

3. Who discovered that the earth moves round the sun?
A. Newton B. Galileo
C. Copernicus D. All are true

4. One horse power is equal to:
A. 546 watts B. 64 watts
C. 89 watts D. 746 watts

5. A parsec is the unit of:
A. time
B. orbital speed
C. distance
D. pressure

6. The law which gives definition of force is:
A. second law of motion
B. third law of motion
C. first law of motion
D. Newton's law of gravitation

7. Newton is the absolute unit of force in
A. M.K.S. system
B. C.G.S. system
C. Both of these
D. None of these

8. The instrument used for measuring radiant energy is:
A. Bolometer
B. Thermopile
C. Radiometer
D. All are true

9. While catching a cricket ball the player moves his hands down. This he does so as to:
A. gain energy
B. provide greater impulse
C. gain time
D. make a graceful show

10. Planets move round the sun due to:
A. gravitational attraction between the sun and the plantes
B. centrifugal force
C. mutual attraction and repulsion between the sun and the planet
D. centripetal force

11. Which of the following is a C.G.S. unit of heat?
A. Therm
B. Calorie
C. Erg
D. Thermal capacity

12. When water vapour condenses on air or dust particles.
A. fog is formed
B. frost is formed
C. hailstone is formed
D. mist is formed

13. Inertia is the property of:
A. strength B. volume
C. matter D. mass

14. Sound waves are not propagated longitudinally in:
A. solids

B. mixture of gases
C. air
D. vacuum

15. Which instrument is used for measuring air pressure?
A. Polarimeter
B. Hygrometer
C. Hydrometer
D. Barometer

16. Which law is associated with the rise of balloon in air?
A. Newton's law of motion
B. Archimedies law
C. Gravitational law
D. Kepler's law

17. Which of the following is an example of crystalline solid?
A. Glass B. Plastics
C. Salt D. Quartz

18. A needle sinks in water while an iron ship floats on it because of:
A. Newton's law of motion
B. Gravitational law
C. Law of floatation
D. All of these

19. Sound is produced due to:
A. impact
B. superposition of waves
C. vibration of a body
D. wave in the medium

20. Inside a solid, transmission of sound waves is possible because of:
A. transverse wave only
B. longitudinal wave only
C. neither of the waves
D. longitudinal as well as transverse waves

21. Sound from a distant source can be heard more distinctly:
A. at dawn
B. at midnight
C. in the evening
D. at noon

22. Sound travels fastest in:
A. O_2 B. CO_2
C. H_2 D. Air

23. Marching troops while crossing bridges etc. are asked to get out of step. This is to:
A. let the soldier have rest
B. save the bridge from forced vibrations
C. save the bridges from vibrations
D. none of the above

24. During lightening, it is safer:
A. to sit near the lighting coducting rod
B. to sit under a tree
C. to sit in a car
D. to lie in an open field

25. A mirage is observed because:
A. total internal reflection of light from bright sand
B. the refractive index of the atmosphere increase with height
C. the refractive index of the atmosphere decreases with height
D. the refractive index remains constant with height

26. The instrument used for seeing very small objects is called:
A. Epidiascope
B. Microscope

C. Compound microscope
D. Periscope

27. Eclipses indicate:
A. reflection of light
B. diffraction of light
C. rectilinear propagation of light
D. scattering of light

28. A well cut diamond appears bright because of its:
A. emission of light by the diamond
B. hardness
C. absorption of light is least for light for any colour
D. high refractive index

29. A person standing in front of a mirror finds his image larger than himself. This implies that the mirror is:
A. convex
B. plane
C. cylindrical with bluging side outwards
D. concave

30. Defect of the eye on account of which the eye cannot form a point image is called:
A. Myopia
B. Astigmatism
C. Hypermetropia
D. Presbyopia

31. When the moon is near horizon it appears bigger. This is due to:
A. diffraction
B. optical illusion
C. atmospheric refraction
D. scattering of light

32. The light which travels through glass with minimum speed is of:
A. blue colour
B. green colour
C. red colour
D. violet colour

33. Long-sightedness can be cured by using:
A. convexo-concave lens
B. convex lens
C. concavo-convex lens
D. concave lens

34. A sudden decrease in the barometer shows:
A. arrival of rain
B. fine weather
C. dry weather
D. arrival of storm/cyclone

35. Telegraph was invented by:
A. Enhorse B. Morse
C. Graham Bell D. Rontgen

36. A transformer is used:
A. to supply a suitable D.C. voltage
B. to transform electrical energy
C. to convert an A.C. into D.C.
D. to supply suitable A.C. voltage

37. In radio therapy, X-rays are used to:
A. detect cancer
B. detect bone fracture
C. detect heart disease
D. treat cancer control

38. Receiver of telephone converts:
A. electrical energy into sound energy
B. sound energy into electrical energy

C. electrical energy into mechanical energy
D. mechanical energy into electrical energy

39. Glass is:
A. an amorphous solid
B. a crystalline solid
C. less elastic solid
D. not an elastic solid

40. Gramophone was invented by:
A. Kundt
B. Graham Bell
C. Edison
D. Quincke

41. Mercury is used instead of water in a barometer because mercury:
A. has a high boiling point
B. has a much higher density
C. is a metal
D. is a good conductor of electricity

42. An explosion on the surface of moon:
A. can be heard in more time than on earth
B. can be heard
C. can not be heard at all
D. can be heard in the less time than on the earth

43. Safety fuses consist of wires of:
A. high resistance and low melting point
B. low resistance and high melting point
C. low resistance and low melting point
D. high resistance and high melting point

44. Radar is:
A. a device for detection of speed & directions of distant object
B. a type of telephone
C. an instrument for measuring light
D. an instrument for measuring speed

45. The function of the weight valve in a pressure cooker is:
A. to maintain the pressure of air
B. to increase the temperature of the contents
C. to increase the pressure of steam
D. to maintain the required cooking pressure

46. The tape recorder records sound in the form of:
A. electrical energy
B. magnetic field on the tape
C. variable resistance
D. sound waves held on the tab

47. Springs are made of steel because it is:
A. unaffected by moisture
B. strong
C. elastic
D. more cohesive

48. Blue colour of sky is due to:
A. diffraction
B. polarisation
C. interference
D. scattering of sunlight by air molecules

49. The best propagator of sound is:
A. air
B. moist gas
C. gas
D. metals

50. A substance which recovers its original shape and size after the removal of the external force is said to be:

A. elastic B. brittle
C. rigid D. plastic

51. Lightening conductor:

A. absorbs the charge
B. conduct the charge to the cloud
C. conducts the charge to the atmosphere
D. conducts the charge to the earth

52. An instrument used for measuring the illuminating power of source is called:

A. galvanometer
B. photometer
C. ammeter
D. photocell

53. Water in an earthen pot becomes cool after some time. This is due to:

A. decrease in average kinetic energy of water molecules
B. increase in average potential energy of water molecules
C. absorption of heat by the pot
D. decrease in average potential energy of water molecules

54. Combustion of candle is a/an:

A. exothermic reaction
B. physical change
C. endothermic reaction
D. none of these

55. A substance which cannot be broken further is called:

A. compound
B. mixture
C. element
D. none of these

56. Which of the following is a compound?

A. Air B. Bronze
C. Cane sugar D. Milk

57. A substance formed by chemical combination is known as:

A. element
B. mixture
C. compound
D. none of these

58. Which of the following is an element?

A. Plastic B. Alcohol
C. Gold D. Ice

59. Soil is a/an:

A. element
B. mixture
C. compound
D. none of these

60. Brass is a/an:

A. compound B. element
C. mixture D. alloy

61. Sulphur is readily soluble in:

A. water
B. alcohol
C. carbon dioxide
D. benzene

62. The method used for separating sand from water is:

A. sublimation
B. distillation
C. filteration
D. evaporation

63. Permanent hardness of water can be removed by:

A. boiling

B. adding lime
C. permutit
D. none of these

64. The temperature at which water expands is:
A. above 4°C
B. below 4°C
C. 0°C
D. none of these

65. Water gas is a mixture of:
A. $CO_2 + H_2O$
B. $CO + H_2$
C. $CO + N_2$
D. $CO_2 + H_2$

66. Density of heavy water is:
A. more than that of ordinary water
B. equal to that of ordinary water
C. less than that of ordinary water
D. one

67. Temporary hardness of water is due to presence of bicarbonates of:
A. Ca and Mg
B. Ba and Sr
C. Na and K
D. None of thse

68. When soap is added to hard water:
A. It is difficult to get lather
B. It lathers readily
C. It has no effect
D. None of these

69. Heavy water is manufactured in India at:
A. Nangal
B. Delhi
C. Kolkata
D. None of these

70. Boiling point of heavy water is:
A. 100°C B. 99°C
C. 110°C D. 101.4°C

71. Which of the following compounds is used as a moderator in nuclear reactors?
A. Nitrogen
B. Heavy water
C. Heavy hydrogen
D. None of these

72. Number of isotopes of hydrogen is:
A. 1 B. 2
C. 3 D. 4

73. Atomic hydrogen has a life period of:
A. fraction of second
B. one minute
C. one hour
D. one day

74. In filling airships, hydrogen has been replaced by:
A. nitrogen B. helium
C. oxygen D. argon

75. The isotopes of hydrogen contain different number of:
A. electrons
B. protons
C. neutrons
D. none of these

76. Which one of the following gases is present in the greatest proportion is dry air?
A. Nitrogen
B. Oxygen
C. Carbon dioxide
D. Argon

77. The formula of ozone is:
A. O B. O_2
C. O_3 D. O_4

78. Nitrogen was discovered by:
A. Scheele
B. Lavoiser
C. D. Rutherford
D. Cavendish

79. Nitrous oxide is known as:
A. tear gas
B. laughing gas
C. producer gas
D. mustard gas

80. The crystalline form of carbon is:
A. coke B. gas carbon
C. coal D. diomond

81. The gas used in extinguishing fire is:
A. SO_2 B. NO
C. CO_2 D. H_2

82. Carbon is:
A. metal
B. non-metal
C. metalloid
D. none of these

83. A constituent of gun powder which is also a reducing agent is:
A. KNO_3 B. C
C. $CaCO_3$ D. KCO_3

84. Reducing agent is a substance which can:
A. accept electrons
B. accept protons
C. donate electrons
D. donate protons

85. Which is the most powerful reducing agent?
A. F^- B. Cl^-
C. Br^- D. I^-

86. The acid present in lemons and oranges is:
A. Acetic acid
B. Hydrocloric acid
C. Nitric acid
D. Oxalic acid

87. Graphite is a good conductor of electricity due to presence of:
A. bonded electrons
B. mobile electrons
C. strong C-C bond
D. none of these

88. The existence of an element in two or more forms in the same physical state is called:
A. anisotropy
B. enanitotropy
C. allotropy
D. isomorphism

89. Which one of the following types of glass is used for making laboratory apparatus?
A. Flint-glass B. Pyrex glass
C. Soda lime D. jena glass

90. Fuels like alcohol, liquid hydrogen, liquid ammonia, kerosene oil, hydrazine, etc. constitute:
A. liquid propellants
B. solid propellants
C. gas propellants
D. none of these

91. The important raw material for paint is:
A. Pigment B. glucose
C. methane D. sugar

92. Which one of the following substances is most combustible?
A. Wood
B. Phosphorous
C. Paraffine
D. Potassium

93. Paper is prepared from:
A. Cellulose B. Sugar
C. Urea D. Ethane

94. The name electron was suggested for the first time by:
A. Stoney B. Rutherford
C. Crooke D. Bohr

95. The electron has:
A. positive charge
B. negative charge
C. zero charge
D. –2 charge

96. The nucleus of the atom contains:
A. neutrons and electrons
B. neutrons and protons
C. protons and electrons
D. protons, electrons and neutrons

97. The cathode rays are:
A. electrons
B. protons
C. neutrons
D. alpha particles

98. Dry ice is:
A. Steam
B. Solidified CO_2
C. Water
D. None of these

99. Which one of the following is a thermoplastic polymer?
A. nylon
B. teflon
C. polyethylene
D. all are correct

100. Fixation of atmospheric nitrogen means:
A. conversion of nitrogen into useful compounds
B. liquification of nitrogen
C. preparation of nitrogen
D. none of these

101. Metallurgy is the process of:
A. mining of ore
B. crushing of the ore
C. extraction of the metal from the ore profitably
D. none of these

102. Stainless steel is:
A. non-metal B. metal
C. an alloy D. metalloid

103. Which of the following is a continuous source of energy?
A. Oil B. Natural gas
C. Wood D. Sun

104. Which of the following metals occur in the native state?
A. Gold B. Calcium
C. Magnesium D. Sodium

105. Marble is:
A. $CaCO_3$ B. $MgCO_3$
C. Na_2CO_3 D. $NaHCO_3$

106. Which of the following is an allotrop of carbon?
A. silver B. gold
C. platinum D. diamond

107. Which of the following is used in a safety match?
A. gun powder
B. rhombic sulphur
C. red phosphorus
D. white phosphorus

108. Who discovered the cell?
A. Schleiden and Schwann
B. Bedle and Tantam
C. Robert Hooke
D. A. Fleming

109. The essential aspects of living beings are:
A. Molecular basis
B. Energy changes
C. Reproduction, adaptation and death
D. All of the above

110. Which one of the following elements give the organic nature to protoplasmic contents?
A. Hydrogen B. Nitrogen
C. Sodium D. Carbon

111. Which one of the following form the blue print for future information?
A. RNA B. DNA
C. ATP D. ADP

112. Which of the following compounds is most important for the origin of life?
A. Vitamins
B. Proteins
C. Nucleotides
D. Nucleic acids

113. Life first originated in:
A. Water
B. Soil
C. Air
D. None of the above

114. The branch of biology in which the study about the cells is called:
A. Cell biology
B. Microbiology
C. Biochemistry
D. Cytology

115. The result of successful metabolic activities is:
A. growth
B. death
C. excretion
D. reproduction

116. What has been placed between living and non-living?
A. Viruses
B. *Paramoecium*
C. *Euglena*
D. *Amoeba*

117. The structure which constitutes the basic structural and functional unit of all living beings is:
A. Cell B. Tissue
C. Atom D. Molecule

118. Which of the following is the smallest organism that can be observed under microscope?
A. Bacterium B. Fungi
C. Algae D. Lichen

119. Which of the following is a connective tissue?
A. Bone B. Cell
C. Organelle D. Blood

120. The tissue that conducts water and minerals in plant is:
A. Xylem B. Cambium
C. Phloem D. Chlorophyll

121. The tissue in plants responsible for conduction of food is named as:
A. Xylem B. Phloem
C. Cambium D. Pith

122. Largest cell in the human body is:
A. Nerve cell
B. Liver cell
C. Epithelial cell
D. None of the above

123. Which of the following animal produces largest eggs?
A. Whale B. Rabit
C. Kiwi D. Ostrich

124. Cellulose is present in:
A. Nucleus
B. Cell wall of plants
C. Chlorophyll
D. Cytoplasm

125. In plants, respiration occurs in:
A. growing tissues
B. all living cells
C. cell wall
D. xylem and phloem

126. The power house of a cell is:
A. Golgi complex
B. Ribosomes
C. Mitochondria
D. None of the above

127. The organelle associated with protein synthesis in a cell is:
A. Mitochondria
B. Lysosomes
C. Ribosomes
D. Chromosomes

128. Biological oxidation of enzymes occur in:
A. Golgi complex
B. Ribosomes
C. Mitochondria
D. None of the above

129. Blood is a:
A. Connective tissue
B. Muscular tissue
C. Epithelial tissue
D. None of the above

130. Bacteria is an example of:
A. Eukaryotic cell
B. Prokaryotic cell
C. Connective tissue
D. Muscular tissue

131. DNA structure was discovered by:
A. Wastson and Crick
B. Robert Brown
C. Charles Darwin
D. None of the above

132. Gibberellins produces:
A. growth in roots
B. elongation in roots
C. young leaves near the shoot tip
D. none of the above

133. The largest part of the brain is:
A. Cerebrum
B. Conjunctiva
C. Cerebellum
D. None of the above

134. Which element is present in maximum amount in the human body?
A. Nitrogen
B. Phosphorus
C. Oxygen
D. Carbon

135. RBCs are formed in the:
A. Liver B. Spleen
C. Bone marrowD. Heart

136. Bile is secreted by the:
A. Heart B. Stomach
C. Liver D. Lungs

137. Which endocrine gland is called as 'Master gland'?
A. Thyroid
B. Adrenal
C. Pituitary
D. None of the above

138. In humans, digestion of food is completed in the:
A. Stomach
B. Rectum
C. Oesophagus
D. Small intestine

139. Vitamins are carried to all parts of the body mainly by:
A. Fibrinogen
B. Heparin
C. Haemoglobin
D. Plasma

140. Blood pressure of normal man is:
A. 100/100 mm Hg
B. 120/80 mm Hg
C. 140/90 mm Hg
D. None of the above

141. Pulmonary artery carries blood from:
A. Heart to kidney
B. Heart to brain
C. Heart to lungs
D. None of the above

142. Universal recipient is the person with the blood group:
A. A B. B
C. AB D. O

143. A kidney stone is formed by:
A. Calcium carbonate
B. Inorganic substances
C. Deposition of uric acid crystals and salts in kidney and pelvis
D. Deposition of blood in blood vessels

144. Which part of the donor's eye is used for grafting in order to cure certain cases of blindness?
A. Retina and lens
B. Cornea only
C. Retina and cornea
D. Retina only

145. The strongest bone in the human body is:
A. Thigh bone
B. Ischium
C. Public symphysis
D. Iliae bone

146. Pathology is the branch of science which deals with the:
A. Fungi
B. Diseases
C. Viruses
D. None of the above

147. The energy is stored in a cell in the form of:
A. DNA and RNA
B. DNA only
C. ATP
D. ADP and DNA

148. Most common source of energy in a biological system is:
A. ATP B. ADP
C. RNA D. DNA

149. The starch and sugar are source of:
A. Fats
B. Carbohydrates
C. Hormones
D. Vitamins

150. The richest sources of protein are:
A. Pulses B. Fruits
C. Vegetables D. Sugar

151. The green leafy vegetables are main sources of:
A. Proteins
B. Minerals
C. Carbohydrates
D. Enzymes

152. In general, fruits are rich in:
A. Vitamin D B. Proteins
C. Vitamin C D. Vitamin A

153. The vitamin manufactured in the skin is:
A. Vitamin A B. Vitamin B
C. Vitamin C D. Vitamin D

154. The major component of bones and teeth is:
A. Calcium
B. Calcium carbonate
C. Potassium
D. Calcium phosphate

155. The nitrogen and sulphur is required by organisms for the formation of:
A. Vitamins
B. Hormones
C. Enzymes
D. None of the above

156. Failure of blood clotting is due to deficiency of:
A. Vitamin A B. Vitamin B
C. Vitamin E D. Vitamin K

157. The nearest planet to the earth is:
A. Earth B. Venus
C. Jupiter D. Mercury

158. The distance of the planets from the sun in the increasing order is:
A. Earth, Mars, Venus, Jupiter
B. Mercury, Venus, Earth, Mars
C. Mars, Earth, Mercury, Venus
D. None of the above

159. When a man circles round the earth in a satellite then:
A. Mass and weight of the man become zero
B. Mass and weight remain constant
C. Mass remains constant but weight becomes zero
D. None of the above

160. Gravitational pull is more at the:
A. Equator B. Poles
C. Mountains D. Oceans

161. The weight of an object at the poles is:
A. Less than at the equator
B. Greater than at the equator
C. Same as the equator
D. All of the above

162. By which method the energy of the sun generated?
A. Nuclear fusion
B. Nuclear fission
C. Radioactive reaction
D. Nuclear radiation

163. Halley's comet reappears in every:
A. 76 years B. 75 years
C. 70 years D. 100 years

164. The closest planet to the sun is:
A. Venus B. Mercury
C. Saturn D. Pluto

165. The Evening star and the morning star is generally called for:
A. Moon
B. Sun
C. Neptune
D. Venus

166. The Red planet is called for:
A. Venus
B. Jupiter
C. Mars
D. Saturn

167. The second largest planet is:
A. Mars
B. Earth
C. Saturn
D. None of the above

168. Alpha, Beta, Gamma, Delta and Epsilon rings are found in:
A. Saturn
B. Uranus
C. Neptune
D. Jupiter

169. Triton is related to:
A. Neptune
B. Uranus
C. Mars
D. Mercury

170. First Indian to reach space is:
A. Sq. Ldr. Rakesh Sharma
B. Wg. Camd. Ramesh Sharma
C. Col. Yuri Gagarin
D. None of the above

171. Vaccination was used for the first time by :
A. Edward Jenner
B. Marie Bichat
C. Robert Brown
D. None of the above

172. Penicillin is discovered by:
A. Karl Landsteiner
B. Alexander Fleming
C. Paul Muller
D. None of the above

173. Fountain Pen was discovered by:
A. T.A. Edison
B. W. Murdock
C. L.E. Waterman
D. None of the above

174. Mendel is regarded as:
A. Father of genetics
B. Father of Botany
C. Father of Lichenology
D. None of the above

175. Egg is a rich source of:
A. Vitamin C
B. Fats
C. Hormones
D. Protein

176. The only source of energy for humans is:
A. Food
B. Minerals
C. Vitamins
D. None of the above

177. Proteins, fats and carbohydrates are called:
A. Macro nutrients
B. Micro nutrients
C. Minor nutrients
D. None of the above

178. Which of the following food stuff not contains fats?
A. Butter
B. Egg

C. Potato
D. None of the above

179. Which of the following minerals formed the haemoglobin of blood?
A. Calcium
B. Iron
C. Magnesium
D. Manganese

180. The oranges contain which nutrient of the following:
A. Proteins
B. Sugar
C. Carbohydrates
D. Fats

181. A passenger in a moving train tosses a coin which falls behind him. This shows that the motion of train is:
A. accelerated
B. uniform
C. retarded
D. along circular track

182. 'When a hanging carpet is beaten with a stick, the dust particles start coming out of it'. This phenomenon can be best explained by making use of:
A. Newton's third law of motion
B. Newton's law of gravitation
C. Newton's first law of motion
D. Newton's second law of motion

183. The rockets work on the principle of conservation of:
A. mass
B. energy
C. momentum
D. velocity

184. The product of petroleum used to drive heavy vehicles like trucks is ....
A. petrol
B. kerosene
C. diesel
D. petroleum gas

185. The value of g on the surface of the moon:
A. is the same as on the earth
B. is less than that on the earth
C. is more than that on the earth
D. keeps changing day by day

186. The atmosphere consisting of a large number of gases is held to the earth by:
A. winds
B. clouds
C. earth's magnetic field
D. gravity

187. The value of acceleration due to gravity of earth:
A. is the same on equator and poles
B. is the least on poles
C. is the least on equator
D. increases from pole to equator

188. When an object falls freely towards the earth, then its total energy:
A. increases
B. decreases
C. remains constant
D. first increases and then decreases

189. Which one of the following is not the unit of energy?
A. joule
B. newton-meter
C. kilowatt
D. kilowatt-hour

190. The commercial unit of energy is:
A. watt
B. watt-hour
C. kilowatt-hour
D. kilowatt

191. The device which converts mechanical energy into energy which runs our microwave oven is:
A. electric motor
B. alternator
C. turbine
D. electric heater

192. Which one of the following does not consist of transverse waves?
A. light emitted by a CFL
B. TV signals from a satellite
C. ripples on the surface of a pond
D. musical notes of an orchestra

193. The maximum speed of vibrations which produce audible sound will be in:
A. dry air
B. sea water
C. ground glass
D. human blood

194. The sound waves travel fastest:
A. in solids
B. in liquids
C. in gases
D. in vacuum

195. In SONAR we use:
A. ultrasonic waves
B. infrasonic waves
C. radio waves
D. audible sound waves

196. Which kind of sound is produced in an earthquake before the main shock wave begins?
A. ultrasound
B. infrasound
C. audible sound
D. none of the above

197. One of the following can hear infrasound. This one is:
A. dog
B. bat
C. rhinoceros
D. humans

198. Which of the following device does not work on the multiple reflections of sound waves?
A. stethoscope
B. hydrophone
C. soundboard
D. megaphone

199. The main constituent of petroleum gas is:
A. methane
B. ethane
C. butane
D. propane

200. The natural gas consists mainly of:
A. methane
B. ethane
C. propane
D. butane

ANSWERS

1	2	3	4	5	6	7	8	9	10
A	B	C	D	C	C	A	A	B	A
11	12	13	14	15	16	17	18	19	20
C	D	C	D	D	B	C	C	C	A
21	22	23	24	25	26	27	28	29	30
B	C	C	D	A	B	C	D	D	B
31	32	33	34	35	36	37	38	39	40
B	D	B	D	B	D	D	A	A	C
41	42	43	44	45	46	47	48	49	50
B	C	A	A	D	B	C	D	D	A
51	52	53	54	55	56	57	58	59	60
D	B	A	A	D	C	C	C	B	D
61	62	63	64	65	66	67	68	69	70
C	C	C	B	B	A	A	A	A	D
71	72	73	74	75	76	77	78	79	80
B	C	A	B	C	A	C	C	B	D
81	82	83	84	85	86	87	88	89	90
C	B	B	C	D	C	B	C	B	A
91	92	93	94	95	96	97	98	99	100
A	B	A	A	B	B	A	B	D	A
101	102	103	104	105	106	107	108	109	110
C	C	D	A	A	D	C	C	D	D
111	112	113	114	115	116	117	118	119	120
B	C	A	D	A	A	A	A	D	A
121	122	123	124	125	126	127	128	129	130
B	A	D	B	B	C	C	C	A	B
131	132	133	134	135	136	137	138	139	140
A	C	A	B	C	C	D	A	D	B
141	142	143	144	145	146	147	148	149	150
C	C	C	B	A	B	C	A	B	A
151	152	153	154	155	156	157	158	159	160
B	C	D	B	C	D	B	B	C	B
161	162	163	164	165	166	167	168	169	170
B	A	A	B	D	C	C	B	A	A
171	172	173	174	175	176	177	178	179	180
A	B	C	A	D	A	A	C	B	B
181	182	183	184	185	186	187	188	189	190
A	C	C	C	B	D	C	C	C	C
191	192	193	194	195	196	197	198	199	200
B	D	C	A	A	B	C	B	C	A

COMPUTER

1. The main purpose of the supercomputer is
A. high speed calculations
B. weather forecasting
C. data Retrieval operations
D. None of the above

2. What are the two essential parts of the Computer?
A. Keyboard and Mouse
B. Hardware and Software
C. Printer and Screen
D. Monitor and Keyboard

3. Future Generation computers will be based on
A. Online processing
B. Artificial intelligence
C. Time sharing
D. None of the above

4. The basic operations performed by a computers are
A. arithmetic operation
B. logical operation
C. storage and relative
D. All of the above

5. Supercomputer were primarily designed by
A. Seymour Cray
B. IBM
C. Hewlett-Packard
D. C-DAC

6. The floppy drive have
A. Magnetic coating
B. Silver coating
C. Gold coating
D. Lead coating

7. IC chips was used in
A. first generation
B. second generation
C. third generation
D. fourth generation

8. Macromedia is a name of a company related with
A. Hardware B. Software
C. Peripherals D. Services

9. The personal-computer industry was started by
A. IBM B. Apple
C. Compaq D. HCL

10. *X-MP* is Models of
A. microcomputer
B. Minicomputer
C. Mainframe Computer
D. Supercomputer

11. Which is used for manufacturing chips?
A. Bus
B. Control unit
C. Semiconductors
D. A and B only

12. Modem is a/an ———.
A. input device
B. output device
C. both A and B
D. storage device

13. ——— is an input device used for playing computer games.
A. Scanner
B. Joystick
C. Light pen
D. Microphone

14. The output that is printed on paper is called
A. hard copy

B. soft copy
C. both A and B
D. None of these

15. In which kind of printers, a light beam is used to print?
A. Dot-matrix printers
B. Line printers
C. Inkjet printers
D. Laser printers

16. Mouse, Keyboard, Monitor and Printer etc. are examples of
A. Software
B. Memory
C. Peripherals
D. CPU

17. Which is not an input device?
A. CRT (Cathode Ray Tube)
B. Optical scanners
C. Voice recognition devices
D. COM (Computer Micro film)

18. A disadvantage of the laser printer is
A. It is quieter than an impact printer
B. It is very slow
C. The output is of a lower quality
D. None of these

19. Which of the following is classified as an impact printer?
A. Jet printer
B. Daisy wheel printer
C. Thermal printer
D. Laser printer

20. In a computer system, which device is functionally opposite of a keyboard?
A. Mouse B. Trackball
C. Printer D. Joystick

21. What is the name of the screen symbol that shows the placement of the next character?
A. Mouse
B. Cursor
C. Trackball
D. Graphic tablet

22. Many engineers and architects use a different type of pen called a
A. Computer pen
B. Light pen
C. Logical pen
D. Pointer pen

23. A peripheral device in which the storage medium used in magnetic tape is
A. Keyboard
B. VDU
C. Punched card
D. Tape deck

24. A mouse is this kind of device.
A. Input B. Output
C. Network D. Storage

25. What are the units used to count the speed of a printer?
A. CPM B. DPI
C. PPM D. BIT

26. Cursor is a
A. Pixel
B. Thin blinking line
C. Pointing device
D. None of the above

27. Which of the following is not an output device?
A. Scanner
B. Printer
C. Flat Screen
D. None of these

28. A file can be created using _____ command.

A. Save B. Open
C. New D. Edit

29. Which of the following is not applications software?

A. Word processing
B. Spreadsheet
C. UNIX
D. Desktop publishing

30. MOS stands for

A. Metal Oxide Semiconductor
B. Most Often Store
C. Method Organised Stack
D. None of the above

31. A Compiler is _____

A. a combination of computer hardware
B. a program which translates machine code into hight level language
C. a program which translates high-level language to a machine code
D. None of the above

32. Computer software includes

A. Application software
B. System software
C. Both A and B
D. All of the above

33. How many bits are there in a byte?

A. 2 B. 4
C. 16 D. 8

34. Which of the following software is System Software?

A. Word Processor
B. Compiler
C. Database System
D. Web Browser

35. Programs are executed on the basis of a priority number in a-

A. Batch processing system
B. Multiprogramming
C. Time sharing
D. None of these

36. The primary function of an operating system is

A. Memory Management
B. Process Manangement
C. Disks and I/O device Management
D. All of the above

37. Which one of the following is not an operating system?

A. UNIX B. Windows
C. XENIX D. APPLE

38. Which one of the following is not a function of operating system of PC?

A. Addition and substruction
B. Control the hardware
C. Provids a platform for application software
D. Interprets the user commands

39. The core of UNIX opeating system is called

A. Kernel
B. Karnel
C. Kannal
D. None of the above

40. ....is not a multiprogramming operating system.

A. Windows B. DOS
C. UNIX D. LINUX

41. The LINUX operating system was first developed in the year

A. 1980 B. 1991
C. 1992 D. 1995

42. ....transforms one interface into another interface
A. Hardware
B. Software
C. Data
D. None of the above

43. MTBF means
A. Mean Time Before Failure
B. Master Time Buffer Feature
C. Most Treated Buffer Time
D. Master Test Board Feature

44. Swapping
A. works best with may many small partitions
B. allows many programs to use memory simultaneously
C. allows each program in turn to use the memory
D. does not work with overlaying

45. Generally modem speeds are measured in
A. bps B. kbps
C. Mbps D. MIPS

46. Which of the following controls the method of iterection between users and operating system
A. User interface
B. Translator
C. Plateform
D. Screen saver

47. Copyrighted software that can be used for free is ________
A. shareware B. freeware
C. groupware D. e-mail

48. To make a notebook act as a desktop model, the notebook can be connected to a ______ which is connected to a monitor and other devices.
A. bay
B. docking station
C. port
D. network

49. The software tools that enable a user to interact with a computer for specific purposes are known as _____
A. Hardware
B. Networked Software
C. Shareware
D. Application

50. A _____ shares hardware, software, and data among authorized users.
A. network B. protocol
C. hyperlink D. transmitter

51. Computer is a:
A. device which performs arithmetic and logical operations
B. device which performs arithmetic operations only
C. memory device
D. calculating device

52. The term 'PC' means:
A. Private Computer
B. Personal Calculator
C. Personal Computer
D. Professional Computer

53. 'SMPS' stands for:
A. Simple Monochrome Powerful Supply
B. Simple Machine Power Support
C. Switch Mode Power Supply
D. Switch Machine Power Station

54. Memory Unit of a Computer is a:
A. Internal Part
B. External Part
C. Both of the above
D. None of the above

55. Maximum digits in Binary Number System are:
A. 1 B. 10
C. 2 D. 4

56. CPU stand for:
A. Central Programming Unit
B. Central Processing Unit
C. Central Programming Understanding
D. Central Processing Understanding

57. Control Unit is the part of:
A. CPU
B. Input
C. Output
D. None of these

58. The first instrument that was used for calculations, was:
A. ENIAC
B. ABACUS
C. Analytical Engine
D. EDSAC

59. Gottfried Leibnitz a famous mathematician who improved on Pascal's Machine was a:
A. British B. American
C. German D. Japanese

60. An Englishman known as the father of computer is:
A. Blaise Pascal
B. Leibnitz
C. Charles Babbage
D. J.P. Eckert

61. Period of first generation computer was:
A. 1956-1970 B. 1925-1935
C. 1946-1955 D. 1930-1940

62. Which one is a Secondary Memory of the computer?
A. RAM B. ROM
C. Registers D. Floppy

63. Which one is not a Package?
A. BASIC B. dBase
C. Word Perfect D. Page Maker

64. What does 'CLS' command in DOS stand for?
A. Clear the line
B. Clear the screen
C. Clear the memory
D. None of the above

65. A set of data is known as:
A. Field
B. Record
C. File
D. None of the above

66. IBM stands for:
A. International Business Machine
B. Inter Business Mechanism
C. Internal Business Management
D. None of the above

67. 1 KB is equal to:
A. 1000 bytes
B. 10,000 bytes
C. 1024 bytes
D. 1240 bytes

68. Printer is:
A. Output Unit
B. Input Unit
C. Both of the above
D. None of the above

69. One byte is equal to:
A. 8 bits B. 16 bits
C. 32 bits D. 64 bits

70. Unprocessed fact is known as:
A. data B. datum
C. file D. field

71. Collection of fields is known as:
A. record
B. data
C. file
D. None of these

72. 'logs' and 'bones' was invented by:
A. John Napier
B. Charles Babbage
C. Blaise Pascal
D. Gottfried Leibnitz

73. Adding Machine was invented by:
A. John Napier
B. Charles Babbage
C. Blaise Pascal
D. Gottfried Leibnitz

74. Computer:
A. accepts the information
B. manipulates that information
C. displays the result
D. All of the above are true

75. Main memory is also known as .....memory.
A. primary
B. secondary
C. auxiliary
D. None of the above

76. EDSAC was invented in:
A. 1947 B. 1936
C. 1940 D. 1955

77. ALU abbreviated for:
A. Arithmetic and Logic Unit
B. Additive and Logic Unit
C. Arithmetic and Learning Unit
D. Auxiliary Learning Unit

78. MICR stand for:
A. Magnetic Ink Character Recognition
B. Magnetic Input Character Reader
C. Magnetic Ink Character Reader
D. Magnetic Input Character Recognition

79. What is data?
A. Processed fact
B. Unprocessed fact
C. Numbers and Characters
D. None of the above

80. 'Collection of records' is known as:
A. file B. data
C. fields D. datum

81. Speed of Line Printer is measured in:
A. LPM B. DPM
C. CPS D. PPM

82. Speed of Laser Printer is measured in:
A. LPM B. DPM
C. CPM D. PPM

83. 'Index hole' is related to:
A. Hard Disk
B. Floppy Disk
C. Printer
D. CPU

84. The period from 1976 to present is known as:
A. third generation computer
B. fifth generation computer
C. sixth generation computer
D. fourth generation computer

85. 'BASIC' is a:
A. Language
B. Package
C. Operating System
D. None of the above

86. Which of the following is not a language?
A. Basic B. Cobol
C. Unix D. Pascal

87. What is fox pro?
A. Package
B. Programming Language
C. Operating System
D. None of the above

88. Monitor of a computer is:
A. output device
B. input device
C. input/output device
D. None of the above

89. OCR stands for:
A. Optical Character Recognition
B. Oriental Character Reader
C. Optical Character Reading
D. Oriented Character Reference

90. RAM stands for:
A. Random Access Memory
B. Read Access Memory
C. Read Arithmetic Memory
D. None of the above

91. ROM is abbreviated for:
A. Read Only Memory
B. Random Only Memory
C. Read Oriented Memory
D. Random Oriented Memory

92. 'Tabulating Machine', invented by Charles Babbage, was named as:
A. Analytical Calculator
B. Babbage's Machine
C. Analytical Machine
D. Analytical Engine

93. Unit of Memory is:
A. Bit B. Byte
C. KB D. RAM

94. Out of given items which one is not related to computer?
A. MDR B. RAM
C. MICR D. LCA

95. ENIAC is:
A. first generation computer
B. second generation computer
C. third generation computer
D. fourth generation computer

96. LED stands for:
A. Light Emission Disk
B. Low Emission Diode
C. Light Emitting Diode
D. None of the above

97. Daisy Wheel Printer is:
A. Character Printer
B. Line Printer
C. Page Printer
D. None of the above

98. Laser Printer is:
A. Character Printer
B. Line Printer
C. Page Printer
D. None of the above

99. Floppy Disk is a:
A. Hardware component
B. Software
C. Utility Package
D. Secondary Storage Device

100. Error correction is also known as:
A. Interpreting
B. Debugging
C. Compiling
D. None of the above

ANSWERS

1	2	3	4	5	6	7	8	9	10
A	D	B	D	A	A	C	B	A	D
11	**12**	**13**	**14**	**15**	**16**	**17**	**18**	**19**	**20**
C	C	B	A	D	C	D	D	B	C
21	**22**	**23**	**24**	**25**	**26**	**27**	**28**	**29**	**30**
B	B	D	A	C	C	A	C	C	A
31	**32**	**33**	**34**	**35**	**36**	**37**	**38**	**39**	**40**
C	C	D	B	B	D	D	A	A	B
41	**42**	**43**	**44**	**45**	**46**	**47**	**48**	**49**	**50**
B	B	A	C	C	B	B	B	D	A
51	**52**	**53**	**54**	**55**	**56**	**57**	**58**	**59**	**60**
A	C	C	A	C	B	A	B	C	C
61	**62**	**63**	**64**	**65**	**66**	**67**	**68**	**69**	**70**
C	D	A	B	A	A	C	A	A	A
71	**72**	**73**	**74**	**75**	**76**	**77**	**78**	**79**	**80**
A	A	C	D	A	A	A	A	A	A
81	**82**	**83**	**84**	**85**	**86**	**87**	**88**	**89**	**90**
A	D	B	D	A	C	B	A	A	A
91	**92**	**93**	**94**	**95**	**96**	**97**	**98**	**99**	**100**
A	D	B	D	A	C	A	C	D	B

MISCELLANEOUS

1. Which country is not in Europe?
   A. Netherlands B. Belgium
   C. Lebanon D. Sweden
2. Which one of these countries is not in South America?
   A. Perù B. Paraguay
   C. Mexico D. Brazil
3. Which one of these countries has no coast line?
   A. Pakistan B. Hungary
   C. Spain D. Sweden
4. Which one of these countries is not in Scandinavia?
   A. Denmark B. Luxembourg
   C. Sweden D. Norway
5. Which one of the following cities is not a seaport?
   A. Sydney
   B. Southampton
   C. Rome
   D. Mumbai
6. What is the official language of the Argentina?
   A. Italian B. Spanish
   C. Portuguese D. German
7. What was the earlier name of Ghana?
   A. The Ivory Coast
   B. Thg Gold Coast
   C. Malabar
   D. The Levant
8. Which country is not in Africa?
   A. Zanzibar
   B. Ghana
   C. Trinidad and Tobago
   D. Sudan
9. When did the Russian Revolution take Place?
   A. 1812 B. 1848
   C. 1917 D. 1939
10. Africa's three best known lakes–Victoria, Tanganyika and Nyasa–are located in:
    A. Niger B. Tanzania
    C. Kenya D. Zambia
11. Which one of the following was a UN Trust Territory administered by the USA and became Independent in 1994 and became the 185th UN member in 1994 itself?
    A. Palau
    B. Panama
    C. Papua New Guinea
    D. Peru
12. Which country is referred to as 'The Land of the Midnight Sun'?
    A. Iceland B. Scotland
    C. Sweden D. Norway
13. Nicaragua is situated in:
    A. North America
    B. South America
    C. Central America
    D. None of the above
14. Which of the following countries is not a member of SAARC?
    A. Sri Lanka
    B. Bangladesh
    C. Myanmar
    D. Pakistan

15. Which city is called the 'City of Seven Hills'?
A. Oslo B. NewYork
C. Tokyo D. Rome

16. The capital of Vietnam is:
A. Ho Chi Minh City
B. Hanoi
C. Ankara
D. Kampala

17. Which one of the following countries receive the most acid rain?
A. China B. Japan
C. Norway D. U.S.A.

18. Which one of the following is not a capital city?
A. Sophia
B. Ho Chi Minh City
C. Panama City
D. Paraguay

19. Cuba is nicknamed as:
A. Cockpit of Europe
B. Hermit Kingdom
C. Land of the Golden Fleece
D. Sugar Bowl of the world

20. Falkland Islands are in:
A. Pacific
B. Antarctica
C. South Atlantic
D. North Atlantic

21. The country more than half of which lies below sea level and which is one of the most densely populated countries in the world is:
A. Sweden
B. Norway
C. Netherlands
D. Kenya

22. Netherland's currency is:
A. Peso B. Pesata
C. Rupiah D. Euro

23. Which of the following is not a fruit, although it is consumed as fruit?
A. Apple B. Pea pod
C. Rhubarb D. Banana

24. Aeroflot belongs to:
A. Japan B. Spain
C. Thailand D. Russia

25. 'Izvestia' is a newspaper published from:
A. USA B. Yugoslavia
C. Japan D. Russia

26. 'Shishu', 'Tarun' and 'Kishore' named interprises are associated with:
A. SBI
B. IDBI
C. MUDRA Bank
D. NABARD

27. Which one of the following was formerly known as Dutch Guyana?
A. Thailand B. Taiwan
C. Surinam D. Tonga

28. Which one of the following is popularly known as the Isle of Cloves?
A. Zanzibar B. Tanganyika
C. Zambia D. Namibia

29. 38th Parallel is the boundary line between:
A. Germany and France
B. USA and Canada
C. Germany and Poland
D. North Korea and South Korea

30. The largest of the Nordic countries is:
A. Norway B. Finland
C. Sweden D. Denmark

31. The most populous of the Nordic countries is:
A. Switzerland B. Norway
C. Sweden D. Denmark

32. Which strait separates Europe from Africa:
A. Bosperns B. Gibraltar
C. Dover D. Bering

33. Maoris are the people of which of the following countries?
A. Greenland
B. New Zealand
C. Norway
D. Indonesia

34. Who was the first President of USA?
A. Abraham Lincon
B. Wilson Woodrow
C. Thomas Jefferson
D. George Washington

35. Capital of Guatemala is obtained by putting the word 'city' after it. The capital of which of the following countries is obtained in such way:
A. Taiwan B. Mexico
C. Laos D. Ghana

36. Two beautiful Japanese cities were the 'first' to be destroyed by atom bomb–one was Nagasaki. Which was other?
A. Tokyo
B. Yokohama
C. Fujiyama
D. Hiroshima

37. Famous Leaning Tower of Pisa is in:
A. Italy B. Greece
C. Cyprus D. Turkiye

38. Vatican City is the residence of:
A. Pope
B. British Queen
C. French President
D. Cyprus President

39. River .... is a collective name of seven rivers.
A. Ghaghara B. Kosi
C. Gandak D. Gomti

40. International Date Line is fixed along the meridian of:
A. 90° B. 15°
C. 180° D. 45°

41. Arakan Yoma is located in:
A. Myanmar B. India
C. Nepal D. Bhutan

42. Belize is a/an:
A. African country
B. European country
C. North American country
D. Central American country

43. The city of Los Angeles is famous for:
A. film studios
B. golden beaches
C. rocket launching station
D. natural beauty

44. Bangladesh came into existence in December 1971. Formerly it was known as:
A. East Bengal
B. Banga
C. Brahmadesh
D. East Pakistan

45. Which of the following countries has introduced 'direct democracy'?
A. Switzerland B. Sweden
C. Finland D. Denmark

46. Which nation is never allowed to fly its flag at half-post?
A. Saudi Arabia
B. Turkiye
C. Morocco
D. Libya

47. Which one of the following countries is famous for dairy farming?
A. Denmark B. Netherlands
C. England D. France

48. Taungya agriculture is practised in:
A. Myanmar B. Japan
C. New Zealand D. Philippines

49. The only land locked country in South-east Asia is:
A. Laos B. Thailand
C. Malaysia D. Cambodia

50. The largest in the world in respect of area is:
A. China B. India
C. Russia D. USA

51. 'Sejm' is the name of Parliament of:
A. Netherlands B. Poland
C. Serbia D. Greece

52. 'White Lily' is the emblem of:
A. Italy B. Greece
C. Cyprus D. Guinea

53. 'Dirham' is the currency of:
A. Malta B. Iran
C. Morocco D. Libya

54. 'Land of White Elephant' is the surname assigned to:
A. Japan B. Thailand
C. Bhutan D. Nepal

55. 'Cockpit of Europe' is the title assigned to:
A. Netherlands B. Belgium
C. New York D. Finland

56. Kremlin in Moscow is:
A. The seat of the government
B. A temple representing ancient archaeological remains
C. The name of a university site in Moscow
D. Lennis tomb

57. 'Abadan' is the famous oil town of:
A. Iraq
B. Iran
C. Jordan
D. Saudi Arabia

58. Tirana is the capital of a country known as:
A. Serbia B. Hungry
C. Afghanistan D. Albania

59. Which of these is the smallest state in Europe?
A. Vatican City
B. Monaco
C. Andorra
D. Luxembourg

60. Which one of the following places in UK is famous for cutlery?
A. New Castle
B. Birmingham
C. Manchester
D. Sheffield

61. Which is the part of Computer System?
A. Accounting System
B. Notebook
C. Hardware
D. Tools

62. Which of these nations has the largest percentage of persons in the armed forces?
A. Iran B. Iraq
C. Israel D. Syria

63. Shatt-al-Arab demarcates the boundaries of:
A. Syria and Turkey
B. Iraq and Saudi Arabia
C. Iran and Afghanistan
D. Iraq and Iran

64. Which of the following countries does use Zloty as its currency?
A. Zanzibar B. Ireland
C. Poland D. Jordan

65. Which is the largest city in China?
A. Shanghai B. Canton
C. Peking D. Nanking

66. Which is input device in computer?
A. Mouse
B. Punch Card
C. Scanner
D. All of these

67. Antara is an important news agency of:
A. Indonesia B. China
C. Japan D. Cuba

68. Madagascar, the world's fourths largest islands lies in the:
A. Pacific Ocean
B. Atlantic Ocean
C. Indian Ocean
D. Carribean Sea

69. Niagra Falls is situated in:
A. South America
B. Africa
C. India
D. North America

70. The writer who refused the Nobel Prize for literature was:
A. Winston Churchill
B. Jean Paul Sartre
C. Boris Pasternak
D. Prem Chand

71. Which is the highest award of National distinction for exceptional work in the field of art, literature, science, sports and public service in India?
A. Nehru Award
B. Jnanpith Award
C. Magsaysay Award
D. Bharat Ratna Award

72. Bharatiya Jnanpith Award is given annually for:
A. outstanding contribution to Indian literature
B. outstanding contribution towards promotion of international understanding, goodwill and friendship among the people of the world
C. outstanding contribution in dance and drama
D. outstanding contribution to promotion of Hindi literature

73. Arjuna Award is given to individuals for:
A. outstanding contribution to Indian literature
B. outstanding contribution towards promotion of international understanding, goodwill and friendship among the people of the world
C. showing bravery in the face of enemy attack
D. outstanding contribution for enhancing the glory of the game

74. Dr. B.C. Roy Award is given every year:
A. in recognition of contribution in different branches of medicine
B. for outstanding research and service to agriculture
C. in recognition of contribution in different branches of science
D. for high quality research in social sciences

75. When were Nobel Prizes instituted:
A. 1901 B. 1905
C. 1896 D. 1834

76. In which year was Pulitzer Prize established?
A. 1917 B. 1907
C. 1901 D. 1947

77. Kalinga Award is given annually by:
A. Govt of Odisha
B. Govt of India
C. UNESCO
D. Jointly by the government of India and Bangladesh

78. In which year was the Nobel Prize for Economics announced for the first time?
A. 1919 B. 1969
C. 1970 D. 1974

79. The Nobel Academic Committee that awards Nobel Prizes is based in:
A. USA
B. UK
C. Sweden
D. Switzerland

80. National sport of Australia is:
A. Football B. Cricket
C. Hockey D. Tennis

81. What is the length of a cricket pitch?
A. 22 feets B. 34 feets
C. 22 yards D. 54 feets

82. Wimbledon is associated with:
A. Bridge B. Hockey
C. Golf D. Tennis

83. The term 'Stone-walling' is associated with:
A. Cricket B. Billiards
C. Boxing D. Hockey

84. Ryder cup is the famous trophy of:
A. Golf B. Chess
C. Boxing D. Billiards

85. With which game are the terms bull's eye, muzzle and plug associated?
A. Billiards B. Solitaire
C. Shooting D. Rowing

86. Olympic Games (summer) are held every.....
A. 2 years
B. 4 years
C. As decided by IOC
D. 6 years

87. There are .... players in a Polo team.
A. 4 B. 7
C. 11 D. 5

88. Swaythling Cup is associated with:
A. Table Tennis
B. Lawn Tennis
C. Polo
D. Hockey

89. How many players are taken in a Basketball team?
A. 4 B. 5
C. 6 D. 8

90. The Davis Cup is associated with:
A. Tennis
B. Lawn Tennis
C. Boxing
D. Football

91. 'Eagle' is a term used in:
A. Golf B. Tennis
C. Billiards D. Volleyball

92. 'Queensberry Rules' is the name given to the rules in:
A. Cricket B. Tennis
C. Boxing D. Hockey

93. Ranji Trophy is associated with:
A. Tennis
B. Cricket
C. Badminton
D. Hockey

94. In which sport do you have bails?
A. Squash B. Cricket
C. Ice hockey D. Polo

95. The term 'Finesse' is associated with:
A. Football B. Shooting
C. Bridge D. Badminton

96. What is the national game of the USA?
A. Cricket B. Soccer
C. Baseball D. Billiards

97. The first Olympiad in Greece was held in the year:
A. 986 BC B. 776 BC
C. 1,122 BC D. 122 BC

98. Lord's is associated with:
A. Hockey B. Cricket
C. Tennis D. Polo

99. Subrato Cup is related to:
A. Badminton B. Hockey
C. Football D. Polo

100. Mohan Bagan is associated with:
A. Cricket B. Hockey
C. Soccer D. Racing

101. Baron Pierre de Coubertin, father of the modern Olympic Games, belongs to:
A. Greece B. USA
C. France D. Italy

102. The term 'Muzzle' is associated with which sport?
A. Archery B. Shooting
C. Boxing D. Judo

103. Longest recognised swimming course in the world is:
A. Palk strait

B. Dardenelles Strait
C. English Channel
D. Magellan Strait

104. The Winter Olympic came into being in:
A. 1896 B. 1916
C. 1924 D. 1939

105. What is the distance of running in a marathon race?
A. 26 miles
B. 26 miles 405 yards
C. 26 miles 385 yards
D. 26 miles 180 yards

106. In which game the term 'Tee' is used?
A. Chess B. Golf
C. Billiards D. Snooker

107. The first Asian Games were held in:
A. New Delhi in 1951
B. Bangkok in 1952
C. Singapore in 1952
D. Kuala Lumpur in 1952

108. Amongst the following pick out the one associated with hockey only:
A. Short corner B. Dribble
C. Bully D. Hat trick

109. Merdeka Cup is associated with:
A. Hockey B. Tennis
C. Football D. Badminton

110. The weight of the cricket ball is approximately:
A. 3 oz B. 4 oz
C. 5½ oz D. 6 oz

111. M.F. Hussain was a famous:
A. Poet B. Musician
C. Painter D. Journalist

112. Tulsi Das lived during the reign of:
A. Babur B. Shahjahan
C. Aurangzeb D. Akbar

113. Who among the following was not an astronomer?
A. Bana Bhatt
B. Varahamihira
C. Arya Bhatta
D. Bhaskaracharya

114. M.K. Gandhi was born on October 2. Another famous *Indian* also born on this day was:
A. Sardar Patel
B. Lal Bahadur Shastri
C. Rabindra Nath Tagore
D. Rajendra Prasad

115. Megasthenese was:
A. an Spartan Emperor's ambassador at the court of Chandragupta
B. a Greek philosopher
C. the envoy of Seleucus at the court of Chandragupta. He was a Greek
D. a Greek Geometrician traveller

116. Charak was a renowned:
A. Historian
B. Physician
C. Minister
D. Astronomer

117. Who founded the Indian National Congress?
A. W.C. Bannerjee
B. A.O. Hume
C. Sardar Patel
D. Subhash Chandra Bose

118. Tansen, before joining the court of Akbar was associated with the court of:
A. Maharaja Banur
B. Maharaja Udaipur
C. Maharaja Rewa
D. Maharaja Jodhpur

119. 'Father of History' is the name given to:
A. Herodotus
B. Megasthenese
C. John Rey
D. Ibn Batuta

120. The first US President who visited India, was:
A. J.F. Kennedy
B. D.Eisenhower
C. Jimmy Carter
D. George Washington

121. The first person who sailed around the world was:
A. Robert Pierre
B. Magellan
C. Captain Cook
D. None of these

122. The first PM to have resigned without attending a Parliament session, was:
A. Charan Singh
B. Lal Bahadur Shastri
C. Morarji Desai
D. Indira Gandhi

123. Valentina Tereshkova is famous for being the:
A. first woman pilot
B. first woman in space
C. first woman on the moon
D. first female engineer

124. Who was called by the epithet "Desh Bandhu" during the struggle for freedom?
A. Chittaranjan Das
B. Lala Lajpat Rai
C. M.K. Gandhi
D. Bhagat Singh

125. C. Funk's name has been associated with the research of which of the following?
A. Vitamins
B. Proteins
C. Minerals
D. Carbohydrates

126. Who defined democracy as a "Government of the people, by the people and for the people?"
A. Ruskin
B. Abraham Lincoln
C. Mahatma Gandhi
D. Aristotle

127. 'Lion of Punjab' is the nickname assigned to:
A. Bipin Chandra Pal
B. Lala Lajpat Rai
C. Sardar Ajit Singh
D. None of these

128. 'Anna' was the abbreviated name of:
A. C.N. Annadurai
B. T. Prakasam
C. C. Rajagopalachari
D. None of these

129. 'Frontier Gandhi' was the nickname of:
A. Mahatma Gandhi
B. Khan Abdul Ghaffar Khan
C. Vinoba Bhave
D. None of these

130. Who advocated 'Rama Rajya'?
A. Aurobindo Ghosh
B. G.K. Gokhale
C. Shyama Prasad Mukherjee
D. Mahatma Gandhi

131. "Freedom is my birth right". Name the famous Indian national leader who gave this slogan.
A. Ranade B. Tilak
C. Nehru D. Gandhi

132. Who said: "Give me somewhere to stand, and I will move the world?"
A. Archimedes B. Newton
C. Galileo D. Einstein

133. Who first propounded the Theory of Population?
A. Darwin
B. Malthus
C. Marshal Ricardo
D. Adam Smith

134. The social reformer of Maharashtra who became famous by the Pen-name of "Lokhitawadi" was:
A. Gopal Hari Deshmukh
B. Krishna Shastri Chaplunkar
C. Bal Gangadhar Tilak
D. Atmaram Panduranga

135. Which instrument was played by Bismillah Khan?
A. Flute B. Tabla
C. Shehnai D. Sarod

136. Bismark was:
A. German Statesman, the first chancellor of modern German empire
B. a noted Prussian statesman
C. a great inventor of early 20th century who classified human blood into various groups
D. an Emperor of France before the World War I

137. The 'little corporal' is the nickname of:
A. Lal Bahadur Shastri
B. Mahatma Gandhi
C. Napoleon Bonaparte
D. Bismark

138. Ravi Shankar was specialised in playing:
A. Flute B. Sarod
C. Shehnai D. Sitar

139. Begum Akhtar was associated with:
A. Ghazals
B. Thumri
C. Bhajans
D. Playback singing

140. Mrs Junko Tabei, created history on May 16, 1975 by becoming the world's first woman to reach the 8,848 metre (29,002 ft) high Everest peak. She belonged to which of the following countries?
A. Japan B. Tibet
C. Thailand D. Nepal

141. In which field of art is Indrani Rehman well-known:
A. Music (Vocal)
B. Music (Instrumental)
C. Dancing
D. Painting

142. Ahmad Jan Thirakawa was known for his mastery in:
A. Sarod
B. Veena
C. Tabla
D. Kathak Dance

143. Fuehrer is the nickname of:
A. Mussolini B. Rommel
C. Napoleon D. Hitler

144. Which of the following disciples of Dayananda Saraswati set up the Dayananda Anglo-Vedic College at Lahore?
A. Lala Lajpat Rai
B. Pandit Guru Dutt
C. Swami Shradhananda
D. Lala Hansraj

145. Zuben Mehta is a famous........
A. Lyricist
B. Violinist
C. Kathak Dancer
D. Musician

146. Michael Angelo was a famous artist, poet, painter, sculptor, architect of Italy. He can rightly be called a 'brother' to:
A. Picasso
B. Van Gogh
C. M.F. Hussain
D. Leonardo da Vinci

147. Who wrote the book 'The Insider'?
A. Khushwant Singh
B. Salman Rushdie
C. Arun Shorie
D. P.V. Narasimha Rao

148. The author of 'Arthashastra' is:
A. Banabhatta
B. Vagabhatta
C. Kautilya
D. Vatsayayan

149. The book 'Prison Diary' was written by:
A. Mahatma Gandhi
B. V.D. Savarkar
C. Jayaprakash Narayan
D. Morarji Desai

150. The Tamil Ramayana was the work of:
A. Tenali Ram
B. Kamban
C. Andal
D. Jayangondat

151. Panchatantra was written by:
A. Vishnu Sharma
B. Ved Vyas
C. Valmiki
D. None of the above

152. Mahabharata was written by:
A. Ved Vyas
B. Valmiki
C. Tulsidas
D. None of these

153. The Meghdoot was written by:
A. Humayun Kabir
B. Khushwant Singh
C. Kalidas
D. Banabhatta

154. 'Eternal India' is the book written by:
A. Dr. Radhakrishnan
B. Maharshi Mahesh Yogi
C. Acharya Rajneesh
D. Mrs. Indira Gandhi

155. Arundhati Roy received Booker Prize for her book:
A. Tamas

B. A Suitable Boy
C. The God of Small Things
D. Lajja

156. Author of the book 'Origin of Species' was:
A. Karl Marx
B. Charles Darwin
C. Newton
D. T.A. Edison

157. Homer was the greatest poet of language namely:
A. Greek B. Latin
C. English D. Spanish

158. The Mid Summer Night's Dream was written by:
A. Wordsworth
B. Shakespeare
C. T.S. Eliot
D. Bernard Shaw

159. The noted work of Surdas is:
A. Krishna Charit
B. Sursagar
C. Sukhsagar
D. Bhagwad Gita

160. The first History book was written by:
A. Othelo
B. Julius Caesar
C. Herodotus
D. Aristotle

161. UNCTAD is:
A. International Development Agency
B. UN Agency for Third World Development
C. UN Conference on Trade and Development
D. Agency for the Promotion of Science and Technology

162. The secretariat of SAARC is located at:
A. Colombo B. Dhaka
C. Kathmandu D. New Delhi

163. OPEC stands for:
A. Oil Producing European Countries
B. Organization of Petroleum Exporting Countries
C. Oil and Petroleum Exploring Countries
D. Organization of Pacific Exploring Countries

164. Headquarters of the 'Organization of African Union' is located at:
A. Nairobi B. Cairo
C. Addis Ababa D. Harare

165. The headquarters of the UN University is located at:
A. Geneva B. Bonn
C. Tokyo D. New York

166. The charter of the UN was signed on June 26, 1945 at:
A. Geneva
B. San Francisco
C. California
D. Paris

167. The United Nations Day is observed annually on:
A. November 14
B. October 24
C. October 2
D. October 30

168. Which of the following is not a subsidiary agency of the United Nations?
A. ICAO B. IAEA
C. WHO D. IRC

169. Which country is not a member of ASEAN?
A. Indonesia
B. India
C. Singapore
D. Philippines

170. Single out the false statement pertaining to the International Court of Justice:
A. Its judges are elected
B. Its decisions are not enforceable
C. It is the principal judicial organ of the United Nations
D. In case of non-implementation of the decision the further redressal of national grievances is not feasible

171. The International Court of Justice holds its sessions at its headquarters in:
A. Lake Success
B. Amsterdam
C. The Hague
D. Paris

172. When was the League of Nations formed?
A. 1914
B. 1920
C. 1935
D. 1945

173. Out of a total strength of 15, the number of permanent members of the security council is:
A. Four B. Ten
C. Eleven D. Five

174. When was the World Bank founded?
A. 1941 B. 1913
C. 1947 D. 1945

175. The abbreviation 'OAS' stands for:
A. The Organisation of Asian States
B. The Organisation of African States
C. The Organisation of American States
D. The Organisation of Armed Servicemen

176. The Secretary General of the UN:
A. is appointed by the General Assembly
B. is appointed by the General Assembly on the recommendation of the Security Council
C. is appointed by the Security Council
D. is appointed by the Security Council on the recommendation of the General Assembly

177. The Ist woman president of United Nations General Assembly was:
A. Margaret Thatcher
B. Vijaya Laxmi Pandit
C. Eleanor Roosvelt
D. Sirimavo Bandaranaike

178. The charter of UN was signed in:
A. February 1945
B. April 1945
C. June 1945
D. October 1945

179. Most of the Odissi performances are based on a famous 12th century poem, *Geet Govinda*, written by:

A. Jaidev
B. Vidyapati
C. Chaitanya
D. None of these

180. According to Bhagavatism the cause of all human sins is:

A. Lobha (greed)
B. Asatya (falsehood)
C. Avidya (ignorance)
D. Maya (illusion)

181. Which of the following erected the nine storeyed Tower of Victory (Jaya Stambh) to commemorate his victory over Mohammed Khilji of Malwa in 1440?

A. Rana Pratap
B. Rana Sanga
C. Rana Kumbha
D. Rana Udai Singh

182. The first Indian musician who have sung before the United Nations is:

A. Hirabai Barodekar
B. Begum Akhtar
C. M.S. Subbulakshmi
D. Siddheswari Devi

183. The beginning of Saivism can be traced to the .... period.

A. Harappan B. Later Vedic
C. Mauryan D. Kushana

184. The Kandhar inscription were written in....script.

A. Kharosthi
B. Greek
C. Aramaic
D. Both B and C

185. The most important and main musical instrument in *Nautanki* form of folk theatre, is:

A. Nagara B. Tabla
C. Flute D. Mohuri

186. The largest cattle fair in Asia that lasts for a month, takes place at:

A. Pushkar B. Nauchandi
C. Sonepur D. Bateshwar

187. The Desert Festival, an annual event in Rajasthan that displays local folk arts and culture, aerobatics, camel races, is held at:

A. Jodhpur B. Jaisalmer
C. Barmer D. Bikaner

188. *Garba*, a popular folk dance, is associated with:

A. Rajasthan
B. Andhra Pradesh
C. Himachal Pradesh
D. Gujarat

189. *Giddha*, a popular folk dance of Punjab, is performed by:

A. men alone
B. women alone
C. men and women together
D. men and women in separate groups

190. Which of the following sects gave woman an important place in their cult and instituted orders of female ascetic?

A. Jains
B. Buddhists
C. Ajivikas
D. Tantric sects

191. The Pala King who founded the Vikramsila University was:
A. Dharmapala B. Devapala
C. Narayanpal D. Ranapal

192. The place where Lord Krishna explained the philosophy of *Bhagwad Gita* is:
A. Mathura B. Dwarka
C. Kurukshetra D. Gokul

193. Which of the following festivals is not a harvest festival of India?
A. Onam
B. Pongal
C. Bhogali Bihu
D. Sarhul

194. *Jatakas* are the sacred books of the:
A. Vaishnavas B. Jains
C. Buddhists D. Shaivas

195. Which one of the following was the founder of the *Advaita* system of philosophy?
A. Ramanuja
B. Ramananda
C. Kumaril Bhatt
D. Shankaracharya

196. The Ajanta painting belongs to the:
A. Harappan period
B. Mauryan period
C. Buddhist period
D. Gupta period

197. Kautilya's Arthashastra is a treatise on:
A. economic theories
B. statecraft and diplomacy
C. warcraft
D. None of the above

198. *Pungi* dance belongs to:
A. Sikkim
B. Jammu & Kashmir
C. Manipur
D. Himachal Pradesh

199. Sanchi in Madhya Pradesh is famous for:
A. rock-cut temples
B. cave paintings
C. stupas
D. Ashoka's rock edicts

200. In Hinayana Buddhism, the practice was to represent Buddha not by his image but by certain symbols like:
A. lotus
B. wheel
C. foot print
D. All the three above

201. The Konark Sun Temple, a living monument of glorious past, was conceived as a chariot. It was built in the:
A. 14th century
B. 12th century
C. 8th century
D. 10th century

202. The main feature of Dravida style of temple architecture was:
A. Shikhara B. Vimana
C. Gopuram D. Mandapa

203. The Sangam literature is written in:
A. Sanskrit B. Brahmi
C. Tamil D. Hindi

204. The capital of the Pandavas was:
A. Indraprastha
B. Kurukshetra

C. Hastinapur
D. None of the above

205. According to a legend Lord Krishna lifted Mount Govardhana to crush the pride of:
A. Duryodhana
B. Kansa
C. Indra
D. None of these

206. Who built the rock-cut temples at Mahabalipuram?
A. Narasimha Varman
B. Raja Simha Varman
C. Mahendra Varman
D. None of the three above

207. *Gangaur* festival is held in honour of:
A. Saraswati
B. Ganesh
C. Parvati
D. Radha

208. The *Vedic* deity *Indra* was the God of:
A. wind B. light
C. thunder D. seas

209. Mahavira, the founder of Jainism was called *Jina*, which means:
A. ghost
B. preacher
C. conqueror
D. free from fetters

210. There were four great preachers of Vaishnavism. Three of them were Nimbarka, Ramanuja and Madhava. The fourth was:
A. Vallabha
B. Shankaracharya
C. Jayadeva
D. Vidyapati

211. Which of the following cities figures prominently in Meghdoot of Kalidasa?
A. Amaravati B. Vaishali
C. Ujjaini D. Taxila

212. The Kumbha Mela comes round once in:
A. 7 years B. 5 years
C. 10 years D. 12 years

213. The message of *Bhagwad Gita* is:
A. virtue triumphs in the end
B. god helps those who help themselves
C. do your duty without desire for reward
D. None of the three above

214. Which one of the following can be said to be the artistic achievements of King Ashoka?
A. Stupas
B. Pillars
C. Caves
D. All of the above

215. The Barabar Hills, the cave dwellings of Ashokan era, are situated near:
A. Patna B. Gaya
C. Sarnath D. Allahabad

216. Which one of the following schools of sculpture thrived during the post Ashokan period?
A. Gandhara
B. Mathura
C. Amravati
D. All of the above

217. The Gupta Age saw brilliant developments in respect of:
A. architecture
B. sculpture
C. paintings
D. All the above

218. The real beginning of the temple architecture in northern India was made on the time of:
A. Mauryas B. Guptas
C. Kushanas D. Chandelas

219. In which of the following languages did Krishnadeva Raya write Amuktamalyada, his magnum opus?
A. Sanskrit B. Tamil
C. Kannada D. Telugu

220. The history of architecture and sculpture in south India begins with the:
A. Pallavas B. Chalukyas
C. Cholas D. Pandyas

221. The best known example of the Hoyasala style of temple is found at:
A. Halebid
B. Ajanta
C. Karle
D. None of the above

222. Stupas were solid domes of brick or stone masonary built to commemorate a noted event or a sacred spot. According to tradition king Ashoka built around .... stupas.
A. 840 B. 84
C. 8,400 D. 1,000

223. The great Siva temple at Tanjore which is the 'largest, highest and the most ambitious' religious structure in India was built by the:
A. Pallavas B. Cholas
C. Solankis D. Hoyasalas

224. Chola paintings of the eleventh century AD have been discovered in the Rajarajeshwara temple at:
A. Tanjore
B. Mahabalipuram
C. Mysore
D. Vijayanagar

225. The author of Vinay Patrika is...
A. Tulsidas
B. Kabir
C. Chaitanaya
D. Lord Buddha's disciple Ananda

226. Buddha delivered his first sermon at:
A. Vaishali B. Sarnath
C. Kashmir D. Pataliputra

227. Which of the following kings was a follower of Buddha?
A. Kanishka
B. Ashoka
C. Harshvardhana
D. All of the above

228. The architecture of the Ashokan period gained in magnificence, as for the first time:
A. stone was employed instead of wood
B. wood was used instead of stone
C. burnt bricks were used for the first time
D. none of the above

229. The Chaitya Hall at Karle represents a magnificent example of:
A. cave architecture
B. the use of capital
C. mural paintings
D. none of the above

230. Hindustani music was largely influenced by:
A. Arbo-Persian Music
B. Persian music
C. Central Asian traditions
D. All of the above

ANSWERS

1	**2**	**3**	**4**	**5**	**6**	**7**	**8**	**9**	**10**
C	C	B	B	C	B	B	C	C	B
11	**12**	**13**	**14**	**15**	**16**	**17**	**18**	**19**	**20**
A	D	C	C	D	B	C	B	D	C
21	**22**	**23**	**24**	**25**	**26**	**27**	**28**	**29**	**30**
C	D	C	D	D	C	C	A	D	C
31	**32**	**33**	**34**	**35**	**36**	**37**	**38**	**39**	**40**
C	B	B	D	B	D	A	A	B	C
41	**42**	**43**	**44**	**45**	**46**	**47**	**48**	**49**	**50**
A	D	A	D	A	A	A	A	A	C
51	**52**	**53**	**54**	**55**	**56**	**57**	**58**	**59**	**60**
B	A	C	B	B	A	B	D	A	A
61	**62**	**63**	**64**	**65**	**66**	**67**	**68**	**69**	**70**
C	C	D	C	A	D	A	C	D	B
71	**72**	**73**	**74**	**75**	**76**	**77**	**78**	**79**	**80**
D	A	D	A	A	A	C	B	C	B
81	**82**	**83**	**84**	**85**	**86**	**87**	**88**	**89**	**90**
C	D	A	A	C	B	A	A	B	B
91	**92**	**93**	**94**	**95**	**96**	**97**	**98**	**99**	**100**
A	C	B	B	C	C	B	B	C	C
101	**102**	**103**	**104**	**105**	**106**	**107**	**108**	**109**	**110**
C	B	C	C	C	B	A	C	C	C
111	**112**	**113**	**114**	**115**	**116**	**117**	**118**	**119**	**120**
C	D	A	B	C	B	B	C	A	B
121	**122**	**123**	**124**	**125**	**126**	**127**	**128**	**129**	**130**
B	A	B	A	A	B	B	A	B	D

131	132	133	134	135	136	137	138	139	140
B	A	B	A	C	A	C	D	A	A
141	142	143	144	145	146	147	148	149	150
C	C	D	D	D	D	D	C	C	B
151	152	153	154	155	156	157	158	159	160
A	A	C	D	C	B	A	B	B	C
161	162	163	164	165	166	167	168	169	170
C	C	B	C	C	B	B	D	B	B
171	172	173	174	175	176	177	178	179	180
C	B	D	C	C	B	B	C	A	C
181	182	183	184	185	186	187	188	189	190
C	C	A	D	A	C	B	D	B	D
191	192	193	194	195	196	197	198	199	200
A	C	D	C	D	D	B	D	C	D
201	202	203	204	205	206	207	208	209	210
B	C	C	A	C	A	C	C	C	A
211	212	213	214	215	216	217	218	219	220
C	D	C	D	B	D	D	B	D	A
221	222	223	224	225	226	227	228	229	230
A	C	B	A	A	B	D	A	A	A